# LOOK WHERE YOU'RE GOING

To Ken
with very best wishes
Paddy Briggs

THE LIFE OF
ALAN PICKERING

# LOOK WHERE YOU'RE GOING

PADDY BRIGGS

First published in Great Britain in 2018 by
Biteback Publishing Ltd
Westminster Tower
3 Albert Embankment
London SE1 7SP


ISBN 978-1-78590-243-7

10 9 8 7 6 5 4 3 2 1

A CIP catalogue record for this book is available from the British Library.

Set in Asobe Caslon Pro and Gill Sans Pro

Printed and bound in Great Britain by
CPI Group (UK) Ltd, Croydon CR0 4YY

*To Ann*

# CONTENTS


| | | |
|---|---|---|
| Foreword *by Alistair Darling* | | ix |
| Acknowledgements | | xiii |
| Introduction | | 1 |
| Chapter 1 | Childhood | 21 |
| Chapter 2 | Learning and Earning | 39 |
| Chapter 3 | Union Man | 55 |
| Chapter 4 | A Sporting Life | 95 |
| Chapter 5 | Living with Disability | 109 |
| Chapter 6 | Pensions Authority | 129 |
| Chapter 7 | The Pickering Report | 159 |
| Chapter 8 | New Beginnings | 205 |
| Chapter 9 | The Sport of Kings | 223 |
| Afterword *by Alan Pickering CBE* | 'If I'd Known Then What I Know Now…' | 243 |
| Appendix 1 | The Pickering Review – Terms of Reference | 257 |
| Appendix 2 | The Pickering Review – Executive Summary | 259 |
| Bibliography | | 269 |
| Index | | 273 |

# FOREWORD
## BY ALISTAIR DARLING

This is the story of a remarkable man. On leaving school Alan Pickering started work as a junior clerk with British Railways. His mother was adamant that he should get a good 'pensionable' job. He went on to take a degree at Newcastle University before joining the Electrical, Electronic, Telecommunications and Plumbing Union. They needed someone to look at pensions policy. So he did. Over the next two decades he was an acknowledged expert on the subject whose views were sought by employers, unions and governments.

He became the chair of the National Association of Pension Funds and, along the way – as a result of a boyhood love of horse racing – became a racehorse owner himself. Naturally, he then became active in the governance of the racing industry as well.

His early experience of working in a collective spirit, coupled with his technical knowledge of how pensions work, made him a formidable advocate for the idea that if we help each other we can help ourselves.

I first met Alan when I was Secretary of State for Work and Pensions in 2001. I had recently introduced reforms to the pensions system that were designed to boost the amount of money people could retire on. But I was very conscious that the post-war mainstay of pensioners' income – the 'defined benefit' or occupational pension – was by then in sharp decline.

I wanted to see what we could do to halt that. So I turned to someone who not only knew what he was talking about, but was firmly rooted in the belief that the joint endeavour of the individual employee and the employer was an essential part of the pensions landscape.

So this book is about pensions and about the politics of pensions, too. It also addresses the paradox that lies therein: a pension is as important to people as anything else they do in life, yet politicians of every party have too often taken an oddly detached interest in the subject. This is particularly strange, as it dominated political thinking immediately before the First World War, and was later seen as an essential part of the welfare state created in the aftermath of the Second World War.

As Alan Pickering observes, the idea that you can save enough in thirty years to cover yourself for the next forty years does not make sense. The great advantage of the occupational pension was that the employee saved and, crucially, the employer contributed too.

Today we have a millennial generation who are the first to find themselves less well off than their parents. The unspoken deal that each generation would do better than the last, and so provide for themselves, has been severely dented – if not broken.

Now people will have many jobs between starting out and retirement. But there is another problem: incomes are being squeezed. We are asking people to pay for their education, bring up their own children, and save for longer retirement than previous generations. The basic principle is that the more you can save, the more you'll get. The underlying level of funded pension saving is falling, not rising, to meet the demographic changes we face.

This book is aptly entitled *Look Where You're Going*. If only we would. The pension system that was designed to fit the twentieth century reflected its demographic. It was also built on an employment pattern that has changed radically.

Alan Pickering was prepared to confront government with what it needed to do. So in looking back over the past fifty years, let's see if we can learn the lesson of what happens when government fails to act or makes the wrong calls. The next generation is growing up at a time of great economic and political uncertainty. We owe it to them to get the right pensions architecture in place.

*Alistair Darling*
*Lord Darling of Roulanish*

# ACKNOWLEDGEMENTS

I received assistance from a large number of people in the course of writing this book – not least from the publisher, Biteback. Iain Dale encouraged me at the start and Olivia Beattie and Stephanie Carey have been a source of good advice throughout. Steph edited the book with immense skill, coping with my eccentric punctuation, unreliable spelling and addiction to inappropriate capital letters and curious footnotes. In early discussions about the scope of the book we discussed whether my helping Alan Pickering with an autobiography in the first person would be preferable to an independent biography in the third person. Alan's preference, as was mine, was to write the latter. This was because we wanted, throughout the book, to include the views, memories and stories of the people who have known Alan over the years. The biography format makes this easier. For me, part of the pleasure of writing the book has been the face-to-face and telephone interviews I have conducted with a large number and wide range of people. Almost everybody I wanted to talk to was prepared to help – in itself a mark of the regard in which Alan is held. The publisher was tolerant when it became clear that this approach, though thorough, was time-consuming!

The key contributor to the biography was Alan Pickering himself. I am immensely grateful to him for having the confidence in me at the start. This was based (I must admit) on fairly flimsy evidence. I had written one biography before[1] and had taught myself a way of doing this which seemed to work – I broadly followed the same approach for this much bigger project. I had also been writing on pensions for some years as a journalist. This came about from my growing interest in the subject of workplace pensions as a trustee director of the very large Shell Contributory Pension Fund. I didn't claim to be a pensions expert – but I knew the subject pretty well.

Alan and I had around fifteen conversations about his life over the course of nearly two years. We did this mostly chronologically though there were one or two specialist subjects which warranted special treatment. Alan's memory is prodigious, so whether we were talking about his childhood in York or much more recent events he could recall them with extraordinary clarity. He also pointed me towards those who could comment and, as I have said, most were very happy to do so. Christine Pickering and Jenny

1 *John Shepherd: The Loyal Cavalier* (London: ACS Publications, 2009).

Davie were always available to help and their contributions have been vital. My wife, Ann, has been the first proofreader of every chapter, and was a great encouragement – never complaining when I locked myself away from domestic duties to 'work'.

The modern biographer has tools that were not available even twenty years ago – not least the plethora of material on the internet. It is immensely valuable to be able to retrieve contemporary newspaper and magazine reports of events, and I probably read – and sometimes quoted – from virtually every British newspaper and broadcast media as well as specialist pensions magazine. Hansard is also available online and to be able to read, and in some cases quote from, debates in the House of Commons was extremely valuable in a book which is in no small measure about the interface of politics and pensions. Some subjects/chapters leant themselves more to desktop research – others demanded personal interviews. Both approaches were invaluable. The following list, approximately in chapter order, of those who helped me is not comprehensive – my apologies to those I left out and thanks to everyone:

York Library, Exhall Grange School, Max Coates, Sylvia Thompson, National Railway Museum, York, York's Chocolate Story, John Spellar MP, Lew Britz, Dave Rogers, Michael Mosley, Robert Burgon, Geoff Whitlow, Mike Peel, Mike Cronin, Richard Akroyd, Joanne Segars, Adrian Waddingham, Lord Alistair Darling of Roulanish, Sir Steve Webb, Mark Heholt, Peter Ford, Stephen Timms MP, (Lord) David Willetts,

Henry Tapper, Steve Delo, Karen Jones, Ed Vaughan, Jamie Spencer, Simon Holt, Charlie Liverton, Luke Morris, Richard Wayman, Helen Grieve.

# INTRODUCTION

This is a book about politics. That said, please don't put it aside and look for something less dull. The reason it's about politics is that through much of his life Alan Pickering operated on the cusp of the political world: in a trade union, throughout his long and distinguished career in pensions and even in his various roles in the world of horse racing. For Alan, the truism that 'politics is the art of the possible' was apparent almost every day in each of these areas. As he put it in May 2007, 'Pensions and politics are inextricably linked since they each deal with the allocation of resources between competing priorities. It is forlorn to call for the separation of pensions and politics.'[2] So Alan has always had to be a political animal, but a rather subtle and bipartisan one. Former Conservative Cabinet minister David Willetts

2 Article in *Professional Pensions*, May 2007.

told me that he had assumed that Alan was of the left but that whatever his political beliefs were deep down they never intruded into his work on pensions. Early career Work and Pensions civil servant Mark Heholt divulged that a Labour minister, in his cups one day, called Alan a 'Bloody Tory'. He wasn't of course; he had no party affiliation at all. The urge to be objective is one that politicians say they seek, and maybe they do some of the time, but often, when push comes to shove, they retreat to their political comfort zone. In Chapter 7 we see how Alan Pickering strove to be objective when working on his eponymous pensions report; he built alliances across the political spectrum – from Frank Field to Peter Lilley and most stops in between. He discussed alternatives with employers, trade unions and other stakeholders, and believed he had a fairly high degree of 'buy in' for his proposals. But in the House of Commons, when discussing the newly published report on launch day in 2002, the opposition parties reverted to type and the Labour government's response was lukewarm. Had the 'art of the possible' been inadvertently breached? Perhaps it had.

The thread that holds Alan Pickering's life together and which is at the heart of this book is occupational pensions. If politics can be dull for the non-addict, then pensions may be even duller. But when you have a man as passionate about the topic as Alan Pickering as the subject of your biography, this cannot be the case. As we shall see in Chapters 2 and 3 Alan's first involvement in pensions happened by chance back in 1974, when he was asked to attend a pensions meeting at Hawker Siddeley by his then manager at the Electrical, Electronic, Telecommunications and Plumbing Union (EETPU), John Spellar. Not to put too fine a point on it, but nobody else was available, and at the time pensions was not a high-profile subject for the union – although that it is not to say it was completely unfamiliar as a subject to Alan. His father's job at the railways brought a good pension with it and his mother was insistent that when Alan started work, his job, like his father's, should be pensionable. The world of pensions is familiar, of course, to those who work in it or close to it, but in order to help the non-specialist reader it may be helpful briefly to summarise the elements of that world before we begin to tell Alan's story in detail.

The story of Alan Pickering is also the story of what we might call the 'rise and fall of occupational pensions in the UK' – an account of how, in the space of three score years and ten, we created and then destroyed occupational pensions. As senior actuary Adrian Waddingham puts it, 'The proud British pension scheme which was the envy of Europe disappeared.' Gradually, over a period of some decades after the war, employers in the private sector, matched by those in the public sector (albeit with somewhat different systems), built pension entitlement into their employment offers.

When I joined a Shell company at eighteen in 1964 I joined a defined benefit (DB) pension scheme. The promise was that on my retirement – probably at sixty but possibly earlier – I would receive for the rest of my life a pension which was equivalent to a proportion of my final salary. In my case (and typically) it would be 1/54th of my final salary for each year of service. So, if I retired at sixty that would be 42/54ths, or 78 per cent. Other schemes were slightly less generous than this but broadly in the same ball park. The benefit I would get at sixty was 'defined'. As I approached retirement age I knew exactly what my pension would be, give or take a bob or two. To fund the scheme I paid around 5 or 6 per cent of my salary into the pension fund – the fund that administered the scheme. And Shell paid the rest to keep the fund solvent. These company contribution amounts would vary over the years with the fund's actuaries advising at any one time what contributions (if any) were required to be made to match the fund's liabilities – now, and in the future. The fund grew over time: partly through organic growth of the company and partly through shrewd investment in bonds, equities, property and other investments. Liabilities grew as well but in the years of plenty they were well matched by asset growth. In his early years at the EETPU Alan Pickering became a pensions expert – he understood how DB schemes worked, supported union officials and members in any collective bargaining that took place with employers on pensions matters. A key task was often to expand the benefits from a pension fund by making them open to all (many had started out as predominantly white-collar worker funds). He also helped trustees of the funds – many of whom were union members – to perform their trustee role properly.

Over his twenty years at the EETPU Alan saw the continued 'rise' of the pension fund as here described. The cultural change which gradually took place institutionalised the norm that employees in such 'contributory' schemes would forego a small amount of their income over the years in order to pay for their retirement – and their employers would accept the responsibility for underwriting the financial health of the scheme in perpetuity. In 1991 there was a shock to the pensions establishment when the Robert Maxwell scandal broke. Maxwell was a crook who had plundered his companies' pension funds to shore up his failing businesses. It was fraud on a grand scale, but it highlighted several deficiencies in the regulatory environment for pensions. Successive governments would later change the rules surrounding pension funds and, as we shall see in Chapter 6, Alan Pickering was gradually playing a more prominent part in the wider pensions world. He had left the union after twenty years in 1992 to join the actuarial firm (and pensions specialists) R. Watson and Sons. In 1986 he had become active in the National Association of Pension Funds (NAPF), and this continued after he joined Watson's. This involvement was key in his move towards his subsequent prominence in the pensions world.

In the 1990s the relatively benign world of workplace pensions received a series of shocks – starting with Maxwell and the legislative reaction to it, which was, with the benefit of hindsight, excessive. Later, the then financial strength of DB schemes prompted the Chancellor of the Exchequer, Gordon Brown, in his first Budget in 1997 to remove one of their tax benefits, so damaging the schemes' financial viability somewhat (see Chapter 7). And then, by the late 1990s, a combination of economic, political and stock market events suddenly threw the whole basis of DB scheme pensions into question at a time when Alan Pickering was chairman of the NAPF. This 'perfect storm' was as swift as it was intense, as John Pierson and Martin Thomas explain in their *Dictionary of Social Work*: 'This has not been helped by the way employers have started to retreat from occupational pension provision or imposing changes on pensions schemes.' The British government was caught unprepared for this storm but in the autumn of 2001 Alan Pickering was essentially asked to review what could be done to save DB schemes. His report, 'A Simpler Way to Better Pensions', 'recommended [some] deregulation of occupational pensions and the optional removal of [some] guaranteed benefits, survivors' benefits and other features ... as a means of giving employers incentives to maintain occupational pension provision'. We will see the story of the Pickering Report in Chapter 7. Suffice to say there was not the political will to take drastic action and the consequence was that, within a few years, virtually all DB pensions schemes had been closed to new members and, whilst the funds themselves were required by law to stay in existence to serve the needs of current members, they became 'heritage funds', and commenced what would be a long-drawn-out, but unavoidable, decline.

In the sad story of the downfall of DB schemes we should

look at what, nominally at least, came along to replace them. A 'defined contribution' (DC) or 'money purchase' pension scheme is a very different animal to the DB schemes it generally supplanted, and we will discuss these in Chapter 8. In essence, the former are not really pension schemes at all, but workplace savings, and certainly not comparable with DB. As former Conservative minister David Willetts said, 'Adair Turner's Pensions Commission[3] (2002–05) was the last chance to rescue some of DB but Turner said that by then that battle had been lost.' Willetts believes that 'with more flexibility we might have been able to rescue some of DB'. (Alan Pickering agrees with this – but the die had already been cast by Turner.)

If 'all work and no play makes Jack a dull boy' is a truism of choice in respect of Alan Pickering, then we will certainly see how maintaining a healthy work–life balance has always been his way – since long before talking about the need for such a balance became fashionable. Not that there was ever a chance that Alan would be 'dull boy'; though a certain Yorkshire dourness can be part of the Pickering brand, he always had a smile. Most of this book is, inevitably, about Alan the 'pensions guru' – indeed, few would question the statement that he has become Britain's leading expert in the field of workplace pensions. That said, this is not a biography about someone whose brain is full of facts, or even about how someone who, having those facts at

3 The Pensions Commission, chaired by Adair Turner, was set up in 2002 to review the UK private pension system and long-term savings.

his fingertips, combines them with the skill to know how to use them. The Pickering story is deeper and more nuanced than that. Expertise is arguably the foundation of Alan's life and work, but on top of this is a natural gift for building on that knowledge base. If intelligence has generally got Alan a seat at the table, it's what he does when he's at the table that keeps him there.

In parallel to Alan Pickering's pensions career have run a number of areas of activity that mostly have little or no connection with his day job. As this book is published Alan is approaching his seventieth birthday, and it is tempting to act out the 'one man in his time plays many parts' cliché; the 'seven ages of Man'. But in truth this would be a misreading of his life. Yes, there have been many parts, but they have not really been sequential; rather, concurrent. In the first chapter we look at how his childhood profoundly affected all that was to follow. Alan's mother (a key figure in more than just his early life) banned the phrase 'Poor Alan' when it became obvious that weak eyesight was going to be a problem. Fading vision was not allowed to be an excuse for anything. And nor was it going to be a limiting factor in what he decided to do either – not if he could help it. Could he get a university degree despite the fact that reading textbooks was a struggle? Could he secure a job in the rather cerebral research department of a major trade union? Could he compete at close to the highest club level in athletics, despite the fact that he might need help even to run in the right direction? Could he rise to the top in areas as diverse as the worlds of pensions and horse racing? We shall see how he could do all these things – and much more.

The compartmentalising of Alan's successful professional career is such that many people in the other worlds in which he participates (and excels) have no idea what his 'day job' is. When he was awarded a CBE, Alan took to Buckingham Palace his wife, Christine, and his business amanuensis, Jenny Davie, as well as his old friend of more than thirty years from the world of athletics, Mike Cronin. When I talked with Cronin whilst researching this book, he said that he had no idea at all about Alan's professional life: 'He's something in the City, isn't he?' We will see in Chapter 4 how competitive athletics in various guises has been part of Alan's life since he was a teenager, and how this and his other interests have never impacted upon Alan's professional life. In Chapter 9 we look at how Alan's love of the 'sport of kings' has been a part of his world for fifty years. But, again, people I spoke to involved in British horse racing – including at the very highest level – were largely unaware that their friend and colleague was also a leading figure in pensions – a 'grandee', as one pensions magazine called him recently. 'I didn't know Alan's work was in pensions,' said Nick Rust, chief executive of the British Horseracing Authority, when I spoke with him about Alan's involvement in the world of horse racing governance. The compartmentalisation is such that there has never been a conflict between Alan's private life and his public identity. However, the personal qualities – innate and learned – that he possesses are applied in the same way whether he is interacting at the highest tier of government (see Chapter 7 on the Pickering Report) or whether he is part of the two-man team negotiating with the Professional Jockeys Association on behalf of racehorse owners in respect of riding fees (see Chapter 9). A clue as to the nature of these personal qualities can be found in the citation when Alan was given a 'Gold Award' for an outstanding industry contribution by Investment Pensions Europe (IPE) in 2004.

> Europe was given the 'Pickering treatment' of down-to-earth common sense and political realism. Shibboleths and fuzzy thinking do not form any part of his thought processes and utterances, which combine with a continuous reaching out for the common ground within Europe's very disparate pensions systems … even the French found their system lauded, which may have been a surprise to them…

Traditional biographies look at 'the man and his work', and that is certainly a large part of Alan's life. Alan's mother, Betty, was a key influence throughout his life until her death in January 1999. And his father's struggle with kidney disease before his early death in 1978 at the age of fifty-five was something that he had to cope with as an only child. For three years before her death Betty suffered from dementia. Her neighbour Sylvia Thompson recalls how Alan was assiduous in visiting her and in arranging for her to go to a care home, despite living over 200 miles away.

He was a dutiful son, but also a loving one, and it is clear that his mother was a major influence on him. As, of course, is his wife, Christine. Alan and Christine married in 1982 and have therefore been together over thirty-five years, and she has been the rock at home without which all of the rest would probably have been impossible. The marriage has been childless by choice (both of their wishes) and there have been few dramas. In their later years there have been no grandchildren to dote over or provide childcare cover for – much to their relief. The garden at the house in Hayes (and an allotment nearby) is something that gives them both pleasure and is conventional enough even if the rest of the story is exceptional. And since Alan jumped a few steps up the remuneration ladder when he became a partner at Watson Wyatt, some of this comparative largesse (that wasn't spent of horses) has contributed towards luxury holidays with Christine in Barbados – now for as long as two months a year. But if this, combined with racehorse ownership (which Christine also enjoys), sounds like fat-cat indulgence, nothing could be further from the truth. Alan and Christine live modestly in Hayes; still in the house that they bought when they were married in 1982. The house is a convenient metaphor for Alan himself – sensible, unpretentious and deliberately un-showy.

In researching this biography I spoke with over forty people who ranged across the social spectrum and all, I think, spoke freely to me. But whether a champion jockey, a marathon runner, a trade union activist, a leader in the world of pensions or a former Secretary of State, there are common themes. One is, I think, that for all of them Alan Pickering remains something of an enigma. Obviously Christine and Jenny Davie come closest to explaining the mystery. Christine says she witnessed an 'emerging genius' in their early time together and that his default position was always 'I can cope' – even though sometimes he clearly couldn't. This has never led to a row: 'Alan won't argue,' she says, and Jenny agrees: 'He is always calm and won't say anything that will upset anyone.' Early on, when it was increasingly apparent that Alan's eyesight really was fading quickly, Christine said strongly, 'You've got to stand up and admit that you've got a problem and that you need help.' For Jenny, an initial task was to get reasonably up to speed on pensions. She says how well even then Alan explained the subject using layman's terms. His early years in trustee training were important for learning by doing. Especially when he reached the height of his profession, Alan's clarity of expression was something referred to by almost everyone who knew him.

Alan is unimpressed by hierarchy. When he was working on the Pickering Report (see Chapter 7), it was experts he sought to surround himself with and the dialogue he had with politicians and others in the world of pensions was deeply knowledge-based. But, surrounding this know-how, there was a pragmatic and cleverly political packaging. As we shall see, Alan's messages to individuals were consistent with one another, but not always the same: he knew well before the cliché became common how to press the hot buttons of those he dealt with. To be scrupulously polite and to treat a stable lad in the same way as he would treat a member of the Cabinet (without kow-towing to anyone) sounds improbable but, having spoken with both during the course of writing this book, I have no doubt that it is true. There is, incidentally, nothing contrived about this behaviour; it all seems perfectly natural.

Memory is vital when you are blind and even more so when you are operating at the top of your profession and where everyone else is sighted. Alan is a master of the meeting: be it a trustee board, a British Horseracing Authority Committee or the club officers at the Blackheath & Bromley Harriers. Colleagues from these organisations now take for granted that Alan will be the best prepared for a meeting and that, if he is the chairman (which he often is), he will know the agenda, know who is present and have a sixth sense for knowing when someone is keen to speak but hasn't had an opportunity to do so. Jenny says that he can remember the details of correspondence from 'months back'. Memory also applies to travel, and I once had Alan explain a route between A and B to me which I then followed using the visual stimuli like buildings and other features that he had given me – even though he had never seen them.

If his memory is very good, his ability to speak coherently in public without notes or visual prompts is remarkable. Whether or not Alan actually commits a speech to memory having already formulated the content is not clear. I think, having heard him in action a few times, that he knows his subject matter and his natural capability to choose and order words creates the speech for him. In our keyboard age this is a rare skill but also an old fashioned one. Speaking in proper sentences with little or no written prompts was not an uncommon skill until recently. Speaking directly to a secretary or into a Dictaphone was not unusual in my early years in business in the 1960s and was the norm during my father's career in the immediate post-war period. Winston Churchill, one of the most prolific writers of the twentieth century, dictated virtually all that he wrote. So for Alan to speak at a conference or at a meeting is not dissimilar to giving dictation – though even Churchill had written notes to keep his mind on track. Alan Pickering's mind is a mystery and a phenomenon. During the interviews which are at the core of this book he would dig deep to recall in considerable detail events from his life stretching back over sixty or more years. These memories do include some visual ones, as Alan's eyesight did not finally slip away until he was in his twenties. But his recall of events later in life was no less vivid – except that it is the sounds and smells and feel of surroundings that is remembered rather than how they looked.

This is not a book about how a disabled man overcomes his disability. Of course, such a story could be written, but we took the decision to cover the subject of Alan's blindness in just one chapter – Chapter 5 – and only refer to it elsewhere when relevant (most of the time it is not). In my interview with Alistair

Darling it was only at the end that we realised that neither of us had mentioned Alan's blindness. This was not some sensitivity to avoid touching on a difficult subject. It was because, as Darling put it, he 'was not aware of Alan's blindness'. This does not mean, of course, that he didn't know Alan was blind; what it means is that it was never a factor. Hardly any other interviewee dwelt on this either. That's not to say that there weren't frequent 'how the hell does he do that?' moments though. As we saw previously, when Alan chairs a meeting he knows who is there, where they are sitting and when they want to make a contribution. Perhaps it is a sixth sense. Perhaps is it the result of years of adaptation, during which Alan had to develop techniques to enable him to perform at least as well as a sighted colleague. Jenny Davie's role should not be underestimated here. They have been together as partners in business for thirty years and she now instinctively knows how to prompt Alan when necessary. This may be as simple as whispering 'hand' to him when someone sees Alan and comes up to him, hand outstretched. Jenny makes a huge impression on everyone with her subtle, understated and vital support. It was the leader of the EETPU, Eric Hammond, who was the first senior person to arrange for Jenny to travel with Alan and give him support back in the late 1980s, and every employer ever since has taken them as a package. Jenny describes how Alan absorbs documents. She reads them to him and he will get the drift and ask her to skip things that he sees will not be relevant.

When someone succeeds despite disability there is sometimes a sense of over-compensation – doing things, or doing them in a particular way, just to prove that you can. Stephen Pollard quotes David Blunkett, in his eponymous biography of the politician, as having said,

> I sometimes think that I am trying to overprove myself. Sometimes I think to myself, are you doing this to prove a point to yourself? I don't think so any more, however. I don't need to. At the beginning, certainly, I had to break through barriers… but a lot now is simply about confidence.[4]

I think that this applies also, but to a lesser extent, to his fellow Yorkshireman Alan Pickering. Though the disability is the same, their personalities are different, and I have seen few, if any, signs of a lack of confidence anywhere in Alan's story. He was, in his own words, 'adapting to unselfconsciously coping'. This does not suggest arrogance or any lack of ambition. Jenny says he is 'a striver, determined and stubborn. He won't be beaten.' Over the pages of this book you will find many examples of that.

If this is not primarily a book about how a disabled man overcomes his disabilities and triumphs, it is also not a book about how a boy from humble origins does the same. You will see in Chapter 1 that Alan was born to working-class parents in

4 Stephen Pollard, *David Blunkett* (London: Hodder & Stoughton, 2005).

the city of York. His father was a railwayman and his mother worked on the production line at Rowntree's chocolates. But this was not the working-class environment of a manufacturing or a mining town. Alan's first house is an end-of-terrace property in a quiet cul-de-sac and his parents bought it with a mortgage. We are not in the back-to-back workers' houses of a mill town or a mining village here – this is not 'Where there's muck there's brass' territory. And there are no landlords to worry about. Similarly, at no point in their lives did Frank or Betty ever have to make use of welfare over and above a family allowance. In this respect the influences on the child were father to the man. Betty Pickering ran the household budget carefully and, comparatively limited though it was, Alan wanted for nothing. Many of those I spoke to commented on Alan's Yorkshireness – usually with a passing reference to his accent, and his careful and droll way of speaking. Pollard describes how a friend of David Blunkett characterised him as believing that 'humour and levity help in an argument', and Alan Pickering would, I think, agree.

The key moment in Alan's early life was when it was recommended that he go, at the age of eleven, to a special school in Coventry. The school had customised facilities and teaching for those with handicaps – but that was not the main reason that Alan was selected to go there. In fact, the teachers at his first school realised that Alan was intellectually gifted, and the local education authority agreed. There was a combination of need and opportunity in the choice. The special focus of the school would help him cope with his handicap but also ensure that his innate intelligence was built upon. This continued beyond A levels when he went to university in 1969. He studied as a normal student and at times it was an uphill battle. Others helped him (especially his mother) with textbooks that were an increasing struggle to read. The respectable degree that he achieved helped him on the next step of his journey – into full-time employment that was appropriate in regard to his skills and intelligence, with the offer of a job at the EETPU.

How we appear to others, particularly in later life, is in part influenced by who we have become, what roles we perform and have performed and the reputation we bring with us. It is difficult to decouple the man from the evidence of his work and his life. But, as far as Alan Pickering is concerned, many of those I spoke to in writing this book volunteered a view which went beyond the CV – and it was always an admiring one. The chairman of the defined contribution master trust, 'The People's Pension' (of which Alan is a trustee), called him the 'Albus Dumbledore of pensions' (author J. K. Rowling said of Dumbledore that he 'knows pretty much everything' about the Harry Potter universe but regrets 'that he has always had to be the one who knew, and who had the burden of knowing'). Former government minister and opposition Work and Pensions spokesman at the time of the Pickering Report, David Willetts, summed up the man he saw beneath the surface of his public persona as a 'pensions guru':

> Alan is a slightly old-fashioned figure. He has a northern gritty integrity which makes him dignified but never a bore. Indeed, he is often lively with a good sense of humour. What he exudes is a certain sort of moral authority. It is communitarian, Beveridgean, friendly society, working-class mutual support type at heart. This led to his admirable and paternalistic view of pensions and to his support for proper (defined benefit) workplace pensions. Today our society is much more individualistic – defined contribution (money purchase) 'pensions' are the embodiment of that individualism. Many would see DB harping back to a gentler, more collective, age.

The source of Alan's character – certainly of his 'northern gritty integrity' was his childhood in the city of York. And it is to York that we now journey to begin the story.

## CHAPTER 1

# CHILDHOOD

*Ever since my childhood I've had the view that I know where I'm going, and if some people want to come with me, that's a bonus.*

Like every part of the United Kingdom, the city of York was emerging slowly from the bleakness of war and austerity when Alan Michael Pickering was born there on Saturday 4 December 1948. The National Health Service, that towering achievement of the Attlee government, had come into effect in July of that year, and it was in what had recently become an NHS hospital that Pickering was born. Acomb Maternity Hospital was situated in Acomb Hall – a once stately home dating back to the late eighteenth century which had been acquired by York Corporation to be a maternity hospital in 1922 and expanded in 1946 to cope with the post-war baby boom. Alan was certainly a baby-boomer – one of the nearly 1,000 children born at Acomb in 1948. He was a 'Saturday's child' – those who traditionally have to 'work hard for their living' – and, as we shall see, he was to be no exception to this rule. Alan's father, Frank, and his mother, Betty (née Chapman), had met at a dance and were married in 1946. Alan was their first and, as it turned out, only child. They lived at the time in rented rooms at 6 Mount Parade, close to the centre of the city and to the railway works, where Frank was employed as a clerk. Betty Pickering had been a heavy smoker but the maternity hospital made her give up cigarettes and she never smoked again.

Frank Pickering had been born in 1922, and grew up in Cloughton, a Yorkshire coastal village a few miles north of Scarborough, where his father was the local joiner and undertaker. Frank was a railway fan from a very early age and Cloughton had a station on the Scarborough & Whitby Railway – just one stop from the end of the line. When he left Scarborough High School for Boys in 1937, Frank got a job on the railways and was posted, to his great delight, to Pickering station on the line of the London and North Eastern Railway (LNER) – just twenty miles inland from Cloughton. In 1939 this enthusiastic young railway clerk knew that the outbreak of war meant that he would have to join up – he chose the navy because, he later said, he couldn't face the prospect of fighting hand to hand with German railwaymen. At school he had been a talented cricketer; once sharing an opening partnership of 500 with his schoolmate Ted Lester (who became a professional with Yorkshire) – Frank scored fifty of the runs. Frank served in the Royal Navy for the duration of the war, including on the HMS *Whitesand Bay,* where another of his talents came to the fore. Although a quietly spoken and even introverted man, he had a gift for music hall patter – a raconteur in the Stanley Holloway style. And it was as a storyteller on board the ship that he teamed up with a fellow wireless operator, Harry Carpenter, in a double act. Carpenter was to become famous as a sports commentator after the war, but during it he and Frank were close as friends and performers. After service they lost touch but Frank continued his stage career – albeit only on the sidelines. His style was laconic, with some slapstick and a rather 'off the wall' sense of humour. As with his cricket, Frank was probably good enough to have earned a living with his comedy,[5] but he was cautious and preferred the certainty of the railways to the precarity of other options.

York's history as a railway town stretches back to the very early days as Britain's railway system began to be built. Stephenson routed his Newcastle to London line through the city and by the mid-nineteenth century it was, after London, Britain's largest railway centre and a major employer. In addition to the railway itself, there was also a large carriage works employing over 3,000 workers, and Frank Pickering was one of more than 10,000 employees serving the railway business in its various forms. Railway

5 Frank continued to perform at the York Empire in the 1950s and occasionally he would 'do a turn' in a concert party when the family was on holiday. Alan remembers one occasion at the Merton Hotel in Jersey when he and a fellow amateur performer did a slapstick double act dressed as painters and decorators for the popular children's television programme *All Your Own*.

work was regular and pensioned, and in the post-war era of austerity, this, along with his inherited love of trains and everything surrounding them, was why Frank chose a railway career.

The largest employer in York after the railways was the chocolate giant Rowntree & Co. Rowntree's employed nearly 8,000 people at the time of Alan's birth – one of them his mother, Betty. Betty Chapman had been born in 1925 in the city. Her mother had been a thatcher in Driffield some thirty miles to the east of the city and Betty was one of seven daughters. After her husband's early death Betty's mother went into domestic service and the family struggled, but Betty managed to get into a good secondary school and afterwards, during the war, she had worked in munitions. It was after her marriage and the birth of Alan that she joined Rowntree's, where her job boxing sweets on the production line was well below her level of ability – but it was well-paid, pensionable and comparatively secure.

In 1949 the Pickerings moved from Mount Parade to 28 Lesley Avenue just off the Fulford Road – a house they bought with a mortgage which they were eventually able to pay off early. Frank and Betty, with safe and reasonably paid jobs, were establishing a sound foundation on which to raise a family. They were financially cautious and avoided debt – and saved what spare money they did have. This was not untypical of those times in York, but it was also a result of concerns about what they saw as potential threats to their situation. During the war Frank had a kidney operation, but this had not been entirely successful and there was concern that kidney problems would recur. Another concern was that Betty's job at Rowntree's was, in those uncertain times and with sweets rationing still in place (it was to continue until 1953), not wholly secure. Rowntree's, for all their deserved reputation as a good employer, operated a piecework pay system and the demand (depressed by rationing) was cyclical; there were frequent lay-offs. Rowntree's was opposed to the unionisation of staff and there was something of a cabal in the chocolate industry, with pay, terms and conditions being fixed between the manufacturers. And it had only been during the war that the company had abandoned its policy of not employing married women. So, whilst paternalist, as befitted its Quaker roots, Rowntree's was not always as progressive in its employment practices as it might have been.

The house in Lesley Avenue had been built during the housing construction boom of the mid-1930s; it is a cul-de-sac, and No. 28 is an end-of-terrace property near the far end of the road. With no passing traffic it was a quiet and safe location in which to bring up a toddler. At home Alan recalls that his house had a distinctive smell – especially on washing day, when the tub washing machine would have to cope with oil and grease from the engine shed as well as chocolate from Rowntree's production line. The Fulford Road connects York with the village of Fulford just a couple of miles south of the city. Although a suburb of the city, Fulford Road had been a distinct community since Victorian times. It was quite genteel and usually elected

Conservatives to the council – though there was a flourishing Working Men's Club as well. One of the main features of the area was the presence of the army at 'Imphal Barracks' – the home of (what was then) the East Yorkshire Regiment (The Duke of York's Own). The barracks were just around the corner from Lesley Avenue.

In 1951, as part of the Festival of Britain, York put on its famous 'Mystery Plays'[6] cycle, and these celebrations were to be followed by a decade of reconstruction and renovation in the city as economic growth picked up after the austerity years. Wages for both Frank and Betty increased steadily and whilst hardly living affluently, Alan grew up in a home which wanted for nothing important. Only the bigger consumer durables like a washing machine were bought with debt, usually from a 'club book' – a catalogue which included the opportunity to pay off the purchase over twenty weeks. Otherwise, Alan's model railway (the bug was inherited early) was only added to once the money for a new coach or an engine had been saved.

The end of Lesley Avenue was something of a playground as Alan played safely with other children of the baby boom. He was a healthy child: vaccinated against TB in 1953 (and later against polio), but it was soon to become apparent that there was a problem. His mother had noticed when he was about three

---

6 The York Mystery Plays, traditionally presented on the feast day of Corpus Christi, are a Middle English cycle of forty-eight plays covering sacred history from the Creation to the Last Judgement.

years old that he wasn't able to see as well as the other children in the street. He was taken to an eye specialist where the first testing was rudimentary at best. The doctor threw a safety pin on the ground and asked Alan to pick it up. He couldn't see it at all. It was clear that he had limited peripheral vision and that he was struggling to see properly in low light. Further examinations were to follow when 'people in white coats shone lights in [his] eyes', but it was to be some time before his condition was diagnosed as retinitis pigmentosa (RP).[7]

As it became clear that Alan had a serious sight problem, and that it would deteriorate, his parents took the decision not to tell him: 'All the way through my childhood my parents pushed me to the limits to be normal.' This was partly denial but mainly because they didn't want him 'chucking in the towel'. Alluding to the gospel, Alan says, 'Be not anxious for the morrow for the morrow will be anxious for itself. Sufficient unto the day is the evil thereof.' Or, more colloquially, 'Crack on – who knows what the future will bring. Together we'll try and make you as normal as you can be.'

Up until the age of five, young Alan was fairly well integrated with other children in the street, albeit something of a loner: 'If it came to a choice of kicking a football with somebody

---

7 'Retinitis pigmentosa (RP) is the name given to a group of inherited disorders that affect the light-sensitive part of the eye (the retina). It is the most common inherited eye condition, affecting 1 in 4,000 people. All types of RP result in progressive loss of the cells in the retina that detect light (photoreceptor cells). Ultimately they all lead to sight loss, and some will lead to blindness.' (Fight for Sight, eye research charity)

else or kicking the ball against the wall, I would normally do the latter.' There were no nursery schools at the time and few formal community activities. With both of his parents in full-time employment, Alan's grandmother – the redoubtable thatcher originally from Driffield who now lived in York – would look after the young boy. His mode of transport was his parents' bicycles – on the crossbar of his father's or on the back seat of his mother's (York is fairly flat and the bicycle is the preferred means of transport). His grandma was a tough nut – a strict disciplinarian who demanded respect. Alan's aunts – her daughters – all worked at Rowntree's along with his mother. Mrs Chapman would take Alan to the city's main recreation area – Corporation Park – or shopping with her in the city, the highlight being a sausage roll from Wright's, the butcher in Bridge Street. As the hooter sounded at Rowntree's the women would cycle away at speed – in Betty's case heading for her mother's house to pick up her son. Alan himself had a three-wheeler which he soon outgrew and was later replaced by a shiny green Raleigh (financed by a Rowntree's profit share), on which he explored the city and its surroundings. (Alan says today that if he regained his sight the thing he would most like to do is ride a bike again.) He also had a 'trolley' – a 'bogie' cart made with old pram wheels, which was especially good on the few downhill stretches in the city.

In January 1954, at the age of five, Alan had reached school age. His weak sight and the likelihood that it would continue to deteriorate meant that admission to a conventional school would be problematic. The decision was taken to send him to Fulford Open Air School – a special school which had been opened on the Fulford Road in 1920 for 'physically defective children' (especially those with TB) and which included a 'partially sighted' class. The premise of these schools was that children who would struggle to survive in an ordinary school would benefit from a healthy 'open air' life (including resting on 'lunchtime beds' outdoors, even on the coldest days), a proper diet (augmented in Alan's case by unlimited Kit Kats from Rowntree's) and physical education. When Alan Pickering joined the school there were four age-based classes in addition to the one for partially sighted children between the ages of five and fifteen run by Miss Jean Noble. Miss Noble was a dedicated teacher who had a good record in raising the ambitions of her charges. She had a broad range of interests, all of which she shared with her pupils – including horse riding and music. The class size was small (fifteen) and Miss Noble had the skill to spot the pupils' strengths and weaknesses. Her teaching method was personal and not blackboard-based. In Alan's case Miss Noble realised that he was different in that he was clearly highly intelligent and quick to learn – so she taught him braille and touch typing.

Whilst Fulford Open Air School was proving beneficial to Alan (largely because of his teacher), there was still an assumption that children with sight difficulties like his could not be expected to have a normal life and career. There was an inherent limit to aspirations which stigmatised the children and curbed their opportunities from the start. And away from the school his fellow young residents of the Lesley Avenue area could be cruel about his disability and the fact that it made him unlike them. He went to a different school and that left him susceptible to jokes and mockery – he was made to feel something of an outlier and there was a stigma attached to this. He was different in other ways as well – and these were often positives things. His father's job at the railways allowed the family to travel around the country on a 'railwayman's pass', and this also took them to the Channel Islands and to mainland Europe. He recalls visiting Innsbruck, Salzburg and especially San Remo, where he was shocked by the poverty – something that was to influence his politics in due course. But, marginalised though he sometimes was at home, he did not lack self-confidence at school. His first experience of public speaking was to tell his class about his trip to Austria – further confirmation that if he had 'special needs' they were likely to be because of his intelligence and ability, not a lack of them.

Miss Noble and other teachers at Fulford School realised that at nine Alan needed more than the school could offer. Despite the bullying, and his handicap, he was socially adjusted beyond his years and he was writing a diary, reading newspapers and going to football matches, and was encouraged by his parents to follow normal boyish pursuits like these. Almost inevitably he became a trainspotter at a time when his father had become a roster clerk in the engine shed – the father–son relationship, which had been good from the start, was by now very strong – this kindly man was 'more like a brother', says Alan today. There was a meeting with the local education department where Worcester College – a specialist school for the blind – was considered along with other options. They chose to seek entry to Exhall Grange School just outside Coventry – a boarding school which had been the first purpose-built institution for partially sighted children to be opened in the United Kingdom. Frank and Betty were somewhat reluctant but saw that the idea was likely to be right for their clever young son – and that there was nothing available in the York area that could match the quality of education and specialist care available at Exhall Grange. Alan was admitted to the school in 1960 at the age of eleven, and for the next seven years it was to be not only his second home but the crucial foundation of all that was to follow.

Exhall Grange is situated some five miles north of the city of Coventry in the leafy village of Ash Green. It had been founded in 1951 and from the start it reflected the aims of its founders to provide education for partially sighted children. The most influential of its founders was George Marshall, who, after a brief period as deputy head, became headmaster in 1953, and it was he who was crucially influential throughout Alan Pickering's years at the school. Marshall was an innovative teacher as well as a dedicated campaigner. He founded the Partially Sighted Society, which actively sought to remove any stigma attached to blindness or partial blindness. In the year of Alan's arrival Exhall

Grange added a grammar school department (a decisive factor in the choice of the school for him) – one of the first formal recognitions in the British education system that sight disability need not be a limitation on a child's potential for academic achievement. Alan Pickering was to stay in touch with George Marshall after he had left the school – especially when he found his sight deteriorating further in his early twenties. Alan had not then realised that the RP condition was progressive and he felt that he needed advice from Marshall, who was by that time an expert (if a non-medical one). He was worried that he wasn't putting enough effort into coping with the problem. Marshall was the one who explained to him that the disease was progressive and that it had nothing to do with how hard he tried to make it better, but that Alan would certainly be fully blind within years.

Exhall Grange was predominantly a boarding school, and Alan was thus away from home on his own for the first time, sleeping in a dormitory in one of the four boys' houses (there were also two houses for girls). In total the school had 360 pupils at the time – most of them boarders. He was not the first boarding school boy to want to go home after his first month there. He had developed nerves-related asthma, and worse was to follow when, in the sick bay, he was slippered for some minor offence. Slippering, a relatively minor form of corporal punishment (but an undignified and painful one), was common at the school at the time. Indeed, the disciplinary regime was generally quite tough, following the then norms in public schools – and Alan was to encounter it again in that first term. He was accused of dropping litter and slippered once more but some other pupils knew that this was an injustice and stood up for him, pointing out that he had been in the sick bay at the time the littering occurred. Alan says today that the support of his fellow boys was crucial – he was for a time the 'most popular boy in the school'. Another lesson came when he joined in the mocking of a teacher whom the boys saw as being weak – Alan dropped an apple core on his head. Another teacher took Alan aside and told him, 'You might think this man is weak but he was the bravest man in a tank in the desert during the war – he had been shot to pieces.' Alan admits this sobering experience had a great effect on him. He knew that children could be cruel – especially if you were different and you were treated as such. But, he now says, you should try never to pre-judge – a good example of how one of Alan's strengths in later life – his calm and considerate approach to others – had origins in his childhood.

The educational standards at Exhall Grange were high and there was a need for streaming as the IQ levels of the pupils ranged between 40 and 160. There was regular testing and Alan always came out at the high end of the curve – this had been crucial in the decision of the York Education Authority to fund his place at the school. He had initially been placed in the second year, but this was a bit too stretching even for him and he reverted to his normal age group class. He was to pass eight O levels – but not science, which the school didn't teach – and later he secured two

A levels: a B in History and a D in French. These were respectable grades for the time and would have been sufficient to secure university entry.

In 1967, aged eighteen, Alan Pickering was at a crossroads. He had achieved a great deal – not just in his studies, but in terms of coping with a daunting and increasingly difficult handicap. He had more than survived away from home, both academically and in respect of the development of his personality and approach to life. At the school he had become interested in politics – the 1964 and 1966 elections had taken place whilst he was there and Britain had a Labour government and a Yorkshireman as Prime Minister. Many of his teachers had been Labour supporters in those heady times, including Alan's housemaster, Mr Wilson, who was the brother of the Coventry Labour MP, William Wilson. Alan recalls that Wilson and his fellow teachers were much more than 'just' academics and were also crucial in developing a wider understanding in their pupils – including of politics. The school (which had been broadening its pupil mix to include children with handicaps other than those that were sight-related) welcomed a wide range of people from all around the country, including many from deprived backgrounds, and Alan saw that some disabilities were unquestionably based on social class. Whilst the institution of the school was strong, its pupils and staff were far from homogenous, and this was a crucial learning experience.

Alan's father, gentle soul that he was, was a Liberal, but his much more forthright mother was dyed-in-the-wool Labour. It was to the Labour Party that Alan turned on leaving school. Max Coates, then a schoolmaster as well as a Labour Party activist and chairman of Fishergate Ward, recalls the young Alan's enthusiasm. He does not think that Alan was particularly politically ambitious – he just wanted to do his bit canvassing and the like, and take part in the social aspects of being a member of the local party. Alan joined Coates at the Working Men's Club and it was there that he took up racewalking, which was a tradition among such clubs in the area. Alan showed talent and did not lack effort. He would walk with his friend Max, who kept him on the right track by cycling alongside him, warning him of obstacles ahead that Alan's tunnel vision might not pick up. Coates recollects Alan being stoical about his sight defect at the time – not just in his racewalking, but also socially, at places like the 'Cats Whiskers Club' with its raised dance floor and darkened room. This was slightly hazardous as the edges of the raised floor were not very visible to Alan. He recalls Alan teetering perilously on the brink on one occasion whilst 'Whiter Shade of Pale' was playing, with his dance partner nowhere to be seen.

However, the main decision that Alan Pickering had to make on leaving school was whether or not to apply for university. He decided against it in the end because, he says, he wanted to 'prove that he was normal in a normal environment' – in a job, that is. He had also been away from home for seven years, so some time with his parents and friends at Fulford Road was appealing.

Paul Chrystal, in *York in the 1960s: Ten Years That Changed a City*, describes York in that era as emerging

> from the greyness of the largely derelict 1950s into a technicolour world of increasing personal freedom and growing disposable incomes allowing some to spend their money on labour-saving white goods, ubiquitous cars and on foreign food and holidays, in supermarkets and voguish department stores and in record shops.

Whilst there may be a touch of hyperbole in this, York clearly did reflect to some extent the 'never had it so good' and, later, 'swinging' times seen elsewhere in Britain. But York was not really a radical or progressive town. In the mid-1960s over 50 per cent of the workforce (predominantly women) was in the chocolate industry (at Rowntree's and Terry's), whereas only around 15 per cent working in the railways at British Railways and at the railways carriage and wagon works were women. Rowntree's was booming and in 1967 the eastern and north-eastern regions of British Railways merged and relocated from London to York – so both of Alan Pickering's now middle-aged parents were in jobs which appeared secure. But, whilst there was no industrial poverty in the city, there had been little movement of new industry to it. At one point the Ford Motor Company had been considering building a factory in the city, but the local employers, especially Rowntree's, stopped it. Chocolate and the railways were the dominant industries, therefore, and Alan was likely to follow his father into a job in the latter.

Alan's father was unsurprisingly positive about his son's wish to follow him into the railways. There was no 'inside track' – nor a need for one. But at his interview he learned that his prospects were limited because of his disability and his father was told, 'We'll give your lad a chance but you must realise that he's never going to progress – he'll start as a junior clerk and that will be the end of it.' If anything was going to provoke Alan to prove them wrong, this was it. He wanted to show that – failing eyesight aside – he was capable of being a 'normal man in a normal environment'.

So Alan Pickering joined the railways as a clerk – a job that he found undemanding but which he worked at with dedication. Elsewhere, he started to attend York races regularly. He had first been to the races at the Ebor meeting when he was in his early teens and he had caught the racing bug. He liked the social diversity of the sport (as it was then) and he liked the horses. A relative of a neighbour managed a stud farm which Alan visited sometimes, meeting along the way great trainers like Vincent O'Brien and Noel Murless.

If racing was to become something of a religious experience for young Alan Pickering – a developing passion which we will follow as the years roll by – more conventional religion was not to be part of his life any more than it was for his parents. York, with its minster and its archbishop, is one of Britain's great Christian centres. He says that his father had an 'instinctive faith' but that his mother, anti-establishment as she was, was not religious. That said, she did ask him to attend a Methodist Sunday school and gave him his bus fare to do so. Alan usually hid under the seat on the bus and saved the fare, which he would put away for a rainy day. But neither the Sunday school nor the mandatory morning assembly at Exhall Grange gave Alan a 'religious moment', though he believes, with Harold Wilson,[8] that Methodism and socialism do relate – so perhaps the Sunday school teachings were not entirely wasted.

By the age of twenty, Alan Pickering was clearly marking time a little. He knew that he had potential and that he had the right attitude to succeed, and he also knew that, as a clerk in a conservative and restrictive workplace, this was unlikely to happen. And, finally, he knew that he was damned if he was going to let the small matter of progressively deteriorating eyesight stand in his way. He was soon to realise that a little more education was to be the route to test the reality of his ambitions.

8 Wilson said that the labour movement 'owed more to Methodism than to Marx'.

CHAPTER 2

# LEARNING AND EARNING

*Money saved is empowerment – and if you are empowered you can choose your personal balance between the twin goals of independence and achievement.*

## WORK, AND LIFE OUTSIDE WORK, IN THE EARLY YEARS

In 1969 Alan Pickering stood on the cusp of the familiar and the unknown. He had peaked early in his ambition to work in the railways and in his wish to prove that he could do a normal job in a normal environment after years in a special institution. The railways were in his blood from his childhood trainspotting at York station and his visits with his father to engine sheds – he had long been learning about trains. Because of his eyesight, the rules had to be bent to get him a job, as clerks had to pass the same eyesight tests as train drivers. The job was initially mundane – basic clerical tasks, running messages, making the tea and checking typing. He was, ironically, mostly doing things which required good eyesight (which he of course did not have) rather than a good brain (which he certainly did). But gradually his supervisors saw that he had potential and he was promoted into a position which supported those seeking to use computers for railway scheduling. The computer people knew little about the railways, and the railway people knew little about computers, so Alan fell into a role which interfaced between these two groups. He did a course on the then fairly new 'critical path analysis' (CPA) project management tool, which uses network analysis to help project managers handle complex and time-sensitive operations and which became very relevant to railway scheduling. An understanding of CPA was to stay with him, and help him, for the rest of his life.

Away from the railways Alan was able to take the initiative and become active in things which did exercise his brain and which allowed him to 'punch above his weight'. He studied successfully for an A level in economics at a local education centre. The Labour Party in York's Fishergate Ward brought him on to their committee and there he fell under the wing of local university lecturer Michael Meacher, whom he was to succeed as the ward's branch treasurer. Meacher was soon to become an

MP and later was something of a left-wing firebrand. His roots were advantaged – he had attended an independent school in Hertfordshire and graduated from Oxford – but in York he lectured on social administration and did research into areas such as social deprivation. Although Alan Pickering was ten years his younger, Meacher clearly saw something special in this eager young man and helped him. His encouragement was crucial to Alan's early development. Alan attended the Labour Party conference – it was a difficult time, with Trotskyists infiltrating the party and with the party in government struggling, not just with this enemy within, but also with difficult economic and political times. Labour also helped by sending him to weekend schools; at one of which, in Scarborough, he met David Blunkett – also a tyro in the party and totally blind. They shared the county of their birth, but at that time Alan was still partially sighted and was keen to avoid 'Blindism' – so whilst he shared Blunkett's politics and background, the two Yorkshiremen did not form any personal links solely because of their shared disability.

The learning at Labour Party events was matched by Alan Pickering's involvement as a member of the Transport Salaried Staffs' Association (TSSA). This white-collar union worked alongside (and always battling against) the much larger National Union of Railwaymen (NUR) and Associated Society of Locomotive Engineers and Firemen (ASLEF), and included employees ranging from managers to clerks. As with the Labour Party, the union ran weekend schools which he attended and there was an annual conference in Weymouth which as a very young delegate he joined in 1968 – the year of the Labour government's Transport Act. He made an impression with a well-received speech, but a degree of naivety about conference procedures (he refused to follow custom and remit the motion) meant that he lost the vote. Nonetheless, he had been noticed. At one trade union weekend school he found himself sharing a dormitory with members of rival mining unions who delighted in Billy Bunteresque pillow fights. These experiences positioned Alan as an open-minded apprentice politician – but he was not a 'class warrior'. He also saw that, increasingly, kudos in the Labour Party was going to the better educated activists – especially graduates. The numbers of university graduates in Britain grew rapidly in the 1960s (the annual figures more than doubled over the decade) and many new Labour MPs (like Michael Meacher) were beneficiaries of a university education.

In 1968 Alan Pickering attended a trade union summer school at Ruskin College, Oxford. According to their website, Ruskin had been founded 'to provide university-standard education for working-class people to empower them to act more effectively on behalf of working-class communities and organisations such as trade unions, political parties, cooperative societies and working men's institutes.' Many labour movement activists, including Jack Ashley, John Prescott, Dennis Skinner, George Woodcock and Norman Willis, studied there. Alan enjoyed the summer school and later resolved to apply for entrance to the college to study for a degree – he didn't see why he should defer to graduates in the Labour Party or anywhere else. The application had to be made to the TUC and, rather ironically given his modest origins, Alan, with his three A levels and his obviously high IQ, was seen as being over-qualified and his application was turned down. Michael Meacher thought that Alan should make a normal application to university and helped him complete the necessary UCCA (Universities Central Council on Admissions) application. His first choice was Newcastle, which had been an independent university since breaking away from Durham in 1963. It was a research institution and had already a good academic reputation. His chosen course was Politics and Social Administration – a choice no doubt influenced by Meacher, who was a lecturer in the subject at York. Newcastle is around an hour by train from York – sufficiently far for Alan to be independent but close enough for him to be able to bring his laundry home at weekends.

The two and a half years between Alan Pickering leaving Exhall Grange special school in 1967 and late 1969, when he started at university, set the foundation for much that he was to achieve in later years. Part of this was intellectual stimulation from the various Labour Party, trade union and personal initiatives he undertook. He was keen to explore his capabilities and to test himself in environments away from the railway workplace. He filled in some of the gaps in his education and saw the need to do more of this. But he also grew in confidence in very adult environments – he learned at the coal face about human relationships but also decided that if he needed to push himself beyond what was expected of him, he was able to do this. Today he sees an important part of his life as having to pursue both independence and achievement and, over time, to get the changing balance right between these two goals. Independence was crucial as he moved from the fairly closeted environment of a special school to the big wide world of employment. But along with this there had to be achievement both for the inherent satisfaction it brought and also as a pathway to future success. Alan's disability was ever-present as these factors played themselves off against each other. Gradually failing eyesight could have resulted in Alan becoming less independent and more reliant on others. Similarly, this disadvantage could have inhibited his potential to achieve. At university the struggle to read and write was considerable, and it slowed Alan down, much to his irritation at times. But his parents' decision not to tell him that it was almost certain that he would eventually lose his sight completely was perhaps a wise one – not that Alan is any sort of quitter, as his life as a whole has shown. In those years between school and university ('gap years', he calls them), Alan realised that he needed to make his education on a par with other people, but he was also competitive in other areas as well. He believed that to be physically fit helped his mental state, and his road walking was a key part of this. Other sports are more difficult if your eyesight is weak, but walking, with the special help of his walking companion Max

Coates, was invaluable. He was also a keen spectator at York City Football Club (at that time in the fourth division of the Football League) and at York Rugby League Club, which was no more successful than its footballing counterpart. In the summer he travelled to watch Yorkshire cricket around the county – the team, county champions seven times between 1959 and 1968, was rather more successful than the York football teams (both codes).

Alan Pickering launched himself firmly into the unknown by going to Newcastle University. Of course this is true of all of us at that moment to some extent, and Alan did have the advantage that he had already spent many years away from home at Exhall Grange. And, as we have seen, he had also taken the initiative to move outside his comfort zone by getting involved with the Labour Party and the TSSA. But the life of an undergraduate at an institution which made few, if any, concessions to those with disabilities (at that time) was a step further. Underpinning his plans was the support of his parents and their confidence that he could succeed. And part of that help was the inculcation of a prudent approach to money.

## THRIFTINESS IS NEXT TO GODLINESS

Mr and Mrs Pickering took the view that taking care of your money was a worthy trait close to godliness – and they especially dinned into young Alan the virtue of looking after whatever money he had and of saving. Both his parents came from modest backgrounds, but whilst there were social divisions in York in those years, there was no financial jealousy. They never felt disadvantaged, and although they might see that they had 'betters' in a social sense (they lived in a small house near the Fulford Road, whilst those with the big money lived in Heslington Lane[9]), there was no envy. They knew the reality that 'money goes to money' and that it was easier to get a job or a house if you already had one. These financial truisms Alan learned very early in life. On his first day at Fulford School he had in his pocket half a crown for his school dinners, and sixpence to open an account with the Yorkshire Penny Bank. Even before that, birthday and Christmas presents had been National Savings products, premium bonds and postal orders. He had a child's account at the Dewsbury Building Society and he learned how to eke out his pocket money, and to save. His parents had a very loving relationship and the only subject about which they did occasionally bicker was money. His mother was canny with the allowance she had – the purse strings were firmly in her hands. His father was instinctively more generous, but it was clear who was in charge.

At Exhall Grange, money was scarce for many pupils and there was a bias to prudency. Pocket money was not generous and a bit of ingenuity was necessary if sufficient funds were to be available

---

9 Heslington Lane is in a conservation area, close to the university and Fulford Golf Club, and one of the most desirable residential enclaves in York. It is less than a mile from the Pickering home in Lesley Avenue.

for tuck shop visits. Luckily, Alan hit on a scheme that supplemented his pocket money. He set up a sort of lending library of books which he describes as 'mildly pornographic' (one step on from Mills & Boon). These he bought for 3/6d and loaned out for 1/6d. He clearly knew his adolescent market and became popular. He also traded in football programmes and had the knack of turning over his stock at a decent margin. The income from these mini businesses he kept in his glasses case, to be spent at the weekend at the pictures or on pie and double chips at the Wimpy Bar.

On leaving school Alan's prudent mother wanted above all for him to have a pensionable job, and on his first day at the railways in 1967, he joined their pension scheme. His first weekly pay packet was £8/12/10d[10] and this was delivered, in a wicker basket, to him and his fellow workers. Following behind the wages clerk was, firstly, a man from National Savings, which, he says, brought Alan face to face with inequality. Those who could afford it bought the stamps with Prince Charles on them and which cost 2/6d, whilst those with more limited funds had to settle for Princess Anne at 6d. Next came the man from Provident Mutual[11] with his savings products, and finally a collector from 'War on Want', who tapped the consciences of Alan and his workmates in seeking a donation.

---

10 This was a little under half the average weekly wage and is roughly equivalent to £150 in 2018 terms.

11 Provident Mutual Life Assurance Association had been established 'for the purpose of affording to clerks and others the means of making a provision for themselves in old age, for their families at their decease, and an endowment for their children.'

Whilst the family, especially his mother, was the main stimulus for Alan's early financial discretion, it was also a factor of time and place. The first credit cards in Britain had been introduced in 1966, but the explosion of consumer credit that they betokened was many years away. As we have seen, his parents had used credit only for the purchase of the larger consumer durables and debt was anathema to them. Part of the Yorkshire character has always been thriftiness ('You can't spend it until you've got it') and it is not for nothing that many of England's major savings institutions (especially the biggest building societies like Halifax, Bradford & Bingley, Leeds and Skipton) originated in the county. Alan sees his financial prudency as being part nature, the Yorkshireman's natural frugality, and part nurture, inherited at his mother's knee. There was also the fact that in York at that time there was not a lot to do with extra money – not many picture houses or restaurants and no need to travel too far for holidays when Scarborough was just down the road. If his parents had earned twenty times what they did they wouldn't have known what to do with the money. That said, his mother in particular saw the inequalities around her, and whilst she did not feel personally disadvantaged she could see that others undoubtedly were. She became politically active and was a champion of the underdog – of those whom she saw as having been short-changed in life. She was not envious for herself, but she saw that the world ought to be more equal than it was. She was a true egalitarian at heart, and a battler. For Alan, to be exposed to these feelings in his teens inspired him not just to take an active role in local politics at that time, but also for the rest of his life.

Frank Pickering supplemented his income from the railways with various part-time and casual jobs. He picked fruit and the famous 'Duke of York' potato at harvest time and had a paper round on Sundays. Alan helped with this when he could – he says that strawberry picking was the hardest job he ever did. The paper round was to the many villages within reach of York, where the canny Yorkshire farmers had to be persuaded to pay a delivery charge for the service. This small business was made possible by Frank's purchase of a car; a stubborn Vauxhall Wyvern bought for £25 was soon replaced with a more reliable Ford Anglia. The car was more a practical necessity than a luxury and not used much for holidays, where free travel on the railways was the preferred mode of transport.

Alan worked for over two years before he went to university, and the savings he made over those years gave him an advantage. For Alan, to have not only a good grant at Newcastle because of the relative modesty of his parents' earnings, but other sources of funds as well, was empowering.

## UNIVERSITY

In 1969 Newcastle was still a young university, though its original constituent colleges stretched back to the nineteenth century. It was, and is, on a central campus site just to the north-west of the city centre. Alan Pickering was not keen to live on campus in student accommodation, so he and four other like-minded students found lodgings across the Tyne in Gateshead. This worked well – at least initially. Gateshead's nearby library was open in the evenings and it was there that he studied. He was inevitably a slow reader due to his weak eyesight, although this may in fact have helped his learning. Once he had read something he usually was able to remember it. In December he reached twenty-one years of age and a party with his housemates and other friends became a little over-celebratory and led to the parting of the ways with his strict landlady. The next term he and his friends moved to Benwell, which was in the then more deprived western part of the city, and over the next three years they rented accommodation – mostly from landlords who were members of the growing Asian community. They saw similar activities to those of the notorious T. Dan Smith and his partners in corruption Andrew Cunningham and John Poulson, who were very active in Newcastle at that time – particularly in the West End area where Alan and his friends now lived. The university was a mile and a half away – a walk through housing estates and close to St James' Park, the home of Newcastle United. For Alan there were long days at university and evenings in the library. He studied Politics and Social Administration which included Sociology, Economics and Statistics. He also went to lectures, especially from visiting speakers, on subjects outside his specialism. Politicians, scientists and businessmen talked to students at these events and

Alan was an active participant. Newcastle had a reputation at the time as a 'smokestack city' and it was certainly a good place to be for a Social Studies student – all human life was there, or nearby. The early 1970s were troubled times politically, with huge ideological clashes underway. But apart from one march against unemployment with Vic Feather (general secretary of the TUC 1969–73), Alan was not active politically at university (though he continued to be back home in York when he could). He says that his goal was to get an 'education as well as a degree'. It was not all work and no play, however, and he formed a friendship with another student whom he describes as being a 'fellow student of mankind' and with whom he tried, every Friday evening, to visit twelve pubs and have a half pint in each. He also joined the Ramblers Association and kept himself fit at a gym club.

Alan Pickering took his finals in 1972 and graduated with a 2:2 degree. He had enjoyed his studies and been helped at weekends and during vacations by his mother, who had read textbooks to him. His fellow students also helped, though this was always subtle and his disability was never really discussed. Alan says that he was 'adapting to unselfconsciously coping' – to not complaining or making a fuss. Certainly the university and the teaching staff made no allowances for the fact that reading and writing was difficult. He had written a dissertation on the 'Railway Trade Unions in York' as part of his final studies and this was awarded a distinction. In preparing this work he had been permitted to see the unions close up and observe how they debated not just terms and conditions for their members locally, but wider political issues. It had been a 'good university education', with lecturers of the quality of the sociologist Norman Dennis[12] and political historian Ben Pimlott. Alan feels that he made the most of it and that it provided learning that has stayed with him – in particular, he feels that his two years or so of employment and political activism had provided him with a study framework and a sense of discipline that might not have existed otherwise. He had never seen university as a 'meal ticket' – he had not gone there to make himself more employable, at least not directly so. Looking back, he does not see himself as a conventional student – more as a 'railwayman topping up his education'. This was not primarily a materialistic choice – though he does say that 'learning leads to earning'. Where that earning would be was the next decision he was going to have to make.

At nearly twenty-four, with a decent degree under his belt and with solid employment and extra-curricular experience behind him, Alan now had to make a decision which was likely to influence the rest of his life. The options seemed to be to stay in academia and emulate his friend, Michael Meacher, in becoming a lecturer, to join the civil service (particularly the Department of Employment) or to work for a trade union. He chose the last option.

---

12 In 2011, author Peter Hitchens described Dennis, who had died in 2010 at the age of eighty-one, as 'one of the most articulate and ferocious defenders of morals and justice in recent times'.

## JOINING THE EETPU

The Electrical, Electronic, Telecommunications and Plumbing Union (EETPU) was formed in July 1968 with the merger of the Electrical Trades Union and the Plumbing Trades Union. Its leader was Frank Chapple, whose philosophy appealed to Alan Pickering. Chapple had a 'vision of enhancement and advancement by education' – there had to be more selflessness, as well as pragmatism and the pursuit of empowerment. For Chapple, the role of the unions was not to 'drive a wedge between the classes', but to pursue 'equality in the workplace'. There was idealism and plenty of altruism, but an underlying logic as well. Shared accountability across the workforce (not 'them and us') was likely to create a heathier work environment and a more successful and competitive enterprise. It was these characteristics which drew Alan Pickering to the EETPU and its leader when the possibility of a job came up. Personally, it was a huge step, not just in terms of the challenges of the job, but the fact that he would have to move south – and a long way south at that. The union's office was in Bromley, Greater London; a commuter town in leafy suburbia and a million miles away from Yorkshire. It was at a time when the rigid distinctions between the 'white collar' and 'blue collar' classes of worker remained firmly in place, and when these distinctions were characterised not just by very different remuneration and benefits, but also by different pension offers – for many employees at least.

For twenty years Alan Pickering was to be an employee of the EEPTU, and early on in those two decades he moved, almost accidentally, into that area – pensions – which was to make his name. On Derby Day in 1974 the aircraft manufacturer Hawker Siddeley was holding a meeting about its pension scheme which the EEPTU was invited to attend. For various reasons, the usual union staff were unable to go, so Alan stood in. He was instantly attracted to the subject and very quickly became the EEPTU's pensions expert – and one of only two or three at the time in the whole union movement. The value of having a pension promised, or making provision for oneself, he had, as we have seen, learned at his mother's knee. He was emotionally and intellectually the right person to look after the interest of the union's 435,000 members in this area. In fact, as we shall also see, helping members with their finances and planning for the future was not to be confined to pensions alone. Insurance, home loans, accident and death benefits were all developed – for every employee and not just, as had historically been the case, for white-collar workers. But this is for the future. For now, let's leave this determined 23-year-old Yorkshireman emerging from Bromley South station in August 1972, blinking a little in the sunshine, but confident that this latest step would enable him to apply the strong values in life that were gradually forming the man.

## CHAPTER 3

# UNION MAN

### SO LONG AS YOU WANT TO WORK HERE THERE WILL BE A JOB FOR YOU

As we have seen, Alan Pickering had decided that a career in the trade union movement was appealing and that he wanted to go straight into this on graduation in 1972, when he would be a few months from his twenty-fourth birthday. A conversation with Jack Peel, the general secretary of the National Union of Dyers, Bleachers and Textile Workers (a very northern institution based in Bradford, and as such perhaps a more natural home for Alan), had confirmed this ambition – and there was a possible job there. Another option resulted from a letter to the Electrical, Electronic, Telecommunications and Plumbing Union (EETPU), which in August 1971 offered him an interview at the union's head office at Hayes Court in Bromley.

The interview panel was Lewis (Lew) Britz, who headed the union's research department, and his deputy, John Spellar. Spellar recalls that the union 'never advertised for staff', but built its team, particularly in the area of research, by looking for people with 'a spark and intuition and understanding'. Some of the department's staff were graduates – Spellar himself had studied PPE at Oxford – but they also looked for those with some experience of the world of work. He says that his prospective university degree, and the couple of years' experience working on the railways, stood him in good stead. At the interview, which was to last an hour, Britz asked Alan about his studies and was impressed by the fact that he was writing a thesis on the Railwaymen's Union in York. 'He said to me', says Britz, 'that no matter how big nor how small the union branch was there were never more than twenty people turned up to meetings. That is exactly right. I wanted to give him a job on the spot. He was very impressive in the interview.' Britz recalls that Alan mentioned his eyesight problem and that he might eventually lose his sight entirely. Alan says that, in contrast to the railways, where weak sight was likely to be a limiting factor on the jobs that would be offered, he was pleased to find that at the union this was not the case. Britz says that Alan's 'north country honesty' was apparent at the interview and that he later came to greatly appreciate that this, combined with his 'very northern sense of humour and practical approach to things', made him such a valued colleague.

The interview led to a job offer – to work as a research officer in Lew Britz's research department at a starting salary of £1,500 per annum.[13] Back at Newcastle Alan completed his studies and graduated with honours – he regarded himself as being in a better position than many students, with a job to go to at a salary that seemed to be a bit higher than many of his fellow graduates. He also felt strongly that although his degree had been the nominal goal of the past three years, his time at university had given him the personal confidence to engage successfully away from the familiar world of his childhood – and it had shown him that, despite his worsening disability, he could compete intellectually and attitudinally with those without the debilitating burden of weak sight. Moreover, the job was going to be adventure enough, but to leave his Yorkshire home – perhaps permanently – was to be an even bigger step, despite his years at Exhall Grange School having, to some extent, prepared him for this. But this was London, or at least its suburbs – and who knew what hazards lurked? Alan and his parents came south and together they found Alan a 'box room' in Cambridge Road, Bromley North. At only £21 a month it did not eat too heavily into his gross income of £125 a month. Hayes Court was a little over three miles away and the 119 bus connected home and work.

In 1972, the rather modern (for the times) EEPTU was very much the product of its general secretary, the legendary

---

13 This compares with average wages in 1972 of around £2,000. In 2018 terms it is equivalent to around £19,000, which is also roughly equivalent to present-day graduate starting salaries.

ex-communist-turned-red-hunter, Frank Chapple, and his soulmate, the union president (from 1963), Les Cannon. Its precursor organisation (prior to the merger with the Plumbers in 1968), the Electrical Trades Union, had been transformed by a moderate leadership team as soon as they had overcome the domination of Communists who had bedevilled the union in the 1950s and '60s. That era had also been institutionally corrupt, which had led to a long-drawn-out legal battle over ballot rigging – eventually resolved in a High Court judgment in 1961. On taking over as general secretary Chapple modernised the union, and this included a focus on proper research. A photograph from 1968 (in John Lloyd's *Light & Liberty: The History of the EETPU*) shows Les Cannon lecturing on research at the union's training centre in Esher Place – a lecture which presciently looked at the need for structure and application in research as well as the need to use new materials and processes. These principles applied across the industries in which the union's members worked, but it applied equally to the union itself.

Alan Pickering says that the EETPU's politics were part of its attraction. Within the world of the Labour Party and the trade union movement the reformed EETPU was branded by some as 'right-wing', but this distorts and over-simplifies its character. Frank Chapple put it simply but persuasively in *Sparks Fly! A Trade Union Life*: 'Ordinary members [of the union] don't belong to the union, the union belongs to them. I am their man.' Rather than define the union on the left–right spectrum, it is perhaps better to look at it as modern instead of hidebound, as pragmatic instead of dogmatic. That said, there was no doubt that, as Philip Bassett puts it in *Strike Free: New Industrial Relations in Britain*, 'The EETPU is the arch-bastion of the trade union and Labour Party right.' Lew Britz (like Frank Chapple, once a Communist, then one of the leaders of the reform movement in the early 1960s) saw Alan at the time of his recruitment as 'mainstream Labour; a socialist but not a left-winger', although Alan's good friend and fellow research department employee, Dave Rogers, says that when he first met him, in 1975, Alan was 'very left-wing. He wore a Russian hat, but he mellowed over the years. He epitomised the southerner's view of a Yorkshireman.' It was certainly, as Rogers puts it, a 'highly politicised atmosphere', and there was an expectation that the union's officers would play a part in the wider political world – essentially in the Labour Party.

From the start Alan Pickering made an impression at the EETPU. Along with the rest of his (mainly) young colleagues, the tasks he was asked to complete were fairly random – the assumption was that each member of the department had the intellect and ability to carry out research tasks without close supervision. Lew Britz says that above all they wanted 'talented people' and that they managed to 'collar a great many capable people to work with us'. Britz was not a hands-on manager of the department and says that his main role was to spot both the aptitude and the interests of each of his staff and build on that. John Spellar was a 'glutton for work and loved the political rough and tumble'. John Lloyd, another Oxbridge graduate, was more academic and cerebral. Dave Rogers had an electrical engineering degree as well as work experience at Portsmouth Dockyard and so tended to get the technical briefs – and so on. Rogers says that this flexible and pragmatic approach extended across the union and that, for example, the national officers were exceptionally able; mostly appointed rather than elected, they were Frank Chapple's 'praetorian guard'. Alan soon fitted into this world. There were no house rules in respect of behaviour or work style (though a collar and tie was mandatory) and few templates for how research was to be conducted. Other than the need for thoroughness and professionalism, the approach on each project was left to the man charged with it (and they were all men). This flowed from the top. Dave Rogers describes Frank Chapple as 'rough and ready, but strategically brilliant', and says that he 'took a great interest in the research department'. Chapple saw the need to have an intellectually powerful resource at his command if he was to continue to realise his ambition of creating the most modern of trade unions. This was partly a factor, as John Spellar puts it, of the EETPU 'having to cover so many different industries, each of which lived in subtly different worlds'. You could not assume, for example, that the same imperatives applied to a plumber and to a lift engineer (the latter lived in a particularly strange world of their own). The goal was professionalism, and this was based on a systematic approach to learning. The union was the first to have its own training college and to have specialist resources in such areas as work study, new technology and, eventually, as we shall see, pensions.

Alan Pickering's early role in the research department was a general one. He and his young colleagues were given fairly haphazardly assigned tasks involving analysis of issues from (mostly) secondary sources – publications of all types which, in this pre-internet era, were all paper-based. For Alan this was a challenge – at the time he could read slowly, but the facility that his fellow researchers had to rapidly skim printed material was not open to him. The union's leadership was sympathetic and helped by acquiring a reading aid machine, which increased text size and reversed it – reading white off black was easier for the partially sighted. From the start it was apparent that Alan was personally compensating for his reading difficulties by developing a prodigious memory. John Spellar says that he saw Alan 'developing an enormous ability to retain vast amounts of information in very complicated areas' – reading was tough for him so the need to retain information without having to re-read it was vital.

The research department team had youth and intelligence in common but in other ways the employees were quite different from one another – which led to healthy debate. They would read the newspapers when they got to the office to look for stories or features relevant to the union and its members. Then there would be a gathering around the tea trolley where the conversation was inevitably political. The learning curve was steep for everyone in the team, in part because politics is not a rational science, and in part because the times were febrile. In the first two years of Edward Heath's Conservative government (1970/71), unemployment had reached over a million for the first time in the post-war era and there was industrial and social unrest. By 1973, exacerbated by the quadrupling of oil prices in October of that year, the economy was in recession and a three-day week was in place. The implications of this for the trade union movement were self-evident, and when the miners threatened another strike Heath called an election. Many members of the EETPU in the electricity supply industry supported the miners, although this backing was not to last. Friction between the miners and the electricity workers was not helped by the hostility of Frank Chapple and the EETPU leadership towards Arthur Scargill and the other miners' leaders. The feeling held by the electricians, of being the aristocracy of the working class, had repercussions within their own union and, as a result, the plumbers began to feel themselves to be second-class citizens by comparison. Chapple and his colleagues had the foresight to see that new technology was likely to radically change the role of traditional electricians – they were going to need to upgrade their skills. And the EETPU was going to provide them with the training to do this. By 1979 this policy had driven the growth of the union and membership peaked at over 440,000 – the product of an aggressive approach to recruitment based on the premise that the union had something unique to offer prospective members. In the coming decade, despite a difficult political climate for trade unions, this offer to members was to be further enhanced. With income running at around £12 million at that time and a healthy operating surplus, this was also a union with a solid financial basis from which to expand.

Although times were feverish, in 1974 the real action at the union was at the top, with Frank Chapple playing a major part in a TUC initiative asking that the miners be treated as a special case. But in the research department, tea-trolley banter aside, the focus continued to be on speech-writing, the preparation of policy papers and representing the union on such bodies as the industry-specific 'Economic Development Committees' (the 'Little Neddies') under the auspices of the National Economic Development Council (NEDC). These brought together management, trade unions and government on economic matters, and for Alan and his colleagues there was valuable learning and exposure – though whether the committees actually achieved anything is another question. For Alan, exploring London as he attended meetings and found his way around was a bonus – the images of the great city, the Thames and its barges, the fine buildings and the great sports facilities were to stay with him in his memory even when the real views were no longer available to him. There was, he says, a welcome 'clear end to the working day' – unlike at university, where he always felt the need to study. But that working day could also be informally extended in the pubs of Bromley – 'The New Inn' opposite Hayes station was one of the watering holes to which he, Dave Rogers and (after 1975)

Michael Mosley would repair. But before Mosley arrived Alan's career at the union had been given a focus which was to change his life when he became the EETPU's pensions expert.

The 1974 Epsom Derby on 5 June was won by Snow Knight at the long odds of 50/1. Less remarked at the time was Alan Pickering's attendance at a meeting on the same day at the aircraft manufacturer Hawker Siddeley (makers of the famous Trident and Harrier aircraft, among many others) to discuss pensions. Alan was no more equipped at the time to engage in this field than he or his colleagues were on any other subject – at least not as 'experts'. At that moment in time, pensions was not a particularly high-profile subject in the world of employment, but this was soon to change – first with the Social Security Pensions Act introduced by the returning Labour government in 1975, and then, in the 1980s, with radical changes to this act made by Margaret Thatcher's administration. To the EETPU it was clear that issues relating to pensions were going to be high on the agenda in the years ahead – not least because trade unions were increasingly to provide some member-nominated trustees to pension fund boards. It was becoming apparent that the provision of occupational pensions was not a disconnected by-product of an employer's compensation package for staff, but an important element of it. In the same way that electricians had to upgrade their skills to cope with new technology, so those involved in collective bargaining in a trade union would also need to become very informed on pensions policy.

The new pensions act was to come into force in April 1978. D. G. Johnson, of the Institute and Faculty of Actuaries, described it as follows: 'The new Earnings-Related State Pension Scheme (SERPS) … represented the product of more than fifteen years' efforts to establish a meaningful earnings-related supplement to the flat-rate basic State pension.' SERPS offered occupational pensions a much larger part in the country's pension structure than ever before. Crucially, members of schemes could be 'contracted out' of SERPS, in which case employers would pay reduced National Insurance contributions. It was the employer (sponsor) and pension fund's choice of either providing benefits on top of the state scheme or of contracting out and providing pensions in place of the earnings-related part of the state pension.

It was in keeping with the EETPU's ambition to be the most modern and member-focused union in Britain that they would allocate significant resources to pensions matters – and Alan Pickering was to be the primary resource. Frank Chapple would say that 'The state pension should be the foundation on which we can build' – the key word being 'build'. If the state pension covered the basic physiological and safety needs in the Maslow[14] hierarchy (the 'foundation'), then occupational pensions should, at the very least, protect the worker's lifestyle in retirement. The union was in a particularly well-placed position, at least in the

14 Maslow's hierarchy of needs is a motivational theory in psychology comprising a five-tier model of human needs, often depicted as hierarchical levels within a pyramid with physiological and safety needs at the lowest level.

trade union movement, in respect of pension matters. Many of the union's members, employees of major private sector firms or in the public sector, were members of defined benefit (usually final salary) pension schemes. And most plumbing sector members were to become part of the 'Plumbing & Mechanical Services (UK) Industry Pension Scheme'– an innovative scheme established in 1975 which not only provided the usual DB scheme benefits but was also portable – an asset in this very employment fluid sector.

Whilst many EETPU members were part of occupational pension schemes many more were not. In lots of companies the provision of pensions in a defined benefit pension scheme had been restricted to white-collar workers – not usually union members. As Frank Chapple said in 1979, 'In my early days as a trade unionist, pensions were the preserve of a privileged elite and the nearest that most workers came to such a scheme was the weekly premium to secure a decent burial.'[15] This had been gradually changing and would be given a major boost by the new act. By allowing blue-collar workers to join a DB scheme and contracting out of SERPS, employers could actually *save* money – not least because life expectancy on retirement for them was (then) lower than for white-collar workers. It was clear that a pension was now to be an important and negotiable component of the employee contract.

15 Introduction to the 'Negotiators Guide to Pensions', published in April 1979 by the EETPU research department, written by Alan Pickering.

Pensions have generally been an area of public policy where the search for consensus has been the norm. Barbara Castle's act of 1975 was not a radical shift from what her Conservative predecessor Sir Keith Joseph had proposed in 1973, and, indeed, partly built on it – both gave a predominant role in pensions provision to occupational pensions. As we shall see, this bipartisanship was to be shattered during the Thatcher years, but in the 1970s pensions were not a big area of political conflict. No doubt for this reason there was relief at the top of the union when Alan Pickering, as John Spellar put it, 'picked up the pensions baton and ran with it'. Spellar says that to a highly political animal like him, pensions were a bit 'boring', and the fact that Alan was readily 'dealing with pension schemes across the country and soon knew all the ins and outs' was a big bonus for the union.

By 1974 John Spellar headed the research department, with Lew Britz having gone to manage the union's largest operational office covering London and the south-east. Later in the year he had a challenging staff issue to deal with. Alan Pickering was increasingly concerned about the fact that his eyesight had now deteriorated to a level which made normal work processes very difficult. Early in 1975, concerned that this would hinder him from doing his job properly, he wrote a letter of resignation from the union. Spellar immediately consulted Frank Chapple, who said with characteristic bluntness, 'We're not going to let him go. So long as Alan wants to work here there will be a job for him.' The letter was torn up. Chapple, who had strong links to the American trade union movement (and who had in part modelled the modern EETPU on American unions), used his contacts to see whether medical science in the United States was more advanced and could help Alan's retinitis pigmentosa condition. Sadly this was not to be the case, but the story reinforces the fact that even at this early stage in his EETPU career Alan was valued.

When Alan Pickering took on the pensions brief there was little, if any, formal pensions training available. Learning for him was initially – of necessity – on the job. However, in 1976, four bodies – the National Association of Pension Funds (NAPF), the Society of Pension Consultants (SPC), the Association of Consulting Actuaries (ACA) and the Association of British Insurers (ABI) – formed the 'Pensions Management Institute' (PMI), of which Alan was to become a founder member. He was one of the first to study for PMI qualifications. Dave Rogers remembers the invigilator from the PMI coming to Hayes Court for Alan's examination and that Alan dictated his answers to the questions to Frank Chapple's secretary, who was a very fast typist. His exam results included a special award from the institute as well as the qualification of 'Associate of the Pensions Management Institute', which allowed him to place the letters APMI after his name. Alan became associated with the world of pensions at a time when the field was becoming increasingly aware of the need for professionalism – and especially that lay trustees need training to help them do their job. This was to become one of his main focuses in the years to come, and hundreds of shop stewards and others were to attend trustee training courses run by Alan.

In 1975 Michael Mosley, a graduate like Alan Pickering from a northern university and a Yorkshireman to boot, came to Hayes Court for an interview about a possible job in the research department. The interview was conducted by John Spellar, with Alan, now effectively Spellar's deputy, alongside him. Whilst Spellar probed Mosley's politics (he was well to the left of the EETPU norm and had been an activist supporting the Shrewsbury pickets[16] as a student), he recalls that Alan was very tough and 'a bit glum' in his questioning. Mosley, who was very articulate, stood his ground against this 'blunt bugger from the north', but was pretty sure that he had 'blown the interview'. In fact, he was offered a job and took his place alongside the other young Turks in the research department. Mosley was to be given the 'health and safety' brief at the union and his launch of an 'H&S Bulletin' for members was to be the first in the trade union movement. He and Alan became firm friends, united by their Yorkshire roots and love of the occasional pint after work. Although 'different characters', both enjoyed cricket and other sports so it was not just politics that dominated their chats at the pub. At these meetings Dave Rogers would invariably come along as well – a southerner who says that when they first met 'Alan had never met anyone from south of Barnsley'. The three

16 Twenty-four building workers picketed building sites in Shrewsbury and were prosecuted in 1973. They became known as the 'Shrewsbury 24', and six of them were imprisoned.

were close for many years – there was a degree of mutual admiration present. Mosley says that Alan 'could take a subject and give you a really straight and unbiased conclusion about it. He had intellectual rigour and integrity, was straight down the line and was never a "plotter". He never let politics get in the way of what he saw to be the truth.' Mosley recalls that when they first met Alan was a little restricted in his experiences and patterned in his behaviour. He said that he went to the same café every day for his tea and had never been to an 'ethnic' restaurant. A pizzeria in Bromley was to be the breakthrough here.

His place in the union secure, and with a job in respect of pensions that he welcomed, Alan set about not just his work but his life with determination. As much as possible, he was persistent in not letting his disability get in the way of what he wanted to do. Mosley recalls that he would not use a white cane or consider a guide dog, and came to rely on his extraordinary memory to help him get around: 'He could learn a new route almost instantly and commit it to memory', and at this time – the mid- to late 1970s – he did not like his arm being taken by a walking companion so Mosley learned to walk slightly behind him, only offering guidance when necessary. When Alan was on his own he might encounter problems if routes had altered significantly. It was this that once led to his falling off the platform at London Bridge station. He lifted himself back up immediately; his arms strengthened from the gym, he levered himself back up in a moment. At work, he realised that he couldn't 'wing it 'or 'live a lie' – in other words, if his sight was inhibiting him in a particular area, he sought help – which was readily offered. Colleagues, especially Mike Mosley, would read documents to him, and this, he believes, was the spur to the development of his ultra-retentive memory. He also developed proficiency with dictating, mostly using a Dictaphone.

As his knowledge of pensions grew Alan became gradually more useful to the national officers of the union to provide support in negotiations and discussions with employers. The 1975 act had transformed pensions and employers had decisions to make – particularly over contracting out of SERPS. The union gained kudos by having an expert on the subject – and one with no particular axe to grind. The long-in-the-tooth, experienced officers and other trade unionists came to respect Alan's knowledge, and he was generally deferred to in employer discussions and internal training events. This seems to have happened quickly and whilst he was still only in his twenties. It is no exaggeration to say he became a valued and unique resource at this time. He understood the technicalities of pensions and could convert them into everyday speech. He also, in early 1979, prepared a ground-breaking (in the trade union world) 'Negotiators Guide to Pensions', which opens with the sentence, 'Those involved in industrial relations can no longer ignore the subject of pensions.' This presciently also said that when factories close or companies merge the 'pensions dimension' must be 'taken into account'. And Alan also took the fight to those who used their 'ideological loyalty to the concept of state pension provision to justify a failure to take seriously the subject of occupational pension schemes' – strong stuff from a young man of just thirty, with only six years' experience in the EETPU (although he was fully endorsed by his general secretary).

The EETPU was, as its name suggests, a union for electricians and plumbers, and the latter, although the junior partner numerically, had a particular advantage from a pensions perspective. In 1975 employers in the plumbing sector, through their employer associations, decided to set up a pension scheme – 'The Plumbing Industry Pension Scheme' (PIPS) – with the aim of providing pension benefits for all employees of firms engaged in the industry. This defined benefit scheme offered deferred benefits (pensions) on retirement based on career average earnings. The scheme was and is operated and administered by a trustee company, Plumbing Pensions (UK) Ltd. One of the original reasons for setting up this innovative scheme was the peripatetic nature of many workers in the plumbing sector. At the time the scheme was set up pension entitlements in workplace schemes were not transferable if a worker changed employer – this was very disadvantageous to the plumbers – but under the new scheme they could change from job to job whilst staying in the same pension scheme. The trustee board comprised a 50/50 mix between employers and the trade union (the EETPU). Robert Burgon, who worked for the Scottish employers association, was asked to take on, in addition, the pensions manager responsibilities for the fund. In March 1981 Alan Pickering was appointed by the EETPU to become a trustee of the PIPS as one of the union's allocation. At first there was a concern, remembers Burgon, that Alan was 'not a plumber', and also that he had been nominated by the union rather than elected by its members. These concerns, says Burgon, were soon dispelled as all the trustees saw that Alan's 'pensions knowledge, plus his integrity and his ability to work through difficult and challenging issues in an unassuming manner', made him the ideal trustee. With hands-on experience as a trustee, the role was also beneficial to Alan personally in helping him build on his pensions knowledge in a very practical context. A trustee has a special and legal responsibility to look after the interests of a fund's members, and that, he found, concentrated his mind. Alan stayed as a trustee for the remainder of his time with the EETPU, and then, when he moved into the private sector, he continued in the role, eventually becoming the independent chairman in June 2001 – a position he still holds for this (now) £1.8 billion fund with 37,000 members.

By 1978 Alan had firmly established his position in the EETPU, and it was at this time that he took some crucial steps in his personal life. His father had died in January and both before and after this event he had been travelling to York to support his mother. At around the same time as this, he started, after some initial reluctance, to use a long white cane when walking. And, as we shall see, it was about this time that his relationship with Christine Tull (a fellow employee of the union when they met in 1974) started to blossom. It would eventually lead to their marriage in 1982.

The union was keen for its officers to be active in Labour Party politics and, whilst this was never a top priority for Alan, he was happy to play a part at the local level. He stood twice in elections to Bromley Council for the Martins Hill & Town ward – a leafy and not very promising part (for Labour) of the overall very middle-class and Conservative area that Bromley is. In 1978 he secured a respectable 730 votes, but this was over a thousand behind the inevitably elected Conservatives. In that year he also started to play an active part in the National Association of Pension Funds by becoming the secretary of its West London branch. He also moved house, leaving his rented box room in Bromley North and buying a flat in Sherborne Court, Elmers End Road, Anerley. This was still (just) in the Bromley borough but it was in what was then (and now) one of the council's few Labour wards – Penge & Cator.

MARTINS HILL & TOWN, RAVENSBOURNE

| | | |
|---|---|---|
| **Walker, William F. D.** | Con | 1,866 |
| **Wilkinson, Anthony M.** | Con | 1,739 |
| Pickering, Alan M. | Lab | 730 |
| Yates, Gordon T. | Lab | 728 |
| Dewdney, Philip E. | Lib | 296 |
| Birchmore, Margaret E. | Lib | 296 |

The first half of the 1970s in Britain saw Prime Minister Edward Heath losing office when he unsuccessfully took on a trade union in February 1974, and the end of the decade saw this repeated when the 'Winter of Discontent' was a main factor in James Callaghan's defeat in May 1979. But, as we have seen, among this turmoil the pensions sector progressed in a seemingly bipartisan way. In his 'Negotiators Guide', Alan Pickering clearly expected the foundation laid by the 1975 act to endure. He said, 'The new state scheme, which commenced in April 1978, enshrines the principle of a partnership between itself and good occupational pension schemes. Because of the stance taken by both major political parties, such a partnership seems likely to exist for the foreseeable future.' Sadly, this was to prove not to be the case.

Frank Chapple was later to describe the situation that prevailed in early 1979 in graphic terms: 'I have never seen such intense hostility from the general public and from most trade union members towards the unions.' Margaret Thatcher's government was to pursue the defeat of trade union power – the 'enemy within' – in the context which Chapple described. Rightly or wrongly, she felt empowered to seek to defeat not just her main antagonists in the National Union of Mineworkers, but the wider union movement as a whole. Whilst her government's approach to pensions cannot be seen directly in this connection – away from collectivism, in favour of free markets and libertarian – the ideological drivers were the same. It is not a coincidence that the EETPU's membership peaked in 1979 and fell away (by 17 per cent) over the next decade – ironically at a time when, in respect of its modus operandi, political moderation and member focus, it was far ahead of the pack. Chapple, in his valedictory memoirs *Sparks Fly*, published in 1984, had been proud of the union's then achievements in respect of member services:

> Our services to the members are second to none. We run residential education and training centres at Esher, Surrey, and Cudham, Kent, and have spent £900,000 in the past three years on redevelopment there. We have recently become the first union in Europe to develop our own new technology training and we have highly efficient research, legal and work-study departments. We provide full-time officials to run our large branches and we have a network of twenty-eight local area offices. We increasingly cater for managerial and technical membership, a major growth area of the future. All these services owe nothing to the idea that trade unions are there to smash capitalism. They are designed to uphold the rights and dignity of our members in their reasonable demands for a fair deal at work and for improved living standards.

When Frank Chapple stood down as general secretary of the EETPU in 1984, he said that he left knowing that the union was 'industrially and politically robust and healthy, financially sound and … the most democratic of all Britain's trade unions'. Part of that special status was the attention to member services that he had pioneered and which his successor, Eric Hammond, was to expand.

In his history of the EETPU John Lloyd says that by the late 1980s the union had broadened 'the benefits associated with trade union membership away from the negative, if vital, protection against disaster that the old "benefits" represented. Nowadays, the union's benefits are positive benefits aimed at raising the standard of living of individual members and their families – a complete change from past practice.' Alan Pickering had been central to this. In 1982 he had authored a sixteen-page 'Guide to Retirement' for EETPU members, which covered not just pensions but investment, social activities, making a will etc. As with so many of the union's initiatives at the time, this was genuinely innovative. Then, in addition to his work on pensions, he was asked to head up a new 'Membership Services Department', which, Lloyd says, 'had grown out of Alan Pickering's increasingly sophisticated advice service to pension negotiators and union pensioners'. In his 1987 book, *Strike Free*, on the new industrial relations climate of the mid 1980s, Philip Bassett (then labour editor of the *Financial Times*) describes this at length:

> The EETPU does not just concentrate on its members' working lives. As well as bargaining on their pay and conditions, unions have always provided a range of services for their members. Traditionally, these have been mainly in areas like death

> or sickness benefit. In January 1986 the EETPU launched a unique, comprehensive package of financial benefits providing advantageous rates on services ranging from unit trusts to vehicle breakdown and recovery. Eric Hammond says the move is 'breaking entirely new ground for the British trade union movement. Once again we are in the vanguard of change.' Negotiated by Alan Pickering, the EETPU's deputy research head, the services offered include a special introduction to the Halifax Building Society for mortgages, with some fixed-price legal conveyancing; 20 per cent discount on Cornhill house insurance; special price membership of Octagon, a leading non-AA/RAC car breakdown service; preferential savings rates with the Bradford & Bingley Building Society; a 2 per cent bonus issue of units with M&G, Britain's largest unit trust group; a new policy with Provident Mutual providing for buy-outs when members leave occupational pension schemes; employer insurance for members who set up their own businesses; and share advice using a firm of London stockbrokers.

Not surprisingly, financial services (and other) providers were enthusiastic about the union's 'Money-Wise' (as it was branded) affinity products initiative that, under Alan Pickering's management, the EETPU had launched. A captive market of 400,000 was very attractive indeed. Bassett also writes how Bob Clarke, of Octagon Recovery, said, 'The union appears to be doing something for their members, as opposed to engaging in political infighting.' However, not everyone in the union was entirely supportive of what was underway. When the package was extended to include an offer on private healthcare, this proved to be a step too far for Alan Pickering's friend Michael Mosley. He protested and threatened to resign, but Frank Chapple offered a compromise that Mosley need not be present when the subject was discussed with employers. Mosley pondered whether this was too much of a concession of his principles, and consulted Alan, who argued that 'for the good of all of us' he should accept Chapple's offer, which he did. Around the same time of the launch of 'Money-Wise', the union, under Alan's direction, arranged the largest ever distribution of kidney donor cards to over 435,000 union members and their families. And the unions' newspaper, *Contact*, increasingly contained practical advice to members on financial and other matters under the heading 'Cashpoint' – this was under Alan's byline and he answered questions on a range of financial matters.

The EETPU set itself apart from other unions not just because of the overriding principle of 'Money-Wise', but because of its initiatives on training, its support for accepting government funding for union ballots[17] and its pioneering of non-strike agreements. This is summarised by Paul Willman, Timothy Morris and Beverly Aston in *Union Business: Trade Union Organisation*

17 The EEPTU was ahead of the game in having a centralised and computerised membership register, which facilitated union ballots as well as providing an easy way for the union to communicate directly with its members.

*and Financial Reform in the Thatcher Years*, which was an analysis of the changing role of unions in the 1980s:

> EETPU is a highly competitive union. Its populist policies are based on a philosophy of responding to members' wishes which set it both against certain political stances taken by TUC affiliates and against any regulatory mechanism ... Its benefits are cost effective and are designed to both attract and retain members. Its efficiency in financial management supports both benefit and recruitment expenditure while enabling the union to compete effectively in the membership market. In this sense, financial management, financial strategy, and union objectives are in close alignment.

The friendship between Michael Mosley and Alan Pickering, which, as we have seen, was built on their Yorkshire roots and their common love of sport and 'proper ale', was important to both of them. They were different characters – Mosley had strong opinions and usually expressed them. But, he says, Alan applied discipline and logic to everything: 'He could take a subject and give you a really straight conclusion which was not biased in any way.' Mosley's girlfriend, Jackie, whom he had met at university, still lived in the north, but by 1979 they had decided to get married, and Michael asked Alan to be his best man. On the day of the wedding Alan had gone to his friend's flat and not seen some bicycles propped up in the hall – he tumbled over them and his trousers became covered with oil. This did not faze him, however, and he performed his duties well – including giving a speech full of dry humour and a touch of subtle innuendo. Mosley recalls that Alan's shoes were the last of a job lot of eight identical pairs he had bought at a bargain price ten years earlier. As a fellow Yorkshireman he admired his best man's thriftiness.

Alan himself had known Christine Tull for a few years and they had been a 'couple' at the Mosley's September wedding. Christine was a local girl who had joined the EETPU in the late 1960s in the typing pool – she recalls that at their first 'date' Alan had bought her a pint, though he did not stretch to a pie as well. For family reasons Christine had to move away from the area (to the south coast) for a time, but the relationship survived this. During these years Christine came with Alan to visit his parents in York from time to time and had been supportive of him at the time of his father's illness and death in 1978.[18] It was an eight-year courtship which was not without its uncertainties. Michael Mosley recalls Alan saying he was concerned about marriage and particularly the idea of children. Not only would there be a burden on Christine due to his increasing blindness, but it was a hereditary condition and there was a possibility of it being passed on to children or grandchildren. As it happened, Christine was, as she puts it, 'not a children person', so the issue didn't

18 Frank Pickering's kidney problems had worsened, and a kidney dialysis machine was installed in his home. A kidney donor was found and the operation had been successful in itself, but unfortunately the strain on his other organs had been too great and he died at the age of fifty-five.

arise, though she says today that she thinks 'Alan would have made a lovely dad'. In 1982, three years after the Mosley wedding, Alan and Christine were to get married themselves, with Michael now performing the best man duties. The ceremony was in St John's Church Penge, with the reception at the clubhouse of Blackheath Harriers in Hayes (as we shall see, athletics had become a passion for Alan by this time and the Harriers were his club). In the run-up to the wedding Alan and Christine had been looking for a house,[19] and they had found one in Hayes Hill Road, Hayes – not far from Hayes Court and close to the station. The house purchase documents had to be signed just before the day of the wedding and Christine recalls that when she stood at the front of the church, having walked down the aisle, Alan leant across to her and said, 'Did you sign the papers?'

During these years at the EETPU Alan kept himself fit and busy away from Hayes Court. As we shall see in Chapter 4, this included competitive racewalking and running, and even winter sports (including, in 1984, the London marathon and cross-country skiing in Norway), as well as a personal commitment to fitness with regular work-outs in the gym and on the track at the Crystal Palace National Sports Centre. Geoff Whitlow, who had joined the research department at the EETPU in 1981, believes that Alan's commitment to athletics and his resolution to compete at the highest level was in part determination not to let

19 The house is a pleasant Tudor-style semi-detached in a leafy lane in the west Kent commuter belt. Alan and Christine still live there today.

the fact that one of his senses was impaired be made worse by things (like fitness) that he could control.

## PENSIONS IN THE 1980S

Whilst the EETPU was modernising throughout the 1980s, this was in a climate which was increasingly difficult for the trade union movement. However, much of the legislation of the early part of the decade, which outlawed the 'closed shop' and required secret postal ballots before strike action, was not contentious for the union (despite this, it was less sanguine about the attack on 'secondary picketing' and on union membership at GCHQ). Reducing the power of the unions was one thing, but the overall Thatcherite ideology had implications that were far broader that just trade union rights and practices. Essentially, Margaret Thatcher and her ministers were libertarians who believed, to a fault, in personal freedoms rather than collectivism. A trade union is by definition a collective – but so are employer associations and, crucially, pension schemes. Modern societies around the world are public/private partnerships – the private sector could not operate without public sector services and the public sector needs a raft of goods and services that are provided by the private sector. And, overall, there has to be a degree of regulation to ensure that everything works as smoothly, fairly and legally as possible. A pension scheme is a classic example, and Barbara Castle's 1975 act – which had only been operating for little over a year when Mrs Thatcher came to power – was, as we have seen, bedding in well. The DB schemes emerging after the 1975 act were far from broken – but the Thatcher government decided for ideological reasons to fix them anyway. Nothing changed during the new administration's first term, and when Thatcher was re-elected with an overall majority of 144 seats in 1983, it was under a manifesto that said very little about pensions:

> Over 11.5 million people – half the working population – are now covered by occupational pension schemes. We will consider how the pension rights of 'early leavers', people who change jobs, can be better protected and how their members may be given fuller information about their pension schemes.

The issues of protecting the rights of 'early leavers' and of the scope for portable pensions were ones that pension professionals and institutions like the NAPF were actively considering, so this manifesto commitment was as uncontroversial as it was limited. There was no commitment radically to change occupational pensions, so when, during this post-1983 second term, this began to happen, the pensions industry was surprised. Ideology was at work here. Mrs Thatcher's anti-collectivism bias spread to any sector where she could see individual rights being diminished. This ideology favoured, for example, private housing ahead of council housing and small business ahead of large. It favoured, of course, the private sector rather than the public sector and then this was extended to a bias for personal pensions ahead of collective schemes. Alan Pickering's objection to this last imperative was not because he personally had an opposite ideology to that of the government. Neither he nor the union he worked for were tub-thumping collectivist socialists opposed to the private sector (in which most of the union's members worked, of course). But when, in 1986, the Financial Services Act introduced personal pensions, making changes to the contracting-out rules to stop employers requiring employees to join occupational schemes, it was clear that an unheralded and unmandated change to workplace pensions was to be instituted because of a belief that DB schemes were 'welfare statism'. The government launched an advertising campaign which portrayed existing defined benefit schemes as a straitjacket and encouraged – and even incentivised – scheme members to consider a personal pension instead. Alan says that at the time he had become sufficiently savvy on pensions to take the view that this was one area where collectivism is better than individualism. It was much easier to plan a pension at the level of a company or industry than it was for each individual to be turned into a 'do-it-yourself pension consultant'. In effect, as Kevin LeGrand (then head of pensions policy at a large HR consultancy) later put it, 'No one at the time seemed to realise the average man in the street wasn't equipped to deal with the freedom in relation to … a pension scheme.'[20] Alan

20 'How the Thatcher Government changed occupational pensions in the 1980s' by Jonathan Stapleton in *Professional Pensions* magazine, April 2015.

himself said at the time that it was 'ironic that the only people available, if not able, to give definitive advice are those with a product to sell and with no obligation to disclose their remuneration from doing so'.[21] The apparent flexibility of the new system, with its ideology of freedom-of-choice, was to lead to a massive misselling scandal – a scandal that 'is estimated to have cost insurers and financial advisers £11.8 billion in compensation payments'.[22] Aggressive salesmen lured pension fund members away from good-quality workplace pensions, which undermined DB schemes and damaged the reputation of the financial services sector. In June 1988 Alan was invited to write in the staff magazine of United Engineering Steels (UES), which had a £180 million final salary pension scheme. He said with characteristic directness that 'Those who turn their back on the UES Scheme [by opting for a personal pension] could jeopardise their own and their family's future.' He went even further: 'such schemes are anything but "personal". They are off-the-peg packages sold by ... commission-hungry salesmen.'

The personal pensions scandal was not the only thing that changed the pensions climate at that time. In 1985 the government forced sponsors to inflation-proof pensions and in 1989 schemes were obliged to pay men a pension at the same (earlier) age as women. These were both admirable changes in themselves though they added liabilities which, combined with

21 'Pity the Poor Personnel Manager', *The Actuary* (R. Watson and Sons magazine), 1990.
22 Jonathan Stapleton, ibid.

other changes, were to be unhelpful to the schemes' overall financial health. The 1986 act also required pension schemes with a high funding ratio (ratio of assets to liabilities) to make taxable payments back to the fund's sponsor and to take contribution holidays. Whilst raising revenues for the Treasury, the taxation of scheme surpluses damaged the health of funds, which more prudently would have used the accumulated surpluses to insure against the risk of future asset losses or liability increases (both of which were later to happen). John Spellar looks back on those years with a politician's scorn: 'What the hell were the government actuaries doing getting it so wrong?'

The changes of the 1980s, which had increased the complexity of the world of pensions by increasing choice and removing some of the previous certainties, placed an extra burden on Alan Pickering in trying to protect the interests of the union's members and in its relationship with employers. Almost overnight, or so it seemed, the recently established and well-received basis of occupational pensions, with its link to the state pension and boosted by the facility to contract out of SERPS, was deemed to need radical change. The complexities of pensions were made more complicated by this politically motivated new initiative. Geoff Whitlow watched how Alan coped with this: 'Alan's technical work on pensions was the epitome of what the EETPU was about. He didn't wave placards – however much he may have disagreed with the changes. He set himself the task of understanding the detail of this new world of pensions better than any employer. He wanted to make sure that the trustees from the union were as well-informed as they could be.'

As we have seen, whilst the climate for trade unions in the 1980s became increasingly tempestuous, the EETPU was not deflected from its goal of being ever more members-focused – of creating an organisation that prospective members would select where they had a choice. At its most controversial, in 1985 and beyond, this included facilitating rather than obstructing (as some in other unions wished it to do) the move to, and modus operandi of, newspaper publisher Rupert Murdoch's News International at Wapping. This and other similar disputes were to lead to the union's expulsion from the TUC, and it meant that the climate within which Alan Pickering and his colleagues were working at Hayes Court was highly charged. Although it would be an exaggeration to say that under the new general secretary, Eric Hammond, there was a 'siege mentality' (Hammond was a self-confessed union rebel), these were certainly febrile times.

Alan's work at the EETPU and his wider involvement in pensions, both from his engagement with employers and his trustee work, led, in 1986, to his election to the council of the National Association of Pension Funds (NAPF). This was a signal that the wider realm of pensions was getting to know him and that he could operate out of the narrower sphere of the EETPU and the trade union movement. This was helped by Alan's now frequent contributions to pensions literature and attendance at conferences – often as a speaker. His speeches ranged across subjects and were often characteristically forthright. Speaking at a series of seminars arranged by the Prudential Group at the end of the 1980s,[23] Alan was both frank and prescient:

> Philosophically, this government has more in common with nineteenth-century liberalism than with its Tory predecessors. It sees big business as a distortion of the way the free market should operate. When it came to power, it thought personal finance was dominated by some monopoly suppliers who needed shaking up. If you look back to 1979, I think that what personal finance looked like then is very different to what we find today ... much of the legislation ... is based on the misconception that a pension plan is an investment. I don't think it is. It is an insurance, and should be seen as such.

At the same seminar Alan presented money purchase (defined contribution) pension schemes as 'a form of savings rather than a guaranteed form of protection', and forecast that future growth would occur 'in the personal pensions market rather than in the corporate sector'. He wasn't wrong.

Alan Pickering's dual role as the pensions guru/head of membership services at the EETPU – whilst increasingly being a 'go-to' man on pensions more generally – was becoming demanding in one particular respect: the need to read an enormous

23 *Pensions Schemes – the End of the Road*, Prudential Corporate Pensions, 1989.

amount of literature at a time when his eyesight had virtually gone. The union was sympathetic. The fact that Alan was becoming something of a public figure, often giving the trade union view at pensions conferences, reflected well on the EETPU and, importantly, showed that the unions, at a time when they were something of a bête noir in the public eye, not to mention for the Prime Minister, were not out of their depth on complex issues like pensions. Eric Hammond realised that the current random arrangement of readers to support Alan was not satisfactory, so he authorised the recruitment of an assistant for him. In April 1988 Jenny Davie took up the job. Jenny was an experienced secretarial worker who had both full-time and part-time experience under her belt. She and Alan hit it off almost immediately and an enduring, productive and unique working partnership began (twenty-nine years and counting at the time of writing). Jenny remembers her first impressions – not least how Alan could dictate a five-page letter or magazine article in impeccable style and grammar when the only references were in his head. She was in effect to become his amanuensis – a role which goes a long way beyond purely secretarial duties. Over the years Jenny was to accompany Alan on many of his trips to conferences and they also, crucially, developed a way of working under which she was effectively his eyes – especially, of course, for the study of complex and often voluminous pensions literature. Alan's prodigious memory combined with his determination and occasional stubbornness made him formidable, and at meetings and conferences it seemed to Jenny even in those early years together that Alan's disability was almost incidental, and did not get in the way of what he wanted to do.

In 1989 Jenny worked under Alan's supervision on the EETPU centenary charity, which, thanks to Frank Chapple's overall direction, was to raise and distribute £250,000 for disabled children who would benefit from electrical or electronic equipment. And she was soon also to provide support across a range of Alan's activities – from membership services and affinity products to his pensions trustee and pensions negotiations roles.

Under Eric Hammond the EETPU was perhaps moving in a less assured direction than it had under his predecessor. Lew Britz was not a fan of Hammond ('Hammond was wrong about almost everything') and there were some tensions which had not been present under Chapple. One of the more bizarre conflicts came in 1987, when Hammond commissioned Dave Rogers and John Lloyd to find a country property which, he said, could be run as a 'Robin Hood venture where the money earned from its weekday use as a conference centre is used to subsidise weekend and summer holidays for union members'.[24] Buxted Park in Sussex was bought from the Sheikh of Abu Dhabi for £6 million. This could be seen as an addition to the Membership Services offer, although the venture did not come directly under Alan Pickering's control – for which he may in retrospect be grateful.

24 John Lloyd, *Light & Liberty: The History of the EETPU* (London: Weidenfeld & Nicolson, 1990).

When the project ran into difficulties with cost overruns on necessary work Hammond asked that the modest EETPU pension fund (of which Alan was a trustee) be asked to help by the union taking a 'contributions holiday'. The £1 million this saved was diverted to shore up the failing project. At the time this was a mini scandal at Hayes Court, with factions developing and the abrasive Lew Britz often in full flight. Alan was, Britz says, totally loyal to Hammond, although he reflects that this was not one of the union's golden moments. (Buxted Park was later sold at a loss in 1994.)

The 1980s changed the trade union movement and the pensions industry dramatically and, as it turned out, largely irreversibly. In 1989 the EETPU commenced negotiations with the Amalgamated Engineering Union (AEU) about a possible merger. The AEU was about twice the size of the EETPU (but had lost a third of its members in the 1980s) and the merged union would be the second largest in the UK, with over a million members. The initial negotiations floundered, but three years later they succeeded and the new union – the Amalgamated Engineering and Electrical Union (AEEU) – was formed. It was this development which prompted Alan to think about his own future. At the age of forty-three he decided that a change of direction would be beneficial. He left in May 1992, he says, 'at the height of his marketability' – essentially feeling that he had a special combination of knowledge and practical experience that was sellable to the private sector in the world of pensions. He was right.

R. Watson & Sons, the world's oldest actuarial firm, made him an offer and said that he could create his own role at the firm. The boy from Lesley Avenue, York had come a long way – but the journey ahead was to be even more exciting and surprising than the one he had already undertaken.

## CHAPTER 4

# A SPORTING LIFE

*Being physically fit would give me the confidence to deal with whatever life threw at me.*

York, the city of Alan Pickering's birth, has a long sporting tradition. As we shall see in Chapter 9, York Races are perhaps the most famous of its sporting institutions, stretching back more than 300 years. Early exposure to York racecourse as a child was to be the foundation of Alan's love of the sport. But the city of his childhood also had football (York City) and rugby league (York) teams – both of rather a moderate standard – and had produced a number of notable swimmers. Alan's first attendance at a professional sports event was watching York City Reserves against Whitby Town in the North Riding Cup at the age of eight – his parents were later to allow him to brave the challenge of the 10,000-plus crowds of the first team matches.

He also enjoyed rugby league, though his gentle father thought that the game was rather too violent and stayed away. Cricket was the happy summer attraction, with Scarborough, just forty miles away, hosting two or three first-class games towards the end of the season. It was a six-hitter's paradise and young Alan sat in the front of the pavilion as Fred Trueman would try to land sixes in his mother-in-law's backyard close to the ground. Leeds, the home of Yorkshire County Cricket Club, was even closer – less than an hour away on the bus – and Alan became a junior member in time to see them win their first county championship for ten years in 1959, with a team that had a few of English cricket's great post-war legends in it – including Ray Illingworth, Brian Close and Trueman.

The family supported young Alan's growing love of things sporting. His father, as we have seen, was a fine cricketer, and his mother had been a decent tennis player in her youth. Alan wanted to be sportingly active from an early age, but the twin handicaps of nervous asthma and weak eyesight limited him, forcing him to be selective in what he did. He knew that to be fit would help his asthma as well as give him the self-confidence to deal with his eyesight problems. Team sports were always going to be difficult, so as a child cricket and football were confined to invented games in the street. He played cricket by himself and made up a scoring system – six if the ball cleared the neighbours' hedge, for example. Mr Ford, the neighbour, who was a painter and decorator, painted Alan's brown leather football white so that he could see it more easily, but his worsening tunnel vision meant that he could only play a kick-about game with one other person. His parents encouraged him, bowling to him in the garden in the summer and kicking a ball with him in the winter months. Fulford Open Air School was a mile and a half away, so there was three miles of walking for his fitness every day. When the family had a holiday away from home for the first time in the late 1950s (on a caravan site in Dawlish, Devon), Alan relished walking along the coast. 'The lad is a good walker,' commented another holidaymaker – quite presciently as it turned out. Back home, and aged five, he started cycling on a three-wheeler, graduating via a second-hand two-wheeler to, at the age of twelve, his brand-new green Raleigh. He also swam – something that can be intimidating for someone with poor eyesight – but says that he was 'a bit too rigid' for swimming ever to be a sport of choice.

At the age of eleven Alan transferred to board at the special school Exhall Grange in Coventry. This had good sports facilities, including a gymnasium and football pitches. By now Alan's sight was such that he could only kick a ball around on his own or one-to-one with another boy. There was a spectrum of disability at the school and Alan was at the more restricted end of this in respect of eyesight. He looked for alternatives to the team games and found it in the gym, where he started weight training, helped by the teacher Mr Jones, who guided him to help build up his technique and strength. Alan was, he says, 'competitive against myself' – an early indication that in sport as well as in life he wasn't going to let his failing sight hamper him if he could. He even bought a set of chest expanders – he wasn't going to have the sand kicked in his face on the beach. With weight training he was the school's star pupil, and won a trophy for being the best in the club. The school had good athletics as well as the gym – including cross-country running, which, at fifteen, Alan also took up despite the limitations of his sight and asthma problems. He trained for the race by running a figure-of-eight course around lampposts at night. The hazards of this manifested themselves when he ran into a lamppost one evening and had to receive treatment in casualty at Coventry Hospital. To finish a very tired twenty-fourth out of one hundred competitors, despite his handicaps, was an achievement of which he was proud – not least because he surprised a few doubtful teachers and fellow pupils.

After his school years Alan Pickering was to maintain a fitness regime that lasts to this day. When working at the railways, during his dinner hour he used the gym facilities at the Railway Institute which was nearby his workplace – augmented by a couple of pints of Tartan Bitter to avoid dehydration. He continued with his weight training and also took to running before work. Later, at university, he started circuit training – working out on every weekday. He says his goal was to avoid being seen as a 'soft-bellied' intellectual and to be at least as fit as the rugby players with whom he shared a house. He did not do any competitive sport at university, but he was clearly building a basis of personal fitness, and a fitness regime, that would work for him in the years to come.

On Easter Monday 1972 Alan had his first competitive road walk. The Fulford Working Men's Club (WMC), which Alan had joined, had a tradition of road walking – as did many such clubs in the north, and, as we have seen, he had started to participate with his friend Max Coates riding alongside him on a bicycle and helping keep him on a straight path. But the Easter Monday event was competitive, and rules and a handicap system applied. One of these was that a new competitor – an unknown quantity – had to start last (a place usually reserved for the fastest walker). In his first race Alan was the fastest on the day and overhauled all but two of his fellow competitors. There is a special technique for competitive walking that Alan took to immediately. If your vison is impaired it is safer than running, and the need to ground the heel rather than the toes first is also helpful for those with eyesight problems. Max Coates was permitted to ride alongside Alan and to guide him, but not to 'pace' him, and over the next two years Alan (who by now had moved south) continued to return for the club's bank holiday events. The club was always helpful to him, recognising his special needs, and he became one of their star performers.

At his new home and place of work in Bromley, Alan Pickering decided to look for a club at which he could continue his walking and perhaps broaden his athletics involvement. Just down the road from his place of work at the EETPU in Hayes is the home of what was then the Blackheath Harriers Athletic Club. One day in 1974 Alan turned up at the club's premises and met the then membership secretary, Mike Peel, and shortly afterwards he joined the club. One of the attractions was that the Blackheath Harriers had an association with the Surrey Walking Club, which effectively meant that the club was the Harriers' 'Walking Club' section. Both Blackheath Harriers and the Surrey Walking Club were longstanding clubs in the area – stretching back in both cases to the nineteenth century. Indeed, both were leaders in British athletics as the sport changed and events became more structured and subject to standards and rules. Both clubs produced Olympians – among them 1964 medal-winning walker Paul Nihill and the great mile runner Sydney Wooderson. Alan's membership of the clubs, and participation in their events, was not without a rather typically English minor controversy. Blackheath Harriers was part of the athletics establishment headed by the Amateur Athletic Association (the 'three As'). The racewalking that Alan had done in Yorkshire had not been in events under AAA jurisdiction. This was because some of the WMC event participants had received money for taking part in other sports (mainly rugby league) and this, at the time, disqualified the races from being official AAA events. So, absurd though it now seems, Alan's personal amateur status could have been under threat if he had continued to take part in such non-AAA events in the north.

Notwithstanding its establishment character, Mike Peel recalls that around the time that he and Alan Pickering joined

Blackheath Harriers, the sport of athletics was changing in that the dominance of university-educated athletes (often from public schools) was giving way to a more balanced social mix. Mike Cronin, a long-established Blackheath member and talented cross-country and long-distance runner, recalls Alan's early time at the club and how he would guide him in training. This was to be the foundation of a lifelong friendship which continues to this day. Dicky Green, a Surrey Walking Club member, suggested that in races Alan followed his black-and-white shirt, which also worked well. Throughout that time, and subsequently, Alan was not a 'blind athlete' but an 'athlete who was blind' – a crucial distinction. His only participation in 'blind' events was to come in the mid-1980s, when he joined the Metropolitan Sports Club for the Blind,[25] which arranged cross-country skiing ('Langlaufen') events in Norway in which he participated twice. In 1976 Alan decided that he would try to become a 'Centurion' – the ultimate achievement for a race walker, giving membership of the Brotherhood of Centurions, a club for those who have completed a distance of 100 miles within twenty-four hours. He succeeded – becoming the 579th British Centurion after having completed the necessary 403 laps at Woodford Athletics track in 22 hours, 1 minute and 35 seconds. He had followed a white line on the track and refreshed himself with Rowntree's jellies, carrots and peanuts. His parents were there to cheer him

25 Now 'Metro Blind Sport' – a charity established in 1973 which aims 'to open doors to sport for all vision impaired people, regardless of age or sporting ability'.

on. Charity walks, including the 38-mile Hastings-to-Brighton event, were to follow, with money being raised for kidney charities in memory of his father.

Mike Cronin says that the mental side of training and running (or walking) is just as important as the obvious need for physical fitness. You need to be mentally tough, and it is in this area that Alan Pickering has a particular strength. Along with this fortitude is a resolve to succeed but also a similar determination not to be a burden. It was concerns in this area that led Alan to not renew his membership of Blackheath Harriers in 1981, despite his having had 'two active years of Kent League involvement' for the club. In his resignation letter he said that he would 'still be keeping fit at the Palace',[26] and that he had 'taken up cycling on a tandem'. This resignation was similar to the one offered to the EETPU (see Chapter 3) in that, deep down, it was driven by his wish not to let his disability be something that others would have to cope with. In fact, as at the union, the help that Alan was given by friends like Mike Cronin and Mike Peel and many others was given willingly, and both say that they were as much beneficiaries of the arrangements as Alan was, both in respect of the friendships and the satisfaction that came from helping. Alan re-joined the club within two years, had his wedding reception at the clubhouse in 1982, and has been a member ever since, and was club president in 1992/93.

26 Crystal Palace Sports Centre, which was near Alan's home in Anerley.

On 29 March 1981 just over 7,000 participants took part in the first ever London marathon. Among them was Mike Peel, who was one of some thirty Blackheath Harriers taking part. He ran the race again in 1982 and 1983 (when thirty-nine Blackheath Harriers members participated) and finished in under three hours. In making plans for his fourth London marathon in 1984, Peel suggested to Alan that he take part, and offered to help him prepare and to run with him. By this time Alan had perfected the art of running long distance with a partner. They would be held together by a six-inch length of red cord which Peel had made and which was quite loosely placed over his right wrist and Alan's left. Could this be maintained for twenty-six miles? There seemed to be no reason why not, but fitness would be critical. Alan and Mike worked out a preparation programme which included track and road work and taking part in a ten-mile road race and a half-marathon. On the day of the London marathon, 13 May 1984, they joined some 20,000 other runners with the aim of finishing the course in around four hours. (On his own, Peel was among the best of the club athlete participants – certainly in his age group – having run it in 2 hours 40 minutes in 1981 at the age of forty. So running in tandem would take some eighty minutes off his best time.) The challenge was guiding Alan through a huge number of competitors – some of whom would stop dead in their tracks without warning. As they ran Peel gave Alan a running commentary with directional instructions and encouragement. It was, of course, a tough race, and it was not without its wobbles along the way. John Bryant, in his definitive book, *The London Marathon*, describes the physiological stresses of a marathon: 'sometimes, however determined a runner might be, the body can take it no more, and giving up is the only option'. This happens usually around the eighteenth mile, where runners often 'hit the wall' – a 'physiological and mental breaking point that lurks around every corner after the eighteen-mile mark … every yard beyond the wall is a fight between courage and collapse'. But Alan and Mike did not collapse, and the official photograph shows the pair of them, Mike Peel competitor number B767 and Alan Pickering number 8135, finishing in 4 hours, 15 minutes and 35 seconds. This was a 'gun to tape' time, and if you take off the time spent at the start after the gun had gone off, but before the crowds spread out and running could commence, the actual time was around ten minutes over their four-hour goal. No doubt, as Bryant puts it, they reached 'the finish high on a wave of excitement and adrenalin, their agony dulled by endorphins, the chemicals released by the brain to deaden pain'. Alan, like many of the competitors, ran to raise money for a charity – in his case, one which helped handicapped children. He says that as he fought the pain the image of one handicapped girl, Chantelle, whom the charity had helped, was in his mind and spurred him on.

Marathon running is a strange obsession – a sport which for the vast majority of those running is about taking part and not about winning. Indeed, the result that all but the elite athletes seek is to finish. Alan Pickering was to run two more London marathons – one with his friend and training partner, fellow Blackheath Harrier Mike Cronin, and the other with Colin Poole – another Blackheath athlete. They also competed in the even more gruelling 'Seven Sisters' marathon, which passes through undulating terrain in the South Downs and includes fourteen gates along the way – and fifteen consecutive Hastings half-marathons. Cronin, who is six years Alan's senior, says that for both of them it is certainly addictive, but that the real key to their long athletics association is that it is an important part of their personal friendship. He says that athletics – especially long distance like marathon running – is very revealing of personality and character. Alan Pickering is, he says, a 'tough individual' who listens to his running partner (as he has to) but keeps his own counsel. His loyalty is such that he virtually never discusses individuals, and if he disagrees with something, he is subtle in how he handles it. The basis of this enduring friendship has been sustained with twice-weekly fitness/training runs and by the mutual support they have given each other – in athletics and in life – for thirty years or more. It was marked when Cronin was invited to be one of Alan's three guests to witness his CBE presentation in Buckingham Palace in January 2003.

Alan Pickering ran further marathons in New York in 1994 and Boston in 1997 – the former with Hilary Newton, who was the postwoman in the village of Wadhurst, where she worked for the charity Talking Newspapers. Boston, the oldest marathon of all, normally has stringent entry rules but these were relaxed for their centenary event in 1997, allowing Alan, by now nearly fifty, to take part, running again with Colin Poole. The 'riding on a tandem' that Alan had referred to in his letter to Blackheath Harriers in 1981 had been the beginning of a long association with Brian Skelton – for nineteen years they went cycling around the hills and dales of west Kent and they rode in five London-to-Brighton cycle races (on three occasions cycling there and back). They only gave up not when they once hit a cow but when, much later, the tandem frame broke. Alan is keen to stress that he didn't give up the tandem cycling – it was the bike that threw in the towel.

Both Mike Peel and Mike Cronin recall that Alan Pickering was a very good and popular president of their club back in 1992/93, attending all the events and using his knowledge of business and finance to good effect in the club's interest. More than twenty years on Blackheath & Bromley Harriers have called upon Alan again as they change their structure to one with charitable status and trustees – he became chairman of the new trustee board in March 2017 and is leading some significant changes at the club, including a move to a new location and the creation of improved facilities at Norman Park Athletics Track on the Hayes/Bromley Road.

Alan Pickering's active participation in sport and his personal commitment over three decades to a training regime that allows him to compete at a good level have been key elements in the development of his character. He has always enjoyed physical effort – from sawing wood and working as a labourer at York racecourse as a young man to gardening and working on his allotment in later life. And, of course, in his structured approach to fitness in the gym and on the training track. As in other walks of life, he has achieved a great deal – but he is keen to stress how much he has owed to others. His parents were always encouraging, as have been his wife Christine and his long-standing business partner Jenny Davie. But in his sporting life, the friends who walked or ran or cycled with him, helping him to overcome his physical handicap both practically and emotionally, were the most important of all. Alan says that he likes to compartmentalise his life, and you sense that his sporting life has rarely interfered with his business life – or vice-versa. The achievements in both worlds (and, as we shall see, in the world of horse racing) stand largely on their own – based on positive thinking, listening to others, and plenty of practice and training. But the determination to succeed, and the acceptance that the attainment of that success will only happen if there is some surrendering of his natural (and often stubborn) bias towards independence, has been crucial. In his sporting life there has been no giving up of a dominant self-confidence and a strong sense of self-belief – but Alan readily admits that he would not have achieved anything without the help and encouragement always so willingly given by others.

## CHAPTER 5

# LIVING WITH DISABILITY

*There are a million things we can achieve. Having an impairment might reduce them down to 500,000.*

John Humphrys was in a characteristically belligerent mood. Alan Pickering had recently been appointed as chairman of the National Association of Pension Funds – one of the small number of really top jobs in the world of occupational pensions in Britain. It was in May 1999, at his first big conference as chairman. 'How can someone with a disability like yours – who is totally blind – chair an association like this?' This was what Humphrys had been hired to do: ask the difficult question. 'Well, John,' says Alan, 'I don't see myself as having a disability. Blindness is a characteristic – like being tall or having blonde hair – I don't have a chip on my shoulder about it and I'm sure that nobody else will have either.' Cue applause.

Alan was of course being a tad disingenuous. Nearly two million people in the UK live with sight loss that has a significant impact on their daily lives – and only a third of them are in regular employment. For every Ian Fraser[27] or David Blunkett[28] or Alan Pickering, there are a thousand blind people whose horizons have been limited by their disability, whose independence has been restricted and whose opportunity to achieve has been inhibited. But from the moment that it was clear that something was wrong when Alan was about three years old, neither he nor the three women who have helped him achieve – his mother, Betty, his wife, Christine, and his work helpmate and friend, Jenny Davie – have let weak sight, which became blindness, restrict him any more than it needed to. And, remarkably, that has not been very much. As Alan puts it, 'A disability might reduce the things you can achieve by half – but that still leaves quite a lot. But you have to push yourself. I would not wish ever to have had to apologise for under-achievement – or to have had to make excuses.'

As we have seen, the cause of Alan Pickering's blindness is a degenerative condition known as retinitis pigmentosa (RP).[29]

27 Ian Fraser, Baron Fraser of Lonsdale, (1897–1974) was a British politician, a governor of the BBC and a successful businessman despite having been blinded in the First World War. He also became chairman of St Dunstan's, a charity for blind servicemen.

28 David Blunkett, Lord Blunkett, (born 1947) is a British politician who has been blind since birth, and who became Education and Employment Secretary, Home Secretary and Work and Pensions Secretary in the Labour governments of 1997–2005.

29 It is estimated that around 1.5 million people worldwide suffer from retinitis pigmentosa, for which there is no known cure.

The Canadian writer Ryan Knighton (another sufferer) describes it in his book, *Cockeyed: A Memoir*:

> Because of a gene mutation, one I was born with, my retina had begun to scar itself and decay. Little holes were developing in my vision and had been developing for some time. Soon they would expand like blurry pools, band together, and narrow me into the slightest tunnel of sight. Later … that last silver of functional retina would eclipse too [and] I would be legally blind within a few years.

Betty Pickering did not tell her son about the diagnosis and he did not know of it fully until informed by a local hospital (later confirmed by Moorfields Eye Hospital) in the 1970s when he was in his twenties. Betty Pickering was, as Alan puts it, a 'flinty' person who knew that for him to succeed he must only surrender any of his independence after a struggle and not set his sights too low just because to achieve would be more difficult as a result of his disability. From the start she made him do everything a child with normal sight would do. He tied his own shoelaces, walked on his own to and from school, went out in the dark when he could see very little at all. Night blindness is the first stage of the retinal deterioration of RP and it indicates the certain onset of the deterioration of the retina and the erosion of peripheral vision. Whether Betty knew this completely is unclear – she was certainly not going to settle for it, and nor would she let Alan.

Betty believed that he must not 'drop out of the race' and that he should be as independent as possible – even if that brought dangers for a stumbling small boy, especially at night. Alan could see lights but not what they illuminated – it was a precursor of what was to be his daytime life without sight twenty years later, though at the time, of course, he did not know that. For Betty, independence was the norm, and her coping mechanisms were self-generated – there was no counselling available in the early 1950s, no 'special needs' help. And there was family pride and honour to uphold as well. His first school was Fulford Open Air School, but this was situated close to what was in those less politically correct times called a 'backward school' – young Alan had his problems, but he was certainly not backward, and Betty made sure the neighbours knew it. When the children in the street mocked Alan about his weak sight – 'You'll be blind when you're sixteen' – she gave as good as she received: 'It's rubbish. Don't listen. You'll not go blind.' There was an element of denial in this, of course, and Betty never really came to terms with the progressive deterioration in his eyesight and was never to be totally honest with him about the prognosis. It was almost as if accepting the reality would have meant giving in to it.

The teachers at Fulford School knew that in Alan they had a pupil who would soon outgrow what they were able to teach and that being in a class for those with sight problems and of mixed age (five to fifteen) and ability was not going to help him. Betty Pickering, understanding that education was the best ticket for independence and achievement, was to be the main driving force through his school years. She reluctantly agreed with the teachers that a move away from home to Exhall Grange in Coventry would be beneficial – this was to be the essential foundation for his later studies at Newcastle University. Betty was not sure that, having established himself in his (pensionable) job at British Railways (and having started to take an interest in politics and the trade union movement), he should give this up for further education. But she helped him by reading to him during his university years and when he achieved his degree she was proud that her son was the first in either her or her husband's family ever to do this – and she was also fully to support his move south to take up the EETPU job. Few concessions had been made to his disability at school or university, and the fact that he attended educational establishments which were not confined to, or especially designed for, blind children, and that his mother pushed him to be as normal as possible, set the foundation for Alan's attitude for the future. There was, as we have seen, one phrase which Betty would never use, and which was banned in his company – that was 'Poor Alan'. No such defeatism or self-pity was ever allowed. There was nothing he could do about his fading eyesight, but he would nevertheless strive to be as independent as he could be at all times. And this drivingly independent young man was to aspire to achieve at the highest level – with no excuses along the way. He says today that at first he felt that if he was on a journey it was easier on his own, and this led him consciously to reject help and group activities. At university he was the first in the canteen for lunch to avoid the crowds – a small piece of coping that was both about avoiding having to rely on others and about not putting himself too much in a situation where his handicap would be a hindrance to himself, or to others. But, with age, he has become more self-confident, which, somewhat paradoxically, has meant a greater willingness to work with others and to accept help which as a young man he might have rejected.

Ryan Knighton has written that 'Taking up a white cane is perhaps the most dispiriting thing a newly blinded person goes through … it is a form of confession and defeat … A cane is a permanent commitment to blindness, more final than a diagnosis, even.' So when, in 1978, Alan Pickering started to use a white cane for the first time at the age of nearly thirty, it was more than just a mobility aid – it was a symbol of the reality of his condition. He had, he now admits, been stubborn in not taking up the white cane earlier. His default response had hitherto always been not to accept help so as not to be reminded, or to have to admit, that he was different. The white cane was to change that. It was a symbol that he was indeed different and signified that help might be welcomed – a tough but crucial change in his approach. So, after a few 'arguments with lampposts', he had crossed this threshold and thought that if he was going to do it, he'd better do it properly. Bromley Council provided training in the use of a white cane and Alan was allocated to a Mrs Kirby, who taught him the art. A cane was selected – roughly chest-high in length

– and Alan was shown how it collapsed into four segments when necessary, and that it could be reassembled with a flick of the handle. He was taught to step forward with his left foot and to sweep the cane from left to right – the trick was not to drag the cane but to lift it and to sweep. The sweeping picked up obstacles and stopped you from walking into them. Over about seven lessons spread over four weeks Alan gradually became proficient in the white cane art. The cane is, as John Hull puts it in *Notes on Blindness*, 'an extension of [the blind person's] perception … of the world … [a perception that] is confined to the reach of his body and to any extension of it … such as a cane'. Alan would learn to trust his cane, how to use it on staircases and steps (with a different approach necessary for going up and coming down). These are the practical techniques that make a white cane such an invaluable aid. Mrs Kirby's help also extended to some very useful advice. He was instructed to treat every street, however familiar, as if he was walking down it for the first time. The most dangerous thing is often the most familiar – walking to the station in the morning along a route he has done a thousand times. Something might have changed overnight and it is hazardous to assume it hasn't. You must always concentrate. Because you need to swing your cane from side to side, you must always walk down the middle of every path (not down the side) without tapping along the wall, and always count the number of steps on routes. And, of course, always use the white cane to navigate. The more subtle changes which come from using a white cane are to do with the reactions of others. On a train, for example, with his cane in his briefcase Alan is not really identifiable as anything other than another commuter – one who prefers to listen through headphones to a tape than read a book. But on the street or the station platform, with cane in hand he is the blind man who might need help. At first this was difficult, and Alan admits that it took years before he came to terms with the reality of the benefits that accepting help from others would bring. And he never discussed his use of a white cane with his mother. There was, from his youngest years, a determination on the part of his mother to see Alan as normal as possible. To discuss the use of the white cane would have jeopardised this, so there was an unspoken agreement that they wouldn't mention it.

Today Alan has long since become used to people offering to help. These casual and random offers to assist come mostly when Alan is travelling – either during his commute to his office in the City or on his frequent trips around Britain and overseas. They come from a wide variety of people and there is no pattern to it. In London the population is diverse, and Alan relishes the fact that people from all over the world and from all walks of life might help him across the street or up the steps at the tube. Once, a man in a pinstripe suit and a bowler hat even guided him from Mansion House station down Garlick Hill. This has become so much part of his life that he has realised that he often accepts help even when he doesn't really need it. This is, he says, so that the helper is encouraged to help the next person who might need it rather more than he does. Alan, of course, doesn't see those who cross to the other side of the road or turn away, though occasionally there will be an inadvertent brush with someone who often hasn't seen him. One day he accidently bumped into a woman in a hurry at Waterloo station. In fluent Surrey, she told him that he should 'Look where you're going', to which he responded, sotto voce, 'If only I could.' The lady was not to know that years later she would give this book its title! The late astronomer Patrick Moore once offered him help and went a mile out of his way to guide him. Alan recognised his voice but Moore didn't introduce himself – just offered a welcome arm. Alan says that he often hears a good story in the five minutes or so that his anonymous helper walks with him and that it is only very occasionally that they panic and leave him stranded in the middle of the road. Although Alan is very well known in his specialist world he is not sufficiently in the public eye to be recognised; the help he gets is sincere, and does not come from someone looking for five minutes of fame with a celebrity. So help that was consciously rejected forty years ago is now openly welcomed – not least because it is never sought. Alan can hardly ask people for help if he can't see them. But if they offer help he might say, 'Can I borrow your elbow?', as he has found that this is the easiest way for him and the helper to move forwards. The worst thing is when he feels someone 'shadowing' him – following behind in case he shows he obviously needs help – by banging into a lamppost presumably. In such circumstances Alan thinks to himself, 'Either clear off, or come and help me.'

David Blunkett famously had a series of guide dogs, and his story is in no small part their story as well as his. But having a guide dog is far from universal among blind people, and Alan Pickering has never considered it. He would agree with Ryan Knighton, who feels similarly on the subject: 'It's one thing to commit to a stick and another to cling to a muddy sidekick named Wally. A dog even eliminates one liberty. To a degree you can hide blindness, selectively show and conceal your white cane, but you can't hide a golden retriever.' Alan says that as a child, although they had cats and other pets, they had never had dogs – they were not a 'doggy family'. Interestingly, Bromley Council never suggested it when he sought mobility help and, he says, his business lifestyle – the itinerant nature of his work and his extensive travel – would have made it difficult. Like Knighton, he says that whilst he can fold up his white cane and put it away, a dog would have been a very visible badge signalling his disability. To have had a dog might have widened his range of friends (many people like dogs, even if they don't like their owners), but dogs need looking after and he is happy he stuck with just his white cane.

Negotiating your way around a city like London is often a challenge for the sighted, but imagine what it must be like if there are no visual clues to guide you. Surprisingly, Alan found it much easier than he had expected. The trains, the Underground and the buses all have announcements indicating the destination of the train and each station as it arrives; a real boon to the blind or partially sighted. And stations are also easier to navigate – most have tactile paving along the edge of platforms to help the blind find their way. But accidents can happen. In 2014 rebuilding work was underway at Embankment station and this disoriented Alan and he fell onto the track. He swiftly levered himself back onto the platform and when a lady asked if he needed help, he took out a clothes brush from his briefcase and asked her to brush him down. (He was on his way to a committee meeting of the British Horseracing Authority, and they don't do scruffy.) A couple of weeks later, a woman, thinking she was being helpful, grabbed his arm and he fell between the train and the track at Charing Cross. His white stick was bent and he had to get a taxi to the RNIB to buy another one.

Whilst this kind of help is unpredictable (but nearly always welcome), the ongoing and permanent support that comes from having a sighted partner is at another level. As Ryan Knighton puts it, 'A blind person and a sighted person can come to an intimacy few are given. Imagine you only see the world through the eyes and the words of another … [one who] sees for me the way I would have wanted to'. Alan had, and has, two such partners. His wife, Christine, covers the 'home front' – she says that the crucial moment for Alan in respect of his disability came when he 'stood up and admitted that he had a problem and that he needed help'. It was, she says, only really then that he moved away from a dogged independence to an acceptance that she and others could help, and that they wanted to. Thirty-five years on, the couple have long since settled into a way of life within which Christine has made room not only for the fact of Alan's blindness, but also for his fierce independence and the fact that he is a successful (and busy) man at the top of his profession. Gradually, says Christine, Alan's philosophy emerged: 'if you have a problem and there's a cure for it, then sort it. If there isn't a solution, then move on and don't go on about it.' She says that she is on her own a lot – she doesn't mind her own company – but that they enjoy a lot of quality time together as well. There is still, all these years on, an engaging pride (even awe) when Christine talks about how she sees Alan not letting his disability get in his way. At the everyday level she makes sure that Alan 'looks right' when he leaves the house (matching socks and a well-tied tie). She admires his astonishing self-confidence and his computer-like memory. He remembers phone numbers from years back, can memorise a map before a journey despite not being able to see it. She is clearly proud that his personality, though forthright at times, is such that they never row. This is not a conventional marriage, but one in which the various roles are prescribed and long-since established. But, put simply, it works.

Alan Pickering's relationship with his business colleague (and 'best friend'), Jenny Davie, stretches back to 1988 at the EETPU. She has since moved with him to Watson's and now BESTrustees. The partnership is a close one, which, as with his marriage, has clearly defined roles. It certainly goes beyond that of Jenny 'just' being Alan's eyes in his professional life (although that is of course her primary duty). That it is supremely effective is illustrated by the fact that his employers after the EETPU happily employed them both as a team – a rarity for employers today, but the benefits of this arrangement clearly exceed the costs.

Jenny accompanies Alan to meetings that he attends and chairs. She prepares him so that he can memorise the agenda and recognise the attendees even though he cannot see them. He can sense people's moods even though he can't see visual clues – a shuffle in the seat will often reveal somebody's wish to say something, and there is a bit of sixth sense about the fact that Alan often spots this. When Alan speaks in public at conferences Jenny will help him prepare by speaking to him from the corners of the room so he can scope the surroundings in his mind. She will also tell him where people are sitting so that he can turn to them as he speaks. At a drinks reception she will help him 'work the room' – tell him who he might want to talk to and who it is better to ignore. They have what Alan calls an 'uncanny empathy', and the relationship is multidimensional. Jenny is quietly spoken, quite reserved, fiercely intelligent and kind. She says that in the past people who didn't know Alan might have seen him as being a bit rude – though they will certainly think he has mellowed today. On his way up the often greasy pole Alan may well have had to fight – though he is never over-competitive. His wins are intellectual and attributable to what he believes to be right, not to his being able to shout the loudest.

When a sense as crucial as sight is missing something has to compensate. It is a bit of a myth that there is some physiological compensation taking place which heightens the other senses. What happens is that if you lose your sight the brain allocates a task to other senses which it would previously have given to sight. Ryan Knighton uses the example of 'recognising people' – you have to use smell (the perfume they wear) or their voice, where previously you would have recognised them from their appearance. The neurologist Oliver Sachs writes in his Foreword to John M. Hull's *Touching the Rock*, 'As vision, and inner vision, disappear other modes of perception become more intense and important, most especially those of hearing and touch.' Alan says that he will hear announcements ahead of sighted people not because his hearing is better, but because he is more disciplined in the use of his senses. He can hear audible messages well ('You hear things because you have to') and his memory and brain help him process them. He is also very methodical and analytical in responding to the stimuli picked up by the senses he does have. That discipline is often remarked upon – 'There are people who think I was born in an East German engineering factory,' he says.

Most of us are profoundly ignorant of what it must be like to be blind. So, for example, Alan has often heard the comment: 'It must be better never to have seen than to have lost your sight.' The reverse, he says, is true. Although Alan's sight was never good – he was, he says, never able to see faces clearly, so he does not have, like John Hull, two groups of people he knows: 'those with faces, and those without faces'. But he does have clear memories of colour and size and of places, which help him visualise things in a way that somebody who was blind from birth would not be able to do. If he is told that someone is wearing a red dress he knows what red is, and if something is 'higher than a London bus' he knows what that means. If he goes to a cricket match he can visualise the ground and the players in his mind. If he 'watches' a football match or a horse race on television he visualises the action from the commentary (though he 'sees' it in black and white). It is arguably true that the most important thing about Alan's life is not that he lost his sight in his twenties, but that up until then he had had it, albeit imperfectly. When a sighted person meets somebody new, most, if not all of their initial impressions are from the appearance of the individual. This is not something you can unlearn, however much you might want to. For Alan, this does not apply. Another frequent question is: 'If you had all your senses and you had to give up one, which would it be?' Here Alan unequivocally chooses to give up his sight – 'It's a very lonely world if you can't hear,' he says. 'A blind person can interact with other people in a way that is more difficult for a deaf person.' Touch is important – to navigate with a white cane or to tell the time on his tactile watch and a thousand other things. Some blind people like to touch someone's face to try and understand what they look like. Alan does not do this and wouldn't want to. He will sometimes ask a sighted companion about people he meets: 'Is he tidy?' – a rather Yorkshire-sounding question which Alan says is not judgemental. Though he admits that if the answer is 'He's wearing shorts', he may be disillusioned ('People in York never wore shorts').

At the time that Alan started work, first with the railways and then later at the EETPU, the stereotype of 'jobs that blind people could do' was prevalent – as, of course, was the reverse: jobs that blind people could *not* do. Alan had been told unequivocally that his prospects were limited at British Railways because of his disability. And when Frank Chapple told him that he would always have a job at the union, the unspoken meaning here was that, if all else failed, he would have a 'blind person's job' as a telephonist or similar. Well, as we have seen, Alan succeeded at many tasks which might not traditionally have been viewed as being possible for someone with a sight handicap, but once he undertook them, that prejudice disappeared. He wasn't the first blind marathon runner – but he was one of the first. When he says that he 'wasn't going to let blindness stand in his way', he of course does not mean that he could do everything that a sighted person could do. The point is that whilst blindness narrows his options, it far from removes them entirely. As Alan puts it, he was naturally blessed with a good brain and memory – and a good mouth, which, combined with a white cane, a tactile watch, a high degree of determination and helpful partners, allowed him to compete with the best. Although he learned Braille as a child, he has not used it as an adult, and prefers to 'read' from recorded audio sources – or to be read to. He prefers to dictate either to a voice recorder or directly to a secretary rather than using an adapted typewriter or keyboard.

The advances in the treatment of blind people in modern times have been considerable – as have their opportunities. But the fact remains that the Alan Pickerings and the David Blunketts are among the few exceptions at the top of business and politics. They can be role models, and Alan, who clearly sets a good example, has very proactively worked for blind charities and other support organisations. He tells a story about how, in his early forties, he was asked by a local church to speak at a holiday they were arranging for blind people. This he did, but, characteristically, he took the position that it was better to accept the challenge of being a blind person in the real world rather than narrowing his horizons to a world only inhabited by those with visual impairment. So he talked about his work, about marathon running, about cross-country skiing and so on. He has generously given his time to help the Talking Newspapers and Calibre charities, which provide audio versions of books, newspapers and magazines. For forty years, Talking Newspapers & Magazines has provided audio renditions of more than 200 publications, and Alan has been an avid consumer. In 2007 he said that these included business magazines like *The Economist* and the *Investors Chronicle*, as well as the *Sporting Life Weekender*, which was one of the gateways to his growing interest in the world of horse racing. 'Talking Newspapers gave me the independence to read what I wanted when I wanted,'[30] he said. Alan supported the charity in a number of ways, including a sponsored walk around Goodwood Racecourse in May 2007. But, in the main, Alan does not (as he puts it) 'do blind' – though he has been interviewed a couple of times on the BBC radio programme *In Touch* by presenter Peter White – coincidentally an old acquaintance from York. On the whole, however, Alan is not involved with charities or other activities which are specifically focused on the needs of the blind or partially sighted.

The BBC once had a sister programme to *In Touch* for people with wider disabilities: *Does He Take Sugar* – a clever title referring to the phenomenon that people often assume that an individual with a disability is unable to interact normally. John Hull describes this: 'I went out with my elder daughter for lunch ... The waiters would not address any remark to me. Everything was said to Imogen.' Alan Pickering has also experienced this but says that he has long since ceased to take offence. He has mellowed in other ways as well, and doesn't view accepting help as a sign of failure. So when he returns to the beach from the sea and can't find where he left his towel, he'll ask for help. Similarly, the need for cooperation is long since inculcated into his way of working and in his recreation. At work he and Jenny have established a partnership, and on the allotment and in the garden he has his tasks and so does Christine – and they complement

30 Talking Newspapers publications catalogue, 2007.

one another. The great poet John Milton, who was completely blind by the time he was in his fifties, wrote, 'To be blind is not miserable; not to be able to bear blindness, that is miserable.' Bearing an affliction manfully is one thing – but to find a way around it and succeed is something else. As we have seen, Alan Pickering describes the task as maintaining the right balance between independence and achievement – in essence, to retain independence where possible, but to be prepared to surrender some of it if necessary. It's a pragmatic trade-off. To be successful you need to independently pursue your goals. But if you try to do it alone – especially if you have a severe handicap – it will be counter-productive. As that other great poet, John Donne, put it:

> No man is an island,
> Entire of itself;
> Every man is a piece of the continent,
> A part of the main.

## CHAPTER 6

# PENSIONS AUTHORITY

*No longer can people argue that pensions and politics do not mix.*

In May 2017 Alan Pickering won the award for 'Greatest Single Contribution to Occupational Pensions (1998–2017)' at the Professional Pensions 2017 UK Pension Awards. It was a well-acclaimed tribute to the role he had played for more than twenty years after leaving the EETPU in 1992. A key part of this had included interface with the political world. When he wrote an article in *Pensions World* magazine in October 1989, which included the statement at the beginning of this chapter, he was being characteristically prescient. The next two decades were to see a revolution in the world of employment pensions, in which politics was central and Alan was increasingly to be a major player.

At the end of Chapter 3 we saw Alan Pickering, in May 1992,

about to move to the private sector from the Electrical, Electronic, Telecommunications and Plumbing Union after twenty years of service. He calls those union years an 'apprenticeship', though in fact his learning about the pensions industry was much less attributable to his employer (though they gave him the opportunity) than it was to his own initiative, ambition and drive. At forty-three he believed he was (as we have seen) at the 'height of his marketability'. That was a canny assessment. The offer to a prospective employer was given substance, in particular, by Alan's membership of the council of the National Association of Pension Funds, a role that brought him into contact with fund managers, pension providers, the investment community and many other stakeholders in the pensions world. Also in that realm were the actuarial partnerships that advised funds on, in particular, the liability side of the schemes' financial statements. He had also written extensively for specialist publications and spoken often at NAPF and other conferences and events. The two leading pensions support specialists were the (mainly) actuarial advisers Bacon & Woodrow and R. Watson & Sons, and Alan wrote to the senior partners at both to enquire whether there might be a job for him. Both were keen, but Watson's were prepared to create a job for him immediately – and also to employ Jenny Davie as well. The dream team was to stay together throughout the next twenty years – and beyond. Richard Akroyd, a senior colleague at Watson's over much of Alan's time there, says that Jenny was crucial support and 'did a brilliant job over a long period' – a view many others have endorsed. Alan himself says that she is his eyes – but also often his brain and always his antennae, picking up signals he might miss on his own. Alan's immediate salary hike was a handy £8,000 as he moved from £36,000 at the union to £44,000[31] at Watson's.

Alan's move to Watson's in 1992 came at a time when workplace pensions were very much in the public arena. The end of the 1980s had seen the 'Big Bang' in the City and the associated launch in 1988 of 'personal pension plans' (PPP), which brought with them misselling on a huge scale.[32] Also, in 1990, the 'Barber judgment' had required pension schemes to equalise benefits between men and women; this was a major change with significant implications for fund finances. In November the following year there was the coming to light of the fraud perpetrated by Robert Maxwell, who had systematically plundered the Mirror Group Newspapers' pension fund – 'Maxwell was theft, not abuse,' says Alan Pickering today. The aftershocks of this crime dominated the world of pensions and led to the 1995 Pension Act, as well as to extended debate both before the act was passed and after about the extent to which the regulation of pension funds was desirable. As we shall see, Alan Pickering was to be a key player in that debate.

---

31 Equivalent to £73,000 in 2018 terms.

32 Politicians involved continued to be in denial about these events years later. John Major was Minister of State for Social Security in 1986/87 and wrote in his memoirs (published in 1999) about the 'liberalisation of the private pension market' and boasted that, as a result, 'Over six million people were to take out personal pension plans, with well over £200bn held in them.' No mention there of the misselling scandal that occurred in the late 1980s and early 1990s, when commission-hungry salesmen wrongly advised as many as two million people to opt out of occupational schemes and take out personal pensions.

Watson's was, in Alan Pickering's words, a 'blue-blooded' partnership – the aristocracy of the actuarial world. When Alan joined in 1992 as a 'senior consultant', the company was on the cusp of change from the era of when actuaries virtually told a client what to do to one where they actually delivered what the client wanted. This is no subtle change, and for it to happen there needed a more shared accountability between client and consultant. At Watson's, Alan became key to this, and Richard Akroyd tells of the innumerable situations where his style was quietly (but authoritatively) conducive to problem-solving – even where the issue had at the outset seemed insoluble. He was, as he now puts it, in a niche at a convergence between the pensions professional (the actuary or the investment adviser), the client (the fund sponsor), the fund's trustees and the client's employees and pensioners – the members of the pension fund. The trustee was a key player and Alan had practical experience in this area which he brought to Watson's. He remained a trustee of the Plumbing Industry Pensions Scheme, and although this had originally been linked to his EETPU job, the union was happy for him to continue now he was at Watson's. This was unusual, to say the least, but mostly uncontroversial. Robert Burgon, long-time director of the plumbing fund, says that the scheme was keen to have Alan continuing his trustee role because of 'his pensions knowledge plus his ability to work through difficult and challenging issues in an unassuming manner'.

Trustee training was already from his time at the EETPU

one of Alan Pickering's most important (and marketable) skills. Following Maxwell there was a strong drive to improve trustees' knowledge and expertise and, building on his work in this area at the union, Alan developed this. Training included the specialists – on trustee law, investment, liability management etc. But Alan's niche was to pull all of this together, recognising that different categories of trustee had different training needs. A company-nominated trustee was not, for example, the same as a union-elected member-nominated trustee, and in developing training packages, Alan addressed this. Some of this training was general, with trustees from a number of different funds coming together. Some was more specific and was based around the structure of individual funds; he 'tweaked the content' to meet the needs as appropriate. An important element was the political arena in which pensions played out. Pensions and politics were inextricably mixed, and trustees needed to understand and respond to this. Joanne Segars, for many years the CEO of the National Association of Pension Funds, says that a politician's time horizon was a maximum of five years, whereas pensions policy had to be consistent over a long time period – and be resistant to the vicissitudes of political change. The Maxwell case was 'seismic' and it led to many people losing faith in company pension schemes. It was in this context that trustee training was crucial – not least because Maxwell led to urgent legislation which culminated in the 1995 Pension Act. Richard Akroyd says that Alan was clear that the 'Trustee job is not to be an expert in all areas but to be able to challenge the experts' – specific training could provide the necessary know-how to allow a challenge to be made, but it was, in Alan's view, far from just being about the things a trustee needs to know. It was about having the confidence to participate actively even if you weren't exactly an expert in any specific area. His own personality as a 'non-expert' underpinned this. The distinguished actuary Adrian Waddingham says, 'Alan was never an actuary but he had a wonderful way of communicating pensions issues in a practical way that people could relate to.'

Trustee training, including running seminars as well as more formal pensions skills training, was an important part of Alan Pickering's initial job at Watson's, but he never had a job description or even an official title. He was a 'senior consultant' initially but his role as an ambassador for the company grew as he became a regular at pensions and financial services conferences and other events. He says that in his first year or so as a conference speaker he tended to get the late 'graveyard' spot, but as his fame grew he was brought on earlier in the programme. He was, he says, quite ambitious. He had a good salary plus some bonuses, but his goal was to become a partner, which would certainly bring financial rewards, but for Alan it was, he says, more to be part of the 'ownership structure' – to have firm confirmation that he 'slotted in'. This seems never to have been in doubt.

Watson's is a client service organisation and for Alan Pickering this meant hands-on involvement in a variety of client service activities. In some cases, and especially for the bigger clients, this could be quite comprehensive. An example was Esso Petroleum, which was then the UK subsidiary of the Exxon Corporation (now ExxonMobil). Esso was a major employer in the UK, with a large defined benefit scheme. The issues playing out in the early 1990s were diverse. One of these was the need to bring together all of the employees under a single pensions umbrella (what is referred to as 'single status', removing the historic white-collar/blue-collar distinctions). The fact that the scheme was in surplus helped to support the creation of a single scheme, but it also brought challenges. For instance, under Nigel Lawson's chancellorship, fund surpluses would be liable to tax (he thought that schemes were abusing their tax advantages). Politics was right in the centre of the pensions world and good employers, like Esso, were struggling to know what to do in the light of legislation. Alan Pickering said to them, 'Whose surplus is it anyway?' (the answer is the fund members'). So contribution holidays (which would benefit only the sponsor) were arguably less defensible than benefit improvements which would advantage the employees and potentially pensioners. As an American corporation, Esso was reluctant to index pensions to inflation, so increases were discretionary under their trust deed. (Alan sees this as an interesting ideological difference: Americans think that people cause inflation whereas in Britain we tend to think it is down to governments.) These issues, the discussion of which involved Alan Pickering actively, showed the growing complexity that trustees had to wrestle with at that time. It wasn't going to get any easier.

The Thatcher/Lawson ideology had been against defined benefit workplace pension schemes, which they saw as 'privatised social security'. What we can now see as the beginning of the slow death of defined benefit schemes had begun in 1988, when Nigel Lawson decided to tax pension fund surpluses to prevent companies using pension funds for tax avoidance. This was a heavy blow as it ignored the fact that the reason funds needed surpluses was because they required them to provide for future payments. The balance between actives (employees) and pensioners in the funds changed over time. This balance was changed in an accelerated way as employers undertook industrial restructuring (reducing staff numbers considerably) by giving early retirement benefits – which were, of course, paid for by the pension scheme. This changed peoples' expectations – if your friend had retired early with a generous pension fund, well, why couldn't you? But post-Maxwell – and under a somewhat different political regime with John Major's premiership and the less doctrinaire and less pensions-hostile chancellorship of Ken Clarke – it was decided that extensive new controls were necessary. The Secretary of State for Social Security (which included pensions) was Peter Lilley, whom Alan Pickering describes as a 'free market right-winger', but even he could see that the light-touch regulation which allowed Maxwell to thrive had to change. With hindsight, the government overreacted. They appointed Roy Goode, professor of law at Oxford University, to look at pensions law in the light of the Maxwell scandal – he recommended a new pensions act which significantly increased the amount and extent of regulation: the Pensions Act 1995. Alan Pickering was to become vice-chairman of the NAPF in 1997 – the very year that the new act came into effect. Looking back, he says that it was clear that the act was overkill – that it introduced a far too tight regulatory structure. It introduced a 'minimum funding requirement' as well as requiring fund sponsors to underwrite fully index-linked pension increases (up to 5 per cent per annum). These rules, along with such benefits as spouse cover, added substantially to the costs of providing pensions. They were also compulsory; there was no flexibility to allow for leeway in times of low financial returns for the fund, for example. Alan Pickering says that requiring guarantees (e.g. of annual pension increments) was too restrictive: 'What they should have done to respond to Maxwell', he now says, 'was have a one-line piece of legislation that said that every pension scheme should have an independent custodian which would hold investments entirely separately and also have "best endeavours" in respect of annual increments rather than a rigid index-linked system'. He also believes that there should have been greater flexibility to allow different schemes to design a modus operandi that was right for them. At the time, Alan Pickering, just a few years into his career at Watson's, was encouraged by his employer to play an active part at the juncture between the world of pensions and that of politics. Richard Akroyd says that Watson's was corporately 'careful about taking positions' in a world that was ever more combative, but that Alan Pickering gradually increased his credibility, in part through his even-handedness, but also because he was prepared to take a personal position – he did not duck issues because they were contentious. His role was, in some cases, to bring employer and employee (usually with the trade union) together – a good example was at Scottish & Newcastle Breweries, where he was asked by the management to sit on the employee consultative committee to advise on pensions matters. Industrial relations at the company were 'tribal' at the time and Pickering performed his 'Honest Al' role – and Watson's was paid for him to do this.

In the run-up to the 1997 general election, which restored Labour to power after eighteen years, the political turbulence was intense. Pensions were for a time a battleground during the campaign, with Labour claiming that further 'reforms' proposed in the Conservative manifesto would involve the abolition of the state pension. This was a canard, but illustrative of the way that pensions (traditionally thought of as rather a dull subject) could be weaponised by politicians on both sides of the argument. And in the year of the election, the 1995 act came into force and, as we have seen, Alan Pickering became vice-chairman of the NAPF. He was well known in NAPF circles, having been secretary and then chairman of the organisation's west London group for fifteen years and also chairman of its national tax committee and the association's treasurer. He set out his stall at the Pensions Management Institute annual conference in November 1997, where he launched the idea that 'a pension is all about insurance and nothing about investment. Most of the problems which we have encountered in recent years have been caused by those who fail to appreciate this basic concept.' He also warned that 'members were at risk in an environment riddled with options' and questioned the need for 'turning every adult citizen into a financial wizard' and, in a theme that was to resonate strongly in the years to come, he regretted the 'needless complexity which had fed through into significant under-provision for those who were in greatest need of a pension'. Early in his first term Tony Blair took the important step of appointing the country's first ever dedicated 'pensions minister', John Denham, who took office in July 1998. It was to be a job with a rapid turnover – Denham was in the job for five months; his successor Stephen Timms for six; though the next appointee Jeff Rooker held office for almost two years up to the 2001 general election. By then, Alan Pickering had moved onto the chairmanship of the NAPF.

Alan Pickering describes his two-year term as NAPF chairman (1999–2001) as being the 'peak of his career'. It was certainly a role for which he was eminently suited. He was, he says, in a characteristically blunt expression, a 'pig in muck' at the NAPF. Alan was in his fiftieth year on election as chairman, with seven years of solid experience of the private sector to add to his twenty working (mostly) on pensions matters at the EETPU. He had by then realised his ambition to become a partner at Watson's (which he later described as 'one of the proudest moments of my career'[33]). It was also a move which helped his finances to such an extent that he was able, in 1998, to buy his first racehorse, Alan's Dream. Adrian Waddingham describes the quite febrile economic and political times into which Alan was plunged in his NAPF role:

> 1997 had been a watershed year with the Bank of England having been made independent and with interest rates falling. The stock market was struggling and Gordon Brown had made the tax change that prevented trustees from reclaiming tax deducted at source on dividends – copying what Norman Lamont had done three years earlier. In addition the inflation protection of the 1995 act (and the cost of regulation) had significantly pushed up the cost of DB pensions. At the same time accounting conventions were changed so that companies had to record pensions liabilities on their balance sheets.

The world of pensions – in part a subset of the financial services sector and in part, at the time, a component of companies' compensation packages – can be confusing to the onlooker. There are many interests at stake and they do not necessarily all seek similar outcomes. This was recognised in the creation of a 'joint

33 Interview in *Money Marketing*, May 2000.

occupational working group' comprising, along with the NAPF, the Association of Consulting Actuaries, the Association of British Insurers, the Association of Pensions Lawyers and the Society of Pensions Consultants. The group had access to government departments – primarily the Department of Work and Pensions. Along with his NAPF responsibilities Alan Pickering was asked to be chairman of this working group – a role in which, according to Adrian Waddingham, he was 'very effective', having gained '100 per cent support' from the group's participants. He says that across the group there was unanimity that 'politicians were killing the pensions goose through over-prescription and over-regulation'. The conventional wisdom of the times was that the damaging outcomes of the changes made in the 1995 act were 'unintended consequences of a well-intentioned development'. Alan Pickering rejects this; the consequences may have been unintended, but they were based on what he calls 'lousy decision-making'.

As chairman of the NAPF, Alan Pickering was to have regular platforms at conferences and elsewhere to speak his mind – as well as direct access to politicians and civil servants. He wanted, as a minimum, to try to ensure 'the government's pensions proposals don't damage that part of the system that is working well'.[34] It was a role he relished. There was some campaigning zeal here as well: 'The problem in Britain is under-provision, not

34 Interview in *Pensions Age*, June 1999.

over-provision, and we shouldn't be discouraging people from making as much advance provision as they can.'[35] On taking office he said in an interview for *Pensions Week*[36] that his priority was developing 'a close relationship between the NAPF centrally and our members. Our greatest failing is not telling our members what we're doing.' He also emphasised the 'need to ensure that the relationship with the government is productive ... the NAPF already has a good working relationship with the Department of Social Security ... [we] want to develop a similar relationship with the Treasury.' In the same interview he also appeared cautious about what was the Blair government's idea of 'stakeholder pensions':[37] 'My real fear', he said, 'is that stakeholder pensions will crowd out other forms of pensions provisions that might have been better. It may result in a "dumbing down" of pensions.' This echoes the views of his predecessor as NAPF chairman, Peter Murray, who was to state at the NAPF annual conference in 1999, 'Our view is that one major effect of the [stakeholder pension] proposals will be to undermine occupational pension provision in the UK. Employers will feel it is easier and more cost-effective to offer access to a stakeholder pension that an occupational scheme for their employees.'

That Alan Pickering was going to lead a pragmatic charge at

35 Interview in *Pensions Age*, ibid.
36 January 1999.
37 Stakeholder pensions were defined contribution schemes designed to encourage greater long-term saving for retirement, particularly among those on lower earnings, with low minimum contributions and caps on charges.

the NAPF was clear in another interview he gave on becoming chairman.[38] A goal he declared at that time was 'to try and improve the relationship between trustees and fund managers to make sure people don't hire and fire managers on unduly short-term criteria'. Asked what he would do if he was pensions minister, he said:

> First I would ring the head of policy to get someone to crawl through every clause and regulation for which we have been responsible since the war. Anything which has passed its sell-by date should be bonfired ... and I will get my departmental secretary to ring his counterpart at the Treasury. He will be invited to put out-dated revenue rules on the bonfire...

Alan also said that pensions planning needs to be 'over a thirty-year time horizon – no room for short-term book balancing'. He said in an interview with *Financial News*[39] that 'Chancellors seem to be more interested in just balancing this year's books and politicians are making annual budgets in the context of pensions schemes with thirty-, forty- or fifty-year time horizons.' His most controversial statement on the subject was about the state pension:

> By 2035, people should have to wait until they are seventy before they qualify, sixty-five is no longer old, and if we have to

38 *Pensions World*, January 1999.
39 December 1998.

> wait until we are seventy before getting our old-age pension, there will be the resources to make the basic state pension a firm foundation upon which everyone can build their private pension provision.

He also presciently said, 'I do not think it is possible for people [in defined contribution schemes] to create enough wealth between the ages of twenty-five and fifty-five to keep them going for the rest of their lives.'

That Alan would challenge conventional wisdoms was clear from an interview he gave to *Pensions Management*[40] a few months into his tenure as NAPF chairman, at the time of the association's annual conference:

> The government has not yet seen the light to allow people to join more than one [pension] scheme. The thing that went wrong in 1998 is that people were forced to choose between occupational pensions and personal pensions. There is also a lack of desire to simplify the occupational pensions system which is complicated by the understandable knee-jerk reaction to Maxwell.

Around the same time he took a robust stance against a government proposal to compel pension scheme trustees to declare

40 May 1999.

their views on ethical investment, which, he believed, could at some point in the future lead to trustees facing pressure to avoid investing in industries such as pharmaceuticals, oil, drinks and tobacco. This was a good example of Alan's pragmatism and his recognition of the overriding need for pension fund trustees to feel free to pursue an investment strategy free of over-regulation. And, at the 1999 NAPF conference, he courageously took a swipe at Gordon Brown's Treasury. He told John Humphrys,

> The sad thing is that the Treasury, both in its ministers and its civil servants, think that they are a cut above everybody else, and that they know best ... we have to lobby all year round and create an environment where the Treasury will find it hard to raid pension schemes.[41]

Later in 1999 Alan Pickering returned to his 'retire at seventy theme'. In a conference in Monaco he said, 'In 1948 people retiring at sixty-five could expect to live for nine years. Today life expectancy stretches another twenty years. Putting people out to pasture at sixty-five not only means that the country is missing out on years of potentially productive labour, but means a rising pensions bill for the state.' He also argued that women's retirement age should rise to be in line with that of men.[42] (In November 1999 the Social Security Secretary, Alistair Darling,

---

41 *Pensions World*, July 1999.
42 *The Times*, 5 October 1999.

said at the TUC pensions conference that the government had no plans to raise the retirement age.)

It was clear that the world of pensions had a spokesman who was rather different from those who had previously been in such a role. The specialist periodical *Professional Pensions* summed up the mood in October 1999:

> In his short time in the hot seat at the NAPF, chairman Alan Pickering has shown a refreshing willingness to express forthright views on nitty-gritty issues ... Under Pickering, the NAPF seems almost to be taking on a think-tank role – thinking the unthinkable by putting forward radical ideas for debate ... the NAPF seems to have widened its vision and is to be congratulated for doing so ... Alan Pickering has done a good job in getting people thinking.[43]

And pensions doyen Henry Tapper agrees:

> It was a great time and Alan was so full of energy – the whole place ticked when he was there. Politically it was a highly charged time; with Gordon Brown's 'tax raids', all kinds of things seemed to be happening. Conferences at that time were febrile events ... which Alan had to cope with when pensions had a great deal of clout.

43 *Professional Pensions*, October 1999.

At around this time another leading pensions magazine, *Pensions Management,* gave Alan their 'Pensions Personality of the Year Award' – picked by a readers' poll. They said that Alan had 'put the issue of underprovision for retirement firmly on the news agenda'. They also said that he had demonstrated 'his desire to inject some badly needed realism into the pensions debate'.[44] That realism also included Alan's attack, in November 1999, on the government's 'stakeholder pension' plans, which he graphically labelled 'pensions apartheid', under which one form of pension provision – good occupational schemes – would be available to the better off whilst poorer workers contributed to a stakeholder scheme. He called good occupational (defined benefit) schemes 'the welfare success of the 20th century' because of their inclusiveness, embracing high- and low-income workers within the same company.[45] The NAPF was keen to persuade the government to allow concurrent membership of DB schemes and stakeholder pensions.

Less than a year into his chairmanship, and Alan Pickering had changed the NAPF such that, as *Pensions Week* magazine put it, 'the NAPF has started looking like a trade body ready to meet the challenges of the changing pensions environment. Let's hope they can keep it up.'[46] The importance of the NAPF cannot be overstated. Neither the Confederation of British Industries

44 *Pensions Management,* November 1999.
45 *Financial Times,* 18 November 1999.
46 *Pensions Week,* 22 November 1999.

(CBI) nor the Institute of Directors (IOD), Alan now says, 'ever tooled up in respect of pensions'. Whilst some of the employers' associations were active and the TUC played a strong hand, it was the NAPF who set the pensions agenda. But the big opportunity for radical change was to be missed by successive Labour governments – a source of great regret for Alan – because 'With a big majority Tony Blair could have got the unpopular pensions changes out of the way. Gordon Brown took no interest in pensions.' (*Professional Pensions* went even further and said 'suspicions remain that Brown is not a fan of the occupational pensions movement and that whatever emerges under the new regime will not be to its advantage'.[47]) Certainly Brown's changes to the tax regime penalised DB schemes – but that was not the main reason for the DB scheme's demise, as we shall see.

At the turn of the millennium, we have Alan Pickering firmly in his seat at the NAPF, Jeff Rooker as the latest occupant of the swivelling pensions minister seat and Frank Field (who had been charged by Blair with thinking the unthinkable of welfare reform) festering angrily on the back benches. The 1995 Pensions Act had been in place for three years. It was clear that the requirement fully to index-link pensions and the introduction of a 'minimum funding requirement' (MFR) were substantially adding to DB pensions costs. Increases in longevity (the 'demographic time bomb' in the argot of the time) exacerbated the

47 *Professional Pensions*, 16 December 1999.

problem, and the inevitable slow decline of DB schemes gathered pace. Add to this, as Tom Ross of Aon Consulting said in *Pensions Age* in 1999, 'There is a huge disincentive ... for [anyone] to save anything for retirement ... because if they do their sums they will know that all they are doing is reducing their future means-tested benefits.'[48] At the same time, the magazine published their list of the '100 most influential people in pensions', as voted for by its readership. This had Gordon Brown at num ber 6, Julian Farrand (the pensions ombudsman) at number 2 – and Alan Pickering at number 1. The boy with weak sight, from a small house in a modest suburb of York, had come a long way.

The arrival of the year 2000 prompted 'agendas for the new millennium' across many subjects, and pensions was no exception. Alan Pickering, now the most respected commentator on UK pensions, gave his own views. He sketched out a brave new world under which

> retirement would be an outmoded concept ... we would lead full and active lives from the day we were born to the day we died. Learning would be a lifetime experience and we would phase in and phase out of full-time employment ... Pensions that come with the job would be praised ... the state would remain a provider of pensions for the poor and for everyone

48 Tom Ross, Aon Consulting, December 1999. Reported in *Pensions Age*.

> else in respect of the first tranche of their later-life income. Politics should be left to politicians, not pension fund trustees.

He was also to say that certain changes to pensions were urgently necessary – not least the scrapping of the MFR for workplace pension funds.[49] At the 2000 NAPF conference he made a plea for the depoliticising of pensions, saying, 'Party politics must be kept out of pensions if the private sector is to shoulder the burden the electorate might have once expected the state to bear. The timescales associated with pensions transcend the electoral cycle.' This latter remark was to underpin Alan's approach in the years to come when he was further engaged with government and the pensions industry to manage change. He was increasingly firm in his belief that 'ageism should be removed from the workplace' and so opposed nascent ideas that government was thinking of banning early retirement for the under-55s. He was, as we have seen, particularly strong in emphasising the dangers of a two-tier pension system:

> We have to ram home the message to the government that occupational pensions cover the whole spectrum of individuals, including blue-collar workers. We take every opportunity when meeting ministers and speaking to other representatives of the chattering classes to make sure they see that occupational

49 Interview in *Pensions and Investment*, January 2000.

> pensions are doing a good job – [they] benefit the rich and the not so rich.[50]

At the beginning of his second year as NAPF chairman Alan Pickering would go on to say, 'There is a real danger that some employers who are finding pension schemes too complex will respond to government interference and offer [new employees] stakeholder instead [under which there] is no obligation to offer contributions.'[51] This remark presciently foreshadowed the move away from a defined benefit pensions offer to defined contribution – something that was to dominate pensions activity over the years to come. He defined what, after a year as chairman, he saw as NAPF's role: 'The aim is to create an environment in which employer-sponsored pension provision can flourish; a legislative environment, a political environment, a tax environment which is all supportive of funded occupational pensions schemes.'[52] He also at that time reinforced his views of the state pension:

> The state in Britain has never really provided an adequate income in retirement. It's always been a basement-level provider, a foundation on which to build. I for one hope that the state will continue to be a pension provider and not just a pension regulator. I think that the state can cost effectively provide

50 Interview in *Money Marketing*, 11 May 2000.
51 Interview in *Money Marketing*, ibid.
52 EMAnetwork, June 2000.

> the first tranche of pension for all of us to make sure that we all have the foundation upon which to build ... we don't want to have all our pension depending on funded and privately invested pension schemes.[53]

In July 2000 the NAPF's campaign to allow employees earning less than £30,000 a year to contribute to both their company pension and a personal or stakeholder pension succeeded – a move which Alan Pickering said was the 'single most important decision announced by the government in its pension review'. A more technical area of concern later in the year was the government actuary's department calculation of 'contracting out rebate rates' for 2002–07. In his position as chairman of the joint working group (JWG) on occupational pensions, Alan wrote to the pensions minister saying the proposals 'could jeopardise the government's policy objectives for pensions provision'.[54] The JWG argued that the rebate level should be set so that there is no doubt that contracting out was the best option. These two cases further illustrate the breadth of issues and complexity of the subject – and of the important part that the NAPF and other professional bodies played at the time. Pensions were increasingly in the public arena and Alan Pickering welcomed this: 'pensions and politics are each concerned with the allocation of scarce resources between competing priorities, the heightened political

53 EMAnetwork, ibid.
54 *Professional Pensions*, November 2000.

debate about all aspects of the current pensions scene is welcome ... [post Maxwell] folk now realise that pension schemes have to be run in accordance with good business practice'.[55]

If ever there was an example of the need for 'good business practice', it was the scandal surrounding the near collapse of the Equitable Life Assurance Society, which broke during Alan Pickering's term of office as NAPF chairman. The NAPF's focus was on the role of the Financial Services Authority regulator – in January 2001 Alan Pickering asked for a meeting with the regulator 'to answer questions about whether it should have acted sooner and whether it was spreading itself too thinly by taking on more tasks than it could carry out properly'.[56] Alan was concerned, as the media reported, that the Equitable affair could do damage to 'savings in general and pensions in particular'. The author of City comment in the *Daily Telegraph* said, 'Mr Pickering commands as few battalions as the Pope, but he is at least trying to push the debate forward before it's too late.'[57] A particular concern for the NAPF was the role that Equitable played as a provider of additional voluntary contributions (AVC), which are a form of pensions 'top up' – the Equitable had 65 per cent of this market. Alan Pickering urged AVC policyholders to 'contact their trustees before taking any action, such as suspending contributions', adding, 'The person to be frightened of is the

55 Magazine of the Pensions Management Institute, November 2000.

56 *Daily Telegraph*, 6 January 2001.

57 *Daily Telegraph*, ibid.

salesman who tells you that there is an open-and-shut case for going down a particular route.'[58] This intervention is interesting in that Alan was in 'Honest Al' mode rather than speaking as chairman of the NAPF and drawing on his long experience of trusteeship in commenting.

Early in 2001 the negative aspects of the 'minimum funding requirement' for pension funds were firmly in the spotlight. In particular, a debate about what should replace the unsatisfactory MFR was underway. Alan Pickering saw the issue at the heart of pensions provision: would employers be prepared 'to pay a contribution to a scheme of any sort or simply act as a facilitator for the collection of employees contributions'? He was emphasising that the future choice was not (just) between defined benefit and defined contribution/stakeholder schemes, but whether employers would make any sort of funding commitment at all for pensions. But first the MFR had to be suspended he said – very emphatically. The MFR was, in his words, 'having adverse consequences for both UK equity investment and DB pension schemes. It is having precisely the opposite effect to that intended.' The MFR was abolished in the 2001 Budget ('A godsend,' commented Alan Pickering at the time). He was in sprightly form after the Budget and, in a light-hearted Q&A, when asked who the most influential person in the pensions industry was, he answered, 'The Grim Reaper.' He also revealed

58 *Financial Times*, 13 January 2001.

that his ideal dinner guests would be 'Dolly Parton and Nelson Mandela', and that his perfect holiday would be 'One week in Scarborough and two weeks in Barbados'.[59]

As Alan Pickering's term as NAPF chairman was drawing to a close in the autumn of 2001, he took the opportunity to nail his colours again to the mast about the ideal pension system for the modern age. It would, he said, be based on four cornerstones: 'Diversity, inclusiveness, stability and simplicity.' The system should encompass both the state and the many forms of private pension. It should be seen as a 'valuable part of our social fabric'. It should be stable so that it is planned for 'decades rather than months', and simple 'because we need to engage employers and the electorate and avoid wasting scarce resources on mere compliance'.[60] It immediately became apparent that this credo was to be attractive – and not just to the pensions industry, or in the United Kingdom.

In 2000 Alan Pickering was elected a vice-chairman of the European Federation for Retirement Provision (EFRP), and in 2001 he became its chairman. It was a body set up to encourage mutual debate and cooperation between European pensions groups and policymakers – a move of particular importance as the EU members instituted steps towards harmonisation of pensions activities and legislation across the union. He says that in the past the UK had

59 *Professional Pensions*, 15 March 2001.
60 *PMI News*, September 2001.

tended to lecture Europeans, saying that we had comparatively good occupational pensions (in the DB scheme heyday), which had meant that the UK financial services community was not well-liked in the rest of Europe. The European model was more skewed to state pensions which were significantly better than British ones, although this was changing.

Despite some previous antipathy to the British the EFRP welcomed Alan – in part, he thinks, because he was seen as a buffer between the French and the Germans. Speaking in December 2001 he applied the 'four cornerstones' principle to Europe as well as the UK:

> We have to be inclusive in such a way that there are not rich people's pensions and poor people's pensions ... I think that an inclusive pension system can oil the wheels of European economic development [but] I hope that we can learn the lessons of the UK where the system has become over bureaucratic ... you mustn't over-regulate the private sector ... beyond ensuring that there are adequate standards of conduct.

On the EU's proposed 'pensions directive'[61] he said, 'I would like to see a directive that is enabling at country and pan-European

61 The EU's IORP (Institutions for Occupational Retirement Provision) directive was introduced in 2003 and sought to establish a system of regulation of IORPs (or occupational pension funds) that was common across the European Union. The stated aim was to foster a single market in IORPs and thereby encourage cross-border provision.

level by recognising that pension rights in one country can be transported to another.'

The abolition of the MFR had been one of the many recommendations of the Myners Report into institutional investment which was published in March 2001. The report was made for the Treasury but commented in detail on the investment aspects of the pensions sector. Alan Pickering says the DWP 'wanted their own version' – broadly, a 'review of private pensions legislation to result in a package of options for simplification'. In September 2001 he was on the Eurostar from London to Brussels for a meeting of the EFRP. His mobile phone rang. It was Alistair Darling, the Secretary of State for Work and Pensions; he asked Alan whether he would chair the proposed pensions legislation review. Alan accepted and an announcement was made in which Darling said,

> I am delighted that Alan Pickering has agreed to lead this review. Alan will bring an independent but realistic approach to the task. He will be relying on input from across the industry to make the review a success and I would encourage everyone with a contribution to make to engage with Alan and his team.

The story of 'A Simpler Way to Better Pensions' – which became known as the Pickering Report – and its aftermath is told in the next chapter of Alan's story.

CHAPTER 7

# THE PICKERING REPORT

*Alan Pickering was very, very committed to the idea that people should have properly funded pensions.* – Alistair Darling

In *The Burden of Power: Countdown to Iraq*, part of his extensive published diaries of his time in No. 10, Alastair Campbell's entry for Thursday 11 July 2002 includes the following:

> Tony Blair spoke briefly [in Cabinet] about pensions and asked for a note. Gordon Brown, very deliberately as part of the current style vs substance line they [Brown and his supporters] were running, said that he would be happy to provide a note on this for the Cabinet but 'It's very important that we focus on next year not next week'. In other words he was long term, Tony Blair was short term.

This vignette is interesting. 11 July 2002 was the day that Alan Pickering's 'A Simpler Way to Better Pensions' was published. As we shall see, the launch was dominated in the media by recommendations in respect of widows' (survivors') pension rights and pensions in payment indexation. Alan Pickering had been challenged on the BBC's *Today* programme about the former in particular, and the media hounds were baying. An *Evening Standard* headline that read: 'Pickering provokes pensions fury' was to follow. You will search in vain for much mention of the subject of pensions elsewhere in Campbell's diaries, and in the two reputable biographies of Tony Blair by John Rentoul and Anthony Seldon (*Blair*, 2004) there is only one reference. Seldon says that in the run-up to the 1997 election Labour's 'pensions policy was left in a muddle'. Blair's out-of-the-blue request to Brown for a 'note' was no doubt prompted by the subject briefly being in the media – and Brown's put-down was a response to this. Blair was only worried about image and tactics, the Chancellor implied, whereas he was concerned with strategy. Brown was certainly right that pensions is a very long-term subject, requiring consistency and consensus, though there was some disingenuous humbug in play as well – as we shall also see.

## WHY THE PICKERING REVIEW WAS NECESSARY

When Labour took office on 2 May pensions reform was not high on the agenda, although it had featured in the party's 1997 election manifesto:

Frank Pickering

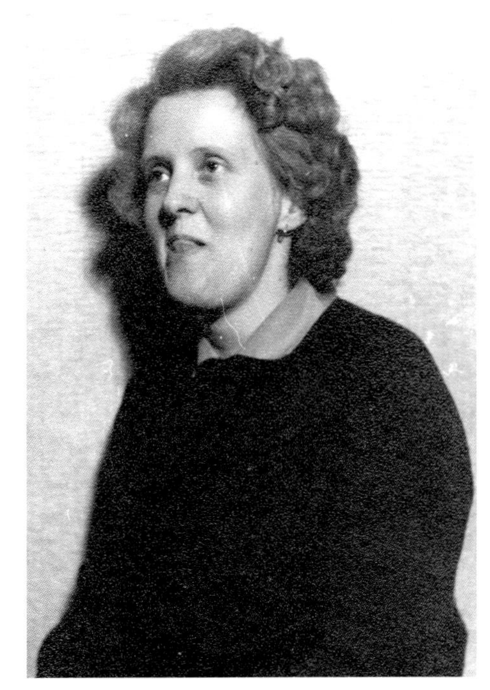

Betty Pickering

LEFT Alan's parents' wedding

BELOW LEFT Alan as a baby

BELOW RIGHT Keen reader

The Pickering family around 1955

Look where you're going

Street cricket

Early horse encounter

28 Lesley Avenue, York

Teenage Alan

Alan and Christine at Michael Mosley's wedding, 1979

University student, 1971

A bearded Alan in 1973 after competing in the seven-mile York INL (Working Men's Club) annual walking race – he finished 24th out of the 53 taking part

Competing at Thames Valley Harriers in 1977

Alan and Christine at their wedding, 11 September 1982

Speaking at a Prudential seminar, 1989

Jenny and Alan at the launch of the EETPU Centenary Fund for Disabled Young People in October 1989

Alan presents the Pickering Report in July 2002 © PA IMAGES

A simpler way to better pensions

An independent report by Alan Pickering

The Pickering Report

Alan receives the CBE in 2004

Robin Hoods Bay, winner of the Winter Derby 2014 with owners Alan and Christine Pickering, jockey Luke Morris and stable lass Anna Szustakiewicz © MARK CRANHAM, *RACING POST*

The next generation: Alan's mare, Primrose Valley, and her foal, Bobby © COLIN WHYMAN

Alan with his mother, 1959

Alan and Christine, 2018 © COLIN WHYMAN

Jenny and Alan, 2018 © COLIN WHYMAN

The provision of adequate pensions in old age is a major challenge for the future ... we propose a partnership between public and private provision, and a balance between income sourced from tax and invested savings. The basic state pension will be retained as the foundation of pension provision. It will be increased at least in line with prices ... We will reform the Financial Services Act so that the scandal of pension mis-selling – 600,000 pensions mis-sold and only 7,000 people compensated to date – will not happen again.

Too many people in work, particularly those on low and modest incomes and with changing patterns of employment, cannot join good-value second pension schemes. Labour will create a new framework – stakeholder pensions – to meet this need. We will encourage new partnerships between financial service companies, employers and employees to develop these pension schemes ... Labour will promote choice in pension provision.

We will support and strengthen the framework for occupational pensions. Personal pensions, appropriately regulated, will remain a good option for many. Labour will retain SERPS as an option for those who wish to remain within it ... We will set up a review of the central areas of insecurity for elderly people: all aspects of the basic pension and its value, second pensions including SERPS, and community care. The review will ensure that the views of pensioners are heard. Our watchword in developing policy for pensions and long-term care will be to build consensus among all interested parties.

Like much of the New Labour philosophy, this was fairly non-ideological in tone and content. The ministers charged with delivering the promise were Harriet Harman, as Secretary of State for Social Security, and her Minister of State for Welfare Reform, Frank Field. Field was an interesting choice – a maverick with a strong social conscience who had always, since his first election to Parliament in 1979, put what he believed to be right ahead of party loyalty. He was asked to 'go away and think the unthinkable on welfare reform and on pensions'. Harman did not wait to hear Field's wisdom and in July 1997 launched an official review of pensions provision which would cover 'all aspects of the basic pension and its value and second pensions, including the State Earnings Related Pension [SERPS]; to build a sustainable consensus for the long-term future of pensions; and to publish the government's proposals for further consultation in the first part of 1998.' She established a ten-person 'Pension Provision Group' (PPG) headed by Tom Ross of Aon Consulting, which included representatives of the insurance industry and of other employers as well as the trade unions. John Denham, then Parliamentary Under Secretary of State at the Department of Social Security (who was the following year to replace Frank Field as Minister of State for Pensions), said in the House of Commons that the government hoped that the PPG would 'provide the essential background to take forward our case for value-for-money stakeholder pensions, to bring better value-for-money, flexible pensions to those who cannot join an employer's occupational scheme at present'.

Despite Harriet Harman's statements that 'the failure over the last two decades to develop an adequate pensions strategy has resulted in widening inequalities among pensioners', and that 'too many of our older citizens do not enjoy security in retirement', the climate for occupational pensions in 1997 was in fact relatively benign. It was certainly true that Maxwell had been a shock to the system, but the continued growth in the stock market[62] for a decade or more, combined with a base interest rate of between 5 per cent and 7 per cent over the same period, had meant that DB pension schemes were in many cases comfortably in surplus. Funds took contribution holidays to avoid excessive surpluses which, following Nigel Lawson's Budget in 1988, could have been taxed. Annuity rates were also attractive, which meant that DC (money purchase) schemes benefited. A combination of the index-linked state pension and SERPS paid out more than any state system in the UK had before. As we have seen in Chapter 6, Alan Pickering at the NAPF was to warn against complacency, and in particular he was concerned that there was a widening gap between the 'haves' and the 'have nots'. But he feels today that these 'clarion calls' were not really listened to by government. He says that Peter Lilley (Secretary of State for Social Security 1992–97) 'found it easier to have a backward-looking review prompted mainly by Maxwell rather than a forward-looking assessment of what needed to be done'.

62 The FTSE was at 4495 on 2 May – ten years earlier it had stood at 2050.

And the new government was initially similar – Alan would agree with the words of a leading financial journalist, Alex Brummer, who would later say in his book, *The Great Pensions Robbery*, that 'pensions should have been high on the new government's agenda … New Labour were in an excellent position to make pensions fit for purpose in the new millennium on the horizon'. Steve Webb, then the Liberal Democrat pensions spokesman, agrees: 'With a majority of 100 plus the Blair government didn't need to build consensus if they didn't want to. All-party support was not so important in those days.'

Gordon Brown's first Budget was presented on 2 July 1997. In it he made an announcement with profound implications for pensions:

> The present system of tax credits encourages companies to pay out dividends rather than reinvest their profits. That cannot be the best way of encouraging investment for the long term, as was acknowledged by the previous government. Many pension funds are in substantial surplus and at present many companies are enjoying pension holidays, so this is the right time to undertake a long-needed reform. The previous government cut tax credits paid to funds and companies, so with immediate effect I propose to abolish tax credits paid to pension funds and companies.

William Hague, the Leader of the Opposition, was swift to comment in the Budget debate:

> For many people, their pension is the single biggest saving that they will ever build up, and every word that we heard today about advance corporation tax was another hammer blow against pensions and savings – another savings tax from the government. Pensions are one of our great success stories. The United Kingdom has built up more than £650 billion in pension funds – more than those of all the other European Union countries put together. We understand why the Chancellor has gone for ACT[63] … The change means that pension funds will be able to claim less tax back, so their revenue will be lower, their growth will be lower, pensions will be smaller and pensioners will be worse off … It is a smash-and-grab raid on pension funds in this country, and it is a cynical betrayal of the millions who have built up pensions and now see them devalued.

The 'smash-and-grab raid' was to remain a cause célèbre for a long time. In the four years leading up to 2001, when Alan Pickering was asked to conduct his review, some £20 billion which would have been accrued by pensions schemes went to the Treasury instead. The issue was revived ten years later, after new information about the lead-up to the decision emerged. Alan, who had been vice-chairman of the NAPF in 1997 when they had advised against abolishing the tax credits, said in 2007 that Gordon Brown was not solely responsible. He told the BBC,

63 Advanced Corporation Tax.

'Many senior Treasury policy officials felt that people joined pension schemes to save tax, rather than save for their retirement, so pension schemes had been on the Treasury's hit list for some time.' There had been an 'unholy alliance' between Treasury civil servants, who wanted to finish off the job started by Mr Lamont, and Mr Brown, who wanted to 'raise some money quite quickly'. In 1997 the total assets of DB schemes were about £1 trillion, so an annual loss of £5 billion (0.5 per cent), whilst significant, was arguably not the disaster some have painted it to be. Gordon Brown's claim in his recent autobiography, *My Life, Our Times*, that his being accused 'of taxing pension funds and thus ruining final-salary pensions' was 'unfair' is a reasonable one. But that it was, along with other factors, a contributory influence cannot be denied. That said, Alistair Darling, who took over as Secretary of State for Work and Pensions in July 1998, says that when initially in that job he had felt that in the pensions world, whilst there was some concern, it wasn't widespread. 'Nobody beat a path to my door to complain.' Darling's shadow minister, David Willetts, agrees: 'There was a belief that [the pensions crisis] was all due to Gordon Brown's tax. Although he did extract some revenue from pensions at a bad moment I didn't think that was the only or even the chief culprit.'

By July 1998 the Frank Field Review had imploded. Field had struggled for breath within the refined air of being close to the top of government (an unfamiliar position for this generally dissident politician). It is possible that telling Gordon Brown that his 'pensions plans will create chaos' did not endear him to the Chancellor. And the Prime Minister was not over warm either to proposals that would have seen the end of the second tier state pension and introduced a compulsion for everyone to save privately, with the government paying in for the poor. Field's proposed 'reforms' had a cost ticket of £10 billion per annum. 'Only £10 billion, Frank?' Tony Blair is alleged to have said.[64] In the department Field had battled with Harriet Harman and when he left she was to go as well. Alistair Darling took over from Harman and said that his 'first objective was to stabilise what was not far off civil war'.

Darling inherited Harman's pensions review as well as Field's Green Paper, 'New Ambitions for Our Country: A New Contract for Welfare', which had set out the framework to the government's programme of welfare reform. The Pensions Green Paper, significantly altered after Field's departure, was published in December 1998. It proposed a new structure for pensions, including a new 'state second pension' to reduce the extent to which low earners have to rely on means-tested benefits. This new scheme was seen to be, as Nicholas Timmins put it, 'more redistributive [because] as it slowly matures it helps the lower-paid more. But its rules are close to unfathomable.' The Green Paper also outlined the framework for the new stakeholder pension schemes and included changes to the regulatory framework for occupational and

64 Nicholas Timmins, 'Labour's troubled history of pension reform', *Financial Times*, November 2005.

personal pensions. The Welfare Reform and Pensions Act 1999 which followed made a number of detailed changes to pensions regulations, but it was primarily concerned with the introduction of stakeholder pensions.

At the beginning of the new millennium the economic graphs – especially the stock exchange indices – stood at an all-time high.[65] The pensions industry at large was generally unconcerned – indeed, a study published by Birkbeck College[66] in June 2000 concluded:

> The UK is one of the few countries in Europe that is not facing a serious pensions crisis. The reasons for this are straightforward: state pensions ... are amongst the lowest in Europe, the UK has a long-standing funded private pension sector, its population is ageing less rapidly than elsewhere in Europe and its governments have taken measures to prevent a pension crisis developing. These measures have involved making systematic cuts in unfunded state pension provision and increasingly transferring the burden of providing pensions to the funded private sector.

With hindsight, this conclusion can be seen as complacent, but, to be fair, the author, one of Britain's most distinguished pensions academics, did signal warnings for the pensions sector in the report. Nevertheless, his assertion about the health of the

65 6,800 in September 2000.
66 'Two decades of Pension Reform in the UK', David Blake, Pensions Institute, Birkbeck College, University of London, June 2000.

industry was widely believed. Life expectancy at the age of sixty-five was increasing year on year – retirees were living longer, something of great interest to pension funds as a key component of their liability calculations. This had risen from around thirteen years in 1980 to around eighteen years by 2000, with the expectation that this could increase further to as high as twenty-five or even thirty years by 2030. This is a complex area with significant differences occurring across gender and region and social class, but around 2000–01, with unfortunate timing, it became apparent that longevity changes had been generally underestimated by actuaries.

In 2000–01 the so-called 'dot-com bubble' burst and the stock market crashed, interest rates started to fall and it became apparent that mortality assumptions made by actuaries had been too low for too long. The impact of the changes to advanced corporation tax and regulatory changes from the 1995 Pensions Act began to be felt and the Equitable Life Assurance Society's years of mismanagement finally came to a head in a nearly calamitous collapse. Coincidentally, at the same time, those responsible for international accounting standards moved to require that pensions liabilities should be shown on balance sheets (FRS18) – that is to say they were to be regarded as material information in respect of a company's financial standing.[67]

---

67 NAPF chairman Peter Thompson said in early 2002: 'Some 95 per cent of our members have told us that providing an occupational pension takes up more company resources compared with five years ago. This new accounting standard could be the final factor which keeps employers from providing traditional final pay pension schemes.' Interviewed by Antonia Senior, *The Times*, 23 February 2002.

As we have seen, the regulatory consequences of the 1995 Pension Act were beginning to be understood – dealing with layer upon layer of regulation added significant costs to the administration of a defined benefit pensions scheme. The combination of all of these factors was bad news for pension funds and their members. Worse still, there was a very real risk that employers would be reluctant to provide benefits in a world where they did not have to – and if the individual employee sees turmoil in the pensions world they may be wary of participating. As Alistair Darling put it,

> One of the biggest mistakes ever made was removing the obligation to be in a pension scheme – when Chancellor Nigel Lawson made it easier to opt out, that was a huge mistake. Human nature dictates that often money in hand can be seen as better than saving for tomorrow.

During the 1990s the pensions sector had been careering along, but as we saw in Chapter 6, by the time Alan Pickering rose to the top of the NAPF as vice-chairman and then chairman, there were worrying signs of decline. The number of active members in DB schemes had fallen from 5.5 million at the beginning of the decade to 4.7 million at its end. The government had inhibited the freedoms of fund managers and trustees and added significantly to the costs of running a pension fund. David Willetts says, 'Successive governments had over-regulated pensions. We learned the wrong lessons from Maxwell. We were providing so many protections and enhancements for members of occupational pension schemes there was a real danger that employers would give up on the whole project.' The perfect storm was completed by the stock market falls, interest rate rises and challenging economic circumstances of the first two years of the new millennium. And in Britain at government level there was a degree of confusion about what to do and a tendency to respond to short-term crises (of all kinds) rather than create strategic solutions. As Alistair Darling puts it, 'So much of government policy is reactive rather than proactive.'

The perfect storm of 2000–01 was to shake any complacency out of the system for good. Early in 2000 some commentators signalled their concern about stakeholder pensions. Alastair Ross Goobey of Hermes said, 'No matter how well intentioned the government's stakeholder pension provision is, it cannot offer the level of income in retirement that will satisfy the reasonable expectations of the population.'[68] Alan Pickering agreed, saying before the NAPF conference in May that year that stakeholder pensions could lead to lower retirement benefits for many: 'the employer is under no obligation to offer contributions'.[69] And Goobey added that 'the greatest future threat to any defined benefit pension scheme is its possible long-term cost to the sponsor', and that a move to a defined contribution scheme would mean that 'in most cases [they would] not have high

68 Investment Pensions Europe – IPE January 2000.
69 *Money Marketing*, 11 May 2000.

enough contributions from employer and employee to offer the levels of pension a traditional DB scheme has been able to offer.' All these factors led Nicholas Timmins to say that at that time (in 2001), 'Final salary schemes [were] closing to new members in droves.'[70] The BT scheme (one of Britain's largest) did this that year and many were to follow. In 2000, 'Eighteen British companies closed their pay-linked schemes [to new members] ... last year [2001] that number grew to forty-six.'[71] (By early 2002 the actuary Hewitt Bacon & Woodrow was to report that 'fewer than four in ten salary-related schemes were then open to new members.'[72]) As actuary Adrian Waddingham puts it,

> There are three big risks when you are saving for retirement: Investment return, inflation and longevity. Changes in these factors can add enormously to the cost of pensions. In a DB scheme these risks are covered by the employer and increasingly there was reluctance among employers to continue to do this.

The political dimension was in play as well. Lib Dem DWP spokesman Steve Webb said, 'Growing numbers of firms are being driven out of providing good-quality pensions and the government is sitting idly by. The pensions of a whole generation

70 Nicholas Timmins, ibid.
71 National Association of Pension Funds, as reported by Antonia Senior in *The Times*, 23 February 2002.
72 Liz Dolan in the *Daily Telegraph*, 17 July 2002.

are now at risk.'[73] This was a little unfair; Steve knew that at the time, in February 2002, Alan Pickering was hard at work.

In July 2001, Ian McCartney, who, after the general election, had become Alistair Darling's fourth Minister of State for Pensions in three years, said,

> I am committed to improving the position of older people, indeed as pensions minister, one of my objectives is to modernise the pensions system ... to make a real difference for both today's and tomorrow's pensioners. Choosing the right pension scheme is one of the most important decisions that an individual will make in their lifetime.[74]

This was a solid declaration of faith, and clearly he was signalling the likelihood of a review. However, by talking about the 'choice' of a pension scheme there was a (perhaps unwitting) reference to money purchase schemes (for which there may be choice) rather than defined benefit (where there isn't).

Alistair Darling sums up the situation as follows:

> When the economy is growing you can mask a lot of underlying problems. When things slow down you see them emerge and you see the defects in the system. The actuaries had taken the view that as a lot of pension funds were in surplus therefore

73 Steve Webb, as reported by Antonia Senior in *The Times*, 23 February 2002.
74 *Lancashire Telegraph*, 13 July 2001.

it was permissible to cut contributions. This was in part a response to shareholder pressure. But pensions are a long-term promise and the misselling of personal pensions had added to the disillusionment that many people felt. There was no doubt that a two-tier system was emerging.

## THE BRIEF TO ALAN PICKERING, AND THE TERMS OF REFERENCE

The 'perfect' storm for occupational pensions happened quickly – well within a year of David Blake's confident assertion in his report for Birkbeck that Britain was 'not facing a pensions crisis'. Whilst recriminations were already being made and guilty parties were being identified, in reality it was a combination of circumstances: some avoidable, others not. However, despite pensions taking a rather higher public profile than before, this was not reflected in the Labour Party's manifesto for the June 2001 general election, where there was no mention of growing concerns for workplace pensions or of pensions policy. Labour won the election comfortably with few significant changes to their House of Commons position and with a renewed strong majority.

Ian McCartney's promise to 'modernise' the pensions system was a reflection of a growing awareness in government of the need for change. The 9/11 attacks also had their impact, at least in the short term, on the world of pensions. As a *Daily Mail* article summed up,

> Major British companies will have to pour billions of pounds

> into pension funds damaged by the stock market falls of the past 20 months. And at least one has asked the official watchdog, the Occupational Pensions Regulatory Authority, for more time to make up its fund shortfall so it can meet commitments to pensioners [and] has also urged the National Association of Pension Funds to support a suspension of some of the rules on fund solvency to let it rebuild the fund … Even before the share price plunge after the US attacks, the pension funds of at least 10 names in the FTSE 100 index, including Tesco, BT, ICI and Scottish & Newcastle, were not fully funded, says pensions consultancy Bacon & Woodrow. A further fifteen big firms, including Kingfisher, Cable & Wireless and Dixons, were only fractionally above solvency levels.[75]

It was all these factors which led Alistair Darling, confirmed in his job as Secretary of State for Work and Pensions rather than for Social Security, to commission Alan Pickering to carry out his review and to make that phone call inviting Alan to head up the work and make recommendations. In choosing Alan he was clearly looking above all to find a solution to the DB scheme 'crisis', as Alan, both from his NAPF roles and because of his personal belief, was a staunch supporter of defined benefit pensions, which, as we have seen, had fairly precipitously come to be under threat. With Alan briefed to

---

75 'Pensions crunch for blue-chips', Lisa Buckingham, *Daily Mail*, 30 September 2001.

direct the pensions review, the government was also looking at simplifying the pensions tax system, which would also lead to a report in 2002.[76] There were, therefore, two parallel work streams from the Treasury (on tax) and on pensions sponsored by the DWP. Alan recalls that this worked well not least because the Chancellor, Gordon Brown, and the DWP Secretary of State, Alistair Darling, were then close and collaborated well together. In addition to these two streams the businessman Ron Sandler had been commissioned to investigate and advise on the savings industry, and his findings would appear just two days before the Pickering Report was unveiled. Alan's report recognised the links between the tax simplification study and the Sandler savings review and acknowledged that the review team 'worked closely' with these two study teams.

Alistair Darling today explains why he chose Alan Pickering:

> Alan's interest in and commitment to pensions he learned literally on the shop floor. He had direct experience and was dedicated to the idea that people should have properly funded pensions. He was, as a result, very keen on DB schemes and the trustee system. At the NAPF many of its leaders came from the pensions industry, but Alan was different to them and as a result was particularly able to influence things. The NAPF was an influential body (which is not the case with all

76 'Simplifying the taxation of pensions: increasing choice and flexibility for all', December 2002.

> industry bodies) and it was fortuitous that he was there for two years at a time when we were all trying to bring some sense to pensions policy. Alan had a passionate feel for the subject and at the same time he knew what he was talking about – in my experience in the world of politics he was, as a result, a fairly rare bird. In public life there is often a great gulf between those who had theoretical knowledge and those who had practical experience. Alan had both as well as a real feel for what people do in practice and why they do it. He understood human nature and was worldly. He was also genuinely independent and driven by his own experience and was someone whose judgment I would trust. He would be willing to point out where there were flaws in the present system without fear or favour.

Alan's commitment to DB was infectious. Pensions guru Henry Tapper, who had spent the early part of his career selling money purchase pensions for Eagle Star, says that when he met Alan he became convinced that DB was a 'fairer way to do things'.

David Willetts agrees with Alistair Darling's assessment of Alan's commitment and objective knowledge:

> One could have proper conversations with Alan – I learned a lot from him and he gave generously of his time as I shared with him some of the issues I was focusing on. As a shadow minister you have to operate without civil servants' advice. Some people are very partisan and others will only give advice

> to government. Alan was never partisan – I assumed that deep down he was a Labour supporter but he was always objective.

Alan's successor as chairman of the NAPF, Peter Thompson, was also enthusiastic about the appointment, saying that Alan Pickering was ideally suited to the task: 'Alan has extensive experience and a great breadth of understanding of pensions issues. We will be happy to put the knowledge and expertise of the NAPF at Alan's disposal in helping to bring about the much-needed simplification of pensions legislation.'[77] Thompson also concurred with the definition of the problem as being one of pensions complexity: 'We get two strong messages from our members. One is about cost, and one is about complexity. I hope that this review will be able to do something about the complexity.'[78]

The government announcement of his appointment was as follows:

> The government has today appointed Alan Pickering to undertake a comprehensive review of private pensions legislation to result in a package of options for simplification.

Alistair Darling commented:

> The government is determined to simplify the pensions policy

77 'Pickering to lead UK pensions simplification drive', ii-Q news, 26 September 2001.
78 Antonia Senior in *The Times*, 27 September 2001.

> system to make it easier to understand and to reduce costs. Complexity makes it difficult for pension scheme members to understand how their pension scheme is run and provides scope for bad practice to continue undetected. The government is committed to working with the pensions industry and consumer organisations to achieve simplification of the regulatory framework for pensions where this can be done without harming scheme members' interests. This will provide greater transparency for scheme members and will help employers by reducing the administrative burden on pension schemes.
>
> I am delighted that Alan Pickering has agreed to lead this review. Alan will bring an independent but realistic approach to the task. He will be relying on input from across the industry to make the review a success and I would encourage everyone with a contribution to make to engage with Alan and his team.

The terms of reference of the review (see Appendix 1) included the need to cover legislation, the regulatory framework and simplification of all types. It required delivery of proposals by July 2002. It required the proposals to protect pension scheme members, take account of economic and exchequer tax effects, of the Myners Rerport on the minimum funding requirement and of the five-yearly review of OPRA (Occupational Pensions Regulatory Authority).

The reaction to Alan's appointment to head up the review was generally welcomed, albeit with a degree of cynicism in some quarters, especially the media. The formidable Patience Wheatcroft said in *The Times*[79] that it was 'noble of Alan Pickering to undertake the exercise ... but the government is expert at organising investigations into the pensions industry. It is what happens next which counts.' She added that stakeholder pensions 'can hardly be said to have fulfilled the original stated aim. Instead, plenty of wealthy individuals are setting up stakeholders for their offspring, whilst those who were not likely to have a "decent, secure income in retirement" [the claim in the Pensions Green Paper of 1998] are still no nearer.' But she still felt Alan was the right person: 'He knows much of what needs to be done to simplify the pensions maze and begin to make it more understandable to the people.'

Alan Pickering himself was clear of the task ahead: 'Even full-time professionals don't understand the system at the moment ... this is not an overall review of government policy. But ministers will have to decide whether complication is a price worth paying for their policy ends.'[80]

## GETTING DOWN TO WORK

Alistair Darling was the sponsor of the Pickering Report, and he was to be one of Alan's main sounding boards in the coming

79 'Let's have some actions on pensions now', *The Times*, 27 September 2001.
80 Antonia Senior, ibid.

months. They had an early exchange of views. Alan stated his position to the Secretary of State:

> There is a fortress mentality in the world of pensions which is giving more and more protection to the pension 'haves' and making it more difficult for the 'have nots' to come inside the fortress. Not only is current private pensions policy misguided, but we should also be looking at problems in the state pension system. The basic state pension doesn't lift someone above the government's own definition of the basic poverty line. It doesn't pay people on the margin to save for a pension because all they are doing is denying themselves access to means-tested benefits if they do. The policy is not fit for purpose and it is the state pension which is the weak link.

In response to this Darling clarified what he wanted Alan to do:

> We are where we are. Write me a report quickly. Knock off the low hanging fruit in terms of simplification and raise your ideas about policy. I will support the simplification proposals – please keep me in the loop overall. The recommendations should be cost neutral but if there is some levelling down for some to enable levelling up for others that is fine.

He also reassured Alan that he was seen as being 'professionally and politically acceptable to both the Treasury and the DWP'.

Having clarified his brief and been encouraged both by Alistair Darling's personal support and by his complimentary public statements about his suitability for the task, Alan set about establishing his team and modus operandi. From his discussions with Darling it was clear to him that the character of his review was to be highly independent; it would be presented not as an official government/DWP document but as an 'independent report'. He wouldn't work within the department. 'They didn't give me an office – or even a biscuit,' he says, though he stresses this is not a complaint. He was happy to operate as a free spirit and not be hidebound by any civil service structure or rules.

The first appointment to what was to be Alan's nine-person team was Mark Heholt, an early career civil servant who had already progressed quite rapidly in the DWP. He regarded it as 'an unusual opportunity to work outside of the civil service/government'. He had been in the loop prior to Alan's appointment, although he was not a pensions expert, and confirms that the department wanted the review to be conducted outside of the daily pressures of the political arena. Alan, he says, was seen as having 'genuine expertise'. Prior to the setting up of the review, pensions had been raising its profile as an area of concern, to which, Heholt says, they now had a response: 'We're on the case.' Interestingly, he recalls that at the time there was a general view among civil servants working on pensions that 'companies had not paid much attention to pensions prior to 2000–01' and that they had been at fault for 'not building up surpluses' when they could. Mark was the only member of the team, apart from Alan, who was full-time.

The other members of the review team who played a major part in its work came from a range of backgrounds. Margaret Craig had worked in the financial services industry since 1979 and was with the ABI (Association of British Insurers) – the trade association for Britain's insurance industry. Peter Ford was on the main committee of the Association of Pension Lawyers and was to be the primary source of legal advice. 'There was', he says, 'layer upon layer of regulation – it was like a layer cake, and it was clear that the whole compliance regime needed change and simplification. A lot of the regulations were impenetrable and there were new ones all the time. There was a need to remove some of the protection.' Chris Dallard was an actuary with Hewitt Bacon & Woodrow and was to provide the actuarial input into the review. Adrian Furnell, who worked for the IBM Pensions Trust, gave an employer's view. Along with Heholt, Craig, Ford and Dallard were the key team members supporting Alan Pickering. Although not officially a member of the team, Jenny Davie continued to support Alan and was a crucial aid to him – especially in helping ensure that he could be aware of the masses of paper that flooded his desk.

The construct of the review team was, Mark Heholt says, 'lean and mean'. The need to deliver within nine months predicated that this could not be work that would risk paralysis by analysis. There are no graphs, tables or complex calculations in the report and there was no economic modelling. Peter Ford says that the team was fully aware of the pressure on DB schemes from the start: 'The regulatory consequences of the 1995 act, the disappearance of fund surpluses, the emphasis on compliance for compliance's sake, the impenetrability of much of the regulation, the need to stop legislating for minutiae…' He also says that the risk that employers would walk away from schemes was very real: 'How do we encourage employers to still provide benefits in a world where they are not obliged to?' Greater consistency over time was also a goal. As Alistair Darling put it, 'If people think the [pensions] deal is going to change, you can't blame them for not putting in. The chopping and changing of the 1990s was unhelpful.'

Over the course of the nine months of the review the team 'received almost 100 written contributions … from organisations and a similar number from individuals [and] had face-to-face meetings with around 30 key organisations such as the Confederation of British Industry, Trades Union Congress and Consumers' Association to discuss their views as they emerged'.[81] Alan stresses the non-partisan nature of the work; from his own recent NAPF roles he knew all the key players across both the civil service and politics as well as in the pensions industry itself. Darling was, as we have seen, key in his 'encouragement to think radically', but across the political spectrum there was also encouragement from

81 Alan Pickering, Foreword to 'A Simpler Way to Better Pensions', July 2002.

Conservatives like Peter Lilley and David Willetts and Liberal Democrats like Steve Webb. As Alan put it, 'Political buy-in has been critical in our desire to obtain considered input from the wider community.' But, as senior actuary Adrian Waddingham succinctly states, 'The prime motivation for politicians is not to make good things happen but to stop bad things from happening.' This is the same as Alistair Darling's view that government is so often 'reactive not proactive'.

Mark Heholt says that, from his experience in the civil service, when reviews or studies are commissioned, there are two common approaches. The first is to 'understand the directions in which government is minded to move and ride that'. The second is to 'be firm in what you believe and hope that the government can be persuaded'. He says Alan Pickering took the second route: 'Even if some of his suggestions were to fly in the face of government thinking, he'd still make them. Alan was trying to change the terms of the debate a bit – to set the weather.' That said, there were regular meetings with Alistair Darling and Ian McCartney, so government opinion was certainly consulted constantly. However, as Peter Ford puts it,

> No ideas were off the table, but Alan knew that the report could not be a 'government thing'. There could be no [party] political agenda. Core principles which are cross-party had to be stated. That is not to say that precisely the same message had to be communicated to all. When Alan presented key material

to people of different political persuasions he nuanced it. He would emphasise what he knew what they would be looking for.

Ford also describes Alan's style in the frequent meetings: 'He always came across as measured and thoughtful. This engagement style meant that people always welcomed the opportunity to discuss things they were really concerned with.'

The overarching complexity of pensions laws and regulations was the main concern, and there were some 'low-hanging fruit to be picked'. So much of the 'regulatory protection was too copper-bottomed it created a wall with some inside and others not', according to Peter Ford. Taking into account the costs often involved in conforming to the rules led many sponsors to ask, 'How can we afford to pay for this?' In addition to the 'perfect storm', there was accelerating social change as well. The defined benefit/final salary pension schemes had emerged at a time when most employees stayed with one company for life. In these circumstances the employer would quite logically conclude that there was a duty of care throughout the forty-plus years of employment and beyond. But entering the new millennium, that paradigm, whilst it was still not uncommon, was far from the norm. This was to be acknowledged in the recommendations, which argued for 'much easier pension transfer rules'.[82]

The Pickering Report came out of a review which followed

82 'The Pickering Report', Executive Summary, p. xi.

the classic model of input-process-output – with the report and its linked presentations and debates being the 'output'. We have seen that the 'input' included the identification of the problem(s), the scope decided by government and the many and varied contributions made by pensions specialists, politicians and other third parties. The 'process' involved a dynamic evaluation in which nothing was off the table and in which devil's advocacy played an important part. The 'devil' was often Alan himself, and Peter Ford says that in doing this Alan had the ability to rise above the detail and look at an issue from a strategic standpoint, sometimes known as 'Helicopter Quality' – the ability to see both the minute detail and a very broad overview. Crucially, the process also included the need to challenge conventional wisdoms. Among these was the challenge to the fact that politicians had chosen to convert a 'best endeavours' paradigm for pensions (under which there is flexibility and discretion) to one based on guarantees. For example, pensions in payment may be increased in line with inflation under the former regime, but such increases became mandatory in the Pensions Act 1995. There was much discussion of this and many of the other guarantees during the process stage of the review. Mark Heholt recalls that the review team worked well together and there were few disagreements. As the work progressed, and the likely direction of the recommendations became clear, there was deliberately no testing of ideas within the DWP. This was to keep the character of the review as an independent one – commissioned by government but not bound to follow any government preconceptions in its recommendations. As former pensions minister Stephen Timms MP puts it, 'We wanted someone who understood the subject to come up with his best ideas and then politicians can decide what to implement.' That said, Peter Ford believes that there was an underlying pragmatism to the recommendations and that although 'no ideas were off the table, the report was not going to be too radical'.

The Pickering Report was published on 11 July 2002. In the run-up to its publication Alan had floated a few ideas in public which tested the temperature of the water. In particular, he endorsed a suggestion from the centre-left think tank, the Institute for Public Policy Research, which called for the state retirement age to be raised to sixty-seven, and repeated his contention that 'You just can't create enough wealth in 30 years of work to support 40 years of retirement.'[83] He also flagged that he intended to 'strip away unnecessary and costly regulation' and that he wanted to create a system that is 'tinker proof against future political interference'.[84]

## THE PICKERING REPORT – RECOMMENDATIONS

In Appendix 2 the five-page Executive Summary of the Pickering Report summarises the recommendations of Alan Pickering

83 'Carry on working to 70 says state pension guru', Antonia Senior, *The Times*, 8 March 2002.
84 Antonia Senior, ibid.

and his team. These recommendations are partly behavioural in tone, as well as in some cases fairly detailed – suggesting both broader improvements and specific changes to be made. The goal of the review is described as: 'to identify ways to make it easier for employers to provide good-quality pensions for their employees, easier for commercial providers to sell appropriate products to appropriate people, and easier for individuals to accumulate pensions benefits.' This mission statement clearly reflects the scope that determined the work areas of the team from the start. Alan Pickering wanted, as he says in his Foreword, to be 'both radical and workable', and to accept that they needed to 'balance the interests of those who are in pensions schemes and those who are not; unduly ambitious protection for the former may raise the entry stakes for the latter'. Among the more specific recommendations we can highlight here:

- The proposal for a 'new kind of regulator'
- All trust-based schemes should have one third of trustees nominated by pensions scheme members
- A more 'targeted' approach to communicating with members
- The same level of protection for both workplace (DB) and marketplace (DC) schemes
- A substantial reduction in generic pension products as a result of greater streamlining
- Employers should be allowed to make membership of their pension scheme a condition of employment (if they wish to)

- There should be immediate 'vesting' in all types of pension arrangements
- There should be easier pension transfer rules
- The requirement to increase pensions payments in line with prices (indexation) should be removed
- The requirement for schemes to provide survivors' benefits (e.g. widows' pensions) should be removed
- The requirement for schemes to offer death in service and incapacity benefits should be removed
- It should be easier for employers to re-shape pension arrangements in the light of contemporary economic circumstances.

The final four recommendations listed here would undoubtedly be contentious. Alan Pickering to some extent pre-empted this by explaining that they considered some existing requirements to be 'over-prescriptive' and that they were 'a contributory factor in employers switching from defined benefit (DB) to defined contribution (DC) schemes'. As far as the option to avoid indexation was concerned, he said, 'the reduction in cost for future accrual might persuade an employer to continue offering a defined DB scheme rather than switching to DC'. The same applied to the survivor's benefit recommendation, and here he added, 'many couples would prefer to make arrangements to ensure they both have an independent income in retirement, rather than relying on derived rights'. Here Alan was relating one of the modern-day social changes that, with both partners working for all or some of their lives, the concept of the 'sole breadwinner' was fading, and that this applied to pensions as well as to earnings. He emphasised that the team was not calling for the abolition of these benefits – merely an end to compulsory provision.

## THE LAUNCH OF THE PICKERING REPORT AND THE RESPONSE TO IT

On 28 May 2002 the Transport Secretary, Stephen Byers, resigned after weeks of vacillation, finally realising that a long series of errors and gaffes had made his position untenable. His successor was Alistair Darling. Alastair Campbell recorded in his diaries that he and Darling 'had a chat about how to grip his new department and how to avoid being a pawn between Tony Blair and Gordon Brown. Alistair was pleased TB had entrusted him with a pretty big challenge and he intended to get on top of the detail…'

Politics is in part a tale of unintended consequences. The risks of Darling leaving the Department of Work and Pensions just six weeks before the Pickering Report was due to be launched were unlikely to have been discussed at No. 10. Darling reflects phlegmatically on this today:

> It is always a problem when a Secretary of State commissions a piece of work that they feel a sense of ownership for. The new man cannot have that same sense of ownership – it was not

a great time to move, but the railway system was descending into chaos…

He says he had to leave the launch, including the presentation in Parliament, to his successor: 'You can't interfere once you've left.'

That personalities put their stamp on Departments of State is inevitable and indeed desirable. However, in the Blair government (and many other governments before and since), Cabinet governance was weak, which pushed the onus either upwards onto the Prime Minister and his close coterie of advisors (on major matters), or downwards onto the ministers on other issues. As Alistair Darling puts it, 'I think our government would have benefited a bit more if we'd had more Cabinet discussion.' In his memoir, *Back from the Brink*, he adds, 'I sat at the Cabinet table for thirteen years. That should be the forum at which government policy is hammered out … [but] both Tony and Gordon were reluctant to have open discussions if there was any possibility of controversy.' He adds that he is fairly certain that the Pickering Report 'was not discussed in Cabinet'. The point in respect of the launch is, of course, that the first thing the new Secretary of State, Andrew Smith, really knew about any of the detail of pensions policy review was when he took over his new job. He had just six weeks to get up to speed before he spoke in the House of Commons debate on the report.

Alan Pickering sees the replacement of his supporter and mentor, Alistair Darling, by the comparatively unknown Andrew

Smith as very damaging to the review: 'He hadn't been with me on the journey and he didn't have confidence in me or in himself to give some of the regulatory proposals a fair hearing.' It is true that the actual pensions minister under Darling, Ian McCartney, was to stay in his job for another year and would provide continuity. However, although it is usually the case, as Alistair Darling puts it, that the 'Minister of State does the donkey work', in this instance this was less true because of the empathy between Darling and Pickering. McCartney was an able junior minister but Alan had to look elsewhere for creative and original input to the review.

At 1.27 p.m. on 11 July 2002 Andrew Smith made his statement to the House of Commons on the Pickering Report. His opening words thanked the contributors and summarised the main recommendations:

> The report is the culmination of nine months of hard work by Alan Pickering and his team. I should like to thank him and also everyone who took the time and effort to submit their views – some of whom are here today.
>
> In his report, Alan Pickering acknowledges the encouragement that he received not only from my Rt Hon. Friends, the Secretary of State for Transport and the Minister for Pensions, but also from the Rt Hon. Member for Hitchin and Harpenden (Mr Lilley) and the Hon. Members for Havant (Mr Willetts) and for Northavon (Mr Webb).

> Pensions simplification has to be at the heart of any strategy to encourage greater pension provision. We need to deal with the complexities built up over the years by successive governments.
>
> Alan's report makes fifty-two recommendations. The key ones include: a new Pensions Act to consolidate all existing pensions legislation; a new, more proactive, regulator; a better, more targeted approach for communicating with pension scheme members; more flexibility to modify schemes; allowing employers to make membership of their occupational pension scheme a condition of employment; and the ending of compulsory indexation for defined benefit pensions; and compulsory survivors' benefits.

Smith emphasised the cross-party nature of the review and name-checked Peter Lilley, David Willetts and Steve Webb. He went on:

> We wanted Alan Pickering to present a strong challenge to the degree of regulation around private pensions. He has done that – he has made some valuable proposals for simplifying pensions legislation and reducing administrative burdens on both schemes and employers, cutting costs and simplifying choices for individuals.

He was also swift to torpedo two of the more controversial of the Pickering recommendations:

> Alan also recommends an end to compulsory indexation of pensions and removal of compulsory survivors' benefits as a condition of contracting out. On first reading, those proposals are not attractive. They go against the drive of the past thirty years to price protect pensions and to enhance survivors' benefits, but again, in the light of the report, we will need to look carefully at all the consequences.

Notwithstanding the promise to 'look carefully', it was quite clear that government wasn't going down that particular path. Smith concluded:

> Alan Pickering's proposals are radical, ambitious and pragmatic. I urge Hon. Members, the public, employers, trade unions and pension providers – all those whose partnership is essential for effective pension reform – to give them full and constructive consideration. The government certainly will. The acid tests for the Green Paper must be increasing the level of savings for retirement and making a secure occupational pension accessible to as many people as possible.

David Willetts then spoke for the Conservatives. He also complimented Alan Pickering and welcomed the report:

> The starting point of the debate has to be a frank recognition of the scale of the problem that faces funded pensions.

> For years, ministers have been shockingly complacent, saying that everything was all right when it clearly was not, and citing statistics that they have since admitted were seriously misleading. The Secretary of State should accept the stark warning in Alan Pickering's report that '...without change, the current trajectory suggests less private pension provision in the future.'

Willets's contribution was very party political in character – much of it a critical backward look at Labour policy since 1997, rather than a forward look at what to do next. Smith replied, not unreasonably,

> The truth is that we have only to read the Pickering Report to see the number of measures that he suggests need to be tackled that were actually the product of legislation passed by the previous Conservative administration, albeit often with the best of intentions. One of our problems is that layer upon layer of complexity and regulation has been built up in response to short-term events, and that has left us all with a huge long-term problem.

For the Liberal Democrats, Steve Webb said that he

> welcomed the fact that Alan Pickering is seeking to create an all-party consensus on pensions structures, and I can confirm

> to the Secretary of State that, if he decides to approach prospective legislation in that way, the Liberal Democrats will certainly play a full and constructive part.
>
> I want to raise two areas of concern: I disagree with Alan Pickering in that I do not believe that benefits for widows, or the post-retirement raising of pensions, are 'bells and whistles'. In our view – and, I sense, in the Secretary of State's view – they are an integral part of what pensions should be. Given that many old pensioners – the poorest pensioners in the land – are often elderly widows, can it be right to undermine provision for widows or to have more pensions frozen for twenty years of retirement? I do not believe so, and I hope that the Secretary of State will confirm his intention to look very sceptically at that proposal.

Not surprisingly, the Secretary of State confirmed that he would do just that:

> The Hon. Gentleman mentioned a description of survivors' benefits as 'bells and whistles'. It is certainly not a description that I would use – such benefits are valued features of current schemes…

Notwithstanding his short time in the post Andrew Smith had done a good job in presenting the Pickering Report to Parliament. He announced that a Green Paper would appear later in the year in response to the report and to other inputs (including the Sandler savings review), but he also pretty categorically ruled out two of Alan Pickering's recommendations. Willetts and Webb retreated to their party comfort zones although the continued debate was actually fairly unpartisan, with informed contributions from Frank Field, Archy Kirkwood, James Arbuthnot and others.

Steve Webb's reference to 'bells and whistles' (and Andrew Smith's swift disassociation from the phrase) was a reference to events earlier in the day. At 6 a.m. Alan Pickering had been picked up in a BBC car which took him the studio from which the *Today* programme was transmitted live. At 7.10 a.m. Martha Kearney went for the jugular about widows' pensions: 'What's this report that says that widows' pensions will no longer be paid? ... You regard a widow's pension as a bell or a whistle?' Alan had responded: 'It is not for Parliament to tell employers if they want bells and whistles or not. It is for employers and employees to make that decision. They should design the scheme that suits them.'[85] Alan agrees today that there was a certain naivety in the use of the 'bells and whistles' phrase. David Willetts concurs:

> I was willing as opposition spokesman not to criticise something that was properly done by a respected expert like Alan – I hope that he took from me that there wouldn't be cheap

85 *Glasgow Herald*, 12 July 2002.

> shots from the opposition about his recommendations. The route he took by recommending that scheme costs be reduced by reducing 'extra' benefits I had actively encouraged him to take. But the 'bells and whistles' descriptor was an unusual mistake from someone who was normally so sure-footed.

In response to the question as to whether, had Alistair Darling still been the minister, he might have told Alan, in preparation for the launch, not to use the phrase, Willetts says today, 'That makes sense. The person who set up the process wasn't there to guide the ship home.'

The following day the press inevitably focused on the 'bells and whistles' phrase. Alan was of course undoubtedly right in his assertion that 'pensions promises were often imposed by well-meaning or interfering politicians.'[86] The balance of this was uncontroversial to a pensions professional. But to the popular press it was dynamite. Similarly, the recommendation to remove the mandatory linking of pensions to inflation caused what the *Daily Mail* called 'fury': 'Pickering's review has prompted fury with its controversial proposal to axe the rules protecting pensions against inflation.'[87] The unions which Alan had carefully cultivated during his review soundings phrase also went ballistic. John Edmonds of the GMB general union said, 'We could be looking at the biggest pensions rip-off in history ... the government has

86 *The Guardian*, 12 July 2002.
87 *Daily Mail*, 12 July 2002.

turned to an industry insider who is trying to make it possible for employers to renege on any pensions responsibility.' And former union leader Rodney Bickerstaffe (also president of the National Pensioners Convention) said of the report, 'It will sentence future generations of pensioners to a retirement on means-tested benefits and charitable hand-outs.' Even Frank Field was quoted as saying on BBC Radio that 'people on low incomes would simply be unable to save for retirement'.[88]

A couple of days after the launch Alan Pickering appeared on the BBC radio programme *Money Box*[89] to be interviewed by Paul Lewis. Lewis, inevitably, focused on the headline issues of pension indexation and widows' pensions. Lewis asked him if 'he'd been disappointed by the largely negative response that his ideas had received'. Alan gave a measured reply: 'Many people have given widespread support for most of what I'm suggesting. Ultimately society has to decide; if society wants big pensions it's got to make big contributions.' Lewis said that this was a 'fair point' but pressed Alan on the two 'radical changes' proposed. Alan came out fighting: 'Much of the publicity has focused on silver-haired widows [but] in the current state of the law survivors' pensions could [apply] to a six-foot-three, 25-year-old Premier League centre-forward ... let's allocate resources to where resources are needed.' Alan also

88 *The Guardian*, ibid.

89 Transcript from *Money Box*, BBC Radio 4, 13 July 2002.

clarified that a change to the indexation rules would 'in no way affect those who have already retired'.

In that *Money Box* programme Paul Lewis also interviewed Donald Duval, the president of the Society of Pensions Consultants, who commented, 'The basic problem with the Pickering review is it's not sufficiently radical ... those employers who are going to close schemes will carry on doing so.' He felt that Alan's remit had been 'too narrow'. This was a position also taken by pensions expert Ros Altmann.[90] Altmann regretted that DC schemes had not really been part of the brief. She said that DC 'is, after all, the way pensions in the future will be provided, whether we like it or not.' Although she wished the scope had been wider and the recommendations as a result more comprehensive, Altmann did support a number of Alan's proposals, including reducing the number of pensions products requiring immediate vesting, the idea for a 'safe harbour' product, the abolition of the difference between 'protected' and 'non-protected' rights, the focus on less prescriptive, unified legislation and improving communication to members.

Hillary Clinton has said, 'If you believe you can make a difference, not just in politics, in public service ... then you have to be prepared to accept that you are not going to get 100 per cent approval.' This is the reality of the political world. For Alan, who certainly understood this truism, the response was not to

90 Ros Altmann, blog, July 2002.

temper what he believed to be right with an attempt at conciliatory pragmatism. Ultimately, the politics had to be managed by the politicians.

As we saw in the story at the beginning of this chapter, at the very top, political actions can often be reactive. Tony Blair was suddenly aware of pensions on 11 July 2002 because the subject was headline news. And headlines reflect not the detail of very complex subjects such as pensions, but what sells newspapers and makes a 'good story'. Within a few days the media had moved on to something else and a much more measured response by the pensions community emerged. On 18 July government put to bed (lest anyone doubted their position) the indexation and survivors' pensions issue. In response to a (possibly planted) question in the House of Commons from Jim Cousins MP – 'Is it government policy to continue those public sector schemes on a final salary basis, including survivor benefits and indexation of the pension once in payment?' – the Financial Secretary to the Treasury, Ruth Kelly, replied, 'The Pickering review … proposed some changes in what it is compulsory for employers to offer in their pension schemes … at first sight some of them, especially those on compulsory indexation and survivors' benefits, do not seem attractive.' This was repeating what Andrew Smith had said on 11 July, and as far as government was concerned it was the end of the matter.

Mark Heholt says that, from his then position at the DWP, 'In government generally people thought that the Pickering

Report was a balanced and well-thought-out piece of work and it was welcomed. It did shape the debate and influence subsequent legislation.' He also says that the fact that the report was independent allowed ministers to see the public response before jumping – the government was very concerned with image. Peter Ford agrees: 'If the media response had been warm then it would have been the government's report and if the media response had been "what a load of old tosh", it would have been Alan's report.' Ford says that nobody in the review team had been allocated the task of managing the communications and the DWP supplied no real structure. Alan Pickering agrees: 'Everything recommended was deliverable given a proper launch.' Stephen Timms MP says that he thought that the report was 'objective, but not necessarily what most ministers wanted to hear'.

In fact, the media response was selective – the mass media went for the headlines but the more specialist outlets recognised not just the value of the report but that it would, in considerable measure, influence the future – via the publication of the Green Paper and its aftermath. With the benefit of hindsight, one can see that actually many non-headline-grabbing changes happened and pensions were simplified. The introduction of The Pensions Regulator in 2005 was a direct consequence of Alan Pickering's recommendations. But Alan still regrets that more of the recommendations were not instigated. Robert Burgon of Plumbing Pensions (UK) Ltd says that 'most of Alan's recommendations were common sense – more should have been implemented'. Adrian Waddingham agrees: 'After the Pickering Report they should have put Alan in the House of Lords and made him pensions minister.'

Alistair Darling says today that 'the Pickering Report was a good job of work and it moved things along. You don't always get credit on day one,' and, as an epitaph, that is probably one that Alan would settle for. The review also directly led to Alan Pickering's award of the CBE in January 2004, and it was Mark Heholt who wrote the citation. In doing this he was asked to show 'how a candidate has changed things, brought distinction to British life or enhanced the UK's reputation in their area or activity'. Mark says it was not difficult to show how Alan had ticked all three boxes.

CHAPTER 8

# NEW BEGINNINGS

*Lifetime achievement awards are a bit of a double-edged sword. They suggest that you've done okay but are nearing the end. For my part, I like to think there's a lot of life in the old dog yet.*[91]

When, much to his delight, two of his racehorses gave birth to foals in early 2018, Alan Pickering saw a certain symbolism to these events taking place in what is his seventieth year. They were new beginnings – again. Not that he dwells too much on age – however thick and fast come the awards which pay tribute to his decades of service.

At the end of Chapter 7 we saw the publication of the Pickering Report and the comment from Stephen Timms MP that the report was 'objective, but not necessarily what most ministers

91 Alan Pickering on receiving a 'Trustee Lifetime Achievement Award' in July 2013.

wanted to hear'. But it did turn out to be what Steve Webb calls, 'the last chance saloon for defined benefit schemes'. David Willetts calls it a 'missed opportunity', and senior actuary Adrian Waddingham agrees: 'The Pickering Report was too honest for the government's liking and didn't get the support it should have had from the politicians who commissioned it.' Alan himself says that he couldn't 'give the government the silver bullet they wanted'. Perhaps nobody could have. This is in part because in order to modernise the pensions system there would inevitably have to have been winners and losers, and 'the winners don't say thank you and the losers cut up rough'. This is the political reality, and the Blair government in 2002, despite its huge parliamentary majority and the weakness of the opposition, didn't want to antagonise potential losers – especially if among them were, as Alan puts it, 'the natural recipients of sympathy'. In *The Pinch: How the Baby Boomers Took Their Children's Future*, David Willetts calls a pension an 'intergenerational contract in its most explicit form' and suggests that it was the baby boomer generation that ducked the opportunity to provide for their children and grandchildren as generously as they themselves had been provided for. This is the 'fortress mentality' that, as Alan Pickering puts it, 'meant that fewer and fewer people were benefiting from good-quality schemes'. He feels that the furore over the 'bells and whistles' surrounding widows' entitlements and pensions in payment indexation (some of it couched in unhelpful 'class war' phraseology) could have been avoided. As he puts it, he included carefully thought-through trade-offs in the recommendations – increasing the employers' contribution in schemes from 3 per cent to 4 per cent in return (indirectly) for deregulation, for example. Alan did spend the rest of 2002 making the case for the report's recommendations, and some of what he argued did find its way into action. But there were also to be more weighty reports from Lord Turner[92] and from the Parliamentary and Health Service Ombudsman,[93] among other studies, and the momentum of change from defined benefit/final salary pensions to workplace savings could not be stopped. For Adrian Waddingham this was a disappointing outcome: 'When the pendulum swings it goes from one extreme to the other. From pensions that were the envy of Europe to cheap and cheerful money purchase. There was no centre ground.' The financial editor of *The Times* put it more starkly again back in March 2004: 'The real problem is that most of the next generation has been excluded from guaranteed occupational pensions in the private sector ... [they are] too costly and risky for most employers.'[94]

In June 2005 Alan was philosophical about the Pickering Report but still proud of its achievements: '[There was] an inability on my part to prove that less prescription would lead to more pension ... but much progress was made, e.g. tax simplifications, a new kind of regulator and the removal of many of the constraints

92 'A New Pension Settlement for the Twenty-First Century', Pensions Commission 2005/2006.

93 'Trusting in the Pensions Promise', March 2006.

94 'Brown isolated on pensions', Graham Searjeant, *The Times*, 12 March 2004.

on how defined contribution pots might be deployed.'[95] But later in the year he revealed that there had been some dirty tricks back in 2002: 'Two days before my report was published, it was selectively leaked, and it was obvious that the leak had come from government sources. By the time the report was published, I was already busy defending the unpalatable bits that had been leaked.'[96]

But David Willetts's 'selfish' baby boomers are not, in truth, much affected by these dramatic changes. And that is why Alan Pickering's role as a guru on workplace pensions did not cease to be important despite the decline of DB pensions. Although virtually all DB schemes are closed to new members, these plans still manage 82 per cent of the UK's pension funds' assets today – around £2 trillion.[97] And these funds have to be managed for the benefit of their members, however privileged some of these members may be seen to be. In fact, although DB schemes have been a boon to all who receive them, across the pensioner population as a whole the receipts per individual are modest.[98] Only a small proportion of the fortunate baby boomers can be seen as fat cats. And pensions have not disappeared from the government's responsibilities or from their ministers' to-do list. Proportionate regulation is part of this and Alan Pickering

95 *PMI News*, June 2005.
96 *The Independent*, 26 November 2005.
97 Willis Towers Watson 2017.
98 The average weekly occupational pension in 2014 was £222 (£11,500 per annum). (Pensions Policy Institute.)

sees that his recommendations in respect of the future regulation of pension schemes to have been one of his review's most important achievements. The establishment of The Pensions Regulator (TPR) was a direct consequence of the review. This is how TPR described its function in April 2006, after one year in existence:

> In 2002 the Pickering report called for simplification of the regulatory framework for pensions. This was followed in December 2002 by the Quinquennial Review of the Occupational Pensions Regulatory Authority (Opra) and in June 2003 by the pensions Green Paper *Simplicity, security and choice: working and saving for retirement*. Both these documents, and the National Audit Office's report on Opra, supported the Pickering report's recommendation for change in pensions regulation and the establishment of a 'new kind of regulator': outcome and customer focused; and transparent, proportionate and risk-based in its approach.
>
> The Pensions Regulator was launched on 6 April 2005. We regulate work-based pensions. Our vision is to improve confidence in work-based pensions by protecting the benefits of scheme members and encouraging high standards of good practice in the running of schemes. Our objectives are in the Pensions Act 2004. They are to protect the benefits of work-based pension scheme members; to reduce the risk of situations arising which may lead to calls on the Pension

> Protection Fund; and to promote the good administration of work-based pension schemes.[99]

Both in the Pickering Report and in his subsequent involvement in the setting up of TPR, Alan Pickering sought to tread a balance between regulation and freedom and also between self-regulation and legislation. In a paper on Pensions Policy for the Adam Smith Institute in the spring of 2004, he said, 'Pension Regulation ... should [not] be expected to deliver absolute consumer security ... [they] should be encouraged to develop an approach to regulation which is risk-based and principle-based.'[100] Alan had practical hands-on experience of regulation from his membership of the (then) Occupational Pensions Board from 1991 to 1997 as well as an in-depth knowledge of the subject from his review. It was, therefore, no surprise when he was asked to become a non-executive board member of TPR in February 2005. He was pleased to have the opportunity – he says that it is rare for report writers to be involved in the implementation of their recommendations. He was on record as believing that there was a temptation for all regulators to over-regulate and from the start he wanted TPR not to do this. One commentator said at the time that Alan's appointment 'assuaged industry fears over heavy-handed regulation', pointing

99 The Pensions Regulator Medium Term Strategy, April 2006.
100 'Pensions Policy – How Government can get us saving again', Adam Smith Institute, Spring 2004.

out that he had 'publicly condemned the 1995 Pensions Act which had imposed such a heavy burden of regulation on pension schemes that it has been one of the factors to some employers' unwillingness to carry on pension schemes'.[101]

Alan was to be a two-term member of the TPR, which he sees as performing a vital function: 'In any sector where there is an asymmetry of knowledge between provider and the consumer there is a need for regulation so long as it is risk-based and proportionate and it is designed to improve outcomes.' This was not to be regulation for regulation's sake, but for the customer's; in Alan's view the regulator's role is to 'educate, enable and enforce'. There were a few operational issues to resolve and a few principles to sort out, such as: should TPR be combined with the Pension Protection Fund (PPF),[102] for example? (It was decided this would not be the case.) But over most of his seven years as a member of TPR board Alan believes the regulator was at the 'cutting edge' in terms of its work and performance. Clearly his unique blend of experience was valuable to them, but his exposure to the wide variety of issues TPR encountered was also useful to him in his main career.

Alan's day job was still at Watson Wyatt, where he had a distinctive role in support of the business. Most consultancies in

101 *Professional Pensions*, February 2005.

102 'The Pension Protection Fund was established to pay compensation to members of eligible defined benefit pension schemes, when there is a qualifying insolvency event in relation to the employer and where there are insufficient assets in the pension scheme to cover Pension Protection Fund levels of compensation.' (PPF website.)

the financial services sector judge performance in respect of fee income. The more a consultant generates income by serving his clients well the better he is seen as performing. Alan was different. He had been close to the centres of power – at least those centres dealing with occupational pensions – and not just in the UK. In his European role as chairman of the European Federation for Retirement Provision (EFRP) he steered the pensions directive (Institutions for Occupational Retirement Provision) through the EU's adoption progress to successful acceptance by the council of ministers. As Investment Pensions Europe had put it when awarding Alan the 'Gold Award for Outstanding Industry Contribution' in 2004 (one of many he received around this time), 'This was the culmination of a decade's work for the association and required a deft pair of hands at the EFRP's tiller to ensure that the directive came through the arduous birth rites involving the EC, the European Parliament and the Council of Ministers...'[103]

As a partner at Watson Wyatt Alan was available to support his colleagues with specific client responsibilities (the ones that generated the fee income) and, as you might imagine, he did this often. For a client to hear from someone who had been, and still was, close to the political and other centres of power in Britain and in Europe on the subject of pensions was highly valuable – particularly for those clients wrestling with a changing regulatory environment and for those with a pan-European business.

103 IPE Awards 2004.

As we have seen, Alan Pickering's early life in pensions had involved trustee training at the EETPU. Later, as a trustee himself of the Plumbing Industry Pension Scheme (since 1981), he had been exposed to most of the issues that trustees of DB schemes have to deal with. In 2005 he warned about over-complexity: 'If trustees have to understand the detailed "how" rather than the more strategic "what" and "why", the future for lay trustees may be bleak and our pensions system is likely to be much poorer as a consequence.'[104] This was a response to 'reams of regulation' about which Alan had been forthright: 'We're selling trustees short by expecting them to be knowledgeable of this legislative garbage.' Some fund sponsors are unhelpfully critical of trustees, seeing them as 'vagabonds who are trying to take money out of the business'. His views were to become increasingly robust – and prescient: 'Politicians no longer put adult manifestos before the electorate, preferring to rely on bland platitudes,' he said in May 2007,[105] 'policy is made on the hoof ... this means that long-term pension policy is made through the rear-view mirror rather than through the windscreen.' He called for a 'labour market which is blind to age, so folk of all ages have access to learning and earning opportunities. We need a simple state pension which provides a guarantee against absolute poverty in old age ... and we need a market for pension savings which is proportionately regulated...'

104 Speech to Pensions Management Institute June 2005, reported in *Professional Pensions*.
105 Article in *Professional Pensions*, May 2007.

By 2008 Alan had evolved into the 'go-to' man on pensions for conference organisers, magazine editors and for others across the financial services sector. He was busy – not to mention with his parallel lives in athletics, horse racing and charities. But, active though he was at sixty, he began to feel that he needed a new challenge, and to that end, he had an amicable discussion with his senior colleague and fellow partner at Watson's Richard Akroyd. He said to Akroyd that the world of the professional trustee appealed to him – Watson's had considered branching out into this area themselves but had concluded that there were too many potential client conflicts. Akroyd had been chairman of Watson's' own pension fund and Alan had been one of his fellow directors, so he had seen for himself what he now calls the 'most professional expert trustee around' in action. So, when Alan told him that he had been approached by BESTrustees about becoming their chairman, he understood why Alan wanted to be at the centre of the trustee world in what would be the final phase of his career. Akroyd's view of the role of the trustee is that it is 'not to be an expert in all areas but to be able to challenge the experts', and there was nobody better qualified to do this than Alan Pickering. Describing the move, Alan said, 'It is time for a fresh challenge. I have been advising trustees for most of my career so it's exciting that I'm about to become one. It must be every coach's dream to leave the touchline and join the team…'[106] Watson Wyatt were

106 Investment and Pensions Europe, August 2008

sad to see him go and paid a touching tribute: 'I cannot think of anyone at WW who is held in higher regard or affection by colleagues and clients.'[107]

The role of 'independent trustee' was growing at the time that Alan Pickering moved to be one – and BESTrustees was one of the leading firms. Having an independent professional trustee on a pension fund board was increasingly being seen as an effective way of raising the level of technical knowledge on the board and of bringing best practice to bear on the board's governance role. In addition, the professional trustee has 'more availability than the lay trustee, each of whom also has a day job'. It is a sign of Alan's commitment to the role that he chose to study at the Pensions Management Institute for an award in Pension Trusteeship, which he gained in March 2010. The attraction of the job at BESTrustees was twofold. To be non-executive chairman of a significant and growing player in an area that interested him was in itself appealing. But at the same time he found building a client portfolio and taking on specific trusteeship roles was a very hands-on and satisfying project as well. Among Alan's varied trusteeship clients (eight in total) are the very large Aviva scheme, the not-for-profit defined contribution master trust, People's Pension Scheme (PPS), the Royal Pharmaceutical Society, Kellogg's and the now £2 billion Plumbing Industry Scheme, of which he has been a trustee for thirty-seven years – much of

107 Internal email from Mark Stewart, head of European Benefits Group, Watson Wyatt, to colleagues.

which he has spent as chairman. He says that one of the key roles for any independent trustee is to bring experience from one scheme to another – the schemes are all different, but they probably face similar challenges, so cross-fertilisation of experience is invaluable. It is important never to undermine the confidence of the lay trustee. Here clearly Alan has a training/mentoring role, a link back to his first involvement in pensions training in the mid-1970s. Steve Delo, the chairman of the PPS, says that Alan is always pragmatic and tries to ensure that the board doesn't get bogged down in detail. And Karen Jones of the £15 billion Aviva scheme similarly says that he is 'never side-tracked'.

Aviva and the PPS illustrate the changing world of workplace pensions that Alan Pickering now operates in. Aviva, following mergers between General Accident, Commercial Union, Norwich Union and a number of other firms, is one of the largest players in the financial services sector and has a very large pension scheme to match. This not only includes the £15 billion defined benefit fund but also a major £1.2 billion money purchase scheme. As a trustee Alan has a role to play in both strategies, and Karen Jones says that he brings an even-handed approach to each and believes that the trust environment is 'ideally suited to DC', but that, despite his background as a strong supporter of DB, he is an 'excellent chairman' of the DC committee. Alan says that he sees his Aviva role as bringing a measure of 'street sanity' to a board composed of 'very clever people'. The PPS is a rapidly growing master trust and is the largest auto-enrolment pension scheme in the private sector, with nearly three million members and assets of over £2 billion. Auto-enrolment[108] has driven PPS's growth and will continue to do so. Steve Delo says that the so-called pensions freedoms forced a change of direction for investment strategy and that Alan's advice on this has been crucial, just as it has been in determining how to cope with the upcoming increases in minimum contribution levels for auto-enrolment schemes.

Karen Jones of Aviva says that 'relationship management is the key to the success of running a pension scheme', and that this is a particular forte of Alan Pickering: 'His experience and wisdom is vital but as important is the perspective he brings.' Alan himself says that part of his personal 'continuing professional development' is the need to look forward and not be a 'defender of the past'. That said, there are few more qualified than he to put present-day issues like auto-enrolment in the context of pensions history. Alan's job at BESTrustees is a full-time role – especially so given his trusteeship responsibilities – but he has continued to play a more general role on pensions and retirement matters. Whilst still at Watson's he became chairman of the financial literacy charity, Life Academy, whose time, he says, 'had really come'. However, as the public sector was a major funder and significant customer, the charity became a victim of spending cuts and it hit the buffers. Another appointment was

108 Under the Pensions Act 2008, every employer in the UK must put certain staff into a pension scheme and contribute towards it. This is called 'automatic enrolment'. Anyone who employs at least one person as an employer has certain legal duties in this respect.

to the board of the Kosovo Pensions Savings Trust, who had 'their own version of auto-enrolment'. He had, he says, some 'enjoyable and enlightening trips to Pristina, where it was interesting to compare Kosovan pension politics with those of the UK'. Another role was in connection with the privatisation of the Royal Mail, wherein the government took historic pension liabilities of the Royal Mail statutory pension scheme onto the public books. A governance group was established to oversee the delivery of these benefits and Alan was appointed the inaugural chairman in March 2012.

Asked for his views of the current political and pensions scene, Alan is characteristically knowledgeable and forthright. His overriding belief, one that has been a theme throughout his life, is the fact that pensions and politics are inextricably intertwined. But in a 24-hour news environment the absolute need to take a long-term view on pensions can be lost. For example, select committees, which were originally designed by Richard Crossman and others to 'hold the executive to account' by scrutinising government departments and influencing government work and decision-making, are increasingly serving as a forum for public debate. Where they were meant to be retrospective, they are now often involved in current issues – including the Work and Pensions Select Committee, where, in Alan's view, it is 'not good politics to see Frank Field[109] pontificating on a daily basis'.

---

109 The chairman of the Work and Pensions Select Committee.

As far as the world of pensions is concerned, Alan says that

> the most gratifying thing about the pensions scene today is that there is an acknowledgment that there is a role for the state to play. Only the state can provide a guarantee against absolute poverty in old age but Parliament must retain the ability to determine what 'absolute poverty' is and also to decide what is old age. One of the major achievements of Steve Webb and the coalition government was to bring in a simple, single universal state pension that provides old people with a basic income which is above the means-tested level. Up until then the means-tested level was above the level of the basic state pension, and for people on the margin there was no incentive to save.
>
> The most disappointing thing is that the quality workplace pensions that were gradually spreading through the 1980s and 1990s through DB schemes based on 'best endeavour' rather than 'guarantee' have withered – mainly because of the costs to employers. Not least is the increase in future costs [liabilities] consequential on improved longevity. I still think that a workplace-defined benefit pension scheme is the most cost-effective way of building on the basic state pension. With a basic state pension the taxpayer takes the risk. In a workplace DB scheme the shareholder takes the risk. But, in a DC scheme, the saver takes the risk. The reality is that taxpayers and shareholders have broader shoulders to weather storms and can also

> deliver, pound for pound, a retirement income much more cost-effectively than can individuals through DC schemes (even if you had the same level of contributions to such schemes as to DB, which is not the case). You cannot employ assets as efficiently in a DC environment as in a DB. The splintering of the private pension system in Britain has been a massive own goal. None of the new products – financial literacy, auto-enrolment – will provide a quality outcome. DC schemes are a workplace 'savings account', not a pension scheme. Until 2014 there was a fig leaf which ensured that DC scheme savings would always become pensions with the requirement to convert savings into an annuity which would provide an income stream for life. But 'pension freedoms'[110] tore up that fig leaf.

As this biography has tried to show, Alan Pickering has always had a hinterland – a term which goes beyond hobbies. In the final chapter we will look at that hinterland outside of his professional life: the world of horse racing. But, as we reflect on Alan's long-standing leadership role in the world of pensions, it is perhaps appropriate to look again at Albus Dumbledore, as we did in the Introduction. Dumbledore said, 'It is a curious thing, Harry, but perhaps those who are best suited to power are those who have never sought it. Those who, like you,

110 Prior to the 2015 budget, which introduced 'Pension Freedoms', most pensioners were required to buy an annuity with their money purchase scheme savings to guarantee them an income for life. In 2015 the government introduced new rules which broadly permitted pensions to be withdrawn at any time and in any amount and for any purpose.

have leadership thrust upon them, and take up the mantle because they must, and find to their own surprise that they wear it well.'[III]

III J. K. Rowling, *Harry Potter and the Deathly Hallows* (London: Bloomsbury Books, 2007).

CHAPTER 9

# THE SPORT OF KINGS

*Mr Pickering always leaves you with a smile on your face. He's a very intelligent person; much too intelligent to be in horse racing*
– Jamie Spencer, twice champion jockey

On 22 March 2014 the six-year-old bay gelding 'Robin Hoods Bay', ridden by Luke Morris, won the Winter Derby at Lingfield Park racecourse. The Winter Derby is one of the leading British flat races on an all-weather track – a Group 3 race[112] which, in 2014, delivered £56,710 to the winning owner. The horse that had finished second in the same race the previous year was trained by the Newmarket-based Ed Vaughan and was owned by one Mr Alan Pickering.

112 In Europe, highly rated flat races are graded into one of three levels:
Group 1 – Classics and other races of major international importance
Group 2 – Less important international races
Group 3 – Primarily important domestic races

Forty-four years before Robin Hoods Bay's triumph at Lingfield the same Alan Pickering had been looking for a job in the summer vacation from his studies at Newcastle University. An obvious option was at York racecourse, which Alan had been visiting for some years and where an initial interest in the sport of kings had been stimulated. York is seen as the 'Ascot of the North'. It's a course which takes pride in looking good, and the offer of a job as a gardener's labourer – part of a team whose role was to maintain the Ascot look – was attractive, despite the modest wage of 4/6d an hour.[113]

York racecourse is situated on the 'Knavesmire' – a large area to the south of the city and across the River Ouse from Alan's childhood home near Fulford Road.[114] Alan's next-door neighbour, George Ford, had family connections in horse racing, so throughout his childhood there was regular racing talk, and the television and wireless were often tuned to a racing transmission. Alan's first view of the Knavesmire came when his parents took him to a field close to the course from which you could watch the racing for nothing. Later, another neighbour, Jessie Teal, who had inherited a love of the sport from her father, took Alan to the course proper and they became regulars in the cheapest of the enclosures, where he gained a good grounding in the sport and the intricacies of betting with the Tote.[115] Funnily enough,

113 Equivalent to £2.22 in 2018 terms.

114 In those days it was a long way around via the city centre to get across the river – now the Millennium Bridge cuts the journey for the pedestrian down by half.

115 At the time the Tote was the national (government-owned) bookmaker.

it was Alan who introduced his parents to horse racing, not the other way round. His father became keen and acquired the betting bug – one good week allowed him to treat himself to an expensive camera. This was a short-lived experiment though, and Frank Pickering soon realised that it was the bookies, not he, who were the winners and that it was better to stick to his financially secure job on the railways. But the love of racing was shared by Alan and his parents and they visited many of the racetracks of Yorkshire together. Alan recalls that one Boxing Day at Wetherby it was too cold for him and his dad even to eat their favourite pork pies.

When Alan went to boarding school in Coventry he maintained his interest in racing and frequently watched races on television or listened to wireless commentaries and even managed to inveigle his father to occasionally place bets for him. So when that summer job at York racecourse came up in 1970, his love of the sport was well ingrained. It was hard work – which he enjoyed. He relished the heavy-lifting jobs and was a good employee. A bonus of the position was that he could watch the races from the best enclosures. The well-heeled and well-dressed aristocrats, whose base was the posh 'Tattersalls' enclosure, tolerated the lad in his gardeners' overalls. Alan recalls that it was so smart and hierarchical that one of the few women on the race committee, Lady Otham, had her own lavatory with a sign on the door signifying clearly that this was not a facility for other ladies who might have drifted into the enclosure, but just for her. Although the gardens were the main work area, Alan also worked on general menial tasks – including cleaning up after the horses in the parade ring. One of his high points was in 1970 when the Group 2 Gimcrack Stakes (a six-furlong sprint for two-year-olds) was held in August. There had been a torrential overnight downpour which had turned the going (the ground) into a quagmire. Entered for the race was Mill Reef, who had impressed in his first few races of his first year but whose trainer wanted to scratch him because of the conditions. However, Mill Reef's owner, the famous American Paul Mellon, said, 'Let him run, I've a feeling it will be all right.' Mill Reef, showing an astonishing turn of speed, won by ten lengths. Some horse. Alan Pickering not only witnessed this extraordinary race but cleaned up after Mill Reef in the parade ring before the start – one of the rituals of a day at the races not enjoyed by everyone, certainly few in Tattersalls. Alan was to return to the Knavesmire in 1971 and there is no doubt that these two summers, which included close proximity to some great horses, were crucial in the development of his love of the sport.

As we have seen in Chapter 3, Alan Pickering started work at the EETPU in August 1972, and visits to York racecourse were to be more curtailed in the years to come. But his love of racing continued – he bet on the ITV7 (£1.05 on an accumulator bet where serious money could be won if you correctly chose the winners of seven races) and was a regular visitor to the betting shops of Bromley. However, after a while, although his love of racing continued, he stopped gambling on the sport. He says today that it 'made small amounts of money too important. If after an afternoon you were two shillings to the good you were euphoric and if you were two shillings in deficit you were suicidal. This made two shillings too important.'

It is at the racecourse itself that for Alan Pickering racing really comes alive. A race afternoon is not just horses flashing by you; it is a series of successive rituals, six or seven short stories each with a beginning, middle and end – albeit very compressed. Above all there is the interaction with the horses. And in the years ahead Alan Pickering was to move from interacting with horses at a distance to being as close as you can get without riding them. Interaction with the jockeys is also important – being an owner takes you to the heart of the sport. Alan mentions that three-time champion jockey Ryan Moore has ridden and won on his horses and he knows him well: 'You wouldn't get that close to Wayne Rooney or Lewis Hamilton.' Horse racing is not just for the aristocracy and the very wealthy, and never has been, but racehorse ownership is – or at least it was until shared ownership as part of a syndicate or a racing club came along in the late 1980s. This innovation came especially from the trainer Martin Pipe, who formed the Martin Pipe Racing Club (a successor to the Pipe-Scudamore Racing Club) to make racehorse ownership more accessible.[116] Pipe was a champion National Hunt

116 Pipe and his associate Peter Scudamore were pioneers in multiple ownership of racehorses and had a number of syndicate and co-ownership models.

trainer (for events such as the Grand National, which he won in 1994 with Miinnehoma)[117] as well as a forerunner in shared ownership, and Alan entered this part of the sport by becoming one of his syndicate members. The outlay was modest but it was a real introduction into the world of the racehorse owner. Initially the syndicate was twenty strong and Alan felt fairly close to the action – and the horses. There were visits to Pipe's stables in Taunton and this gave Alan, he felt, a new closeness to the sport. But this changed when a much larger syndicate was formed and Alan looked for another way to be involved as an owner. The opportunity came when he heard that a top Newmarket trainer on the flat, Alec Stewart, was setting up a syndicate. Alan contacted the stable and was surprised when Stewart himself called back. The syndicate, to be called 'Racing for Gold', would have twelve members and five horses initially. The cost was a modest £2,000 per year per member. You might get around £700 per annum back in prize money and there was openness from the start. Joining the syndicate was not an investment but an entry ticket to the world of owning horses. Stewart treated him and his fellow syndicate members well: 'I was treated like a king and shown all the same courtesy as a sole owner. The horses were good quality (which is not always the case with syndicates).'

By the late 1990s Alan Pickering had become a partner at what was now Watson Wyatt LLP. This recognition of his value

117 'With 4,180 winners to his credit, [Martin Pipe] is easily the most successful trainer in the history of the sport', *Daily Telegraph*, 1 May 2006.

to the firm was accompanied by a significant uplift in his remuneration from profit sharing. Suddenly the out-of-reach dream of being a racehorse owner became a reality and via Alec Stewart he acquired his first horse, which he appropriately named 'Alan's Dream'. The horse cost £25,000 as a yearling, which was to be the most Alan ever paid for a single horse. Alan's Dream grew quickly and it became clear that such a potentially large horse would be suited to National Hunt jump racing far more than he would be to the flat. Alan had part-owned some jump horses in his days with Martin Pipe but now wished to concentrate on the flat, so he sold Alan's Dream as a two-year-old. Renamed 'Harrovian', he was to have quite a successful jump career for the flamboyant owner Ivan Straker.

Alan's first runner was at Newmarket in April 2001 – 'Yorkshire Grey' was not destined to be a star either under Alan's ownership (eleven starts) or after he sold him in July 2003. But he was the first to carry Alan's distinctive yellow and blue colours[118] and as such has a special place in his racing memory. Alan's first winner was to come in his fourth year as an owner, in 2004. The horse was called 'Mr Velocity' after a Scarborough speedboat (many of Alan's horses have since had names with Yorkshire connections). The race was at Redcar and the prize was £3,376. Even better was to follow in September, when the same horse, this time with the famous Kieren Fallon back in the saddle, won the Chanton Group

118 The racing colours are taken from the flag of Barbados, which has been Alan and Christine Pickering's holiday destination of choice for twenty years.

Handicap at Epsom and earned a tidy £9,791. There was another win at Musselburgh that month – the horse covered Alan's costs for him that year, winning over £26,000 in prize money. Between Alan's first win in June and the win at Epsom, Alec Stewart, Alan's mentor on all things horse-related, died at the age of forty-nine and his assistant trainer, Ed Vaughan, took over the stables. Ed has been Alan's sole trainer ever since. There is clearly a very close partnership and a high degree of mutual admiration between the two men. Vaughan says that Alan is unusual in that he is always philosophical about the outcome of races, win or lose. Not all owners are the same! Vaughan thinks this is probably because 'Alan has learned more about life than any of us' – an insightful observation. He complements Alan's personality in that both of them are prepared to take their time and work with a horse fully to explore its potential. It's a tough world at times and passions can run high, but Ed Vaughan says that in all their time together he and Alan 'have never had a cross word' and that Alan 'never tries to second-guess me and always takes my advice'. They also share the belief that the 'horse always comes first' – again, not something that all owners (or trainers for that matter) share.

By 2006 five of Alan Pickering's horses competed around the country, and the following year two horses, Cosmic Destiny and Convivial Spirit, were to bring him five wins – his most in any one year at that time. By now Alan was an owner to be reckoned with. Between his first runner in 2001 and the 2017 season, Alan has had twenty-seven horses which have competed 478 times in races in British flat racing, he has had forty-nine winners and has won over £438,000 in prize money. Against this it is wise to remember that to have seven horses in training, as he did in his peak year of 2015, will incur a cost of at least £175,000 per annum. So what sort of racing man is Alan Pickering? And how has the sport become such a passion for someone who cannot directly enjoy what for most people is the attraction – the colour and the tension of watching a race? As racing commentator Simon Holt puts it, 'racing is such a visual sport'. A clue comes from the chief executive of the Racehorse Owners Association, Charlie Liverton, who says, 'owners are owners because of the horses' – but can you have a relationship with a horse if you cannot see it? Alan Pickering is in no doubt that you can. He looks back to that first win with Mr Velocity back in 2004:

> The nearest thing to a horse being a human we have owned was Mr Velocity.[119] When he won at Redcar I went into the winners' enclosure and when I was close to him he leant on me so that I knew he was there. We were standing shoulder to shoulder. I'm not a romantic, but I did feel that that horse knew that by leaning on me he was showing me that he wanted to be as close to me as he could get.

119 Ed Vaughan describes Mr Velocity as a 'lovely horse with a wonderful temperament. He was everybody's favourite.'

Racing commentator Simon Holt says that

> some people have telepathy with horses and a bond develops, and horses often act in a kindly way when they sense that someone has a weakness of some sort. They have an inner sensitivity which often makes them gentle with small children – they can also sometimes be almost inexplicably on the same wavelength as adults they want to be kind to.

Racing journalist Peter Thomas hit the nail on the head describing Alan's ambitions in the sport back in 2007: 'Just because he's living in the dark, don't make the mistake of thinking he's living in the past as well. [For him] the future is bright, and the present has a warm glow to it.'[120]

Almost any role in the world of horse racing is 'riding a roller coaster', as Simon Holt puts it. But to be the owner is perhaps potentially the most satisfying – as well as being all too often disappointing, even tragic. On 7 August 2009 Alan Pickering's bay mare 'Miss Tikitiboo' was entered in the Blindley Heath Handicap at Lingfield Park. Jamie Spencer had taken her to 3rd on the same course in her last-but-one run and, at three years old, with seven races under her belt, she was learning her trade. She was an attractive-looking horse with big ears who stood out in a crowd. During the race, she was coming round the bend

120 'Talking Horses', interview by Peter Thomas in the *Racing Post*, August 2007.

and was kicked by another horse. She tripped and the commentator said, 'Miss Tikitiboo has gone wrong' – perhaps the most chilling words any owner can hear. Alan's mobile phone rang and it was Ed Vaughan, who was not at the course but who had been called by the on-course vet to say that the horse's leg was broken; she was in pain and the recommendation was that she had to be put down. Alan agreed instantly. He then went to the Weighing Room where the jockey, Ian Mongan, was waiting for him. Mongan is an experienced Lingfield jockey and no blame for the tragedy fell upon him. It is a rare event in flat racing (and especially compared to the jumps of course) but, as Simon Holt says, 'Horses are fragile animals. They have huge bodies on four thin limbs and accidents can happen.' Alan says that the clerk of the course looked after him and provided what he calls 'impressive bereavement counselling'. But Alan's principal concern was for the horse's groom, who had to take an empty horsebox back to Newmarket.

The relationship between the horse and its stakeholders – trainer, owner, jockey, stable lads and the public at large – can be an emotional one, and it usually is. Racing is a business – and a very large one. But for owners it will virtually always be a business which never turns a profit. The atmosphere of a race day is addictive, and for the owner the close proximity to both the horses and the human participants who make it all work is everything. Alan says that his long involvement as an owner has given him special friendships with many in that unique world.

The jockeys are the ones who, on the day, can turn probable failure into unexpected success, and Alan's affection for them is reciprocated. 'Mr Pickering is as gracious in defeat as he is in victory – he takes a great interest in the sport and racing is lucky to have him,' says Jamie Spencer. His fellow jockey, Luke Morris, agrees: 'He is a very understanding man. He knows exactly what every horse might be able to do. But he leaves the job up to you and has every confidence in the people, like me, that he employs.'

Alan Pickering's record as an owner follows a steep learning curve from 2001 through to the years 2013 and 2014, over which he was to have sixteen winners from his fine horses, Robin Hoods Bay and Flamborough Breeze, and five others. Alan was not Robin Hoods Bay's first owner, but he acquired him as a two-year-old when his then owner, against trainer Ed Vaughan's advice, decided to sell him. Alan bought the bay gelding for 2,500 guineas.[121] His first run was in November 2010 and he gradually improved and had his first win, at Kempton Park, in May 2011. Over the winter of 2012–13, and in the run-up to the Winter Derby at Lingfield Park in March 2013 (for which he was being prepared), he had some good races and was rarely out of the places – including some good wins with Luke Morris on board. But on the derby day itself Morris was not available to Alan, so Jim Crowley rode him to a good second place against the favourite. The odds of 12/1 were good for the each-way punter. Over

121 A guinea is the equivalent of one pound and one shilling – or £1.05 in decimal currency. It is still commonly used in horse racing.

the next year Robin Hoods Bay had a special win at Haydock in August in the 'Better Prices On Goals Galore' handicap where, in a strong run in the closing furlongs, Luke Morris brought him home to land a 25/1 win, bagging a handy £32,345 for Alan Pickering – his biggest win to date. Robin Hoods Bay ran five more times over the winter, earning another handy £12,000 on the all-weather track at Lingfield in February with Luke Morris riding again. The Winter Derby beckoned on 22 March – could Robin Hoods Bay go one better than in 2013 and win?

It was a cool, windy and rainy day at Lingfield Park on 22 March 2014, and there was a strong field for the Winter Derby; among them the previous year's winner, Farraaj and Windhoek, trained by Saeed bin Suroor for the elite Godolphin stable. Luke Morris says that

> the all-weather track at Lingfield on that day suited horses racing from off the pace, but as they approached the final stages it wasn't the plan for Robin Hoods Bay to be quite that far back. But I found that I could pick off the horses that had gone fast early on, and I came up on the outside and got the job done.

The horse had shown a remarkable turn of speed and the time of 2 minutes 1.25 seconds was seen by the experts as very quick. The win was, according to Simon Holt, one of trainer Ed Vaughan's very best, and the prize money of £56,710 was comfortably Alan Pickering's biggest pot. 'Ed did a very good job,' says Holt, the horse was not fundamentally that sound, but very talented, and Ed brought him on and treated him with great care. Ed's stable is not the biggest in Newmarket, but horses often get more attention in a smaller yard and a lot of owners – including Alan Pickering – prefer this. There is loyalty received and given – and this has helped the success.

After the Winter Derby Robin Hoods Bay was to have two more races in 2014, but it became clear that he was not consistently sound enough to continue to race and he was retired, having won eight races, £135,322 in first-place prize money and a further £55,020 in place money. He was retrained as a riding horse by the Moorcroft Racehorse Welfare Centre – a charity Alan's supports. He is, says Richard Wayman (British Horseracing Authority's chief operating officer), 'passionate about the well-being of racehorses on retirement. He often gives a retiring horse he owns to a riding stables rather than putting them in the sales where they could face an uncertain future.'

Alan's love of horses and the world of horse racing was to have a new outlet when he decided to extend his racing interest into thoroughbred breeding. His brood mare, Cosmic Destiny, a five-furlong specialist, has produced four foals – two of which, Primrose Valley and Costa Filey, have had nine winners between them. Simon Holt says that Cosmic Destiny is a rather particular horse who only likes one stallion, Pastoral Pursuits – a rare example of monogamy in horse racing (at least on the distaff side). The stud farm, Pantile Stud, in Soham, Cambridgeshire, has looked after Alan's breeding interests, and two of the horses born there have now had foals of their own.[122] As with his relationship with Ed Vaughan, Alan has a loyal and close relationship with the Stud and its manager, Bo Hicks-Little.

Alan Pickering's status as a serious player in the world of horse racing was perhaps inevitably to lead to involvement in the governance of the sport. As he would say, 'Whenever I'm involved with something I like to pay my way.' Horse racing is Britain's second largest spectator sport (after football), with seven million people going to race meetings every year – there is at least one meeting around the country almost every day of the year. On around one hundred days every year there are meetings at which the attendance exceeds 70,000 – making racing a serious business. But its profits have not been as healthy as they should be despite the '£3.8 billion annual contribution to UK PLC'. The then newly appointed chairman of the British Horseracing Authority (BHA), Steve Harman, said in 2013 that

> returns to owners, at average 23p in the pound, are unacceptable and are detrimentally affecting the horse population, fixture list and jobs [and that] many mid-range trainers, with say twenty to fifty horses, struggle to make ends meet. Many jockeys outside

122 Primrose Valley has a foal called Bridlington Bobby – so the Yorkshire connection remains, despite him having been born in Suffolk.

> the top twenty make little money. Many smaller owner-breeders struggle [and] many racecourses make low returns.[123]

Alan's involvement in the governance of horse racing was initially to be as a member of the fourteen-strong board of the Racehorse Owners Association (ROA), which, as the name suggests, looks after the interests of the 8,000 British horserace owners.

The ROA was the logical vehicle through which Alan could move into racing governance, but becoming a member of the board did not happen overnight. He stood for election on five occasions (securing only eighty-three votes on his first attempt) before finally being chosen in 2011. In his manifesto in 2007 (his second year as a candidate) he said, 'If you vote for me you would be electing a stayer with vision' – no doubt a characteristic response to one or two newspaper articles with headlines like 'Blind man backs himself to win a place on the ROA Council'. Upon being elected, he declared, 'I am a tryer. This is my fifth attempt to seek a place on the council – last year I came fourth but they only paid out on three places – I hope to gain some black type[124] this time.' He did. Former ROA chief executive Richard Wayman says that Alan's perseverance was unusual – candidate board members usually give up after a couple of failures. The ROA is an 'owners union', and one of the key organisations in British horse racing. Within a few years Alan was asked by his fellow board members

123 Speech to the Gimcrack Club at York racecourse, reported in the *Daily Telegraph*.
124 'Black type' refers to a winning bet, whereas 'red type' refers to a losing bet.

to become the ROA's vice president. Wayman says he has an 'impressive grasp of the subject matter of racing. His understanding of the politics and how people behave shows great wisdom and he is a wise counsel.' Current chief executive Charlie Liverton says that Alan has a 'remarkably clear mind and vision' and that if discussions get bogged down Alan can 'always bring it back to the point'. One instance was when, as a member of the Gold Standards Committee, which determines the minimum standards owners should expect at race meetings, Alan was able to pacify some rebellious syndicate managers. 'Alan can make you feel that he's "been there, done that,"' says Liverton. 'He makes you feel that he's been in your shoes. But he also sees the bigger picture and understands the needs of all the various players.' It was these qualities which led to Alan being asked to chair the ROA's Race Day Committee.

One of Alan Pickering's key roles on the ROA board has been to take the lead with the chief executive in the annual negotiation of riding fees with the Professional Jockeys Association (PJA). Here, Liverton says, Alan's 'personal qualities, clarity of mind, nerves of steel and his engaging and never confrontational style are effective. It also helps that he's very good with numbers.' Richard Wayman mentions that he negotiated the introduction of a 40 per cent fee to apply if a jockey had been engaged for a ride but the horse had to be withdrawn.[125] This, and other

125 Flat race jockeys are paid a flat fee of around £140 per ride, plus around 7 per cent of winnings. The rewards for those (around 150 racers) who aren't at the very top are modest.

qualities, mean he is respected by those who ride for him, and in the small world of the professional jockey he is clearly seen, not as a 'boss's man', but as one who is fair to both sides.

The ROA is, as we have seen, one of the bodies coordinated with the others by the BHA, which is both the representative body and the regulator of the sport. The BHA asked Alan Pickering to be a member of its Rules Committee, which covers an extraordinary diversity of rules and regulations in the sport. These range from those applying to commercial sponsorship, technical specifications, medical treatment, procedures for jockeys to follow and many more. Nick Rust, the BHA's chief executive, says that Alan brings to this role a 'moral compass' and that he always takes a reasonable position:

> He is from the horsemen [as the owners are often called] but he is not partisan. So many people cannot take off the one hat that they are wearing for one moment. Alan is different. When there isn't much common sense around Alan has it in bucket loads. He is always on top of papers and documents despite his disability and we never have to make allowances for him. He has shaped our rules and made a conscientious and positive contribution to racing.

For Alan Pickering every day that he goes racing (now a hundred times a year) is a pleasure. To own horses is a privilege. Winners are an added bonus. As with his day job in pensions there are enormous complexities – not least where rules are concerned, but the same principles apply. He favours rules within clear principles rather than tight prescription. As with pensions there is a bias, if a problem occurs, to slip into 'something must be done' mode – to reach for the rule book and rewrite it. This is not Alan's way. His love of the sport makes his occasional criticisms of it all the more pertinent. Asked what he disliked about racing in September 2013, he was blunt:

> Arrogance. Many racing people have been successful in other walks of life, which can give rise to a degree of arrogance. I remember a trainer once telling me that owners should stay out of the big issues in racing – I think that racing needs to be very careful about denigrating its clients in that way.[126]

The worlds of pensions and horse racing are seemingly poles apart. For Alan Pickering, his success in the former enabled him to fulfil a dream in the latter. But this is neither a rich man's indulgence nor a whim. Whilst Alan obviously relishes being well known and respected in the sport, fame is not the spur. The draw for him is the camaraderie and the smells and the sounds and the tension of what is conventionally seen as a very visual sport. When Alan has a horse running, commentator Simon Holt gives what he calls a 'radio commentary' in respect of Alan's

---

126 *Thoroughbred Owner and Breeder*, September 2013.

runner. Whether the public at large spots that one horse gets a few extra mentions even if it is not at the head of the field is doubtful. But you can be sure that the mind's eye of Alan Pickering was brilliantly illuminated when, at Lingfield in 2014, Robin Hoods Bay made that run that jockey Luke Morris so modestly describes: 'I came on the outside and got the job done.' Come to think of it, that's a description that equally applies to the remarkable life and work of Alan Pickering.

AFTERWORD

# 'IF I'D KNOWN THEN WHAT I KNOW NOW...'

## BY ALAN PICKERING CBE

'Look where you're going!' So said the harassed lady who collided with my white cane as we each traversed the busy Waterloo station concourse during the evening rush hour. If that lady is reading this, she can be reassured that I do not hold a grudge. Her explosion probably owed more to shock than anger.

That lady has been in a minority among those fellow travellers with whom I have come into contact along life's way. Never is there a journey devoid of a helpful elbow. Although Patrick Moore may have been the owner of the most famous elbow, I have touched thousands of people from every corner of the globe. They share their intimate secrets with me as if I was their priest or social worker. With some, I have a recurring relationship, whilst with most I enjoy a one-walk relationship. They all brighten my day and remind me how wonderful humankind can be.

Throughout my life I have pursued two objectives, which are simultaneously complementary and conflicting. Independence and achievement have been my goals. Initially, independence reigned supreme and that target was often seen as an achievement in itself. However, the blind pursuit of that objective would have restricted the other achievements to which I might aspire. Independence has to be curtailed if maximum achievement is to be attained. I could not have achieved anything without the help of others. To the thousands of commuters to whom I have already referred must be added many more friendly folk with whom I have had longer-lasting relationships. Three ladies deserve special mention. These are my mother, Betty, my wife, Christine, and my best friend, Jenny.

Although saying that my mother was in denial is going too far, she was unwilling to make any compromises in order to give me an easy ride. Whilst she probably knew I could never see in the dark, she insisted that I went out at night if that was helpful in our pursuit of normality. Ironically, she was more worried when I went out in the fog. This might have been an acknowledgement that, whilst I could hack it, others might not see me.

In sending me off to boarding school, she made a painful sacrifice. Furthermore, she did not like the idea of sending me to a different school to that attended by the children of her friends and workmates. She did, however, value the importance of a good education. Later on, she took a different view when I chose to give up a pensionable job on the railway in order to attend Newcastle University as a mature student. Among her fears were that I would abandon beer in favour of wine and newspapers in favour of books. Above all, although she did not articulate it as such, she too bought into the need to balance independence and achievement. She provided me with a double helping of the former knowing that achievements would surely follow.

At our wedding in St John's Church Penge, the Reverend Smith asked rhetorically, 'Christine, do you really know what you are taking on?' I like to think that the Reverend Smith would be pleased to see me fulfilling my role as gardener's labourer on the family allotment. Christine, like my mother, has read more pension publications than is healthy. If either of them had remembered a tiny fraction of what they had read, membership of the Pensions Management Institute would be guaranteed.

Being well-turned-out is important to me. Over the years, strangers have come up to me saying, 'You may not know this but you look really smart.' This is definitely preferable to 'You are a bit of a scruff but what else can you expect from a blind person.' Each day when I leave the house I know that, thanks to Christine, I am well-turned-out.

Jenny and I met in April 1988 when we were both working for the EETPU. Both Frank Chapple and Eric Hammond, the two union general secretaries whose tenure coincided with our employment, held me in sufficient regard to minimise the risk that

I might come a cropper whilst travelling the world on behalf of the union. They encouraged Jenny to travel with me whenever her family commitments permitted. The rest, as they say, is history.

We have continued to travel the world for the past thirty years and have always changed jobs simultaneously. Each time, the prospective employer has been willing to give me a job so long as Jenny comes as part of the package. There are those – friends among them – who would say that Jenny is the target whilst I am the makeweight.

Most people born with an infirmity face the dilemma of choosing how to balance independence and achievement. For my part, I do not regard sight loss as a disability, but treat it as a characteristic. Although I have maintained a watching brief as medical science progresses, the pursuit of a personal cure has never been on my agenda. Life is too short to spend time on such a quest.

Being different to others was at its most challenging during my childhood. Children can be very cruel. In my case, this cruelty manifested itself in the taunts from local children who said that I would be blind before I reached sixteen. I did not believe them since my parents had not told me that retinitis pigmentosa was a progressive disease, although it was not a case of 'will I go blind?' but 'when will I go blind?' My parents felt that if I had known this, I might have thrown in the towel.

I abandoned education at the age of eighteen in order to prove my normality by following in my father's footsteps working for the railway. As we have seen in this book, the railway employers were not very enlightened and only gave me a job with restricted opportunities because of the family connection. This attitude heightened my political awareness and I found that trade union and Labour Party activity in York gave me the hope of advancement that the railway was unwilling to offer.

In the late 1960s, the barrier to political advancement was not lack of sight but lack of education. Already, educated folk were supplanting blue-collar workers in many representative roles. Again, I did not want to be a second-class citizen.

I replaced Michael Meacher as the treasurer of my Labour Party ward. He was, at the time, a lecturer at York University. Our paths were to cross many years later when he was pensions minister and I was a bit of a pensions buff. I shall be eternally grateful to him for his guidance in helping me swap a pensionable job on the railway for a degree course at Newcastle University.

In those days, it was not trendy to put Newcastle down as your first choice. As a result, I was offered an unconditional acceptance. They did not know that my sight was limited in advance, but were extremely helpful in mitigating the impact during my three-year course. All my fellow students were similarly supportive.

One of the lecturers in my department, Mr McCloud, was blind, and so other members of the departmental team had first-hand experience of how to help such people. Many years later, there was an ironic parallel when I was working closely with

Alistair Darling. Alistair knew exactly what to say and what not to do. No doubt I was the beneficiary of the experience that Alistair had gained whilst sitting around the Cabinet table with David Blunkett.

My two summertime work placements whilst at university involved being a gardener at York racecourse. This brought together two of my passions and meant that I was working with folk who, academically at least, were at the opposite end of the spectrum to the student population of Newcastle. Again, they were kindness itself and welcomed me back a second time round knowing that what I lacked in vision I would make up for in hard work. They were more than happy for me to do the heavy lifting and back-bending jobs.

Again, the union was willing to go the extra mile in helping me come to terms with sight loss. Indeed, Frank Chapple worked tirelessly to leverage his US contacts in order to find a cure. Jenny and I had the honour of working with Lord Chapple when, despite his own failing health, he chaired the EETPU Centenary Fund which Jenny and I ran. Together, we raised and spent £250,000, providing electronic and electrical aids to help disabled youngsters fulfil their potential.

From then on, life became much easier as I could no longer hide my disability. Fortunately, most people who mattered did not see it as a standalone feature. Indeed, asking if I wanted to borrow an umbrella became commonplace. I regarded this as a compliment even though, if more forethought had been given, people would have realised that you cannot carry a briefcase in one hand, a white stick in the other and still find room for an umbrella. More importantly, me and an umbrella would have been a lethal combination for the fellow travellers with whom I came into contact.

Chairing meetings is what I now do for a living. Many of these meetings can easily accommodate me flying solo. Others – especially the more challenging ones – require the presence of a pair of eyes. When Jenny is around, she fulfils this role. When this is not possible, I ask those who I am chairing to wave at a designated individual if they want to participate, since trying to catch my eye would be a waste of time.

As we have seen in Chapter 4, sport has loomed large on my radar. Sport as a participant has been a natural follow-on from a childhood desire to use physical fitness as a means of overcoming asthma. In later life, it has provided another opportunity to prove that I was able to participate in a wide range of activities in spite of a visual impairment. In some ways, that impairment has been an asset rather than a liability. Without it, I would not have been able to take part in cross-country skiing, run marathons, ride tandems, and engage in racewalking and hobie cat sailing.

All of these activities have been accomplished with the help of others. Only the cross-country skiing was undertaken in the confines of a visually handicapped group. Whilst I have extreme admiration for such groups, my segregated schooling had always given me a preference for taking part in events aimed at the wider public.

Perhaps my greatest achievement as an active sportsman was becoming a Centurion, which involved racewalking more than 100 miles in twenty-four hours. Perhaps the most satisfying activity was participating in working men's clubs' racewalking events around the streets of York. Not only did I do quite well, I became an acknowledged part of the local community.

When I moved south I had to choose between unauthorised racewalking in York and officially recognised events in the south. The only real difference was transparency. In York, the events were tainted by officialdom because amateurs like me were competing with ex-rugby league players who had received a pittance for playing rugby for York. Down south the shamateurs were often being rewarded more handsomely by receiving tangible prizes that could easily be exchanged for money. Because I had more opportunity down south, I had to forsake my home town. This still rankles.

The skills of my day job have always interacted with my sporting activities. I was president of Blackheath Harriers in 1993 and in 2017 became chairman of the trustee board responsible for all activities of Blackheath & Bromley AC.

I watched live sport for longer than was merited by my failing eyesight. However, standing on the terraces watching York City or York Rugby League provided much more involved excitement than could be gained from listening to wireless commentaries. I now make use of the latter and feel that I can see every movement. A general point here is that, contrary to popular belief, having lost sight is always preferable to never having had sight. At least I know what a red football shirt looks like.

Cricket was another sport that I enjoyed watching. Use of binoculars meant that I could keep track of the scoreboard. I will cherish wonderful memories of cricket close to the sea at Scarborough and in the raucous cauldron that was Headingley.

I started watching horse racing as soon as I became a teenager. After rugby league and football, horse racing was the third most popular sport in York. Racing has played a major part in my life ever since. More recently, my love of politics and fanaticism for racing have overlapped. Such overlap is a common feature of my life.

My parents were both interested in politics, my mother Labour and my father Liberal. As we have already seen, I became politically engaged in York whilst working on the railway. I had, however, developed my knowledge of politics whilst at school in Coventry, where one of the teachers was a Labour councillor. We always had mock general elections at school and I was always the candidate or candidate's agent.

Whilst living in York, I was an office-bearer in both the ward and constituency parties. Every year, I enjoyed canvassing with those of a similar mind. Once you had knocked on the first door, the rest became enjoyable and a fruitful source of anecdotes. It is true – there is nowt so queer as folk.

When I moved south, I stood twice for election to Bromley Council. Although I stood no chance, a salt-of-the-earth running mate, Tom Yates, did get elected when the Tory vote was split. He became a splendid ward councillor.

Whilst working for the union, I chose union work over party politics. The latter began to ring hollow when you had to say that everything your party stood for was good whilst the other lot never talked any sense.

One of the attractions to union work was the belief that, for every problem, there was a solution. Ironically, this philosophy backfired on me when I applied to join the Samaritans. I undertook the training course and my enthusiasm for the role grew steadily. At the end, for a variety of reasons, I was turned down. Although the leader was not supposed to be explicit in accounting for my failure, he did say that for many of the Samaritans' clients, no solutions existed for the problems that they face.

Given my penchant for politics, it comes as no surprise that I pursued the politics of pensions once my career went down that route. The National Association of Pension Funds was the key umbrella organisation with which the government consulted on all aspects of workplace pensions. I was elected to the NAPF council at the first attempt but failed in my first endeavour to become NAPF chairman. I was successful the second time round and took considerable pride in the office, which gave me an opportunity to interact with politicians at the highest level at a time when pensions were a hot topic. Reference has been made elsewhere to my chairmanship of the European equivalent. Similarly, this was a source of personal satisfaction that representatives from many different countries elected me, a Brit, to a leadership role, even though the British had a habit of criticising the rest of Europe for not doing what we did in regard to pensions.

The combination of political awareness and pensions knowledge was one of the reasons why Alistair Darling asked me to write a report for the government. Whilst the ostensible aim was to simplify the system, the underlying project was to search for ways in which we might turn the tide of the closure of defined benefit pension schemes. Chapter 7 shows how this was a challenge too far. We should have done this in the 1990s, when things were going well, but those of us in the know were aware that significant changes were needed if the prize of defined benefit provision so recently won by the masses was not to be squandered. It was much easier for politicians of the day to focus retrospectively on the Maxwell scandal than to look forward. The 1997 election gave Labour such a big majority that they were guaranteed at least two terms of office. Difficult decisions taken during the first term would have borne fruit during the second term. No such decisions were taken.

In Chapter 9 we saw how my love of racing overlapped with my interest in politics. I never ever thought I would own a racehorse, let alone one, Robin Hoods Bay, who would win the Winter Derby, which is the most important flat race of the all-weather season taking place at my beloved Lingfield Park. The trainer-jockey combination of Ed Vaughan and Luke Morris brought Robin Hoods Bay home at odds of 12/1. Holding the trophy aloft, I felt as though York City had won the cup, York Rugby League had beaten St Helens and Yorkshire County Cricket Club had become champions. Sixty years of sporting involvement had culminated in a ten-furlong race that had lasted just over two minutes, which would provide memories that live as long as I do.

I love all aspects of racing and wanted to give something back. For me, that meant seeking election to the governing body of the Racehorse Owners Association. In sport, if at first you do not succeed, try, try and try again. It took me five attempts to gain election to the ROA board. Once there, however, I soon became a member of the executive committee and was honoured in 2016 when I was elected vice-chairman.

Another honour that meant a great deal for me was the award of a CBE in 2004. Christine, Jenny and my running friend, Mike Cronin, went to Buckingham Palace to meet the Queen. I enjoyed my thirty seconds of banter during which Her Majesty shared some of her financial secrets with me.

Have I missed out on anything through not being able to see? Until recently I always said it would be nice to see the people sitting around me on the underground train. However, when Jenny told me that many of the men were wearing shorts and some of the women were covered in graffiti, I decided it was a good miss.

If I had known then what I know now, would I have done

anything differently? Yes – I would have succumbed to the use of a white cane earlier than I did. Before using such a cane I was dicing with danger and often giving the impression of being stand-offish and obnoxious. At the very least, the white cane would have dialled down the level of danger. And, what's more, it would have widened my social circle much earlier, as my fellow travellers would be aware that I was not deliberately stand-offish. The jury is still out as far as obnoxious is concerned.

*Alan Pickering*
*Summer 2018*

## APPENDIX I

# THE PICKERING REVIEW

### TERMS OF REFERENCE

*The review was announced in September 2001. The following were the Terms of Reference that the Review Team worked to.*

The simplification team will be led by a senior pensions industry figure with seconded Department for Work and Pensions (DWP) officials and outside experts in support.

*The review will:*

- Carry out a comprehensive review of DWP private pensions legislation to identify a package of options for simplification and the reduction of compliance costs
- Consider the principles behind the legislation as well as the

processes and ensure that the law is proportionate to the policy purpose

- Consider the means by which the regulatory framework is enforced
- Identify areas of simplification which can be achieved by secondary legislation and identify more fundamental reforms to be achieved by primary legislation
- Report to the Secretary of State by July 2002 with proposals for simplifying the regulatory framework that do not compromise the security of individuals' investments

*The review will have regard to:*

- The need to maintain effective protection for pension scheme members
- Wider economic and exchequer effects
- The links with, and impacts on, tax rules and the Inland Revenue Review
- The separate work to implement the recommendations of the Myners review and to reform the Minimum Funding Requirement
- The work of the forthcoming five-yearly review of the Occupational Pensions Regulatory Authority

## APPENDIX 2

# THE PICKERING REVIEW

### EXECUTIVE SUMMARY: OUR GOAL

Our overall objective in carrying out this review is to identify ways to make it easier for employers to provide good-quality pensions for their employees, easier for commercial providers to sell appropriate products to appropriate people, and easier for individuals to accumulate pension benefits. We have sought to identify ways to make the private pensions framework more efficient, whilst at the same time ensuring that pension scheme members are properly protected and can have confidence in the system.

In order to implement our suggested changes, we propose a new Pensions Act which should repeal or consolidate all existing Department for Work and Pensions (DWP) private pensions legislation.

## KEY THEMES AND RECOMMENDATIONS

Three key themes have emerged during our review.

*Theme 1 – A proportionate regulatory environment*

We propose that four principles should sit at the top of the new Pensions Act and that future legislative changes should be judged against those principles.

Our proposed principles are:

i. Each statutory requirement (whether set out in primary or secondary legislation) should include a statement of that legislation's underlying policy aim
ii. Statutory requirements should focus on the objective to be achieved rather than the process needed to achieve it
iii. Statutory requirements should be proportionate to the stated policy aim and should avoid unnecessary complexity
iv. Each new piece of pensions legislation should not be considered in isolation, but should have regard to the existing law applicable to pension arrangements

There should be mainly non-prescriptive primary legislation underneath these principles.

We recommend some prescriptive primary legislation where that makes things clearer and simpler: where there is only one sensible course of action, it should be specified.

We propose a new kind of regulator. This organisation would be more pro-active than the existing Occupational Pensions Regulatory Authority and it would act as an adviser as well as a regulator.

We think that the regulatory regime should place greater reliance on professionals exercising and backing their judgement.

There should be a small number of Codes of Practice/Guidance Notes. Most of these would be drafted by the regulator, in consultation with interested parties. A few would be drafted by appropriate professional bodies and authorised by the regulator/adviser; in a few cases, it might be more appropriate for guidance to be authorised by the government.

We have concluded that pensions are too complex, even in our proposed simplified world, for most consumers to act as do-it-yourself regulators. They need help from a regulator, scheme professionals and organisations whose function it is to look after the interests of their members. In this context we believe too much emphasis has been placed on the disclosure of information to members. Provision of information is important but not a panacea. We recommend a much more targeted approach to communicating with scheme members that focuses more on key pieces of information and does not overload them with information that only causes confusion. But, at the same time, we think that full, detailed information should be available to those who want it, particularly those such as trade union representatives or others whose function it is to look after pension scheme members' interests.

All trust-based schemes (apart from centralised or

industry-wide schemes) should be required to have one-third of their trustees nominated by pension scheme members, ending the current opt-out. However, we will propose no legislative prescription on how schemes must bring that objective to fruition.

*Theme 2 – 'A pension is a pension is a pension'*

We think that employers and commercial providers should be treated even-handedly by the regulatory framework: pension scheme members deserve the same level of protection, irrespective of whether their pension comes via the workplace or the marketplace.

Likewise, we think that small and large employers or schemes should be treated even-handedly by the regulatory framework. Again, pension scheme members in either case deserve the same level of protection.

We think that greater streamlining of both Inland Revenue and DWP legislation should lead to a substantial reduction in the number of generic pension products, which would go a long way towards simplifying the whole pensions landscape.

We have aimed to eradicate as many differences between the rules governing occupational pensions and individual pensions as possible.

*Theme 3 – More pension less prescription*

*More pension*

The objective of the following proposals is to enable individuals to build up as much pension as possible during their working lives.

Employers should be allowed to make membership of their pension scheme a condition of employment if they so wish. We think this provision should include traditional occupational pensions and other employer-sponsored pensions such as stakeholders, personal pensions or group personal pensions where the employer is making a contribution of at least, say, 4 per cent of the employee's pensionable salary.

There should be immediate vesting in all types of pension arrangement (once someone becomes a member). This will be particularly beneficial for younger people who have a greater tendency than older people to change jobs frequently and who, under current rules, may work for many years without accruing any pension.

There should be much easier pension transfer rules. We offer a proposal which would enable trustees to transfer small amounts of accrued pension into 'safe harbour' products, where the scheme member does not object or make a voluntary transfer within a set period of time. This will alleviate the administrative implications of immediate vesting.

*Modern benefits*

At present, occupational pension schemes and certain elements of contracted-out personal pension schemes are required to provide very specific types of benefit. We think it is right that schemes which want to contract out should be required to provide minimum standards but we think that the existing requirements are overly prescriptive and are a contributory factor in employers switching from defined benefit to defined contribution schemes, often cutting contributions and contracting back into the state scheme. The following proposals aim to reduce prescription and to modernise pension benefits, to give more choice and allow individuals, employers and commercial providers to determine the best type of pension to meet their circumstances.

The government should remove the requirement for occupational pensions and the protected-rights element of personal pensions to increase pensions in payment in line with prices (this would not affect those who are already drawing a pension and any benefits which have accrued but are not yet in payment would be subject to an equivalence test). In defined contribution arrangements, this does not mean a change in the value of benefits but to the 'shape' of the annuity that is purchased with the member's money-purchase retirement fund, generally leaving the member with more choice. In defined benefit schemes, the reduction in cost for future accrual might persuade an employer to continue offering a defined benefit scheme, rather than switching to a defined contribution scheme and cutting contributions. Individuals should be free to determine the pension benefit – either with or without indexation – with their employer or commercial providers. Individuals should be able to shop around in the marketplace for the pension which suits their circumstances and requirements. In the workplace, the pension is part of the remuneration package and we would expect individuals considering job offers to take that into account and for trade unions and staff associations to include pension provision in remuneration negotiations with employers. We look at the possibility of retrospective changes in this area in the report.

The requirement for schemes to provide survivors' benefits should be removed (including defined benefit and money-purchase arrangements). We think that, in the modern world, many couples would prefer to make arrangements to ensure they both have an independent income in retirement, rather than relying on derived rights (the only current requirement is in relation to spouses). Again, whether or not the pension has survivors' benefits attached should be determined by the individual and their employer or commercial provider.

A new simplified reference scheme test should be introduced to simplify contracting out.

In occupational defined benefit schemes, we recommend the optional removal of Guaranteed Minimum Pensions and their replacement by a retrospective reference scheme equivalence test.

For other contracted-out pensions, we propose the abolition of the current distinction between the form of benefits deriving from National Insurance Contribution rebates and that derived from other contributions.

It is important that employers keep their pension promise. However, we also think it should be easier for employers to re-shape pension arrangements in the light of contemporary economic or other circumstances. This might seem to be a consumer loss but it is better than an employer faced with unsustainable costs in their defined benefit schemes having to close the scheme altogether. A careful balance needs to be struck here between giving employers the right to amend pensions in the light of changed circumstances and their responsibility to keep their pension promise. Our proposals seek to strike a fair balance.

## LINKS TO THE SANDLER AND INLAND REVENUE REVIEWS

The remit of our review was to recommend changes to the private pensions legislation for which DWP is responsible. However, the pensions regulatory landscape is also shaped by the Financial Services Authority (FSA) and tax rules. In drafting this report, we have worked closely with the Sandler and Inland Revenue review teams and we hope that the recommendations from all three reviews will dovetail effectively.

## CONCLUSION

It is sometimes argued that pension system efficiency on the one hand and consumer protection on the other are mutually exclusive. We do not believe this is the case. Consumers have an interest in efficient systems which do not waste money on unnecessary bureaucracy; and employers and commercial pension providers need the public to have confidence in the pension system and pension products. We believe that our recommendations strike the right balance and can make a real impact in helping to increase pension provision in the UK.

# BIBLIOGRAPHY

Bassett, Philip, *Strike Free: New Industrial Relations in Britain*, Macmillan, 1986

Blunkett, David, *On a Clear Day*, Michael O'Mara Books, 1995

—, *The Blunkett Tapes: My Life in the Bear Pit*, Bloomsbury, 2006

Bower, Tom, *Maxwell: The Final Verdict*, HarperCollins, 1995

Brown, Gordon, *My Life, Our Times*, The Bodley Head, 2017

Brummer, Alex, *The Great Pensions Robbery: How New Labour Betrayed Retirement*, Random House Business, 2011

Bryant, John, *The London Marathon: The History of the Greatest Race on Earth*, Arrow Books, 2006

Butler, David, *British Political Facts since 1979*, Palgrave Macmillan, 2006

—, *The British General Election of 1997*, Palgrave Macmillan, 1997

Cadbury, Deborah, *Chocolate Wars: From Cadbury to Kraft – 200 Years of Sweet Success and Bitter Rivalry*, HarperCollins, 2011

Campbell, Alastair, *Power and Responsibility*, Arrow Books, 2011
—, *Power and the People*, Arrow Books, 2012
—, *The Burden of Power: Countdown to Iraq*, Arrow Books, 2013
Carpenter, Harry, *Where's Harry?: My Story*, Pelham Books, 1992
Chapple, Frank, *Sparks Fly!: A Trade Union Life*, Michael Joseph, 1984
Chrystal, Paul, *Chocolate: The British Chocolate Industry*, Shire Publications, 2011
Darling, Alistair, *Back from the Brink: 1,000 Days at Number 11*, Atlantic Books, 2011
Delaney, Juliana, *York's Chocolate Story*, Continuum Attractions
Ezra, Don, *The Retirement Plan Solution: The Reinvention of Defined Contribution*, Wiley, 2009
Freeman, Andrew, *All you need to know about being a Pension Fund Trustee*, Longtail, 2006
Hammond, Eric, *Maverick: The Life of a Union Rebel*, Weidenfeld & Nicolson, 1992
Hayter, Dianne, *Fightback!: Labour's Traditional Right in the 1970s and 1980s*, Manchester University Press, 2005
Hull, John, *Notes on Blindness*, Profile Books, 2017
Keegan, William, *The Prudence of Mr Gordon Brown*, Wiley, 2004
Knighton, Ryan, *Cockeyed: A Memoir of Blindness*, Atlantic Books, 2007
Lloyd, John, *Light and Liberty: A History of the EETPU*, Weidenfeld & Nicolson, 1990

Lowther, Richard, *Horses in Training*, Raceform, 2017

Mount, Ferdinand, *Mind the Gap: Class in Britain Now*, Short Books, 2004

Nuttgens, Patrick, *The History of York*, Blackthorn Press, 2007

Oborne, Peter, *Alastair Campbell: New Labour and the Rise of the Media Class*, Aurum, 2004

—, *The Rise of Political Lying*, Free Press, 2005

Parliamentary Ombudsman, *Trusting in the Pensions Promise*, The Stationery Office, 2006

Pensions Provisions Group, *We all need pensions: The Prospects for Pension Provision*, The Stationery Office, 1998

Performance and Innovation Unit, *Winning the Generation Game*, The Stationery Office, 2000

Pickering, Alan, *A Simpler Way to Better Pensions*, The Stationery Office, 2002

Pipe, Martin, *The Champion Trainer's Story*, Headline, 1992

Pollard, Stephen, *David Blunkett*, Hodder & Stoughton, 2005

Rentoul, John, *Tony Blair: Prime Minister*, Little, Brown, 2001

Sampson, Anthony, *Who Runs This Place?: The Anatomy of Britain in the 21st Century*, John Murray, 2004

Sanctuary, Brian, *Sleeping in the Snow: The Story of York's Open Air Schools*, Quacks Books, 2001

Seldon, Anthony, *Blair*, Free Press, 2004

Tett, Gillian, *Fool's Gold*, Little, Brown, 2009

Thomas, Martin, *Dictionary of Social Work: The Definitive A to Z of Social Work and Social Care*, Collins Educational, 1995

Turner, Adair, *Second Report of the Pensions Commission*, The Stationery Office, 2005
Wheatcroft, Geoffrey, *Yo, Blair!*, Politico's, 2007
Willetts, David, *The Pinch*, Atlantic Books, 2010
Willman, Paul, *Union Business*, Cambridge University Press, 1993

# INDEX

Acomb Maternity Hospital 21–2
Adam Smith Institute 210
Additional Voluntary Contributions (AVC) 153–4
Akroyd, Richard xv, 130, 138, 214
Alan's Dream (horse) 229
Amalgamated Engineering and Electrical Union (AEEU) 92
Amalgamated Engineering Union (AEU) 92
Amateur Athletic Association (AAA) 100
Aon Consulting 149, 162
Arbuthnot, James 198
Ashley, Jack 42
Associated Society of Locomotive Engineers and Firemen (ASLEF) 41
Association of British Insurers (ABI) 68, 141, 183
Association of Consulting Actuaries (ACA) 68, 141
Association of Pensions Lawyers 141, 183
Aston, Beverly
 *Union Business: Trade Union Organisation and Financial Reform in the Thatcher Years* 79–80
Attlee, Clement 21
Aviva 216, 217

Bacon & Woodrow 130
Bassett, Philip 77–8
 *Strike Free: New Industrial Relations in Britain* 59
BESTrustees 215, 217
Better Prices on Goals Galore Handicap 235
Bickerstaffe, Rodney 200
Birkbeck College 168, 174
Blackheath & Bromley Harriers 13, 250
 Blackheath Harriers Athletic Club 100–101, 105, 250
Blair, Tony 139, 142, 164, 160, 167, 191–2
Blake, David 174
Blindley Heath Handicap 232
Blunkett, David 16, 41, 125
Boston Marathon 105
Bradford & Bingley Building Society 48

British Broadcasting Corporation (BBC) 165–6, 200
In Touch 126
Money Box 200–201
Today Programme 160, 198
British Horseracing Authority (BHA) 9, 13, 119, 236–8, 240
Rules Committee 240
British Railways ix, 36, 113
British Telecom (BT) 172, 175
Britz, Lew xv, 57, 59, 67, 91–2
Bromley Council 74, 114–15, 252
Brotherhood of Centurions, The 101, 250
Brown, Gordon 148, 165–7, 176, 191–2
Budget (1997) 5–6, 164
Budget (2001) 154–5
*My Life, Our Times* 166
Brummer, Alex
*Great Pensions Robbery: How New Labour Betrayed Retirement, The* 164
Burgon, Robert 72, 203–4
Byers, Stephen
Secretary of State for Transport 191

Calibre 125
Callaghan, James 75
Campbell, Alastair 191
*Burden of Power: Countdown to Iraq, The* 159–60
Cannon, Les 58
Carpenter, Harry 23
Castle, Barbara 67, 83–4
Chanton Group Handicap 229–30
Chapple, Frank 58–9, 65–6, 75, 91, 124
EETPU Secretary General 53, 76–7
*Sparks Fly! A Trade Union Life* 58–9
Charles, Prince of Wales 47
Chrystal, Paul
*York in the 1960s: Ten Years That Changed a City* 36
Churchill, Winston 14
Clarke, Bob 78–9
Clinton, Hillary 201–2
Close, Brian 96
Coates, Max xv, 35, 44–5, 99
Confederation of British Industries (CBI) 147–8, 184
Conservative Party 25–6, 64, 67, 74, 138–9
members of 1–2, 185, 195–6
Consumers' Association 184
*Contact* 79
Convivial Spirit (horse) 230
Cosmic Destiny (horse) 230, 236
Costa Filey (horse) 236
Cousins, Jim 202
Coventry Hospital 98
Cronin, Mike xv, 101–2, 106
Crossman, Richard 218
Crowley, Jim 234
Cunningham, Andrew 50

*Daily Mail* 174–5, 199
*Daily Telegraph* 153
Dallard, Chris 183
Darling, Lord Alistair xv, 14–15, 170–71, 173–4, 176–82, 184–5, 191–3, 199, 204, 248, 253
*Back from the Brink: 1000 Days at Number 11* 192
Secretary of State for Transport 191
Secretary of State for Work and Pensions 157, 166, 175–6
Social Security Secretary 145–6
Davie, Jenny xv, 12, 90–91, 107, 110, 120–21, 130, 183, 244, 248, 254
defined benefit (DB) pension scheme 3–4, 6–7, 66, 84–6, 147–9, 154, 163, 166, 170, 177, 184, 189–90, 208, 213, 216, 219–20
defined contribution (DC) pension scheme 7, 163, 189–90, 201, 216, 219–20
Delo, Steve xvi, 217
chairman of PPS 216
Denham, John 139
Dennis, Norman 52

Dewsbury Building Society 46
Donne, John 127
dot-com bubble (2000–2001) 169
Duval, Donald
  president of SPC 201

Eagle Star 177
Earnings-Related State Pension Scheme (SERPS) 65–6, 71, 87, 161–2
East Yorkshire Regiment 26
*Economist, The* 125
Edmonds, John 199
Electrical, Electronic, Telecommunications and Plumbing Union (EETPU) ix, 4, 15, 18, 55–60, 62, 68, 72, 79–80, 83, 87–8, 91, 99–100, 102, 120, 124, 129–30, 139–40, 213, 226, 245
  as Electrical Trades Union 58
  Centenary Fund 248
  formation of (1968) 53
  pension fund 92
Epsom racecourse 230
Equitable Life Assurance Society 153, 169
European Federation for Retirement Provision (EFRP) 155–6, 212
European Parliament 212
European Union (EU)
  member states of 155
  pensions policies of 156–7
Eurostar 157
*Evening Standard* 160
Exhall Grange School 31–3, 38, 46–7, 57, 97, 113
Exxon Corporation/ExxonMobil
  Esso Petroleum 135

Feather, Vic
  TUC Secretary General 51
Festival of Britain (1951) 26
Field, Frank 148, 166–7, 198, 200, 218
  Minister of State for Social Security 162
  'New Ambitions for Our Country: A New Contract for Welfare' 167–8
*Financial News* 143
Financial Services Act (1986) 85
Financial Services Authority (FSA) 153, 266
*Financial Times* 77–8
First World War (1914–18) x
Flamborough Breeze (horse) 234
Ford Motor Company 36
Ford, Peter xvi, 183–8
Fulford Open Air School 29, 97, 112–13
Furnell, Adrian 183

GMB (Trade Union) 199
Gold Standards Committee 239
Goobey, Alastair Ross 171–2
Goode, Roy 137
Government Communication Headquarters (GCHQ) 83
Grand National 228
Green, Dicky 101
Grieve, Helen xvi
Guaranteed Minimum Pensions 265

Hague, William 164–5
Hammond, Eric 15, 88, 90–92
Harman, Harriet 167
  Secretary of State for Social Security 162–3
Harman, Steve
  chairman of BHA 237–8
Hawker Siddeley 54, 64
Heath, Edward
  administration of 62
Heholt, Mark xv–xvi, 2, 182–5, 187, 202–4
Hermes 171
Hewitt Bacon & Woodrow 172 183
Hicks-Little, Bo 237
HMS *Whitesand Bay* 23
Holloway, Stanley 23
Holt, Simon xvi, 232, 235–6, 241
House of Commons xv, 2, 174, 192–6, 202

Hull, John 126
*Notes on Blindness: A Journey Through the Dark* 115
*Touching the Rock: An Experience of Blindness* 122
Humphrys, John 109

Illingworth, Ray 96
Imperial Chemical Industries (ICI) 175
Institute and Faculty of Actuaries 65
Institute for Public Policy Research 188
Institute of Directors (IOD) 148
Investment Pensions Europe (IPE) 10, 212
Gold Award for Outstanding Contribution 212
*Investors Chronicle* 125

Johnson, D. G. 65
Joint Working Group (JWG)
Occupational Pensions 152
Jones, Karen xvi, 217
Joseph, Sir Keith 67

Kearney, Martha 198
Kellogg's 215
Kelly, Ruth
Financial Secretary to Treasury 202
Kempton Park racecourse 234
Kirby, Mrs 114–16
Kirkwood, Archy 198
Knighton, Ryan 114, 118, 122
*Cockeyed: A Memoir of Blindness,* 111
Kosovo Pensions Savings Trust 218

Labour Party 2, 34–5, 40–42, 45, 58–9, 64, 74–5, 138, 148, 160, 160–62, 164, 174, 196, 247, 251, 253,
Lamont, Norman 166
Lawson, Nigel 135–6
Budget (1988) 163
Leeds Building Society 48
LeGrand, Kevin 85
Lester, Ted 22–3
Lewis, Paul 200–201
Liberal Democrat Party 164, 172–3, 185, 196, 251
Lilley, Peter 2, 185, 193–4
Secretary of State for Social Security 136, 163
Lingfield Park racecourse 232, 234–5, 254
Liverton, Charlie xvi, 239
chief executive of Racehorse Owners Association 231
Lloyd, John 60, 91
*Light & Liberty: The History of EETPU* 58, 77
London and North Eastern Railway (LNER) 22
London Marathon 104–5

Major, John 136
Marshall, George 31
founder of Partially Sighted Society 31
Martin Pipe Racing Club 227–8
Maxwell, Robert 133–4, 163–4, 170–71
Mirror Group pension fund scandal 5, 131, 253
McCartney, Ian 185, 193
Minister of State for Work and Pensions 173
McCloud, Mr 247–8
Meacher, Michael 40–42, 52, 247
Mellon, Paul 226
Metropolitan Sports Club for the Blind 101
Miinnehoma (horse) 228
Mill Reef (horse) 226
Milton, John 127
minimum funding requirement (MFR) 148, 150, 154, 157
Mirror Group Newspapers 5, 131
Miss Tikitiboo (horse) 232
Monaco 145–6
Mongan, Ian 233

Moorcroft Racehorse Welfare Centre 236
Moore, Patrick 117, 243
Moore, Ryan 227
Moorfields Eye Hospital 111
Morris, Luke xvi, 223, 242, 254
Morris, Timothy
  *Union Business: Trade Union Organisation and Financial Reform in the Thatcher Years* 79–80
Mosley Michael xv, 64, 69–71, 79–82
Mr Velocity (horse) 231–2
Murdoch, Rupert 88–9
Murless, Noel 37
Murray, Peter
  chairman of NAPF 142
Myners Report (2001) 157, 179

National Association of Pension Funds (NAPF) ix, 5–6, 68, 74, 84, 88, 109, 130, 133, 137,138, 141–4, 145, 148, 150–5, 163, 165–6, 170, 171, 175, 178, 184, 252
National Audit Office (NAO) 209
National Economic Development Council (NEDC)
  Economic Development Committees 63
National Health Service (NHS) 21
National Hunt 227–9
National Insurance Contribution 265
National Pensioners Convention 200
National Union of Dyers, Bleachers and Textile Workers
  members of 55
National Union of Mineworkers (NUM) 75
National Union of Railwaymen (NUR) 41
Negotiators Guide to Pensions (1979) 71–2, 75
Newcastle United Football Club 50
Newcastle University ix, 49–50, 57, 98, 245, 247
News International 88–9
Newton, Hilary 105
Noble, Jean 29
Norman Park Athletics Track 106
Norway 101

O'Brien, Vincent 37
Occupational Pensions Board 210
Occupational Pensions Regulatory Authority (OPRA) 175, 179–80, 261
  Quinquennial Review 209
Octagon Recovery 78–9
oil price crisis (1973) 62
Otham, Lady 225
Oxford University 56
  faculty of 137
  Ruskin College 42

Pantile Stud Farm 237
Partially Sighted Society 31
Pastoral Pursuits (horse) 236–7
Peel, Jack
  general secretary of National Union of Dyers, Bleachers and Textile Workers 55
Peel, Mike xv, 102
  participant in London Marathon (1981) 103–4
Pension Protection Fund 210
Pensions Act (1995) 133–4, 169–70, 187, 194, 211
Pensions Act (2004) 209, 259
*Pensions Age* 149
Pensions Management Institute (PMI) 68, 245
  annual conference (1997) 139
  Pension Trusteeship Award 215
*Pensions Management* 144, 147
  Pensions Personality of the Year Award 147
Pensions Protection Fund (PPF) 211
Pensions Provision Group (PPG) 162
Pensions Regulator, The (TPR) 209–10
  personnel of 210

*Pensions Week* 142
*Pensions World* 129
People's Pension Scheme (PPS) 215–17
  personnel of 216
personal pension plans (PPP) 131
personal pensions scandal (1985) 86–7
Pickering, Alan
  awarded CBE (2003) 105, 204
  birth 21
  career at British Railways 39ff
  career at the EETPU 55ff
  career at R. Watson and Sons 5, 130–32, 134, 137–8
  career at Watson Wyatt 211–15, 228–9
  career at BESTrustees 215ff
  chairman of NAPF 139–45, 151, 153–5, 178, 252
  education of 28–32, 43, 49–52, 98, 112–13
  family of 8–11, 16–17, 27–8, 34–5, 37, 107, 110, 119–20, 244
  horses owned by/interest in governance of horseracing 223–4, 229–36, 238–41
  marathons run by 104–6
  marriage 82
  president of NAPF 109
  recipient of 'Greatest Single Contribution to Occupational Pensions (1998–2017)' 129
  role in DB pension scheme development 4–5, 8
  trusteeships held by 215–16
  vice-chairman of NAPF 137, 165–6, 170–71
Pickering (née Chapman), Betty 22, 24, 26, 31, 111
  death of (1999) 10
  family of 17, 45–6, 110, 244
Pickering, Christine xiv, 9, 11–12, 81–2, 107, 119–20, 245, 254
Pickering, Frank 22–6, 31, 49
  death of 102
  family of 17, 34–5, 37, 45–6
Pickering Report 12, 18, 157, 176, 180–81, 186–8, 193–5, 202–3, 205–8, 257–67
  Executive Summary 188–90
Pierson, John
  *Dictionary of Social Work: The Definitive A to Z of Social Work and Social Care* 6
Pimlott, Ben 52
Pipe, Martin 227–8
Pipe-Scudamore Racing Club 227
Plumbing Industry Pensions Scheme 132, 213, 215–16
  Plumbing & Mechanical Services (UK) Industry Pension Scheme 66
Plumbing Pensions (UK) Ltd 72
  personnel of 203
Pollard, Stephen
  *David Blunkett* 16
Poole, Colin 105–6
Poulson, John 50
Prescott, John 42
Primrose Valley (horse) 236
Professional Jockeys Association (PJA) 10, 239
*Professional Pensions* 146
Prudential Group 89–90

R. Watson and Sons 5, 92–3, 130–32, 134, 137–8
Racehorse Owner Association (ROA) 231, 238–9
  Race Day Committee 239
Railwaymen's Union 56
Rentoul, John 160
retinitis pigmentosa (RP) 27, 68, 110–11
Robin Hoods Bay (horse) 223–4, 234–5, 242, 253–4
Rogers, Dave xv, 59–60, 63–4, 69, 91
Rooker, Jeff 139
Ross, Tom 149, 162
Rowling, J. K. 18
  *Harry Potter* (media franchise) 220–21
Rowntree & Co. 24, 28, 36–7, 101–2

Royal Mail
  statutory pension scheme 218
Royal National Institute for the Blind (RNIB) 119
Royal Pharmaceutical Society 215
Rust, Nick 9, 240

Sandler and Inland Revenue 266
Scarborough & Whitby Railway 22
Scargill, Arthur 62
Scottish & Newcastle Breweries 138, 175
Second World War (1939–45) x, 25
Segars, Joanne xv
  CEO of NAPF 133
Seldon, Anthony 160
Shell Contributory Pension Fund xiv
Skinner, Dennis 42
Skipton Building Society 48
Smith, Andrew 192–8
  Secretary of State for Work and Pensions 192
Smith, Rev. 245
Smith, T. Dan 50
Social Security Pensions Act (1974) 64
Society of Pensions Consultants (SPC) 68, 201
Spellar MP, John xv, 3, 56, 59–60, 67, 69
Spencer, Jamie xvi
*Sporting Life Weekender* 125
St Helens and Yorkshire County Cricket Club 254
state pension 151–2
Stewart, Alec 228, 230
Surrey Walking Club 100–101
bin Suroor, Saeed 235

Talking Newspapers 105, 125–6
Tapper, Henry xvi, 146–7
Teal, Jessie 224
Tesco 175
Thatcher, Margaret 67, 83–5, 136
  administration of 64
  industrial policy of 75
Thomas, Martin
  *Dictionary of Social Work: The Definitive A to Z of Social Work and Social Care* 6
Thomas, Peter 232
Thompson, Peter 178
Thompson, Sylvia 10
*Times, The* 180, 207
Timmins, Nicholas 167–8, 172
Timms MP, Stephen xvi, 139, 205–6
Trade Union Congress (TUC) 43, 63, 88, 148, 184
  members of 51
  Pensions Conference 146
Transport Act (1968) 42
Transport Salaried Staffs' Association (TSSA) 41, 45
Trueman, Fred 96
Tull, Christine 73–4, 81
Turner, Lord Adair 207
  Pensions Committee (2002–5) 7

United Arab Emirates (UAE)
  Abu Dhabi 91
United Engineering Steels (UES) 86
Universities Central Council on Admissions (UCCA) 43

Vaughan, Ed xvi, 223, 230, 233, 235, 237, 254

Waddingham, Adrian xv, 3, 134, 140, 172, 185, 204, 206
Watson Wyatt (WW) 11, 214–15
  personnel of 211–14, 228–9
Wayman, Richard xvi, 236, 238–40
Webb, Sir Steve xv, 164, 172–3, 185, 193–4, 196–8, 206, 219
Welfare Reform and Pensions Act (1999) 168
Wheatcroft, Patience 180
Whitby Town Cricket Club 95–6
Whitlow, Geoff xv, 82–3, 87–8

Willetts, Lord David xvi, 1–2, 7, 18, 166, 170–71, 177–8, 185, 193–6, 198–9, 208
*Pinch: How the Baby Boomers Took Their Children's Future – And Why They Should Give It Back, The* 206–7
Willis, Norman 42
Willman, Paul
*Union Business: Trade Union Organisation and Financial Reform in the Thatcher Years* 79–80
Wilson, Harold 38
Winter Derby 223–4, 234–5, 253–4
Winter of Discontent (1974) 75
Woodcock, George 42
Worcester College 31
Work and Pensions Select Committee 218
Working Men's Club (WMC) 26, 35
Fulford 99

York City Football Club 45
York City Reserves 95–6
York Corporation 21
York Education Authority 33
York Racecourse 225, 248
York Rugby League Club 45, 250–51, 254
Yorkshire County Cricket Club 96
Yorkshire Penny Bank 46

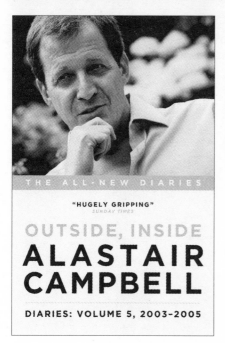

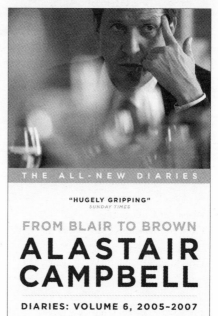

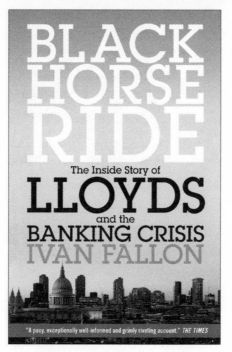

# War
# or
# Peace?

Published by the Christian Studies Press,
The Old School, High Street, Coton, Cambridge CB23 7PL.

First published as e-book 2014,
Printed 2015 by Createspace.


Webwords: Why World War One? We can Disarm the World. Why We War. War or Peace? WOP. War to Peace. World Multilateral Disarmament. The long failure of western arms. Two World Wars - One Cause.

**Key words**: Peace, war, arms trade, the economics of arms, the merchants of death, munitions, militarism, Mulliner Scare, Fascism, Nazis, the United States' Fascist Coup Attempt, First World War, Second World War, World Multilateral Disarmament.

**Key Names**: Krupp, Armstrong, Schneider, Vickers, Gladstone, Zacharoff, Nobel, Tolstoy, Doukobors, Tsar Nicholas, Fisher, Lloyd George, Hardie, Lópes, Shaw, Bannerman, Von Moltke, Churchill, Grey, Ponsonby, Von Tirpitz, Beresford, Wilhelm II, Balfour, Von Papen, Skoda, Passy, Jaures, Von Suttner, Addams, Benedict XV, Du Pont, Thyssen, Wilson, Cavell, Morgan, Rockerfeller, Bush, Lenin, Stalin, Trotsky, Cecil, Noel-Baker, Nye, Robertson, Shearer, Hoover, Zinoviev, Thurin, Henderson, Hankey, Vansittart, Simon, Marley, Stimson, Lansbury, Litvinoff, Nalodny, Attlee, Baldwin, Englebrecht, Hanighen, Nietzsche, Grotz, Ansaldo, de Wendel, Mosley, Hess, Hitler, Ford, Von Schleicher, Hugenberg, Roosevelt, Butler, McGuire, Schacht, Farben, Morgenthau, Kennedy, Schmitz, Teagle, Harriman, Bechtel, McCone, Speer, McGuire, Shouse, Raskob, Bush, Walker, Davis, Clark, Murphy, Smith, Dulles.

ISBN 1-903576-02-4

# Contents: WAR OR PEACE? (WOP)

Introduction.

Volume 1. MANUFACTURING THE FIRST WORLD WAR.

*PART I. THE INDUSTRY OF WAR EMERGES*
1. The Start of the Industrial Arms Trade. 7
2. The Big Boys - Krupp, Schneider, Armstrong, Vickers. 18
3. Moving politicians into line –the British Naval Lobby. 33
4. Exporting Militarism. 42

*PART II. WHY WORLD WAR ONE?*
5. Weapons lead to War. 53
6. The Build-up and Pressure of Arms. 63
7. The Mulliner Panic and British Militarism. 73
8. Krupp, Von Tirpitz and the Kaiser. 96
9. The Attempts for Peace. 115
10. The Great War Boom. 145

*PART III. THE WAR TO END ALL WARS?*
11. Learning from History? A Review. 171
12. Christianity and Peace. 179

Volume Two: PULLING THE STRINGS OF FASCISM.

*PART IV. SUPERPOWER MILITARISM*
13. The United States learns Militarism. 187
14. Teaching Russia Militarism. 204

*PART V. DEFEATING PEACE.*
15. Peace and Disarmament or Arms and War? 220
16. The Politics leading to the Geneva Disarmament Conference. 240
17. The Great 1932 Geneva Disarmament Conference. 257

*PART VI. THE MILITARY-INDUSTRIAL COMPLEX AS THE DRIVER OF FASCISM.*
18. Looking behind Fascism. 286
19. Fascism in Italy, Japan, France and Britain. 301
20. Those behind the Nazi War Machine. 316
21. The American Fascist Coup Attempt. 341

*PART VII. ARMING THE WORLD – THE SECOND WORLD WAR.*
22. The Second World War: the fully armed World Economy. 369
23. The Second World War inside our Heads. 392

The Short Version. 400

Postscript. 411

Chapters in War to Peace. Vols. Three and Four. 413

Chronology. 415

Index. 465

Endnotes. 475

**Introduction.**

This book seems a big chunk to bite off, but it is not really. It tells of the accumulation of power by the arms companies and the military over the last hundred and fifty years. This story is also the history of war. The book suggests selling arms has been the *engine* of war throughout this period, in particular producing the two World Wars. There are twists and turns in the tale, but the underlying process is clear. Arms and their promotion cause war. You merely have to see if you think the case is made.

This understanding questions the way the West has operated in the modern era. We are told weapons make us safe, when they produce wars and rumours of wars. The industry of arms causes unlimited devastation yet we continue with it, because the munitions people hide the evidence gathered here. The book probably understates the pressure, corruption, insider influence over politicians, media manipulation, fear and distortion by which this industry has obtained its power, because much is still hidden, but the general picture is clear and available through multiple sources. Perhaps, it has messed up the world.

There is nothing original in the argument. It was fully stated and accepted throughout much of the world in the twenties and thirties, but then buried because the arms companies and military arranged another World War. Since then it has been covered up much of the time and this gathering of the evidence develops it further than previous studies. Chapters 7, 17 and 18-21 are especially pregnant with the theme.

This book stops at the end of the Second World War. The second, War to Peace, takes the same story to the present. The deeper point of both, through providing the historical evidence of our failure, is to suggest that world-wide multilateral disarmament is practical, good and relatively easy compared to arming and fighting wars.

There is a short 2% précis of the full argument of the book at the end, (which you might want to start with) and a useful chronology.

## Volume One: MANUFACTURING THE FIRST WORLD WAR.

*In the twentieth century, something like two hundred million people have been killed in war-related deaths in a multitude of wars. They occur so often that we have become fatalistic towards them, yet they are not inevitable, but caused. Among the reasons for war, one requires much fuller analysis. It is the growth of industrial arms companies. They are in the business of sales and need wars to survive and grow. They emerged in the 19$^{th}$ century and looked to create a market for their weapons. They used mass production and needed large scale conflict. Over decades, arms manufacturers like Krupp, Armstrong, Vickers, Schneider, Du Pont, Skoda and others plied their trade. A series of wars kept them profitable and expanding. It was not long before they moved into a place of political influence and exported militarism throughout the world. They became the confidents of emperors, rulers, generals and prime ministers. Every war strengthened their position and soon they were powerful players in international affairs.*

*In Volume One we look at the way these companies encouraged wars, until the world was set up their way. They then played the dominant role in precipitating the Great War. The First World War made them the biggest industry on the planet, replete with profits and not looking to give up their work as the merchants of death.*

## Part I. THE INDUSTRY OF WAR EMERGES.

*Before the 19th Century weapons were largely a craft industry and mainly orientated to a national market. Often the state met its own military needs directly. Then in the mid-19th century industrial arms companies began to emerge. They needed constant reliable markets to grow and spread the idea of militarisation through their exports and sales. Soon they began to have influence in domestic and international politics. They knew how to promote their wares and grew into large-scale industrial enterprises in Britain, France, Austro-Hungary, Russia, Germany and the United States.*

# Chapter One: The Start of the Industrial Arms Trade.

### The Napoleonic Wars.

We begin in 1789 with the French Revolution and twenty five years of European War. On the 14th July, 1789, the Bastille, a large weapon and ammunition cache and a small prison, was stormed and the guns passed around. The French aristocracy was ousted. Conflict spread, as it often does. Soon Europe was plunged into a war which affected everybody either in the price of bread or sometimes more directly because they were killed. Goya who had once painted the Spanish aristocracy in full pomp moved to painting "The Third of May, 1808", showing the horrific massacre of Spanish peasants by French riflemen. During twenty five years of war from 1789 to 1815 something like four or five million people died, often brutally - an average of 200,000 a year.

It was a time of intense militarisation. The weapons which probably did the most damage were the artillery – brass cannon that were moved around by horses and fired into the bodies of advancing soldiers. Vast numbers of muskets, rifles, bayonets, lances and especially swords were used in close quarter combat by millions of soldiers. They all needed to be made. Already there were quarters in every major nation making these weapons in workshops which were still largely craft organisations, and for twenty five years they were in full production. Birmingham was a hive of hot iron working, turning out over a thousand muskets a day.[1] Small weapons are capable of amazing levels of mass destruction and throughout Europe people suffered year after year. The end of the Wars, when Napoleon had been killed by the arsenic in his wallpaper, was marked by famine, loss, poverty and devastation, and the continent longed for peace. After 1815, war was firmly off the agenda.

This Quarter Century War was about empire, intense nationalism and patriotism, the control of people and plunder. There was no great discontinuity between these motives and later ones when weapons were industrially available. But in another sense wars did become different; there were local streams which turned into the world's greatest industrial river. The industrial production of steel weapons began its journey. The factory based munitions people were aiming at permanent manufacture and steady demand, and they learned to control their market. What do weapons' manufacturers do when wars are over? Suddenly there are too many swords and guns, and nobody wants to commission any more; there is a deep recession. After 1815 the crafted weapons centres of Europe atrophied as demand fell. But what if this industry could become permanent, constantly supplying weapons in a world-wide market? How do you keep these factories in business? What if arms companies could facilitate war and the rumour of wars. In 1815 such a thought was largely unthought, but by 1915 the munitions companies had the systems in place. If you need a war, you have to find one. They were in business, what would become the biggest business of all.

**A Time of Relative Peace in Europe, 1815 - 1853.**

By and large peace emerged in Europe for forty years or so between 1815 and 1853, apart from some smaller skirmishes. During periods like this the scale of weapon production closes down, armed forces shrink and people get used to peace. Threats and war scares diminish and people forget what war is like. This is the era when Thomas Hood wrote his poem, Faithless Nellie Gray.

Ben Battle was a soldier bold
And used to wars alarms,
But a cannon ball took off his legs
So he lay down his arms.

Now, as they bore him off the field,
Said he, "Let others shoot,
For here I leave my second leg,
And the Forty-second Foot!"

but when he returned home, he was cruelly deserted by his betrothed, faithless Nellie Gray.

Said she, "I loved a soldier once
For he was blithe and brave
But I will never have a man
With both legs in the grave!

"Why then," said she, "you've lost the feet
Of legs in war's alarms,
And now you can not wear your shoes
Upon your feats of arms!"

You need some distance from war to make these kinds of jokes about it. The demand for weapons was now low. New industries got underway – cotton, wool, railways, pottery, soap, cutlery, ironware and all kinds of industries began to supply the things that ordinary people needed in their lives.

There were still two outlets for weapons. Britain and the other countries of Europe were winning colonies, and gun and cannon did the job. This trade survived and even grew, spreading its own mayhem. A particularly evil war in China following the Opium War cost millions of lives, where many were shot. Gun exports to Americans who were "pacifying", i.e. shooting, the Indians, increased as they expanded their territory westwards. Other colonies "needed" guns in order to keep the natives in their place. Guns make empires.

The second outlet was more subtle. The wealthy, landowning establishments began to recognise that they needed weapons to quell the revolutionary masses who might eye their land, wealth and political power. The dangers heralded by the French Revolution meant the rich would always pay for the weapons they needed the keep the "sans culottes", the revolutionaries, in their place and they wanted armies under their control to defend themselves. The revolutions which occurred throughout Europe in 1848-9 hardened this attitude. In country after country urban masses took to the streets to protest against their rulers and against their poverty, lack of bread or lack of democratic rights. At the end of June 1848 it was soldiers on the streets of Paris who stood between the aristocrats and their demise. The regimes which put these marches and insurrections down were usually privileged – landowners, aristocracy, capitalists and the rich. They perceived that they needed weapons to defend their property, whether they were Prussian Junkers, French aristocrats or British Tories. The Iron Duke, the Duke of Wellington, was a Tory figurehead to defend privilege against the revolting poor. Somewhere in their heads there was an understanding that weapons were needed, not just to shoot grouse and pheasants, but to keep the masses in their place. A presumptive alliance developed between the privileged and the manufacturers who would supply the weapons to keep them safe.

And so, nearly unnoticed within the industrial revolution, a new kind of weapons' manufacturer began to emerge - not strongly before 1850 - but increasingly thereafter - producing iron, brass and steel mass-produced weapons. Initially, they were small producers, dwarfed by other areas of production. Steel can also be transformed into railways, bridges, cutlery, girders, bicycles, factory machinery, boats, ploughs and coaches; so there was no necessity to make weapons. But some manufacturers saw a market they could develop and went for it. One of these was Alfried Krupp.

**Steel and the young Alfred Krupp.**

Crucible steel first emerged in the City of Sheffield as a kind of craft industry, a guarded monopoly from the 1740s for the rest of the century. Some of it was used in hand weapons and other luxury items and gradually the industry grew in the forges of the Don Valley and its reputation spread. By the early 19th century there was a wider European competition to make good steel and break this monopoly which the people of Sheffield guarded avidly. In the 1830s a young Alfried Krupp of Essen was trying to produce crucible steel but had not really mastered the process. He travelled to Sheffield in 1838 in an early example of industrial espionage.[2] In boots and spurs he hung around the great forges to see what information he could pick up - not really good gear for spying. We can imagine the conversation as Alfried stood outside, and the man at the factory gate said, "O've heeard at hah yo wantn a chap to sho ya throot factoriz, an sitch ioik." and Alfried answered "Ya, bitte! Wo machen Sie Stahl?" The man at the gate must have been a bit suspicious, realised that he was not a tourist and limited his access. They called him, "the Baron" and he did not learn the Sheffield secrets of crucible steel, although he got a good sense of what steel production was like. He enjoyed his time there and became an Anglophile, changing his name to Alfred, after Alfred the Great, in benign acknowledgement of the English. Krupp had no hint of hatred to the English. Yet on the whole the visit was a failure, and Alfred had to work out how to make good steel himself.

He was a man obsessed by the technology of steel and by money. His father had died in 1826 trying to create a steel firm but failing spectacularly, leaving the family precariously in debt. He, young Alfried, only ten when his father died, had to put the family business together again and make enough money to fulfil his father's ambition and look after his mother and siblings. Tenaciously, this goal ruled his life; it was hard, obsessive work. Gradually he gathered the innovations necessary for good steel manufacture from beginning to end. Die Firma Krupp grew; it was autocratic in organisation, workers were looked after well and expected to be supremely loyal. They were known as "the

Kruppianer", the loyal workers of Essen. Here's the celebratory poem recited when a statue of Alfred was raised later, just to continue the poetic quality of this book.

"Let us raise our glasses
Drinking to the firm's good state,
Which for all its working masses
Helps in every blow of fate.
The firm is our father,
I would want to add,
We are all Kruppianer rather
And that's not too bad."

It may sound better in German, but probably not.[3] This was paternalistic capitalism in its purest form: Krupp would do well by them if they gave him unconditional commitment. Only once did it waver, as we see later.

After a while Alfred had thoroughly mastered steel manufacture. At the 1851 Great International Exhibition at Crystal Palace he exhibited a much admired cast steel field gun and an even more gawped-at ingot of steel weighing 4,300lb. Sheffield ironmasters had managed a 2,400lb block of steel, but it had been dwarfed by the newcomer's lump. Krupp was good at self-promotion, and he had arrived on the international scene as a steel manufacturer. Still his single smart cannon on a mahogany base did not get orders. It was a sign of the possible direction of his company, but he could not sell the new gun. At this stage Alfred had a lot of possible products in mind – steel railway wheels, cutlery and cannon. The railway wheels brought in the money and became the symbol of "Die Firma Krupp". It seemed they were the way to go. The workforce moved above a thousand and mainly built railway wheels, axles, lines and equipment in the factory complex in Essen.

**Ordinary People and the Crimean War.**

The abiding attitude of most ordinary people to war is that they abhor it and seek to avoid it. This was no less true of people in 1853. They knew that after the battle, men lie moaning, dying in agony with horrific open wounds, victims of barbaric behaviour between individuals and states. The sixth commandment, "You shall not kill", had forbidden the taking of life some three and a half thousand years back at the time of Moses, and it was now God's accepted word to the Christian world in Europe. It was written on the walls of most churches and learned by millions from childhood as a command from God to uphold the sanctity of human life for everyone. It made complete sense. If you do not want to be killed, don't kill others.

But in Prussia, St. Petersburg, Paris and London there were politicians who had learned statecraft and had found ways round the commandment by working out how many dead bodies they could cope with in their strategies of warfare. They were too sophisticated to take the Sixth Commandment seriously. Instead, the militarists looked to the Roman Empire, Napoleon, Wellington, Nelson and others for their inspiration; they believed in might, military tactics and the deployment of soldiers, whether in Paris, London or Berlin. They were like the Wellington, Napoleon or von Blücher who surveyed the battle scene and calculated the strategy and what might be the likely losses among the poor sods who were actually doing the fighting, and whether they could win. This was the business of militarism. Generals have to be prepared to bury the Sixth Commandment as part of their corporate culture.

The Crimean War of 1853-6 was between the Russian Empire and a coalition of France, Britain and the Ottoman Empire. Like many wars, it is not clear why it happened. Its presenting cause, rather ironically in view of the Christian understanding mentioned above, was squabbles about who should be in control of the "holy places" in Jerusalem. Britain and France, supposedly Christian countries, became allies of the Ottoman Empire, supposedly Muslim, in opposing Russia, supposedly Christian, about Muslim occupation of the "holy places" which, of course, were actually Jewish. The real issue, however, was worries France and Britain had that Russia was pushing down in the Black Sea area to expand her vast domain and become Europe's superpower. Many wars start merely through calculations of military power. Each state weighed the balance of power, and acted accordingly. It was the first major European war for thirty eight years – a big gap. It opened up a strong new demand for weapons, and firms in each country suddenly expanded their output and profits. Battleships were still made of wood, but they began to use steam.

On the Russian side Tolstoy was one of the officers in the war and from his experiences looked back to write *War and Peace,* supposedly the world's greatest novel. We shall look at the way Tolstoy changed later. It was a bloody and pointless war resulting in half a million casualties. Or rather, we must call them deaths. The word, "casualty" with its meaning of accident, unintended or by-product, is a dishonest word. We might not intend *our* soldiers to be killed, but we try uncasually to kill the others. The dead, too, before we harden to the numbers, we remember, are individuals like each of us, half a million, more than the whole population of Liverpool, killed for a trivial outcome and largely by calculations of power. The kind of war the Crimea was is conveyed by cavalry charging with swords, hoping to sweep all before them by cutting up infantry, who retort with artillery and muskets. The speed of reloading was crucial. If you could not reload fast enough the Hussars on horses would carve you down dead. This book will not be macabre, but we must reverence every death and injury. Tolstoy describes a man in hospital in Sevastopol in December 1854 with an amputated leg. "it struck me in the leg, just as if I had stepped into a hole, - and behold, I had no leg."

Yet the military did not have it all their own way, for there were two views of the War. The real hero of the Crimean War was Florence Nightingale, the gentle mender of bodies. She was quite clear where she stood. One of her most famous sayings was: "I stand at the altar of the murdered men, and, while I live, I fight their cause." That is fairly unequivocal. Moreover, the public knew what was happening. *The Times* reporter, William Howard Russell and a photographer, Roger Fenton, sent back direct accounts and pictures of the war; so this was no longer war according to the generals. The public perception was, especially in incidents like the Charge of the Light Brigade, of the waste and destruction of war and the stupidity of the generals, although the event was also cloaked in heroism. Some questioned empire, worked to end slavery, focussed on Christian mission and abhorred violence. Patriotism was the normal way of silencing these questions. Tennyson summed up this contradiction in *The Charge of the Light Brigade.*

Forward, the Light Brigade!"
Was there a man dismay'd?
Not tho' the soldier knew
Some one had blunder'd.
Theirs not to make reply,
Theirs not to reason why,
Theirs but to do and die.
Into the valley of Death
Rode the six hundred.

Cannon to right of them,
Cannon to left of them,
Cannon in front of them
Volley'd and thunder'd;
Storm'd at with shot and shell,
Boldly they rode and well,
Into the jaws of Death,
Into the mouth of hell
Rode the six hundred.

But, of course, we are all free to reason why, and rather than honouring the charge they made, may conclude that this kind of warfare is madness on horseback. The generals had goofed in producing cannon fodder, even though it was some kind of victory. Meanwhile the munitions' manufacturers were busy.

**The British Gun Trade.**

At the beginning of the Crimean War the British arms industry had two centres, one in Birmingham and the other in London. In Birmingham hundreds of workshops were turning out the weapons on which the British Empire depended, and they were also exported throughout the world. Between 1851 and 1861 six million guns were proofed in Birmingham, many for the Crimea and for export to America.[4] As well as supplying for the Crimean War between 1853-6, Birmingham made guns for the American Civil War of 1861-5, giving more or less fifteen years of uninterrupted expansion. It became the gun capital of the world. Many of the small firms coalesced into BSA, the Birmingham Small Arms Company, which could then handle big contracts. Noel-Baker records the case of Mr Goodman, the Chairman of the Birmingham Small Arms Company announcing in 1863 that he had sold 50,000 rifles to the Grand Vizier of the Turkish Empire, with the help of the British Ambassador.[5] Presumably, the Ambassador was not particularly worried that they might lead to the massacres of the Armenians which started in the 1870s and 1880s. Already the British state was facilitating the arms trade through its ambassadors and politicians, a pattern which would continue. By 1868 BSA had become the largest small arms manufacturer in Europe.

Yet the munitions' success in the Crimean War also occurred in London. The dominant British weapon was the Enfield rifled musket, or rifle, as it came to be called. It was manufactured in large quantities partly so that there was a standard weapon for British troops. Grooves, or rifling, in the barrel improved the shot. Enfield in North London, near where I used to live, was the location of the Royal Small Arms Factory, set up during the Napoleonic Wars. It was not far, for obvious reasons, from the Waltham Abbey Royal Gun Powder Factory. Another great Government factory complex was the Royal Woolwich Arsenal, which had a stronger naval focus. It is now more known for its football team, Arsenal – the Gunners, who later moved north of the Thames and found a less destructive way of shooting. These were government owned factories directed by the Board of Ordnance. Government factories could produce a more systematic, uniform pattern of weapons than the huge variety emerging from the Birmingham gun shops, and were therefore more efficient for running an empire. In other words, this was a nationalised industry, controlled by the War Office, and was an era *before* weapons were mainly sold by commercial enterprise. The British *state* was equipping its army and navy for whatever military activity it undertook. Yet, at the same time, when the American Civil War was underway Enfield rifles were sold to both sides in millions. It easily became commercial.

At this time it was still debateable whether a cavalry charge could win over the slow loading muskets. Cannon could be captured and turned against their previous owners and riflemen could be mowed down by charging horses. But really this was the era when manufactured guns and artillery were becoming the decisive instruments of war. Russell, *The Times* Correspondent, described the way in which the "Thin Red Line" of the Argyle and Sutherland Highlanders on the 24th October, 1854 defeated the massive Russian cavalry charge at the battle of Balaklava with two lines of muskets.[6] It was the moment when rifles and cannon could finally defeat the charging soldier, although this lesson was still unlearned in the futile attacks across no-man's land in the First World War. With the Crimean War and then the American Civil War the weapons' manufacturers were back in business. The industrial arms trade had arrived.

# Chapter Two: The Big Boys - Krupp, Schneider, Armstrong and Vickers.

**Krupp's arms sales get going.**

Krupp was an onlooker in both these wars. At this stage he could not even convince the Prussian army to buy his weapons. Though he demonstrated the superiority of his steel cannon to the Prussian tin-hats, they stubbornly preferred the old bronze cannon they had always relied on. Steel weapons' manufacturing was not yet on a roll. His trade in arms gradually got underway through avid salesmanship. Englebrecht and Hanighen, who later wrote the important book, *The Merchants of Death,* convey the frustrations well.

> Progress, however, was still exasperatingly slow. The military refused to be budged from their conservative ideas. Not until 1849 did the Prussian Artillery Testing Committee agree to test his gun, and even then no orders were forthcoming. But Krupp was doggedly persistent. He exhibited his gun at all industrial exhibitions, together with his other crucible steel products. He went to London in 1851 and received the award of the highest distinction. He exhibited at Munich in 1854 and in Paris in 1855. He presented his gun to the Prussian king, Frederick William IV, in spite of the open opposition of military circles. Results were completely lacking.
>
> Finally in 1856 there was a rift in the clouds. The khedive of Egypt, Saïd Pasha, decided that the Krupp cannon were all that their manufacturer claimed for them and he placed the first substantial order for the guns. This was immediately followed by a French order for 300 cannon, but the order was cancelled due to lack of funds. The French were later to regret this lack of funds and indifference to Krupp products.[7]

The point about the French was only partially true; there were another two reasons for the failure to sell to the French. At the 1855 Paris World Exhibition, France's answer to the great Crystal Palace show in 1851, Krupp freighted over an even more massive ingot of steel, 100,000 lbs of the hard stuff, as a kind of virility symbol. The great monster performed by crashing through the main floor of the Exhibition Hall, which slightly undermined the French reputation for making floors and probably piqued them slightly. Nevertheless, people were impressed and Napoleon III was very taken with Krupp's new cast steel twelve pounder cannon. He thought about buying, but was dissuaded by the French arms producer, Schneider, who did not like Krupp selling on their home patch. Krupp's sales were weak throughout the 1850s with only the order from Egypt. Railway wheels sold much better. It is quite sensible to conclude at this stage that Krupp was more concerned about keeping his business flourishing selling railway wheels than he was in selling arms.

Indeed, throughout this study the manufacturers are probably more committed to making money than they are to producing weapons which kill. The latter is merely an unfortunate consequence of this particular market. As late as January, 1859 Alfred wondered about giving up cannon production altogether, but then came an order. Wilhelm I, about to become King of Prussia, whom Krupp had been courting for a decade by showing him round the works at Essen with much obsequiousness, at last ordered 300 six pounder cannon. Krupp, bowing and scraping to Wilhelm, was off on cannon production. In the early 1860s he also sold guns to Russia, Belgium, Holland, Spain, Switzerland, Austria and England.[8] Krupp's relationship with Kaiser William I was crucial. Krupp would give him the best weapons and an empire. William I would give him money. Always Krupp charged way over the odds, leaving funds for hospitality, house building, gifts, profits and investment.

Alfred Krupp was not nationalistic, except when it suited him to be. He sold to the Austro-Hungarian Empire, with whom Prussia fought in 1866, much to the annoyance of Bismarck. He was also prepared to sell to Britain. In 1862-3 he was approached by the British Government to supply guns. His response was, "Why should England not obtain the material from her friends abroad, until her own industries can make it?"[9] Nor at this stage were Krupp's guns dominant. Several of his cannon blew up in the 1866 Austro-Prussian War, but Krupp got new orders through the influence of William I.[10] His insistence on selling cannon to anyone is well conveyed in his response to the Prussian War Minister, von Roon, who in March 1866 asked him not to deliver guns to Bavaria. Krupp's response was, "I know very little about the political situation. I am getting quietly on with my work. If I cannot do so without upsetting the balance between patriotism and integrity, I shall cease work altogether, sell my works and live as an independent man of means." In translation the letter is saying, "Get off my back and get lost. I'll sell where I want to."[11] In 1867 at the Paris International Exhibition, he gave William I a great monster of a cannon worth 150,000 thalers.[12] Gifts prepared the ground and contracts would follow later. Alfred tried a further time to sell cannon to the French in the 1860s, which in view of the up and coming Franco-Prussian War in 1870 was a little ironic. Moreover, it seemed as though they had placed a big order. Yet, again, moves behind the scenes from the French arms firm of Schneider scotched the deal when it looked as though it was signed. Otherwise the Germans would have been mowed down by Krupp cannon in 1870.

Of course, Krupp was not the only German munitions manufacturer. The Mauser Company, led by Paul Mauser, became famous in rifle production. Again they sold internationally, often modifying the design to suit their purchaser and to experiment in model development. As well as producing for Prussia and Germany, there was a Turkish, a Serbian, a Belgian, an Argentine and a Spanish model of Mauser rifle. The design was also passed on to the Birmingham Small Arms Company, showing how these arms companies interlinked and co-operated. The Mausers bought by the Spanish allowed the Americans to be outgunned for a while in Cuba, to their annoyance, and also caused similar problems during the Boer War for the British. In 1898 a standard Mauser rifle came to be developed which was extensively used in the Great War. Mausers were an internationally traded weapon sold throughout the globe. The trade was more important than patriotism.

**Schneider – Le Creusot and the French arms trade.**

Schneider, sounding German but actually French, was another of the major players in this trade of destruction, and we must dwell with them for a moment. As in Britain the French State had arms manufacturing facilities at St Etienne and Tulle, but in 1836 the firm, Schneider-Le Creusot, was founded by the Schneider brothers, Adolphe and Eugène, who also started the firm's ability in steel manufacturing. The company dominated French railway and weapons' manufacture as Krupp was to come to dominate the German scene. It expanded by supplying arms for the Crimea in 1854 and was behind much French colonial conquest. It was good at early all-steel armour plating for battleships. There were other French arms manufacturers. The famous Chassepot rifle was made by the Manufacture d'Armes de St. Etienne and other companies, and under licence to Britain. It was enormously successful; its bullets flattened out as it hit the body and inflicted far more serious injuries, as the dum-dum bullets used in the Indian Mutiny did. Interestingly, the use of dum-dum bullets was outlawed after 1898 after German protests that they were inhumane, because they inflicted more injury. Merely shooting people in the head, it seems, remained humane – slight inconsistency there. During the 1850s and 1860s the French arms industry seemed successful and continued to export, but it had not undertaken the full development of steel, and so its weapons were technically inferior to the German ones. When the Franco-Prussian War arrived, the defeat was also a defeat for French weapons as the massive strong Krupp cannon pounded Paris without reprisal.

Initially the great defeat in the Franco-Prussian War, which we examine shortly, was a big set-back, but the French munitions industry bounced back, with Schneider and the other companies determined to produce the best weapons for the next conflict with Germany and claim back their export markets. Weapons companies are often not overcome by military loss, because the lesson from defeat, if you discount the possibility of peace, is that you need better weapons next time. By 1914 Schneider was producing the 75mm field gun which was probably the most successful rapid-firing cannon during the First World War. It also produced a vast array of other weapons including two massive 520mm (20 inch) howitzers. One of these was captured by the Germans later and transported to Russia to bombard them, but a shell exploded in the barrel and it never worked. Schneider had another trick in their box. Around 1900 the company began combining bank loans from French banks with the purchase of weapons. That meant that you did not have to pay for them until later, perhaps when you had won the war. It made sales much easier and persuaded states to buy weapons they could not really afford. Moreover, it was the banks who took the risk of the loans and not the arms' companies. The idea was sold to the banks as a lucrative loan to a foreign power guaranteed by the state who had sold the weapons, and to the buying state as a loan against future profit that the arms might yield. This model of buy now, pay later, became a standard ploy in selling arms, and it also brought munitions and banking interests in bed together. They remained in bed for an awfully long time. The arms company is paid immediately, and then the loan may or may not be repaid to the bank at a later date. If you win the war, you cough up; if you lose, you default. In 1906 Schneider sold guns to Bulgaria linked to a loan floated on the Paris money-market. The loan was not repaid and the guns killed French troops in WW1.

But this was not the biggest loan. Vast quantities of weapons were sold to Russia on the basis of loans of sixteen billion francs raised on the Paris money market in the period leading up to the Great War as Russia sought to have the most advanced arms of the period. Schneider exported the arms; they were paid for by the loans which were never repaid after the Russian revolution of 1917. So the French paid for Schneider's exports to Russia because the bankers did not see the Communist Revolution coming. Other sums were loaned to Mexico, Greece, Serbia, Turkey, Roumania and Japan. So, substantially, the French public financed Schneider's international arms trade. The enormous Schneider 1877 steam hammer still sits in the centre of Le Creusot, showing the scale of their heavy engineering. It was largely French guns which made the Boer War so difficult for Britain. Since British guns in the possession of the Boers also made it difficult, we could hardly complain.

By the end of the century this French company was a strong rival to Krupp and one of the international cartel managing the weapons' business, for these great companies were not only rivals, but also knew how to co-operate to further their joint business. In October, 1894, partly under the impetus of producing "Harvey Steel" under patent, the companies Vickers, Cammell, John Brown, Dillinger, Hütten, Krupp, Acières de la Marine, Schneider, Chatillon, Bethlehem and Carnegie formed a syndicate to control prices and to divide foreign orders by drawing lots. The syndicate operated in third party countries, not in Britain, Germany, France and America.[13] They were working together to arm the world.

**The Franco-Prussian War of 1870**

The Franco-Prussian War turned out to be Krupp's salvation. The French were goaded into the war by Bismarck, and the move reflected Prussia's knowledge of its military power and the quality of its steel artillery. At the start most people thought the war would be a walk-over for the French with their battle-experienced troops and reputation. But as the confrontation opened up, although it was a long and bloody conflict, it became clear that Krupp's cannon power was decisive. Eventually, when von Moltke had surrounded Paris and had the French under siege, he used some massive guns that Krupp had specially supplied to pound Paris into submission. This was a time of humiliation for France as William I crowned himself Emperor of Germany at Versailles, but it was especially the time when Krupp cannon were seen as overwhelmingly successful. The London *Daily News* report from Archibald Forbes, a veteran war correspondent, was as follows: "the terrible ghastliness of those dead transcended anything I had ever seen, or even dreamt of ... slaughtered with missiles of terrible weight, shattered into fragments by explosions of many pounds of powder, mangled and torn by massive fragments of iron."[14] This was a time when industrial carnage was new. It was a bit tough for the victims, but for Krupp it was a time of instant success. From now on orders for guns would pour in from all over the world and he could readily support a workforce of 10,000, a large private mansion, and yet more work on instruments of death.

The Franco-Prussian War was a deeper loss than the immediate death and destruction, although about 170,000 died and a further 240,000 were seriously wounded. The people of Paris experienced famine as their city was besieged and pounded with cannon, and the destruction of centuries of buildings took place. Really, of course, the German Empire, proclaimed at Versailles in an obvious insult, could not occupy France permanently. Germany imposed an indemnity of five billion francs on the French, justifying the reprisal of reparations later at Versailles after the First World War. It therefore helped the trajectory towards the First and Second World War. The deeper tragedy was that France and Germany then did not trust one another for the following eighty years after having had 55 years of peace; they remained habitual enemies. They were each to lose millions of people killed by one another in two World Wars. Like all wars they dwell in the heads of people for a lifetime, and each side remembers war either as victory justifying weapons and murder, or as defeat requiring weapons and revenge. As always, the only victors in war are the munitions' people.

Alfred Krupp, and the other arms manufacturers, sublimated the consequences of using these weapons. He closed his mind to carnage and refused to discuss the fact that his cannon were mutilating bodies on a vast scale. The politics and actual use of weapons was not his business; he was only selling them. Their use was someone else's concern. Of course, their use was his concern. He meticulously studied whether they penetrated armour, how they exploded, hit their targets, and fragmented into bodies, but the outcome happened far away on some battlefield and could be mentally neutralised. Deaths, injuries and destruction were not to be discussed and the process was to be seen as a technical adjunct of statecraft, where the military made the decisions of war and peace...

except too much peace was dangerous to the arms trade and politicians may need encouraging in another direction. Arms were a business to make profit and pay the workers and Krupp remained mentally frozen throughout his life onto that task. In this he was no different from any of the others within the business. Someone's head might be blown off, but you had to be able to shrug your shoulders. Krupp's focus was on making weapons, a sumptuous house with two hundred and twenty rooms, high status and the financial rewards of the business. All other considerations had to be out of bounds. We will see later some of the effects of this on Alfred's family.

**The Impetus for an International Trade in Weapons.**

Previously, states made weapons only for themselves. The British had not sold many yew bows to the French, nor had the Spanish sold galleons to the British, because you did not want your enemy to have weapons which could be used against you. This argument strongly retains its logical and practical power, but the weapons' manufacturers from the beginning wanted to be able to sell to *anyone* for profit; they wanted an international market. The home market is not always stable. During long periods without aggression the home market declines, and after rapid expansion during wars demand falls at the end of them; munitions companies are likely to find themselves with low domestic orders. In contrast, if the companies can sell anywhere, they are more likely to have full order books. Selling weapons internationally was the key for all the arms manufacturers. They went about it avidly.

The trade involved courting the rulers and the military of faraway countries, usually with gifts and a carefully crafted version of the superiority of this particular weapon and the dangers of being without it. Key figures could be bribed. Contacts were often schmoozed in secret, or the embassies were used to provide a sufficiently grand occasion for arms sales to be discussed. Entertainment was key, and somewhere was needed at home to impress the foreign dignitary. At Krupp's great ugly Villa Hügel vast numbers of people were entertained and lavish events were put on. Soon we will meet Sir William Armstrong. His great Cragside House had a Japanese room to impress his Japanese guests into buying battleships. Everywhere soft bribery was practiced. "If I am nice to you, you will buy my weapons, won't you?" The appeal was often to royalty, to the people at the top, to a few eminent military people who could swing the big order, not to the elected representatives. This was not a democratic business. The key was always to get orders; rulers were lured into buying far more weapons than they would otherwise by hospitality, bribes, scares and courting the generals. Once militarized, a state would continue buying for decades. Selling anywhere world-wide had spin-off benefits. It generated rumours of war. If your neighbour buys 200 cannon, you wonder why and are frightened into buying some yourself. Salesmen promoted competitive buying, or arms races, as they have come to be known. In an arms race you never hit the tape; you go on and on until you drop from exhaustion. More than this, if arms are sold abroad, you end up selling more at home, because external threats are slowly ramped up. Of course, this sometimes created tensions with the domestic state, when weapons sold abroad were used against the home forces. That complaint will recur. But from the 1850s onwards the international arms market for profit appeared and began to militarize the planet.

**The British Cannon and Naval Arms Trade – Armstrong.**

Rifles and smaller firearms were not the only area of British expertise. British cannon development was also strong, partly focussed towards naval cannon, the main element in battleship performance. The key figure in this development was William Armstrong. He started his engineering career building cranes, but then moved to designing cannon. In the mid 1850s he worked with James Naysmith and Isambard Kingdom Brunel to develop a breech-loading, rifled cannon with exploding shells that pushed the technology of cannons way ahead. He strengthened the barrels with a layered construction which made them stronger without increasing the weight. Soon they were the obvious world leaders.[15] Krupp at this stage was behind and did not catch up until, say, the late sixties. In 1858 Armstrong won in a national contest for the best British cannon to back. He beat his rival Whitworth from Openshaw near Manchester, who later funded the Whitworth Art Gallery. The Indian Munity was in progress, and the Armstrong gun was rushed into production. But there were problems. Working the guns proved difficult for the untutored soldiers. Whitworth still pushed his rival cannon, and in October, 1862 the Armstrong contract was terminated. Armstrong decided to join the firm at Elswick, near Newcastle, and uttered a fateful sentence: "From that time the firm had no alternative but to commence a new career, based on foreign support, and it was by that support – and not by government patronage – that the Elswick Ordnance Works was established."[16]

Armstrong developed a brilliant engineering company making guns, rivalling Krupp, and gloating when one of Krupp's guns exploded into pieces. He worked especially with George, Stuart and Hamilton Rendel, sons of his friend, James Rendel. He took George into his home and taught him all the engineering he could. Initially the company could turn out fifty tons of guns a week and they expanded fast, selling to both sides in the American Civil War. Armstrong also sold to Austria, Italy, Spain, Egypt, Denmark, Holland, Chile and Peru in the late eighteen sixties. In 1867 the firm completed two ironclads and was also in the business of battleships.

Here, they swooped ahead. At Elswick Armstrong linked with a shipbuilder Mitchell. Soon they began to produce battleships fully equipped with guns which grew ever bigger with better armour and more powerful engines. They produced the steel, did all the engineering, and soon the British navy could not but buy from them. They were the backbone of British naval supremacy. In 1883 Armstrong and Mitchell built a new yard and began producing the world's biggest and most powerful steel battleships. Armstrong was the same kind of technically obsessed businessman as Krupp. He later merged with his Manchester ordnance rival, Whitworth, to expand the company even more. Soon Armstrong's factories and slipways expanded along the Tyne and he was producing the best warships in the world, fast and efficiently. Sir William Armstrong built himself a magnificent high technology house at Cragside which was the first to have a system of domestic electric lights, and he became a powerful part of the British establishment.

As an aside, here, we note the obvious, that William Armstrong was male, like almost all the other characters who will unfold for the next hundred years. The history of munitions and militarism is also a feminist tract simply because women and their attitudes were not present in the business, and men have always insisted on running the whole military business their way. You may bring up Boudicca and Joan of Arc as counter examples, but they hardly undermine this general conclusion. This was, and remains, a male show and we are handling a strongly gendered way of seeing things – men, guns, war, violence, conquest are a vast cultural nexus which millions of boys and men absorb with their breakfast. The gender point will be made sparingly, though it could be made repeatedly. Militarism is patriarchy.

Armstrong, like Krupp, understood the business of marketing. Once countries wanted the ship and you had sold it, the rest was easy. You sold before you made, unlike in most other industries. He had agents drumming up trade and he knew he had to put on a good show to convince people that his guns and ships were the best. One of his sales agents was Mr. Robert Thompson. He had been special correspondent of *The Times* but found selling arms more lucrative. He exploited tensions between Spain and Portugal (1886-1890), Argentina and Chile (1890-93) and the Chinese and Japanese to land big contracts. He was succeeded by Sir William White who was especially good at playing off the Chinese and Japanese. Soon Armstrong dominated world warship production, but he was not the only big British naval shipyard.

**Vickers and Zaharoff rival Armstrong.**

Another British arms firm was started by Thomas Vickers. It was initially based, after a number of amalgamations, in the Brightside area of Sheffield, close to the present Meadowhall shopping complex just off the M1. Initially, it had been one of the Sheffield crucible steel firms, involved in general engineering, but then it entered the armaments industry somewhat later than Armstrong in the late 1880s initially to supply steel plate for battleships. Again, Tom Vickers was an obsessive engineer. When he was working on a problem, he shut himself up in the works and ate and slept there for weeks. He was a steel man. His brother, Albert, was the entrepreneur, and he linked with Hiram Maxim, an American born inventor, who had invented the first efficient machine gun. It used the recoil from the firing to move on to the next bullet and so was capable of continuous firing. Vickers therefore had another great armaments business within its ambit. Then the company moved from producing steel ships' components and guns to making whole ships, including warships, in the great shipyard at Barrow-in-Furness on the Lancashire coast after an amalgamation in 1897. Around this time, too, Lord Rothschild, the banker, was also investing heavily in the company, and so it was able to expand very quickly. Rothschild's personal appointment to the Board, Sigmund Loewe, who became managing director of Maxim Nordenfelt in 1895, drove the company forward further. It was a clear rival to Armstrong, the second British company which was a world leader in armaments.

Its chief salesman became Basil Zaharoff, the most famous arms salesman of all. Zaharoff was part Greek and part Russian, but was completely at home in any capital of the world. He moved in and drummed up trade seeing kings, princes, prime ministers and field-marshalls. He was the masterly fixer and helped move Vickers towards being the greatest British arms conglomerate. He quickly became a millionaire and central to the development of the company, generating orders and taking his cut. Zaharoff sold Vickers products everywhere with consummate ability. He had mastered most of the selling techniques we looked at earlier, playing off Greece against the Turkish Empire and getting big naval orders from both, and doing the same with Russia and Turkey.[17] Most potent of all, he left wads of notes on clients' desks, to "do the needful" as he described it. He was a bigamist and implied that he worked on many contracts in bed with influential women. By the time of the Great War Vickers was more dynamic internationally even than Armstrong-Mitchell. Basil Zaharoff was knighted, given honours in Paris and an honorary doctorate in civil law by the University of Oxford, some may think because of his ability to evade the law and in return for donations to the University, for he was probably by this time a (dollar) billionaire and the richest man in Europe.[18] When the salesman makes that kind of money you know it is a lucrative business with large profit margins. Zaharoff manoeuvred the biggest arms deals in Europe with the Russians, smarting under their loss to the Japanese, outselling even Schneider.

These and other major companies we shall meet later in what amounted to a flourishing world-wide arms trade, pushed by agents travelling first class throughout the world and expecting to make contact with the military, monarchs and political leaders of all the countries they visited. Often the agents met, compared notes, and did not baulk at working for more than one company.

**Selling weapons and selling war.**

The British arms trade also flourished through what came to be called "arms fairs" like the great Royal Naval Exhibition of 1891. It took up an extensive site not far from where the Chelsea Flower Show is held today with a vast pavilion including galleries covering different weapons, ships and components. It was a fascinating show. There was a 34ft scale model of HMS *Victoria.* The model took ten men four months to build, and showed the thronging crowds what the modern British navy was like. The official catalogue presenting the armaments and other attractions ran to 570 pages and had 5,354 entries. 70,000 of the catalogues were sold, and there were only British entries. The Armstrong gallery was vast, with demonstration of the ability of steel armour to withstand shell penetration and lots of other goodies. After this, potential buyers from around the world knew where to come. The focus of the whole event was to sell and the British were in the lead. There was a Düsseldorf Exhibition in 1902 and others thereafter. They were often called "arms fairs" to show they were jolly occasions for the family, but selling arms became a highly calculated business.

Yet, this industry did not function like the local bread shop. On the whole you know you need bread and go out to buy it. The arms industry had to beat up trade; it had to persuade its customers that they needed these weapons. Weapons, of course, are only useful in war. You cannot use cannon to deliver the post or missiles to go to work. The industry was therefore tuning states up for conflicts and wars. There were hints, scares, guesses at what neighbours were buying, the exploitation of tensions, or the prospects of conquest – not in your face – but suggesting "realpolitik". This is an interesting word - "politics based on realities and material needs, rather than on morals or ideals. [German]" as the Oxford Dictionary defines it. And this was the basic move. War is "real" and the stuff of practical politics, while peace is idealistic and "unreal". This is the underlying illusion of the whole show. War and weapons are realistic, but peace and prosperity are not. Once this ploy had been planted in the mind, selling the goods was child play. Even then wars did not always turn up. Visiting Canadian ministers, Sir Frederick Borden and Louis Brodeur were taken aback by a remark from a Vickers official "the Empire is going to the dogs for lack of a war, and worst of all, there is not even one small war in prospect."[19]

This sales pitch was two-faced in relation to the home nation. One of the great psychological weapons of arms traders is fervent nationalism. At home the arms' traders were nationalists, but abroad they were not. These people were all in the same trade, and they were not going to compete on price and undermine their profits. There were cartel arrangements among Armstrong-Whitworth and Vickers from Britain, Krupp and Dillingen Hüttenwerke from Germany, the Schneider-Creusot Company from France, Skoda from Austro-Hungary, Terni from Italy, Mitsui in Japan, and Bethlehem Steel and Du Pont from the United States. There were other smaller members of the cartel, but it was dominated by the big boys. These men were pals. Often they were in a sell-sell, win-win situation. I'll sell to Greece - you sell to Turkey. At home they seemed patriotic, doing their best for the country, but elsewhere they were combining to milk every contract to the maximum. It is almost a truism that arms contracts are drastically over-priced, and, when orders have been placed, prices can be raised further for extra features. That is partly through cartels, partly to allow room for bribery and partly because governments get locked into projects which require particular technological developments. Arms companies love technological development which gives them an edge. They compete on product and often on bribes, but not price; those are the tacit rules, established well before the twentieth century. Even in war, as we shall see, their greater loyalty was to the arms cartel than to the home nation.

So this industry got underway and expanded into a great international market. Often the companies were good to their workers and the leaders were knighted, but they remained merchants of death. They needed wars, for that was their trade.

# Chapter Three: Moving politicians into line – the British Naval lobby

**The Naval Lobby is in charge.**

Politicians, we assume, shape national and international events, and so in a sense they do. They probably think they choose where they are going, but they do not notice the man at their arm, occasionally steering them a little or suggesting they hurry a little more. Much of this study will be looking at the way the arms companies guide and direct the politicians. Perhaps, when it comes to wars and weapons, the politicians are the puppets we see and the arms companies, and sometimes the military, hold the strings and do the movement. For this military complex to succeed, they need to be inside politics, able to convert the politicians to their way of seeing things and make them cough up big contracts. Often this is done by using the military's interest in better weapons. Generals and admirals are almost automatically in favour of more spending on weapons, battleships, fighters and missiles, and they also predispose the politicians. This system has been so long in place that we can scarcely question it, but question it we must. Here we look at the start of the process of pushing industrial munitions on the politicians, especially in Britain where its development was earliest.

In Britain the shipyards made the running. They were out for battleship orders to produce the great new steel battleships that were making all wooden ships completely obsolete. Steel ships were lighter, because of the greater strength of steel, and also faster and bigger. In the late 19th century the underlying requirement for ruling the empire was naval success and expansion. Rule Britannia, Britannia rule the waves, and for that you need good steel battleships. The Admiralty had considerable self-confidence. Nelson was on his column by the 1850s, and it was understood that the British navy would retain the world dominance it had had for a hundred years. The advent of steel battleships, given Britain's lead in industrialization, meant that this superiority was even more marked. The arms manufacturers in Britain, especially the naval ones, became an efficient pressure group able to dominate the political scene upholding the Empire and Great Britain. How powerful they were can be seen more clearly when they were not fully getting their own way, as occurred later in the 19$^{th}$ century.

You know a system is in control when it succeeds in getting rid of a Prime Minister, especially one as eminent as William Ewart Gladstone. Gladstone was a towering figure, and part of his moral weight grew from opposing imperial injustices; he could champion the Irish against the British, and the Afghan peasant against colonial power, if their cause was just. He represented a vast tranche of middle class Christian morality that wanted to do the right thing and had enormous political clout. But in this case he had met his match.

**Enter, Jackie Fisher.**

In the 1880s and 90s there were three big British naval scares. The cynics among us would say that a naval scare is created by arms companies as a route to getting new orders. The first one arose through articles written by W.T. Stead about the Navy in the *Pall Mall Gazette* in 1884 and it led to the Northbrook programme of naval construction. But that was eclipsed by another one in 1888-9 which focussed on the principle that the British Navy should be bigger than the two next major sea powers. The result was the Naval Defence Act of 1889 with a budget of £21.5 million which funded an additional seventy ships.[20] This was well in excess of what the Navy considered to be necessary, and given the time it took to produce warships, the programme was only just underway when the third crisis broke in 1893. Gladstone was again Prime Minister, a wise old bird at 82, when some of his Cabinet asked for more money to build even more warships. They were prompted by the naval manufacturers, aiming to expand year on year, and the question was what the Grand Old Man would do. At this stage he was like his picture on the wall plates hanging in millions of Victorian homes - hand on chin, skeptical and not easily conned.

This confrontation featured a new figure on the scene. Young Jackie Fisher was appointed Comptroller of the Navy in February, 1892, responsible for all naval supplies. Fisher is a key figure in our story. Although he did full service at sea, he also spent about fifteen years of his life on land, working and thinking about warships and interacting closely with the naval arms manufacturers. As Comptroller, he was the Third Sea Lord, responsible for equipping the navy with its ships, guns and armour. He was an outstanding naval strategist, and his obsession was technical advance. He discussed guns, design, speed, fuel, torpedoes and submarines with everybody and made sure that he was completely abreast of all developments in nautical engineering. He knew the naval manufacturers, and they courted him to become one of them. As Hough reports:

> The offers of wonderful highly paid jobs from armament and shipbuilding companies became increasingly attractive, especially when he was feeling frustrated and bitter. Some of these offers he described as 'really beyond the dreams of avarice'. He received the first as long before as 1887 and almost took it. Lord George Hamilton appealed to his patriotism and helped to persuade him to turn it down. Fisher hated the discomfort of penury on the one hand, and the vulgarity of riches on the other. In moments of financial gloom he cheered himself up by quoting Swift: 'If you want to know what God thinks of riches – look at the people he gives them to.'[21]

Fisher knew what each of the shipyards could do, and also what the best naval strategy was in relation to placing orders. The yards wanted to churn out the ships, but he was out for technological development and superiority in battle. He wanted to cut the numbers of poor quality battleships. He used the adage: "Build few and build fast, each one better than the last!" His focus was on speed, bigger guns, torpedoes, oil-fired ships instead of coal, developed destroyers, turbines and a range of other innovations; he was determined that the British Navy would be the best. Fisher was thus the key figure through more than twenty years of world-leading naval development and we shall meet him again. But at this stage he was merely a young man, part of the naval lobby, and pushing for naval orders.

**British Military Expansion.**

We British think we are likeable people, and it is difficult to see ourselves as others might see us. Yet, in about 1890 Britain was rightly seen as a bombastic, militaristic, dangerous world power. The height of our self-congratulation occurred with reviews of the fleet, when we gathered all our warships together at Spithead. We associate reviews of the fleet with the famous later BBC broadcast in which a man called Woodruffe presumably wearing a dinner jacket and naughtily plied with drinks by his mates gave a beautiful tipsy evening commentary on the event, repeatedly pointing out that the "Fleet is all lit up, lit up in fairy lights. It's all lit up.." followed by more repeats when the lights were switched out saying, "Now the fleet has gawn. It has disappeared..." It is the most intoxicating radio we will ever hear. That classic broadcast was in 1936, but Reviews of the Fleet had been a monumental form of showing off to visiting dignitaries, especially in the late 19th century. They occurred in 1856 with more than a hundred battleships, in 1865 when the French Fleet visited and was observed to be very inferior in armour and guns, in 1867 when we showed off to the Sultan of the Ottoman Empire and the Egyptian ruler, and so it went on in 1876, 1878, and then in 1887 the great Golden Jubilee Fleet Review before Queen Victoria. These were the events which proclaimed Britain's power to the world. No-one else could touch them. Then on the 5-6 August, 1889 Kaiser Wilhelm and Admiral von Tirpitz were entertained by a substantial review of the fleet, watching lines of British battleships steaming past. It is worth reflecting on this event. It was probably here that Kaiser Bill and Von Tirpitz became convinced that Germany, too, needed a big navy and began the naval rivalry which contributed to the Great War. That's what comes of showing off.

The British believed they ruled the waves and the fleet was their means to an empire. It was an industrial-technological lead involving developing iron, and then steel-hulled, ships and big steam engines fired by coal allowing these ships to move from the vagaries of wind to a reliable set of reciprocating engines which would rotate propellers. British battleships went round the world holding the empire together and making it the controlling trading nation of the era. The Empire was based on conquest, and the dominant tool of conquest was the battleship. In 1889 the Naval Defence Act passed in May had provided another £21.5 million over five years to build more battleships. It was a massive level of shipbuilding which would ensure that the Royal Navy was bigger than the two next navies, those of France and Russia for the foreseeable future. At this time Britain built *80%* of the decent sized ships in the world. Its dominance was unassailable, and we could not resist the chance of showing off to other leaders and reminding them that we ruled the world. The Kaiser would know how inferior the German Navy was, small ships, poor technology and completely ineffective. Von Tirpitz similarly was starting on his naval career. He had only recently come to know the Kaiser and was interested in the technology of torpedoes. Confronted with this Grand British Navy, both of them would also covet a half decent navy for Germany, the new coming industrial powerhouse of Europe. Meanwhile, the British naval lobby could not be stopped in its career for orders.

**The 1893 Naval Crisis.**

The supposed crisis of 1893 was triggered by a tragedy in which four hundred sailors lost their lives. This loss of life was appalling and a great sorrow, but at the same time, the event was a catatonically funny error. A naval exercise organized by Vice Admiral Tyron led to the collision of two of Britain's newest battleships, the *Victoria* and *Camperdown*. They turned under Tyron's orders and went head to head at each other and then failed to avoid one another in a more or less nose to nose crunch. The Victoria went down in 13 minutes after collision, which is nearly plastic dingy time. The *Camperdown* was severely flooded, but saved. As we have seen, the *Victoria* was featured at the Royal

Naval Exhibition and bore the name of the Queen; it was a top-of-the-range battleship. The Queen's namesake was not supposed to sink, even when attacked by the enemy, but here a boat playing on the same side sent it to its grave. The event is best reported by that outstanding Scottish poet William McGonagall,

Alas! Now o'er Britannia there hangs a gloom,
Because over 400 British Tars have met with a watery tomb;
Who served aboard the "Victoria", the biggest ship in the navy,
And one of the finest battleships that ever sailed the sea.

And commanded by Sir George Tyron, a noble hero bold,
And his name on his tombstone should be written in letters of gold;
For he was skilful in naval tactics, few men could with him cope,
And he was considered to be the nation's hope.

'Twas on Thursday, the twenty second of June,
And off the coast of Syria, and in the afternoon,
And in the year of our Lord eighteen ninety-three,
That the ill-fated "Victoria" sank to the bottom of the sea.

The "Victoria" sank in fifteen minutes after she was rammed,
In eighty fathoms of water, which was smoothly calmed;
The monster war vessel capsized bottom uppermost,
And, alas, lies buried in the sea totally lost.

The "Victoria" was the flagship of the Mediterranean Fleet,
And was struck by the "Camperdown" when too close they did meet,
While practicing the naval and useful art of war,
How to wheel and discharge their shot at the enemy afar.

Sir George Tyron was on the bridge at the moment of the accident
With folded arms seemingly quite content;
And seeing the vessel couldn't be saved he remained till the last,
And went down with the "Victoria" when all succour was past.

Methinks I see him on the bridge like a hero brave,
And the ship slowly sinking in the briny wave;
And when the men cried, "Save yourselves without delay,"
He told them to save themselves, he felt no dismay.

To spare your tears other verses have been omitted. Presumably, Queen Victoria was not amused at the loss of her namesake. It was an outstanding own goal, making the Admiralty look a fool. "Turn to port! No, I mean starboard. Oh bother!" But, the battleship manufacturers and the navy, partly to draw attention away from their own inadequacy, focussed on the threat to British naval supremacy caused by this event, arguing yet again that we did not have enough ships and scaring the public. Actually, we had plenty of ships and most of them had rudders.

**The Ousting of Gladstone.**

When Gladstone was challenged in the House of Commons on the 19th December, 1893 that British naval supremacy was threatened, he was dismissive, even withering. "To maintain that the situation in which we stand to-day is a situation of emergency and danger is to pronounce an opinion that is irrational and even absurd. It is beyond contention, first of all, that the first-class battleships of Great Britain are at this moment 19 in number; and, secondly, that the first-class battleships of France and Russia are not 19 when added together, but are 14 in number...Finally, if I look at the tonnage in the rough, and speak of the present Navy, I believe the House will be correct in accepting this statement, that we have in battleships at the moment 527,000 tons of fighting material, and that France and Russia together have at this moment but 383,000 tons." It is a response which should have deflated the opposition. What Gladstone said was conclusive, and usually he carried the day, but the naval lobby did not give up.

Fisher and the naval manufacturers were out for more ships; they organized a political coalition including Austen Chamberlain, Lord Spencer, Sir William Harcourt and others to get them ordered.

Soon Gladstone was confronted by a group of senior colleagues asking for another great tranche of naval funds, effectively a pressure group of the naval yards. He dug his heels in and said, "No". The group became powerful enough within the Cabinet to force the issue through and did so. Gladstone could have given way and carried on as Prime Minister, but the Grand Old Man was adamant on the issue and resigned. He saw the future with a clarity which was prophetic. Sir Edward Hamilton recounts his words to Cabinet thus:

> "He again and again said it was not a matter of amount... No. It was a question of policy. Russia and France had gone ahead with their ship-building, solely owing to our Naval programme of 1889 for which we had to thank the late Government; and now we were to 'go one better', thus directly challenging Europe in the race of armaments. It was his conviction that this competitive action of ours would accelerate some great European catastrophe – these vast armaments must lead to some flare up..."[22]

As Roy Jenkins reports, he later added to Hamilton, "If I stood alone in the world on this question, I could not so be moved; so strongly am I convinced that this large increase to the Navy will lead to disaster in Europe – *Europe* is my watchword."[23] Of course, Gladstone was right; the Russian and French navies were relatively weak and the threat non-existent and more ships would be seen as aggressive. The issue sent Gladstone into a depression, probably not because of his own demise, which followed in due course, but because he could see the direction that Europe would take, led by Britain. We had set up the competitive international armaments scene through navy scares, and the pressures of the arms' manufacturers carried the day. This pressure group was powerful enough in the British Government to get rid of perhaps the most dominant Prime Minister the country has ever had. The programme of new naval building amounted to a further £31 million of orders and the Armstrong yard at Elswick complained because it only got an order for five battleships.. Britain was awash with warships and

Gladstone was gone.[24] We had opened up the route to the First World War two decades later.

This removal of Gladstone should bring us up short. To get rid of such a Prime Minister was extraordinary, yet the military-industrial complex was powerful enough to do it. We will see later that it was able in the States to get rid of Presidents and put its own kind into power. The ability of the military-industrial complex to control the politicians in the areas crucial to its own position is astonishing. Gladstone's ejection is the first warning.

## Chapter Four: Exporting Militarism.

### A World-Wide Trade.

None of this book is intellectually challenging; the points are all simple and obvious. This chapter merely points out that arms companies, energetically selling their wares to anyone, spread militarism throughout the world. Buy our arms. Learn how to use them. Now you are militarized. Easy. The process has been going on for over a century and is now much more developed than it was in the 19th century, but already then it was a strong pattern. Here we consider some examples.

### Bribing and Militarising Japan

The spread of militarism often happens after countries are attacked. Every military defeat teaches countries to strive for military dominance. It produces a reverse domino effect; every country knocked over wants to stand up and knock over someone else. So it happened with Japan. Alongside Armstrong and Vickers naval sales to the British Government stood the export trade, and now it became a powerful growth industry. Battleships were exported throughout the globe; one example of this process is especially poignant in relation to the Second World War. Britain militarized Japan. Japan was a vibrant, but quite traditional country, until it faced some bullying by the western military powers in the late 19th century.

In 1853 the United States' Government sent four warships, under Commodore Perry to Uraga Harbour with a letter from the President "requesting" a commercial treaty. The Japanese did not comply and eight months later Commodore Perry turned up with ten ships, and they did comply. At this stage the Japanese actually had a prohibition on building sea-going ships, and so we can see how little of a military threat they were. In 1862 three British people were killed in a skirmish, and the British demanded an indemnity and punishment of the offenders. The Japanese feudal chief involved did not comply, and the next year the British sent in a fleet and bombarded the capital of Satsuma and partly destroyed it. Also in 1863 some Japanese fired on Dutch, French and American vessels in the straits of Shimonoseki, which were really Japanese domestic waters, and as a result in 1864 an allied fleet of nine British, four Dutch and three French warships bombarded Shimonoseki and demanded $3 million in reparations, an excessive demand which was paid by 1875. Since the leader in Shimonoseki was also in rebellion against the Emperor and had also fired at his ships, this was hardly a major international incident in their own territorial waters for which the Japanese could be blamed. In 1868 when two more Europeans were attacked, the Japanese paid an indemnity and ordered the Japanese officers held responsible to commit suicide in front of the European diplomats by disembowelment. In the face of this kind of continual humiliation the Japanese began to conclude that they needed some kind of navy to defend themselves.[25] But Armstrong and Vickers persuaded them to do more.

At the same time Japan began to move into a process of democratization. An edict in 1881 declared the establishment of a national parliament, which actually arrived in 1890. This paralleled the time Japan realized it might be able to buy warships from the British. Not for the last time there was tension between a democratic direction for a nation and one which involved militarism and autocracy. Sadly in Japan the latter won with considerable help from British and other naval suppliers. The process started in 1887, and especially in the 1890s a great line of battleships and cruisers went from the British shipyards to Japan when modern steel battleships were in their early formation. The battleships included *Fuji, Yashima, Shikishima, Hatsuse, Asahi,* and *Mikasa* and the cruisers were *Asama, Tokiwa, Izumo* and *Iwate*. By 1914 Armstrong-Whitworth's alone had supplied 17.[26] John Brown built *Asahi* and other yards were involved. As important as the ships were the guns, and the Japanese received top quality battleship guns which they continued to copy for decades after. These warships were all fully functional by 1902. The cost was vast and it took expenditure away from improving the lot of ordinary people, and was resented by them. At the same time in 1902 an Anglo-Japanese Treaty, and then Alliance, was formed in which Britain and Japan were committed to quite a high degree of mutual support in war if other countries allied with the aggressor. Not for the last time, arms sales seemed to generate a political alliance.[27]

Yet, this was not even normal arms sales, but bribery, for certainly by 1908 a strong British pattern of greasing palms was going on. The lead company in this case was Vickers, probably keen to get in on Armstrong-Whitworth's stomping ground. Matsuo Tsurutaro was an expert in naval shipbuilding friendly with Admiral Matsumoto and the bribes flowed first towards him. But the big fish was Admiral Fujii, who received 210,000 yen in connection with the building of the battle-cruiser *Kongo*. This was illegal under the British Corrupt Practices Act of 1906. Tsurutaro was found out and sentenced to two years' imprisonment, so it was clearly not legal under Japanese law either. In the Court case it came out that Fujii had received ¥300,400 from Vickers, ¥34,100 from Yarrow, ¥17, 300 from Weir and Co. ¥26,900 from Arrol and Co and ¥700 from Siemens; so the bribery was systemic. Siemens-Schuckert was found to have tried to get rid of the Italian captain Ide because he actually made real comparisons of price and quality, that is, he did his job.[28] In summary, we can see that the British naval companies, initially through Armstrong-Whitworth, then Vickers and others led the world in using bribes to get orders, against British law. Zaharoff was at his shadowy work. Other countries' arms traders followed where we led, and bribery became normal throughout the twentieth century, and we do not know the half.

**The Russo-Japanese War**

Shortly after this expansion of the navy, Japan was involved in some difficult disputes with Russia which did not work out, and in February, 1904 Japan severed diplomatic relations and war was declared. Partly, of course, they declared war because they had a strong modern navy and wanted to try it out. It was a war in which Britain would not side with the Russians, because of its alliance with Japan. It was both a land and sea confrontation. The land battles were not decisive, although the Russians got the worse of it at Mukden, losing 97,000 dead to Japan's 45,000 – we think again of the actual personal horror and grief of these levels of casualties. At sea, the Japanese navy succeeded in destroying most of the first Russian navy in and around Port Arthur. The Russians then sent out another fleet sailing all the way round from the Baltic. Famously, the Russians attacked some English drifters off Dogger Bank in the North Sea thinking they were Japanese torpedo boats - not good geography. Britain punished the Russians by sending them round the Cape rather than through the Suez Canal, and so the Japanese probably had time to receive a few more British battleships before the Russians arrived. When the second Russian fleet eventually appeared, it was also defeated by the Japanese. For the first time in the modern era the East - Japan, had defeated the West - Russia, but with the West's weapons.

We shall see later how this event played into the dynamics of world politics in the build up to the Second World War. But the effect of this victory was deep within Japan. The cost of the war was £170 million, a vast sum in those days. It increased the national debt and taxation. This produced quite a strong reaction to the military, and the question was whether the military or the democratic emphasis would win out. The military carried the day, and from then on, with a possible gap in the 1920s, Japan became a strongly militarized economy and an autocratic political state dominated by the military. The arms dealers had turned the direction of a nation. There is not a straight line between British arms sales from 1887 and the events of Pearl Harbour and the War in the Far East, but there is a strong line. We have tended to dramatize Japanese military traditions, but really they learned a lot from us. By threat, bribes and naval aid Britain helped militarize Japan.[29]

**Armstrong –Whitworths and the Selling of Battleships.**

Let us reflect on the development of the munitions trade in the 1880s and 1890s. It had a variety of different specialist groups – small arms, cannon and big guns, explosives, naval craft – and the companies involved, whether they were Nobel, Du Pont, Schneider, Skoda, Krupp or Vickers were international, selling their wares world-wide through strong marketing including bribes and using government support. The scale of the naval arms trade can be judged by the output of Armstrong-Whitworths. It gives us an understanding both of the weight of arms trade output and also its distribution throughout the world. In the period between 1884 up to July 1914 the Company built 141 warships with a total displacement of 620,000 tons. These were the biggest military vessels of the era. A *quarter* of these (36) were for the British State and just under *three-quarters* to foreign states. The distribution of countries was as follows: - Argentina 6, Austria 2, Brazil 13, Chile 13, China 23, Holland 2, Italy 5, Japan 17, Norway 6, Portugal 1, Roumania 1, Russia 8, Spain 2, Turkey 1, USA 1, Siam 1. You may well ask what Austria was doing with two battleships? Presumably, they patrolled up and down the Danube looking for naval invaders, as one would. Clearly, Armstrong was able to get Argentina, Brazil and Chile to distrust one another, and similarly, China and Japan, and we have already seen how Japan and Russia were set in animosity and war.

These sales affected the British Navy. Noel-Baker comments rather archly on the list above as follows. "Thus, in a world where every nation's hand was potentially against every other's; where national safety and well-being were universally held to depend upon national armed strength alone; where mankind, visibly and consciously, was on the verge of Armageddon; and in a country whose Government and people believed that naval power would be the decisive factor for victory or defeat in time of war, the greatest of British Armament Firms sent more than two thirds [actually 74%] of the fighting ships it made to foreign countries.[30]" This example of one company conveys the extent to which Britain was arming the world, or rather 'arming the world. With battleships you could think of having colonies and an empire. Britain did not only have an empire, but sold the idea of empire throughout Europe and wider afield. First buy your battleships and then build your empire. It was a good and successful sales pitch.

**The Paraguayan Example.**

Many countries were militarized. In many other places democracy was not even on the table, and regimes could be corrupted towards war very easily, if you could get at, flatter and subvert one or two rulers. One such example was Paraguay. In 1853 Francisco Solano López came to France, Britain and Italy for eighteen months. He was the son of the President/Dictator and in Paris he linked up with an Irish prostitute, Eliza Lynch, who eventually became his consort back home and gave him five children. The arms dealers found him in Paris and no doubt plied with drink Solano bought arms on a large scale, was committed to dressing his generals in French uniforms and returned home to be Minister for War, building up a strong armoury of imported weapons. He was an easy target for arms dealers because of his vanity and lack of wisdom. Despite his father, Carlos López, giving him strong advice against war, when he became President, militarism defined his rule.

In an insane example of foreign policy he made Paraguay declare war on Brazil, Argentina and Uruguay at the same time in the War of the Triple Alliance between 1864 and 1870. Margaret Hebblethwaite describes the later horror of the war. "By this time his (López) adult army had been virtually eliminated. Undeterred, he sent out an army of 3,500 children under 15 years of age, with moustaches painted on their faces to make them look like grown men, and they were wiped out in the shameful massacre of the Battle of Acosta Ñú in 1869. From there on the pace of retreat quickened, and López resorted to executing thousands of his own people for supposed treachery."[31] The eventual outcome was a bloodbath in which *more than half* of Paraguay's people were slaughtered and estimates of the death toll in the adult male population go over 90%. Paraguay is still under-populated. Lópes died believing in the "greatness of our immolation", but really weapons had led to the genocide of most of a nation. A South American tragedy was hatched in the sales of the arms manufacturers in Paris. It led, through selling weapons to a weak and mentally inadequate leader, to the death of an estimated half a million people. That is what western weapons have been doing around the world ever since.

**The Afghanistan Example.**

Militarisation was a pattern to be often repeated, and it was a long-term trend. The arms traders did a few slick sales to political leaders from some far off country, but the effect of those weapons was long-term gruesome fighting which distorted and destroyed nations. Always, when you probe, the arms dealers have led processes of militarization. Afghanistan has been involved in a guerilla war at the beginning of the twenty first century, and its pacification seems very difficult. But its militarization has been long-term. A million rifles went there from the United States in the nineteen eighties and nineties. But that was not the first stage of militarization. There had been troubles long before in the North West frontier of India, what is now the Afghan border. It was estimated that 140,000 rifles went into the territory in the late $19^{th}$ and early $20^{th}$ century to the tribesmen there. The militarization of Afghanistan has been going on for a century and men have learned to live with a rifle on their shoulders for generations. Not surprisingly, they used them in raids and attacks, what we now call terrorist attacks. The *Times of India* in 1897 called for measures to

> curtail or extinguish a trade which is fraught with such menace to our future peace in the North-West…British influence in the Persian Gulf has not been maintained for centuries in order that the gunmakers of Birmingham should wax wealthy by the stealthy encouragement of the foes of order and good government.[32]

In the light of later events, as bodies still come back from Afghanistan, this becomes a long prophetic statement. Yet, the manufacturers objected to attempts by the British Government to curb this trade. "Prohibitions are usually a farce…our view is that it is better to wink at an evil than to make futile and impossible attempts at its remedy."[33] Of course, there is still the option of a *non-futile* end of exports to these remote areas. Around this time opium growing seems to have arrived first in this area. Drugs and weapons have a long history of intertwinement, often selling one to buy the other. This was not a great part of British history.

**The Philippines.**

Another example of the gratuitous use of arms occurred in the Philippines. It had been a Spanish colony, but the United States offered to help it attain independence as it became embroiled in the war against Spain involving Cuba and the other Spanish colonies. General Dewey made a compact with the Filipino leader which stated that America was looking towards independence for the Philippines and was not interested in colonies. In any case the Filipino rebels had more or less succeeded in defeating the Spanish and declared independence, an end to four hundred years of Spanish domination. However, at home public opinion, led by McKinley who was running a presidential campaign at the time, was for annexation of the Spanish colonies.[34] The policy changed. It was then called "Benevolent Assimilation". The Filipinos were not grateful and did not say, "Welcome! Come and take us over and be our new rulers" but started to fight their double-dealing American invaders. Their leader Aguinaldo had the temerity to point out that the nation that purported to champion oppressed nations around the world was invading them.

They fought strongly. By this stage guns were available in the States on a grand scale. The Gatling gun was in use, capable of mowing down dozens of advancing attackers. The rifle was the Krag-Jorgenson, copied on license from Norway. It was bolt action with a five-shot magazine firing smokeless powder, was simple, reliable, and popular with the troops. It had a knife bayonet. They had Colt .45 revolvers and big guns. The Filipinos had some old rifles, but they had to pass one rifle around between four or five soldiers and were also low on ammunition. They also had knives. Frequently they were mowed down and there were hundreds lying in trenches. But the Filipinos carried on fighting against Benevolent Assimilation using what we would now call guerilla warfare, and the Americans changed the name of their game. They now called it "Pacification". Well, that's much better. We are all in favour of imposed peace. Atrocities were committed, especially under General Otis. These included torture, the "water cure", as well as gratuitous murders. Soldiers who sent information home about these atrocities were court-marshalled. General Arthur MacArthur, father of Douglas MacArthur, whom we shall meet later, was also active in the war. Concentration camps were set up and hundreds of ordinary unarmed Filipinos were mowed down in village after village. Something like a million Filipinos died and the nation was cowered into submission. Well done, America. A number of commissions were set up and eventually in 1934 a law was passed granting the Philippines independence in ten years time after forty five years of colonial occupation. Ironically, President McKinley, who had sanctioned this policy, was shot by an anarchist in 1901 with a .32 calibre Iver-Johnson revolver and also died.

At this stage we should probably admit, whether we are American, English, French, Belgian, Hutu, Japanese, Filipino, Australian, Indian, German, Pakistani, Israeli, Syrian, Egyptian, Paraguayan, Scottish or whatever we are, that we have done atrocious things with weapons - killing and maiming. There is no higher place of self-righteousness from which the sins of another nation or ethnic group can be looked down on. This problem is bigger than all of us. As the Bible insists throughout, We have all sinned.

**The Bigger Picture including Africa**

Gradually, the arms' manufacturers racheted up their influence, their reach, their economic and political power. Japan was won to militarism. Russia, smarting from defeat by the Japanese increased their military expenditure to be greater than anyone else. They imported western arms and even western munitions factories at Putilov and Zarizyn, buying from everyone. The alliance with Japan did not prevent Armstrong and the other British arms dealers from doing all they could to sell arms to Russia. Turkey and Greece were also competitively arming, and both sides could be encouraged to buy.

Other continents were being opened up to the trade. White colonials in Africa needed plenty of guns. The Boers were buying weapons from a number of sources including Martini-Henry rifles made in Enfield and Birmingham, and so the Boers were shooting the British with British weapons; so we could hardly complain. Colonialism was pumping arms into Africa, but the main victims were the native Africans. One obvious focus was the Belgian Congo as it was called. Perhaps 20% of the population of the Congo died through gun-imposed Belgian control, in what has come to be known through Joseph Conrad's novel as *The Heart of Darkness*. In its colonial history the Congo was really a personal fiefdom of Leopold II until 1908. It was an atrocious rule. As rubber became an important raw material natives were sent to gather it from trees. Joe Lusi, of *Heal Africa*, recounts that if they were unable to gather enough during a day to fill a barrel, native workers would be "short-sleeved", that is, their arms would be cut off above the elbow. That was a measure of the barbarity brought by Europe to the Congo and elsewhere. Really, though Conrad does not labour the point, weapons are at the centre of his novel bringing the stench of death. Kurtz has his own collection of guns and they are treated with reverence when he is dying. When finally they are on the steamer, Conrad describes the others as "getting out their rifles with an air of anticipating a jolly lark" shooting at the natives on the bank on the river. Callous gun power is behind the ivory trade and other exploitations driving a vast country towards inner destruction. Belgian guns had been manufactured in Liege for centuries, but in the mid-nineteenth century they centralized and streamlined production. The biggest companies were FN and Établissements Pieper, but they had an arms manufacturing school, Leon Mignon, teaching the apprentices of nearly two hundred companies, and by 1907 the gunsmiths of Liege were turning out 1.5 million guns, and they were voluminously taken to the Congo and also exported throughout Europe.[35]

Everywhere colonial militarism was extending its rule, the rule of the gun and the gunboat, and because it infected all of the colonial powers it must also inflect their relationships with one another, driving them towards war. Above all the powers of Europe were looking to new weapons and increased militarization, moving towards the ultimacy of military control and fulfilling Gladstone's prophecy. Chemical warfare was being discussed. The tank would slowly surplant the horse, which, as Philip Sampson has pointed out, have been a war-bred animal for much of human history. We tend to forget that six million horses died in World War One, usually suffering and rigid with fear. Yet, as the great web grew, it was the British who set the scene and shaped world events. It is strange that countries which claim imperial or super-power status also come to think that they are not responsible for the way things go. With the creep of arms manufacturing and arms trading, a World War was coming, and Britain, full of itself, "Send Us Victorious", was in the thick of generating it. Especially, the weapons' manufacturers, out for their business, were pushing towards war.

# PART II. WHY WORLD WAR ONE?

*Why did the Great War happen? Throughout the world people have gathered round war memorials in the cold wondering why this thing should have been. Some debate about the causes of the First World War focusses on diplomacy, the character of the Kaiser and other politicians and on issues of statecraft. More commentators see an important role for the military - the naval rivalry between Britain and Germany, the German High Command, the military position of Russia, Austro-Hungary, France, Italy and Japan, and see the military build-up as decisive. Here we look especially at the munitions companies and the impetus they generated towards the Great War through proliferating arms and raising scares. Perhaps it was through their success that peace was really confounded.*

## Chapter Five: Weapons lead to War.

**The Underlying Argument.**

For decades students have been writing essays on the origins of the First World War. Most commentators point out that the causes are not mainly located in happenings at Sarajevo but in bigger European national rivalries. We can note that when Archduke Ferdinand was shot, it was with a Belgian-made Fabrique Nationale M1900 semi-automatic pistol, a product of the arms trade which had migrated to Serbia. Yet that was symptom rather than underlying cause. Many essays focus on imperialism, nationalism and the Social Darwinist idea of the struggle of the races. They look in detail at Bismarck, the Kaiser, Asquith and Lloyd George, the Czar and the failing Austro-Hungarian Empire. They consider the diplomatic interaction between Metternich, Grey and others. Though these are parts of the events leading to the War, they may not be the most seminal causes of the events which occurred.

Most commentators also recognize the importance of military rivalry - the British-German naval rivalry reflected in the Dreadnoughts, the German fear of Russia's growing armed strength and the preparation of both the French and German armies to face one another. Yet even these rivalries occurred within a bigger framework, namely the marketing and salesmanship of industrial munitions. Here we examine the part played by the arms manufacturers in pushing towards the Great War. We consider the case that *arms manufacturers and sellers decisively shaped the situation which led to the Great War and many other wars.* When war came, it was more or less expected, because the build-up of arms had been so intense, and could not continue without war some time or another. The imperatives of arms led the way to war. Germany wanted to attack Russia because she believed that Russia's munitions development was not yet up to speed. Britain was quite willing to engage with Germany because she knew she for the time being had an overwhelming superiority in battleships, and so it goes on. The calculations and fears about weapons really precipitated the event, and the arms companies ran the show from behind the scenes. Sooner or later weapons cause wars.

Some interpretations are nationally focussed. Most British people probably believe that the war was not really *our* fault, but was mainly caused by German aggression. But perhaps Britain contributed more than she concedes. Maybe, the underlying point is not whether Germany or Britain (or France, Russia or Austro-Hungary) was mainly to blame, but what pressure was brought to bear by the arms manufacturers and the military within all of these states. Krupp, now the biggest industrial enterprise in Europe, stood behind Von Tirpitz and the army, while Armstrong, Vickers and others stood behind the British Government. Similarly, in France, Schneider and the Dreyfusards were pushing a right-wing militarism and arming for conflict, while in Russia the Tsar was also marching out of control to the tune of the arms' manufacturers of Britain and France, as well as of Russia. Actually in most countries leading politicians who fought to prevent the war, but they were powerless when faced with the intrigue, creation of distrust, military antagonism and preparedness for war which grew through the arms manufacturers and the expansion of arms. Thus, the weight of explanation lies with the munitions people and the way they shaped the politicians. So it was and has continued to be. This explanation is not new, but the most common among statesmen and people after 1918. Strangely in 2014, it is largely sublimated and ignored.

**Undershaft and his Ilk.**

George Bernard Shaw made this very observation in his play *Major Barbara,* written in 1905 close to the time when the Great War was formed, for usually wars are engineered a decade or more before they take place. Prescience is always worth a bit more. In the play, the arms manufacturer, Undershaft, tussles with the Salvation Army lass, Major Barbara, each on their own terms. Undershaft was probably based on a combination of Krupp and Basil Zaharoff. He responds to his son, a hopeful politician, thus:

UNDERSHAFT [with a touch of brutality] "The government of your country! I am the government of your country: I, and Lazarus. Do you suppose that you and half a dozen amateurs like you, sitting in a row in that foolish gabble shop, can govern Undershaft and Lazarus? No, my friend: you will do what pays US. You will make war when it suits us, and keep peace when it doesn't. You will find out that trade requires certain measures when we have decided on those measures. When I want anything to keep my dividends up, you will discover that my want is a national need. When other people want something to keep my dividends down, you will call out the police and military. And in return you shall have the support and applause of my newspapers, and the delight of imagining that you are a great statesman. Government of your country! Be off with you, my boy, and play with your caucuses and leading articles and historic parties and great leaders and burning questions and the rest of your toys. I am going back to my counting house to pay the piper and call the tune."

Shaw here was speaking the unspoken. The arms traders, of course, did not let on that they were running the show. It was done quietly. They may also not have been hoping for what we now know as World War One. Indeed, nobody could have known what it would be like. But they knew that war does not harm their business and put no obstacles in its way. When war arrives suddenly everyone wants weapons and seemingly without concern for the price. War is Wonderful for arms companies! The peacemakers lagged way behind and were easily outplayed; they were outsiders while Krupp and Armstrong were consummate insiders, effectively for war, day in and day out. There was nothing inevitable about this War, except that the agendas of the arms manufacturers and the ethos they created came to shape international politics and popular culture. The First World War was the munitions industry's first great success.

**The Conclusion of the Prime Minister, Campbell Bannerman.**

The role played by the arms industry was not just Shaw's verdict, but the conclusion of many of those who were best qualified to judge. Someone else who made the point, well before the event, was the Liberal, Sir Henry Campbell-Bannerman, British Prime Minister from 5th December, 1905 to 6th April, 1908. He was MP for Stirling Burghs, had been Minister for War and opposed the Concentration Camps in the Second Boer War as "barbarous".[36] He said in his first speech as Liberal Prime Minister in 1905, "I hold that the growth of armaments is a great danger to the peace of the world. A policy of huge armaments keeps alive and stimulates and feeds the belief that force is the best, if not the only, solution of international differences."[37] Campbell-Bannerman tried to keep political control of this danger in the key period between 1905 and 1908, backed by Lloyd George, Churchill and others who saw the danger. He tried to cut the level of armaments in Britain and elsewhere, but resigned on the 3rd April, 1908 from ill-health and died nineteen days later. The cap on military expenditure was defeated by the munitions people, especially the naval interests after his death. Yet, here we see Campbell-Bannerman's prophetic awareness. He, like Gladstone a decade and a half earlier, saw the problem coming.

He did succeed for a while in cutting the military budget and in Jackie Fisher had a figure at the Admiralty who could make these cuts work. Yet, the anger and cunning of the great munitions companies at this move was such that they made sure their agenda and not Campbell-Bannerman's would win.

**Lloyd George's Analysis.**

We have looked at two Prime Ministers, and now come to the third. Lloyd George was Chancellor of the Exchequer during the build-up to the Great War. In 1911 his Budget introduced unemployment, old age and sickness insurance, a super-tax on the rich and created the structure for a vibrant, more equal economy. He was unbellicose, but looked to the peaceful development of Britain. When eventually war came, simply through his competence he became Minister of Munitions and then Prime Minister. He is generally estimated to have turned Britain around in fighting the conflict and came out of the war with laurels. As the architect of victory, he did not need excuses and was also most deeply acquainted with all aspects of the Great War. His own conclusion brings into focus the intertwining of munitions and the military. Let us listen to his account.

> Whilst diplomacy desired peace and worked for it by confused and bewildered methods, there were powerful elements in every community that thirsted for war. The Military Chiefs, high and low, in at least three of the countries principally concerned were not averse from putting their theories, plans, and hopes to the test. In Germany...military sentiment counted for a great deal. I am inclined to believe, after a careful perusal of the evidence, that it was a decisive factor. The Kaiser had, owing to certain incidents and indiscretions, lost much of his popularity. His popularity with his Army was definitely on the wane. They realised that he had not the heart of a soldier, and that he was not the man who would lead them into battle if he could avoid a fight. The Crown Prince was their favourite. The Kaiser was becoming sensitive to this rather contemptuous opinion formed of his courage by the Army he idolised. He knew that any symptom of shrinking or shuddering at the prospect of a great fight would finally forfeit the last

remnant of respect for him in the breasts of the soldiers he adored. This he could not face...

Von Moltke replied that it was too late, as all the preparations had been made on the assumption that the German Army would immediately march through Belgium and capture Paris in a given time. In Austria and Russia the High Command were finally responsible for the War. They insisted on mobilisation whilst not unhopeful negotiations were still going on. Austrian mobilisation led to Russia mobilising her army so as to prevent any surprise movement across the frontier. Austria mobilised to strike at Serbia. Russia mobilised for a counterblow. When the Kaiser, frightened by the thunder clouds, intervened personally with the Tsar to avert war, he begged " Nicky " to cancel his Decree which had already gone forth, for the mobilisation of the Russian army. The Tsar was willing to accede to this not unreasonable request, but the army leaders assured him that the " technical " difficulties of cancellation and even of partial demobilisation were insuperable. It was thus that the military chiefs in the leading countries of the Continent thrust the nations into war, whilst their impotent statesmen were still fumbling for Peace. Each army believed in its own invincibility and was anxious to demonstrate it.

The French Army, on the other hand, were equally confident of their powers. They believed they had the best gun in the field the famous soixante-quinze and they were not far wrong. It is not the first time that rapture over the possession of a new military invention has made a nation less averse from war. The French had also great confidence in the training given to their officers and in the fine quality of their troops. They knew their organisation was excellent and they had the inevitable " plan." There never was a time since 1870 when the French Army had less fear of its great rival. The Russians had improved their Army in equipment and organisation since their defeat in Manchuria. They felt infinitely superior to the Austrian Army, and deemed

> themselves quite a match for what was left of the German Army, after the better half of it had marched to the East. Generals in this frame of mind hungered for war and had no difficulty in manoeuvring statesmen who did not know their own minds into positions where war became inevitable. Thus great armaments made war.[38]

This was clearly Lloyd George's long settled conclusion.

**Winston Churchill on Cutting Arms.**

A fourth Prime Minister, though not until much later in changed circumstances, was Winston Churchill, who worked at the Board of Trade with Lloyd George. At this stage he was sceptical of the increase in military budgets both at home and in other states and not at all like the later simplified version of him. He strongly opposed the bellicose attitudes towards Germany. This is Churchill on the 15th April, 1909.

> I have left the most monstrous error to the last. [After speaking about the "cries of cowardice" of the naval lobby wanting more battleships and stressing the impossibility of Germany building them secretly and quickly – "Such ideas are childish."] It is this – that there is a profound antagonism of interests between the British and the German nations which can only be resolved by a supreme trial of strength towards which the tides of destiny are irresistibly bearing us... It is not true. There is no natural antagonism between the interests of the British and German peoples... If a serious antagonism is gradually created between the two peoples, it will not be because of the workings of any natural or impersonal forces, but through the vicious activity of a comparatively small number of individuals in both countries and the culpable credulity of a larger class.[39]

The "vicious" minority was the munitions lobby. He was fighting the process of competitive arming and was working for peace and reductions in military budgets.

Churchill saw the general principle that expenditure on weapons and the military produces its own crisis. He understood military build-up as being the precipitant of war through economic forces five years before it happened. Especially interesting is his analysis in a Cabinet Paper of 3rd November, 1909 made as President of the Board of Trade. He perceived the German increase in debt created by arms expenditure, including naval expenditure, as pushing it towards war because of the fiscal crisis that would ensue from an outlay of £105m in ten years. You cannot spend money at this rate without provoking an economic crisis. He states:

> These circumstances force the conclusion that a period of severe internal strain approaches in Germany. Will the tension be relieved by moderation or snapped by calculated violence? Will the policy of the German Government be to soothe the internal situation, or to find an escape from it in external adventure? There can be no doubt that both courses are open...But one of the two courses must be taken soon."

In other words, the economic costs of arms drive towards war because State debt becomes unsustainable. Churchill adds in his history, "This is, I think, the first sinister impression that I was ever led to record."[40] But he could see both sides of the picture. At Frome on the 27th January, 1910 he addressed the way the Conservative Party had pandered to the naval lobby.

> The attitude of the Conservative Party with regard to the Navy has been a disgrace to that party. It was the most contemptible policy ever pursued by a great party; it was a policy of trying to raise a panic without reason, a policy of trying to raise ill-will between two great nations without cause, a policy of decrying and belittling the fleet and of trying to get money out of the pockets of the weak and the poor. It was the lowest depths to which any great party had ever sunk.[41]

In a final attempt to address this problem Churchill in early 1912 proposed a "naval holiday" where both Germany and Britain ceased building battleships and both countries could get off the treadmill of expenditure and calm down, but it was not accepted. It is interesting that Churchill, no anti-militarist, recognizes the pressure that military expenditure places on the state by building towards an economic crisis.

**Lord Edward Grey.**

Perhaps the most qualified of all to reflect was Lord Grey, who was Secretary of State for Foreign Affairs in the decade preceding the start of the First World War and involved in all the diplomacy with Germany. He experienced directly everything that was involved in the build-up to the War, and his conclusion therefore carries great weight. It was as follows.

> "The moral is obvious; it is that great armaments lead inevitably to war. If there are armaments on one side, there must be armaments on other sides…
>
> "The increase of armaments that is intended in each nation to produce consciousness of strength, and a sense of security, does not produce these effects. On the contrary, it produces a consciousness of the strength of other nations and a sense of fear. Fear begets suspicion and distrust and evil imaginings of all sorts…
>
> "But, although all this [diplomatic difficulties with Germany] be true, it is not in my opinion the real and final account of the origin of the Great War. The enormous growth of armaments in Europe, the sense of insecurity and fear caused by them – it was these that made war inevitable. This, it seems to me, is the truest reading of history, and the lesson that the present should be learning from the past in the interests of future peace, the warning to be handed on to those who come after us."[42]

Grey's expertise was matters of state and political negotiation. He met all the statesmen of all the other belligerent nations, yet for him the decisive "real and final account of the origin of the Great War" was munitions and the build-up of arms.

**The Overall Conclusion.**

These are not sudden opinions, but considered and decisive reflections by the most experienced major British figures in foreign affairs including, with Gladstone, four Prime Ministers. *They all conclude that buying weapons and building up arms pushed all of the countries concerned towards the Great War. Conversely, if all these weapons were not needed for war, then they were useless and a crisis of militarism must emerge. This did not happen, because war ensued.* This understanding of the Great War by Gladstone, Campbell-Bannerman, Lloyd George, Churchill and Lord Grey is not easily gainsaid. The point was perhaps most directly made by Arthur Ponsonby, MP in the Commons debate when War was being faced on 3rd August, 1914.

> The balance of power is responsible for this—this mad desire to keep up an impossibility in Europe, to try and divide the two sections of Europe into an armed camp, glaring at one another with suspicion and hostility and hatred, and arming all the time, and bleeding the people to pay for the armaments. Since I have been in this House I have every year protested against the growth in the expenditure upon armaments. Every year it has mounted up and up, and old women of both sexes have told us that the best way to prepare to maintain peace is to prepare for war. This is what they have led us to—those who were foolish enough to believe it. It was inevitable that if Europe continued to arm, if every nation bled the people in order to furnish new ships and new guns, to grind all the people who devote their energy, their labour, and their enterprise to one sole object, the preparation for war, war will take place.[43]

Indeed, the evidence for the part played by this build-up of weapons grew stronger in later decades. But now it is usually ignored, because the historians focus on the politicians and the military. Yet, as we shall see, it is the arms makers who give the military their power, and it is their accumulated self-promotion that provides the impetus towards war not just immediately in 1914, but building up for the previous three decades. Let us examine, not just the broad sweep of the argument, but the detailed process through which it came to pass.

# Chapter Six: The Build-up and Pressure of Arms.

## European Economic Militarisation.

We are talking about the decisions which led to the deaths and injuries of tens of millions of people, an event of still untold tragedy. Clearly, thousands of little moves were part of this process, and they were not all one way. There were peace movements, pulling away from war. Many tried to cut military expenditure. Politicians worked hard to avoid conflict. The play of forces leading to war was complex and in some ways finely balanced. But the pre-war build up of arms was not finely balanced. It was continuously one way apart from a short dip in the mid-1900s and it was backed by a pattern of fear-mongering engendered by the munitions people and their backers. Britain, France, Germany, Austro-Hungary, Italy, Russia and Japan all increased their military expenditure many times in the lead-up to war.

This decisive trend in the expansion in arms and arms expenditure can be seen in the table below. We are looking at more than three decades of continual growth in arms, prompted by the munitions companies, leading all the nations involved to trust in weapons and fighting rather than peace and mutuality. This table alone sets out the main driver towards the Great War. It occurred against a background where military expenditure throughout Europe had been low and ordinary economic development had happened. Here are the relative defence expenditures of the key nations at intervals before the outbreak of war. Because prices were falling during this period the figures understate the expansion, especially in 1908.

**Defence expenditure in £'s millions[44]**

| | 1858 | 1883 | 1908 | 1913 |
|---|---|---|---|---|
| **Britain** | 23 | 28 | 59 | 77 |
| **France** | 19 | 31 | 44 | 82 |
| **Germany** | 5 | 20 | 59 | 100 |
| **Italy** | 2 | 12 | 18 | 29 |

| | | | | |
|---|---|---|---|---|
| **Austria** | **11** | **13** | **21** | **24** |
| **Russia** | **19** | **36** | **60** | **92** |
| **Total** | **79** | **140** | **261** | **404** |

This shows an increase in armaments of something like twice the level of growth in national income over five decades. Britain led the way earlier, rivalled by France and Russia in the 1880s, reflecting Gladstone's observations. Germany moved through and caught Britain up in 1908, although with heavier army than navy expenditure. Russia, Germany and France grew substantially up until 1913. Any one of these countries experiencing expansion must have felt impelled towards war, but in fact they all did. The rise in the last five years from a very high level was more than 50%. Arms expenditure by the main European powers increased more than five and a half times between 1858 and 1913 in real terms. This heavy growth in arms expenditure mainly led to the First World War, and, as we shall see, it was strongly promoted by the munitions companies. Sadly, the build-up of growth in 1913-14 was to be followed by a war which kept the munitions' companies burgeoning in the greatest crescendo of militarism the world had ever seen.

**How Arms Cause Wars.**

The way military expansion led to the Great War operated through a number of economic and political consequences. These are standard throughout modern history, and we shall see them repeatedly in action.

First, though not most important, is Churchill's argument that there is a fiscal crisis with increasing military expenditure. When economies militarize, they travel in a direction that takes resources away from industry and consumers. Necessarily there are increases in national debt and taxation, and loss to other areas of government expenditure. As a result the economies tend to become unstable and unsustainable. Either military expenditure must contract sharply, or there must be war. If war had not occurred in 1914, the German,

Russian, Britain and French regimes would have faced a general economic crisis through a larger national debt and unsustainable militarisation. The USSR faced a similar economic crisis in 1990 when it fell apart under the economic strain of its military budget. Military economies fail, as we shall repeatedly see, because of the effect *on the state* of vast parasitic expenditure on useless arms.

Second, added to this, is the fact that a military boom must lead to a recession *for the arms companies and the military,* unless there is war. War has been talked up for a decade and demand for arms has increased, but then nothing happens and politicians can work out that it is better to spend money on other things. The munitions companies and the military therefore become caught in a need for war, and increase their pressure, because demand for their products will otherwise collapse, and they will be in long-term recession. At the end of an arms race, the munitions people and the military will be in crisis *unless* they find an enemy. For them a war is the way out; it also prevents their product from seeming useless.

Third, weapons destroy trust, as they clearly did in 1914; countries which had previously lived together amicably, draw back in distrust when stiff with weapons. Europe was a rich quilt of intertwined relationships in 1900. Yet, it is difficult to shake hands with a person holding a gun in the other hand. Weapons are always relational, *and one primary cause of the Great War was not the fight over territory or ideology, but tensions caused by the possession of weapons.* Germany did not trust Russia, France or Britain. Italy did not trust Germany, Austro-Hungary or France. Russia did not trust Britain, because it had backed Japan or Germany. Britain did not trust France, Germany, Russia or anyone who might threaten their Empire including the Boers, the Indians, the Sudanese, Afghans, Burmese, Tibetans and other groups around the globe. The French did not trust Germany and their closest ally was perfidious Albion, justifiably so seen. All these relationships were made more suspicious and tense by the weapons, battleships, rifles, cannon, troops which each state was building up. If two countries could get together against a third, then the third needed twice the arms of the other two, and the perceived need for militarization became even stronger. This pattern is voluminously evident among all the powers. In this obvious sense, weapons caused the War. We shall look at some of these dynamics later, but historians have pored over them for decades, and the basic point is obvious.

Fourth, the growth of arms conditions people to think of war and conflict. It is presented as an option in international diplomacy. Strategy becomes military, not diplomatic. Britain knew the German navy was getting more powerful, but Germany knew Russia was becoming more powerful still; both predisposed towards war. Politicians were pressured by weapons into making military calculations paramount; thus weapons create a self-fulfilling policy by changing political culture.

Fifth, at a basic level, weapons are pointless unless you use them; you have to find work for these white elephants or they are seen as a stupid waste of money. This especially affects the military. If armed forces grow, and train, and receive new weapons which they learn to operate, and are consulted by politicians, they will declare their preparedness for war and their ability to wage war otherwise they are not credible. The status of the military depends in the end on having wars, and therefore, sooner or later, they must have one, or they finish up like the Grand Old Duke of York (whom we will one day realize was a canny old bird half way to sanity).

Sixth, the expansion of armaments increases the power of the military within governments. Through all kinds of institutional arrangements, buildings, committees and procedures governments can be militarized. The military presence in Edwardian London was immense. Admiralty Arch, between Trafalgar Square and the Mall was finished in 1913. What we now know as the Old War Office on Whitehall was built between 1899 and 1906 using 30,000 tons of stone and fifty million bricks. And the title of the building was important. During the 19$^{th}$ century it was the War and Colonial Office. At this time Britain was looking towards making colonial wars normal. In 1903-4 Lord Curzon, ruling India for no particular reason, decided to invade Tibet for no particular reason, except that the Dalai Lama did not invite him to tea. A force went in under a lout called Younghusband with Maxim guns, mowed down the

Tibetans even when they were running away without weapons, leaving soldiers sick at what they had done. The troops stormed Lhasa, and imposed a treaty of the Tibetans effectively making Britain the controlling power. We made them pay an indemnity for having resisted our invasion – appalling failure to appreciate what we would do for them, no respect for pith helmets, don't you know. The same attitude prevailed at all the other borders of Empire. We were into War because we had the weapons to do it.

Seventh, states begin to bargain on the basis of their military strength rather than what is fair, right and good. There is a pride in the attitudes of all nations and a resentment towards other powers which makes international negotiations brittle. The Agadir Crisis in July, 1911, where it looked as though Germany was seeking a naval base in North Africa, was one such point, but there were many other surrounding the German Naval Law, British and French colonial conquests and the sheer self-importance of states with military might. Arms are seen as creating the right to dominate and an automatic arrogance reflected in the self-importance of senior military uniforms.

Eighth, weapon proliferation increases the possibility that conflict will break out somewhere and precipitate a more general war; local conflicts grow. If not Sarajevo, then elsewhere... All of these processes contributed to the emergence of the Great War, and other wars. Put more crudely, the munitions people and the military constructed the pro-conditions for war and they got what they wanted.

**The Routes of Influence.**

The munitions companies could do this because they had direct routes to politicians and State decision-making. The evidence in the next few chapters is substantial, but understated. A lot of the relevant information is hidden. In November 1927 the elderly Sir Basil Zaharoff made a fire of 58 years of diaries detailing his contacts with many of the world's politicians, scribing whom he met, worked with and bribed. That evidence went up in smoke. But there is still plenty lying around. Dash uncovers another source of evidence of Zaharoff the consummate political insider.

> "Derby's entries record high-level contacts: "Zaharoff came to see me today," he wrote to a former Prime Minister, Lord Balfour, in August 1918, "and told me of conversations he had had with you, the King and [the then Prime Minister] Lloyd George." [45]

This was in the context of offering advice about continuing the Great War to the very end for there were a number of peace initiatives and it was not always clear that the war would go on, but Zedzed seemed keen to advise that it should. It's an impressive list, even though Zaharoff was boasting. And other evidence is about. There were machinations over France and Germany. So, in 1907 Zaharoff wrote from Germany to France to get one of his Vickers mates to put out a press release about a military build-up in Germany. It was published in the French papers, created an instant fuss about French re-armament, which was in turn reported in the German Reichstag and helped increase *their* vote for military spending. Zedzed was pulling two sets of strings.

The arms moguls usually had access to their national political decision-makers – Krupp directly to the Kaiser and Von Tirpitz, Armstrong to the Cabinet, the Comité des Forges to the French political and media elite. Tooley details the insider status of Schneider:

> Similarly, the Schneider family of the French company Schneider-Creusot came out of the French defeat at Prussia's hands in 1871 with huge profits. Having supported Napoleon III, the company was now equally supportive of the various Third Republic governments, especially those of a nationalist coloring. Meanwhile, the company relied on the state to suppress strikes and manage discontent at its factories, as it supplied the army with weapons. The Schneiders eventually managed to place one of their own, Eugene Schneider, in the Chamber of Deputies, where he served throughout a period crucial to arms makers: 1900 to 1925.[46]

They discussed weapons with Ministers of War, Prime Ministers, Presidents and Generals. They were insiders, with the state depending on them for the weapons it needed and receiving advice about weapons development. Not to have imported weapons meant greater security of supply, especially if a war started, and it was a relationship which Directors of Ordnance valued highly.

Then, the arms dealers had access to the rulers in other nations. The Tsar was drowning in arms dealers and Armstrong's house, Cragside, was visited by the Shah of Persia, the King of Siam, the Prime Minister of China, the Prince of Wales and many other politicians world-wide. Vickers is usually associated with Zacharoff, but they had other fine executive salesmen: - Sigmund Loewe, acquired with help from the Rothschilds, Trevor Dawson, experienced in every area of munitions, Vincent Caillard, who had served in the Ottoman Empire and had languages and intelligence work. Francis Barker helped look after Russia, and Stephen Dardier worked on Italy and Spain.[47] They travelled, were linked in with bankers, formed intimate relationships with rulers and generals and brought in the contracts.

Third, the arms companies operated through the military. We shall repeatedly come across the revolving door – the manufacturers go to the military and they employ the military who are insiders, friends, club-members, intermarried with the people who will dish out the contracts or push for more weapons. The munitions people sell their wares, not to people who pay for them, but to the military who want to push up their military budget and war office people whose pension they might provide. Clearly the munitions people and the military are natural allies. They want the best equipment, the new weapons and the largest quantity of arms possible. Often when the military speak about equipment, they are primed by the munitions people. Sometimes, as with Jackie Fisher, military procurement is independent, but Fisher was punished for his independence by being sacked. Usually, the military wholly played the tune of the munitions people, by bribes or by conviction. Shortly we see Von Tirpitz pushing Krupp's Navy. Conventionally, militarism means the domination of military agendas in government, but, as we have already seen, usually it is the munitions companies who supply the pressure for the military to grow with big battleships, bigger guns, air power, machine guns and other advanced instruments of death. It was these salesmen, not the users, who mainly ran the show.

Fourth, especially before the First World War, these groups set out to change public opinion. They funded pressure groups like the British Navy League, the German version - the Flottenverein, and newspapers to promote armament to the public and opinion formers. It was the most sophisticated propaganda the world had seen at this stage. In 1908 the British Navy League spawned another group, the Imperial Maritime League, to push even harder for naval expenditure. The message was that the Navy made us strong and safe and "Pax Britannia" kept the world at peace. "Pax Britannia" was, of course, us conquering the world and winning an empire. The key message was for a big naval budget. They also had influence within the Press. Often Press Lords owned armaments shares, and a war scare gave them a windfall profit. General Smuts, a great measured statesman and also obviously a General, concluded in 1918 as follows: "The Press, influenced by the large profits and advertising enterprise of the armaments firms, whips up public opinion on every imaginable occasion; small foreign incidents are written up and magnified into grave international situations affecting the pacific relations of States, and the war temperature is artificially raised and kept up." Smuts' evaluation is authoritative. The word, "jingoism" was coined around sending a British fleet to resist Russia in 1878.

Fifth, we do not know the scale of bribery and corruption throughout the military system, but it was going on. Armstrong and Zaharoff distributed largesse in part to be accepted by the political establishment, but all kinds of other gifts, hospitality, job offers and movements of funds took place, aside money on desks to keep politicians loyal to the munitions' cause. We are invited to presume that bribery did not operate within the honest British system; it is more likely that it was just good-mannered bribery.

**Munitions and Buying into War.**

None of this process is complex. Weapons are made to win wars and buying weapons is buying into the *process* of war. It is a whole package. Now we try to justify militarism and disguise what is going on by calling it "defence". True, shields and bunkers are defence, but rifles, bombs, gas, howitzers, grenades, flame-throwers, tanks, battleships, destroyers, bayonets and machine guns are attack. Most weapons are constructed to win wars by killing and destroying the enemy. Buying weapons involves putting your mouth where your money is. If you have bought these things, then you have to talk as though this process makes some sense, as though using them is a reasonable option. If you mouth says so, then your brain must so think, at least in part. You think a number of moves like talking up enemies, thinking of winning or losing, backing certain weapons and being optimistic about war. We can see all of these processes operating in relation to the First World War. It would be over by Christmas. No side formed any clear conception of what it would lose, and each new weapon was trumpeted as decisive. Yet, the underlying reality was of a vast tranche of people who bought into the business of war at different levels – as soldiers, designers, welders, generals, politicians, sailors. It was, if not their raison d'être, their reason for work. They were predisposed to the business of war; sooner or later it would happen.

The Kaiser's Memoirs show part of this process – in the shipyards. He praises the man who deeply influenced him - the Emperor of Germany – to build a navy.

> Admiral von Tirpitz worked with tireless energy. Encouraged and fired with enthusiasm by him, the German shipbuilding yards went at the great problem, filled with German audacity, and solved it with positively brilliant results, greatly outdistancing their foreign competitors. The admirable technical endowment of the German engineers, as well as the better education of the German working-classes, contributed in full measure towards this achievement. Consultations, conferences, reports to me, service trips to all

> shipbuilding yards, were the daily bread of the indefatigable Tirpitz. But the tremendous trouble and work were richly rewarded.[48]

Yet, the picture is not quite right. The politician is praising the militarist, the Admiral, but behind the militarist is the munitions man. It was Krupp, not von Tirpitz, who was really running these yards day in and day out. Von Tirpitz might be strutting around giving directions, when the Kaiser was about, but the shipyards were Krupp's domain. He had developed battleship armour, guns and building. He had secured the contracts. He pushed for and organized the expansion. They were his workers and the business of building warships was his vision. He had started it and Von Tirpitz had come on board later. Behind the uniforms, it was Krupp's show and he was building a navy at considerable profit. Ultimately, he needed these battleships to be used. Munitions, military, politics - but the greatest of these was munitions. It was the munitions push in both the navy and the army that set the clock ticking for war.

# Chapter Seven: The Mulliner Panic and British Militarism.

## The Build-up of the Arms Race.

In the next two chapters we look at the British and German contributions to this process. The point is not to apportion blame, although blame for wrongdoing is a real part of the picture, but merely to point out the simple lesson that if world-wide catastrophe was the next village down the road, both states were driving there, and the car engines were the munitions/military people. Lloyd George was the most powerful politician in Britain and the Prime Minister who actually won the War. He had a deserved reputation as a war leader and had successfully organized munitions during the War. So for him to reflect that it was the "wasteful, ruinous, suicidal competition in armaments... those bloated armaments which are the curse and the disgrace of our civilisation,"[49] is sobering. This was not self-pleading, but anger at what had actually happened. Nor was he excluding Britain from this judgment. Indeed, that was partly his focus. When later in 1936 Lloyd George gave evidence to the Royal Commission his contribution was as follows:

> There was a good deal of direct, and even more indirect, propaganda conducted by these enterprises [Arms Firms]. Sometimes it took the subtle form of inculcating the horrors of war with suggestions that people must prepare to protect themselves against them. It more often took the form of an exaggeration of the preparations made by other countries, with more than a hint that they were directed against our security. The pre-1914 Government had an illustration of the latter method. They would remember the Dreadnought panic. The naval programme of Germany was exaggerated in the Press and on the platform. There was an exaggeration as to the number of ships being built and the size of the guns...

> A Cabinet Committee was appointed to investigate all the facts with regard to German shipbuilding and German guns. The armaments firms tendered evidence in their possession, based on secret evidence which they had received – all of the most alarmist character. They had already passed it on to the Admiralty. This demonstrated that the Germans were laying down ships considerably in excess of their published statutory naval plan. There was no doubt that this evidence considerably influenced the Cabinet. It turned out to be completely inaccurate.[50]

Shortly, we shall examine the process to which Lloyd George refers, the Dreadnought Panic. Others were similarly upset. Lord Welby, Head of the Civil Service, said before the Great War referring to the British scene: "We are in the hands of an organisation of crooks. They are politicians, generals, manufacturers of armaments and journalists. All of them are anxious for unlimited expenditure and go on inventing scares to terrify the public and to terrify Ministers of the Crown."[51] Again, Welby and Lloyd George were not potty radicals, but sober, experienced, mature statesmen. Why were they so adamantly angry at the munitions' companies? We need to go back a few years to get the full picture of British military development.

**The Boer War, or the British War Against the Boers.**

The Second Boer War started on the 11th October, 1899. It was a major colonial war and occurred when the munitions companies, especially Vickers, were already well supplied with orders. It was fought when the world had been discussing peace at the first Hague Conference in the summer, and the rest of the world was not happy with this belligerence. The Boers were Dutch by origin, and Holland was especially upset. Why we were fighting the War? Essentially, gold had been discovered in Witwatersrand and diamonds in Kimberley. Cecil Rhodes and others were busy exploiting them and bringing in loads of "uitlanders" (Dutch for "foreigners") into the area. They were mainly British migrants, who were beginning to swamp the already established Boer farmers, although there is some irony in the Dutch calling incomers "foreigners". The Boers were upset because this was obviously becoming another British colonial take-over. They had been assured of the independence of the Transvaal and the Orange Free State at the end of the First Boer War, but the word of perfidious Albion was not worth much. Rhodes was scheming for a take-over all the time and in 1895 organised the Jameson Raid which was a blatant attempt to invade and take over Johannesburg. After this Paul Kruger imported 37,000 Mauser rifles and 40-50 million rounds of ammunition, and so the Boers were prepared for what followed.

The main presenting issue of dissention later was full, immediate voting rights for the immigrants. There were negotiations. Lord Milner was British High Commissioner and he believed there could be no hope of peace with the permanent subjection of the British to the Dutch in the independent republics. Presumably he thought there could be permanent peace with the subjection of the Dutch to the British, because we are nice chaps. There were negotiations in June, 1899 in Bloemfontein, but they failed, to Milner's satisfaction. In September the British Colonial Secretary, Joseph Chamberlain, demanded full voting rights in the Transvaal and began marshalling troops on the border. Paul Kruger, President of the South African Republic, issued an ultimatum on 9th October 1899, giving the British government 48 hours to withdraw all their troops from the borders of the Transvaal and the Orange Free State. It was not met and the Transvaal and Orange Free State declared war on the British Government. It was a war which Rhodes, Milner and the War and Colonial Office wanted. There were murmurs about Boers using slaves, although Morton summarizes the evidence that this was not a real concern: "Existing studies of the Transvaal have dismissed the notion that slave raiding and slavery were part of Boer state policy. Beginning with Agar-Hamilton's *Native Policy of the Voortrekkers* (1928), the literature has certainly conceded that such practices existed in the SAR, but concluded that they were localized, isolated and erratic. In Walker's words, the 'trekkers as a body were certainly neither slavers nor slave owners.'"[52] So the British fighting against Boer slavery was a suitable fiction for a colonial take-over, not a real concern. Opposition to slavery, it seemed, did not extend to the use of native labour in the deep British gold and diamond mines. Here there was no "slavery". The native workers and the imported Chinese coolies were merely charged a poll tax which they could only meet through receiving wages and paying back a third of their low wages in tax. Occasionally they might want to go back to their families or die from exhaustion. It was the usual British hypocrisy writ large.

The Boer War was a vicious event. The Boers had weapons, mainly bought from the Germans including the Mauser rifles and Krupp artillery. But they also included four Big Toms, made by Schneider at Le Creusot. They could fire a 94lb shell six miles and the Boers had plenty of shells.[53] So the Boers could attack the British effectively in the field and in towns, and besieged Ladysmith, Mafeking and Kimberley. Eventually British re-enforcements in troops and weapons arrived. Still they lost to the Boers, and yet more were called for until an army of 180,000 was assembled. Lords Roberts and Kitchener took over direction of the War, and eventually relieved Baden-Powell in Mafeking where he was probably practising knots.

The British then undertook a "scorched earth" policy, destroying thousands of Boer farms. They also used Concentration Camps, pretending at one stage that they were voluntary. There were about 120,000 prisoners in the camps and about a quarter of them, especially children, died through starvation, disease and cold. Gradually, the evidence emerged through Emily Hobhouse and Millicent Fawcett and later more natives were interned and suffered. The War cost some 75,000 lives, including 22,000 British soldiers. It was perceived in the wider world as a pitiless, inhumane war carried out as part of a world-wide push for colonial control by an aggressive militaristic regime.

In October, 1900, while it was still being fought, there was the "Khaki Election" surrounded by false language and dishonesty. In the Conservative Manifesto the Marquess of Salisbury said, "In due time those [South African] territories will doubtless enjoy the benignant colonial policy which this country has pursued for half a century, and whose brilliant fruit may be discerned in the affection that so many of our colonies have displayed to the mother country during the recent war." Concentration camps were studiously ignored. He added, "The brilliant success of Lord Roberts and his Army must not blind us to the fact that the war has disclosed imperfections in our own armour of defence which, but for it, might have remained unnoticed. It will be among the most urgent duties of Parliament and the Government, now that peace is apparently restored, to investigate and remove the defects our military system in the light of scientific progress and the experience of other Powers." This, of course, was coded language for saying that earlier battles had been lost and there had been a sudden need for lots of weapons. The Conservatives, boosted by jingoism, were returned with a larger majority. The War ended in May, 1902.

Behind the scenes, this was bonanza time for the British munitions companies. Vickers, especially, profited. It brought up factories and shipyards and both increased capacity and integrated its operations so that it could make arms from start to finish. Between 1898 and 1902 its issued capital rose by 246%.[54] It made an agreement with Nobel in July 1900 to supply explosives and ammunition cheaply and linked with Beardmore and Co. of Glasgow. It signed up for all the contracts it could and more and surged in output and profits beyond Armstrong. Suddenly, demand mushroomed and Vickers was intent on meeting the demand. Barrow's capacity was doubled. The Sheffield gun-shop could push out hundreds of pieces of artillery a year and Erith and Dartford pushed out vast quantities of weapons. Vickers produced 42% of the weapons bought by Britain in the War and became the dominant producer, a true mega-company in arms production.[55] The cost of the Boer War exceeded Treasury projections by twenty five times and amounted to £250 million, an enormous sum in those days.[56] A lot of this money went to the expanded munitions companies who looked for permanent levels of sales at these levels, especially for the new machine guns, and Britain had had a long practice run at war and the procurement of weapons a decade before the Great War was to happen. She was perceived as the most belligerent nation in Europe. The arms companies had orders and they wanted more.

**The Small Naval Recession.**

The story the rest of this chapter sets out is the one to which Lloyd George refers, normally called "the Dreadnaught Panic". The munitions people and especially the naval lobby created a national scare about the Germans, starting in 1906, which eventually dominated Parliament and the press by the summer of 1909 and fed into all the developments that followed. It was widely reported in Germany, and because Germans knew that the accusations being made were untrue and because they seemed to come from within the British Government and Navy, it undermined the possibility of trust between Britain and Germany. It also resulted in a more rapid expansion of the two fleets and a presumption that war would follow.

As we have seen, the rule of thumb was that the British navy should be bigger and better than the next two navies in the world, and this generated a big flow of naval orders from the time of Gladstone's demise onwards. However, naval strategy was also a matter of weighing dominance in different areas of the world, including the Far East, Suez and the Mediterranean. Here the British suddenly enjoyed some fortunate developments which helped their position considerably. In 1902 following the British naval yards' construction of a Japanese Navy which we have already described, the British and the Japanese concluded a Treaty. This offered Britain the chance of withdrawing from the Far East and its Chinese interests and concentrating its fleets closer to home. Within a couple of years this alliance offered another bonus, because the Russo-Japanese War of 1903-4 ended with the destruction of two of the three Russian fleets in the Far East. Since Russia was one of Britain's strongest potential naval rivals, the two navy standard was now easy to reach. Another change made things even better for Britain. The French Navy faced a number of set-backs which weakened it. The *Brennus* was damaged in a collision in 1900 and in turn sunk the *Framée,* shrinking the smaller French force. Other ships had faults and weaknesses, and another potential rival had disappeared. It is ironic that the two so-called threats that Gladstone was asked to respond to had disappeared a decade later. Suddenly the British Navy was overwhelmingly dominant with a surplus of ships. The Naval Budget could be cut.

As a result Naval Expenditure on new construction fell: 1903-4 £10.8m, 1904-5 £10.1m, 1905-6 £7.8m, 1906-7 £8.4m, 1907-8 £7.5m, 1908-9 £7.1m.[57] This reduction in demand, of over 30%, occurring as it did against a long rising trend, was a set-back for the naval yards. It was, of course, in tune with Campbell-Bannerman's thinking. The naval munitions companies did not like this naval recession one bit, and set to address it.

They did a number of things. First, they went gunning for Fisher and the Liberals who were pursuing this policy of limited battleship building. Fisher, of course, had earlier been a close ally of Armstrong and the other naval manufacturers, but now he was now less popular, as we explain below. Second, they began a concerted propaganda campaign to make sure through scares and publicity that warship building was cranked up. After all they had got rid of Gladstone, so a reversal of policy here should not be difficult. In Britain the Navy League had been formed in 1894 as a pressure group and public front for the battleship manufacturers. It was funded by them to push for a high budget for battleship building as more or less the first modern organized political lobby. It had publications, meetings, pressure group tactics and a big presence throughout the country to make the Navy popular. Everyone was encouraged to be strongly for the Navy, the source of Britain's pre-eminence and to make sure that we continued to rule the waves. (Incidentally, "Rule, Britannia! Britannia rule the waves: Britons never will be slaves" written in 1740 by James Thomson and set to music by Thomas Arne was always a bit hypocritical when Britain spent much of the next sixty years making slaves of millions in Africa, but the British never let a bit of hypocrisy get in the way of a good song.)

The Navy League's aim was to promote the building of yet more battleships; it was the pre-eminent pressure group requiring the loyalty of ministers and MPs, far ahead of all other lobbying organisations. The membership grew from about ten thousand shortly after its formation to a hundred thousand by 1914. Loyalty to the Navy could even sell cigarettes. Players and other companies featured Navy Cut cigarettes, featuring a sailor with "Hero" on his hat and HMS Britannia and Dreadnought in the background. The Navy League questioned candidates at elections to see whether they supported a strong navy and gave financial support to those candidates who did. Through it Armstrong, Vickers and the other firms were able to sway public discussion, political debate and present military spending as the only viable policy for Britain and the Empire. But they still had a small naval recession to cope with around 1905.

**Sir Jackie Fisher – First Sea Lord.**

The British Navy was now run by Sir Jackie Fisher as he had advanced to become First Sea Lord in October 1904. He had both an intimate knowledge of the naval manufacturers and knew what he wanted out of them. When he was appointed, he hit the ground running, modernizing and insisting on the best quality for his fleet, getting rid of a whole range of old and obsolete ships – 154 were scrapped including 17 battleships. He focussed on technological developments including torpedoes and submarines, artillery and turbines and introduced a level of collaboration with the naval munitions companies that was unprecedented. He knew their business from the inside, because of his time as Comptroller. This meant that he worked strongly with the naval companies, pushing technology and bargaining for the best ships. He was his own man, and not a soft touch for the naval manufacturers. With Fisher in charge the British navy improved vastly.

He wanted technological dominance, and identified it with a new class of battleships, the Dreadnought Class. The idea had partly started with the Japanese who laid down an all big gun dreadnought type ship, the Satsuma, equipped with 12 inch Armstrong guns and built at the Yokosuka Naval Arsenal five months before the first British Dreadnought was laid down on the slipway. Fisher moved to do something better. The building of the first Dreadnought by Armstrong was spectacular. It was begun in December, 1905 and completed in a year, an unprecedented speed of manufacture, and launched by King Edward on the 6th December, 1906. It was a fast, all big-gun battleship which was meant to be intimidating to the Germans and others. It raised the stakes, not least because popular claims were made that it alone could wipe out the whole German navy, obviously an idea that did not appeal to the Germans. Opinion on this move to Dreadnoughts was divided. In 1905 Britain had a fleet of 50 first class battleships, but this new class of ship seemed to make them obsolete. The Dreadnoughts were bigger and a few knots faster, but they did not turn out to be as decisive in the First World War as was earlier thought. The building of the Dreadnought increased tension with Germany and was seen as a kind of challenge. It also meant a slow-down in naval building while the new technologies were mastered. But the general opinion was and is that Fisher was doing what a First Sea Lord in that situation should do, if his navy was to remain dominant. We might add that this technological dominance proved more perceived than actual. The first Dreadnought failed to successfully attack any ship other than ramming an early submarine, and was sold for scrap for £44,000 in 1921. Probably its significance was over-rated, pumped up by the manufacturer - Armstrong.

The Dreadnought provided one irresistible tale that we must break off to tell. It occurred in 1910. Four members of the Bloomsbury Group including Duncan Grant and Virginia Woolf dressed up as Abyssinian princes, and were put on a special train from Paddington by "Cholmondley of the Foreign Office", really Horace de Vere Cole, the architect of the jape, to buy a battleship. They were welcomed by Admiral Sir William May, handed out visiting cards printed in Swahili and kept intoning the words "Bunga Bunga" whenever they were impressed by the Dreadnought's guns and fittings and because their Swahili was limited. They failed to purchase the battleship or to be recognized and sent a picture of themselves to the *Daily Mail,* bearded, turbanned and darkened, while everyone tut-tutted that such a thing could happen.[58] It showed that the arms manufacturers were happy to sell battleships to anyone.

All the commentaries focus on the Dreadnoughts, but this was not the key element in Fisher's strategy. He was for quality rather than quantity and looked at a lot of technical improvements, especially moving from coal to oil powered vessels. He understood naval obsolescence in an industry that had moved into perpetual technical innovation. He also knew the shipyards and knew that if they had guaranteed orders, he would not get the technical developments he wanted. He conveyed his position passionately in a letter to Churchill in 1912 when the latter had funding responsibilities for the Navy.

> THE GREAT SECRET IS TO PUT OFF TO THE VERY LAST HOUR THE SHIP (big or little) *that you mean to build* (or PERHAPS NOT BUILD HER AT ALL!). You see all your rivals plans fully developed, their vessels started beyond recall, and then in each individual answer to each such rival vessel you plunge with a design 50% better! Knowing that your rapid shipbuilding and command of money will enable you to have your vessel fit to fight as soon if not sooner than the rival vessel... so don't be a damned ass and deliberately lay down a ship which you know is obsolete. [59]

Fisher was driving for the very best navy Britain could have. He wanted twelve to sixteen inch guns and all of his warships to go over 30 knots and be driven by oil and not coal. He was the greatest naval professional in British history, reshaping every aspect of the fleet. The number of Dreadnoughts built by Britain fell from four in 1905 to three in 1906 and two in 1907 as Fisher carried out his policy. It was one which on its own would not provoke the Germans by pushing up the numbers of battleships, but it also did not make the shipyards happy. They were struggling for orders.

**Armstrong and Beresford against Fisher.**

There was another bit of the picture. In January, 1906 the Liberals formed the new Government after the election with Sir Henry Campbell Bannerman as Prime Minister. As we have seen, he was aware of the danger of a munitions build-up. His policy was to try to reduce naval expenditure and curtail the escalation of battleship building. For a while there was a strong attempt to curb the competitive building of battleships. During this period Churchill, a Liberal, describes himself as leaning "to the side of those who would restrain the froward both in foreign policy and armaments." [60] The deliberations in the Liberal Cabinet of the time were firm towards Germany, but not belligerent and there was a political attempt to moderate naval building. In Germany there were also many who were opposed to militarism. Campbell-Bannerman was Prime Minister until 6th April, 1908 and this policy lasted until he died and was replaced by Asquith. But, during this time, the munitions' people organized to make sure that their policies won. Like Undershaft, they were going to be in control.

They acted on a number of fronts. First they moved to get rid of Fisher. This was odd, because almost everyone acknowledged that he was an outstanding First Sea Lord, perhaps the greatest Britain has ever had. But he was not ordering battleships, and we know why. A whispering campaign started against him. The front man was Lord Charles Beresford who wanted to become First Sea Lord and criticized Fisher's moves whenever possible. Beresford was a Conservative MP and also an Admiral. He also happened to be chairman of an armament steel firm, Henry Andrew and Co and on the executive committee of the National Aerial Defence Association, the air version of the Navy League.[61] So, he was a front man for the munitions lobby. Also behind Beresford was George Elliot Armstrong with strong naval interests. In July 1906 with the new Liberal Government a 50% cut in the capital ship construction for the 1907-8 estimates was announced to Parliament. Fisher was happy with this, because he knew from reports that the building of the Dreadnought had made the Germans postpone their battleship building for eighteen months and rework the design and it would take them some time to do so. They also faced the need to widen the Kiel Canal to take the bigger ships that were now being built at the cost of £12 million, another cruel economic burden. So Fisher was happy to wait, knowing that the Kiel Canal problem was a real headache for von Tirpitz.

But Beresford was not happy. Armstrong's camp was gung ho for orders and Fisher, seemingly his man, was not coming up with the goods. He therefore set about constructing another power base that would deliver the required orders. The effect was astonishing. Beresford, the Navy League, the arms manufacturers and the popular press made an outcry about these cuts and began to attack Fisher. Suddenly Fisher, the great Sea Lord, was threatened and in fear of losing his job. His correspondence is full of puzzled awareness of the danger that Armstrong, Beresford and the others in the big naval spending camp posed to him, but he could not effectively counter their propaganda. Fisher's strategy left him open to the people who just wanted battleships turned out to keep the profits rolling. He was safe in this policy for a couple of years but then in March 1908 the position changed again. A new Navy Law increased Germany's battleship building programme by 25% over the next five years and this was an opportunity to arouse a clamour for more ships. Fisher was moving his policy anyway, and asked for the reinstatement of another battleship in the estimates in early 1908. Beresford made charges against the Admiralty in October, 1908 and even succeeded in getting Fisher subjected to an official inquiry, at which Fisher was exonerated. By this time, as we shall see below, the events to which Lloyd George made reference were underway, and another scare had guaranteed that naval building would pick up. Fisher, despite a sound building programme, was now being criticized, along with the Government, from another quarter. Eventually Armstrong got his way and Fisher was sufficiently undermined to be slowly forced out of his job as First Sea Lord. The munitions men got rid of him. The arms manufacturers wanted someone who was unequivocally on their side. There was some irony in the position of the person who had helped get rid of Gladstone himself being booted out by inferior men, but that is what happened.

**Background to the Dreadnought Panic – enter Mr Mulliner.**

Now we move to look at the other naval firms. Vickers and Armstrong, whom we have already met, were the strongest companies and the advances in technology associated with the Dreadnaught building programme lay with them. But the Dreadnought panic was created by quite a minor and desperate figure in the naval munitions business - Mr Herbert Hall Mulliner. He was an industrialist, involved in munitions since the Boer War, in partnership in the Wigley-Mulliner Engineering Co. which moved from Birmingham to Coventry around 1900. Three big shipyards, John Brown, Cammell Laird and Fairfield were also building warships, but needed a good artillery factory to build the great guns necessary to complete world class battleships. John Brown bought the Coventry Ordnance Works in 1904[62] and then set up an agreement with Cammell Laird and Fairfield Shipbuilding for joint production of naval guns at Coventry together with a big erecting department at Scotstoun. John Brown owned half, and the other two yards a quarter, of the Coventry firm.[63] The Coventry Ordnance Works were tooled up with big lathes and the other machine tools needed to make the biggest naval guns. This would enable these three yards to compete with Armstrong and Vickers in the full production of the most advanced battleships. However, it did not quite work out that way. With the Russian and French navies off the radar, the need for naval expansion slackened, and business was not so buoyant in the shipyards and ordnance factories. In fact John Brown, Cammell Laird and Fairfield received no orders for battleships or cruisers and the main plant at Coventry remained completely idle. The new Managing Director at the Coventry Ordnance Works was Mr Mulliner, who now becomes a chief actor in the drama.

Mr Mulliner faced an uphill task. He was dependent on John Brown, Cammell Laird and Fairfield getting orders and they were not receiving them. He would calculate that in a while these three companies would find a Managing Director doing no work a luxury they could not afford. We can sympathize with him as he twiddled his thumbs. But he did not stay twiddling his thumbs. Mr. Mulliner desperately needed some orders through 1905 and the beginning of 1906 and he set out to create them. In May, 1906 he wrote to the War Office and to the Admiralty. In his letter he said that there was an "enormous expenditure going on at Krupp's for the purpose of manufacturing very large naval guns and mountings quickly."[64] He estimated the investment figure at £3 million. He went on, "their whole scheme seems to be speed of production. For instance they are making immensely powerful lathes which will bore and turn a 12 inch gun simultaneously, which they estimate will save at least half the time. They seem to have ordered five machines for turning up the roller paths and turntables for very large mountings, each of these machines costing £5,300; there is nothing nearly so good in this country. These extensions etc. will give them a possibility of output far in excess of the whole capacity in Great Britain." Here was the letter of a desperate man. We note that Krupp, obsessively secretive since the time of Alfred, were not going to explain their technological developments to anybody, let alone Mulliner. We also note that German Dreadnaught production remained stubbornly slow right through and into the War. The speed was entirely imagined. This was clearly scare talk about a massive German Dreadnought fleet to drum up orders for the Coventry Ordnance Works.

Where did Mulliner's supposed information come from? It seems to be from one of his employees, Mr Carpmael. Consider, for example, the number of machines. Sir Reginald Bacon, Director of Naval Ordnance, was also approached by Mr Mulliner. His version reported to the Royal Commission in 1935 was: "Mr Mulliner came back from Coventry and told me that Krupp had got orders for – I think I am right in saying – four circular planes, particular machines with very big base dimensions."[65] So was it five or four? Also reporting later was Mr Carpmael in 1934 in a letter to the *Times* when the issue became controversial. He reported having gone to Krupp's works to see a large boring machine for machining gun turn-tables before purchasing it for the Coventry works. "I visited the works of the German firm, and saw parts of six machines in course of construction for Krupp's." So was it four, five or six? Since

Carpmael saw only the parts, some confusion might be understandable, but this had all the signs of a cobbled together story. Carpmael, no doubt under Mr Mulliner's instructions, also said: "Krupp's with these machines, and other machines to balance the output, could have turned out the armaments for more than six Dreadnoughts a year."[66]

Whether Mr Mulliner primed Mr Carpmael or however he constructed his scare story, we do not know, but the main question was whether it was true or not. First we consider the speed of construction, which Mr Mulliner expressed as the key to the process. Using Andrew Toppan's total list of German Dreadnoughts with their specification, the average time from laying down the keel to the warship becoming operational was *over three years* right through into the War. Given the original British Dreadnaught was built in a year and a day between 2nd October, 1905 and the 3rd October, 1906, German warship building remained very much slower and probably more thorough than the British. [67] We also know the very outcome of the ships Mulliner was talking about. Von Tirpitz in June 1906 felt compelled to ask for an increased budget in the Navy Bill to move to Dreadnought type, naval construction. The keels for four such ships were laid down in June to August 1907 and they were completed three years later, the earliest in May, 1910, and then not with turbine engines. Three years remained the time taken to build German battleships right up to the World War, and so there does not seem to be any increased speed of output or advanced planning for expansion in May 1906 when Mulliner wrote his letter. Further, we know that Krupp's workforce actually declined around this time. It was 64,353 on 1st January, 1907, had fallen to 63,171 on 1st January, 1909 and increased by 3,200 by the end of November in 1909.[68] The supposed expansion of work at Krupp's asserted by Mulliner did not happen during the period concerned, but only in late 1909.

Mulliner pestered the Admiralty, the War Office, the Imperial Committee of Defence and many others with his supposed information during 1906, but no-one would believe him. His claims were investigated by the Admiralty, a sophisticated and well-informed organization, and by a Cabinet Committee, but they did not find in 1906 any evidence of German expansion beyond what they knew about, as Lloyd George noted earlier. They had their own reliable informants and spies and knew Mulliner was being inaccurate in the hope of generating orders. He got nowhere. Meanwhile, in 1907 Cammell Laird, one of Mulliner's contributing firms, was charged with "irregularities" in their dealings with the Admiralty and the War Office and were struck off the list of Navy contractors until they reformed their management and working practices. The chairman and other directors resigned and Cammell Laird were making losses. Mulliner was in a very difficult position.

**The Kaiser Tries to Calm Things Down.**

The Kaiser visited England each year to sail at Cowes for a family re-union. He had had a good relationship with his grandmother Victoria and his cousins, King Edward and Tsar Nicholas. He spoke English without an accent and felt himself familiar with the English people, more than perhaps he was. When he sent a letter, he would expect to be understood and trusted. In February, 1908, there was constant political propaganda, agitating to secure higher Naval estimates and trying to raise a scare against the Germans. The naval groups used terms like "the German peril" and the "German challenge to British Naval Supremacy." Kaiser Bill wrote a letter to Lord Tweedmouth, First Lord of the Admiralty, addressing the so-called German challenge and trying to calm things down. He stated: "This phrase [the German challenge to British naval supremacy], if not repudiated or corrected, sown broadcast over the country and daily dinned into British ears, might in the end produce most deplorable results. I therefore deem it advisable, as Admiral of the Fleet, to lay some facts before you, to enable you to see clearly. It is absolutely nonsensical and untrue that the German Naval Bill is to provide a Navy meant as a challenge to British supremacy..." He explains that Britain should be free to have whatever Navy is needs for its world-wide Empire, the greatest trade of the world... whether it be sixty or ninety or a hundred battleships that would make no difference and certainly no change in the German Naval Bill. May the numbers be as you think fit, but people would be very thankful over here if at last Germany was left out of the discussion. For it is very galling to the Germans to see their country continually held up as the sole danger and menace to Britain by the whole press of the different contenting parties.." Thus far it was a good letter.

Then occurs a bit of imperious impatience, a nice put-down of Lord Esher who had been at the Board of Works looking after the Royal Palaces. "In the letter Lord Esher caused to be published a short time ago he wrote, 'that every German from the Emperor down to the last man, wished for the downfall of Lord Fisher'. Now I am at a loss to tell whether the supervision of the foundations and drains of the Royal Palaces is apt to qualify somebody for the judgment of naval affairs in general. As far as regards German affairs naval, the phrase is a piece of unmitigated balderdash..." The Kaiser had a certain style and was rightly attacking paranoia, and probably Lord Esher was better at drains, but he was not gaining friends. Wilhelm added that British naval supremacy would be unchallenged for generations to come.. The Kaiser's previous letter was leaked shortly after Colonel Repington, the *Times'* military correspondent, wrote an article "Under Which King?" claiming the Kaiser was trying to influence British military policy. Lord Esher was on every Imperial Defence Committee around and probably was not well-disposed to the Kaiser. The situation was even more complicated in that Colonel Charles à Court Repington, to give him his full name, had a running battle with Jackie Fisher and looked very much like the Kaiser..

The conclusions would probably be that the Kaiser was stating what was largely true, he was a bit too caustic, but that the Navy lobby was stirring up the German scare dramatically to get their orders for more ships. They knew how to see the Kaiser off with a bit more hate.

**The 1909 Dreadnaught Panic.**

By this time Mulliner was desperate. Between 1906-9 Cammell Laird, John Brown and Fairfield had no battleship or cruiser orders and Mr. Mulliner was the Managing Director of a vast new munitions factory which was completely idle. In early 1908 he tried again to increase the navy's spending. He approached the Admiralty, seeing Admirals Fisher, Jellicoe and Bacon, but they failed to respond, although there was a further German increase in naval spending announced in November. Fisher was still confident and biding his time. Yet now the Beresford camp was gunning for Fisher, hoping that the First Sea Lord would be replaced by Beresford himself. Mulliner went public with letters to *The Times* and with a series of visits to politicians. He set out to create a monumental scare, buoyed up by the increase in German armaments that had occurred eighteen months after his allegations, while pretending that he had been accurate all along and was acting in the national interest. In the Spring and Summer of 1909 there was storm of propaganda promoted by Mulliner and taken up by others. This time the exaggerations stuck. The opposition leader, A.J. Balfour, fed by an MP, Mr Samuel Roberts, who happened to be a Director of Cammell Laird, raised the alarm and demanded that eight Dreadnoughts be put on the blocks as soon as possible.

The newspapers were a big part of this scare. The *Daily Express* ran a serial about a possible German invasion of England, and a play about a German invasion of England was a great success in the West End. Soon, the *Daily Mail* was saying that the Germany can now turn out one Dreadnought *a month,* fully equipped and armed.[69] So we know the actual building time was three years, not the one month asserted in the *Daily Mail.* The *Mail* was claiming 2.8% of the actual time needed. It was 97.2% wrong – so much for its accuracy. It was the scare to end all scares. The Germans were coming and the famous demand for eight Dreadnoughts – "We want eight and we won't wait" was repeated like a mantra by the military backing press. The Government and everybody else capitulated and the eight Dreadnoughts were ordered.

We need to be aware of how these events must have appeared to the Germans at this time. We remember that Kaiser Wilhelm was Queen Victoria's grandson and quite warm towards Britain. He wanted a strong navy, but not one to rival Britain's and von Tirpitz saw a navy not in terms of conquest or invasion, but as helping maintain the balance of power and guaranteeing that Britain would not fight Germany. The Dreadnought launch had been a shock to the Germans, because it was completed in a year and also because there were statements in the English press that this one ship could wipe out the entire German navy. That made them touchy and worried about a possible first strike against their navy. It underlines why there was pressure for Dreadnought level German shipbuilding. But then the Mulliner naval scare was especially astonishing to the Germans because they did not know it was insinuated by Mulliner. From their point of view it was a British naval move, stirring up untrue statements about German naval building. Von Tirpitz conveyed how the British were coming over to them. "The Navy Scare, which Fisher now set going, offended in our opinion against good manners in international relations, because the Admiralty and many members of the Cabinet did not hesitate to stir up their country with exaggerated and false statements regarding our building programme.. In the Spring of 1909 Admiral Fisher even admitted quite frankly to our naval attaché that the Navy scare was nothing more than one of the usual manœuvres to prepare Parliament and the nation for the acceptance of bigger Naval estimates."[70] Actually, of course, Fisher was saying that the scare had been mounted *against* him by his opponents, but it was interpreted as a deliberate British Government and Navy lie.

The Kaiser and von Tirpitz were nonplussed by the situation. Here was misunderstanding which would help to start a World War. The Kaiser saw the notes of a meeting between Metternich, the German Ambassador, Sir Edward Grey and Lloyd George on the naval rivalry and added his private comments as follows: He describes England's "tendency to see phantoms"... Ship building "has not been speeded up" On naval rivalry: "Does not exist! Ours is limited by law." On British determination to preserve naval superiority: "They have it three times over already." A powerful German fleet: "Will never be powerful compared with England!" On slowing the tempo of German fleet building: "We have no fast tempo."[71] Those are the comments of a man who is not thinking of undertaking rivalry with the English fleet in July 1908. We will see why the date matters later. This was the point at which German trust of the British broke down, for obvious reasons.

Meanwhile in Britain the naval scare ran its course. Key was Arthur Balfour, the defeated Conservative Prime Minister and in this episode a small man. He predicted that "there is no doubt" that the Germans will have 13 Dreadnoughts by the 1st of April 1911. Actually, they did not have 13, but 5. This is even a bad throw on a darts board. He also said the probability was that on 1st of April, 1912, the Germans would have 21 or perhaps even 25. Actually, they had 9. The claims were wild and dangerous. At this stage the Admiralty fell in with the campaign. They claimed that 17 German Dreadnoughts in March 1912 were a possibility and 13 a certainty. Nine was the certainty. The British Naval League kept the campaign going until the Government fell in line. Churchill gives a laconic commentary on the process.

> In the end a curious and characteristic solution was reached. The admiralty had demanded six ships: the economists offered four: and we finally compromised on eight. However, five out of the eight were not ready before "the danger year" of 1912 had passed peacefully away.[72]

His further commentary on the episode was,

> The gloomy Admiralty anticipations were in no respect fulfilled in the year 1912. The British margin was found to be ample in that year. There were no secret Dreadnoughts, nor had Admiral Tirpitz made any untrue statement in respect of major construction.[73]

This was true, but when the panic really took hold the Government gave in and did expand its Dreadnought programme drastically so that even Cammell Laird got orders. The panic had succeeded, the Naval Lobby won, and it communicated to the Germans that the British could not be trusted.

There is a sequel to the history of Mr Mulliner. The Admiralty was so angry at the falsehoods he had stirred up that they made clear to the directors at the Coventry Ordnance Works that the company would get no orders until he left the works. Their tenders had been turned down in 1907 and 1908. As Mulliner himself said, "There seemed no alternative but for me to retire". He did, and the Coventry Ordnance Works and the parent shipyards then did get big orders from the Admiralty. Clearly, the Admiralty was determined that Mr Mulliner himself did not benefit at all by naval expansion. They must have been genuinely disgusted by his campaign.[74] Mr Mulliner pursued other business interests and became a connoisseur and collector of English furniture, writing *The Decorative Arts in England 1660-1780.*

This great scare was important, because it marks the point when German trust of Britain was destroyed and the possibility of a stable military situation was gone. Later, Churchill proposed a naval holiday when both sides just stopped building Dreadnoughts. It was a good idea and honestly meant, but it was too late. It was now impossible for Germany and England to agree because mistrust had been sown and was bearing its bitter fruit. There were no secret Dreadnoughts. So why were the British inventing them except to secure orders? The British Navy was going to be totally dominant for the foreseeable future. The scare weakened the diplomatic position of Count Paul Wolff Metternich (Ambassador to Britain who later strongly opposed the Armenian massacres) and the diplomatic descent into the First World War was in place with the politicians really defeated by the process. "We want eight and we won't wait" was British jingoism at its worst, manipulated by the arms dealers, who now, for real, were going to be the merchants of death.

**Scare in the Air.**

There is another strand to the scare business. We have noted that Beresford was on the executive committee of the National Aerial Defence Association who were beginning to build military aircraft. All the normal suspects were there – the Birmingham Small Arms Company, Cammell Laird, Vickers and others. "Beginning" is the word, for Bleriot was the first to cross the Channel in a small biplane on the 25th July, 1909. These organizations, too, needed a scare. The first opportunity was the possibility of airship attacks. At the time Count Zeppelin was trying to sell airships. One crashed in 1908, observed in Germany by Lloyd George, but people had worked out that the prevailing westerlies in Britain made it difficult to float them over to Britain; it was like swimming upstream. Shooting airships was also rather easier than getting grouse, so they were not really a threat. Nevertheless, a scare developed through the Press out of nothing. Any Norfolk or Suffolk man a bit tiddly on his bike who saw something strange was reported in the Press, and there were even sightings in Wales and surprise, surprise in New Zealand. One of these turned out to be lads putting a pumpkin with a candle in it on a pole at night.

It would be funny were it not also the case that Sir John Barlow, the Liberal MP for Frome, on the 19th May, 1909, asked the Minister for War about information on the 66,000 trained German soldiers who were hiding in England and the 50,000 Mauser rifles and 7.5 million cartridges hidden in London. They were, of course, hiding in his head. This was the stuff of scares and the National Aerial League fanned the flames. A second scare took place in 1913. The reality was a bit different. In the Great War a few Zeppelin raids took place. One, operating in strong winds and thinking that East Dereham, a nice sleepy town in Norfolk, was Hull in Yorkshire, dropped a bomb on the 8th September, 1915 near the White Lion Pub in Church Street to the astonishment of the regulars. "Oi'd jist ordered a pint, when that bugger splooded all oover Dereham, and oid payed frit." A few people were killed and injured, also in King's Lynn and Yarmouth, but it was not a national crisis. Shooting down large inflammable slow moving sausages was great fun for the early airline pilots, and Zeppelins became another obsolete military technology.[75] The scare was so much hot air, set up for orders.

**Reflection.**

The British arms manufacturers made sure they were fully occupied and expanding up to the First World War through lies, pressure and drumming up fear. The Naval Scare from 1906-8 was dishonest, mainly led by Mulliner, and contributed to German mistrust of Britain and intense naval rivalry. The Press fuelled distrust. The attack on Fisher was similar, merely to get more orders, but in fact generating an unwarranted fear of the German navy; actually the output of British warships was strong and resulted in an overwhelming dominance which kept German ships in port thoughout the War after Jutland. As a result of these scares war talk became normal. For example, in October 1908 the *National Review* published a report that the Kaiser had already drafted an excuse for a sudden, immanent attack on the British fleet.[76] Of course, he had not. Arms made people think about superior power. They made calculations and strategies of conflict. They prepared plans for fighting. Intense nationalism was encouraged by the Navy League, funded by the arms companies. Expenditure skewed towards militarism. The great budgets of Lloyd George addressing poverty and inequality were partly underfunded before and during the Great War. As well as the peace dividend, there is the arms penalty. It was welfare or warfare, not both, and the arms companies chose warfare. Time and time again, when the direction is set by weapons purchases, the outcome is war. The policy is led by arms manufacturers and sellers, even when, like Mulliner, they do not personally get what they want. British arms manufacturers contributed strongly to the origins of the Great War.

The arms trade, far from being passive, has shaped political history. The direction of this process is no less than wicked, though often it is careless wickedness. The arms firms were out for profits. They were not too concerned about how they got them or what the consequences of their operations were. It was probably not intended that their trade will end in filling war cemeteries and trenches with millions of bodies, but they did. Countless more were injured, and many soldiers later sat in shell-shock unable to express to their families the horrors of what they had seen. They were killed and injured by weapons intended to kill and to maim. The arms manufacturers were in the long run cadaver manufacturers. The correct conclusion is that they themselves needed eradicating, though without any harm to their persons, limbs or innards. Grey's maxim, "Great armaments lead to war" may contain different sordid details, but it was the definitive understanding of the Great War. In 1918 millions of people now understood this to be so.

# Chapter Eight: Krupp, Von Tirpitz and the Kaiser.

## Rethinking German militarism.

German ideological nationalism and militarism are usually understood in Britain to be behind the Great War. It is a view that suits us and allows us not to reflect on British militarism. But Germany was not really much different from ourselves. Germans, emerging into democracy, were also defeated by a similar munitions' led group of Krupp, the Kaiser and von Tirpitz. The problem, as in Britain, was the ability of the munitions' people to orchestrate and advance military policy against other groups which were more democratic and were challenging the world of Krupp. Prussia was, of course, militaristic, and the victory over France in 1870 led to the crowning of Wilhelm I at Versailles as German Emperor, but the new German nation moved on from this start. In 1900 it was becoming well educated, with outstanding advances in science, theology, technology, history, sociology, economics and the arts. It had a vibrant economy with a growth in manufacturing which was becoming the best in the world and attracted streams of immigrants looking for good work. Social Democracy and Christian social teaching were influencing politics and opening up democratic ways of seeing things and shaping institutions. It had no far flung empire and was concentrating on its own development.

We have looked at Krupp, but it was only one firm, and aside its relationship with the Kaiser and Von Tirpitz, was not widely liked. A new economic future was opening up for the German nation which did not involve militarism and war. Indeed, when we reflect that the two World Wars took out perhaps two decades of development, we can see just how strong German potential was. There were two possible directions of development – peaceful or militaristic – which would it be?

## German Naval Vested Interests.

Germany, for obvious reasons, was not a state with strong naval traditions. Its development is generally associated with Admiral von Tirpitz, who pushed for a strong German navy for twenty years before the actual War. He was responsible for a series of Fleet Laws laying down the expansion of the Navy planned through to 1920 which aimed to develop a world quality fleet. Kaiser Wilhelm was also keen on the idea, probably out of vanity and to impress his English and Russian cousins. He worked closely with von Tirpitz. As we have seen, both went to the Spithead Review of the Navy and probably got the idea there. The idea of developing a fleet was not straightforward, and many German leaders and the army were critical of it. Germany is largely landlocked apart from the Hamburg area and although it looked to acquire some colonies, the idea of expansion, of "lebensraum", was not really an issue before the First World War. Rather Germany was importing labour from all over the place to man her burgeoning industry. The rationale for the fleet was rather just to copy Britain. Its Baltic location somewhat limited its possibilities, especially in winter. Germany was classically more concerned with its army than its navy. But this changed under von Tirpitz's influence. He took up the post of State Secretary to the Navy in 1896-7, after Gladstone's prediction, and wanted to build a world class navy. It was not easy getting the budgets through the Bundestag, because of opposition from the Socialists and those who thought it was a waste, but von Tirpitz persevered. How many ships were to be built was laid down well beforehand and published for all the world to see, so that everyone knew what was happening.

The responsibility for the growth of the Navy is normally laid on von Tirpitz and the Kaiser, rather than the manufacturer, but actually the lead was taken by Krupp before von Tirpitz was on the scene. Only Krupp could build a German Navy and he it was who had the idea for one. He had developed and engineered the armoured steel for the hull and the guns. He was out on his own in terms of German naval production. He constructed the great Germania shipyard in Kiel, purchased in 1896 before von Tirpitz really got going. Already a decade or so before that, in order to build battleships, Krupp concentrated on developing what came to be known as Krupp armour, creating the world's biggest armour plate rolling mill, using nickel steel, for plating battleships. It was an outstanding success and in 1890 Krupp was producing this armour for Friedrich Hollman, von Tirpitz's predecessor, and it was obviously a technical breakthrough. Krupp absorbed another company, Gruson, and extended his naval competence further. It was he who pushed the possibility of building a navy, not Hollman, and he met with limited support from the older man as he got the new German Navy underway. When von Tirpitz arrived on the scene, Krupp had more support. He could deliver a world class navy, and von Tirpitz was more proactive. Actually relations between Krupp and von Tirpitz were sometimes quite prickly. That was partly because Krupp took profits of something like 50% on his armour plating; he was building battleships and dreadnoughts for money not love.[77] German battleships cost something like 30% more than British ones, and a lot of that money went to Krupp. Yet the Kaiser with his strong relationship both to Krupp and von Tirpitz, and his love of the Navy – he sailed at the Cowes Regatta in England each year – held this obsessive trinity together and Krupp knew that battleship building was good business.

In order to sell the navy publicly Krupp and von Tirpitz used the tool which had been developed in Britain. The German Navy League, the Flottenverein, formed in 1898 went further than its British namesake. It grew to a million or so members, with publications, local groups, meetings and lectures. It even tried to raise funds in the United States. It every way possible it kept pressure on the politicians to make the German Navy strong. The crescendo of propaganda put out by the Flottenverein and other similar organizations lay behind the ability of von Tirpitz and Krupp to expand the navy against considerable democratic opposition. Krupp owned the Berlin newspapers the *Neueste Nachrichten* and the *Post,* and they pumped out pro-armament disinformation. He ran a propaganda machine. One Sunday in February 1898 he gave a lunch for 250 people – mostly the Ministers, aristocracy and members of Parliament – the food and decorations were lavish, and they were entertained by actors, Tyrolean singers, black minstrels and an Italian concert party.[78] All the decisions makers were going to have plenty of butter with their guns. Any rumour or silly statement could be brought into the arena. So an article in the *English Saturday Review* in 1897 which said that if Germany were "swept away tomorrow, every Englishman would be the richer" and ended with the words, "Germania delenda est" - Germany must be destroyed. It was given maximum coverage to back the expansion of the German fleet. Of course, there were other silly English people saying anti-German things, and their importance was puffed up to provide propaganda against the British Navy. As in Britain a German invasion had been invented, so the spectre of a British invasion was raised in plays, the media, speeches and pamphlets by those who wanted to increase military expenditure, and it was successful, most of the time.[79] Thus, the influence of von Tirpitz was present, but he was preceded and outdone by Krupp who supplied the equipment, technology, the propaganda machine and the shipyards.

**Inside Von Tirpitz's Head.**

It sometimes helps to get inside other people's heads and see things their way. Von Tirpitz in his Memoirs conveys his attitude to the British, true after it had hardened by the war, but it is interesting to hear it. Here is one seeming rant:

> You Anglo-Saxons, on the other hand, enslave the peoples, body and soul. See, ye peoples of the earth, how many of you have already sunk more or less to the helpless conditions of vassals, and how much greater the danger will be in the years to come. Thus we are fighting for the freedom of the world against the strangling tyranny of the Anglo-Saxons.
>
> You Anglo-Saxons call us militarists and autocrats, whilst amongst yourselves you have established for the maintenance of your own fighting spirit the most absolute dictatorship that history has known.[80]

His point was that the British had been subjugating people's around the globe with Maxim guns to mow down the natives and establish their Empire. Concentration camps in the Boer War and acquiring colonial servants on a large scale could be seen as less benign than we usually manage in our exculpatory arrogance.

It would have been good if we had not given Von Tirpitz the raw materials for his rant, but unfortunately the Anglo-Saxons have a history of "Land of Hope and Gory". They looked to the Mother of the Free, but supervised slavery and servitude on a large scale even into the twentieth century. The Grand Admiral has a point, even as he obsessed about his Navy.

**The Kaiser and the Krupp Family.**

The relationship between Krupp and the Kaiser Wilhelm II was crucial to German militarism. It was a close one, although intimacy between two such stiff men was largely shared salutes. Wilhelm regularly attended the Krupp works, saw the weapons manufacture and was given elaborate pageants which were a bit like Wagner's operas. He was constantly assured of Fritz Krupp's devoted service to the All-Highest, as Wilhelm was routinely known. This relationship, largely outside the Democratic processes of German politics, allowed Wilhelm to continue his autocratic way. His power base was the military, and the military's success was down to Krupp. The relationship became even more interdependent in the twentieth century.

Krupp was now run by Friedrich Krupp, or Fritz as he was known, who succeeded his father, Alfred in 1887. Alfred had indoctrinated him in the ways of munitions, requiring him to read all his father's voluminous notes on the business of making weapons. He continued to develop the firm and expand its operations. He had a seat in the Reichstag from 1893-8 to represent Krupp's interests, but did not go down well in debates. The firm flourished. From 1887 to 1899 the number of employees increased from 13,000 to 25,000 and the scientific and technological competence of the Essen operation grew enormously. It was close to being the biggest firm in the world. Then, after decades of obsessive work Fritz began to relax. However, his holidays on the island of Capri were not quite normal. He entertained a lot of young men and boys in homosexual parties which soon became talked about in Italy and beyond, especially his relationship to Adolfo Schiano, an 18 year old barber and musician. This activity was illegal under German law and when the fairly lurid news of it got out into the press, raised by the German Socialists, the Krupp Empire was in crisis. Fritz hid himself away and his wife, Margarethe, appealed to the Kaiser in some distress to sort things out, and she was promptly locked up in a lunatic asylum, though she was as sanity itself. At this point on 22nd November, 1902, Fritz died, probably by suicide, and the Krupp empire, always a family firm, was in complete crisis. The Kaiser worked hard to support the family and die Firma Krupp, labelling the homosexual orgies as "false accusations" and insisting that everyone accepted his account of the situation though he knew it to be untrue. Krupp must be saved at all costs.

Margarethe, now removed from the asylum, and still as sane as ever, took over running the firm, Krupp. She did this with some wisdom and humanity, but for a number of years expansion was off the agenda. But this was not good enough for the Kaiser. Clearly, die Firma Krupp had to be run by a man. In the next generation Bertha Krupp was next in line to succeed to the family business, and she was a woman. Wilhelm, no feminist, directly intervened and solved this problem by marrying her off. He found an obsessive minor bureaucrat who could run the Krupp enterprise and effectively arranged the marriage. Gustav von Bolen and Halbach was married to Bertha on 15th October, 1906, and Gustav slowly took up the reins of Krupp, and produced six sons to secure the succession, which also took up time. There was therefore a bit of a lull in the growth of die Firma Krupp during the period of the Mulliner Scare, again showing the inaccuracy of Mulliner's prognostications. In the end Bertha's only contribution to the munitions' industry was to give her name to a big cannon. Thus Kaiser Wilhelm nurtured the Krupp family through this crisis in a very personal way, but he, too, knew that he needed Krupp as much as they needed him; it was *his* company in the face of a lot of democratic opposition…

**Tolstoy and Kaiser Wilhelm.**

The links between Krupp munitions, the military and the Kaiser are easy to show, but it is worth at this stage taking a more distant view of the conception of military power which the Kaiser had developed. We listen to Leo Tolstoy, recognized as the world's greatest novelist, who looked at the Kaiser after he had rethought his earlier partial glorification of war in *War and Peace*. He exposed him and held him to ridicule in the early 1890s nailing the underlying attitudes of militarism. Tolstoy had come to see clearly the structure of militarism and autocracy. It involved the use of violence to secure wealth and control over the labour of others, and he lambasted the German ruler as an example of this way of seeing things. Tolstoy was writing in 1893, twenty years before the Great War, but he sees with absolute clarity the inner direction of this ideology. He addresses a situation where the Kaiser is giving a speech to a company of new recruits and identifies the way in which soldiers must obey unconditionally and even become ready to move to murder when they are given orders. "All manifest a readiness to kill their brothers and even their fathers, at the order of the first misguided man who wears a red and gold livery, asking only when and whom they are to be ordered to kill..." Soldiers must sell their souls by being ready to murder when their commanders see fit. It is an attitude we now pass over in silence, but Tolstoy will not be silent. It is, of course, best to tell the event in Tolstoy's words.

> "The German Emperor has recently explained with minute precision the character and vocation of a soldier, having distinguished, thanked and rewarded a private for killing a defenseless prisoner who attempted to escape. In thanking and rewarding a man for an act which is looked upon even by men of the lowest type of morality as base and cowardly, Wilhelm pointed out that the principal duty of a soldier and one most highly prized by the authorities, is that of an executioner, - not like the professional executioners who put to death condemned prisoners only, but an

executioner of the innocent men whom his superiors order him to kill.

Yet more. In 1891, this same Wilhelm, the *infant terrible* of State authority, who expresses what other men only venture to think, in a talk with certain soldiers, uttered publicly the following words, which were repeated the next day in thousands of papers: -

> 'Recruits!.. You have taken the oath of allegiance to *me*; this means, children of my guards, that you are now *my* soldiers, that you have given yourselves up to me, body and soul.
>
> 'But one enemy exists for you – *my* enemy. With the present socialistic intrigues *it may happen that I shall command you to shoot your own relatives, you brothers, even your parents* (from which may God preserve us!), *and then you are in duty bound to obey my orders unhesitatingly'*

This man expresses what is known, but carefully concealed by all wise rulers. He says outright that the men who serve in the army serve him and his advantage, and should be ready for that purpose to kill their brothers and fathers.

Roughly but distinctly he lays bare all the horror of the crime for which men who become soldiers prepare themselves, - all that abyss of self-abasement into which they fling themselves when they promise obedience. Like a bold hypotizer, he tests the depth of the slumber; he applies red-hot iron to the sleeper's body; it smokes and shrivels, but the sleeper does not awaken.

Poor, sick, miserable man, intoxicated with power, who by these words, insults all that is sacred to men of modern civilization! And we, Christians, liberals, men of culture, so far from feeling indignant, at this insult, pass it over in silence."[81]

Tolstoy probably did not later take a holiday in Berlin, but the point is clear. The "poor, sick, miserable man", Kaiser Wilhelm, was embedded in militarism, and given sufficient perceived threat from "Great" Britain, his default mode would be to override the views of others and require unquestioning loyalty. The links between militarism and autocracy in the person of the Kaiser were deep; Tolstoy had the Kaiser's soul on his pen. But Germany was bigger than the Kaiser.

**The Democratic Opposition.**

Those exerting military pressure did not have things all their own way in Germany. There were peace movements which we examine later and a solid democratic opposition to military expansionism. The Social Democrats, especially Karl Liebknecht and Rosa Luxembourg amounted to a strong, principled opposition to naval militarism. Liebknecht wrote a book *Militarism and Antimilitarism,* which led to him being arrested in 1907 and imprisoned for 18 months, illustrating the title. In 1908 he was magnificently elected to the Prussian Parliament, although still in prison. But, apart from this radical opposition, a wider democratic weight was against naval expansion. Krupp had been quite strongly criticized since the 1890s, and especially at the time of the homosexual scandal and Fritz's death. Between 1907 and 1912, the crucial period we have been examining, the Social Democrats, firmly critical of the military, moved to being the biggest party in the Reichstag with 110 seats. Many opposed the sheer cost of military expenditure. There was also strong criticism of the naval lobby on the understanding that Germany did not need a navy and this was just a wasted expenditure, given other possible uses of the money. Perhaps we need to re-evaluate the weight of this anti-militaristic sentiment in Germany. It was far stronger than is usually allowed, and the militaristic group was on the defensive under attack from the Social Democrats and some other democratic groups.

This opposition comes out clearly in the Zabern affair. Zabern, or Saverne, was a town in Alsace Lorraine with strong

Social Democrat and French sympathies. In response to some local military bullying the townspeople protested, and there were two courts martial on soldiers who had behaved badly. Then a Lieutenant von Forstner, a nasty piece of work, had an altercation with a lame shoemaker and cut him down with his sword. It created an outburst of abhorrance throughout Germany and he was court martialled, but then acquitted for supposedly acting in "self defence." It was an obvious whitewash and there was a further national uproar and a debate in the Reichstag on 4-6th December, 1913 against the Chancellor, with heavy criticism of Emperor Wilhelm as well. A vote of censure was passed by an overwhelming majority of 293 to 54, and an attempt was made to vote down the Chancellor's salary and thus put him out of office, but it was defeated. To have a vote like this against the military faction and the Kaiser in 1913 just before the outbreak of the Great War shows how strong the democratic opposition to militarism was. It showed the Kaiser and the military party what a rough ride they were likely to face in future normal democratic politics. A war and appeal to patriotism was much easier.[82] When the arms manufacturers and the military are under attack, then they are at their most dangerous.

**Militarism and the German High Command.**

Even when we focus on the military, they are not necessarily militaristic. People who may die in battle tend not to embrace it with open arms, although as "Oh what a lovely War!" conveyed to us, the generals and strategists who make decisions about wars usually will not be at the front or fear for their life. Still, the military may not be propelling a nation towards war, especially when they know their comrades will die in droves. Nor are soldiers filled with animosity towards their potential adversaries.

One interesting example is Franz von Papen, who was later to become German Chancellor. It is trivial, but shows the extent to which these people did not seem to think about or expect war. Before the Great War von Papen was part of the elite Army General Staff, which would lead the attack after 1914. In his autobiography he waxes lyrical about his visit to Britain in 1904 to have some

English hunting after reading Whyte-Melville's "wonderful books on riding in England, particularly his *Market Harborough*" No passports were needed. He visited his friend, Campbell, who lived in Windsor and marvellously enjoyed hunting with the Shire packs in the Queen's, Quorn, Belvoir, Pytchley and Mr Fernie's hunts. Von Papen adds,

> I paid another short visit to England in November, 1913, just before I left Germany for Washington. This time I had been asked by the Kaiser's Master of the Horse, Count Westfalen, to accompany him in search of some stud horses. We were invited to ride with Lord Annaly's pack and I remember being impressed by a wonderful grey. When we asked its owner whether the horse could be bought for the Kaiser, his answer was: "Not even for the King of England, sir!"

It is clear that Franz von Papan, enjoying dinners at London clubs, had no hint of personal animosity towards the English and enjoyed his English hunting a few months before the Great War. Similarly, Von Papen's wife in a happy marriage was from a French family and he had French in-laws and was deeply internationalist. The imperative to war was not with him a matter of personal antipathy or ethnic hatred. [83] Of course, the High Command was instrumental in the final decision-making, after the Kaiser's blank cheque to Austro-Hungary, but the explanation of avid anti-Britishness again bears re-examination.

**The Kaiser and Going to War.**

The political build-up to the Great War has been pored over for a century, and especially the Kaiser's contribution to it. He was an autocratic German military figure as head of the armed forces, but as Lloyd George has already implied even the Kaiser was ambiguous. He was intimately linked to the British royal family. His mother was Queen Victoria's daughter, Vicky; he loved his grandmother and the Isle of Wight and see-sawed in his militarism. He was hardly a warmonger. As Barbara Morgan notes, "Twice Moltke broke down in tears of frustration before he was able to finally convince the Kaiser to give the order for mobilization."[84] The German Imperial War Council on the 8th December, 1912 with the Kaiser, von Tirpitz, Admiral von Müller, General von Moltke, Admiral von Heeringen and General von Lyncker was obviously a strategic meeting, but it was probably one to delay the possibility of war until the widening of the Kiel canal was complete in 1914. The Kaiser was to fight his cousins, Tsar Nicholas and George V with deep regret. They were all good chums, swapping uniforms and linking up regularly. He had repeatedly tried for peace. On the 14th February, 1908 he wrote to Lord Tweedmouth trying his best to convey that the German Naval Bill was no menace to British naval supremacy.

In view of what we know about the Dreadnought scare, it is easy to understand the Kaiser's position in his later interview with the *Daily Telegraph* on 28th October, 1908, when he famously said the English were "mad, mad as March hares". He thought the suspicion roused in Britain in the "We want eight and we won't wait" campaign was entirely misplaced. It was mad to think like that. He was an avid friend of Britain, close to his "revered grandmother", Victoria, and keen to avoid other countries ganging up on Britain during the Boer War and even prepared to give advice to the British military on how to conduct the Boer War! He was trying to stem the popular antipathy in both Britain and Germany. Gradually, this position as Britain's friend, undoubtedly genuinely meant in 1908, was eroded by the breakdown of trust and the weakening of his own position in Germany. Wilhelm felt intimate with the English, as he sailed and hunted with his English relatives, but trust was decaying. He was going to face the assassination of Archduke Ferdinand, heir to another imperial throne in the Austro-Hungarian Empire, and his links with the British had been tried.

**The Serbian-Skoda Arms Deal and the Pig War.**

The immediate origins of the War occurred in Serbia. There, too, arms sales directly drove the route towards conflict. The shooting at Sarajevo of Archduke Ferdinand of Austro-Hungary receives all the publicity, but it was another arms dispute that really drove the conflict between Austro-Hungary and Serbia. At its centre was Skoda, another of the really big munitions companies, primarily supplying the Austro-Hungarian Empire. Its main factory was at Pilsen, south west of Prague. It was taken over by Emil Skoda in 1869 and fashioned into a large steel and weapons unit, strongly supported and promoted by the Austro-Hungarian State, especially the Royal family. It was making weapons for an empire and was in the top league along with Vickers, Armstrong, Schneider and Krupp. In the decade before the First World War, Serbia was under considerable pressure from Austro-Hungary to buy Skoda field and mountain guns. Skoda wanted this sale in what was effectively their back yard and set out to get the order, using diplomatic pressure from the Austro-Hungarian State. In May 1903 the king of Serbia, Alexander Obrenovich and his wife were assassinated by a group of junior army officers, and replaced by King Peter I. This was supposed to be linked in some murky way with the Skoda arms deal which was on the point of being made. But the deal did not happen. The king was murdered and Skoda did not get the deal. As Grant points out in his study *Rulers, guns and money*, "Indeed, Skoda's fortune was so tightly bound up with the fate of the king that Trappen [Skoda's General Director] was the last civilian to speak with the king before the king's murder." [85] Probably, the new armed junta was worried that Serbia was becoming too dependent on Austro-Hungarian arms, broke the link and repudiated the order. If you rely on your potential enemy to supply your weapons, you are sunk; anyone can see that. "More shells? Sorry, we are out of stock just now, while our guns are shooting at you. Try us again next year."

When this set back occurred the negotiations for the big order of cannon became more and more tense. The Serbians said the French Schneider 75mm guns or Krupp's cannon were better, but they were also more expensive, and Skoda produced outstanding weapons, especially its large howitzers. In a convoluted pattern of negotiations, Schneider-Le Creusot, Krupp and Skoda and most of the banks of Europe prepared to provide a loan which took a couple of years to bargain. Skoda was now worried; if they did not get the deal, the big boys of western Europe would dominate their local market and they therefore were determined that "their" Government would negotiate hard, which they did. As a result the so-called "Pig War" of 1906-9 broke out. It started out as a customs embargo by Austro-Hungary because they did not like a French proposal to sell arms. They suggested bank loans to pay for their Schneider guns could be repaid by the large-scale export of Serbian pigs. The French got pork and the Serbians got guns. In retaliation the Austrians closed their borders to Serbian pork and tried to bring Serbia into line. Up to that time, selling pork to Austrians was Serbia's major export. The economy suffered badly from the embargo, but then other countries, notably Germany, discovered that they very much liked pork, especially at low prices, and began importing pigs in large quantities. As a result the embargo did not work; for a while Germany and Austro-Hungary had different interests. The Serbians would not give in, and eventually recruited Russia as an ally against Austro-Hungary. The forming of this alliance was almost a practice run for the First World War, when Russia was supporting Serbia against Austro-Hungary. Other munitions tensions were present. For example, Mausers and 50,000 rifle barrels were ordered from the Austrian arms firm, Stehr. But in 1908 in the Pig War, Austro-Hungary suspended delivery of the last 15,000 rifle barrels.[86] If Austro-Hungary used their muscle at this point, they could do so again .

Eventually the "Pig War" merged into the Bosnian Crisis involving Bosnia-Herzegovena and Bulgarian independence, which was even more tense, and by this time the Serbians were adamantly opposed to buying Skoda weapons. This confrontation around weapons' purchase was thus a major contributor to the tension between the two countries directly involved in the outbreak of the Great War. In the build-up to the assassination in 1914 and Austro-Hungary's reaction, Skoda's pressure to sell arms was crucial.[87]

**The High Command's Military Strategy.**

Then, as everyone knows, the assassination took place. It offered the opportunity to Austro-Hungary to attack its troublesome neighbour, Serbia, and it looked to Germany for support so that it did not have outside trouble from Russia or anyone else. The Habsburg Empire claimed it was not seeking territory, and probably the conflict was the result of this long stand-off on arms. The Kaiser was asked for his support, and on the $6^{th}$ July, the Kaiser sent the fateful telegraph through Bethman-Hollweg with the famous last paragraph.

> Finally, as far as concerns Serbia, His Majesty, of course, cannot interfere in the dispute now going on between Austria-Hungary and that country, as it is a matter not within his competence. The Emperor Francis Joseph may, however, rest assured that His Majesty will faithfully stand by Austria-Hungary, as is required by the obligations of his alliance and of his ancient friendship.

The "blank cheque" to Austro-Hungary became the event which turned the handle to open the door to a European War. Even this is understandable given the Kaiser's sympathy with the Austro-Hungarian Emperor Franz-Joseph and the assassination of his son. After all, Emperors must stick together. Wilhelm was an unfortunate individual, locked into the militaristic world of admirals and generals and autocracy from which Germany was departing and he succumbed to an understandable personal loyalty. Yet, this decision was backed by the German High Command, in particular the Minister for War, Erich von Falkenhayn and others who were consulted. In this sense the German High Command wished the conflict to be carried out, initially by Austro-Hungary, but with any necessary German support. They also were willing to fight Russia because they were aware that Russia was unprepared, and might not want to fight at the time. They were the ones who said "Yes" to war.

But this decision needs further analysis. What kind of decision was it? It was not carried out for territory or gain. Rather the underlying German rationale was military strategy and fear. No-one put it better than Lloyd George when trying to calm some British jingoism.

> Look at the position of Germany. Her army is to her what our navy is to us – her sole defence against invasion. She has not got a two power standard. She may have a stronger Army than France, than Russia, than Italy, than Austria, but she is between two great Powers who, in combination, could pour in a vastly greater number of troops than she has. Don't forget that when you wonder why Germany is frightened at alliances and understandings and some sorts of mysterious workings which appear in the Press and hints in "the Times" and "Daily Mail"...Here is Germany in the middle of Europe, with France and Russia on either side, and with a combination of armies greater than hers. Suppose we had a possible combination which would lay us open to invasion – suppose Germany and France, or Germany and Austria, had fleets which, in combination, would be stronger than ours. Would we not be frightened, would we not build, would we not arm? Of course we should. I want our friends, who think that because Germany is a little frightened she really means mischief to us, to remember that she is frightened for a reason which would frighten us in the same circumstances.[88]

Lloyd George's empathy, along with European disarmament, would have prevented the Great War. By 1914 German military strategy had to take into account the possibility of attacks from France and Russia. France was the old enemy known to be re-arming on quite a scale. More than that the Russian Empire had a population of some 170 million compared with Germany's of less than 70 million. As Russia industrialised and armed with the help of both France and Britain, year by year it became a bigger threat to Germany. So the strategy was laid out. Better a war earlier than later. Germany should have the advantage of surprise, because in the long term she had to fight on two fronts, and the Schlieffen Plan whereby she struck in the west before Russia could mobilize in the east were all well understood as the basic German strategy. The obvious point is that these exigencies are all military calculations based on the *possibility* of going to war, but they predisposed the

German High Command towards *initiating* a war. This was merely the outworking of ways of thinking among those who had bought into militarism and war and learned to think in its terms. They had power to precipitate policy for the tens of millions who died and were injured and the hundreds of millions who suffered. That is the warning.

**The Outcome: Austro-Hungary Declares War against Serbia.**

The result of these tensions occurred in July 1914. By this time the Austro-Hungarian military, was led by Count Franz Conrad von Hözendorf, Chief of the General Staff of the Austro-Hungarian Army. He instituted a pattern of intense bullying of Serbia. General Vladimir Giesl, the Austro-Hungarian Minister in Serbia presented the fateful ultimatum at 6pm on July 23rd, 1914, an hour later than the 5pm which was originally intended. Either Serbia would accept or Austro-Hungary would go to war. The 6pm time was because at the later hour the French fleet would have sailed from Kronstadt, and Russia and France would miss the opportunity of immediately arranging co-operative naval action. Thus the military agenda framed even this momentous political event. The ultimatum was presented, demanding a 48 hour, unreserved acceptance to humiliating conditions. Everyone was shocked by the terms of the ultimatum. Pasitch, the Serbian Premier, replied with an answer as conciliatory as he could make it. "We have accepted all that we possibly could. For the rest, we rely on the chivalrous honour of an Austrian general – yourself – with whom we have always been content." Pasitch had hidden his wife and secretary, Von Stork, behind some curtains as witnesses of this fateful conversation. The Serbians had only demurred from allowing Austrian "police", which was code for the Austrian army, from operating freely in Serbia, effectively agreeing to a military take-over, which obviously they could not accept. With these words the ultimatum was taken as rejected and Austro-Hungary went to war, pushed by their own, and the German, military, led by von Moltke.[89] The French fleet sailed on, but the chain whereby other States – Germany, Russia, France, Britain, Italy, the United States and most of the other countries of the world - be drawn into the war was already forged. With Skoda's role in Austro-Hungary and the region, the explosion of the First World War was detonated. This should never have been.

It was worse than this. When Austro-Hungary went to war against Serbia it encountered strong resistance and it engaged in atrocities which are beyond mentioning. The Serbs were treated as "Untermenschen", faced firing squads and were mown down. Archibald Reiss, a Swiss academic criminologist, set about uncovering and recording these events and they were followed by later Nazi brutality. So a whole nation was brutalized beyond our imagination following the declaration of war in 1914, and the effects of that process have come down into later wars and even to the present.

**Calling the Tune and Humming it.**

Austro-Hungary was only one arena. There were similar military pressures in France, Russia, Austro-Hungary and Britain which detonated wars or the possibility of war. Britain undertook the Second Boer War without justification, merely to get colonies full of gold and diamonds. The way it fought that war, with concentration camps and scorched earth policies suggested it was a most aggressive and callous colonial power. The people of the Netherlands were so disgusted with the British conduct of the Boer War that they remained neutral in 1914. Britain demanded a naval supremacy in relation to Germany and everyone else which was self-serving. It armed as fast as all the other nations and armed other nations. We have seen how the Dreadnought Panic must have further conveyed it could not be trusted. All of this implies Britain might have contributed more to causing the war than some recent historians have suggested.

Yet the problem is with the underlying cast of this thinking, looking to the nation which was to blame, whether it was Austro-Hungary, Serbia, Germany, Russia, France or Britain. In all of these countries there was an escalating commitment to buying weapons and expanding the military. It had been going on for three decades, fed by the military promises made by the great munitions' companies – "buy our products and you will win". Sooner or later there was pressure to use these arms, and the pressure was building, especially in the eight years before the 28th July, 1914. Throughout Europe, Armstrong, Vickers, Krupp, Thyssen, Schneider, Nobel-Bofors, Skoda, BSA and many other companies had been producing arms and selling them strongly. They had conveyed that there was a purpose in selling them, and gradually a distrustful armed Europe could not, even by diplomacy, prevent that purpose from coming into effect. They had generated four arms races – the British German naval race and the confrontations between the French-German armies, the German-Russian forces and the Russian, Austro-Hungarian, Turkish and Serbian forces. All of these were bristling with ever more weapons avidly supplied by the weapons merchants. It only needed a spark to ignite these mountains of firepower and the logic of armament would be fulfilled. Tragically, at Sarajevo that happened. The unlimited supply and use of weapons was underway, and the soldiers were to die in their millions.

In 1905 George Bernard Shaw suggested Undershaft, the arms manufacturer, was calling the tune; by 1912-14 most people were humming it from memory. "Great armaments lead to war."

## Chapter Nine: The Attempts for Peace.

**The Peace Movements.**

History is often written by the winners. The peace movements lost their war already in 1914, not 1918, and they tend to have been ignored. They were strongly pulling against the great military trend we have examined, but were dragged along the ground in this tug of war. Yet, perhaps, the losers teach us more. The movements for peace were principled and careful. They were learning and feeling their way. Most of all, they were correct; peace is infinitely better than war.

However, these groups failed. This chapter remains a study in defeat, because, in part, these groups were ineffectual, too late, not savvy about the munitions lobby and impotent in the face of the control of the popular media, especially tabloid newspapers. The peace people were honest and even outstanding people, but their awareness, ability to confront, to create political weight and work for disarmament was not up to the task. This inadequacy was not for want of trying, patience and prayer. They were outplayed and sidelined by the militarists, whose tactics even including paying thugs to break up meetings violently. They lost to weak arguments parroted to success by shallow men; it is sad to conclude that often false assertions win over sound conclusions in the modern media culture. They were also constantly forced onto the back foot by charges of being unpatriotic. It is clear that to prevent and defeat the First World War, surely the greatest victory of all, the peace movements would have had to do something different. As we have seen, the understanding of Prime Ministers Gladstone in 1893 or Campbell Bannerman in 1906 had also not been enough.

But the peace people were surely right. They worked out what was required by the rule of international law, procedures for disarmament, and saw through the militarist agenda. They recognized the weaknesses of imperialism – now, one hundred years later, acknowledged world-wide - and they uncovered the inner strength of peace, of loving the enemy until enmity disappears. They were, and are, the true roots of an international world, and deserved to be studied more than all the fighters and generals and admirals.

There is one other thing about these movements. They can easily be delayed and sidelined. The real enemies - the militarists - distract from the fact that weapons kill and generate wars; they don't play by the same rules, but win behind the scenes. These peace movements worked for decades, but they could not mobilize in 1914. A more coherent peace movement did emerge in the 1930s, but then also it was too late. It peaked after Hitler had come to power, when the opportunity for disarmament had already passed. So we are looking at a failure which has continued a century. Peace movements have to grow and succeed well before crises are imminent.

**The Great Christian Anabaptist Tradition.**

People of peace in the Anabaptist tradition had lived without conflict and refused weaponry or fighting since the time of the Reformation. These people looked at the teaching of Jesus and formed their position on a number of principles. First, they were going to love their enemies and refuse to fight them. Second, they were to be peacemakers, actively setting out to generate peace and reconciliation between people. Third, they refused to be soldiers or to support the State in any actions of warfare. Fourth, they agreed to follow Christ and to reject the State's demands of absolute loyalty, especially in war. Fifth, they believed in the equality of all people created by God and their God-given right to life, irrespective of money or power. These were amazing moves in a normal warring, nationalistic culture in the 16$^{th}$ and 17$^{th}$ centuries, The Quakers, Mennonites and other Anabaptists at the time of the Reformation set out to create and sustain communities of peace capable of confronting the State and its aggression. In these Christian communities, co-operation and sharing were accepted as the basis to living without conflict.

Because they were a threat to the system, they were persecuted and attacked. There is some irony in people of peace being attacked and killed because they are people of peace, and it points up the vindictiveness of aggression, but it also mirrors the treatment of Christ. If someone is systematically for peace, you have got to kill them. When peaceful and truthful people - a deep threat to those with weapons - were attacked, they still maintained that theirs was a better way. George Fox was one such, as he explains. "Justice Bennet sent the constables to press me for a soldier, seeing I would not accept of a command. I told them I was brought off from outward wars. They came down again to give me press-money but I would take none. . . . After a while at night the constables fetched me up again and brought me before the Commissioners, and they said I should go for a soldier, but I told them that I was dead to it. They said I was alive. I told them, "Where envy and hatred are, there is confusion." They offered me money twice, but I would not take it. Then they were wroth, and I was committed close prisoner without bail or main prize."[90] What a man! A trail of men stuck in the nose of the powerful, and they were often imprisoned, yet they were going to obey God's way of peace rather than the presumed power of the State. Even after the Restoration and wide persecution, this way grew in influence throughout Protestant Europe. Mennonites, Swiss Brethren, German Brethren and others were persecuted and moved particularly from the Netherlands through Prussia to Russia and Moravia. Smaller Anabaptist groups remained in the Netherlands, Britain and Italy.

These people of peace also moved to the States - William Penn for example. Sometime, you should visit the Quaker Chapel he attended in Jordans, Chalfont St Giles, Buckinghamshire, where he is also buried; it conveys beautifully how these quiet people met with God. Penn's move to America was not on a mission of conquest. He refused to fight the American Indians and set up the state of Pennsylvania without conflict, making the way for other principled Anabaptist peaceful communities in other States. They disavowed holding, using or manufacturing weapons, and refused to enter military service. The Amish, Mennonite and other pacifist groups formed strong communities in the mid-western States and have become the backbone of modern American pacifism.

Community was a way of life for these people. They built houses together, shared resources, ignored most of the vanities of consumerism and became rich in one another. They valued one another far more than they value things. Their way of life has remained. We remember driving through one of the Amish otherwise car-less areas at about eleven o'clock at night with our children asleep in the back of the car. Surprisingly, the roads were thronged with horses and buggies as families returned from their evening visiting. While most of our contemporary neighbourhoods are full of silent houses where computers and television claim the social space, these were communities in which everyone visited and chatted. Similarly, as guests near Paris, at a gathering of Mennonite communities, we became aware of another small aspect of their community life. When someone wanted to speak to the full gathering, they would quietly raise a hand, rather than shout or clap. The raised hand would be noticed and copied until everyone was quiet and the person could share what they wanted to say with easy audibility. These ways of peace are a relief from the organized barbarity depicted in much of this narrative.

Later peace movements grew from a recognition of the horrors of warfare; some began after the Napoleonic wars. Gradually, they formed coherent movements, especially in the mid-19th century. In 1889 a Peace Conference of all the American nations took place. A key American figure in non-violent resistance was Adin Balou (1803-1890). Also in 1889, the Inter-Parliamentary Union, the fore-runner of the League of Nations, was set up by William Kramer and Frédéric Passy. Passy described the problem vividly. "We are being ruined to enable us to take part in the senseless wars of the future, or to pay the debts left us by the criminal and insane wars and contests of the past. We shall perish with hunger to have success in murder."[91] Those two sentences have not dated. Other key figures established the Universal Peace Conferences which met almost annually until the start of the Second World War. They included Count Komarovsky, Enrico Ferri, Charles Booth, Sir Wilfred Lawson, the Abbé Defourny, Signor Moneta – many key figures who talked eminent sense. Here, indeed, was a substantial international movement which saw the futility of war and militarism.

**Leo Tolstoy**

Perhaps the most important voice for peace came from Leo Tolstoy. Earlier in his life he wrote *War and Peace* based on his experiences in the Crimean War, but set further back in the Napoleonic Wars. It is often described as the world's greatest novel, but Tolstoy effectively repudiated it as too accommodating to war, after he was converted to a fuller view of Christianity. It is interesting how dismissive Tolstoy is of it in *My Confession.*

> In this way fifteen years passed... I continued all the time to write. I had experienced the seductions of authorship, the temptations of an enormous pecuniary reward and of great applause for valueless work, and gave myself up to it as a means of improving my pecuniary position, and of stifling in my soul all questions regarding my own life and life in general.[92]

After some intellectual and scientific rethinking, Tolstoy came to the teachings of Christ and became a Christian espousing especially Christ's teaching on peace and its principial and practical consequences. From henceforth his new perspective can be described as *Peace Not War*. In his book, *The Kingdom of God is within You* he addresses the changes of heart and outlook required by following Christ, accepting the Law of Love for the whole of life and towards everybody. He critically examines the process of militarism, routing it from the field. He profusely uses the arguments of others, quoting Passy: "The heads of governments emphatically affirm that they desire peace, and eagerly emulate each other in their pacific utterances, but almost immediately thereafter they purpose to their legislative assemblies measures for increasing armaments..." "There is military slavery, and it is the worst of all slaveries... it forges chains for the necks of free and strong men to use them as instruments of murder, to make them executioners and butchers of human flesh..." Strong images indeed.

He exposes the shallow arrogance of militarism confident in its right to kill people.

Tolstoy turns the tables. "When people talk of cannibals we smile contemptuously with a sense of superiority to such savages. But who are the true savages?" Tolstoy supplies the answer for all who cannot work it out.

> "Today, with all our wisdom, civilization, with the advancement of science, the degree of philosophy to which the human spirit has attained, we have schools where the art of murder, of aiming with deadly accuracy and killing large numbers of men at a distance, is actually taught, killing poor, harmless devils who have families to support, killing them without even the pretext of law..."
>
> "If it be criminal to kill one man, the killing of numbers cannot be regarded in the light of extenuation; that if it is shameful to steal, it cannot be glorious to lead an invading army."
>
> "Then war comes on the scene, and in six months all the results of twenty years of patient labour and of human genius are gone forever, crushed by victorious generals." "We have seen war. We have seen men maddened; returned to the condition of the brutes, we have seen them kill in wanton sport, out of terror, or for mere bravado and show..."
>
> "Has not the inventor of the wheelbarrow, by the simple and practical contrivance of a wheel and a couple of boards accomplished more than the inventors of modern war?"

And so it goes on - laying out the futility and destruction and waste of militarism as the dead body of a madman is laid out.[93]

Organised murder is always wrong, and Tolstoy tells it as it is. Yet, he does not stop there. He looks at Christianity as it is understood and practiced. His immediate focus is the Russian Orthodox Church, and he questions the compromise and hypocrisy in its leadership and the way ritual and quasi-miracles are practiced in a corruption of the Christian faith. Has the Church itself not been compromised into supporting militarism, even through accepting bribes? Pithily he says, "The disparity between ecclesiastical creeds and the doctrine of Christ is so great that a special effort is required to keep mankind in ignorance." Crucial, for Tolstoy is Christ's teaching against fighting in the Sermon on the Mount which he sees as an absolutely clear repudiation of the way of violence, even when evil has been done.

> "Ye have heard how it is said, an eye for an eye: a tooth for a tooth.
>
> But I say to you, that ye withstand not wrong. But if a man give thee a blow on thy right cheek, turn to him the other.
>
> And if any man will sue thee at the law, and take thy coat from thee, let him have thy cloak also.
>
> And whosoever will compel thee to go a mile, go with him twain.
>
> Give to him that asketh: and from him that would borrow turn not away.
>
> Ye have heard how it is said: thou shalt love thine neighbour, and hate thine enemy.
>
> But I say unto you, love your enemies. Bless them that curse you. Do good to them that hate you. Pray for them which do you wrong, and persecute you,
>
> That ye may be the children of your heavenly Father: for he maketh his sun to arise, on the evil, and on the good, and sendeth his rain on the just and unjust."

Tolstoy deeply understood these words. He pointed out: You cannot love people and kill them. It's difficult to get round that one. This call of Christ's was not just to individuals, but reflected the global purposes of the Kingdom of God. Tolstoy sees it as the way of sanity for humankind, as opposed to the madness that would have fifteen million people in arms and use up half of government expenditure in pointless military maneouvres.

Clearly, this perspective diminished his popularity somewhat with the Russian Orthodox Church. They excommunicated him. The Tsar and the Russian establishment must have seen the truth of what he said, and resented the challenge to their armed dominance. But it was hard to exercise power over somewhere who cared not a whit for Fabergé, the aristocracy, coaches and horses, stately homes or tradition, but preferred peasants, ploughing, talking to pilgrims and walking. Tolstoy gained some of his own inspiration from a pacifist group of Russian Christians called Doukhobors, who had links back into the Anabaptist movement and migrant Prussian Mennonites. They lived, causing no trouble to anybody, yet Tsar Nicholas was determined to conscript them into the armed forces. In Easter 1895 60-70 Doukhobors serving as soldiers threw down their guns and refused to fight because they were Christians. They were fiercely punished, but a couple of months later 7,500 Doukhobors gathered all their guns and burned them in three great piles of weapons singing hymns as the weapons blazed and melted. It must have been one of the great parties of all time and could start a trend even now – gun burning celebrations – bring them on. Tolstoy was much affected by these peasant people. They were punished and imprisoned in Siberia. Many died, but eventually Tsar Nicholas allowed the rest of them to emigrate, if they raised their own passage.

Many surviving Doukhobors finally went to Canada. Tolstoy's son Sergey went with 2,000 of them on their passage, because Tolstoy and others paid for them. The Old Man worked himself to exhaustion writing his novel *Resurrection* in 1898, coughing and haemorrhaging with tuberculosis, but the book was done, the royalties came in and paid the passage of the Doukhobors,[94] along with contributions from Quakers and other groups. It is not surprising that what may *really* be the world's greatest novel should have had such a motive as its impetus. Tolstoy's peace vision moved out from his home at Yasnaya Polyana around the world. At the end of his life he exchanged letters with a young Indian man, Mohandas Karamchand Gandhi, discussing peaceful non-resistance. Gandhi absorbed Tolstoy's pacifism, and bargained with Jan Smuts for a proper status for Indian South Africans, and then later for the end to Indian colonialism. And so the ripples widened.

The reverberations of these events, the peace conferences and Tolstoy's writings spread around Europe and beyond, showing the kind of movement which was underway. The Universal Peace Congresses became practically annual events throughout Europe and beyond, gaining impetus in the urgent bid for world-wide peace.

**The 1890 London Peace Congress Conclusions.**

Tolstoy looked at the 1890 Congress in *The Kingdom of God is within You,* where he reviewed the representatives of the peace movements and expounded their position, adding his own perspectives and relating it to the teachings of Christ. He recounted the principles espoused in the 1890 London Peace Congress. Already by this time the contributors had worked out in some detail what needed to be in place for peace to succeed and the Congress adopted the following proposals:

1. The brotherhood of nations requires all nations' interests to be acknowledged as of identical value.
2. The teaching of Christ on peace and goodwill should be taught in all churches and beyond, especially on the third Sunday in December.
3. History teaching should call the attention of the young to the evils of war and how it has usually been waged for inadequate causes.
4. Militarism is to be excluded from schools.
5. Aboriginal and weaker races should be guarded from injustice, fraud, and seizure of their territories, liberty and property under the principle of the universal rights of man.
6. Warlike prejudices and propaganda should be removed from national politics.
7. There should be an international unification of weights, measures, trade and science.
8. In view of the vast moral and social influence of women, women should form societies for the promotion of international peace.
9. European nations should settle trade and poverty issues in relation to disarmament.

10. A general disarmament is the best guarantee of peace. A Congress of Representatives of all the States of Europe should work out a gradual general disarmament which already seems feasible.
11. It looks to particular nations to take a lead.
12. Peace societies should work to get electors only to support candidates who back Peace, Disarmament and Arbitration.
13. Arbitration should be obligatory in all international controversies, following the example of the International American Conference.

These proposals show the kind of full bodied programme that was already part of the peace movement. All of these principles are coherent and sensible and could work incisively for us today. The people involved in this movement were more strongly for peace than the politicians, but the politicians did feel the power of the movement, especially with Tolstoy's impetus. Tolstoy was merciless in his arguments, pointing to the hollowness of power.

> The attractions of power and all it brings, - riches, honours, luxury, - seem to men really worth struggling for only until they are won, for no sooner does a man hold them within his grasp than they manifest their own emptiness and gradually lose their charm, like clouds lovely and picturesque in outline seen from afar, but no sooner is one enveloped in them than all their beauty vanishes.

He also points out that the scum rises to the top. Many of our problems are our leaders.

> Having learned by experience, sometimes in one generation, sometimes in several, how utterly worthless are the fruits of violence, men abandon these vices acquired by the passion for riches and power, and growing more humane, they lose their positions, being crowded out by others who are less Christian and more wicked; whereupon they fall back into a stratum, which though lower in the social scale, is higher in that of morality, thus increasing the mean level of Christian consciousness. But straightway, the

worse, the rougher, and less Christian elements rise to the surface...[95]

As Tolstoy exposed the hypocrisies of the ruling classes and the Orthodox Church in the name of ordinary Christian teaching, there was increased pressure on them to do something about it. Tolstoy lived his talk, rejecting high society, looking after peasants, ploughing their land, and living a simple life. Here was a man who spent as much effort writing an *ABC* for schoolchildren to learn to read and write as he did on *Anna Karenina,* and who set up the school at Yasnaya Polyana so that peasant kids could have a decent education. The Tsar was under enough moral pressure to allow thousands of Doukhobors to move from prison in Siberia to Canada, and initiate the first world-wide peace conference. The pacifist/disarmament cause was on the move.

**The 1899 Hague Peace Conference.**

The Hague Peace conference met for a couple of months in the summer of the last year of the nineteenth century and involved twenty six states. Delegates included the Emperors of Germany, Austria, China, Russia and the Ottomans, the kings of the Belgians, Denmark, Serbia, Siam, Sweden, Norway, Spain, Portugal, Roumania, Greece and Italy, Queen Victoria and the French and American Presidents or their plenipotentiaries. It established most of the conventions of fighting wars which are observed until this day – proper treatment of prisoners of war, prohibition of pillage, not to attack undefended cities, field hospitals and hospital ships, the white flag, not to kill undefended people and so on. It also set up the principle of not resorting to force and arbitration as a way of settling disputes, and famously established the international Court of the Hague for this purpose. It also tried to eliminate unhumane ways of killing through poisons, expanding or dum dum bullets and aerial bombing (or bombing from balloons as it was quaintly called then). The simple recognition that weapons were inhumane had its foot in the door.

But the establishments of Europe could not change so quickly. The poison gas prohibition was broken in the Great War; countries, especially Germany continued to work on it, even though they had signed to disavow its use. Justifying the practice of hypocrisy is one of the regular skills of the militarists. It can always be covered by the white sheet of national security. Most of the delegates signed the Peace declaration, some with qualifications, but already the military people and arms manufacturers confused any outcome in terms of real disarmament. The people who did not want disarmament were there at the Congress, slowing initiatives and making sure it did not work. The British were a bit reticent about peace. They were gearing up to fight the Second Boer War in October, 1899, when they would annex Transvaal and the Orange Free State and eventually set up concentration camps, so they were unco-operative about peace getting in the way of colonial expansion. The British naval delegate was Jackie Fisher, and he conveyed that the British were for peace, but they also wanted a navy which was twice as strong as anyone else's. Fisher was a Christian, and one wonders what fissures went through his soul as he worked against peace with gentle people of goodwill. The munitions companies were already savvy enough to sabotage peace and make sure that no actual proposals to give up arms manufacturing were passed. Sadly, bombing was not stopped before it really got started, as it could have been at this conference.

Nevertheless, it was an acknowledgement by the "great powers", as they were called, that the way of peace might be the one to follow. It had enough weight to be seen as the first of many, and a second conference was called for 1904 by President Theodore Roosevelt. However, the Russo-Japanese war intervened, engineered in a literal sense by British munitions, and it did not take place then. That War ended with a Peace Agreement supervised by Theodore Roosevelt. There was also a tacit agreement between the United States and Japan that Japan could control Korea while the US ran the Philippines, where the United States had been fighting for a number of years to "pacify" the Philippines, hardly democracy at work. Roosevelt was awarded the Nobel Peace Prize for his pains. Meanwhile, a lot of preparatory work was undertaken for the real peace conference which did not take place until 1907.

**The 1907 Peace Conference.**

The postponed second Peace Conference took place over a four month period in the Summer of 1907 and it had a much more ambitious agenda of actual disarmament. This time 44 states attended, and the main initiator was Teddy Roosevelt. Really, Roosevelt was like the god Janus on peace; he was facing two ways, since he was mainly engaged in a variety of quasi-colonial military enterprises in the Americas. Nevertheless, the Conference had a strong agenda focussing on sorting out quarrels through international arbitration, a good method if it is given a firm framework of international sanctions. Some disputes go way beyond their significance and being forced to hear the other side is no bad idea. The Convention went on with a lot of good work, defining the declaration of war, terms of engagement, neutrality and the position of merchant ships. Key figures at the Conference were Fyodor Martins, a Russian international lawyer, Ruy Barbosa of Brazil and Donald James Mackay heading the British delegation. It also worked at prohibiting unanchored mines, which could become a permanent hazard to shipping and ruled out the naval bombardment of undefended cities and coastlands. It is easy to forget the fact that these two conferences set standards for pursuing war which prevented it becoming even more barbaric than it has been.

Yet the real focus of the Conference was on trying to get delegates to reduce their military budgets, and especially their naval budgets. And here the pattern was already set. Sir Edward Grey was willing to negotiate along with the United Kingdom Cabinet similarly in a limited kind of way, though the pressure from Mulliner and the other arms companies against it was considerable. In the end it was the German unwillingness to have any constraints on *their* naval expansion, given the size of the British navy, which left the Conference without any disarmament results. It became a silly, "if you've got it, we want it" mentality. Or there was another argument. As members of the German delegation said, "If we disarmed what would happen to Krupp's workers?" The answer was that they could work at useful things like railways, cars, cargo boats, bridges, steel frame buildings and all the other things that high quality German engineers have since done. By this time von Tirpitz was established with the Kaiser and with power enough to avoid controls on his Budget. Thus, the last real opportunity, and it was a big opportunity, for disarming the major nations before the Great War and moving nations towards peace and prosperity passed and ended in failure, seven years before Sarajevo.

**The British Peace Movement.**

Behind these developments were national movements of peace before the First World War. Many were Christian. In Britain, during the Napoleonic Wars the Friends of Peace produced Peace Petitions in 1807-8 and inveighed against war profiteering.[96] Later the "nonconformist conscience" was a general voice for peace and influenced Liberal thinking after the 1906 election. Missionaries opposed imperial control and aggression more than is usually reported. But the influence of British Christians, especially Anglicans, at this time was disappointing. They were preoccupied with an emphasis on personal holiness, the Welsh revival, millennialist thinking, denominational rivalry and fundamentalist movements and had no concerted ability to be peacemakers. The weakness of this position is well conveyed by a Baptist recruit to the army writing very honestly in November, 1914 about his compromised position.

> "I was once, alas! a peaceful civilian…schooled in the old Liberal belief that war was impossible, that to launch a Dreadnaught was as absurd as throwing £2 million into the sea. As a Nonconformist I stood for independence and freedom. How many times from public platforms have I exhorted the working classes to regard every German as a brother? Now I am paying for it all. The bugle has sounded, and after a few months under a canvas I emerge a disappointed Liberal, and with no feelings of brotherhood against the Kaiser. However, I am still a strong Baptist!"[97]

The incoherence of this letter from a man who was probably to lose his life to the war is heart-wrenching. At the same time, many Anglicans were unthinking imperial nationalists with the moral backbone of a worm with diarrhoea, and so a coherent Christian witness for peace did not arise. For many the Anglican Church after the Great War was imaged in bishops blessing battleships, hardly a systematic stand for peace.

A key British figure was Keir Hardie, a Scottish politician of great integrity and founder of the Labour Party when it was struggling and small. It had grown among working people while the privileged played tennis and, as a result, millions of socialists and trade union members had a thoughtful distrust of capitalism and a belief in their own political status over against the moneyed elites who had presumed to boss them about for most of their lives. Here was a body of independence and Hardie was its leader. Hardie's own experience of the Boer War taught him what warfare and militarism was really like, and he also understood the power structures of the military establishment. He was a Christian, strongly committed to the peaceful ways of Christ as the direction for his politics. Time after time he proclaimed the wrongness of militarism and war and was frequently vilified for so doing, as he faced attacks from the establishment. Those other Labour politicians who really stood for peace were targeted; they included Ramsey MacDonald, Philip Snowden, Charles Trevelyan, Arthur Ponsonby and Noel Buxton. The munitions men, aided by the media whom they either employed or courted, stirred up the unthinking masses to see conscientious objection as treason and make hatred of the enemy required. And those who do not hate were further hated, just as Jesus was hated for not hating the Romans.

Hardie faced this kind of opposition. He organized collaboration among international socialists and led a Coalition against War with Jaurès of France, Haase of Germany and others. Jean Jaurès was assassinated, shot in the head sitting in a café next to his workplace on the 31st July, 1914, as he tried to organize an international strike against the war, an idea which might just have succeeded in Paris, St Petersburg, Berlin, Vienna and London, and might be useful yet. His murderer wanted the War to go ahead, and got his way. When he was brought to trial in 1919 the murderer was acquitted though obviously guilty and Jaurès' wife had to pay costs. The Socialist International, even though it mobilized a lot of support, failed to prevent the popular march towards war. Hardie found himself shouted down, hooted at and abused by crowds even in his own constituency, so much so that he commented to a friend shortly before his death, "I understand what Christ suffered in Gethsemane as well as any man living." He died in 1915, but his reputation did not.[98] He has represented the integrity of the Labour Party ever since. Other conscientious objectors stood against the war, wearing the taint of being traitors or unwilling to fight. Yet, by the end of the war with millions of dead and injured the rest of the population understood what Hardie and the conchies had been fighting against. Other Labour Party pacifists included George "bleeding heart" Lansbury, another Christian. As editor of the *Daily Herald* he opposed the war, supported pacifists and was charged with sedition and imprisoned. Fenner Brockway, who knew his Reformation radicals, was another imprisoned leader of the time. But they were beaten by the dominant jingoism.

When the War came and conscription was required, some 6,000 people became conscientious objectors, or "conchies". One thousand five hundred were imprisoned and 69 died of ill-treatment there.[99] They were often subjected to degrading treatment, and some went mad. Others served in the Quaker ambulance brigade. A No-Conscription Fellowship was formed mainly made up of Quakers and members of the Independent Labour Party who stated why they had made their choice. The men who signed the main leaflet were Clifford Allen, Edward Grubb, Fenner Brockway, WJ Chamberlain, W.H. Ayles, Morgan Jones, Barratt Brown, John Fletcher, CH Norman and the Rev. Leyton Richards. Other public figures argued against war including Bertrand Russell, Philip Snowden, Maude Royden, Rev. John Clifford and Duncan Grant. They, too, had seen through the appeal of dying for one's country when one's country had helped precipitate an horrific unnecessary conflict. They were defeated, except the truth of events continued to speak for them.

**European Peace movements.**

Apart from Tolstoy and the pacifist movement which he created throughout Europe and beyond, there were other contributors to peace. In France, interestingly, British Quakers, trying to heal the wounds of the Napoleonic wars were significant. Joseph Tregelles Price founded a group called *Le Société des amis de la morale Chrétienne* in 1821 and Priscilla Peckover precipitated the *Association de la Paix par le Droit* (APD) an important group. Later Frédéric Passy saw the possibility of peaceful internationalism and was a great figure. Victor Hugo had a similar vision. Léon Bourgeois and Baron Paul Henri d'Estornelles de Constant, who represented France at the 1899 Hague Conference both received Nobel Peace Prizes.[100] The French socialist movement led by Jaurès was also strongly against war, but they were up against the Anti Dreyfusards who became the leaders of militarism in France.

In Germany, the founder of the Peace movement was Alfred Fried (1864-1921). He helped set up the journal, *Die Waffen nieder!* (Drop your arms!) and set up the German Peace Society in 1892 which was the main focus of peace activity. He also championed Esperanto as a linguistic means of bringing the nations together. He was awarded the Nobel Peace Prize in 1911 and fought comprehensively against the First World War. There were all kinds of initiative. A Lutheran, Siegmund-Schultze at a Christian pacifist conference in Germany met a British Quaker, Henry Hodgkin, and the two of them covenanted in the face of imminent war that "We are one in Christ and can never be at war." The Fellowship of Reconciliation continued to bind German and British pacifists for peace and against war. Alongside the peace movements in Germany and Austria there were other influences within the traditional parties. The Catholic Centre Party was antagonistic towards militarism, but was gradually worn down by accusations that it was not patriotic enough.[101] The Marxist wing of the Social Democrats, led by Karl Liebknecht and Rosa Luxemburg also opposed the war with growing democratic support. By 1913 they were dominating much legislation and had over 13,000 members on regional, municipal and district councils. It was clear that the establishment of the Kaiser and Krupp would soon have to give way to this growth of democratic socialism, but they held out until the war occurred. So, these movements and groups were defeated by the process of war, but not without a struggle.

**A Reflection on Nobel: Peace and Bombing?**

We have mentioned Nobel peace prizes, but Alfred Nobel (1833-96) contained in his person the inconsistencies ambivalence towards war and peace that we are looking at. He sought to go north and south. His father, Immanuel, was an engineer and sold weapons. For a while Alfred was quite interested in poetry, but his father wanted him to be a chemical engineer, and he travelled and linking up with an Italian who had developed nitro-gycerine. It was far more explosive than gunpowder, but unstable. His father went bankrupt and Alfred worked on obsessively until he developed a safe, usable form of nitro-gycerine. During this process an explosion occurred which killed his brother and some other people; nitro-glycerine was clearly more dangerous than poetry. The City Council sent him out of Stockholm for his experiments, lest he do any more damage, and he eventually achieved stable nitro-glycerine (before you ignite it). The result came to be called dynamite and became crucial to military developments, like detonators, bombs and shells, as well as quarrying and road-building. It can be useful, but it depends on where you sell and use it. The big money was in weapons. It was a crucial breakthrough for heavily-damaging warfare.

Countess Bertha Kinsky, later Bertha von Suttner, was his housekeeper, an important friend and strongly critical of the arms race. She talked and corresponded with him a great deal, half converting him from militarism, and wrote a book *Lay Down Arms*, which contributed to the peace movement. Nobel himself was torn between his military inventions and peace. On the one hand he created an explosives empire and on the other he included in his will provision for the Nobel Peace prizes. Von Suttner was one of the people awarded a Peace Prize. Yet, Nobel-Bofors became dominant munitions manufacturers for many countries of Europe and the supplier to all sides of explosives sowing thousands of deaths in the Great War. Alfred Nobel died before the War, but any sober estimate has to conclude that his legacy through bombing outweighed a few peace prizes. Nobel's conscience, or failure of conscience, did not die with him, but carried on in new manifestations of his problem.

**Peace Movements in the United States.**

In the States there were various long-standing pacifist groups including Mennonites, Quakers, Amish and others. There were also important black traditions objecting to war and militarism. A key overall organization was the American Peace Society, especially strong in the 1890s and led by Robert Treat Paine and Dr Benjamin Trueblood. There was also the American Union Against Militarism. The Women's International League for Peace and Freedom showed another dimension of this movement, and Jane Addams, its founder, was awarded the Nobel Peace prize in 1931. The AUAM leaders were Crystal Eastman, Max Eastman, Oswald Villard and Paul Kellogg. They had some significant magazines and journals, and issued a statement of principles, "Towards a Peace That Shall Last." They had some spine to them. But they could not prevent the entry of the United States into the Great War. When J.P.Morgan and Bethlehem Steel and Du Pont pushed towards war, these groups were shouldered aside.

When war came they were also vilified. Especially noteworthy was the attack made on them by President Wilson, not normally seen as a hawk. He identified the entire peace movement with treason and called then agents and dupes of the Imperial German Government. Given he had moved from being the president who was going to keep America out of the War to the one who led them into it, this stridency probably reflected his own conscience. That has to be a good sign. An Espionage Act was passed in June 1917 allowing any literature which might embarrass or hamper the Government in conducting the war to be confiscated. It was a World War One McCarthyite era. It seems the United States for a hundred years has been incapable of handling moral objections to war except by calling them "Communist", reflecting a slight intellectual poverty. A Committee on Public Information controlled the media. Any magazines or newspapers that gave space to the anti-militarists were closed down. They were forbidden to say that the war was wrong, or that the Government is the tool of Wall Street or the munitions makers. Now why would they say that? There were declarations that traitors should be hung from lamp-posts and scores of black people were beaten, lynched, burned and drowned in East St. Louis.[102] Jane Addams was followed by secret agents and otherwise victimized, but walked peace.

**Pope Benedict XV and the Christmas Truce.**

Pope Benedict was elected on the 3rd September, 1914, a month after the Great War hostilities had begun. On the 1st November, 1914 he issued an encyclical, *Ad Beatissimi Apostolorum,* appealing for peace. He described the situation:

> The combatants are the greatest and wealthiest nations of the earth; what wonder, then, if, well provided with the most awful weapons modern military science has devised, they strive to destroy one another with refinements of horror. There is no limit to the measure of ruin and of slaughter; day by day the earth is drenched with newly-shed blood, and is covered with the bodies of the wounded and of the slain. Who would imagine as we see them thus filled with hatred of one another, that they are all of one common stock, all of the same nature, all members of the same human society? Who would recognize brothers, whose Father is in Heaven? Yet, while with numberless troops the furious battle is engaged, the sad cohorts of war, sorrow and distress swoop down upon every city and every home; day by day the mighty number of widows and orphans increases, and with the interruption of communications, trade is at a standstill; agriculture is abandoned; the arts are reduced to inactivity; the wealthy are in difficulties; the poor are reduced to abject misery; all are in distress.

This description is important. The militarists want to win wars; this describes the defeat that war truly is. He reiterates from Christian teaching that the Kingdom of Peace is founded on brotherly love with a sense of the bodily unity of humankind in creation and in relation to Christ, and then he looks at the jealousies, rage and self-love which were driving events. The position of the Catholic Church was of principled neutrality, or non-war, but that was not just neutrality in the sense of not favouring either side, but in the deeper sense of seeing both sides as being able to address their issues of injustice without fighting and resorting to weapons. Benedict deeply opposed war, because the Christian faith did.

In early December 1914, after the horrors of the First Battle of Ypres had taken place, he called for a truce at Christmas, asking that the nations "cease the clang of arms while Christendom celebrates the Feast of the World's Redemption". The Generals were a bit worried. General Sir Horace Smith-Dorrien sent out a warning:

> "It is during this period that the greatest danger to the morale of troops exists. Experience of this and of every other war proves undoubtedly that troops in trenches in close proximity to the enemy slide very easily, if permitted to do so, into a "live and let live" theory of life...officers and men sink into a military lethargy from which it is difficult to arouse them when the moment for great sacrifices again arises...the attitude of our troops can be readily understood and to a certain extent commands sympathy...such an attitude is however most dangerous for it discourages initiative in commanders and destroys the offensive spirit in all ranks...the Corps Commander therefore directs Divisional Commanders to impress on subordinate commanders the absolute necessity of encouraging offensive spirit... friendly intercourse with the enemy, unofficial armistices, however tempting and amusing they may be, are absolutely prohibited"[103]

So, you see how dangerous a "live and let live" theory of life can be. However, the truce took place on the initiative of soldiers, reflected in about thirty brigades on both sides, especially between the Germans and British. Ordinary soldiers at the front in trenches, sang carols, had services, fraternized with the so-called enemy, and the famous football match, which Germany is supposed to have won 3-2, took place among a number of kick-abouts. Germans talked English and the English offered to sing in poor German - nothing changes. Addresses were exchanged. Suddenly, everybody liked it. After all, it was much more pleasant than being killed or cowering in sodden trenches and the enemy were the same pleasant, fearful, young men as ourselves acting under orders. Then word of the peaceful Christmas parties travelled back to headquarters and the generals became agitated. If the soldiers shook hands and went home the War was over. General Sir Horace Smith-Dorrien looked to punish those who were too friendly, got the guns started again, and soon everybody could carry on happily fighting and dying for four more years.

Pope Benedict tried again. He was distrusted by the Germans and the Allies, who each thought he was on the other side, but came up with a proposal on 1st August, 1917, after three years of war and millions more deaths. It involved the following principles:

1. Arms and fighting were to be replaced by the moral force of law.

2. Reciprocal disarmament to a level preventing external aggression was to take place.

3. Where disputes occurred, they should be addressed by arbitration.

4. The principle of the free use of the seas be established.

5. Heavy sanctions were to be applied to those who did not submit to arbitration.[104]

His proposal was not taken up. After all, three years of fighting without winning would make all sides look rather silly. "For King and a Draw" does not have the same ring to it. Even the American Catholic bishops led by Cardinal Gibbons preferred a separatist philosophy of state and faith rather than a proper Catholic understanding of peace.[105] At the armistice Benedict was snubbed by Wilson who refused to allow a Catholic delegate to the Versailles Conference, even though the pope would have been the biggest ally in all that Wilson would try to achieve. Even so, mean motives in all of us destroy the possibility of good. Benedict XV should have been at Versailles; it would have been a very different conference if he had been there. So the Catholic peace initiatives during and after the War for peace were defeated.

**The 1915 International Congress of Women.**

Another important, but ignored, peace initiative occurred early during the Great War. On the 28th April, 1915, some twelve hundred women gathered from twelve countries including Britain, Germany, Austria, Belgium, The United States, Switzerland in the Hague for the third international peace and disarmament Conference. The Netherlands was, of course, a neutral venue. They aimed to stop the Great War through a negotiated peace and establish a system of international law which would outlaw war at all times. They called for the War to stop on the grounds that war should in principle be illegal under international law. The demand made eminent sense. Some 14 million lives were still to be saved and it was already a dead-locked war.

But the delegates went further into a series of principles for addressing war and disarmament, recorded by Freya Baetens in her account of the Congress. [106] First, they required rape as an instrument of war to be addressed – the first time this had been brought up as a matter of principle. They also expressed their solidarity with war victims on all sides, eschewing the normal double standard of regarding one's own casualties as martyrs and the death of enemies as a triumph. They then set up and stated five Principles of Permanent Peace. The first was acceptance of national democratic territorial sovereignty, so that no state could take over the territory of another and its politics. There were to be no military victories. This principle was recognized by the United Nations in 1945, although practised only imperfectly. The second was the mandatory settlement of international disputes by arbitration and courts. The third was that social, moral and economic pressure should follow any state's aggressive military act. Fourth, they lay down that foreign policy should be subject to democratic, rather than autocratic or military, control. Fifth, they voted for the full enfranchisement of women in voting and government. Properly applied, these principles were powerful and way ahead of their time, but the women delegates did not only set up principles, but the institutional framework to implement them.

They advocated the establishment of a "Society of Nations", what later was adopted as the League of Nations format, together with an international court to settle disputes. They also stipulated a process of disarmament in two stages. First the manufacture and trade of weapons was to be in the hands of governments only, removing the profit motive from war, and second, universal disarmament was to take place. The Congress also backed the prohibition of secret treaties, the equivalent of what later came to be known in Britain as the Ponsonby rules. After the Congress, the women leaders went to the governments of the Netherlands, the United Kingdom, Germany, Austria, Hungary, Russia, Switzerland, Italy, the Vatican, Belgium, Norway, Denmark, Sweden and the United States arguing their case and were received at the highest level. It is a measure of the paucity of the opposition to their case that the main concern seemed to be that entering negotiation for an end to the war would be seen as a sign of weakness, a particularly pathetic macho response. The formative power of this great women's initiative carried on, even though its aims were immediately thwarted, into the Treaty of Versailles.

**Defeating Peace.**

In retrospect these initiatives for peace were inadequate, despite the convictions of those involved and the strength of their case and its supporting arguments. They worked out what peace involves and saw through the humbug of the military establishments they were confronting. But, they were not able to fight the militarism of the arms companies and the military in Britain, France, Germany or Russia. They could not mobilize people against mob patriotism and nationalism. They had no real access to power and decision-making within the political system. To put it simply, they were outgunned. They did not wise up to the tactics that would be used by the vipers they were fighting against, ignoring the first half of Jesus' advice in Matthew 10 16. "You must be as shrewd as vipers and as gentle as doves."

In an era when modern democracy was just opening up they were especially outplayed by the links of the munitions people to the popular press. Engelbrecht and Hanighen show the way it worked in France. Russia needed big loans to buy French arms, and it was the Russian Imperial Agent in Paris, Raffalovich, and the French Minister of Finance made sure that the loans would go through by bribing the French Press. Raffalovich's accounts give the flavour.

> "Subventions of the (French) press began in February 1904 at the time of the panic provoked by the outbreak of hostilities in the Far East. Upon request of M. Rouvier, Minister of Finance (later Premier of France), the Russian finance minister opened a credit of 200,000 francs. Money was expended through the agent of the French ministry, M. Lenoir, and continued until the assurance of the 800,000,000 loan.... The internal events in Russia, disturbances, mutinies, and massacres, caused such an uneasy state of mind among French holders of our securities that if the press had been left to itself it would not have failed to upset public opinion still more.... The outlook was so threatening that the Banque de Paris put 50,000 francs at our disposition, which was issued as follows: 10,000 francs to *Havas* Agency, 7,000 francs to Hebrard of *Le Temps*, and 4,000 to *Le Journal* on November 30, and again as much on December 30. The costly sacrifice for *Havas* and *Le Temps* are absolutely necessary... the support for a majority of the press is unfortunately indispensable until the loan is put through... the papers have become greedier.. we must continue 100,000 francs for three months and look forward to paying *Havas* 10,000 for an even longer period."

In 1904 the bribes amounted to 935,785 francs, and in 1905 to 2,014,161. " In ten months the abominable venality of the French press will have absorbed 600,000 francs." In 1906

Raffalovich wrote to say that *Le Temps* had been bribed 100,000 francs in connection with that year's loan. Other items on Raffalovich's account indicated that a sum of 50,000 francs was distributed to *Le Temps, Le Petit Parisien, Le Journal, Figaro, Gaulois,* and *Havas*. Another list requiring 3,796,861 francs, including advertising, was distributed among the following: *Journal des Débats, Echo de Paris, Liberté, Patrie, Eclair, Rappel, Radical, Intransigeant,* and, curiously also, *La Vie Parisienne.*[107]

In other words, the whole of the French Press was bought so that the Schneider arms deal backed by French bank loans could go through on the basis that the French public would not understand how big the revolutionary upheavals in Russia were.

The British Press was similar. Repeatedly the popular press resorted to jingoism to stir up people against supposed enemies and for war and war-like positions. Alfred Harmsworth, later Lord Rothermere, sent a writer to Germany to produce a sixteen part serial for the *Daily Mail* called "Under the Iron Heel". We have seen how correct arguments can be drowned with nonsense and the people of peace can be muzzled, as occurred with the Mulliner Scare and the *Daily Mail.* Eventually, the British and German popular media fanned antagonism with scant regard for the facts, and the new media barons found it sold newspapers like nothing else. This exchange in the Commons on the 8th August, 1914 conveys the problem of even elementary factual accuracy..

> **Mr. JOYNSON-HICKS:** May I ask the Home Secretary a question, of which I have given him private notice: Whether his attention has been called to the statements which appeared in a special edition of the "Daily Mail," published this morning, in regard to a naval battle which was said to have taken place off Holland and which appears to be absolutely untrue in every detail; and whether the Government will be able to take some steps to restrain a paper of this importance from publishing infamous and false war news in order that people may be deluded into buying their paper, thus causing very great hardship and heart-burning to the people who read this news? I am quite sure

> that the Government will do something to stop such infamous conduct.
>
> **Mr McKENNA:** On inquiry at the Admiralty, I learn that there is no foundation whatever for the statement that has appeared in the Press that there has been a great naval battle. This House, I am sure, will join in an expression of condemnation in the strongest terms of the fabrication of false news, which I cannot say, and do not say, in this case was wilfully done, but which might be wilfully done for the purpose of assisting the circulation of a newspaper.[108]

Of course it was wilfully done to advance the circulation of the *Daily Mail* and to pump up jingoism.

The British Government realized as the War went on that it had to manage news and the media to keep a positive image of the war. The famous, "Your country needs you" recruitment posters of Kitchener were an early part of that process, and in 1917 when Lord Beaverbrook of *Daily Express* fame was appointed Minister of Information, a new propaganda machine went into operation for the first time. The only message allowed was that the War was necessary to defeat the evil Hun. All over Europe money was flowing from the arms interests into media outlets, cooking the truth, raising scares, and leading the people of different nations into mindless patriotism. The public were like sheep, kept from information by national security and the military establishment and succumbing to the scary headlines of the tabloids. The military system did not encourage conscience, because it was dangerous. If people start thinking for themselves, anything could happen. Once the conflict has started, those who might object had to be silenced. On the whole, public opinion was as a feather blown by patriotism.

Thus, peace was the aim of many good people, but often it was vaguely meant and had been compromised by nationalism, weapons and war. Most people had not begun to think of what it meant to fight for peace, then or now; they were like draughts players on a chessboard. They needed to wise up, to learn not to be sidelined. They needed to have answers to jingoism, and war scares, and insider politics, and sowing confusion, and discrediting peace movements, and delaying tactics, and using rogue nations, and funding anti-peace movements, and slogans for the masses, and priming conflicts, and covert arms deals, and engendering popular hate and distrust. They also needed to insist on ordered disarmament and on laws making weapons illegal to cut the role of the arms companies. They needed to insist that ordinary democratic voters think these things through and kmow the case against war. They needed to identify all the vested interests who want abundant riches, profits from arms deals and banking, who like to control markets with weapons and retain international control. They needed to face down politicians who insisted on defending us against enemies whom they had helped create. So do we.

The radical failure of peace movements needs to be faced for what it was. Many involved did not understand what the military lobby was and how it played; they were too nice. The armaments people had sewn up their power base and insisted on autocratic and secret government contacts. Weapons procurement was deemed absolutely necessary to guarantee national security. If governments wobbled, the media was fed anxiety raising stories. Charges of national disloyalty and smears were used. Military decisions were kept within small groups of loyal, pre-selected politicians and the decisions were made before the public could do anything about it. Politicians moved to armaments companies to retire and armaments companies had access to departments of defence, the armed forces and cabinet. This was a strong system and peace movements were unable to rock it. It had grown strong and is now even stronger. Unless it is toppled, it will continue. All of this can be said without anything other than honour and respect for members of the armed forces. Indeed, one myth is that peace movements are against the military. Really they are the ones who take the lives and well-being of soldiers most seriously of all by keeping them alive. But the battle to oppose militarism requires rigor and the demolishing of strongholds. Given the chance, the arms companies will undermine peace in every which way. They are the establishment and they expect their way and their will to be done. They will their way through the institutions of government. Be warned.

**Keeping the people out.**

The people can often be easily led by jingoism, but in the Great War they were really kept controlled and also marginalised. The big decisions were taken by the Kaiser, the Tsar, the Austro-Hungarian Emperor, and elite groups in the military. When wars are a possibility, the military tend to take over decisions. Even Sir Edward Grey can be criticized for his secret diplomacy on the issue of the Great War. Yet, if millions of people are going to die in wars, it is arguable that they should have a say in their death.

At present, people do not have much say in war and arms manufacture, even in many "democratic" countries. Never has a government allowed a referendum on a war, because, by and large, the people would vote with their feet away from it, shuffling away in the opposite direction. Conversely, the military and the arms manufacturers have always been strongly allied to autocracy. This is probably true from BC to Blair. The dealers and military have quiet discussions with the men at the top, voicing fears and the need to be firm. When war looms democracy is shut down, and there is rarely a war election not sewn up by patriotism. In wars you have to control the people, eliminate dissent, glorify cannon fodder and glamorize leaders. It is amazing how well it works, unless you lose a war. As United States leaders have found in Vietnam and Iraq, you then have to find a different phrase than "losing the war". It was not really lost; we just forgot where we had put it. A closed military establishment tightly controls matters of war, and the people are kept on the outside. The peace people, especially, are pushed out to the margins, kept away from the levels of power – William Jennings Bryan, Keir Hardie, Karl Liebknecht, Jane Addams, Fenner Brockway, Jean Jaurès will tell you what this means, and Undershaft will voice what the other side normally does not say.

As Emery Reves said, "The fundamental problem of peace is the problem of sovereignty."[109] When the decisions are made, the peacemakers *will not be in charge*. There are no institutions for peace. There is not a Department for Peace, but only a Ministry of

"Defence", which really means a Military Department. The ordinary people and the peacemakers are shut out of the organizations of government. They could have gatherings, marches, rallies (which governments fear) but they do not get their hands on the levers of peacemaking. We have got to work out how to change this. Many statesmen in the inter-war period tried, but they too failed. The scope of the failure should alert us to the size of the task. With arms manufacturers and dealers you probably have to be as wise as serpents, and swallow your prey, rather than being like an adolescent Labrador bitten again by the snake.

Of course, the people can be war-wanting for a while, given the mass media we often have, but Eisenhower's words to Macmillan have deep historic weight: "I believe that the people in the long run are going to do more to promote peace than any governments. Indeed, I think that people want peace so much that one of these days, governments had better get out of their way and let them have it."[110]

## Chapter Ten: The Great War Boom.

### The Great War.

The Great War stands out in human history as one of the cruellist tragedies ever. Millions were killed and injured and it was rightly called a World War because people of almost every nation fought in it and conflict occurred from the Far East to the West. It was, moreover, four years of intense fighting with a fire-power completely unequalled in previous history. Detailed military history of these four years is covered by many fine historians and it is not right to try to elaborate it here. The horrors of the battles, the victories, alliances, defeats, military strategy and different national experiences have been told in many studies. Personal records of the War have been collected by the Imperial War Museum and other agencies. Poets, journalists, historians, novelists and artists have shown us what was going on in this great event when international murder became seen as a good and honourable thing to do. Here we offer the briefest summary of those years of bloody encounter, and instead of looking at the fields of battle, we look to the sidelines where the arms were produced to fuel the conflict.

A brief history of the War might look like this. Serbians fought and repulsed the Austro-Hungarians in the original quarrel. Then, more widespread conflict developed in the Balkans. The Germans came with the Schlieffen Plan through Belgium, aiming to outflank the French and nearly did so, but were eventually held by the French and British. The Russian attacked in the East and made the Germans split their resources. The Russian attacks were vast, but they eventually suffered from lack of munitions and gradually the Germans advanced through Tannenburg and other battles until they hit the Russian winters. In the west the War moved into trench warfare with machine guns, poison gas, barbed wire, howitzers, gas, horses, mud and a series of horrific battles. Marne, Ypres, the Somme, Verdun each produced near a million casualties. The strategies changed. Tanks came in. Aircraft and bombing were used. There were naval confrontations, especially the great battle of

Jutland where Britain lost more ships, but Germany was forced back into port. The German development of submarines was another challenge to the British navy in the Atlantic, but not a decisive one. The Ottoman Empire came into the War on the side of the central powers, and another confrontation took place in the Dardanelles. Conflicts in Egypt and the Near East reflected control of the route to India. There were other wars in the Far East and Africa. The Allies were pushed back and the big German guns were again within reach of Paris.

Meanwhile, the Russians were running out of guns and ammunition and faced the defeat of the Tsarist Imperial System in revolutions in February, 1917 and October, 1917. Following the October Communist revolution, with the Bolsheviks in power, Lenin withdrew completely from the War, saying it was a capitalist, imperial conflict with which he would have nothing to do; the Russians had to accept, for the time being, a humiliating defeat. By now the United States had entered the War and with an increased force against them gradually the Germans were pushed back from Paris. In the Spring of 1918 Ludendorff mounted another sustained attack, but it petered out with the internal German exhaustion of fighting. By the summer of 1918 the Germans were close to internal collapse and the military command knew they had lost and the outcome was now inevitable. The military tried to move responsibility for defeat over to the politicians. The war was over. Germany was defeated. With perhaps sixteen million killed and twenty million injured the world lay devastated by bereavement. There was another level of tragedy. Spanish flu struck a weakened population from January, 1918 to December, 1920, and, across the globe, some further *fifty million to a hundred million died*. The 'flu may have started in a troop camp in Étaples or through Chinese labourers brought over to the Western Front, and it mainly hit the young who died from pneumonia who carried in back home. Encased in tragedy and loss, surrounded by those whose wounds would never heal, the world was full of weeping and the old grieved for the young.

**The Munitions' War.**

Tooley gives some idea of the scope of this munitions fuelled war.

> A few figures will give an idea of the scope of destruction. At the Armistice, the Entente powers on the Western Front and the Italian Front had in their lines 29,315 artillery pieces. Shelling was more-or-less constant along all fronts, especially the Western Front. It intensified with attacks, and the pre-attack explosives expended in shells or mines tended to increase as the war went along. Artillery shells came in many varieties, and by the end of the war, they were raining high explosive, shrapnel, burning heavy metals, gas, and other death-dealing substances down on enemy positions. The zone of destruction on the Western Front alone was roughly 400 miles long by 50 miles wide. Of these roughly 20,000 square miles, some substantial segments remain today so thoroughly impregnated with chemicals, live explosives, and other detritus of war that they are still "red-zoned" by the French government-that is, habitation is simply forbidden, and no economic activity is allowed, except logging in some cases.[111]

Behind all these battles was an industry of war, an industry of blowing people up. As Haythornewaite says, "Estimates range from about 30 to 1,400 shells required, on average, to kill one enemy."[112] That intimates roughly how many shells you had to dodge to stay alive. Especially at Chilwell, near Nottingham, there were hundreds of thousands of shells in sheds waiting to be taken off to the front, with women using sack-barrows to move them around, Behind the War the biggest industry on earth was providing all that was needed for the countless battles and destruction happening at the Front. This was the apotheosis, the final glorification of the munitions ideal, the unlimited use of weapons, no expense spared. The arms manufacturers had achieved their goal, their victory, the purpose of their weapons, the killing of millions.

**What was the point?**

Why did this war happen? For four long years most of Europe was engaged in a conflict which drained manpower, health, food, economic activity. We honour the bravery, selflessness, dying for others and the suffering of millions in doing what many thought was their bounden duty. But if one asked what these great nations were fighting *for,* it is not easy to find the reason. Let us, somewhat lightly, look for an answer.

Some believe it was about patriotism. They were fighting for Der Vaterland or La Patrie. But why should one *fight* for one's country? Is one's country better, because one fights for it? Clearly, it is not. Does it make more sense for Britain, France, Russia and Germany to fight for their country, or not fight for their country? Obviously, it is sensible for us all not to fight for our countries, but to live in them, and it is easy to live in your country when you are not attacking other countries. Fighting for one's country is a half-baked idea.

Is it a question of fighting for territory? Clearly there were some disputes about territory, but the disputes about territory were mainly military – about France, Germany, Russia having a buffer territory against military invasion. At the end of four years of bloody and violent carnage, France was still France, Germany was still Germany and the same was true for the other countries. There would be some losses of territory and reparations for the losers, but that was merely because the cost of the war was so great and Britain and France had big debts to the United States. The War did not sort anything out. Alsace-Lorraine is German-French to this day; indeed the border has more or less disappeared. Moreover, we all work hard to get people from other countries in Europe to come to our territory on holiday. If you want to invade France, buy a house there.

Nor was it even about empire. The states of Europe were busy acquiring colonies in the rest of the world. Germany did not need Lebensraum, but rather a growing workforce for its highly successful industrial development. Colonies were far away and if fighting was to occur, it happened there, as was the case with the

Boer Wars. Though Serbia deserves respect, it would not be correct to say that Germany, France, Russia and Britain were concerned about Serbia as a country or a colony. Nor even was Austro-Hungary. The main source of the spat was Skoda's pressure for an arms deal, and later the murder of the Emperor. Now, of course, the powers of Europe have lost their empires, not through wars, but because they are wrong. There has been a slow defeat for what was humanly untenable in the British, French, German, Belgian, Spanish and Italian empires. Wrongs can be gently defeated.

This War was often presented as good defeating evil. The greatest evil is when someone is killed. Before this Great War almost no-one was killed, but it resulted in millions being killed in every major participant nation. Each state did evil things and each state suffered the wickedness of others. Nor was this the first war when people could learn this lesson. They could have noticed, people had been killed in earlier wars. There was a Hundred Years War. There were the Napoleonic Wars we looked at first in this book. The wars have all been evil. Have they been necessary evils? No, because the wars have not been necessary. The sins of pride, hate, anger and aggression and the desire to enslave that prompted the Great War are sins of humanity and are to be fought in relation to God, not some external enemy. In 1918 these evils were not defeated, but repeated in 1939 in a kind of hammered-in stupidity. This is not the way to defeat evil.

Was it for the future? The words, "When you go home, Tell them of us and say, For your tomorrow, We gave our today", dwell with us, for those men and boys were brave, selfless, dying for others and we honour them. Once the War had started they gave themselves for us. But that was a time-local truth. The War should not have started. If it had not, the world's future would have been far better - without mourning, and injury dominated lives, with better houses, trade, families, education and health. It is stupid to have a war *for the future*. Wars merely generate vast debts and destruction *from the past* which have to be met in the future. War requires recovery for five, ten or twenty years. You do not cut a leg off in order to get better.

Thus, we have to face the fact that there was no reason for this Great War. It should not have started; it was a *mistake*. Europe goofed. Millions dying and injured, making weapons that can kill and destroy, attacking other nations, devastating families and promoting cruelty – it was all a mistake, a tragic mess, a failure of elementary wisdom. But there is one more thing to add. There is only one logic which gave a reason for the Great War. It is the logic of the arms manufacturers - Krupp, Armstrong, Schneider, Vickers, Nobel, Du Pont, Remington, the Putilov Works, Skoda, Ansaldo and others. They were producing weapons for war, and year in year out they were promoting their wares. In order to sell they had to persuade politicians to believe in weapons, and they did. They trained states to use them. They spread distrust, scares, encouraged arms races and promoted the success of their products. The logic: selling weapons depends on wars and the rumours of war. It was *this* logic which won, not because it is good logic, but because sufficient people, especially among the powerful elites chose to believe in it and idolatrously it was give power to determine events. The point of the 1890 London Peace Conference stands. This War was fought only in the logic of arms. There was no other good reason for the War. It was a useless waste.

**The Economic Loss.**

The waste of the Great War can be economically quantified in rough figures. The fighting went on for over four years and grew to involve seventy million armed forces. Those working in munitions and related industries added further tens of millions to this figure. Conservatively, let us say that a hundred million people were involved in fighting a war for four years. That is something like four hundred million man years, possibly nearly a trillion man hours (1,000,000,000,000) devoted to largely destructive activity. That is stupidity beyond belief. That was merely the men. Women, too, wasted their time on the war in more subtle, but no less life consuming ways, and so this figure must be bumped up again. Let us say that throughout Europe and elsewhere 20 million women were engaged in war-related work for a couple of years – probably the number was larger and the time more distributed. Another 40 million women years (80,000,000,000 work hours) went to the war here. And then there is the time needed to put right the property, infrastructure and agricultural damage especially in Russia, Poland, Germany, Belgium and France. A guess would be that 50 million years of work (100,000,000,000 work hours) was so destroyed, another vast tranche of time, probably a large under-estimation. The world would have been better off if the soldiers had spent a trillion hours twiddling their thumbs. What a vast useless, destructive waste!

Of these some 9.7 million combatants died along with about 6.8 million civilians, making over 16 million who died, roughly equal to all the men in England and Wales before the War started. In economic terms, a subsidiary issue to the tragedy of the deaths of these people, but no less real to Europe, was the loss of economic earning power that the deaths of these young men represented. The mainly men who died were aged say from their teens to their thirties. As children they had been brought up for fifteen years by the work and care of others. So, something like two hundred and forty million years of dependence and training for adult work had been cut short by death, involving perhaps forty million years of bereaved work by the old in bringing up the young - a ratio of six children to one carer/teacher overall across their young lives. Thus, another 80,000,000,000 hours of care was wasted. Then, there at is a further waste through the loss of the working lives of the 16 million who died. Their working lives had been cut short by thirty, forty or fifty years so that another input to the world economy was lost. If we conservatively estimate a loss of thirty years, four hundred and eighty million years of future work, nearly a trillion hours (960,000,000,000) had been eradicated in Europe and beyond. Given this level of waste, we need to look no further for much of the privation experienced in Europe and especially Russia, in the twenties and thirties. These are the economic losses, but primarily these were sons, husbands, friends and neighbours who were engulfed in the engine of war. To do justice to all those names on war memorials in villages, towns, churches and cities is not possible.

A further 21 million were seriously wounded, often for life, although this figure is misleading because it focuses only on physical injury; others were traumatized for life in what was called "shell shock" and we now recognize as Post Traumatic Stress Syndrome. If we assume that this decreased their economic effectiveness by 20% for the rest of their working lives, that is another one hundred and twenty six million years (250,000,000,000 hours) wasted, and it too explains why the inter-war European recession was so deep. This is a total economic loss of about three trillion hours of people's labour to the world economy – an horrific figure. Physical economic damage was vast, especially in the east where towns and cities in Russia were routinely destroyed. The western front was mainly across fields and hills, and bombing had not yet become a method of mass destruction, and so this kind of destruction was lower, though still beyond comprehension. The tragedy of this War was written in the lives, families and faces of those who remained, and they were to come out of the war, if they survived, determined that it was to be the War to end all Wars. Recently, I heard of a single one of these tens of millions of injured - a Lancashire man suffering from gas injury, not able to work again properly, and a quiet tragedy within his family for decades after 1918 and still remembered today as such.

**Arms Manufacturing in War.**

Especially in great wars the attention is on the fighting - those who die, the heroes, the victories and the defeats, and this study does not want to detract from these realities. We think of the Somme, or Jutland, or other great battles, and yet in all there were a hundred and fifty major battles in the Great War with soldiers choking on gas, being blown up, cut to pieces, losing limbs and going mad. It is hard to get beyond the immediate horror. Yet there are another set of calculations going on in modern wars and they have to do with the supply of arms and equipment for the battle. Modern warfare is about the production of munitions. The munitions people, the merchants of death, are experiencing a runaway market, bonanza time and unholy profits. They become obscenely bigger. In the First World War, the Great War, as it was known for twenty years, the build-up of arms before the War was nothing compared with the explosion in arms manufacturing which occurred with its outbreak, especially in Britain, France, Germany, Russia and the United States.

Before the war the economies had not been strongly orientated to military expenditure. In 1911 Britain gave 2.3% of its GNP to the military, France 3.3% and Germany only 1.6%, again an indication of how relatively unbellicose the German economy was.[113] But when the war came military expenditure shot up. War economies are boom, boom economies because everybody is working or dying. As a share of GNP, military expenditure went up to 22% in Britain, 43% in France and 20-25% in Germany. *In other words, it encompassed roughly a quarter of the European economy.* This increase is the underlying effect of this war. The military economy in the west expanded from, say, 2.5% to 25%. It is roughly a *tenfold* increase in the military-industrial sector. It had control of a quarter of the European economy. Suddenly arms manufacturers had access to any labour, funds, raw materials and technology they wanted and they were given money or resources on demand. It was bonanza time for them all over Europe with a vast scale of investment, profits, subsidy, speeded up production, output and power; everything was skewed in this one direction. Factories hummed with patriotic workers and weapons poured to the front. Now, of course, what the arms companies were doing was right. It was the patriotic thing to do for Rule Britannia or the German Reich. The military economy had arrived.

It was also a time of unprecendented technical development in arms, for technology was *only* directed towards weapons, and away from all other areas, by the war. On land the development of tanks, guns, large shells and mobile armoured warfare began to replace swords, horses and muskets. In the air warplanes and aerial bombing started to happen. At sea, submarines and torpedoes emerged as significant weapons. Everywhere well paid groups were working at designing and delivering the supposed knock-out weapons. For many that was chemical weapons and both Britain and Germany become committed to producing horrific burns and deaths through air borne chemical weapons. People of both sides felt their skin drop off and their lungs quit working. In war we are told, anything goes. But does it? Nothing remotely justifies this level of inhumanity. Meanwhile other technical developments did not take place.

The military expansion into the economy was unprecedented and marked the direction of the new century. The military grew and it would not shrink voluntarily. It never does. Wars create an entrenched system that is even more difficult to demolish. Relinquishing power amicably is rare.

**Arms Manufacturing in Britain – the State moves in.**

Yet, in Britain it was not fully like this. The British like to think of themselves as cobbling things together at the last moment. Though the Navy was well prepared, there is some truth in the attitude of amateurism in relation to the army. It was nearly disastrous. As Churchill notes, the Navy, with a strong period of battleship construction, went on to double its size during the war, while the army, much less well prepared, had to expand to the equivalent of ten or fifteen fold.[114] But it was not so much the soldiers as the arms that were lacking. Previously the War Office had ordered munitions from companies, often inefficiently, and with little sense of the strategy necessary in a great war. Then in 1915 the Russians who relied on Vickers and Schneider for much of their weaponry and shells faced an acute shortage. The arms manufacturers were swamped with orders from both Britain and Russia and were just not giving the soldiers the explosives and shells to respond to the weapons of Krupp and Skoda. The situation was worse because Kitchener was keen on rationing his troops in their use of shells and did not really see the need to expand output.

Then after a series of defeats Lloyd George moved from the Treasury to a newly formed Ministry of Munitions on the 26th May, 1915. After facing stubborn opposition from Kitchener, Lloyd

George decided to rapidly expand the output of every kind of munition substantially. He had to do a number of things to effect this change. First, he over-rode the War Office. Then he reached out to a whole range of factories outside the established munitions groups to incorporate them in war production. Then, he had to prevent restrictive practices among the workers. This was done by making sure that the munitions capitalists could not make excessive profits. Vickers profits moved from £900,000 in 1913 to only £1,100,000 per year in the years 1914-19.[115] Thus, Britain was the one country in which war profiteering was not excessive. True, the munitions people were well off, but they did not have the money of the Thyssens, Du Ponts and others who would later finance Fascism. Lloyd George also cut alcohol consumption from 89 million gallons of pure alcohol in 1914 to 37 million gallons in 1918, largely by creating weaker beer. Then he moved women into the workforce at a guaranteed minimum wage and directly mobilized factories to produce the output necessary. His machine-gun orders to Eric Geddes, one of his ablest co-workers, were: "Take Kitchener's maximum (four for battalion); square it; multiply that result by two; and when you are in sight of that, double it again for good luck." This gave 32 machine guns per battalion with another 32 for a margin and the fighting could be done properly.[116] Most people knew that these efforts by Lloyd George were the backbone of the British contribution to winning the war, against the elitist inefficiency of the toffs. That was one reason why he was hated later, reflected in the 1922 vote at the Carlton Club.

The deeper significance was that this state-run structure, dismantled after the War, did not leave a vast munitions/military establishment in the 1920s and gave no strong financial base for British Fascism.

**One Side-effect: Weapons Kill your Own.**

As part of this munitions expansion, new explosives factories were quickly created at Gretna, Gadbrook and especially at the Brunner-Mond factory at Silvertown, below the Victoria Dock on the Thames. It produced nine tons of TNT a day, but not all of it got to the front. On 17th January, 1917 about fifty tons of it exploded, killing 73 people and injuring 400 – it could have been far worse – and the whole area was flattened. The biggest factory of all was in Chilwell near Nottingham. In three years the factory produced about nineteen million shells, half the national output, weighing approximately one million tons. In addition 25,000 mines were supplied to the Navy, and 2,500 bombs to the Royal Air Force. Towards the end of the War another munitions plant explosion at Chilwell killed 137 people. Making weapons even kills your own side. As a result of these factories tons of explosives were churned out every day to produce the successful carnage of the Germans. The new Committee created a centralized, direct system for generating weapons on a large scale. As Woodward points out, "no other arrangement would have been adequate to provide munitions on the immense scale with which they were used in 1916, 1917 and 1918. During its existence the Ministry spent over £2,000 million, probably the first time billions appeared in government accounts, and its staff rose to more than 65,000. These are awesome figures. But on the ground new factories, shipyards, depots, stores and manufacturing units sprang up all over the country. There was competition over which kind of weapons would be most effective and most needed. There was a torpedo factory in Weymouth, a shell factory near Crossgates, and so it goes on. The wheeling and dealing which went on to produce the funding for different kinds and makes of weapon are lost in the annals of time, but they must have kept a lot of the 65,000 Defence Ministry people busy. Other war-related industries sprang up. *Half a million* cats were employed as gas detectors and ratters during the War. Who bred and transported them?

Another bit of the picture was the predominance in the munitions workforce of women. More than two million women moved into a wide range of jobs which were part of the war effort, and a lot of these were in munitions. The "Canaries" were women working in TNT factories whose skin was turned dangerously yellow by the work, hence the name. Women at this stage were more pliable, less unionized, required lower pay and thus helped the profits of the arms' manufacturers. At one level it was exploitation. At another, it made the case for Women's Suffrage unavoidable after the War. Quite a few women were killed in regular explosions within the shell loading factories. For example, Annie Bell was killed in a munitions factory in Lancashire; "was it the White Lund Factory in Morecombe?" asks a relative. Much of this military-industrial expansion was later useless and has disappeared, but investment in anything else stopped. Effectively the Government gave orders and supplied the money and the arms manufacturers increased output. The command economy had its first outing in Britain. Other expenditure was pared and the whole economy was geared towards war.[117]

**Socialism and Munitions in Britain.**

Ordinary people's relations with the munitions companies grew more antagonistic as the War continued. The State controlled the workforce and made sure they were paid at a basic level. Strikes were made illegal. Since munitions' workers were not dying on the battlefield, this seemed fair. In effect Socialism and the Trade Union Movement were written out of the script for the duration of the war. The Labour Party was also divided, because Keir Hardie and Lansbury opposed the war as pacifists, while other Labour leaders supported it. Nor was this just a mild disagreement. Hardie was hounded and abused by the militarists. His sons were also conscientious objectors, and when people brought up the subject of his sons going to war, Hardie's response was that he would rather have his adult sons be put against a wall and shot than that they go to war.[118] He meant what he was saying to the end.

At the end of the War, even though profits were controlled, there was considerable anger at the way arms manufacturers had grown rich manufacturing weapons while soldiers died in millions. They were "the merchants of death". The anger also hardened because these people were seen as encouraging the build up to this horrific event. They had taken profits out of the vast expenditures on arms and lived sumptuously of the proceeds compared with everyone else. Many soldiers came back from the War seeing themselves as cannon fodder used by a rich capitalist group of people who were going nowhere near the fighting. Soldiers knew they had been gassed by chemicals, or shot to pieces by cannon or holed by rifles manufactured by a class who did not really care about casualties. They knew existentially that weapons tear people to pieces and that private manufacturers had vested interests in killing them for profits. There was a fundamental sense that this should not be done which settled over the nation, not just for a few months, but powerfully for a decade or more.

Perhaps the most poignant expression of this occurred at the end of an article by Keir Hardie, a man who with open clear conscience had opposed the movement towards and the generation of war. Others would come to this conclusion, but it would still be defeated again. Hardie, months from death in 1915, a hated man, wrote:

> When the war is only a sinking memory of a blood-stained nightmare, and we are again face to face with the real things of life, surely there will be a great and mighty agitation for complete enfranchisement of democracy – men and women alike – and thus win control over both domestic and foreign policy and break the rule of those to whom imperialism and militarism means wealth and power, and install all the peoples of all lands in authority, and thus bring plenty, peace and concord to a long suffering race."[119]

Sadly, Keir Hardie's faith in democracy is not fulfilled yet, because the people are still capable to acting like mindless sheep veering towards war and weapons with a few barks from their leaders, but God is still waiting. Since then the people have shown time and time again that they can be led by the nose into militarism and war. Democracy is an important opponent of war, but we need more than democracy. We need also a wised-up electorate.

**Germany's War Munitions.**

In Germany during the War the arms manufacturers flourished inordinately. They also, it seemed, controlled the media. A report from Sir Horace Rumbold recorded: "A part of the Press of

Austro-Hungary, and nearly all of the press of Germany, is controlled by munitions manufacturers and these raise an outcry the moment they observe a glint of peace beginning to dawn".[120] The dynamic of the arms industry within war was very strong. When wars break out arms manufacturers gain immense influence and power. Much of the time they are working out new ways to kill people, and poison gas was a great chemical growth industry during this time, as we shall see. I.G. Farben was the lead company in the development of poison gas, and doubtless they pressed their products on the military with zeal, but the British manufacturers of poison gas have been airbrushed from history. In every area, production was increased and the munitions companies were encouraged to expand. Companies did well and made big profits from Government contracts as a study by Charles Rist shows well.[121] In 1917 The Benz Car Company was making 15 million marks profit on a capital of 20 million marks, an amazing 75% return on its capital, but Daimler did even better in 1916. Then it made a profit of 12 million marks on a capital of 8 million, a 150% return to capital.

However, all this Government expenditure, not least to Krupp and Thyssen, had to be paid for. The Germans had some assets abroad and some 3 million marks were raised in this way, but most of it was raised at home. There were nine big war loans issued to the banks and they raised just under *one hundred billion marks,* an astonishing amount. There was another 19 billion marks of debt in Treasury bills, held by the banks. They also printed notes. In July 1914 there were two billion marks in notes, and in November 1918 there were 17 billion and a further 10 billion in loan-bureau notes. This reckless pattern continued after the War had ended. The notes had climbed to 36 billion and 13 billion loan bureau notes, making a total of 49.6 billion marks on notes, twenty four times the amount at the beginning of the war. This contributed to inflation which at the end was slightly less than ten times the prewar level of prices, but then reparations and later pressures led to the famous hyperinflation when one gold mark equalled one trillion paper marks in 1923.[122] So we can see the overall financial structure of the German War. The people financed it with an extraordinary level of saving. Much of this went to the munitions companies who were having a bonanza. At the end of the War the savings of the German people became worthless. They paid for an extravagant war through massive inflation and the almost complete loss of their savings held in government debt. In addition, through reparations the German people were asked to pay much of what the British and French had spent, especially on American munitions. It was the hardship and chaos produced by this wartime finance that led to the horror of post-war Germany. The people should always know before a war starts that they will pay for it with their lives, their savings and their poverty. That would rapidly dampen most of their bellicose attitudes. Wars might last five years, but paying for them lasts for twenty.

War industry companies flourished. The massive Thyssen steel company, of whom we shall hear later, produced almost all its output for the war and saw big expansion and profits. Steel was a war business. Thyssen was a rival to Krupp. As Vickers challenged Armstrong, so Thyssen challenged Krupp. In April 1913, August Thyssen helped to get Krupp in trouble over bribing officials in the war ministry; he passed on incriminating documents to the Center Party, hurting Krupp. During the War the company made vast profits but Fritz Thyssen also carefully moved some of his profits into the neutral Netherlands just in case Germany lost so that he would continue to be rich after the War. He knew the war economy was a winner and after the war he looked around for someone who could continue it with this kind of militarism. Early on in 1922-3 or so, he settled on Adolf, paid him as his retainer and gave him the economic clout to employ a load of bullies and make a name for himself to our everlasting cost. So, Thyssen's war time profits set Hitler up in business. Industrialists saw their future bound up with new military contracts, and big pre-war contracts like the widening of the Kiel Canal to let bigger battleships through. The Canal, at large cost, opened on the day Archduke Ferdinand was murdered and was followed by even bigger contracts. Ships, railway lines, chemical weapons, cannon, armour, guns and other military necessities all mushroomed. Many companies of all nations have edited out their war-time activities and processes from company histories, burying them in silence wrapped in "What me gov?", and so much of the actual detail has been hidden, burned or shredded, but these companies became enormous war-rich combines, ready to use their riches at the end of the War for their kind of business.

Primarily, of course, Germany was an army-based military. Much of its military production centred on tanks, guns and other munitions for the army, taking advantage of its output of steel. The impetus for this production was driven by another scare - that of Russia. There was an awareness that Russia with its vast population was industrializing and soon would have the capacity to attack Germany. This was vastly overstated in the First World War, because Russian equipment was inferior and the Russian defeat under the Tsar disastrous. Yet, German output had a problem in that its emphasis on high quality engineering meant that levels of output were not as great as those produced by the cruder methods of other countries. The munitions manufacturers were still more committed to making money than anything else. Krupp was helping manufacture guns for the Russian army in high quality German steel in 1914, and the German firm of Rumpler was selling early aeroplanes to Russia. National loyalty was not paramount at Krupp when profits were to be gained.

**German Post-War Munitions.**

Thus, with the war underway a vast war machine in Germany moved into massive levels of production, making the armaments manufacturers into barons who were rich and powerful people, but at the end of the War at Versailles the manufacture of munitions was absolutely forbidden and their work suddenly ceased. It was a juddering change, but it produced a bunch of determined men who were out to restore the system in which they had flourished most strongly. A statement by Krupp made in 1919 has justly become famous.

> At that time the situation seemed almost hopeless ... the machines were destroyed, the tools were smashed, but the men remained – the men in the construction offices and

workshops, who in happy co-operation had brought the production of guns to its last degree of perfection. Their skill had to be maintained by all means, also their vast funds of knowledge and experience. The decisions I had to make at that time were perhaps the most difficult ones in my life. I wanted and had to maintain Krupp, in spite of all opposition, as an armament plant – although for the distant future... Without arousing any commotion, the necessary measures and preparations were undertaken.[123]

This is chilling. Already in 1919 Gustav Krupp was back in the groove, providing the designs for the next war. He was not alone. Of course, many factories did move over to good civilian production. Cargo and passenger ships replaced battleships and tractors and cars began to flow on the production lines. There was a big genuine reversion to non-military production. But some industrialists hankered after munitions, and they evaded the prohibition on manufacturing armaments in the Treaty of Versailles by exporting production to other countries. The Oerlikon factory in Switzerland was under the control of Krupp. In 1920 the Swedish company Bofors entered into an agreement with Krupp. They also had interests in Austria, the Netherlands, Argentina and Poland. The Junker aircraft factories and chemical weapons works moved to Russia.[124] Thus, again, there was a process of disseminating munitions manufacture throughout Europe and beyond, growing out of the deceit of the German munitions manufacturers. The arms impetus in Germany was not dead.

**The United States' Munitions Lobby.**

The American arms manufacturers could see the vast income and profits waiting for them if the United States entered the War, and they emerged as a strong business lobby in Washington. They were moving from arms sales to domestic arms manufacture. We know the buildings where most of the requisitioning happened. The Main Navy and Munitions buildings dominated Constitution Avenue west of the Washington Monument and were completed and occupied in 1918 before the end of the war. They brought together the groups of arms companies jostling for sales and shortly we shall see who was at the centre of this web applying political pressure. There were groups like the American Defence Society, the American Navy League, the National Security League, the National American Manufacturers and others, who were in the business of pushing for a war that suited their businesses. If America entered the war a vast domestic market for munitions was waiting for them. They knew which side their bread was buttered.

President Wilson, when backing peace, had considerable opposition. We call ex-President Theodore Roosevelt "Progressive", but really he held together a coalition of businessmen, bankers and nationalists who were fairly committed to the war. He called for war in 1915 after the sinking of the Lusitania, which incidentally had munitions on board bound for Britain. Roosevelt also said in 1915, "The man who believes in peace at any price…should instantly move to China. If he stays here, then more manly men will have to defend him, and he is not worth defending."[125] So much for the recipient of the Nobel Peace prize. The Christian pacifist William Jennings Bryan, Secretary of State in Wilson's Cabinet decided he had to resign on 9th July, 1915, because he felt the United States was drifting away from neutrality. You can feel Wilson being moved during this period, as if by the weight of a much heavier pack away from his initial position, and the powerhouse of the scrum was the arms manufacturers. Talk of war in December 1916 sent stock prices soaring, led by the arms company shares. There is a lot of evidence of the power of this coalition to undermine Wilson and those who were for peace. They used money and influence to get what they wanted. As we see more fully soon, the munitions men led the way towards war.

Technically, the question of the supply of arms to the Allies actually caused United States entry to the war. The Germans knew that American arms were defeating them, and new submarines and torpedoes offered them the chance of doing something about it. They sank seven supposedly arms laden ships and the Americans huffed into the conflict. At a number of different levels, *through the sale of arms* the United States entered the First World War.

**After the War – Europe and the Treaty of Versailles.**

After this Great War with every country exhausted, and millions grieving for their dead, especially older parents for their sons, economies ruined and a decade of damage to clear up, victory was declared. It was, of course, hollow, and the armistice had to be vindictive. Versailles has been endlessly debated. Clearly, it was facing two ways. It was a Peace Conference and it was a Revenge Conference. The Peace Conference we look at later. First, we consider Germany. It was forced to cede about 27,000 square miles and 7 million people by the Treaty of Versailles. It was also to lose the Saar coalfields for fifteen years to be followed by a plebiscite. Provisional reparations of twenty billion marks in gold were fixed, as we shall see later, mainly to pay for British and French arms purchases in the United States. The German merchant marine was decimated, and the allies were given most favoured nation rights in German markets for five years. German demilitarisation included an army maximum of 100,000 (still enough to maintain the traditions) and rigid curtailment of navy, arms manufacture and no aircraft. Actually, the demilitarization could have worked, albeit with the counter example of Krupp, because a country without armed forces ceases to think militarily - except when they are invaded. But the French military invasion of the Ruhr destroyed this possibility. It was humiliating and provoked a reaction in favour of the armed forces. Because full German compliance with the Versailles Treaty was required before joining the League, their participation in peace-making was delayed for seven years, another humiliation. Yet, there was more or less complete German disarmament. It was accepted and implemented. If this process had taken place alongside the disarmament of the other European nations, then it would have been permanently successful, because the same rules were coming to apply to everyone. But it was not. The double standard was glaring. Germany must disarm, but the Allies could rearm. Repeatedly the British and French used a "We won the War" response rather than a principled peace-making response.

**The United States, President Wilson and Versailles.**

President Wilson had an authoritative role in the Treaty of Versailles. He was post-colonial in his thinking. The United States had emerged as the world's dominant economy. It had intervened and helped win the War for the Allies and as against the old order of bickering nations, the United States seemed to have a different vision. President Wilson also reverted to his understanding of arms and militarism. Here is Wilson speaking to the Senate on the 10th July, 1919 seeking the ratification of the Treaty of Versailles signed a few days earlier. Wilson saw the need for the League of Nations as the instrument of peace and disarmament. It was a powerful plea.

> It was universally recognized that all the peoples of the world demanded of the Conference that it should create such a continuing concert of free nations as would make wars of aggression and spoliation such as this that has just ended forever impossible. A cry had gone out from every home in every stricken land from which sons and brothers and fathers had gone forth to the great sacrifice that such a sacrifice should never again be exacted. It was manifest why it had been exacted. It had been exacted because one nation desired dominion and other nations had known no means of defence except armaments and alliances. War had lain at the heart of every arrangement of the Europe,—of every arrangement of the world,—that preceded the war. Restive peoples had been told that fleets and armies, which they toiled to sustain, meant peace; and they now knew that they had been lied to: that fleets and armies had been maintained to promote national ambitions and meant war. They knew that no old policy meant anything else but force, force,—always force. And they knew that it was intolerable. Every true heart in the world, and every enlightened judgment demanded that, at whatever cost of independent action, every government that took thought for its people or for justice or for ordered freedom should lend itself to a new purpose and utterly destroy the old order of international politics. Statesmen might see

> difficulties, but the people could see none and could brook no denial. A war in which they had been bled white to beat the terror that lay concealed in every Balance of Power must not end in a mere victory of arms and a new balance. The monster that had resorted to arms must be put in chains that could not be broken. The united power of free nations must put a stop to aggression, and the world must be given peace.[126]

Yet, tragically, this great secure hope was defeated in the United States.

There is a still a deep pall over the United States failure to sign the Covenant or join the League of Nations. It was mainly a combination of the great munitions-banking powers and the Republicans who opposed it. A lot of people had become rich through the War and were very annoyed at the way Wilson was talking about war and about government being hi-jacked by the bosses. They were not going to be pushed into this call for peace and fought against it. The normal reason given for the rejection of the Covenant is American isolationism. Other views emphasize Wilson's failing health, his obstinacy in not accepting compromise, or good speeches by Senator Borah and others. But there was steel in this campaign. Really, the armaments manufacturers were not going to vote themselves out of business and "private societies for the promotion of 'adequate defense'" grew up[127], funded by these manufacturers. They created a vast media and political reaction against disarmament and in favour of those rich from the War. The owners of the press were from a similar stable. There was a Democrat surtax of 65% on the highest incomes during the War, and the Republican business interest was going to get Wilson's attack on the rich out of the way as quickly as possible. So, without much thought, the United States ditched one of the best chances of peace the modern world has had. As a nation it should ask itself why it has made so many thoughtless, poor and damaging decisions in the last hundred years of its history. Frequently it has chosen the wrong Presidents, chosen the wrong allies, scuppered its principles and declared the wrong wars. It is often locked in a shallow self-congratulatory nationalism that undermines its ability to think.

Wilson saw the confrontation with amazing clarity. Immediately after the words above to the Senate on 10/7/1919 he refers to Jesus' words in Matthew 12 that it is not enough merely to sweep an evil away and leave the house empty. It must be replaced by the gentle Spirit of God, otherwise other evils will come back.

> If there was not the will or the intelligence to accomplish that now, there must be *another and a final war* [added italics] and the world must be swept clean of every power that could renew the terror. The League of Nations was not merely an instrument to adjust and remedy old wrongs under a new treaty of peace; it was the only hope for mankind. Again and again has the demon of war been cast out of the house of the peoples and the house swept clean by a treaty of peace; only to prepare a time when he would enter in again with spirits worse than himself. The house must now be given a tenant who could hold it against all such. Convenient, indeed indispensable, as statesmen found the newly planned League of Nations to be for the execution of present plans of peace and reparation, they saw it in a new aspect before their work was finished. They saw it as the main object of the peace, as the only thing that could complete it or make it worth-while. They saw it as the hope of the world, and that hope they did not dare to disappoint. Shall we or any other free people hesitate to accept this great duty? Dare we reject it and break the heart of the world?

Wilson looks to *a final war* to get rid of the munitions people and the militarists, and his enemies saw their possible demise and fought hard, *as they will fight now,* until Wilson was defeated. In the end Wilson fought though ill and dying for what he knew to be true – that America was being offered the leadership of the world for peace. The Senate turned it down led by Lodge and the old Republican establishment, intertwined with banking and arms. The judgment of Lloyd George was, "America has been offered the leadership of the world, but the Senate has tossed the scepter into the sea."[128] The League of Nations was established without the United States participation.

There was still massive hope, but it was not effective in a new way as European nationalism continued after the hurt of the War. France and Britain were locked inside their own patriotism for five or six years before a thaw occurred. By that time Mussolini was in power, showing that Italians were prepared to vote like mentally retarded sheep. Germany was in a crisis of self-belief in its defeat, and salvaged its Volk ego by blaming Jews for losing the War. Politicians were slow to think like statesmen with a concern for the international order. Elections were fought on the basis of narrow national advantages. There was thus a gap in any co-ordinated attempt to address the problem of war. Just as, later, the end of the Cold War occurred without any systematic attempt at disarmament, so the end of the Great War, the War to End all Wars, was followed by a dearth of activity to try to follow it through. Of course, countries were war-weary and incapable of thinking beyond the business of tending the injured and rebuilding lives. Yet this failure was to cost dearly.

**The Spiritual Battle of War or Peace?**

We who have not fought cannot know the horrors of war - to see bones exposed, arteries ripped and life going, to walk past bodies of comrades, to shoot a person dead, to die of poison gas, to sink to death in a submarine. Millions of people suffered deaths like these and millions more brought the injuries and memories home to live open-wound lives. What war *is* has been proved time and time again, though there are industries whose job is to hide the evidence. Victory hides and etherealizes the evidence. The ideology of victory is that we have won. Might is right and because we have won, we are right. The Great War was the biggest expression of the philosophy of patriotism, militarism and war that the world had ever seen. But people's hearts were not in it. At the end they wanted it to be the War to End all Wars.

In 1919 as a result of public subscription a white marble statue of Nurse Edith Cavell was erected outside the National Portrait Gallery in central London not far from Nelson's column and its lions. She tended the sick of both sides and was eventually shot by the Germans. I pause before this statue whenever I pass near it; it draws you. Underneath are written her most well-known words, "Patriotism is not enough. I must have no hatred or enmity towards anyone," reflecting her Christian faith and Jesus' insistence on loving our enemies. She said it shortly before she was shot by the German military. Then your eyes move upwards. Behind, the rather elegant white figure is a monolithic squared stone plinth with the words, "For King and Country" dominating the façade over the statue. You what! The political establishment could not allow her attack on patriotism to stand uncorrected. Of course the words partly reflect the fact that Cavell helped British soldiers get back home, did not hide the fact, and was therefore shot by the Germans. But Patriotism is also the last unassailable weapon of the munitions' people to pull us all into line. It had succeeded in 1914 and it was to succeed again. But Cavell, and we, know that we must have no hatred or enmity towards anyone, especially not expressed in weapons and war. Edith was, and is, right. After the Great War, millions more did know. The weapons of the arms manufacturers had gassed them or removed a limb. They knew there was a system needing systemic defeat. The issue was to defeat war. Decent men and women wanted to change things and rule out the possibility of war. Jingoism met peacemaking, and on the whole the movement through the War was from Elgar's rousing Pomp and Circumstance Marches to the dark, humble commitment of the Cello Concerto.

Yet, the project of peace was difficult and almost doomed from the start. At the end of a war it is most difficult to love your enemies or put to bed the hate adrenalin which so fully drives the process. In France and Britain the movement to make Germany pay was driven by hate, and even Lloyd George succumbed to it for a while. The young, rather verbose Keynes who spent six months in Paris at the Peace Conference describes it thus:

> In this lies the destructive significance of the Peace of Paris. If the European Civil war is to end with France and Italy abusing their momentary victorious power to destroy Germany and Austria-Hungary now prostrate, they invite their own destruction also, being so deeply and inextricably intertwined with their victims by hidden psychic and economic bonds.[129]

That judgment stands the test of time. The vindictiveness of the reparations, the occupation of the Ruhr, and other measures made sure that the underlying sentiment in Germany would be one of resentment, a resentment which clouded and obscured movements towards peace. Defeat was ugly and demeaning and the Germans, too, could not locate their problem with the munitions men. They talked about the Jewish stab in the back and other conspiracies; the issue became why they lost, not who caused the war. Initially, many blamed the military/political complex, tearing the insignia from their uniforms as they returned from defeat. [130] They turned to the Socialism of Rosa Luxemburg and Karl Liebknecht, until they were murdered, but soon the munitions men, punished by Versailles, were reinstated in the German national cause. Rather than real recovery, they would lurch into the National Socialism of Hitler, helped by munitions' money.

# PART III: THE WAR TO END ALL WARS?

*After this great world-wide tragedy the question was whether the world could change direction. Around 1918 there was not only deep mourning, but most of the statesmen of the era had seen that mutual armament was fatally destructive, and they understood something of where the merchants of death had led them. We have seen how President Wilson and other statesmen were determined the change the world order of escalating armaments. But would it change?*

*For, at the same time, the Great War had created the biggest and most profitable industry seen on the planet. It had a momentum towards weapons, and although it would now face a severe recession, it was not easily going to give up on its business. Would the subsequent history be one of disarmament or re-armament?*

## Chapter Eleven: Learning from History? A Review.

**The Understood Problem.**

The question of why the First World War happened has been asked for nearly a hundred years. This study is hardly coming up with an original answer for it was the standard answer in the twenties and thirties. Yet now it has become original and unheard! We recall the answer given by Lord Grey of Falloden, who should know "…the real and final account of the origin of the Great War. The enormous growth of armaments in Europe, the sense of insecurity and fear caused by them – it was these that made war inevitable. This, it seems to me, is the truest reading of history, and the lesson that the present should be learning from the past in the interests of future peace, the warning to be handed on to those who come after us."[131] We have reviewed the long history of the arms manufacturers and seen how they grew into industrial giants in Britain, France, Germany, Austro-Hungary, Sweden and Belgium and the United States all intent on selling weapons, and creating the kind of distrust where weapons were necessary. We have seen the international transmission of arms sales - battleships, cannon, guns and machine guns to Japan, Afghanistan, South Africa, the Congo and to Paraguay. Half of this story has not been told. The growth of armaments caused wars – the Russo-Japanese War, the Afghan wars, the Boer, Zulu and a dozen colonial wars, the 1870 Franco-German War, and many others. If you have bought and acquired weapons in excess of another nation, the temptation to attack increases and calculations of war take place. Otherwise, it would be pointless to buy the weapons in the first place.

So this great culture of armaments and militarization inhabited the major countries of Europe. Russia was weaker because it partly depended on buying in the weapons of France and Britain. Turkey found that three warships it was buying from Britain, the enemy it was shortly to face in the Dardanelles, were requisitioned by Britain in 1914 before they were delivered. Hey Ho. France, Germany, Britain and Austro-Hungary were all making calculations around their armaments and military might. As we have seen it was building into a crescendo of expenditure, which either had to be pointless, or end in war. The Great War was not an unfortunate confluence of events which tripped Europe into conflict, but the outcome of a long build-up of military confrontation. Big events have big causes and the cause of the Great War was the build-up of arms and mistrust over several decades. The trigger could have happened at any time. Thus, as Roch reports, as early as 1911 the organization of the six British divisions movement to France was planned down to a "dix minutes ârret" for soldiers to have a cup of tea. Even more knife-edged, after the Second Moroccan Crisis in 1911 McKenna wisely refused to move his ships until the Cabinet made a decision for or against war, because moving the battleships might immediately precipitate such a war.[132] Europe, primed, with weapons, was like a large box of fireworks with blue touch paper ready to ignite and send the whole box up. The Great War could have been prevented, but not without addressing the arms agenda to which all the major nations had subscribed, especially as their trust of one another was eroded by the messages of the militarists.

So the answer of Gladstone, Campbell-Bannerman, Lloyd George, Churchill and Grey was correct. The war was caused by the build-up of arms, by the agenda created by the private selling and manufacture of arms on an industrial scale. This conclusion is as sharp as flint and as solid as granite. The main problem was the arms manufacturers – Armstrong, BSA, Vickers, Schneider, the gun manufacturers of Liege, Krupp, Rheinmetall, Nobel-Befors, Du Pont, Remington and Skoda promulgating an agenda of weapons with a vested interest in wars and rumours of wars. Promoting belief in weapons, international distrust, military absolutism, a military-industrial complex, armies and navies leads almost inexorably to war. Conversely, addressing the evil of the private manufacture of arms – the post-War call of the Treaty of Versailles, President Wilson, Lloyd George, Lord Cecil, Sir William Robertson and many others - meant ending this industry which as inevitably produces war and death as the tobacco industry produces smoking and cancer. Great armaments cause wars, and eliminating arms sales and possessions allows the way of peace. What would everyone do with this understanding, this truth about war, which pressed so heavily on their hearts and minds?

**Forgetting the Answer.**

We pause to remember this momentous conclusion. We are explaining the cause of the Great War, and even, since most of them died or were injured through arms – shells, machine guns or gas - the direct *cause* of millions of deaths and injuries. This sickening truth will not be sidestepped. The build-up of weapons, promoted by the arms companies, caused the Great War. You will be tired of this repetition. You would think this answer could not be forgotten. But, astonishingly, it has. What causes World Wars? Oh, ah, we've forgotten. This conclusion has been buried and covered over by the very munitions people it identified. This full story is told in the second volume of this narrative. Really it needed two decades of political failure, a Hot World War and Cold War propaganda to drum it out of western culture. But it happened. What was a sharp answer, addressing the problem, became mushy, lost in a cloud of amnesia, especially fogged by naming Hitler and the Nazis. Disarmament was presented, following Churchill's interpretation of the Second World War, as the danger of appeasement, of not having enough weapons to address Fascism. Yet we shall see that the same arms problem underlay the generation of the Second World War and subsequent wars. The input of the munitions companies was sublimated and they are seen as passive, merely doing their job, indeed, their patriotic duty, to supply Spitfires, tanks, submarines, bombers and all the other tools of modern warfare. The supply, promotion and international dissemination of weapons had become legitimated, a patriotic duty, as the arms suppliers became an unquestioned part of the political establishment. It is the biggest whitewash in history, allowing the later dissemination of weapons world-wide without blame or condemnation. We are taught arms make us safe and do not question their purchase or use. The Great Reversal: weapons were the problem, but are now the solution.

So the Great War was not the War to End all Wars, but the initiator of something like 200 million war-related deaths in the following century, an horrific history including the Second World War and genocides, especially the Holocaust. That this whole history might be related to the arms people, the merchants of death, has also been forgotten and overlooked. We have become inured to militarized living and to frequently occurring wars. But perhaps it need not be so. The First and Second World Wars could have *not* happened, if people had been wiser; so it is possible that these millions upon millions of death and trillions of dollars could have been saved. If weapons sold worldwide cause wars, military dictators, create international distrust and open up the possibilities of oppression, they are a dumb option and we can do better.

**Idealism or Realism?**

Over the last hundred years most of us have been brainwashed into believing that disarmament and peace are a distant ideal which cannot be considered in international politics. This mantra conditions us to live with weapons and war as a permanent part of life. We will ask some people to fight for us and pay for the best weapons to make us safe. In 1918 they concluded that if the Great War was to be the War to End All Wars, the world needed to disarm. But that policy failed. It was appeasement. Now stocking weapons makes us safe. Or at least we vaguely hope they will. Disarmament is idealistic, but armament is realistic, a neat ancient Greek dualism. If we are all armed, then we will all be safe and wars will end. In the name of realism, we opt for the American model of everyone sleeping with a gun under their pillow, because that will make us all feel safe, especially on fireworks night.

We ignore all the arguments we have seen arise in relation to the Great War. Weapons destroy the trust between nations. Weapons often produce competitive arms races; if one side has them, the other side wants more. Weapons predispose to war, because that is what weapons are used for. If Germany has a load of howitzers, France will assume they mean war. With weapons, armies and navies the military come to have power within governments and usually they are anti-democratic and autocratic, because militarists tend to debate with guns. The old conclusion, that weapons, rather than preventing wars, cause them, does not go away. Disarmament prevents wars and armaments lead to them, but we have been taught the opposite.

Wars do not work, as we know from the Great War, Iraq, Afghanistan, Syria, the Congo and elsewhere. They cause long term trauma, waste, adversarial politics, social failure and economic disruption. They make problems worse. Often one war follows another, because people learn war. But still we sanctify War. The Russian War in Afghanistan was followed by the United States War in Afghanistan for obvious reasons. Wars cost billions and trillions of dollars. Moreover, with global integration and interdependence it no longer makes sense to have enemies; we are members one of another. Indeed, we are running out of real enemies. It does not make any *real* sense to think of waging war.

More than this, aside the fear the weapons manufacturers generate, how realistic are the threats from other nations? We have seen how the arming of Russia, making her a future threat to Germany and thus made her more in danger of German attack. And Austro-Hungary because she armed and attacked Serbia was attacked and destroyed as an empire by Russia, Italy and the other

Allies. And Germany fearing attack by the Triple Alliance of Russia, France and Britain armed and precipitated attack by invading Belgium, herself to be defeated. Much better, disarm and trust one another. Unarmed countries are safer because they are no threat. No weapons means no threat. No weapons means we are all safe. No weapons for sale in Bristol and Manchester means they are safer places. It's not difficult to work out. Disarmament is practical in making peace and ending conflict. Arming everyone and hoping that conflict does not break out is hopelessly *idealistic*. For all these reasons and more disarmament and peace are *realistic*. Indeed, it is the way most of us function in ordinary life day by day and there is no other way of living than through living with people and getting on without attempting mutual destruction. War turns out to be unrealistic, the source of vast debt and the very disruption of life. A war of two years takes twenty of recovery. Yet as a result of the Great Reversal, despite the lessons of the Great War, we have opted for arms as *realistic.*

**Why Disarmament Doesn't Happen.**

We have come to think disarmament does not work. It failed around 1900-19134, but why? There were dozens of disarmament meetings to get rid of weapons, but usually they were not successful. Here, we face one of the most intellectually challenging bits of this book. As we look back to the Conferences of 1899, or 1906, we see that disarmament does not work because the military are put in charge of the process. The argument goes as follows. When the military are in charge of disarmament, they tend to be against that which they are doing, because their jobs and careers depend on that which they are about to abolish, and so they confound the process and make sure it does not happen. In case that was too difficult, we will envisage the actual situation. Two sides plan disarmament and then they invite a load of generals, admirals, military strategists, defence chiefs, weapons experts and arms manufacturers to work out how disarmament should be done. They cannot do it. They conclude it will not work, and they are still needed for a few more decades. They find a few marginal cuts that will not make much difference, and the mood passes, because disarmament is so difficult. Admirals will not decide to abolish the navy or generals get rid of guns. So, of course, disarmament does not work, because those put in charge of the process do not want it to work. It is like putting the manufacturers of Maserati, Porsche and Aston Martin in charge of rigorously enforcing the speed limit; it will not happen. Disarmament can happen when the militarists, munitions people and defence departments are not in charge.

Then disarmament also does not happen because munitions companies break the rules, keep selling weapons, create distrust and inflame disputes to prevent disarmament happening. They try to destroy disarmament. They do not want to be selling snow shoes in summer. The wars can be internal or external, but their business is to keep us all afraid and allow the sales of weapons to continue. There are powerful groups with an interest in making sure disarmament cannot be thought about. Usually, they are close to and within government, talking up threats, finding enemies and arming them. So disarmament does not work.

**Why Disarmament does Work.**

But, of course, disarmament does work. If I am thinking about buying a gun to take to the office, it helps to know no-one else in the office is allowed a gun. Offices are safe because there are no guns. Conversely, in international affairs nations have all been armed to the hilt and some 200 million have died in war-related deaths and tens of trillions have been wasted through destruction and we constantly worry about whether disarmament works. Disarmament works, because if A and B disarm, then C and D do not need weapons either and the distrust of militarism is deconstructed. Disarmed people think differently. Heavily armed Brits might think of invading France, but unarmed Brits just go there on holiday.

Disarmament works because weapons are made to kill and destroy. They are a threat. We call it defence, but it is attack-defence, pre-emptive strikes, threats, weapons to take out weapons and weapons which defy defence. So the weapons of others threaten us and may well be used against us, as ours might against them. Unused they are a waste. But if we do not have weapons, they are no threat. With disarmament no weapons will be used in war because they do not exist, and the war will not exist. Most of us can work out that one.

Constructing what might have happened is often called counterfactual history. It is imagined and in an obvious sense "unreal". Imagining a world where the Great War did not happen would seem like wish-fulfilment, because it did; the states of the world armed and went to war. Yet the *factual* history mounts the case. The industry of munitions and war, what Eisenhower called, the military-industrial complex, has held steady and repeatedly produced its results. What we are considering here is an enormous accumulation of evidence, with different circumstances, that weapons and militarism produces war. This is not counterfactual history, but strongly evidenced history. In 1904-14 France and Britain helped arm Russia and contributed to the build-up to the Great War. In 2013 because Russia had armed President Assad, he was willing and able savagely to attack those who were looking for reform, bulldozing their lives with tanks and chemicals. The time has come in 2014 to question the presumption that arms make us safe, because the experiment has indubitably not worked dozens of times. Disarmament, nearly tried in 1932, will work, because wars without weapons become games like rugby, football, cricket and chess which we actually enjoy.

## Chapter Twelve: Christianity and Peace.

### Defeating Christianity.

Christianity has been mentioned in this text mainly in relation to some of the figures who featured in the peace movements and other individuals who appear in the narrative. Jackie Fisher was a Christian. In different ways, the Tsar, Florence Nightingale, President Wilson and many in the trenches were. But there is a bigger narrative in this period and it is one of the partial defeat of Christianity.

An earlier part of this story was the way Bismarck undertook to curtail the power of the Church in relation to the new German state. He waged the Kulturkampf to bring church schools and other institutions under the power of the new German state. For Bismarck the allegiance of Catholic churches especially and church schools to the Vatican and Christian teaching compromised the absolutism of the German State, as Christianity challenges all absolutisms. Really, the point at issue was the requirement of unconditional support for the Reich, reflecting the kind of position which had occurred in Prussia earlier. Bismarck was out to defeat the Catholic Church. At the same time German culture was also moving in a secular direction away from Christian teaching. Nietzsche, Wagner and others looked for a German mythology which would supercede the centrality of biblical teaching in the churches. This was partly because the place of Jewish history was resented, but also because ethnic history of the Aryans was seen as more important than the biblical treatment of human origins identifying all people as made in the image of God; it did not fit with the struggle of the races. It was a planned marginalization of Christian teaching in German culture and thought.

This kind of change also occurred in Britain. Not so much Darwin, but Social Darwinism, fitted with the idea of imperial conquest and Anglo-Saxon superiority, and many commentators accepted the inferiority of other races, and even the working classes, against the background of British domination and the extension of the British Empire. Public Schools looked more to the classics of

Greek and Rome, many of them extolling Empire, more than to the Bible and this same classical revival was present in France, and not surprisingly, Italy. So these cultural influences were seeking to push out Christianity as a "weak" set of beliefs for the age and they partially succeeded.

Another part of the Darwinist idea was "of nature red in tooth and claw". It was seen as a universal principle of the war of all against each, and was not difficult as a validation of the British Empire. Noble animals were predators. That was their nature and lions had to kill and eat as part of their destiny. The British were lions. Not surprisingly lions appeared at the bottom of Nelson's column, on stamps and elsewhere as a sign of the self-identity of the British Empire. Of course, many animals eat grass, and we humans do not have to behave like lions or hyenas, but this Darwinist idea was made into a general paradigm for political superiority and inferiority, together with a scorn for human weakness. And so British culture came to the broad intellectual conclusion that it is OK to shoot natives because lions kill impala, and it was taught to question why Jesus had not thought of this before he said, "Blessed are the meek, for they shall inherent the earth." With the Roman Empire all around him, surely he could have worked that one out.

**Christianity and Militarism.**

The time has come to face the empasse between Christianity and militarism. It occurs at many different levels. First, Christian teaching undercuts the common rivalry between tribes, races and nations that is often the currency of war. As opposed to ethnocentric conflict, Christianity insists on the common humanity of all races made in the image of God and therefore equal before God. It even suggests in Genesis 11 that the divisions of races and nations came from misunderstanding, sin and pride. More than this, the prophets deconstruct the idea of national defence and victory. Israel will be defeated and should concentrate on its own righteousness before God. The New Testament allowed no distinction of ethnicity, as Peter and then Paul were taught. Christianity is for people of every tribe, race and nation. There is neither Jew nor Greek before God, in sin and in salvation.

Second, Christianity critiqued the idea of weapons. Frequently in the Old Testament, chariots and war-horses are seen as pagan and destructive and part of the culture which must be rejected. Indeed, when Israel fights, it is often without weapons and with the help of God, as in the escape from Egypt and Gideon's fight in Judges. Then, in a bronze and iron age culture filled with conflict the persistent theme of "swords into ploughshares and spears into pruning hooks" emerges in Isaiah and the other prophets. The purpose of this change is clearly stated; it is so that we learn war no more. With weapons we learn war; without weapons we unlearn war. This principle cleaves through the subject matter of this book and it is made even sharper by Jesus' words, "Those who take the sword will perish by the sword." If you go for weapons, then in the longer term weapons will get you. Christianity, faith in the Prince of Peace, brought with it this necessary attitude to weapons, however compromised the attitudes of particular Christians have been in different periods of history.

Third, Christianity has a clear attitude to empires and imperialism. It begins with the great Jewish narrative of the Old Testament. The Israelites are liberated from Pharoah and the Egyptian empire. Partly, this was because slavery was unjust and oppressive and the Lord heard the groanings of the Israelites. Yet, it was also so people could be free to live before God and know something of God's laws. Abraham Kuyper's summary of this principle – "When you bow the knee to God, you bow the knee to no-one else." – shows the radical opposition to controlling political power which was built into Jewish and Christian understanding. Thoughout the Old Testament the theme continues. Every power aspiring to empire – the Philistines, Egyptians, Babylonians, Assyrians will be brought low. Pride comes before a fall, because overweening political power, using the power of the sword, will crumble. It is obvious why. Do people want a ruler who will threaten and use them to their own ends? No. When they get a chance to get rid of them, they do. Always empires rise and fall.

The greatest imperial confrontation is between Jesus and Rome. When Christians say they believe in the Lord Jesus *Christ* they are saying, Jesus is Lord and not Caesar." They are disassembling all militant imperial rulers who would gain control over others. This was Jesus' third temptation. He was offered all the kingdoms of the world, if he was prepared to accept evil, but he rejected the temptation. So Christianity stands against all the world's empires, including the French, German, Belgian, American, Russian and British. Really, the subtext of much 19th century European politics was the marginalization of Christianity because it was at odds with Empire.

Fourth, Christianity insists on forgiveness, first, with repentance, from God to us, second from person to person and group to group. Our forgiveness in relation to God is found in Christ's death on the cross. Christ was killed by a concatenation of human evils – greed, pride, anger, bribery, force, self-righteousness, hate, cowardice, lies, deceit and complicity in evil. It was all there, as it has been present in much more of human history. Yet, Christ was willing to forgive. "Father, forgive them, they know not what they do." He went beyond human failure with the forgiveness and healing of God. In Christ we are forgiven before God and in turn given the power and requirement to forgive sin. "Forgive our sins, as we forgive those who sin against us." It opens up the possibility of new starts, not just for Peter, the betrayer, after the resurrection, but for all of us, free before God from the power of sin and evil and in relation to our military past. Christ's way of non-reprisal, of reconciliation and friendship between people and nations is there to break the causal chain of evil. It is in the reality of repentance, forgiveness, grace and humility that weapons and war can be buried.

Christianity has the sharpest of edges with militarism. Jesus Christ, God with us, claims to *rule*. He has planted a kingdom and its ground-rule is peace, "Peace be with you", a pattern of rule without compulsion or domination. We enter the kingdom voluntarily and its character is one of welcome and service not domination. Jesus is described as the "Lamb on the throne", the most ludicrously unaggressive image of rule possible. Moreover, the Gospels recount the process whereby Jesus, telling the truth, is got rid of by the powers of his age in order that the established powers of Rome and Jerusalem may retain sway. He is crucified, the most obvious sign of the Roman military power to kill, but, through his resurrection, God's gentle way for humankind is opened up and the agenda of military control is blown up. Christians remember Jesus words *not* to fear those who can kill the body, not easy to obey, but still the deep truth for the world which must conquer aggression and intimidation. They are to be peacemakers, to love enemies, to deconstruct the petty quarrels of greed, anger and control, and they are to return evil for good. As Jesus warned, and this history has exemplified, those who trust and use weapons will perish by them. So the two patterns of rule are there – militarism and empire or the gentle rule of Christ, and as the Roman Empire, the greatest in human history, waned, Christianity continued to grow and spread now to some two billion voluntary citizens over twenty centuries.

But on the way, especially in 1914, it was defeated largely by the inadequacy of the Christians of the age – bishops seeking status, denominations which were sectarian, churchgoers who succumbed to ritual, believers who became small-minded, ordinary believers who could not stand on principle and Christians who were more ethnic than Christian. Some were taken in by "God on our side" and many just floated with the streams of secular culture. The Church was full of failures, as it always is, but these failures cost in the advent of a World War, despite those who swam against the tide - known and unknown - who loved their enemies and returned good for evil. This Christian failure needs acknowledging. It was not the last.

**Victory and Defeat.**

So we have to ask the question: what was the First World War, Victory or Defeat? For some nations, it was technically victory, for France, Britain, the United States, Italy, Belgium, but it was not victory for the many of a generation who had died, been injured or traumatized. Other countries, Germany, Austro-Hungary, Russia, Armenia, Turkey and Serbia had been traumatized beyond what we dare discuss by defeat and the destruction of war. Really, this was defeat for the world and the failure of European civilization.

By 1914 Christianity in Europe had suffered a partial defeat, the possessors and proponents of force had won, and they had their war. But they did not have the truth about this Great War and that was, *it should not have been*. That we now know all too clearly. For a while the Christian witness to war, arms, militarism was too compromised even to carry clarity into the post-war era, but it fought back in the next decade and a half. There were giants of peace and disarmament, and the outcome was in the balance, but the overall impact of the churches in the crucial countries of the post-war settlement was again trying to win the dramatic tryst between War or Peace in the twenties and thirties. This Second World failure not just in war, but also to address war, was revealed even more fatefully in 1939. This we examine in Volume Two.

## Volume Two: PULLING THE STRINGS OF FASCISM.

*After the Great War, the World War, the War to End all Wars, there was deep mourning and a strong determination to change the direction of world politics among both leaders and millions of ordinary people. They had seen the build-up of arms as the War's major cause, and looked towards disarmament, not least in the Treaty of Versailles. Yet disarmament and peace did not quite happen, though it was far closer in the events culminating in the Geneva Disarmament Conference in 1932 than is usually recognized.*

*Two new superpowers emerged. The United States and the USSR who were to dominate twentieth century military history. Each sought, and did not seek, peace, as their military establishments grew.*

*The titanic battle for peace centred on the 1932 Geneva Disarmament Conference, a world event backed by most of the major powers. Yet disarmament did not happen. We examine its world-wide support and why it failed.*

*Ideological Fascism is usually understood to be the origin of the Second World War in Italy, Germany and Japan. Here a different interpretation of Fascism looks at the support it had from those with an agenda for arms production and sales. Strong arms interests were supporting and promoting Fascism. They paid the piper and called the tune.*

*Retrospectively, the cause of World War Two is generally seen through the Churchillian lens of appeasement. Yet, that interpretation only applies to a few years in the late 30s. Instead the Second World War was generated by the defeat of the Peace Movement and by Fascist chaos throughout Europe, both substantially shaped by the funding and support of arms companies, bankers and elites. They controlled the scene after 1932 and led the career towards the Second World War.*

*So in Italy, Japan, Germany, France, Britain, the USSR and the United States the military-industrial complex was again able to produce a race in arms manufacture, a Second World War. The conclusion has to be: TWO WORLD WARS, THE SAME CAUSE – THE ARMS COMPANIES. They again made weapons the dominant world industry, a reality that could not be undone after 1945.*

## PART IV. SUPERPOWER MILITARISM.

*During the era before 1914 Britain, Germany and France had been the dominant munitions states spreading weapons around the world. Suddenly, in the Great War the United States moved to full industrialization around weapons production and became what is now called a "superpower". Two decades later the USSR did the same thing, with America's help, and these two countries became the Superpowers who would dominate the late 20$^{th}$ century. Here we look at how they, too, learned this culture.*

# Chapter Thirteen: The United States learns Militarism.

### Cowboys and Indians.

The United States did not enter the War until the 6$^{th}$ April, 1917, but its importance in all the events and subsequent history requires fuller treatment. We have looked in passing at the First World War weapons bonanza for the States, but something far deeper was going on. Within a few years militarism had taken hold, especially through the munitions companies which supplied the War in Europe. The United States is a vast country with enough resources for everyone and to spare. During the era up to 1939 it had no real external enemies and could have been a beacon of peace, yet despite this, it moved to becoming a military superpower. The munitions people played a significant role in this transition. It was later to become the biggest producer of arms the world has ever known and strongly militaristic. The States prides itself on its status as the 'Good Guy', but this good guy has two holsters and revolvers.

Of course, weapons were already well established. There were long-term systematic massacres of Indian tribes with the gun in most places other than Pennsylvania, where William Penn's Quaker move for peace took place. We might also try to ignore the use of the gun in the slave trade, and in the operation of slavery, but it will not work. Slaves were transported with the gun, kept in check with the weapon, and shot if they tried to escape. Eventually, slavery was fought with the gun in a Civil War which helped get arms manufacturers underway and give a military direction to the economy. The Civil War was a bloody affair, mainly fought with the gun. Some 625,000 people were killed, 50,000 while in prison, and a further 400,000 seriously injured, many of them amputees, so the effects of that war were written on several generations. The gun has become so engrained in American culture that it is difficult for Americans to think without them. Present gun ownership is about one per person across the whole country. The purpose of having a gun well might have been to shoot buffalo, not people, but now few buffalo remain and people are plentiful. Personal defense requires a gun, so that people will be safe in their homes from attack by other people with guns. If we all have guns, we're all safer than if nobody has guns. Right? Political campaigns for the right to own a gun seem able to ignore the fact that about 30,000 people die each year from guns, many from suicide, and a further 75,000 are injured; the United States has the highest homicide rate in the "law-abiding" west. So, the United States has long had a gun-dominated culture.

It also became equipped with bigger weapons. The Gatling Gun, designed in 1861, with a multi-barrel revolving mechanism - provided you cranked it well - fired 200 rounds a minute, allowing fast sequential killing. For some reason its inventor, Dr Richard Gatling, declared it would show how futile war was; that conclusion can be reached without profits from the Gatling gun and a modicum of thought. Naval warships were encouraged by the famous experiments of the Civil War. Cannon and other developments surged in output among Confederates and Republicans. There was another innovator, John Thomson, who worked on a smaller version of the heavy European machine guns. Companies like Bethlehem Steel moved quite strongly towards weapon manufacture and looked to overseas markets. So, as the Great War approached, the United States was already a weapon producing and exporting country on an industrial scale. It was also now marketing across the world.

**The United States Arms the Allies.**

When the War came, the United States moved into a pivotal role in weapon supply. One company was Remington Arms, already expert in 1914 in rifle production. When the European War arrived, they surged in size, building a big complex in Bridgeport, Connecticut covering 76 acres in less than a year; it is now abandoned but still awesome. They had a big contract to supply rifles to the Tsar for the Russian army and when there were strikes for an eight hour day throughout Bridgeport, they quickly gave in so that they could fulfill their lucrative contract.[133] But you could hardly say the workers had a pleasant time. The factory was a lethal place filled with lead powder and with regular explosives and machine accidents. It had 300 ex-soldiers patrolling to keep the workforce at their tasks in case they did not love their work. Nor was the Russian contract straightforward. As the Remington Society notes, Of the 750,000 Mosin-Nagant rifles manufactured by Remington, only 469,951 had been delivered to Russia by February 1917 (when Lenin took over and ended the Russian War). Remington-UMC was facing a horrific economic loss after Russia defaulted on the balance of the weapons but was relieved when the U.S. Government purchased most of the remaining, completed rifles. All the usual elements are there – the war loser defaults and the munitions' company is bailed out by its own government.

The scale of United States' arms production expansion was remarkable. Suddenly whatever was produced could be sold. European munitions purchases from America rose from $40 million in 1914 to $2,340 million in 1918, a *sixty* fold increase, giving an overall total for the European arms trade of *$4 billion* during the War. At the beginning of the twentieth century this was profiteering on an amazing scale. Money could be made more easily than growing grass. This was an industry for those who wanted to be rich fast. Weapons factories sprouted all over the Eastern States - using steel, chemicals, railroads and ships. This sixtyfold increase in arms sales was big, but it was nothing compared to what happened when the United States entered the War in 1917 and required its own weapons. Then, this bonanza increased to a frenzy as this great nation moved for the first time to its own war footing. It became a gigantic armaments factory. This growth put a new culture of hard money-making through arms close to the centre of American life.

**The United States' Entry into the War.**

It is easy to forget how strong the political policy of neutrality was in the States at the beginning of the First World War. Most Americans had fled from Europe and turned their backs, as they thought, on war. The Monroe Doctrine placed a strong political barrier between the States and European disagreements that was easy to understand and seemed workable. "We are not going to be bothered with European quarrels." On the 4th August 1914 President Wilson issued a proclamation of neutrality, and nothing seemed likely to embroil his country in what was a European, not a world war. The United States only had about 100,000 soldiers and throughout 1914, 1915 and 1916 there was no real preparation for engagement in the war thousands of miles away. Peace groups were therefore seemingly in control, winning the challenge of ignoring European belligerence. Politically, this was no passive position. President Wilson was *against* the colonialism which regarded states as possessions of western colonial nations like trophies of war. America was anti-colonial in principle since the War of Independence, and understood war as resulting from the race for territorial gain. It had an anti-imperial, pro self-determination ideology, even if Teddy Roosevelt had strayed from the path and the Indians were treated differently. On 7th November 1916, when the Great War was more than half over, Wilson was re-elected on the slogan, "He kept us out of the War". Next month, he sent a communication to the warring powers suggesting that they come to terms. His epithet was "peace without victory", an interesting slant on what should happen in, or before, most wars. Yet on 6th April, 1917, five months later, the United States had declared unrestricted war on Germany. How did this strong neutral stance of a popular President come to such a quick end?

The position on the supply of weapons by a neutral country was strongly spelled out in the Hague Convention of 1907 convened by Theodore Roosevelt. It included as Section XIII, Article 6, the rights and duties of neutral powers in naval war, ratified by the United States, "The supply, in any manner, directly or indirectly, by a neutral Power to a belligerent Power, of war-ships, ammunition, or war material of any kind whatsoever, is forbidden." That seems fairly conclusive, and it closes down the scope of wars considerably, but the munitions people were quite happy to subvert this position, and the supply of US weapons was soon underway mainly to Britain and France. Weapons factory towns sprang up all over the place, with big profits and well-paid workers, and vast quantities of weapons were being sent to the allies. This was partly by conviction and common ties to Britain, but it is easy to over-estimate that link. There were also lots of people of German origin in the States and the Irish did not exactly love Britain. The reality was more mundane: - British control of the sea would not allow weapons to be exported to Germany or Austria. The British were seizing any vessels, including US vessels, trying to trade with the enemy through neutral ports; so this was policy enforced by the British Navy. Weapons therefore flowed to Britain and its allies and became a vast source of profits for the munitions' men. But these processes do not stand still and by 1916 there were strong pressures emerging, led by the arms traders and bankers, to lead the United States into the Great War.

**Bankers must lend to the winning side.**

The logic was simple. American bankers lent about $2 billion to Britain, France and Russia to pay for armaments. If they lose the war, the banks go under. The banks must lend to the winning side. Therefore the United States must ensure that Britain, France and Russia win. In the Great War there was a two thirds success. Russia lost and went Communist, defaulting on its loans, to the extreme displeasure of the bankers. But Britain and France won; so in theory they could pay up, if they in turn got reparations out of Germany.

What we are discussing here is no new understanding. In 1936 the Nye Commission examined the United States' munitions industry. They scrutinized the process of American entry into the

First World War, and the overall conclusion of Senator Nye was initially carefully tailored not to offend the big magnates. "No member of the Munitions Committee to my knowledge has ever contended that it was the munitions makers who took us to war. But that Committee and its members have said again and again, that it was the war trade and the war boom, shared in by many more than munitions makers, that played the primary part in moving the United States into the war." [134] The Senator is being unduly polite in the first disclaimer, because he could not directly take on these powerful people, yet the second statement more or less means what he is disavowing. The dynamic which took the United States into the Great War largely came from the munitions men and their bankers.

Soon after the war started, Britain was running out of money to pay for munitions, and without loans from the United States, impossible from a position of neutrality, the trade would collapse. Moreover, the bankers had to lend to the winners, because the war losers would default. The arms traders put pressure on the bankers to take up this lucrative business. Again Nye comments more to the point, "Bankers were in the heart and center of a system that made our going to war inevitable. We started in 1914 with a neutrality policy which permitted the sales of arms and munitions to belligerents, but which forbade loans to belligerents. Then in the name of our own business welfare, President Wilson permitted the policy to be stretched to the extent of permitting the House of Morgan to supply the credit needs of the Allies. After this error of neutrality, the road to war was paved and greased for us."[135] In case the message didn't get through, he stated it even more forcefully. "When Americans went into the fray, they little thought that they were there and fighting to save the skins of Americans bankers who had bet too boldly on the outcome of the war and had two billions of dollars of loans to the allies in jeopardy." Unless Britain and France won, J.P. Morgan would go under. The United States' war entry was required by the financial pre-commitment resulting from the arms sales.

**Morgan the Banker and financing War.**

We have already looked at the way in which banking has become locked into international arms dealing. The Rothschilds funded the Napoleonic wars, French banks funded Schneider's sales to Russia, but now we come to the big one. J.P. Morgan and his American banking consortium funded the European War for Britain, France and Russia. Or rather, money went from J.P. Morgan and the banks in America to the arms manufacturers including himself also in America. Morgan was both banker and arms provider; he just moved wads of money over from his right to his left trouser pocket. The money never left the American coast, but paid for American manufactured arms. The arms – ships, howitzers, machine guns, rifles and explosives - went to Britain, France and Russia incurring the debts held by Morgan the Banker. America became, in part, Europe's armory and her bank.

We should consider the House of Morgan further. J.P. Morgan had begun with arms deals. Engelbrecht and Hanighen relate how in 1861 he pulled off a cunning scam foreshadowing his career as a high-class confidence man and his astonishing lack of moral scruples. "In the 1850s, the U.S. army had condemned as obsolete and dangerous some rifles.... These rifles were...sold by auction... [for] between $1 and $2, probably as curios. In 1861, he bought 5,000 of the useless weapons for $3.50 each and sold them back to the Army for $22 apiece, making $92,500, a small fortune. When [General] Frémont's soldiers tried to fire these 'new carbines in perfect condition,' they shot off their own thumbs.... The government refused to pay Morgan's bill. Morgan promptly sued the government.... A special commission... allowed half of [his] claim, and proposed to pay $13.31 a carbine. Morgan... sued [again] ...and the court promptly awarded him the full sum, because 'a contract is sacred'" [136] From this kind of start the House of Morgan moved into international finance, supporting government debt, and financing weapons and war.

When the First World War arrived, debt suddenly became the biggest of big business. Russia needed a loan of $12 million, but it was France and Britain that really opened up the financial possibilities. Over $2 billion of loans were extended to them to pay for the vast quantity of weapons being bought. Indeed, because the allies could not pay back the loans until much later, the bankers, especially J.P. Morgan faced a funding crisis. At one stage Britain owed $400 million on a maturing loan which they could not repay. It was underwritten by J.P. Morgan, which must have made the company very nervous, but the United States' Government suddenly advanced $700 million to Britain, allowing it to continue its war expenditure.

We should note in passing that in the First World War a vast array of debts brought Britain from being a creditor nation with assets all over the world to being a debtor nation owing funds to the United States; we were drastically impoverished. This hardened the Allies approach to the Treaty of Versailles, because they wanted reparations to help meet some of their debts. The indebtedness also led the move from free-trade to interwar protection, because countries had no leeway for a trade deficit. More generally, military and war debt have dominated public finances and been behind most of the financial crises that have occurred in the modern west. Wars are also responsible for the bulk of the internal sovereign debt which western nations have built up and which generate internal financial crises.

Earlier the Federal Reserve Board had been set up by a consortium of bankers including Morgan, Rothschild, Rockefeller, Schiff and others as a coordinating banking system with fractional reserve requirements and mutual guarantees of security. This allowed the bankers to be supported when they hit problems, as they did in the Great War. To bail out the bankers, Wilson's Government raised money through the issue of Liberty Bonds. These were widely advertised by "Uncle Sam" along with a strong appeal to patriotism. Bankers added to the propaganda, saying that thrift was a great public virtue. In the end about $18 billion was raised from the American public in this form.[137] While the loans came in at 3.5% interest or less, the funds were quickly passed on to J.P. Morgan and other companies who were needing money to keep the war-time bonanza sale of arms to Britain and France going;

obviously the House of Morgan charged much higher rates of interest to them. Thus the U.S Government financed a lucrative business for the House of Morgan throughout the latter part of the War, raising money cheaply for Morgan to lend expensively. This process of government validation of the Morgan lending programme allowed the company to make vast profits and emerge from the end of the War as an enormous financial conglomerate.

**Morgan the Blacksmith and Promoting Arms.**

But this was no mere financial pressure, because J.P. Morgan Junior acted as the focus of American militarism and arms production through ownership of US Steel. Morgan the banker was also Morgan the blacksmith but not Morgan the organ, as the Welsh would say. In the new century US Steel was the world's biggest company. It is an interesting story. Andrew Carnegie was a Scottish immigrant who had built up a massive steel company around the Pittsburgh area. Then he had something like a conversion where he moved from making vast amounts of money from steel to philanthropy, building libraries and funding education for ordinary people. It was an amazing pattern of generosity. To undertake this work Carnegie sold his steel firm to J.P. Morgan, supposedly for $100 million less than Morgan was prepared to pay for it, and it became the first $1 billion corporation. With Morgan's links into the arms trade, steel for arms became a strong focus, and Morgan became the hub of a vast pro-military pressure group. He coordinated the right-wing groups that sought to retain a military emphasis against the peaceful emphasis of Wilson at the end of the War. They were out to dump Wilson and get rid of left wing sentiments. They ran the first Red Scare, worried about workers who might copy the Russian Revolution. Morgan formed the American Legion partly to enlist returning troops in the fight against Communism. In 1926 he would also fund Mussolini to the tune of $100 million. This was a seamless ideological position. Morgan had the company which was the supplier of about half of the steel going into all American weapons. He was in there, lock, stock and barrel for right-wing militarism.

There was an ironic sideshow on this financial and military capitalism when an explosion occurred outside the House of Morgan's main offices on 16th September, 1920. It was initially seen as a Communist plot, but the New Castle News reported that the cause was a cart carrying nitro-glycerine moving to help excavate the foundations of the new stock exchange building nearby – a poignant image. The problem was explosives and capitalism, not Communism. Those creating the scare were scared into their own propaganda. Yet this anti-pacifist scare was no joke but part of a more widespread paranoia. John Witt conveys its scale.

> Private and quasi-private patriotism were often as powerful a force as the authority of the state. Ad hoc vigilante gangs and patriots – organizations like the American Defense Society, the American Protective League, the National Liberty League, the Liberty League, the Knights of Liberty, the American Rights League, and the Boy Spies of America – smashed anti-war demonstrations, interrupted pacifist speaking halls, and lynched men suspected of pro-German leanings. The more respectable National Security League held events urging national loyalty and condemning those whom Theodore Roosevelt (who would become increasingly outspoken in his nationalism during the war) called "weaklings, illusionists, materialists, lukewarm Americans and faddists of all the types that vitiate sound nationalism." Security League speakers were supplemented by the thousands of speakers ("Four Minute Men," as they were known) who operated out of the federal government's Committee on Public Information. Headed by former journalist George Creel, the CPI spearheaded a massive propaganda campaign in the form of an extraordinary 75 million pamphlets and as many as 6000 press releases..[138]

It was United States War Department against the peace people. Militarism, munitions, capitalism, banking, state loyalty, and anti-Communist jingoism all combined to set the direction of United States politics for a century, and by and large, they succeeded. Cynics might say that democracy is making sure that one side wins. Many following generations do not know they have been affected by this unrelenting stream of propaganda.

**The Munitions System for War.**

The creation of systems is always powerful. The munitions people, including Remington Arms, United States Steel, Du Pont, Winchester and dozens of others supplied the weapons, or sometimes failed to, and the War Department ordered them to equip the American forces. It had a more or less unlimited budget to throw at whatever was needed. Companies were even asked to provide goods at the price they themselves set. Because demand was so high there was very little possibility of competition in the tenders. It helps to have an overall idea of the types of supply needed. They included Guns of all types, Mobile Field Artillery up to massive howitzers, Railway Artillery – the biggest of all, Motorized Artillery, Sights, Fire Control Apparatus, Explosives, Shells, Mines, Bombs, Propellants, Artillery Ammunition, Tanks, Machine Guns, Service Rifles, Pistols and revolvers, Small Arms Ammunition, Trench warfare Material, Miscellaneous Ordnance Equipment, Navy Ordnance, Airplanes, The Liberty Engine, Other Airplane Engines, Aviation equipment and Armament, Radio telephones, Balloons, Warships and Flying Boats, Toxic Gases, Gas Masks, General Engineering Supplies, Listening Gear and Searchlights, Signal Material, Food, Clothing and Equipage, Miscellaneous Quartermaster Undertakings, Vehicles and Medical Supplies. Any one of these categories required vast expenditure and organization. All of these departments were buying to hand over to the army, navy and emerging air force.

Let us look at one bit of this vast system – the Old Hickory plant for producing smokeless powder, near Nashville, Tennessee. Building the plant cost around $90 million and Du Pont won the contract for setting it up. Benedict Crowell, the Assistant Secretary for War and Director of Munitions 1917-1920 states at one point that "The Du Ponts figured on both jobs, [Old Hickory and another plant] but quoted terms which the Government considered out of reason"[139] So the original asking price must have been much higher. The factory was designed to produce nearly a million pounds of powder a day, more than all the powder mills in the United States in 1914 could turn out in a month. It spread out over 5,000 acres and was probably the biggest factory of its kind ever built with nine powder lines. But, and savour this, it started operation on 1st July, 1918, four months before the end of the war and by the armistice it had only pushed up output to 500,000 a day. In other words it was a big explosive white elephant that on the 11th November, 1918, was of no use to anybody. The Du Ponts pocketed the hefty profit, and moved on. Or, not quite. On the 14th July, 1923 they bought the 500 acre site back for $650,000, less than 1% of the construction cost they had received five years earlier, and built it into a new production facility. Seems a good deal...[140] It was not surprising that Du Pont's profits rose from an average of $6 million in the four years before the War to an average of $58 million during the War and stayed high after it.

**The Bush Family Tree.**

Systems are full of people and families. Indeed, it is the people, and their values and faith, who construct systems, for they always contain human purpose and direction. More than this, people become like their work in the sense that the direction and values of work come to inhabit the souls of those who commit to their workplace – people become healers, teachers, cleaners, organizers, actors, musicians, waiters and watchmen. We focus the spotlight on one man in the War Department mentioned above. Enter Samuel Prescott Bush (1863-1948), the founder of the Bush dynasty. He gives a personal insight into the way the whole system operated.

Samuel Bush worked his way up and then became General Manager of a substantial steel firm, Buckeye Steel Castings. It was owned by Frank Rockefeller and supplied the Harriman railroad companies, of whom we shall hear later, with the castings that joined their coaches. In 1908 Rockefeller retired and Sam became President of Buckeye which we may guess, as the European War approached, looked to munitions for orders. Probably, by 1917 his steel firm was well embedded in making castings for a range of munitions equipment. As a result of this engagement, when the United States entered the Great War, Samuel Bush went to Washington in the early days of the Council for National Defense to help with munitions,[141] and when the War Industries Board was set up under Bernard Baruch at the beginning of 1918, Samuel Bush became Head of the Forging Guns, Ordnance, Small Arms and Ammunition Section responsible for a lot of important war contracts.[142] There is another explanation of how Sam Bush got the job. He happened to be married to Flora Sheldon, and George Sheldon was a Director of Bethlehem Steel Corporation, a dominant American munitions' manufacturer. Sheldon was also Vice-President of the Navy League, the organization agitating for a massive expansion in the Navy. This was an interlocking establishment and having your son in law in the right place was useful. Sam Bush provided contracts and George and his friends were bidding for them, though probably not with a strong sense of price competition.

Later in the War in the fall of 1918 Sam Bush was moved to the Facilities Division which was responsible for the location and construction of new plants for war work. Sam will probably have loosely supervised the building of the Old Hickory Plant mentioned above, though we can't be sure because the records have been carefully destroyed by someone or other, probably other.. He may also have been responsible for their disposal after the War ended. So you can imagine when Du Pont had charged the W.I.B. $90 million for the construction of the plant and received it back at the end of the War for $650,000, the Du Pont family might have sent a box of chocolates over to Sam Bush in gratitude. So, we surmise, Samuel Bush made a lot of money out of the War, and climbed towards the east coast elite.

This was not a one generation involvement. Samuel sent his son, Prescott Bush, to Yale where he joined a group of rich, spoilt, students, and in a prank, is reputed with his mates to have dug up the bones of the Apache Chief, Geronimo, causing not a little annoyance to the tribe who revered him. It's not clear whether they got the right body or were sober when they did it. We don't know how much study he did either. He then went off to the Great War shortly before it ended, and in another jape sent a letter back saying that he had been awarded the Victoria Cross by the British, the Legion of Honour by the French and the Distinguished Service Cross by somebody else. The letter was actually published in a newspaper and taken seriously, and his mother, Flora, had to write to the paper saying it was a prank. The locals did not see the joke and Captain Prescott Bush found himself in a scandal which required his quick exit from Columbus, Ohio. At this stage he was clearly a spoilt, silly young man. Sadly, his mother died in September, 1920 knocked down by a car, and he lost her influence on his life. Soon he was in with the group which would shape his future. They were essentially the sons of fathers who had become rich through war profiteering, and he struck up with the Harriman brothers and a number of others. They would provide him with jobs and a wheeler-dealer view of the world, and his progeny would include two American Presidents.

**Review – two possible ways.**

At the end of the First World War the United States was the richest nation in the world. It had suffered no internal war damage like other countries. It had nearly a million young immigrants a year coming in and pushing west, ready for work and producing the most dynamic economy the world had ever seen. It had the capital to invest in expansion. It also had no enemies against whom it needed to defend itself. It was imbued with Christian teaching among ordinary people. The possibility was there of becoming a beacon peace economy for the next century.

This did not happen for three strategic reasons. First, the United States economy had become rich partly by supplying weapons and loans for the War. It now had a vested interest in War and the possibility of being a peace leader was compromised. The defeat of Wilson and the exclusion of the United States from the League of Nations would freeze the United States from world peace negotiations for a decade, as the dying President understood. Especially important in this pattern were the massive loans made to the Allies. The loans to Russia were gone, as the Communists were not going to pay the capitalist United States, and really Russia lost their war anyway. But the loans to Britain and France were key, and remained to be paid. The Morgan related banks insisted on repayment and therefore these two countries, themselves bankrupt, had to extract reparations from Germany, itself more than bankrupted by the War. So the post-war settlement was frozen around re-paying the United States the cost of its exported weaponry. It was a policy which would carry forward to the Second World War in the raw suffering of Germany in the early 1920s.

But there was a second effect. The war profits from Europe and also from the United States Government moved into the hands of the du Ponts, Morgans, Rockerfellers and Harrimans. The detailed economics of the period are not for this book, but there is a strong line of causality from war profits to the Wall Street Crash. From the excessive profits of the munitions and banking companies during the War came the early speculative funds which fuelled the Stock Exchange bubble. You have excess war profits and what do you do with them? Basically, you cross the road from the offices of J.P. Morgan at 23 Wall Street to the Stock Exchange. There, that didn't take you long did it? The munitions people and bankers in the Great War had become used to a whole range of ways of obtaining easy money and profits. 1914-18 was get rich quick time. This kind of self-interest was translated into the Stock Market boom of the twenties. The big boys set the market expanding and then it was democratized. Six or eight years later the little people were prepared to fall for a get rich quick bubble, but they were hurt and millions lost their jobs. This instability damaged the ability of the United States to lead a stable world economy, especially in the early 30s, when through population movements and income expansion it was set to do so. This, too, helped Fascist groups in many different areas.

The third strategic reason was the continued influence of the munitions people. The system of arms companies and arms traders, international bankers and an expanded military did not just go away. It knew the heady days of the First World War, when profits dropped off trees and its people enjoyed the business of munitions far from the front and the fighting. In the twenties and thirties, demand shrank, but this sector looked for business wherever it could, irrespective of ideology. It was looking for the good days again. We will look at its attempts to re-establish its position against the strong peace movement of the interwar period. In the end, it won, and it was prepared to help create and use Fascism to do so. This is not to say that the arms dealers wanted a further World War. Yet, they did create the forces that undermined the strong possibility of peace. No, that conclusion is too flabby. The arms people did know that their business was war. They were prepared to work towards another massive War for the sake of their business. Again the manufacture and trading of weapons would generate a world-wide cataclysm of destruction – the Second World War..

## Chapter Fourteen: Teaching Russia Militarism.

### Imperial Russia and Revolution.

And so we move to the other Superpower. Russia has been one of the great imperial powers of Europe, subduing a whole range of other ethnic groups across to the Far East and almost encircling the top of the globe. It also pushed south into the innards of Europe threatening other nations from Scandinavia to eastern Asia. It could hardly be called a pacific nation, although most of the population just wanted to be left to get on with life without harassment. Their historic imperial might was typified by a Cossack on horseback, a decisive fighting machine in open countryside, and this model continued through the Crimean War until the First World War when the Russians lost one and a half million horses in battle. Russia also had a substantial navy, located in the North, the Black Sea and Vladivostock, and it had developed military hardware – cannons and guns. We tend to think of the Tsarist regime producing finely jewelled swords rather than effective weapons, but actually, as in Germany, the munitions people in Russia and throughout Europe had access to the Imperial Court and were selling vast quantities of weapons to a strongly militarized state.

The Russo-Japanese War, February 1904 to September 1905, increased this emphasis yet further. The direct costs of the conflict fought half way across the globe, were high, as were the losses of men and equipment, especially in the navy. After the defeat at the hands of Japan, many of the returning soldiers were angry. In order to rebuild their munitions, the Tsar called in Basil Zaharoff to organize the building of a vast munitions complex at Tsaritsyn (which later became Stalingrad) as a subsidiary of Vickers. The internal repression of Russians on Bloody Sunday in January, 1905, signalled the further reliance on arms for internal control. The Russian Government spent voluminously with French, British and other arms manufacturers and these costs had to be reflected in taxes or loans. The October Manifesto of 1905 moved towards universal suffrage and the establishment of the Duma and it could have had a long-term peaceful outcome, but the armed uprisings, partly led by military mutinies, created enough havoc for military repression to follow, and the peaceful outcome was lost to either state repression or armed uprising. The White Revolution became stained with blood and the Tsar was locked into military reliance which ultimately led to his downfall. Moreover, in 1914 Russia flush with a great arsenal of new arms and orders decided to intervene in a quarrel between Austro-Hungary and Serbia and lifted it to the status of a World War. This was an enormous tragedy for Russia, the Tsar, Democracy and the world. It had much of its origin in militarism and the sales push of the British and French arms companies. When the War arrived, the equipment was not all it was supposed to be and Russia frantically sought more weapons and was further accelerated into becoming a militarized state.

The conflict between war and peace was the root conflict. The Tsarist State was behind the times, elitist, not doing enough for ordinary people and not allowing the democratic development of government. It could have set out to help ordinary people, allow representative government and allow the peaceful development of this great nation, but the absolutist Tsar and the militarists largely won.

**Knowing War as it is - Defeat.**

Yet, Russia also had its advocates of peace. Russia has a soul formed on long winter nights of talk and reflection. We have looked at how warmly Leo Tolstoy's pacifism was received, but he had also acquainted the Russian people with the nature of war. He wrote *War and Peace* in the 1860s set back in the Napoleonic Wars, but he had fought in the Crimea and in 1855-6 wrote sketches from Sevastopol which gave everybody an awareness of what war was really like. He showed its hypocrisy, and was effectively one of the best war correspondents, describing both the officer putting on his white gloves and the process of dying with a shell fragment in your chest. Millions of Russians found that you do not unread Tolstoy on war. He insists on confronting the evil and vanity of the process. In "Sevastopol in May", he sets out the scene.

> But Kalugin was an egotist and gifted with nerves of steel; in a word, he was what is called brave. He did not yield to his first sensation, and began to arouse his courage; he recalled to mind a certain adjutant of Napoleon, who, after having given the command to advance, galloped up to Napoleon, his head all covered with blood. "You are wounded?" said Napoleon to him. "I beg your pardon, Sire, I am dead." – and the adjutant fell from his horse and died on the spot. This seemed very fine to him, and he fancied that he somewhat remembered this adjutant.[143]

Then characters actually do die and the horrible nature of war unfolds.

> Hundreds of bodies, freshly smeared with blood, of men who two hours previous had been filled with divers lofty or petty hopes and desires, now lay, with stiffened limbs, in the dewy, flowery valley which separated the bastion from the trenches, and on the level floor of the chapel for the dead in Sevastopol; hundreds of men crawled, twisted, and groaned, with curses and prayers on their parched lips, some amid the corpses in the flower strewn vale, others on stretchers, on cots, and on the blood stained floor of the field-hospital.

As the months move through into August Tolstoy describes the process whereby the Russians are defeated by the French and retreat in defeat. By the end of the account the glory of war is dead, as it rightly should be.

Others were opposing war. Radical socialists were beginning to plot the overthrow of the Tsarist State in the name of the working class. Reformers were trying to move politics to a western democratic model, and other reactionary groups of aristocrats, peasants, churchmen and soldiers were trying to hold the old order together in St Petersburg and Moscow in some kind of peace. Then as democracy was tried, though the decision was on a knife edge, the Great War came. Often the focus is on Rasputin and the Tsar, but the real fulcrum of opposing Germany and Austro-

Hungary lay with the foreign arms companies who praised their own equipment, saw bonanza time ahead and flattered the Russian High Command into confrontation over Serbia. Russia entered the War with its own doctrines of invincibility and high expenditure on munitions. "Everyone knows what happened to Napoleon when he invaded Russia" Yet, the German invasion was devastating. The West tends to underestimate the sheer scale and cost of the war to Russia; 1.7 million soldiers were killed and 5 million injured, especially on the open plains leading towards Moscow, and the heroism of Russian troops usually fighting with inferior or even no effective weapons is beyond telling. Here was endurance and courage to prevent invasion, and so in the end they did, until the Germans had to retreat. Yet the regime was also by now hopelessly wallowing in the debt of war and therefore also going down into the abyss.

**Lenin and Arms.**

The people who fight the war are not always those who win them. Here in Russia, the Bolsheviks - the Communists - had a steadfast policy of not fighting. First, following Marx they understood that militarism was a capitalist enterprise for the economic subjection of other peoples and countries. In this they were and are right beyond ideology; products like oil, opium, tea and uranium are part of a money-making web backed by arms and arms themselves are primarily sold to make money. War was part of international capitalism. The British had subdued the Cape, Calcutta and Hong Kong for commerce and trade, not out of love for the natives. Lenin argued that the Bolsheviks were therefore not going to fight in this capitalist war. This affected the Western munitions companies. Russia had ordered enormous quantities of arms and ammunition from the Remington Arms Company and others. When the Bolsheviks came to power, they just tore up the contract and Remington was left with huge stocks of guns and no hope of payment until they were baled out. That move is part of the American anger at Communism.

Lenin nailed down his opposition to the Great European War in seven theses. First, it was a bourgeois, imperialist and dynastic war; the capitalist classes were fighting it for their own interests, not those of the workers. Second and third, those who support the War betray socialism in other countries. Fourth, *Socialists* who support War have betrayed socialism and destroyed the Socialist International. Fifth, all justifications of the Great War are deceptions. Sixth, it does not matter if the Tsarist monarchy and its army lose, because they oppress the peoples of Poland and elsewhere. Seventh, the *real* war is for a socialist revolution in all countries.[144]. Obviously, these assertions can be addressed, but Lenin was clearly saying that the European War was *their* war, not *our* war. This is an interesting move, because, of course, those who start wars want all of us to own them. When we say, this is "our" war and we are buoyed by nationalism, we will fight, pay and support a war. Lenin cut the link. This is not "our" war. He gets a very bad press in the West, deservedly so, but we must be aware of why he partly so does. The genuine reaction is to a leader who was prepared to use force to come to totalitarian power. In this sense Lenin was evil. But another reaction was mixed up in this. A movement that repudiated war was a threat to the whole military machine, and the best way to remove the threat was to attack it, and require militarism of the other side. There is nothing the munitions people hate so much as those who repudiate their whole way of operating. By and large Lenin had a point. Wars have been linked to capitalism and imperialism for centuries and the underlying pattern of aggression has been located in imperial Britain, Germany, Russia, Austria and France.

Yet, there is also Lenin's belief in force. Tolstoy stood in his way and he hated Tolstoy's pacifism. His essay on Tolstoy when the old man was eighty, *Leo Tolstoy as the mirror of the Russian revolution* ended "Under the hammer blows of the lessons taught by Stolypin, and with undeviating and consistent agitation by the revolutionary Social-Democrats not only the socialist proletariat but also the democratic masses of the peasantry will inevitably advance from their midst more and more steeled fighters who will be less capable of falling into our historical sin of Tolstoyism!" This is verbal garbage not argument, and Lenin was not even consistent. Wasn't fighting a capitalist war Russia's historical sin even according to Lenin? So Tolstoy was right. Russia should not have gone to war. The essay is strong on bombast, but weak on both style and logic. Are you *for* or *against* war, Vladimir? You are against war and for war. So Lenin was a militarist; he was going to fight the *revolutionary* war, not the capitalist one, in military terms. When the Great War was declared Lenin was caught in Austria, Russia's enemy, and was lucky to escape with his life. Nevertheless, he lived by his seventh thesis. He ignored the Great War and concentrated on fighting for the Revolution.

But "fight" is the operative word. The formation of Russian Communism was based on faith in arms. This was the main characteristic that distinguished the Bolsheviks, the Reds, from the Mensheviks, the Whites, in the lead-up to the Revolution. Bolshevik Socialism chose the way of violence, terrorism, murder, bank robberies. It gloated in arms. Lenin despised law, gentleness and peace. He drove for action and that action was armed conflict. After the uprising in December 1905 Lenin commented, "they should have taken to arms more resolutely, energetically and aggressively...Those who do not prepare for armed uprising must be ruthlessly cast out of the ranks of the supporters of the revolution and sent back to the ranks of its enemies, traitors and cowards..."[145] Lenin noticed Stalin as someone committed to armed terror and promoted him. Lenin and Trotsky drove people to fight by shouting, bullying and asserting attack.

Stalin similarly was a man of war; his nickname "Stalin" means "man of steel". His heart was formed in arms. He said in 1905: "What is needed for a real victory? For this three things are needed: first, we need arms, second, we need arms, third, again and again, arms."[146] In was the failure of the Bolshevik USSR that it was founded on this unconditional commitment to arms, first internally in bringing about the revolution, and then externally in fighting others. Here was a militaristic regime in its very formation. Later, the Gulag was a Stalinist system of military control leading to the deaths of millions of people organized by a person who believed in killing. It was as portrayed by Solzhenitsyn - one of the horrors of humanity. Stalin, like Lenin, championed military socialism. They were against war and they were for war.

But there is yet another bit of the picture. The Bolsheviks were fighting, but they were fighting a different war, a class war which they saw as cutting across the nations of the world. They had killed thousands of opponents in the revolution. They wanted to redefine the meaning of war. There were against all other bourgeois governments but for the people. This was a real threat. French forces fighting against the Bolsheviks mutinied against their Government. Working class unrest was present in many western countries. This was an acute threat to the rich capitalist West, and they knew it. They were fighting for control of the workers and were determined to have it. Yet the biggest cost was to Bolshevism and to the working class movement. Rather than a movement of political reform for justice for ordinary working people, which was really incontrovertible, the toffs were able to raise the bogey of armed attack by Communists. Socialism in the west was split, democratic or militarist, to its long-term cost. More than this, Soviet communism was compromised at birth. Those who murder people in war either repent or move through to self-justification, and the self-justification imprisons them. Once you have justified the killing, you cannot easily escape from the expediency of murder. Lenin was as evil as Solzhenitsyn and others have discerned. Worse was Stalin, with a yet stronger doctrine of the expedience of killing, the arrogance that moves above the commandment: You shall not kill. For this reason, we shall kill and instigate the Red Terror. It was here that the Gulag was born. This story is continually one of self-justification, the argument by which the proponent moves beyond the commandment towards "righteous" killing. In the end, self-justification is ideological death.

**Churchill and Russia.**

Yet, there is another angle that tends to be ignored in the West. We focus on the October Revolution (Gregorian calendar), really the

November Revolution, in 1917 and miss what happened later. When the Bolsheviks, the Reds, came to power they, in particular Trotsky, negotiated an armistice over a number of months with Germany and Austro-Hungary. Russia was gasping from exhaustion. Trotsky's declaration as he refused to sign a Treaty is worth repeating.

> "We are removing our armies and our people from the war. Our peasant soldiers must return to their land to cultivate in peace the fields which the Revolution has taken from the landlord and given to the peasants... We are going out of the war. We inform all peoples and their governments of this fact. We are giving the order for a general demobilization of all our armies ...We are waiting in the strong belief that other peoples will soon follow our example.... The governments of Germany and Austro-Hungary are determined to possess lands and peoples by might. We cannot approve violence. We are going out of the war, but we feel compelled to refuse to sign the peace treaty..."[147]

Immediately, the Russians suffered, but Germany's Spring 1918 offensive bolstered by the eastern front troops moving to the west was also the prelude to their final defeat. Meanwhile Lenin and the Bolsheviks, facing acute shortages in the winter, failed to establish a democratic basis for power and to unify the nation. They faced rebellions from different groups out to defend their property and way of life. But more than this, the Communists experienced external aggression, especially from Winston Churchill.

An episode that tends to be overlooked at the end of the First World War is Churchill's role as Minister for War. When the Armistice was signed, there were still all kinds of skirmishes going on and Churchill was assigned to mop things up. Many of these were conflicts between Mensheviks and Bolsheviks in areas of Russia, an internal conflict, but Churchill in effect organized his own large-scale personal war against the Bolsheviks of the Russian Revolution. Though the Great War was supposedly finished, Churchill set up a coordinated effort using troops from all the

Allied countries to "strangle the Bolshevik baby in the cradle" as he so eloquently put it. The attacks of the White (Menshevik) armies in this Civil War were bolstered from the South, East and North-West by Churchill. The Bolsheviks were attacked in Arkangel, Murmansk, North Russia, in the Caucasus, and on the Odessa Front. The Red Army was defending the pre-existing Russian Empire including Finland, the Ukraine, the Baltic Republics and Poland. They were deservedly angry at being under systematic attack by states who had been allies in the Great War, but were prepared to take advantage of the USSR's supposed weakness. This, sadly, was the place where the USSR learned that they must live by force, well before the Stalinist era. The fighting talk of Trotsky grew in this soil.

From the South Churchill pumped a quarter of a million rifles, two hundred field guns, thirty tanks and large numbers of munitions to General Denikin who advanced over a front from Kiev to the Caspian.[148] In the East Admiral Koltchak was supported from Vladivostock in mobilizing the Siberian armies. Churchill in 1919 supplied "nearly a hundred thousand tons of arms, ammunition, equipment and clothing."[149] This vast supply of munitions was no accident and they were easily available with the end of the War. Churchill's attempts in the Commons to describe this aggression as merely created by the difficulties of withdrawal stretched credulity to breaking point. It was personal adventurism from one whose background was Blenheim Palace and the Duke of Marlborough, part of a vicious propertied backlash against those who would seize the property of the rich. Thus the formative experience of Communism was of having the whole military world against them. Churchill's later meetings with Stalin at Yalta and elsewhere reflect it. Churchill knew that Stalin would not trust the cigar in Churchill's mouth, let alone the man, and he tried to apologize. He asked Uncle Joe whether he would forgive him for being so hard on Russia after the Great War, Stalin replied, "God alone forgives..." and for a while they had some kind of working relationship. The Bolsheviks experienced a military onslaught from the allies which convinced them that they could trust no-one. Winston was the earliest origin of the Cold War, as well as the one who named the Iron Curtain.

But, it was worse than this. Russia gives its soul in war. The pacificism of Tolstoy and others had hovered like a dove over that vast land, but had found no resting place. It had lost the War in the Crimea and more recently in fighting the Japanese both on land and sea, and had a sense of military failure. Though its output of iron and steel was expanding fast and it had the world's biggest army, yet, in the Great War it was really again defeated, relying on its winter to rescue it. The Treaty of Brest-Litovsk with the Germans early in 1918 took a third - sixty-two million - of the Russian population away from Russia in a humiliating armistice. It was the rout of the Russian Empire. Though the defeat of Germany partly reversed this process, Churchill's engagement in the Civil War scarcely restored its soul. The number of people killed in the Russian Revolution was enormous, some nine million, many through famine, and the Communist regime was therefore born in blood and knew the deaths of millions. We cannot guess what that meant. Perhaps 80% of the productive capacity of the economy was also destroyed, including farms, and in Russian winters that makes life hell. The lesson was, never, never, never could Russia be defeated again in war and that meant militarization. The dove of peace still found no resting place in this great land.

**Stalin's Military Policy.**

Stalin's political career tells us of his approach to policy and international affairs. He was appointed by Lenin as General Secretary of the Communist Party and began to accrue power to himself as Lenin's health declined. Lenin mistrusted him and made clear in a final letter, effectively his will and testament, that Stalin should not be leader because someone more tolerant, polite and considerate was needed. When Lenin died in January 1924 with the help of Gregory Zinoviev and Lev Kamenev, Stalin gained dominance in the Party and then wiped out all opposition. He was involved in a confrontation with Trotsky who also felt he was too dictatorial and wanted more democracy in the Party. In 1925

Trotsky was removed from the Government, where he had been Chair of the Revolutionary Military Council, and quickly lost power. In October 1926 he was expelled from the Politburo, in November 1927 from the Communist Party, and in January, 1928 he went into internal exile and a year later was expelled from the USSR. Part of Trotsky's vision was for world revolution; he was the ideological firebrand. Stalin, by contrast, was more concerned with life within the Soviet Union. His focus was on national development, on "Socialism in one country", not an externally militaristic agenda.

While the West was going through the traumas of the Great Depression Stalin had three main things on his mind. The first was economic policy. The first Five Year Plan was introduced in 1928 and it involved a centralized model for the development of basic industry – iron and steel, electricity, machine tools and transport. It was a model for the rapid industrialisation of the USSR through central control and heavy investment. Stalin reintroduced pay differentials. In some ways the results were very impressive, with consistent growth which contrasted with the stagnation in Western economies during the same period. Soviet industry recorded a growth rate of 16% per annum between 1929 and 1940, an astonishing achievement. The understanding was that through this non-capitalist economic transformation the USSR would become the dominant world economic power, as it almost did.

At the same time Stalin was fighting to maintain his dictatorial position within the party and nation. He carried out purges against those who disagreed with him. There were the Kulaks (farmers) and Muzhiks (peasant farmers) who opposed Stalin's collectivization of agriculture. They were attacked by the Red Army and starved to death. Then in 1934 he had a disagreement with Sergey Kirov, the Leningrad Party boss. The latter finished up being assassinated. In September 1936 Stalin appointed Nicholai Yezhov as head of the Communist Secret Police who arrested and executed all those who might be seen as Trotsky sympathizers. Shortly after he began a purge of the Red Army which finished by having 30,000 of its members assassinated.

Yezhov and Stalin then carried out purges of anyone who might be an enemy. Something like one in twenty of the population was involved. Finally, Stalin killed those in the Secret Police who knew about the purge, so that he could not be blackmailed by them. Estimates of how many were killed by Stalin's purges vary. They were in excess of twenty million and may have been far higher. They show Stalin so insecure about his internal position that he was prepared to go to any lengths to maintain it.

The third element in Stalin's policy was external militarization, but it was a later element in the picture. After the First World War the USSR still had the population of France, Italy, Germany and the United Kingdom combined. It was a mighty country, one sixth of the world economy. When the leap forward in steel, coal and manufacturing had occurred, Stalin was still relatively unarmed and he faced no obvious military threat. Actual military spending was low in 1929.[150] Stalin did not want militarization until and beyond the arrival of Hitler. These are his words in 1936. "We are pursuing a policy of peace and we are prepared to come to an agreement concerning disarmament, including complete abolition of standing armies, which we declared to the whole world as far back as the time of the Genoa Conference. Here is a basis for agreement in the diplomatic field."[151] Looking at Stalin's position more generally leads one to believe that he meant them. Stalin wanted to grow the USSR through industrialization and not through external wars. The USSR had no thirst for external aggression.

**The United States Arms the USSR.**

While the West faced the Great Slump, the Soviet economy continued to grow. Yet, Stalin saw a war coming as soon as Hitler came to power. Given Adolf's rabid anti-Communist stance, it was not difficult. Stalin's aim was to be armed, to stay out of war as long as possible, and to intervene decisively when the time came. In the early 30s he set out to create that military base. Surprisingly, help came from United States' manufacturers. They were keen for business, especially with their domestic slump, and began selling factories, machine tools and military production lines to manufacture everything from tanks to rifles, and much more besides. It is interesting how little objection American military capitalists had to selling weapons and weapons' production systems to the Communists. There was a strong relationship between tractor factories and tank factories. Tanks have caterpillars and tractors have caterpillars. Step in the Caterpillar Tractor Company. Tanks need armour. Never mind. T-34 tanks were built with several million tons of armour-plate imported from the United States. The Russians received so much help that one construction engineer was awarded the Order of Lenin. Tanks need engines, and so the Chase National Bank of New York (now Chase Manhattan) tried to export a large quantity at $2,000 a throw. With a recession in the USA, the Soviet Union offered an alternative market; gold was coming in from Siberia and the labour camps to pay for imported goods. Tractor factories could make tanks, and Ford and other companies set about exporting the world's best tank production factories to the USSR. The big ones were in Stalingrad, Kharkov, Chelyabinsk and Leningrad. Ford and other companies completely built them. Soon Kharkov was turning out 8-10 tanks a day, and the USSR had the most modern munitions industry in the world courtesy of the USA.

The United States armed the USSR? It is so unthinkable that we need to dwell with the process. The book by Anthony Sutton, *The Best Enemy that Money can Buy*, and his other writings convey the irony of the move and deserve detailed study for the wealth of detail, especially since they continued long after the Cold War was in full swing. Sutton was forced out of the Hoover Institute at Stanford University for detailing these links, and stands out as an independent scholar, prepared to point out the unpalatable. The following selection of western supplied weaponry conveys only some of the vast western contribution to the arming of the USSR through the 1930s into the Cold War.

1. Ford-Gorki military truck assembly plant (1930)

2. The Brandt (Detroit) ZIL assembly plant for anti-aircraft/rocket launch trucks (1929-36)

3. Kama River, the world's largest military truck plant. Big million dollars contracts for Fiat, Gulf and Western, Honeywell, Glidden, Holcroft, Landis and other mainly US firms. Pushed by David Rockefeller (Chase Manhattan), Kissinger, William Casey and others. (1968-73)

4. Computers. Western computer sales, mainly American, to Soviet bloc were running at $40 million annually by late 60s. Obvious military uses..

5. Military aircraft. Martin (full bomber design), Douglas, Vultee among 20 American companies supplying parts, technical assistance for complete planes and aircraft manufacturing plants between 1932-40. Later Rolls Royce, Wright Cyclone and Pratt and Whitney supplied engines, including leading Rolls Royce turbojets.

6. Big Chemical factories in late 30s by Du Pont, Nitrogen Engineering (NY). 50s and 60s fifty chemical plants acquired from West including the firms Monsanto, Occidental Petroleum and others. Chemical weapons components came from Shering, Rhone-Poulenc, Monsanto, ICI (1975-85)

7. The three great USSR tanks factories (Stalingrad, Kharkov and Chelyabinsk) were largely US made by Ford and other companies with some German and British input by a range of other suppliers and engineers. (early 30s).[152]

This process is odd. The people who organized these sales and the banking that went along with it were not closet socialists, but right wing conservatives like David Rockefeller and later Henry Kissinger. It was more or less continuous, before and after the War. They knew the Russians were Communists, and presumably they were aware that these great plants had vast military implications. They were used in the Second World War of course and in the Vietnam War. They helped the USSR's development of nuclear weapons. Why did they do it? It seems these people were used to pushing capital around among the big players and this was merely good business. They felt they could run the show on both sides.

Walter Scott Dunn's conclusion is as follows. "The American built factories and their equipment formed the basis for the Soviet war industry in World War II. These factories, far more efficient in mass production than their German counterparts, made the tanks and other weapons that defeated the Germans." [153] Other evidence for this process emerges in relation to the Spanish Civil War, where there was a United States' embargo on weapons from 8th January, 1937 until the 1st April, 1939 and investigations into where US arms found there came from. The Italian newspaper *Popolo d'Italia* said that "the United States exported arms and munitions totalling upwards of $20,000,000 of which nearly $10,000,000 was bought by the Soviet Union, which in turn sent the arms and munitions to Red Spain."[154] Further, in responses to charges that the United States was directly arming the Red Spanish, secretary of State Hull stated that manufacturing rights for certain types of Boeing, Curtis and Martin planes had been sold by these companies to the Soviet Union.[155] He is hardly likely to be lying. During the depression therefore tank, plane and many other kinds of weapon system were passed wholesale to the Soviet Union by United States companies with Government approval. This process of arming the Communists was undertaken from when the Geneva Peace Conferences were still underway through to the Second World War when Stalin formed a non-aggression treaty with Hitler. It went against the official United States' orientation to the Soviet Union, but Nelson's telescope did its work again. Indeed, later we will see that it was Nelson's binoculars. One eye couldn't see that they were arming the Communists and the other eye couldn't see that they were arming the Nazis and the Fascists. People in the system were closing both eyes. What weapons? Where? They are Communists? Reds? Anticapitalists? When it came to business, these companies inveighed against Socialism and Communism like operatic baritones, while happily jumping into bed with the Reds to sell them arms (to mix metaphors). Good old capitalism armed the Soviets, helped them copy western weapons, gave them the equipment to move fast into Eastern Europe at the end of the Second World War and make the transition to a superpower sitting on the other side of the Cold War. It is time the United States came face to face with its contribution to its own international problems.

**The Militarized USSR.**

Always we focus on Stalin and the supposedly dominant political leaders of the Communist State, but these American military factories, the world's best, became vast industrial complexes, and by the time Hitler had been defeated in 1945 they were as firmly entrenched as the Pentagon was to become in the United States. Stalin was in part being run by the military machine supplied by the United States and the West because its industrialization had taken this form. The United States munitions people had successfully created the next "enemy". The avid anti-Communists had armed the Communists. But we move ahead too fast. Between the two World Wars there was great hope of peace.

# PART V: DEFEATING PEACE.

*The familiar British construction of the inter-war period is of Churchill's warning to re-arm against the coming Fascist challenge, which was ignored through appeasement until it was nearly too late. The reality was actually very different. Between 1918-33, fifteen years of the twenty one inter-war years, there was a world-wide attempt at peace and disarmament backed by popular support, statesmen and some politicians. It was opposed by the arms manufacturers, their bankers, some of the military and some other politicians. These opponents just managed to destroy the Great Geneva Disarmament Conference of 1932. They set in train the re-armament which opened the way for Hitler and led the descent into war. We need to consider the way Churchill and the Conservatives among others ignored this earlier chance to avoid another World War.*

## Chapter Fifteen: Peace and Disarmament or Arms and War?

### The Obscenity of War and the Peace Movement.

Although there were pressures towards militarism, most of the world's population was in a very different place. The end of the First World War involved a worldwide time of grief and remorse. A generation of young men throughout Europe and North America were dead, leaving parents, fiancées, wives and children orphaned and living with loss. The numbers of injured were vast – some living with the after effects of chemical weapons, others without limbs and others blind, deaf or lame. Another great group of people had their hearts and lives seared by what they had witnessed and were "shell-shocked" into withdrawal and silence. Even without the witness of the war poets everyone who thought had to conclude that this Great War was wrong and evil, a failure for humankind of unprecedented levels.

The mourning and weeping of spirit did not just stop there, but developed into a determination, shared by millions, that this war would be the War to End All Wars. It was no accident that the BBC formed in 1922 had as its motto the verse from Isaiah saying, "Nation shall speak peace unto nation." This attitude was held by many. One example is Vera Brittain who served as a nurse during the Great War. Her fiancé Roland Leighton, her friends Victor Richardson and Geoffrey Thurlow and her brother Edward Brittain MC were killed in battle after they had exchanged a stream of letters sharing the experiences of the war[156]. A short poem, "Epitaph on my days in Hospital" conveys her experience of Christ during this period.

I found in you a holy place apart,
Sublime endurance, God in man revealed,
Where mending broken bodies slowly healed
My broken heart.

She became a pacifist joining the Peace Pledge Union and the Anglican Pacifist Fellowship. She was principially unhardened to war and killing and later campaigned against carpet bombing of German cities. In 1970 when she died she had requested that her ashes be spread on the grave of her brother, Edward, saying "...for nearly 50 years much of my heart has been in that Italian village cemetery". Her wishes were carried out by her daughter, Shirley Williams, another warrior for peace. People's whole lives were lived in the sadness of war loss and the determination to prevent it again. Most of the nations wanted actions and structures which would move beyond European rivalries and establish world peace. It was in this spirit that the League of Nations was formed. We have already seen Woodrow Wilson's vision for it.

This great movement for peace almost succeeded. Its ultimate failure is a tragic story, but deeply instructive, because it points to how peace can be subverted. Nation can be pitted against nation. War profiteering can win. The munitions' people can shackle peace movements. Establishments prove incapable of decisive action. The popular press can be easily stirred to stir jingoism and distrust, and hawks without good arguments can succeed because they shout loudest. Even significant structures like the League of Nations can be made impotent, when humbug confuses the simple, and weapons sold to X can create fear in Y and Z. Weapons' manufacturers bleat the necessity of defence until they are heeded. The military need jobs. Aggression and threats are the best ways to promote peace. All of these moves, unaddressed and unexamined, can pull others back into militarism. A successful peace movement needs far more than sentiment. It needs to be rigorous, require observance and honesty, and it needs to know and outplay its enemies. We need to learn again from this enormous failure.

**The Contraction of the Worldwide Munitions' Industry.**

At the end of the First World War the arms companies were the world's biggest industry and rolling in profits, but suddenly they were without demand for their products. There were all kinds of conflicts which carried on after the Armistice, using the vast surfeit of weapons available. Jeremy Black records conflicts in Bukara and Khiva, previously Tsarist protectorates, Outer Mongolia, a revolt in Egypt (1919), in Persia (1921), the Chanak Crisis with Turkey (1922), the French-Druze confrontation in Syria (1925-7), in Morocco (1920-25), Java (1926) and Sumatra (1927). The Italians fought brutally in Libya in 1922 killing perhaps 50,000 civilians and then there were the great confrontations surrounding Russia, including the war with Poland which led to hundreds of thousands of deaths.[157] There were also Churchill's activities in relation to the newly formed USSR. But these conflicts generated no new need for weapons and were small compared with what had gone before. The White Russians were using war surplus. So the arms companies faced an enormous crisis: they were without demand for their products and faced annihilation.

Suddenly the industry had to contract convulsively. Because Germany was forbidden weapons and weapons manufacture, the enemy had disappeared and there was no obvious threat to peace on the horizon. Britain, the United States, France and the other allies were awash with weapons which they did not need. After November 1918 Britain had a surplus valued at £1 billion, including 10,000 aircraft. Germany surrendered 5,000 heavy and field guns, 25,000 machine guns, 3,000 mortars and 1,700 airplanes, adding to the surplus. Some were sold on to other regimes, for example the warlords in China.[158] Others just became fireworks. In August 1920 200 tons of war surplus powder and shells collected by Francis Bannerman exploded on Pollepel Island on the Hudson River in an unscheduled display. We should be aware of the extent to which the munitions' people contracted in a very short time, in Britain as elsewhere. As the economy had been distorted by war, it now needed to readjust to useful industrial output. Of course, they were swimming in profits which they were free to use as they saw fit. They constituted a vast and powerful tranche of capital, but for the immediate future they faced a level of industrial contraction unknown before.

Their response was mixed. One move was into civilian forms of production. Massive opportunities were opening up with the new technologies. The age of oil and electricity was dawning. Refrigeration, cars, radio, bikes, coaches, passenger liners, mass produced newspapers, steel frame buildings, and dozens of other developments made this potentially the most exciting century technologically and industrially that the world had ever seen. It is interesting to see the role of the company, ICI, in this transition. It was formed in 1926 from Brunner Mond (who had run the famous Silvertown explosives factory which did actually explode in the First World War), Nobel Explosives, the United Alkali Company and the British Dyestuffs Corporation. It became Britain's largest company involved in fertilizers, paints, insecticides, plastics, artificial fabrics, plastics, pharmaceuticals, demonstrating that companies could move from munitions to something more useful.

Others hung onto their munitions business and became even more aggressive in seeking business than they had been when it was easy to come by. This involved looking worldwide, stirring up countries to war, bribery and putting intense pressure on politicians, especially through those who were financially linked to the arms business. The Nye Commission's overall conclusions were:

> The Committee finds, under the head of sales methods of the munitions companies, that almost without exception, the American munitions companies investigated have at

times resorted to such unusual approaches, questionable favors and commissions, and methods of "doing the needful" as to constitute, in effect, a form of bribery of foreign governmental officials or of their close friends in order to secure business.

The committee realizes that these were field practices by the agents of the companies, and were apparently in many cases part of a level of competition set by foreign companies, and that the heads of the American companies were, in cases, apparently unaware of their continued existence and shared the committee's distaste and disapprobation of such practices.

The committee accepts the evidence that the same practices are resorted to by European munitions companies, and that the whole process of selling arms abroad thus, in the words of a Colt agent, has "brought into play the most despicable side of human nature; lies, deceit, hypocrisy, greed, and graft occupying a most prominent part in the transactions."

The committee finds such practices on the part of any munitions company, domestic or foreign, to be highly unethical, a discredit to American business, and an unavoidable reflection upon those American governmental agencies which have unwittingly aided in the transactions so contaminated.

The committee finds, further, that not only are such transactions highly unethical, but that they carry within themselves the seeds of disturbance to the peace and stability of those nations in which they take place. In some nations, violent changes of administration might take place immediately upon the revelation of all details of such transactions. Mr. Lammot du Pont stated that the publication of certain du Pont telegrams (not entered in the record) might cause a political repercussion in a certain South American country. At its February 1936 hearings, the committee also suppressed a number of names of agents and the country in which they were operating, in order to avoid such repercussions.

The committee finds, further, that the intense competition among European and American munitions companies with the attendant bribery of governmental officials tends to create a corrupt officialdom, and thereby weaken the remaining democracies of the world at their head.

The committee finds, further, that the constant availability of munitions companies with competitive bribes ready in outstretched hands does not create a situation where the officials involved can, in the nature of things, be as much interested in peace and measures to secure peace as they are in increased armaments.

The committee finds also that there is a very considerable threat to the peace and civic progress of other nations in the success of the munitions makers and of their agents in corrupting the officials of any one nation and thereby selling to that one nation an armament out of proportion to its previous armaments. Whether such extraordinary sales are procured through bribery or through other forms of salesmanship, the effect of such sales is to produce fear, hostility, and greater munitions orders on the part of neighbouring countries, culminating in economic strain and collapse or war.

The committee elsewhere takes note of the contempt of some of the munitions companies for those governmental departments and officials interested in securing peace, and finds here that continual or even occasional corruption of other governments naturally leads to a belief that all governments, including our own, must be controlled by economic forces entirely.[159]

There was an underground desperation among these companies to get back to the days when they could sell to anyone and arms races guaranteed their prosperity. It was not that they were looking for another World War, because they did not think strategically, except about selling weapons. Their motivation was profit, and it drove them wherever there was money. The apostle Paul's dictum that the love of money is the source of all evil gets the emphasis right. The munitions people sold weapons, not to kill people, but to make money. They would not give up on their business, unless they had to.

**The Forming Principles of the League of Nations.**

Meanwhile the politicians were working for disarmament. It was not just the people who had a longing for peace but also statesmen throughout the western world. This was a strong widespread determination. After all the World War had to be seen by any humane person as the greatest political failure in human history, and many of the statesmen had a strong grasp on the fact that militarism was the problem. Lloyd George was asked a question about private munitions at a big conference in the Central Hall, Westminster, on 18th January, 1918 before the War had ended. His answer is significant:

> A delegate inquired whether I would give an undertaking that the production of armaments here (in Britain) should be nationalised, and private profiteering in these engines of destruction brought to an end. My reply was:- All I can say is that, speaking for myself, I am entirely in sympathy with that proposition. I do not think there ought to be any pecuniary incentive to encourage armaments in the world, and I am entirely in sympathy with the spirit of that question."[160]

The phrase, "pecuniary incentive to encourage armaments" cannot be gainsaid. You aim to sell arms which will kill people to make profits. The link between profits and death was well understood. The first move to end the private manufacture of arms came with the formation of the League of Nations at the Treaty of Versailles in 1919 with Woodrow Wilson, the United States' President as the chief architect. It was established by a Covenant, carrying its biblical meaning of an agreement made with God under the norms which should govern human life - as an instrument for world peace, no less. The first seven articles were constitutional, and then armaments were addressed in a series of powerful articles. They are worth quoting in full.

**Article 8.**

**The members of the League recognize that the maintenance of peace requires the reduction of national armaments to the lowest point consistent with national safety and the enforcement by common action of international obligations.**

**The Council, taking account of the geographical situation and circumstances of each State, shall formulate plans for such reduction for the consideration and action of the several Governments. Such plans shall be subject to reconsideration and revision at least every ten years.**

**After these plans shall have been adopted by the several Governments, the limits of armaments therein fixed shall not be exceeded without the concurrence of the Council.**

**The Members of the League agree that the manufacture by private enterprise of munitions and implements of war is open to grave objections. The Council shall advise how the evil effects attendant upon such manufacture can be prevented, due regard being had to the necessities of those Members of the League which are not able to manufacture the munitions and implements of war necessary for their safety.**

**The Members of the League undertake to interchange full and frank information as to the scale of their armaments, their military, naval and air programmes and the condition of such of their industries as are adaptable to war-like purposes.**

**Article 9. A permanent Commission shall be constituted to advise the Council on the execution of the provisions of Articles 1 and 8 and on military, naval and air questions generally.**

Article 10. The Members of the League undertake to respect and preserve as against external aggression the territorial integrity and existing political independence of all members of the League. In case of any such aggression or in case of any threat or danger of such aggression the Council shall advise upon the means by which this obligation shall be fulfilled.

Article 11. Any war or threat of war, whether immediately affecting any of the Members of the League or not, is hereby declared a matter of concern to the whole League, and the League shall take any action that may be deemed wise and effectual to safeguard the peace of nations....

Article 12. the members of the League agree that, if there should arise between them any dispute likely to lead to a rupture they will submit the matter either to arbitration or judicial settlement or to enquiry by the Council....

Article 13. ...judicial settlement, the Court to which the case is referred shall be the Permanent Court of International Justice. The members of the League agree that they will carry out in full good faith any award or decision that may be rendered, and that they will not resort to war against a Member of the League that complies therewith...

Article 14. ... The Council shall formulate and submit to the members of the League for adoption plans for the establishment of a Permanent Court of International Justice....

Article 15. ...Members agree that a dispute not submitted to arbitration or judicial settlement will be submitted to the Council and then the Assembly....

Article 16. Should any member of the League resort to war in disregard of its covenants under Articles 12, 13 or 15, it shall ipso facto be deemed to have committed an act of war against all other Members of the League, which

**hereby undertake immediately to subject it to the severance of all trade or financial relationships...It shall be the duty of the Council in such case to recommend to the several Governments concerned what effective military, naval or air force the members of the League shall contribute to the armed forces to be used to protect the covenants of the League...**

**Article 23. ....will entrust the League with the general supervision of the trade in arms and ammunition with the countries in which the control of this traffic is necessary in the common interest.**

These are deep commitments and it is quite clear that the aim is to eliminate aggression through armaments from all international relationships. We note, too, that this is not pacifism in the sense of vaguely hoping that unilateral declarations of peacefulness will work, or that individual people or nations should renounce fighting. Rather it is an international system of law and justice which prohibits national aggression, and controls the build-up of arms that lead to aggression, as unjust and punishable. As such it is principled common sense. Why should a nation have a right to kill and destroy the people and property of another nation, when universally this is ruled out within nations? If a nation does make war in violation of the Covenant, Article 16 allows for both economic sanctions and common military intervention from other members. There were other provisions against secret treaties, and all in all this was one of the most powerful structures for peaceful world relations that could be envisaged. And even though some nations have compromised and undermined the Covenant, its value and significance have never been destroyed. It was undermined, but this model could be tried again next year and properly implemented as a basis for world peace.

**Carrying out Disarmament.**

Gradually, the League of Nations became a hive for those concerned with disarmament. One key figure was Lord Robert

Cecil, an English Conservative by background and an outstanding statesman for peace. One of his themes was to advocate "qualitative disarmament" whereby all nations move towards giving up aggressive arms, the kind forbidden to the vanquished powers – all big naval and air strike forces and large ground armour – and this way forward became widely accepted. Thus, during the mid 1920s statesmen worked for a general limitation of the armaments of all nations. The Assembly of 1924 established the Geneva Protocol, which made even stronger the commitments under the League of Nations Covenant in ruling out the initiation of war as any kind of option. It also prohibited the use of chemical and biological weapons, though not their manufacture. This commitment held throughout the Second World War despite the availability of these weapons, another major victory for peace. In October 1925 the Treaty of Locarno accepted Germany into the League of Nations and established a strong relationship between Aristide Briand of France, Gustav Stresemann of Germany and Austen Chamberlain of Britain. At this stage it looked as though Germany, welcomed back into the community of nations, was pledged to peace and had turned her back on aggression. The Treaty of Locarno guaranteed the French-German border, reducing another point of earlier tension.

The Kellogg-Briand pact of 1928 was another step towards peace, because it brought back the United States into international affairs, and effectively put her military weight behind the determination to outlaw aggression. It originated with Briand and the United States' Secretary of State Frank Kellogg. Again, it was expanded into a multinational treaty renouncing war as an instrument of national policy. There was widespread support for the Kellogg-Briand Pact's rejection of the recourse to war and a strong impetus towards further disarmament. It was an active policy. Coolidge and Hoover pushed it to a powerful international agreement. Especially, since the countries concerned have not disavowed it, it is worth quoting in full.

**"Article 1--The high contracting parties solemnly declare in the names of their respective peoples that they condemn recourse**

**to war for the solution of international controversies, and renounce it as an instrument of national policy in their relations with one another.**

**"Article 2--The high contracting parties agree that the settlement or solution of all disputes or conflicts of whatever nature or of whatever origin they may be, which may arise among them, shall never be sought except by pacific means."**

The signatories were Australia, Belgium, Canada, Czechoslovakia, France, Germany, Great Britain, India, Irish Free State, Italy, Japan, New Zealand, Poland, Union of South Africa, the United States of America, Afghanistan, Albania, Austria, Bulgaria, China, Cuba, Denmark, Dominican Republic, Egypt, Estonia, Ethiopia, Finland, Guatemala, Hungary, Iceland, Latvia, Liberia, Lithuania, the Netherlands, Nicaragua, Norway, Panama, Portugal, Peru, Rumania, Russia, Kingdom of the Serbs, Croats and Slovenes, Siam, Spain, Sweden, Turkey, Greece, Honduras, Persia, Switzerland, and Venezuela. Moreover, ways of resolving disagreements began to emerge. A conflict in 1925 between Greece and Bulgaria was authoritatively settled by Briand. The move for peace was strong. The League of Nations Union was a popular international movement, backed by local movements which marched and gathered to promote peace. The language, Esperanto, was developed to cross European language barriers. It was seen as a beacon of hope for communication between nations.

**The Arms Companies seem Beaten.**

The two processes were going on. The politicians looked for peace and arms companies were scurrying about looking for business. For a while it looked as though the latter were beaten. The contraction in munitions, the surplus of weapons and the end of military rivalry left them in recession. Some weapons' systems had underperformed in the Great War. Big battleships had turned out to be ineffective and vulnerable to submarines, and orders more or less dried up in the early 1920s. Armstrong and Vickers, with the scuttling of the German Navy at Scarpa Flow, faced an almost complete absence of demand for battleships. They moved from being world dominant to scrabbling around for business, and in 1927 they came together into Vickers-Armstrong to consolidate their business and cut down on their losses. As Mr. Douglas Vickers said at the shareholders meeting in 1926,

> It appears that our armour plate plant here (at Sheffield) will be almost closed down for the year; the cruisers, all that the Washington Conference allows until 1931, carry very little armour, and, as far as can be told, the total requirements of the country would not keep one armour plant even half-employed, and there are five such plants in the country."[161]

Sir Herbert Lawrence, Chairman of Vickers, went a bit further in 1928.

> We have to face the possibility of a further limitation of armaments, and, despite any development of our commercial business which we can bring about, the result would be a serious one for your company.[162]

They were appalled at the impact movements towards peace were having on business, but were slow to convert their works to civilian use. Both passenger and cargo shipping and passenger aircraft were potential growth industries and car manufacture was a growth replacement for tanks and artillery. Arguably, both Vickers and Armstrong missed the boat, because they were in a good position to build passenger liners in the 1920s, but the Italians, French and Germans built them and John Brown launched *Queen Mary* in 1936 and *Queen Elizabeth* in 1938. In waiting for munitions to pick up and the good times to return, Vickers and Armstrong ignored this growth industry.

It was similar in Germany. Krupp in 1927 had substantially converted to civilian output. Some manufacturers tried to break the Versailles restrictions, but to a substantial extent weapons manufacture ended in Germany and inspections made sure that it was so. As Von Klass comments of Krupp, "Now that the transfer to non-military work had been successfully accomplished, the firm was in good shape. The Ordnance department had shrunk to a staff of seven constructors, who had really nothing to do but keep their files and drawings in good order."[163] Krupp fully made the transition to civilian work, making a large variety of good steel products and expanding its technological base, despite the recession. But, as we know, he had not let go of his main ambition in munitions, as the background work on design and the exported factories show. Yet, they were on the defensive. There was a good head of steam for peace and disarmament. In situations like this the arms manufacturers had to look for cracks that could be prized open. They soon appeared.

**The Attempted Sabotage of Naval Disarmament.**

As we have already seen, Woodrow Wilson was undermined by arms manufacturers and hawks of the American right, so that the United States did not join the League of Nations. But the momentum for disarmament was strong even in the United States and with the Republican Party. In 1921 the Republican President Warren Harding set up the Washington Naval Limitation Conference, and in early 1922, thanks especially to the US Secretary of State Charles Hughes, it succeeded in a substantial level of naval disarmament by cutting the numbers of battleships and aircraft carriers by about 40% for the United States, the United Kingdom, Japan, France and Italy. It also established a naval holiday in which no new ones were built. This was a great success and ended the dominance of the great warship building empires. It brought Japan within the orbit of arms limitation. A massive munitions empire in several major countries had been closed or contracted by democratic parties seeking normal peaceful development. The agreement also curtailed some rivalry between the United States and Britain, who were not always as cosy as we like to think. Britain was still a naval empire. Because the existing navy was so strong anyway, Armstrong and Vickers faced a long naval recession and a necessary contraction in the building of battleships.

A further Naval Conference was summoned by President Coolidge in 1927 to stop the building of smaller warships – cruisers, destroyers, torpedo boats and submarines. By this time the naval firms knew how to react. It failed, partly because the US and British proposals clashed, and partly because Lord Jellicoe, sent as the New Zealand delegate, huffed and puffed about the navy needing to protect British merchant ships. Jellicoe's assertions were shot down in flames, but generated a lot of smoke which prevented agreement. Further, the American naval shipbuilding firms paid a professional propagandist, William Shearer, over $20,000 for six weeks work to disrupt the Conference, which he in part achieved. Shearer's dreadful reputation rumbled on and on the 6th September, 1929 President Hoover issued a statement against Shearer's propagandizing which ended:

> "it is obviously against the public interest for those who have financial interest in, or may be engaged in, contracts for the construction of naval vessels to secretly attempt to influence public opinion or public officials by propaganda in favor of larger armaments and attempt to defeat the efforts of the Government in world limitation of such armaments or to employ persons for such purposes. I am making this statement publicly so that there can be no misapprehension of my determination that our present international negotiations shall not be interfered with from such sources and through such methods"[164]

The arms companies grovelled, saying that Shearer was just employed by them to gather information, but they knew they were lying and the damage had been done. The final *coup de grace* to the proposals was supplied by Winston Churchill who refused in Cabinet parity with the United States' Navy and undermined the possibility of progress. At this stage in his life Churchill was all over the place in his military responses.

This evaluation of the way the Conference was sabotaged was widely accepted at the time. *The Times* stated: "It is impossible to avoid the conclusion that there are influences at work which would gladly see the Conference break up amid failure..." It talked about the "farrago of nonsense" spoken by the agents of the arms companies. [165] The U.S. Senatorial Committee (the Nye Committee) reporting in 1936 came to a similar conclusion. "The Geneva Arms Control Conference of 1925 was watched carefully by the American and European munitions makers... the objections of the munitions manufacturers were considered carefully (by the Departments of State and Commerce)... Their agent at Geneva (in 1927) claimed credit for the failure of that conference... The Navy has not denied to the committee that this agent of the shipbuilders was in possession of confidential Navy Department documents during the time of his activity at Geneva." By 1928 the munitions companies knew they had won in relation to this peace conference and the report describes them as "cocky".[166] Noel-Baker is clear that similar pressures were operating in Britain, France, the United States and Germany. The Nye Committee found the munitions companies had "a record of active opposition to such (peace) proposals, of resentment towards them, of contempt for those responsible for them, and of violation of such controls whenever established, and of rich profiting whenever such controls failed."[167] It is a blood-curdling, but perhaps realistic, conclusion that this sinister pressure undermined the effort to disarm and bring peace.

Yet, the result was not quite as the arms companies expected. The Conference failed, and Cecil resigned from the Conservative Government and the League of Nations section of the Foreign Office. In his resignation letter he pointed out that he did not really have the support of the majority of the Cabinet and he was disquieted by the instructions which came from the Government. There was a lot of public annoyance at the failure of the Conference, because vast numbers of people had gone to meetings advocating drastic international reduction of arms. Public opinion in Britain was heavily in favour of Cecil, and when the general election of May 1929 was held, five months before the Wall Street Crash, Labour was returned to power strongly backing disarmament. The new Prime Minister, Ramsey MacDonald looked towards it and had a good agreement with President Hoover to do the same. Arthur Henderson, a key figure in the whole process, was appointed Foreign Secretary and he threw his weight completely behind disarmament. His Parliamentary private secretary was Philip Noel-Baker, MP for Coventry, who had worked in Geneva for years. Lloyd George leading the Liberals was now strongly of the same opinion. There was a London Naval Treaty in April 1930 between the United States, Britain and Japan establishing ratios for smaller ships, and by 1932, despite the recession, a heavy head of steam had built up for substantial disarmament.

**The Weapons Manufacturers Re-emerge – the Example of China.**

Behind the scenes the munitions people gradually got their act together. They had to influence the major nations by destroying attempts at disarmament. That was a political, media and strategic role which we will look at more fully in the next chapter, but they also had to open up any markets available, using all the techniques they had developed for decades, finding areas of strife and making sure that they expanded into more fully armed conflict. They also tried to refocus on aircraft as a more dynamic market. South America offered some contracts, but China was more promising. British companies, along with other munitions' people, looked towards a big civil war there as a lucrative source of orders.

China in 1919 had already been subject to a lot of colonial attacks from Britain, Japan, France, the United States and other western nations looking to dismember it and take the pickings of this great nation. As a result of these pressures it moved towards a pattern of competing warlords as the Manchu dynasty came to an end. The leading warlord, Duan Qirui, had entered the First World War against Germany, but more to develop his own military base. At the end of the World War there was the Shanghai Peace Conference, but when it concluded in June, 1919, it failed to secure the peaceful development of the nation. There had been an Arms Embargo Agreement by the western nations, set up by Britain on the 5th May, 1919 to prevent western arms flooding China and stoking the rivalries of the Warlords, but the arms companies soon began to evade this Agreement, often with the connivance of their governments. Sadly, Britain was among the first. Five months after the Embargo the British Government approved an aircraft agreement between Vickers and Duan Qirui for twenty-four Vimy airplanes and twenty fully equipped Avro biplanes with ten spare engines. A £2 million loan accompanied the sale in October, 1919. Not surprisingly this was seen as hypocritical by other nations. The British Government then disallowed a Handley Page contract, but the stable door was open. Soon Italy sold arms openly and brazenly into China. France, Czechoslovakia, the Netherlands, Denmark, the Soviet Union and Germany, who had not signed the embargo, also sent weapons. The result was utterly predictable. China faced a series of internal wars throughout the twenties which weakened the State and gradually created chaos, opening up the way for a crisis that would occur in 1931-2, the Manchuria Crisis, which would fundamentally undermine the crucial moves towards peace in the Geneva Disarmament Conference. Nor was this crisis a sudden one for Japan. For years, Japan, too, supplied weapons to the Chinese on a large scale – some 35% of the total, fomenting the internal conflict that they would exploit later. One of the weapons used in Manchuria was a tank, the Type 89CHI-RO, a Japanese development of a Vickers Tank bought earlier. Schneider, Skoda and German firms were often exporting arms, including chemical weapons, to China through Hamburg.[168] Why worry about a nation's health and unity when you can sell arms and make money?

What was tried in China was similarly tried across the globe, in South America, Africa and the rest of Asia, but it even that was not enough to compensate for the shuddering lack of demand for weapons in the rich countries of Europe and the United States. A series of amalgamations took place to give some stability to the smaller companies in the acute arms recession. For a while it looked as though long-term peace would break out among the major western powers and the arms manufacturers would be permanently out of business. Moreover, there was strong hostility towards the merchants of death and the private manufacture of arms, and so their public business position was very weak. But when a weapons manufacturer is down, he is rarely out. All he needs to be back in business is a war or a rumour of war. Soon they were planning for growth.

**The Imperative to Sell.**

The arms companies had an imperative to sell. They would say and do most things in order to get orders. Especially, they would assert that arms bring peace. Sir Reginald Bacon, successor to Mr Mulliner at the Coventry Ordnance Works, in his evidence to the Royal Commission said: "Armaments are a check on war, a much greater check than the League of Nations." At least he had the chance to see his theory tested. Within five years the League of Nations had obviously failed and the biggest catastrophe the world has seen up to the present followed after a crazed growth of armaments. The cost of testing Bacon's view was the destruction of the League of Nations. In the next chapter we see how this battle played out. The arms companies wanted competitive arming. As G D H and Margaret Cole point out: "Almost every other commodity is produced in response to a limited demand, so that the sale of a dose of it by one producer means that less of it is to be sold by others. But with armaments this is not the case. If an armament firm succeeds in selling to one country some new and deadly engine of destruction, that is a reason why all the other countries which are its rivals in the armaments race should seek immediately to possess themselves of a quota of the same engine of destruction... The armament firms have been perfectly prepared to sell to anybody, and never happier than when they have been in the satisfying position of selling to both sides in some jolly war which has created a gratifying demand for their products..."[169]

The arms companies were out to generate this kind of market, by scares, pressure, publicity, lies and rumours. They were rampant and uncompromising. As people moved away from the horrors of the First World War, they were quite prepared to create the conditions for another, if it was good for business. Soon sales were generating more sales and their factories were humming, whilst most of the world was longing for disarmament and peace. As the

*Financial News* stated on 20th February, 1936, "Our estimates of the prospects for the heavy armaments companies in particular were clearly such as would, if they were to be realized, justify much higher prices for the shares...The upshot o the matter is that, if our estimates are approximately correct, the prices of the shares in the heavy naval and land armament group have not yet by any means discounted the improved prospects in view."[170] So, military capitalism was looking forward to improved prospects, and sadly, that meant War.

## Chapter Sixteen: The Politics leading to the Geneva Disarmament Conference.

### Slowing Down Disarmament.

The Covenant of the League of Nations required all countries to disarm and from its formation the process was underway with a Commission set up to pursue it. It had been President Wilson's vision and Article 8 insisted that the Council should formulate plans for disarmament. Cecil and others worked at it, and insistently at each Annual meeting of the League a draft programme for a disarmament conference was requested. Sometimes progress was made, but repeatedly the process was stalled. Why was this the case? The obvious answer lay with the victorious powers. The status quo suited them. They remained armed. Germany and Austria remained unarmed. What was the problem? They had a wartime surfeit of arms which could be kept to maintain their position. They wanted to enforce the payment of reparations and armed forces were the obvious way to do it. So the dominant military forces retained their weapons with some rivalry among themselves and enjoyed the status quo without thinking about disarmament too much.

Each country had its own agenda. The United States was slightly worried by Japan and with the Monroe Doctrine understood that through military power it could do more or less what it wanted in the Americas. Moreover, its withdrawal from the League of Nations meant it was introverted in its political concerns mainly coping with a million immigrants a year in its push to the west. France was worried by its security in relation to Germany. It had been overrun in 1870 and nearly in 1914 and was concerned that its neighbour would and could do so again. So, its aim was to keep itself strong and Germany weak. Italy saw its neighbours to the North as the main threat and looked towards an Empire in North Africa. The USSR was mainly concerned with the internal turmoil of revolution in the 1920s and kept its eye on the German aggressor to the West. Japan had emerged unscathed from the War and its military built up control within the Japanese state and looked towards expansion towards mainland China.

Britain was similar. It had status as the main victor in the Great War from the Old World, especially as the United States had withdrawn. At the same time many British leaders, Conservatives especially, were jealous of the United States' new world supremacy. The Empire was still its main preoccupation internationally, and that meant making sure the passage to India, Suez, was secure and the other colonies could be run satisfactorily. Gradually the Empire would morph into the Commonwealth, and the idea of running an empire was becoming dated, as Wilson had shown at the Treaty of Versailles in 1919, but Winston Churchill and others still clung to it strongly. The British Conservative establishment still had no reason for disarmament or grasp of the issue.

The military establishments of all the main victors remained in place, enjoying the position and security of victory, with a surfeit of arms. Disarmament, turkeys voting for Christmas, was not their agenda. They had learned what trench warfare was like in war and they could do exactly the same thing in peace. The dug in against all moves to disarmament. Yet the peace imperative would not go away. As Wilson said on the 11th November, 1918, "The eyes of the people have been opened and they see. The hand of God is laid upon the nations." The world had to do better than the old way. They had to disarm, and the way of peace had its soldiers too in their millions, grieving, fighting, working for swords into ploughshares. The message of the masses was simple – no more weapons, no more wars. The challenge of the military establishments was to make it more complicated.

**Some Dirty British Politics.**

The early years after the War in Britain were preoccupied with internal questions and especially the re-emergence of the Conservatives as the dominant party. The Liberal Party had split during the War with Asquith leading a rather petty rebellion against Lloyd George and the Labour Party was not yet strong, though obviously gaining momentum. The Representation of the

People Act in 1918 gave the vote to all men without property qualifications and to women over 30. Obviously, if you could fight and die for Britain, you deserved to vote in Britain, and the Suffragettes had stopped their campaign to support the War, apart from some Suffragette pacifists. Women had worked in munitions factories. Yet in all of this, the Conservatives moved into power. In 1922 the famous vote of the 1922 Committee signaled the withdrawal of support from Lloyd George and his demise. Yet, Conservative dominance was not easy and their role in relation to disarmament is important.

This old establishment was stolidly and overwhelmingly against international disarmament and, whenever they were able to, they treacled it. On the whole they were rich, hanging onto their land, property and business assets in a world where labourers were suffering unemployment and poverty. They also were old style imperialists and militarists, believing Britain should rule the waves and some would soon have quite a bit of sympathy with Fascism because it would keep socialism and the workers in their place. We look at the two general elections of 6th December 1923 and the 29th October, 1924. Broadly speaking the Labour Party in the early 1920s was strongly for disarmament, while the Conservative Party was against it and provided a home for generals, militarists and believers in ruling through strength. They had affluence, clubs, shoots, luxurious lifestyles, problems with servants and still just about maintained a good supply of port and pheasants. But disarmament was going too far, don't you understand.

On the 6th December, 1923 the General Election produced 258 seats for the Conservatives, 191 for Labour and 158 for the Liberals. The Tories had failed to win on tariff reform and could not come back without a majority. George V sent for Ramsey MacDonald and a minority Labour Government was formed for the first time – an historic government of the workers. It was always going to be temporary and in many ways did little in economic policy, apart from housing, but the Labour Cabinet did help transform world diplomacy with a remarkably new attitude. They made a workable peace with the Russians, after the hostility created by Churchill.

They also worked with the Americans in the Dawes Plan to sort out the animosity between Germany and France arising from reparation payments. This evacuated French troops from the Ruhr, scaled down the immediate payments of reparations and provided an American loan to help meet the payments. They helped the Reichsbank reorganise. Suddenly Germany was in some kind of order. Further, the Ponsonby Rules were enacted whereby no secret treaties can be undertaken. Then Ramsey MacDonald helped formulate the Geneva Protocols which strengthened the peaceful resolution of all international disagreements.

Suddenly the route to peace was opening up. But MacDonald and Labour were batting against other forces. Ramsey MacDonald turned down the advice of the Admiralty and Foreign Office to build a new naval base at Singapore, because that would compromise the move towards peace, but the old guard did not like being refused. There was some – what we would now call – disinformation. Viscount Grey, for example, discovered he was against the Geneva Protocols in a newspaper, when he was not, and other lies were spread. By autumn 1924 the Conservatives had decided that the Labour Government should be ended and forced an election. In other words, Labour was facing the Conservative establishment which was going to keep them out of power if at all possible.

Then, occurred one of the most disgusting events in British electoral history: the so-called Zinoviev letter. The "so-called" reflects the fact that it was not a Zinoviev letter, but a forgery. Four days before the election on the 25th October, 1924 the *Daily Mail* published a letter purporting to be from Grigory Zinoviev, along with Stalin one of the chief leaders in the USSR. He was supposed to have written a letter to the British Communists telling them to rise up against the Government and infiltrate the armed forces and to prepare for revolution. At the time there were only about 3,500 British Communists and their influence was weak. The boy scouts were more dangerous. Communists were deliberately excluded from the Labour Party, which was determined not to have any truck at all with undemocratic politics. Yet the *Mail*'s gloss on the letter was a Red Scare implying that the Labour Government was receiving orders from Moscow, and finished with the conclusion, "Get rid of our shifty Prime Minister", an appalling insult to Ramsey MacDonald.

It turned out that the letter was forged by white Russians in Berlin, carried by the Polish secret service and disseminated within the British Secret Service, the Foreign Office, and to the Conservative Party and the Press, led by the Daily Mail. Where along that trail the impetus for and instigation of the deceit came from we do not fully know. The *Mail*'s headlines on the 25th October were "CIVIL WAR PLOT BY SOCIALISTS' MASTERS. Moscow Order To Our Reds. Great Plot Disclosed Yesterday. Paralyse the Army and Navy. And Mr MacDonald Would lend Russia Our Money". It ignored the fact that the letter was a forgery, that it had nothing remotely to do with Labour, and that Labour was anti-Communist. Some Labour supporters later named the *Daily Mail*, "The Forgers' Gazette". The only true point was that a loan was being negotiated which would allow Russian debts to British subjects, mainly rich individuals, to be repaid. When news of the (forged) letter broke, MacDonald was on the road giving dozens of electoral speeches and was not able to address the Red Scare properly. He was also too protective of his civil servants to expose their ineptitude and anti-Labour bias. The screeching headlines, and rabble rousing speeches from Curzon, Churchill and others made sure that the electorate was led by the nose to give the Conservatives perhaps 50 seats more than they would have had otherwise, although there are disputes about how much difference the so-called Zinoviev letter made. Conservatives - as we might expect - said it made very little difference, taking on themselves the task of speaking for the electorate. The letter "surfaced" at exactly the right time to harm Labour's campaign. Labour lost 40 seats against an otherwise consistent rising trend between 1918 and 1929.

The civil service establishment plotted at different levels to obtain and publicize this forgery; bluntly, they were out to get rid of the Labour Government. The Foreign Office disobeyed its own procedures by publishing the letter and MacDonald's response to the USSR, even though he had not had time to establish its authenticity and had not finished writing the response and signed it off.[171] The Secret Service was probably in on stages of the letter's movement to London. Zinoviev declared the letter to be a hopeless forgery, not just because he hadn't written it, backing his statement by noting the headings were inaccurate, the titles of other signatories were wrong, but ironically because he was actually away on holiday remote from correspondence when the letter was supposed to have been written. The so-called original, including the supposed signatures, was never seen, and the content was an odd amalgam of Zinoviev-like speeches such as forgers would produce. Finally, it would have been a silly thing to write. It would have been even more silly to pass it on to white Russians. The failure of the Foreign Office, MI5 and the Press initially to consider whether it was forgery merely reflected what they wanted to believe. Later experts were quite clear it was a forgery, although there have been a number of fudges in establishment reports alleging that we are not really sure about it because the truth is so damning.

Key in stirring the whole thing up was Donald im Thurn, a kind of ex-spy. The Conservatives agreed to pay £7,500 to him, a small fortune, for making them "aware" of the letter and for delivering it to them. The overall event was cheating on proper democracy, appalling Conservative sleaze, and all the people involved must have had a bad conscience about it. The Conservatives have continued to pretend that it might not have been a forgery or didn't matter, when they knew it was an untrue carve-up. They were happy to disseminate lies to kill Labour's election chances. The outcome was that they were in power for five years with a solid majority when they should not have been. And the result, because the Conservatives were cool on disarmament, was a serious slowing of the peace initiative at the crucial time when it should have advanced.[172] Further, the possibility of good relationships with the USSR was ended, because the Soviets knew the letter and the Red Scare were dishonest, and Churchill was back in the Cabinet. It was a disgusting Conservative election for which the British public have long been owed an apology.

**Slowing Down and Speeding Up the Disarmament Process.**

As a result the Conservative Government was in power until 30th May, 1929. During this period the group working in Geneva became detached from the British Government as the latter showed less interest in the process. Lord Cecil, Noel-Baker, Arthur Henderson and others worked for disarmament, while the Conservative Government though not hostile to disarmament now had Winston Churchill as Chancellor, and he was very cool on the possibility. It rejected the Geneva Protocol in March 1925, at a Cabinet meeting involving Stanley Baldwin, Winston Churchill and with Sir William Hankey as Cabinet Secretary. Hankey's involvement was significant; he was far from a neutral Civil Servant. He had developed the view that war purified a nation and was a deeply convinced militarist right at the centre of government business. He continued to subvert the disarmament process. There were subsequent proposals at the Locarno Conference which were less strong and were agreed by Austen Chamberlain on behalf of the British Government in October 1925, and eventually the League of Nations' Commission got to work preparing for disarmament but with far less encouragement from the Conservatives. The 1925 Geneva Conference was mired. The munitions people and their agents were now organised to minimize and delay moves towards disarmament. There was a drag against the earlier momentum.

So the confrontation was building. By this time the munitions people were organised. The international gunmakers held a conference in Paris and came to an uncompromising resolution: "the Congress has unanimously decided that the private manufacture of arms and munitions cannot be submitted to any regulations other than national police regulations." So there was no doubt where they stood. There had been a delay in the actual Disarmament Conference date. It could have been arranged in February 1931, or even October 1930, but the powers moved slowly, no doubt held back by the military interests. The key German statesman, Gustav Stresemann, had died in October 1929. Fridtjof Nansen, the Norwegian Arctic Explorer, who began the League of

Nations' refugee work and saved the life of millions through his courageous acts, also died in May 1930, probably just of overwork. He had been a strong pacifist. Aristide Briande, several times French Prime Minister and with these two also the recipient of the Nobel Peace Prize, died as the conference got underway. So these great men of peace were not able to shape the conference as it came to fruition. Their absence was an immense loss.

**Parliament after August 1931.**

British domestic politics also played into the scene. A Labour Government was eventually elected in May 1929 by a substantial number of seats, though still a minority. Arthur Henderson as Foreign Secretary re-innervated disarmament. Suddenly Geneva and the Labour Government were singing the same hymn and the impetus towards disarmament was strong. But this was only for two years. When the Labour Government faced the world recession, Ramsey MacDonald, pushed by his civil servants and the May Report of July 1931 agreed to cut its budget expenditure drastically. Effectively, this was a Labour Government being told by civil servants to pursue Conservative policies. The Labour Cabinet split and MacDonald resigned as Prime Minister. In the election of the 24th August 1931 he agreed to stand as the Prime Minister of a new potential National Government with the Conservatives and Liberals. It was seen as the great betrayal of the Labour Movement and created a barrier between MacDonald and Henderson.

In the August election MacDonald won a landslide victory, or rather the Tories did, as 470 Conservatives were returned at the election. Baldwin was the power behind the throne and was surrounded by a quite reactionary troop of Conservative MPs. One of the most depressing occupations is reading Hansard for the early thirties and seeing the appalling level of unawareness in this group. The Commons' debates were poor with few good speakers. So, for example, on the 2nd February, 1932 the otherwise forgettable Mr Hopkinson asked: "Is not the real reason for the stoppage of the work [on a Cunard liner] that the late Labour Government left so few millionaires that there is no demand for luxury ships?" to which Ramsey MacDonald responded with a suitably withering: "I have no objection to putting as many virtues upon the late Labour Government as it can bear, but I cannot say that the late Government was responsible for the condition of millionaires in America." The next day Captain Arthur Hope, apart from informing us that, "we ought to take one bite of the cherry at a time and not go the whole hog", also reflected on the State of the Commons.

> "On Wednesdays the House was also frequently counted out by dinner time. Everybody appeared to look upon Wednesdays and Fridays as non-working days, and they took the opportunity to go off to their constituencies and to their businesses or to play golf and to do anything else they wanted to do, and only a handful of Members was present. Some people have talked about Parliament not having the confidence of the country that it used to have. I think that that is largely true, and it is due to the feeling of a great many people with regard to the futility of certain proceedings in this House."[173]

The young acerbic Nye Bevan's summary in the same debate of the Conservative MP's he faced was not flattering: "But these 400 Members have such a paucity of mind, and have so little contribution to make, that they want to be relieved of any opportunity at all of telling the House and the country what they would do if they had the power to do it." It will have been in an ascerbic Welsh accent implying far more than the words alone. He may well have had a point.

More strategically significant was the loss of Arthur Henderson as Foreign Secretary to be replaced by Sir John Simon. Robert Cecil the benevolent engine of disarmament was seriously weakened in relation to the British Government, although, as we shall see, many of the Conservative statesmen were in favour of disarmament too. The British delegation had lost some backing from the Foreign Secretary and the Government five months before the Conference started.

**Japan and the Manchurian Crisis.**

There was one other cloud over the Disarmament Conference, namely the Manchurian crisis which blew up on 18-19th September, 1931. The League of Nations was meant to settle international disputes. The crisis began in Mukden when a Japanese army unit created disturbances around the South Manchurian railway line and made a bid for control in the region, claiming that they were restoring order. Really it was a disguised attempt by the Japanese military to take over Manchuria. At the time the Japanese military was partly operating independently of the Government with direct access to the Emperor. An incident rousing nationalist fervor in Japan would give the military popular weight, and the disturbance in Manchuria provided this. The aim was to gradually establish a Japanese puppet ruler in the area independent from China.

The incident was reported to the League of Nations by China who impeccably followed the procedure for disputes. Japan tried to obscure what was going on, but faced increasing pressure from both the League, and the United States' President, Herbert Hoover, acting through Henry Stimson and Hugh Wilson. At first the League tried quietly to let Japan pull back, but then its requirements became firmer. There were several problems. The US Vice President Dawes tried to do his own diplomacy, but botched it. The Japanese Government and the Military were at odds, and the British Government, now with Sir John Simon as Foreign Secretary, was soft on Japan, whose military support they might need in the Far East. They deliberately fudged American initiatives. As the MP, Mr. McGovern asked on 15th February, 1932: "Is it the case that, while the British Government are protesting against this conflict, they are encouraging Japan to go ahead behind the scenes?"[174] It was deemed by the Speaker to be an improper question, but it was a good improper question.

Lord Marley pursued the issue of selling weapons later in the year when the arms trade was discussed, and, because it makes clear British duplicity, it is worth quoting at length.

> The British attitude—I am very anxious to draw particular attention to this—was, I venture to say,

lamentable. In the first place the British representative began by a quibble as to the competence of the Committee to consider the suppression of private manufacture at all—a verbal quibble which was referred to the legal section of the Secretariat of the League of Nations, who of course swept it away as entirely without any foundation or justification. The British delegate then suggested that the French delegate was not sincere in his proposal for total suppression. He said he understood that France would not insist on the suppression of private manufacture and that she would be prepared to support mere regulation. In this connection the French delegate at two subsequent meetings denied that entirely and reiterated that he stood by suppression, the complete and absolute suppression of the private manufacture of arms. The British delegate then suggested that the action which Great Britain had taken was already sufficient, and he went on to say that: He felt that a considerable measure of progress would have been registered if all other states followed the example of the United Kingdom and adopted similar measures of control of the private manufacture of arms. It is interesting to know that the Government—presumably he was acting on the instructions of the Government—feel that Great Britain has done all that is necessary.

It is interesting to see, for example, the result of this control in the impartiality with which British armament firms supply equally China and Japan in view of the present state of affairs in Manchuria. For instance, last month British armament firms supplied 40,000 machine gun cartridges to China and 250,000 to Japan. The month before, they supplied 200 machine guns to Japan and 1,500,000 cartridges to China. In August, 500 sets of bombs were supplied to China and fifty machine guns to Japan, while in June 500 bombs were supplied to China and 1,000,000 rounds of machine gun ammunition to Japan. There has been complete impartiality during the past year, although amounts have varied month by month, Japan being sometimes up on the deal and China sometimes up on the deal. I suggest that a control which allows a state of tension between two nations in distant parts of the world to be caused perhaps to rise into a state of war, by means of supplying munitions of war impartially to both sides, is hardly a control with which this Government should be satisfied.[175]

This is appalling. Lord Marley is measured but basically the British were supplying both sides in a conflict where an arms embargo had been explicitly agreed while supplying combatants was also against the League of Nations Covenant. So while formally the Government was pretending to go along with the Geneva Disarmament Conference, it was backing its arms companies in supplying arms both to the aggressor and Japan's opponent. It was as perfidious as a beautician using acid.

**Britain Undermines the United States**

The failure of the United States and Britain to work together amounted to hostility between them. The process began with Mr. Stimson's failure to back a direct investigation of Japan's activities in Manchuria on the 22nd September, 1931. When the League passed a motion demanding the complete evacuation of Manchuria by Japan on the 22nd October, the United States represented by Mr. Stimson did not back it. Then the United States decided to act more firmly. Shortly after this Sir John Simon became Foreign Secretary, and then when the United States issued a strong statement on 7th January, 1932, aiming to strengthen the Disarmament Conference, Britain failed in turn to back it up. Sara Smith's commentary is as follows:

> It was a stunning blow when on Monday, January 11, the London morning papers published the official communiqué of the British Foreign Office backed by the even more specific editorial in the London Times; both the communiqué and the editorial made plain a point of view radically different from that of the United States and offered

encouragement to the Japanese to continue in their predetermined course of action.

> Here then was a tragedy. If Great Britain and the United States could not stand together to prevent aggression, particularly in a part of the world where the interests of both were involved, what possible combination of powers could be expected to do so? … Mr. Stimson writes that the contents of the British communiqué "were such as to be taken by most readers, including – what was most important – the Japanese, as a rebuff to the United States", that Japan was quick to take advantage of this assurance of divided counsels…[176]

Latterly, released papers have suggested that Sir John Simon did try to co-operate, and it may have been Sir Robert Vansittart, the new Permanent Secretary at the Foreign Office who helped create the distance. Whatever the dynamics, this Britain - United States row seemed to be peevishness between a British Conservative elite, accustomed to dominating world politics for a hundred years, and the United States as the parvenu, the new kid on the block. The problem was serious in the Manchuria crisis; it would be a chronic failure at the Disarmament Conference a few weeks later. For these reasons and others, the League of Nations acted indecisively and the issue still hung over them when the Disarmament Conference convened on 2nd February, 1932.

**The Arms Companies, Japan and China**

We have already seen Lord Marley's reference to the arms' companies involvement in Japan and China. In reality the Manchurian Crisis was being driven by the arms companies. They needed a good war and an international event which would drive a coach and horses through the peace conditions of the Versailles treaty. Englebrecht describes what was happening.

> For twenty years this immense country has been the prey of a dozen rascals, real fomenters of war who raise mercenary armies. These armies have European equipment,

> and if anyone wants to know where the equipment comes from he has only to follow in the newspapers the visits of their officers to Creusot, Saint-Etienne, Krupp, and Vickers. The big armament firms provide them abundantly with cannon, machine guns, and munitions, and are paid with the proceeds by the pillage of the provinces. Every general has his sleeping partner whose name can be found in the banks of Hong Kong, Paris, New York, Yokohama, or even Moscow. Simple shifts of capital determine the separation or fusion of armies. The sleeping partners change generals or the generals change sleeping partners. This system has unleashed all the horrors of the Thirty Years War on this unfortunate country.
>
> This gives an excellent background for the recent Japanese venture in Manchuria. As the clouds of war gathered, Shanghai became a large centre of the arms industry. Japanese factories, as noted, sold munitions to the Chinese there. Schneider and Skoda and other leaders in this traffic acquired a huge building in the International Settlement. From this centre public opinion in Japan and China was influenced and made ready for war. Three great journals, one in English, one in Japanese, and one in Chinese, amply supplied by advertising from the munitions makers, began to shriek for war. The English paper, the Shanghai Post, was cynical enough to remark that "a war would undoubtedly be very helpful to many branches of industry."[177]

This orchestration was mentioned by Noel-Baker with an impressive list of arms sales to Japan including 200 million francs of contracts from France including tanks and 4000 bombs, 3 million dollars from Poland, 20,000 bombs from Czechoslovakia, 400,000 rifles from Birmingham, a big consignment of torpedoes from Glasgow and a thumping 180 million dollars of exports from the States. Germany's contribution was about three and a half million pounds of acid for making explosives and Hamburg was used for many of the exports, presumably because it was a free port.[178] Most of the countries of Europe were therefore condoning the export of arms when Article 16 of the Covenant of the League of Nations forbad any trade to an aggressor, and arms would be foremost in the required embargo. The arms companies were therefore acting, and able to act, with impunity in providing the means of killing for the Japanese invasion of China.

When the Manchuria Crisis was being debated in the Commons on 27th February, 1933, Sir John Simon was accused on facing both ways and one pacifist MP Morgan Jones, told the following story about a British factory. "I understand that in a certain factory recently an amusing incident, something like this, took place. I gather that in one part of the factory they are preparing armaments for Japan and in another part, armaments for China, and by an unfortunate chance the Japanese and Chinese representatives arrived at the same factory at the same time, and an unfortunate official pushed both of them into the same room. While they were there they began to discuss what they were being charged for their armaments, and very amicably they came to the conclusion that they would present a joint ultimatum to the firm to reduce the price."[179] The arms companies had a huge vested interest in the Manchurian crisis, and the outcome must have been as they hoped because the Government was allowing the exports and dancing to the tune of the munitions men. It was a big war in the offing between two major powers promising a bonanza of weapons' sales and the Conservative dominated Government was supine.

The crisis cast a deep shadow over the Geneva Conference. Sir John Simon knew that British arms exports to Japan were four times greater than her exports to China. They included machine guns, millions of rounds of ammunition, aircraft and aircraft guns, millions of shells, grenades and bombs, 76 ships, including one 45,000 ton troop carrier. Here was an arms customer we did not want to upset, and if we had sold them, we could not be too picky about how they were used. It showed that munitions anarchy could have its way unaddressed by the great powers and the British Government was too compromised to do anything or to properly back disarmament. If the Governments had stood firm against weapons exports in 1931/2, they could have imposed a proper discipline of peace, but they messed up.

**The Germans and Disarmament.**

Of course, the underlying question was where was Germany in all of this? First, Germany could rightly and legally expect other countries to disarm. The intention of disarmament was built into the post-war settlement. The Statement of the League of Nations makes it clear. "The Members of the League recognise that the maintenance of peace requires the reduction of national armaments..." Germany had explicitly agreed at Versailles to its own disarmament on the grounds that there would be the general reduction of arms as agreed in Article 8 of the League's founding document. In the *negotiations* they asked the question so that it would be absolutely clear. The response of the Allies was equally clear. Their statement was awesome in its intent and direction.

> "The Allied and Associated Powers wish to make it clear that their requirements in regard to Germany armaments were not made solely with the object of rendering it impossible for her to resume her policy of military aggression. They are also the first steps towards that general reduction and limitation of armaments which they seek to bring about as one of the most fruitful preventatives of war, and which it will be one of the first duties of the League of Nations to promote."[180]

So Germany could expect other nations to disarm, and if they did not, Germany could well be aggrieved, and indeed was during the Disarmament Conference. Partly because general disarmament had not proceeded, some German companies had felt able to cheat on arms manufacture and export. Decisive action was needed.

Two factions were involved. The Democrats, Catholics and Socialists largely wanted to disavow war and develop a peaceful German economy; the industrial arms people were increasingly looking to Hitler to solve their disarmament bind. The Nazis achieved much of their leverage in the election of 14th September,

1930 by denouncing the Treaty of Versailles. They had a total 107 seats while the Social Democrats remained substantially the largest Party. The next election was to be on 31st July, 1932 which was a crucial date in relation to the Geneva Disarmament Conference, six months after it started. Any proposal which ended the inequity of German disarmament by also disarming the First World War allies would silence the Nazis. If there was no change, they would do well. There was no change. The Nazis got 230 seats, and were the biggest party, though not in overall power. Even in the election of 6th November, 1932, they fell back to 192 seats with Social Democrats and Communists much stronger. Really whether the Nazis would come to power was on a knife edge. The success of the Geneva Disarmament Conference would disarm the Nazis of their most popular appeal, as many wise people said at the time.

There was yet another bit of the picture. Germany was still - thirteen years after the end of the War - being plagued by demands for reparations, and by 1930 the German economy and banks were reeling. On the 20th July, 1931 President Herbert Hoover, no mean world statesman, proposed a one year moratorium on reparations payments, but it was opposed by the French. If this generous gesture had been accepted then, it would have also weakened the Nazis. Instead, on the 7th January, 1932 Chancellor Heinrich Brüning declared that Germany could not and would not, resume reparations' payments. The international community had again failed to address legitimate German need and fed the resentment on which the Nazis flourished.

Thus, there was a period, especially from 2nd February, 1932 to the 29th July, 1932 when the Geneva Disarmament Conference could easily have undermined Hitler and the Nazis and strongly decreased their chances of coming to power. The window of opportunity lasted almost until 31st January, 1933 when Hitler did actually come to power as Chancellor. Even then if the major states had acted in concert there would have been the possibility of closing down European military competition, as we shall see. When the delegates met on 2nd February, 1932, everything was still possible.

# Chapter Seventeen: The Great 1932 Geneva Disarmament Conference.

## The Great Purpose and the Magnificent Opening.

By 1932 a head of steam for disarmament had grown up world-wide, backed by most of the world's statesmen and by representatives of half the world's population. Surely now nation could speak peace unto nation and orderly disarmament defuse the possibility of war. On the 2nd February, 1932, 60 nations gathered for a Disarmament and Peace Conference at Geneva to try to achieve substantial world disarmament. This was the culmination of a movement which had been forming since 1918 and planned over many years. Millions who had experienced the horrors of war directly, who had lost family members dead or injured, or who had brooded on the waste and destruction of the great European War were determined that it should not happen again. They had laboured, volunteered, held meetings, raised money, gathered evidence, persuaded politicians and voted so that disarmament would happen. In most nations of the world a large number of people were for world disarmament; they were not alone. King George V proclaimed his own hopes:

> "I share to the full the fervent hope and prayer of the Archbishops, Bishops and clergy for the success of the Disarmament Conference at Geneva. I am confident that my governments throughout the British Commonwealth will exert themselves to the uttermost to secure the largest possible measure of general disarmament, and their endeavours will be greatly assisted by your wholehearted support and prayers. I pray that Divine guidance may be with those who, in these anxious days, bear the great responsibility of directing the affairs of our own and of other nations." [181]

It was an extraordinary process of the nations coming together, gathered in genuine goodwill.

The scope of the movement was worldwide. Einstein, who had denounced his own nation for starting the First World War, was a renowned pacifist. So, too, was Mahatma Gandhi, also touring the world, and reflecting the views of Tolstoy, whose influence was still strong. Leaders who supported disarmament in Britain were Lloyd George, Ramsey MacDonald, Arthur Henderson, Viscount Grey, George Lansbury, Dick Sheppard, Donald Soper, Vera Brittain, Bertrand Russell, Arthur Ponsonby, Augustus John, Charles Raven, H. G .Wells, Rabindranath Tagore, Sigmund Freud and many others. These people had influence and respect and were linked to millions of others by speaking, preaching, writing and discussion. As George V's comments above convey, this was majority, orthodox opinion. We needed disarmament and the end of the trade in these murdering weapons. George V was speaking to already open ears around the world. With Kings and Presidents behind this movement, how could it fail? The 1932 Geneva Conference, though it had been a long time coming, had a good head of steam.

**The Tidal Wave for Disarmament.**

The build-up to the Conference in Britain was magnificent. We get the feel of the whole event from Noel-Baker, who took full part in the proceedings.[182] Millions of people responded to the call and went to meetings and rallies on a vast scale and in many different places. In Britain, the League of Nations Union with 600 local branches had meetings in every town and city. Its journal, *Headway*, had a circulation of 80,000, reaching to all the organizers. There was a National Disarmament Committee centralizing the work of a vast range of public bodies. The Archbishop of Canterbury, Anglicans, Catholics, Methodists, Quakers, Presbyterians all showed a strong Christian response. The unions reached millions of workers with the idea. The Co-operative Movement was in the action. Women's movements were marching and gathering for peace and disarmament. The BBC covered it. It was truly a national movement with overwhelming support throughout Britain.

One crowning meeting was a gathering in the Albert Hall of ten thousand people who heard three Prime Ministers speak passionately for disarmament. Ramsay MacDonald, David Lloyd George and Stanley Baldwin, the leaders of the three main British parties all spoke for pursuing disarmament, a level of agreement unknown in British politics on any subject. But the star of the show was Field Marshall Sir William Robertson, or "Wullie" as he was known. He was Chief of Imperial General Staff between 1915 and 1918, one of the key military figures during the Great War. He knew militarism first hand; Wullie's message was uncompromising and stark and is worth quoting at length.

> ten million lives were lost to the world in the last War, and they say that £70 million in money was spent in the preliminary bombardment in the Battle of Ypres; before any infantry left their trenches the sum of £22 million was spent, and the weight of ammunition fired in the first few weeks of that Battle amounted to 480 thousand tons… I do not believe that that represents the use the world can be expected to make of its brains and its resources. I prefer to believe that the majority of people in the world in these days think that war hurts everybody, benefits nobody – except the profiteers - and settles nothing.
>
> As one who has passed pretty well half a century in the study and practice of war, I suggest to you that you should give your support to Disarmament, and do your best to ensure the promotion of peace…[183]

This address by Wullie, and three Prime Ministers, was enough to present the cause, and the over-full Albert Hall resounded with cheers and few believed that with this level of support in Britain, disarmament would be long in coming. Everyone knew what Lord Cecil, Arthur Henderson and others were trying to do.

Moreover, the international response was similarly strong on an even grander scale. The organizations which the different peace movements claimed to include and represent through petitions added up approaching *half the population of the world, a thousand million people.*[184] Vast church gatherings took place. The Catholic Church could mobilize millions and did in many countries campaigning for peace. More than that, it effectively required a disarming response from Geneva. Popes Leo XIII, Pius X, Benedict XV and Pius XI had all spoken for peace, including through the First World War, and they marshalled the Christian arguments for peace and disarmament. Pius XI in his apostolic letter of the "2nd February, 1931 affirmed that the "moral force of Right shall be substituted for the material force of arms." Thousands upon thousands of Christians turned out for disarmament. It culminated in a mass rally of Catholics in Geneva on 7th February, 1932 which was quite clear where it stood. "Rivalry in military preparations between members of the society of nations must be brought to an end."[185] On the 11th February, Pius XI met Mussolini at the Vatican to put the screws on him for disarmament, with notable success. It was a powerful moral imperative for peace from millions of Catholics world-wide. Protestant churches were similarly mobilized. Bishops, Archbishops, Moderators, and ordinary church members campaigned for peace. Arthur Henderson, "Uncle Arthur", the trusted convenor of the Conference, was a Methodist, Cecil an Anglican, Noel-Baker a Quaker, and there were many other church links into proceedings.

Women were especially strong in the process. Mrs Mary Dingman spoke on behalf of *forty five million women* in the Disarmament Committee of Women's Organisations world-wide, and the International Union of Catholic Women's League collected the signatures of an amazing *twenty six million Catholic women* and brought them to the Conference.[186] A Dutch woman, Mrs Steenberghe Engeringhe spoke to the Conference in the opening session conveying how strongly women around the world felt about disarmament. I remember seeing a picture in a book by Michael Fogarty on Christian Democracy. [187] It showed an innumerable crowd of women, and looked at first sight like a Nuremberg rally, but on closer examination it was a vast crowd of young women at a Catholic Action Rally in Brussels. This was a later rally in 1934, when there were still hopes for peace, but I had not realized the scale of Catholic Action input. We hear about the Nuremburg rallies later, but nothing about these great gatherings for peace. The Women's International League for Peace and Freedom, led by the indefatigable Jane Addams, named by the FBI as "the most dangerous woman in America" (what an honour!) brought a petition of *six million signatures* to Geneva, lorryloads of names arriving exhorting the delegates to peace. This was a great women's democratic peace movement.

The Trade Union Movement was similarly involved. The International Federation of Trade Unions had *40 million* paying members. The International Co-operative Alliance represented *85 million families*. Other organizations had encouraged young people to think in terms of peace and reconciliation. In 1932 some 50,000 young people in the Crusade of European Youth for Disarmament walked from all over Europe to Geneva. They came from a variety of Christian organisations carrying banners saying "God's Peace." After long journeys for most of them, they congregated in Geneva in April to present a petition to Arthur Henderson, the President of the World Disarmament Conference.[188] The expectations were extremely high. A decade or more of work by people working for peace in many of the countries throughout the world was now to come to fruition. The hopes of millions hung on these deliberations.

It was also a time when the media were involved. Pathé News, showing in cinemas throughout Britain, filmed the Prime Minister, Ramsey McDonald, just up from his sick-bed with eye trouble legging it up into the single passenger seat of a plane with his parachute in pouring rain and half a gale of wind on his way to Paris and then Geneva. The commentary points out that it shows his enthusiasm for the Conference. Another Pathé Newsreel shows a petition with 2,071,944 signatures being loaded up in London for the Conference sending some of Britain's messages for peace. Arthur Henderson is showed opening the Conference and several thousand Germans are shown marching determined to *prevent* Hitlerism from being in the ascendant there. This was a crescendo of backing for world disarmament conveyed back to the public.

**The Start of the Conference.**

The Conference started on the 2nd February, 1932. Leading figures from all the major countries of the world gathered and took part in preparations. This was an opportune time: governments were looking to cut budgets, since they were in the depth of the Great Depression, and undertaking more expenditure on munitions was the last priority in most people's minds. But beneath the surface there were problems with the way the World Disarmament Conference was set up. Women and unionists had campaigned, millions sent in petitions, but the people who actually turned up were mainly men, government ministers and diplomats, the military and the agents of the munitions companies. There were some exceptions. Miss M.W. Kidd, the President of the Canadian National Council of Women who had collected half a million signatures for peace, weighing nearly a quarter of a ton, went as a Canadian delegate. Mary Wooley, President of Mount Holyoake College from 1901-37, attended with three other women delegates. These five women were greatly outnumbered by the Generals and Admirals. Admirals do not usually vote for a smaller navy and there was to be ample opportunity for these people to create all kinds of local squabbles about different levels of arms reductions.

Lord Cecil opened the proceedings with a great speech, but then he had to withdraw, because he was no longer a member of the Government, a great loss. After the grand statements of the hope for disarmament, the old powers made their proposals. France was willing to disarm provided there would be an international force who would guarantee her safety in relation to Germany. Brüning for Germany wanted to take back home the promise of disarmament equality, including a fairly mild level of French disarmament, to increase his domestic popularity. The Russians, and there is every indication they meant it, were for complete disarmament. The British position followed Lord Cecil's line as Carolyn Kitching summarises:

> "This case, presented by Sir John Simon, was based upon a qualitative disarmament agreement, under which all aggressive weapons should be abolished, and it received

widespread support. The United States advocated a similar line, and for Italy Grandi made a statement 'in favour of abolition of submarines, capital ships, heavy guns, tanks, aggressive aircraft and a revision of the laws for war'. Even Cecil, the most dedicated disarmer, congratulated Simon on his speech, declaring that 'Considering your instructions, I thought it a masterpiece!" Rather than moving proceedings forward, however, the British proposals stopped them completely. The question raised by Simon's proposals was how to define aggressive weapons, and the course of action adopted was to form a sub-committee to discuss the question. This sub-committee was still deep in deliberation when the Conference broke for Easter, with no positive progress having yet been made."[189]

The weakness of this position was that it allowed the armed forces and munitions people to move centre stage to discuss the minutiae, and their thinking was always what was best militarily for their nation. The process was a disaster. If Britain was ahead on tanks, it had less interest in tank disarmament and so on. Sir Dudley Pound presented the battleships and larger cruisers as sacred and untouchable. This study will focus mainly on the British conduct of negotiations, but the other major powers were similarly dominated. So, for example, a French General insisted on arguing that a 70 ton tank, one of the biggest, was "defensive" and therefore should be retained. Noel-Baker points out that this fuss was about a single tank. Moreover in 1939 France still only had one 70 ton tank. It was argument for argument's sake.[190] Nevertheless, Cecil's focus on offensive weapons was not really broken. Clearly, there were weapons, air, sea and land which were crucial in attacking other nations. After Easter it became clear that this committee deadlock needed to be broken. In terms of what we now know about the importance of the German elections on 31st July, 1932, things were getting urgent. There needed to be a breakthrough, and there were two. There was an attempt in April by the German Chancellor Brüning to organize a deal which would suit the French. This was sadly thwarted by French electoral politics, but then President Hoover stepped forward.

**President Hoover's Disarmament Plan.**

The lead in the Conference was taken by President Hoover on the 22nd June, 1932, five weeks before the German elections. Suddenly the leader of the world's most powerful nation was in charge. The United States, since the time of Coolidge had been fully involved in international disarmament negotiations. It was by now the acknowledged world leader. It was critical of the arms companies who had hired agents like Shearer to try to destabilize disarmament. Hoover went into this Conference with enthusiasm. He was a millionaire, peace-loving Quaker who had brilliantly organized aid and recovery from the First World War among 10 million people in Belgium and Northern France. He also had worked closely with President Woodrow Wilson and accepted his awareness that the system of munitions needed confronting. He wrote a book, *The Ordeal of Woodrow Wilson*[191], detailing Wilson's fight for a new world order of disarmament towards the end of his life and it was clear Hoover wanted to continue the process. He knew what he was doing.

When proceedings opened, and after the great formalities as the nations gathered, and after this initial deadlock, Hoover brought together the best proposals for disarmament, put them in a package and gave them his unequivocal support. They were geared towards making all countries safe from weapons of attack. His delegate, Hugh Gibson, presented the proposals in June. Big picture disarmament was back on the table.

His proposals made many delegates gasp. They included the abolition of all tanks, all chemical warfare and all large mobile guns. All land armies were to be cut by *one third*. He further proposed the abolition of all bombing planes, the prohibition by international law of bombardment from the air and the stringent limitation of fighter aircraft. He further proposed the reduction by one third of battleships, by one quarter of aircraft carriers, cruisers, destroyers and destroyers, with an absolute ceiling on submarines of 35,000 tons. It was a swingeing disarmament proposal, but Hoover went further. He was prepared to act. He promised that the United States would scrap over 300,000 tons of their fleet and forgo 50,000 tons of new ships, that they would destroy over a thousand large caliber mobile guns, nine hundred tanks and three hundred bombing aircraft forthwith. These were not only proposals, but the cash was on the table. Hoover concluded,

> "These proposals are simple and direct. They call upon all nations to contribute something. The contribution here proposed will be relative and mutual. I know of nothing that would give more hope for humanity today than the acceptance of such a program with such minor changes as might be necessary. It is folly for the world to go on breaking its back over military expenditure, and the United States is willing to take its share of responsibility by making definite proposals that will relieve the world."[192]

The conference was packed for these announcements. Excitement, frisson and applause marked the announcement, and then the other delegates at the Conference responded.

One of the first delegates was the Russian Litvinoff. He had been preaching general and complete disarmament, but did he mean it? He addressed them with measured approval. These proposals *did not go all the way,* but he intimated that the Russian delegation would be happy to sign this kind of agreement. The German delegate Nadolny also wondered if we could go further, for this would help the Germans to achieve parity by reduction of arms, but he welcomed with warmest sympathy the proposals. Then Signor Grandi spoke for Italy in English saying that after consultation with his Head of State, Mussolini, Italy accepted entirely and in all its parts the disarmament plan submitted by the United States. Grandi had been able to lean on Mussolini, because of Italian public opinion, and there was even talk that he would replace Mussolini as the Italian leader. Spain followed with a Yes. Then there was an adjournment for a couple of weeks. It resumed. Canada, Belgium, Brazil, Turkey, Cuba, Austria, Norway, the

Dominican Republic, Finland, Hungary, Denmark, Mexico, China, Sweden, Estonia, Switzerland, New Zealand, Roumania, Persia, Venezuela and the Argentine all affirmed the Hoover Plan with only Roumania less than very enthusiastic. The last session continued the chorus of assent – the Netherlands, Afghanistan, Lithuania, Columbia, Latvia, Portugal, Bolivia, Bulgaria, Yugoslavia and other countries gave their support.

Peace and disarmament was coming over the horizon. All it needed was strong British support, but the British Government made a lamentable and ultimately disastrous response. While saying that it was broadly in agreement, it did not really support the Hoover Plan. On the 7th July Baldwin's statement in the Commons said that Hoover's proposal should be put alongside the other proposals of Britain and the other major powers; that is, he doomed them to be lost in the morass already existing. Instead of offering a resounding political "Yes" like the other nations and allowing a vast move forward in world disarmament, we started arguing again about details and fudged it. Richard Lamb's conclusion is tart: "British performance at the Conference was deplorable. They arrived without proposals of any kind, and during the proceedings opposed almost all those made by other delegations."[193] It also guaranteed the arrival of Hitler in power in Germany at a time when his support was waning. What a dreadful, seemingly inexplicable event! How could we, the British, do this? It was a titanic event, also in the sense that many of those on board could not spot an iceberg in front of their eyes. Not surprisingly this episode has been expunged from British public history. Let us detail this war and peace fulcrum of the century.

**The British Conservatives Mire Hoover's Disarmament Proposals.**

As we have said, by early 1932 the pro-disarmament Labour Government had broken up and a new National Government had been formed with Ramsey MacDonald as Prime Minister but overwhelmingly made up of Conservative MPs. Really, Stanley Baldwin was in charge. The Foreign Secretary was Sir John Simon, in favour of disarmament, but weak-minded. Amazingly, there was no proper discussion of the content of the Government's position in the Commons, including the Hoover Proposals. Lansbury, Attlee and others tried to get a full debate in the Commons, but were fobbed off by an executive who claimed to handle things their way, being generally pro-disarmament, but having reservations on specific measures. The National Government had such domination in the Commons that they were not really accountable. The British Government response to the Hoover proposals was muffled and carried out behind the scenes. When finally Baldwin made the statement, the Hoover proposals were praised, and the British proposals were said to be very similar, but there were differences which would make long further negotiations necessary. What people looked for was clear. David Grenfell MP made it plain on 12th July, 1932.

> ...he will give the House some encouragement to hope for a further reduction in armaments. The world is asking for such a reduction, but never have we received such scant encouragement. Petitions signed by millions of people have reached the right hon. Gentleman from those who want peace and who are praying for peace, but who so far have been grievously disappointed; and their mortification is all the more bitter because they see another country which has made more advanced proposals than our own Government. I hope the Foreign Secretary will assure us that the Lord President of the Council (Stanley Baldwin) did not speak the last word for the Government the other day, and will give us some encouragement in our task of organising the peace mind in this country, in the hope that there will be a substantial reduction in armaments of all kinds in this and in every other country.[194]

The Government response was small minded. We seemingly agreed to Hoover's abolition of tanks, but then wanted only to abolish tanks over 20 tons, when most of ours were under 20 tons. Other niggling differences were brought up. A clear principled acceptance of Hoover would have led to worldwide disarmament.

Japan could be isolated. France was encouraged by the Locarno agreements and her long term fears could have been addressed. Tardieu's position was that if it was understood that any act of war was deemed to have been committed against the League as a whole and would bring universal reprisals, it was a guarantee with which France could be satisfied. All the other major players were for the Hoover Plan, but the only real sticking point was the Conservatives and military establishment wanting a big navy to police her Empire. If the British had backed Hoover, international action on disarmament would have rolled out, helping domestic budgets and shaping a peaceful world.

Sir John Simon did not lead. Lloyd George's verdict on him was that "Sir John Simon has sat on the fence so long that the iron has entered his soul." Another colleague commented, "His smile shines like the brass plate on a coffin." And a verse went round Whitehall:

"Sir John Simon
Isn't like Timon.
Timon hated mankind.
Sir John doesn't mind."[195]

Sir John did not do his homework on the papers presented, but dithered. He was pressured by the armed forces. Lord Londonderry was apoplectic at the idea that aerial warfare might be outlawed, briefed all the time by Lord Trenchard, former Chief of the Air Staff. Vansittart and Hankey were fighting disarmament all the time from within Cabinet Secretariat steering him away from the Hoover plan. Actually Simon had strong support from MacDonald, Baldwin, Eden, Henderson and others who offered amazing popular backing for disarmament. But he was too scared to go out on a limb and he had no grasp of the historical significance of his role in the Conference. Anthony Eden's verdict was damning. On 14th October, 1933 he wrote, "It is very difficult to feel anything but contempt for the man at these times. It is not only nerves at the speech which we might all suffer or excuse, but I truly believe an utter lack of moral courage."[196] Harold Nicholson was more direct, describing him as "a toad and a worm".[197] Sir John Simon feared his job might be lost, and he produced a muffled negative response in Geneva to protect British military interests and partly to keep 500 conservative MPs liking him. He was still for disarmament, and pointed out what everybody could see; not pushing through disarmament would result in Hitler coming to power and German rearmament. "We have to choose and our choice is very clear. Shall we disarm ourselves, or shall we allow the Germans to re-arm?"[198] Yet, he himself fudged the means for achieving the end; he did not answer his own question.

Along with all of this, most within the vast body of the Conservative Party could not accept disarmament, and Sir John Simon was mindfull (correct spelling) of them. He also had the arms manufacturers who had been ploughing weapons into Japan and China and were obviously against disarmament at his back. Many of the Conservatives were ceremonial soldiers, rear-admirals, colonels and owners of colonial wealth. They thought about the servant problem, gout, their lunch at the club and buying horses. They included men who thought the Charge of the Light Brigade was a triumph, and whose military thinking was shaped by Nelson and the Duke of Wellington. Rear admirals supported the navy. They were against all this disarmament nonsense and there's an end to it. Guns and soldiers were always needed to defend privilege. Hostile to the Hoover Plan, they were more concerned about asking detailed questions in the Commons about the expenditure of the League of Nations on its new Assembly building, a deliberate trivial distraction from the main issue. Thus, mindless British Conservatives opened the way to Hitler and the Second World War.

**The Conference Stalls.**

Still, the Conference went on formulating disarmament proposals, but now the cleanness of reform had gone. There were many closed sessions of discussion, and the arms manufacturers and retired generals were busy. The French had Charles Dumont, the spokesman for Schneider insinuated among their delegates, and the British had Colonel F.G.C. Dawnay, brother of a Vickers' director. They got to work creating dissention and fear. More than this, the situation changed. If disarmament reform had gone through, the Socialist and Centre parties in Germany would have experienced a massive swell of support, but nothing had happened by the time of the election on 31st July, 1932, when the Nazis won 230 seats in Hitler's major breakthrough. The failure at Geneva dominated public perception at the election; Hitler on the edge of power was asked to serve as vice-chancellor under Franz von Papen, but refused in order to wait his chance.

The Conference was supposed to break for summer, but Henderson was asked to work through the summer and aimed to draw up a Resolution summarizing the progress that had been made. Edouard Beneś was responsible for it and would have liked a statement on the proposed cuts to air forces, bombing, tanks mobile land guns and naval armaments, but key players demurred and unanimity was gone. Although a substantial majority voted for the Beneś Resolution, there were enough abstentions and votes against for it not to be solid. The German delegation, now more influenced by Hitler, said that it would temporarily withdraw from the Conference until it was treated with full parity in the disarmament proposals. Still that could have been done, but an agreement did not quite come through. The Resolution signaled the nations' decision for a substantial reduction of armaments in line but Germany voted against the resolution and asked for complete equality in defence, and the wider public saw the declaration as completely inadequate, because the whole process had been fudged.

**The Churches Respond.**

The public was given very little idea of why disarmament had not come through. Everyone seemed for it and yet the statesmen did not achieve the result. The Churches, deeply involved in forming the great disarmament public consensus, were anxious like everyone else and tried to get action to remedy the situation, and they were nearly successful later in the year 1932. Maurice Bowman notes:

> An irresistible trend in Anglo-Saxon opinion became evident. On September 20th, 1932, a delegation led by the

Archbishops of Canterbury and York, the head of the Methodist Church and the General of the Salvation Army was received at the Foreign Office by Prime Minister Ramsey MacDonald and the Foreign Minister, Sir John Simon. It expressed disappointment at the slowness of the Disarmament Conference's work. "the problems involved are of a moral, not a juridical character… The promises given at Versailles, by virtue of which the compulsory disarmament of Germany ought to constitute the first step towards general disarmament have not been fulfilled.… The British Government should formulate a definite disarmament policy based on legal equality among all the League of Nations members. [199]

Their remarks were even more pointed. As Lord Marley reported it, they added,

> We believe that one of the obstacles to disarmament is the vested interests of private armament firms. The Churches must protest against any group of private individuals being allowed a vested interest in the weapons of death and destruction, and we would urge that this traffic be either entirely prohibited or at least strictly controlled by Government licence.[200]

This picked up on the public mood in Britain, mystified by the way the popular, clear call for disarmament had been muddied in Geneva, and the pressure for disarmament was back on the Government.

At this point Stanley Baldwin had a change of heart. Ramsey McDonald, the British Prime Minister, was really quite ill. He was isolated from his erstwhile Labour colleagues, and his speeches became slightly incoherent. Baldwin had to lead. In June, 1932, he had allowed the hawks, Hankey, Vansittart, Eyres-Monsell, Hailsham and Londonderry to scupper Hoover's Plan. Now he saw his mistake.

On 10th November 1932, there was a censure motion in the House of Commons of Sir John Simon's conduct of the disarmament process. Clement Attlee led the debate on the motion: "In the opinion of this House, it is an essential preliminary to the success of the forthcoming World Economic Conference that the British Government should give clear and unequivocal support to an immediate, universal, and substantial reduction of armaments on the basis of equality of status for all nations, and should maintain the principles of the covenant of the League of Nations by supporting the findings of the Lytton Commission on the Sino-Japanese dispute." It was aimed at getting an absolutely clear statement out in the open, and getting action, but after Attlee's speech, Simon, perambulated round the issue. Perhaps the key speech was that of George Lansbury. He addressed Simon directly,

> "This question of disarmament and peace has got to be brought right down to bed rock. Do we really want total disarmament or not? I want total disarmament, and if there is any nation which proposes total disarmament it is the duty of the British Government to support it and get it carried by the other nations. You do not like the Russian proposition, you do not like the Italian proposition. Nobody can please you. And then Mr. Hoover comes along with proposals and they are discussed and talked about, but nothing happens. The right hon. and learned Gentleman makes speeches here and at Geneva but nothing comes of them; and after weeks we have another set of proposals, the French proposals. All I have to say is that if these proposals mean an increase of military forces in Europe, no matter whether they are conscript or voluntary, or militia, if they mean an increase, it is good-bye to disarmament and to peace. There is not a single hon. Member who will not admit that this is absolutely true. Therefore, we cannot be satisfied with what the Foreign Secretary has told us to-day. He has not told us how he proposes to accomplish the first stage or how he proposes to proceed afterwards, and he has not told

us what steps he proposes to take for security amongst nations."

Then Baldwin, the effective Prime Minister behind Sir John Simon, made a famous, and he hoped persuasive, speech. He could not criticize his own Foreign Secretary directly, but he launched into a direct warning about what war would be like. "There is no power on earth that can prevent the man in the street from being bombed. Whatever people may tell him, the bomber will always get through..." Baldwin pointed out that Britain was against gas in the First World War, but then quickly used it. We were against aerial bombing, but quickly used it... He continued, "Fear is a very dangerous thing. It is quite true that it may act as a deterrent in people's minds against war, but it is much more likely to make them want to increase armaments to protect themselves against the terrors that they know may be launched against them. We have to remember that aerial warfare is still in its infancy and its potentialities are incalculable and inconceivable....I am firmly convinced myself, and have been for some time, that, if it were possible, the air forces ought all to have been abolished..." He pointed out that it would be the young who would fight another Great War implying that the older generation who knew what war was like were solidly for disarmament, as indeed they were. He finished, "As I say, the future is in their hands, but when the next war comes and when European civilization is wiped out, as it will be, and by no force more than that force [air bombing], then don't let them lay the blame on the old men. Let them remember that they principally, and they alone, are responsible for the terrors that have fallen on the earth." Baldwin was hardly being fair. He had helped cripple the Hoover initiative. Really, the older generation was the problem, but he was making eddies round Simon's position.

**The Knife-edge in Germany.**

Baldwin's speech made a deep impression throughout the world, and not least in Germany because it set out what war would be like. The hope of Disarmament revived among the great majority of people who longed for it. The German General Election four days earlier had seen a fall in Hitler's support of some two million votes; he was now not a rising star but a falling star. Geneva could send him down. The Germans in the Secretariat of the League on hearing Baldwin's speech all said: "That's the end of Hitler. Let's make a Treaty and we shan't hear of him again."[201] Baldwin followed up his speech without delay. Instructions were sent to Anthony Eden in Geneva to prepare a British plan in the form of a Draft Treaty for World Disarmament on which general agreement could be reached. In the States at the time Hoover and Roosevelt were engaged in a Presidential election, one in which an assassination attempt was made on Roosevelt, and US influence was temporarily muted, even though both Hoover and Roosevelt were strong disarmament people. Yet, gradually even this initiative unravelled. Hankey and Vansittart were doing their work and events were moving in Germany, so that the resolution never came.

This was still before Hitler came to power. The election on the 6th November produced a decline in Nazi seats to 192, but they remained the biggest party. On the 17th November von Papen resigned and Hitler was asked to form a coalition, but failed to get the necessary support, and it was not until 30th January, 1933 that Hitler was unequivocally asked to be Chancellor after General Von Schleicher had served in that post and the German Government had lurched towards his form of militarism. Von Schleicher set up the programme of public works which was later to lead to the WV and autobahns. All during this time Hitler's hold on power was tentative, and disarmament reform could have weakened it further. It is sobering to think that but for the British Conservative vacuum of thought, the tyrant responsible for the deaths of millions could have been marginalized in history.

Later, when disarmament became even more popular Baldwin tuned into it during the next election, but really it was too late. The mindless, often older, Conservatives had scuppered the Hoover proposals and he could not as Conservative leader turn his party to disarmament. The speech damaged Hitler but did not eliminate him, because no actions followed.

**Rethinking the Oxford Union, LSE, Manchester and Aberystwyth Debates.**

It is interesting revisiting an event of February 1933 which reverberated from Baldwin's speech. It mildly hurts to defend Oxford students, but everybody remembers that the Oxford Union agreed the motion, "This House will in no circumstance fight for King and Country." by 275 to 143 votes. The debate took place ten days after Hitler became German Chancellor. After this defeat for patriotism a repeat motion was tried with Randolph Churchill, Winston's son, speaking against it; then the vote was even more overwhelming at 750 to 138. Why did the Oxford students vote like this? Baldwin's words were still echoing; they were being invited to say where they stood. They were facing the ineptitude of the British Government's handling of the Geneva Conference in the light of the international impetus to disarmament. The Oxford student body would be angry and willing to state their disgust at the Government. But more than this, as the words, "in no circumstance" convey, some students, as well as C.E.M. Joad speaking for the motion, were expressing a principled pacifism, an opposition to being roused into nationalism and a commitment to the disarmament agenda. They were reflecting the principles of the Geneva Conference. There was probably sorrow that the Government and the military could have failed in this key chance for world-wide disarmament. They had a right to their opinions; many of them would die through the failure to disarm.

Nor were they alone. At the London School of Economics a similar motion was carried unanimously. Aberystwyth University voted for pacifism 186 to 99. Manchester University voted for pacifism 371 to 196.[202] These were not isolated reactions, but reflected a general understanding among young thinking people that disarmament was necessary for peace and should happen. This dismissive assessment of the failure of the Government was far stronger than is usually allowed, and it seems to be the correct understanding of what had happened.

**Contributing Factors to the Failure of Disarmament – Hankey and Vansittart.**

We could look at the way the Great Disarmament Conference limped through various proposals to an inconclusive end. Decisive action could still have stymied Hitler in 1933.Yet, it failed. That resounding democratic chorus for peace was muted by obscure processes. Noel-Baker identifies four causes of its failure. The first was two extremely powerful Civil Servants who did a lot of damage on the inside of government. Some Civil Servants think they know better and work hard at imposing their perceptions on the politicians. Sir Maurice Hankey was one of these. After the Great War Parliament voted him £25,000 in recognition of the service he had given in promoting victory. He became Secretary to the Cabinet, a new office, and ruled from that administrative position, partly fixated by his own activity in the Great War. He believed in war as a great formative influence on human civilization. As he wrote to Cecil, "Whatever you do, War will come sooner or later, and if you carry disarmament too far, and crush the military spirit, your civilization will go under...Decline of civilization is connected with decline of military spirit."[203] He saw peace as degeneracy and a decline in the virile military spirit and war as the true test of greatness, and he therefore set out to make sure that the disarmament programmes failed from within the central administration of British Government. He tirelessly worked against disarmament from within the Cabinet.

Hankey disliked the League of Nations and its international character and negotiations, because his thinking remained totally rooted in British national identity. He was out of sympathy with Lord Cecil, and was probably one of the reasons why the latter was eased out of government. As Noel-Baker reports, he was intoxicated with his position and angry at nonconformity to his views. He was a man who could do damage.[204] He did much to undermine the Geneva Protocol and the proposed Treaty of Mutual Assistance.

Sir Robert Vansittart was similar in his views. He was Private Secretary to the Prime Minister between 1925 and 1930 and Permanent-Under Secretary at the Foreign Office from 1930-38. He was appointed by Sir Warren Fisher, Head of the Treasury, and another Civil Servant who, with Hankey, was strongly against disarmament. From this position at the Foreign Office, Vansittart, or "Van", as he was known, had great power. He believed in conventional national power politics, had a strong hatred of the Germans and saw war with them as inevitable. He wanted Britain to form an alliance with Mussolini and saw disarmament as undermining this possibility. He disliked all the international negotiations associated with the Geneva Disarmament Conference and of course formed Sir John Simon's pattern of participation in the events. Indeed, it would be quite difficult to disentangle the views of each. The failure of Simon in 1932 might partly be the sabotage of Vansittart.

But Van did not only work through one man. He even persuaded MacDonald, Hugh Dalton and other key Labour politicians to negotiate with Mussolini in March 1933, when participating at the Geneva Conference on his own draft Treaty for disarmament. MacDonald was persuaded by Vansittart to leave Geneva and go off to Rome to meet Mussolini and be impressed by him. Of course, the world, seeing MacDonald travelling away from the Conference to Mussolini, got the impression that MacDonald was not serious about disarmament. Probably that was not so, and MacDonald was being set up and used by Vansittart, a weasely move. These two Civil Servants were poison in the system.

**Failure and the Arms Companies.**

Another cause of the failure was the arms manufacturers' pressure groups and allies. Noel-Baker describes the 1932 Conference process:

> When things were going well, not only were Press attacks made, and not only did they become keener as things went better, but also rumours used to spread like magic through the lobbies of the Conference that the Conference was about to break up, that such and such Great Power delegations had come to an agreement that there must be an adjournment for an indefinite period of time, etc. Now these

rumours did not happen once or twice, but on dozens of occasions, always in a new form, usually connected in an ingenious manner to something which was true, so as to give them an air of verisilimitude. They were very persistent; they were very demoralising; they had every air of being organised, to anyone who followed the matter rather closely, as I did. They always came from no-where; I could never trace the original source. They were always untrue, and I say that with a knowledge of the facts; and I came to the conclusion that there was no doubt whatever that they were in fact the work of paid agents, like Mr. Shearer.[205]

Shearer as we know was an American agent at the 1927 Conference. He was denounced for subverting that conference, but he was back. As *Time* reported on 29th February, 1932, "New and powerful men who appeared at the Geneva Conference last week were Col. William Taylor, representing the du Pont interests (hardly an interest in peace from this explosives giant) and bluff 'Big Navy Bill,' Mr. William B. Shearer." His aim was to subvert, not to observe. Noel-Baker also details how French arms interests mounted a similar campaign to undermine it.[206] (367-9) These agents were professional saboteurs, but they were aided by the third factor.

Many of the sessions were carried out in closed negotiations. This left what the participants said closed to public scrutiny, and if an outcome depended on a committee then it could always be stalled. The results tended to be decided by who could get into the sessions and dominate their outcome. Those representing Britain on the technical committees of the Conference were three Brigadiers, two Colonels, three Majors, one Vice-Admiral, three Captains, three Group-Captains, a Commander and a Squadron-Leader. [207] They were not going to close down the armed forces; turkeys don't vote for Christmas. The military choosing disarmament? It's laughable, were in not that millions would die from these spanners being thrown in the works.

For finally, Noel-Baker points out, there were outright hawks, people who were linked to the arms industry or the military, who were used to having power and influence because of the political-military system, and not going to be sidelined. The inter-relations can all be seen in a map of Whitehall. The centre of the UK Government clusters around Downing Street. But what surrounds it? Next door to Downing Street and the Cabinet Office are the Horse Guards buildings representing the soldiers. Across the road is a vast Ministry of Defence Building with another one further up towards Trafalgar Square often known as the Old War Office, across from the Admiralty. With Cabinet War rooms and other buildings the centre of Government is largely surrounded by militarism, with statues of Kitchener and others keeping an eye on things. The military establishment was largely filled with hawks as dovecots are filled with doves. A reliable verdict on the hawks of the world is that they "have learned how to work in concert, how to reinforce each other and to divide the opposition so as to convert every international arrangement as well as each international crisis into an internal victory for their hard-line approach."[208] Political civil servants, arms manufacturers' agents, closed secret sessions, a hawkish military establishment and bungling politicians saw off the greatest peace movement the world has yet known. The time has come to have another one that really sees the job through.

**Churchill's View of Interwar History.**

During this period Churchill was in some turmoil. He had had a row with Stanley Baldwin and was therefore not in office. He was perhaps the strongest Conservative old-style colonialist and he felt that Baldwin was going soft on India and allowing moves towards independence. He also wanted to defend the navy against any further cuts. He was by conviction a professional militarist. He had been a war correspondent in the Boer War, revelling in the experience. Before and during First World War he was deeply engaged with naval affairs while at the Admiralty and loved his contact with Sir Jackie Fisher. During the Great War his appetite for military adventures led to the Gallipoli landings and other escapades. He is also credited for backing most strongly a military response to the Easter uprising in Ireland. Then, as Minister for War in 1918 he had more or less carried on a private war against the Bolsheviks after the Armistice, and he was quite prepared to bomb the Kurds in 1924 to teach them a lesson. Consistently, he was for using military outcomes and backing military dominance. This was no mere interest, but also a hereditary vein which ran fairly deeply. His biography of the Duke of Marlborough was both focusing on an ancestor with whom he identified and was written in the early 30s at the time we are discussing. His volumes on the First World War reflected the fact that he wanted to study conflict. Gandhi, the pacifist, especially got under his skin. His militarism seemed out of date, and he was not trusted by many in his own party, the Irish and the working class. He was, and became, a complex man, but his orientation towards militarism was clear. He argued for Japan in the Manchurian crisis, and was clearly out of sorts in the debates on disarmament.

But Churchill's importance at this point lies in his overall interpretation of the history of the 1930s. He was keen later to be *the* historical interpreter of the era through which he lived and was surprisingly successful by providing a single package that dominates the thinking of most British people. He stood for the dangers of appeasement in relation to Nazi Germany and the weakness of being unarmed. When Churchill came to write his history of the Second World War, after he had been rejected as Prime Minister in 1945, he tailored the events to the story he wanted to tell, as David Reynolds has shown.[209] So the history we get is the single narrative of *appeasement* and weakness leading to the War, and then the Churchillian understanding of the heroic conflict in the Second World War, where Britain holds back the Nazi tide and the Soviets are more or less forgotten. Indeed, Churchill described the First World War and the Second World War as the "Thirty Year War" trying to convey that there was no other possibility in the twenties and early thirties. This was not only bad history, but also a gloss for his failure to address militarism in this period. Yet, it is a narrative repeated almost every week in British public life and overwhelmingly dominates British people's understanding of its modern military history. Churchill, the historian, achieved this by largely sublimating the 1932 Geneva Disarmament Conference and the opportunity for disarmament throughout the period 1918-1933. In the chapter, "The Locust Years." in *The Gathering Storm,* he presents the coming to Hitler to power before several tangential remarks about the Peace Conference. The jumbled chronology obscures the possibility of disarmament before Hitler came to power and focussed on 1933 when the possibility of a breakthrough was already defeated. Hoover's proposals are not mentioned.[210] As a result 99% of the British public is unaware of the Geneva Conference and our contribution to its failure. It does not exist in the British historical consciousness; try it on your friends.

Churchill's study of the Second World War extends to a million words, and it was this interpretation which became orthodoxy and was projected into the future with Churchill's further attack on the USSR and the need for a Cold War, where strength had to be met by strength. This Churchillian interpretation hangs over our national consciousness. Of course, Churchill the person was far more complicated than this single theme. As we have seen, he distrusted the naval build-up to the First World War, and he also felt that the Second World War could have been avoided. His position rightly changed with the circumstances. He may have been correct about appeasement *after* January, 1933, when Hitler came to power, but before then there were thirteen years to develop peace culminating in the Geneva Disarmament Conference which he largely ignored. Churchill was also correct in that Krupp and some other munitions companies were covertly trying to keep in business by opening factories abroad and by preparing new weapons, but that could have been addressed. He was wrong in that up to July 1932 or later it was possible that munitions companies and their fascist expressions could have been kept from power. Universal disarmament would have excluded them from government, and there was sufficient political support in Germany for the military to be kept small. Churchill, like many of the other

Conservatives, could not think disarmament, and his earlier imperialism contributed to the failure to disarm and live in peace.

**The Peace Ballot.**

So the Disarmament Conference foundered. But the British people did not give up. Indeed, the world public hoped for better and continued to do so in a great emote of longing for disarmament. In 1934-5 a Peace Ballot organized by Robert Cecil in another bid to get disarmament through by popular assent was developed. The Peace Ballot's official backers included the Labour Party, the Liberal Party, the Archbishop of Canterbury, the Archbishop of York (and more than fifty bishops), the Moderator of the General Assembly of the Church of Scotland, the Roman Catholic Archbishop of Liverpool, the President of the National Council of Evangelical Free Churches, the General Secretary of the Baptist Union, the Moderator of the English Presbyterian Church, the Chief Rabbi, and numerous other public figures. Throughout Britain half a million canvassers distributed ballot papers to every household and got 11,559,600 responses, about 95% of the number of those who voted in the 1935 General Election.

The results were astonishing. 93% of these people affirmed that "the manufacture and sale of armaments for private profit should be prohibited by international agreement."[211] The full results were:

1. **Should Great Britain remain a Member of the League of Nations?**

***Yes*, 11,090,387. *No*, 355,883.**

2. **Are you in favour of all-round reduction of armaments by international agreement?**

***Yes*, 10,470,489. *No*, 862,775.**

3. **Are you in favour of an all-round abolition of national military and naval aircraft by international agreement?**

***Yes*, 9,533,558. *No*, 1,689,786.**

4. **Should the manufacture and sale of armaments for private profit be prohibited by international agreement?**

*Yes,* **10,417,329.** *No,* **775,415.**

5. **Do you consider that, if a nation insists on attacking another, the other nations should combine to compel it to stop (a) by economic and non-military measures:** *Yes,* **10,027,608.** *No,* **635,074. (b) if necessary, military measures:** *Yes,* **6,784,368.** *No,* **2,351,981.**

The public was mightily for international control of armaments and war. It was the first time the British public had spoken in an ordered democratic way on any subject and their opinion was decisively for the League and disarmament. When Lord Cecil announced the results in the Albert Hall on 27th June, 1935 it was clearly a vast tide of opinion, far bigger than any parliamentary majority, and no-one could argue about the figures.

**The Conservatives Swing over to Peace and Disarmament.**

Clearly, this was a voting matter and an election was coming in November. People like Vansittart were angry at Cecil and the whole operation, but the Conservative Party leaders then swung to talking about peace, because it was obviously a vote-winner, and they became the "peace party" in the election of 15th November, 1935, which Baldwin won with an overwhelming majority, saying, "I give you my word that there will be no great armaments." These words were candy floss, because the Government was arming fast, and the real possibility of disarmament had gone. This in 1935 was the appeasement that Churchill fulminated against. He had accurately seen the Nazi menace which was now deliberately preparing for war and had to watch his own party going off like Gaderene swine trying to outdo Labour on peace statements, later to be amplified by Neville Chamberlain at Munich. It was all too late, a whoring after peace as a vote winner rather than out of any integrity or understanding.

By now Churchill was right, although he was no fatalist. In the British Library there is a touching letter between the two great statesmen of this drama. It is from Churchill to Lord Robert Cecil, the main architect of the Geneva Conference in 1932 written on the 1st September, 1944 when it was becoming clear that the war which followed would be won, and Churchill looked forward to the United Nations picking up where the League of Nations had failed. He commented as follows,

> My dear Bob... This war could easily have been prevented if the League of Nations had been used with courage and loyalty by the associated nations. Even in 1935 and 1936 there was a chance by making an armed Grand Alliance under the aegis of the League to hold in subjection the rising furies in Germany or at the very least to enter into armed conflict on terms far more favourable than those eventually forced upon us...[212]

Cecil thought disarmament and Churchill thought armed strength, but Winston was far from merely backing arming for war. His thinking was of prevention as late as 1935 and 1936; he also knew the War could have been avoided.

**The Private Manufacturers of Arms lose the Argument, but get their War.**

Peace and disarmament were a very strong popular movement. The private manufacture of arms was seen by statesmen and ordinary people throughout the 20s and 30s as the major precipitant of the war, but one of the issues worth pondering is how slowly this historic conclusion emerged. The awareness came when it was too late. Englebrecht and Hanighen's *The Merchants of Death* was only published in New York in 1934. The Peace Ballot reported in June 1935 was after Hitler was well ensconced. Philip Noel-Baker's *The Private Manufacture of Armaments* was not published until 1936. Already by that time Hitler was ranting as Chancellor and pulling in investment from America to re-arm. The consciousness was strong, but events had moved on.

A decade earlier disarmament could have happened as part of a peace movement, but it did not, for the reasons we have already examined. The history of the century could have been very different. For-profit manufacturing of arms was not understood properly and closed down by the British or anyone else because the overall political consciousness came too late. The good people who labored for peace could be side-lined by the hawks; profit from arms burgeoned and in seven years a Second World War arrived. The conclusion of G. D. H. and Margaret Cole, writing about the Conference in 1933 (in the same year, before it was evident that World War II would follow, and therefore of greater perspicuity) was sobering.

> The concession to Germany had come too late; for it is quite possible that if the claim granted in December had been granted earlier in the year [1932], the Brüning Government would never had fallen, and the advance of the Nazis might have been checked or reversed.[213]

Hitler withdrew from the Geneva Disarmament Conference and the League of Nations on 14th October, 1933, and the peace movement was broken. On such threads hung the deaths of millions. Military interests played a strong part in subsequent rearmament. The UK National Government fell to pieces under its failure at the Conference, and the hawks had won the day. Soon the arms companies of the liberal west were lining up to arm Hitler, Stalin and Mussolini, creating the enemies against whom we would have to fight. This failure should be engrained in the minds of all of us. It was here in the failure to disarm that the bodies and lives of multitudes across the world were ripped apart. But, as yet, less than half the story has been told.

# PART VI: THE MILITARY-INDUSTRIAL COMPLEX AS THE DRIVER OF FASCISM.

*When we think of Fascism, our minds go to ranting, frog-marching movements like those of Mussolini and Hitler with a strong ideology involving racism, the cult of leader, a hatred of Jesus, anti-communism, a drive to world domination and the wicked murder of the Jews. It is the most evil of all modern ideological constructs and rightly most vilified for the Holocaust and other evils. But the history does not allow this distancing. Fascism grew up in most western countries as strong movements competing for power through parties and alliances. Fascism was present in most countries, often supported by elites, and it needs another kind of explanation than merely disgust. It is closer to us than we think.*

*But we are taken in by Fascism at another level. We look to the political leaders, but ignore those who fashioned them. In Japan, Italy, Germany, France, Britain and the United States Fascist movements were partly formed by the arms companies and bankers who had made vast amounts from the Great War, but were now unwanted. This group encouraged, used and funded Fascism to stir up strife on the streets and defeat Socialism. This money gave Fascism its manpower to march and sow disorder, and its opportunity for dominance. It paid the piper, but we only listen to the tune.*

## Chapter Eighteen: Looking behind Fascism.

### The Arrival of Fascism.

Thus far we have looked at the interwar years in terms of the failure of the disarmament movement and the machinations of the arms companies, because these possibilities of peace between 1918 and 1932 have been widely ignored. However, most people associate the interwar years with the growth of Fascism, and we now look at this movement. It is most strongly associated with Mussolini and the Fascists in the twenties and Hitler and the Nazis in the thirties. First, we recall how widespread this movement was.

Fascist movements occurred in most of the countries of the world and arrived at different times in this period.

There are legitimate questions about what constitutes a fascist movement and it is an important debate. Here, for a start, we characterize the ideology in terms of a number of well recognized elements. Fascists believed in militarism rather than democracy, and operated through coups, armed militias and a melding of the military with the state. They had a strong ideology of the leader. They were nationalist and ethnically focussed, normally with a certain "pure" or "master" race and a converse hate race, often the Jews. Social Darwinism, or the struggle of the races, was normally part of their thinking. They were opposed to Communism, Socialism and strong unions, favouring rather the rich corporate leaders. And they had some view of the March of History and their special role in it, normally of national and/or international domination. They wanted mass and corporate responses with people acting together, rather than individually, and had a nationally required ideology which they were prepared to enforce by closing down views other than their own. If we look at the world-wide movements which roughly inhabit these kinds of views we might come up with quite a list of nations, parties, dates and governments involved.

**World-wide Fascist Parties in the Twenties and Thirties.**[214]

**Argentina**: 7 Fascist parties from 1923. The Argentine Patriotic League (anti-Jewish) backed General Uriburu in the military coup of September, 1930. General Peron continued a similar tradition later.

**Australia**: 4 minority Fascist parties. None came to power.

**Austria**: Two parties (1902, 1933) Came to power – Dollfuss in May, 1932.

**Belgium**: Four minority parties 1930 onwards.

**Bulgaria**: Four parties. Zveno founded in 1927 by army officers came to power in 1934 coup.

**Chile:** National Socialist Movement of Chile attempted coup in 1938

**Croatia**: Ustaše founded as terrorist/Fascist group in 1930. Used by Hitler later.

**Czechoslovakia**: National Fascist Community formed in 1926, looked to Italian Fascism. Later Nazi group.

**Denmark**: National Socialist Workers Party modelled on Nazis formed in November, 1930.

**Finland**: Lapua Movement tried coup in February 1932. Succeeded by Patriotic People's Movement.

**France**: We look at in greater detail later. The Faisceau Party formed in November, 1925 led the way, but Action Français took over later.

**Greece**: A number of parties including National Socialists in 1932 led to the rule of Ioannis Metaxis from April 1936 to 1941 in a largely Fascist style of dictatorship.

**Hungary**: The Hungarian National Defence Association or MOVE acted as a paramilitary political force partly against Communists. The Szeged Fascists formed within the army became ruling party under Major General Gömbös as Prime Minister in 1932, who promised not to enact any anti-Jewish laws.

**Northern Ireland:** The Irish Republican Army (IRA) formed in 1914 had Fascist tendencies - an autonomous military command, terrorism, racial identity, a strong leader and the strategy of first making a country ungovernable, a pattern which continued for much of a century.

**Israel**: Brit HaBirionim, the Strongman Alliance, formed in 1930 was a militarist "pure" Jewish reversal of the Italian Fascists.

**Italy**: The National Fascist Party emerged during the First World War and came to power in 1922 after a coup attempt.

**Japan**: A plethora of military inspired Fascist groups existed in Japan as a result of the Russo-Japanese War and the First World War.

**Latvia**: The Pērkonkrusts formed in 1933 were pure Latvian nationalists out to replace Christianity with a Latvian ethnic religion.

**Lithuania**: The Iron Wolf Organisation was a Fascist group formed in 1927, attempted a Fascist coup in 1934.

**Manchuria**: A group called the Russian Fascist Organisation/Party was formed in 1925 obviously against USSR Communism.

**Mexico**: Small anti-socialist Italian-imitating Fascist Party formed in 1923.

**Netherlands:** A number of small Fascist parties developed in the 1930s.

**Norway**: A small Nazi Party, Nasjonal Samling, led by Vikdun Quisling, was formed in May 1933. Collaborated with Nazis. Quisling came to have the reputation of a rat.

**Peru**: The Revolutionary Union led by Lieutenant-Colonel Luis Serro came to power in 1931. It had a Blackshirts military arm. Serro was assassinated in 1933.

**Poland:** Camp of Great Poland (OWP) formed in 1926. Was anti-Jewish, youth militias, etc. Nazi influence later.

**Roumania**: Iron Guard was formed in 1927. It was Fascist and anti-semitic.

**South Africa**: The Nationalist Party founded in 1915 was a Boer ethnic party. It became more extreme when it opposed the United Party of Jan Smuts and developed Apartheid.

**Spain**: General Franco faced with the marginalization of his military position by the Republicans, started the Civil War and then set up an autocratic Fascist style dictatorship supported by Rome and Berlin. At the end of the Civil War there were a quarter of a million people in prison and a further half a million had fled the country.

**Sweden**: The Swedish National Socialists Workers Party was Nazi like but withered as the full Nazi agenda became clear.

**Switzerland**: National Front formed in 1930 was anti-semitic. Other minor Fascist groups.

**United Kingdom**: Small National Fascisti party in 1920s morphed into British Union of Fascists (1932) led by Mosley.

**United States**: The Fascist League of North America formed in 1923 from Italy. Friends of New Germany and German-American Bund in 1933 backed Nazism in the States. Coup attempt in 1934.

**Yugoslavia**: Organisation of Yugoslav Nationalists (ORJUNA) formed in 1921. Anti-Jewish, Communist, Serb, with military wing.

These parties and organizations varied, but they were clearly a world-wide movement. They were present in almost every country of the world including the United States, Canada, Britain, France, Australia and the other allies who fought against this ideology in the Second World War. Fascist-like governments grew in Germany, Italy, Spain, Portugal, Austria, Japan, Albania, Bulgaria, Croatia, Greece and Hungary. They were partly anti-democratic, representing the old established hierarchies who wanted to remain in control, and the capitalists and landed gentry who feared the workers. But there were intersecting attitudes. As many commentators have noted, the USSR, although far to the left of Fascism ideologically, had many similar characteristics: a one party state, a strong military, purges, anti-Semitism, a dictator, and a desire for imperial conquest. In that sense, too, it bought into totalitarian militaristic control. Fascism is a much broader phenomenon than most of us would allow, and it requires an explanation as to why it emerged and became so powerful.

**Explanations of Fascism: Fascism as Ideology.**

It has been frequently seen in ideological terms. It is a movement like Socialism, Liberalism, Conservatism and Nationalism with a set of ideas which appeal to the public in a certain kind of way and gathered support. In some senses that is true. State Corporatism was an important response to economic collapse which had some popular appeal. Mussolini did not make the trains run on time but Volkswagen was, and is, an outstanding company, and it offered a way out of mass unemployment. Of course, nationalism and patriotism, the cheap recourse of politicians throughout the modern era - mere national political selfishness, self-righteousness and self-importance - was the real Fascist vote winner, especially when times were hard. It was often little more than a blind hope in Great Britain, La France, or the Third Reich, a hope as contentless as frog-marching, but it had popular appeal in these early mass elections after a great war. Voters are often not too discerning. This was one of the reasons why Fascism grew. But it was not the main one. Hitler, Mussolini and General Franco did not come to power because they argued their case. Indeed, a strong part of the Fascist agenda was not to argue their case, but to assert their dominance and hate the old style commitment to freely traded views and principles. Its predominant image was of marching in tune to the orders of the leader, without thinking for oneself, putting blind trust in the leader.

Nevertheless, a kind of ideology remained important. Much fine scholarship reflects on the ideologies, structure and character of Fascism, not least its construction of the ideology of the Aryan Race, the idea of leadership in Il Duce or Der Führer, its concept of the march into the future, its fear of modernism, its development of crude Racial Darwinist philosophies, and its state- corporatist philosophy. All of this added up to an important tranche of views, especially because the Nazis and others had the opportunity to try them out. Fascists had stuff in their heads which gave then an unqualified belief in themselves and made them immune to all their wrongs. Ideology was in this sense important to the movements, but it did not bring them to power. We have seen how Hitler used "socialism" as an untied balloon in the Nazi Party title. Fascism was not a matter of ideas and democracy; indeed, it was intent on closing down democracy. It was a matter of power and it needed the levers of power. Money and intimidation were the most important part that power, money and arms…

**Fascism, Nietzsche and Power.**

Most obviously, Fascism changed the meaning of "power", sought to come to "power", and fêted power as leadership, marching and follow my leader. Yet, "power" is a deeply ambiguous concept. As a Christian I look to the power of the Creator, the gentle power of the Holy Spirit to guide us and the reconstruction of human "power" as service, truth, equality before God, freedom, humility and law-abiding living rather than as control over others. That hardly sits well with Fascism, as we now see. Most commentators identify the philosopher, Nietzsche, as the obvious progenitor of the Nazi belief in power, and it is worth having a short reflection on his perspective. His idealized 'Superman' was seen to embody the will to supremacy: a creature of power, might and action, not of thought, faith or reflection. He was the philosopher who most fully engaged with the worship of power and will, rather than understanding and truth. His thinking was forged in his own personal depression, and so this was no easy journey for him. Indeed, it drove him to insanity. But its direction was towards the modern faith in power and control which shaped much of the commitment to militarism in the 20th century.

Nietzsche changed direction and it is worth reflecting on his own journey of thought, which was substantially formed in reaction to Christianity. He despised it, because it was a religion of weakness and submission. The Christian God of commandments, the one who named sin, was a denial of life. He states:

> The Christian conception of God – God as God of the sick, God as spider, God as spirit – is one of the most corrupt conceptions of God arrived at on earth; perhaps it even represents the low-water mark in the descending development of the God type. God degenerated to the contradiction of life, instead of being its transfiguration and eternal Yes! In God a declaration of hostility towards life, nature, the will to life! God the formula for every calumny of "this world", for every lie about the "next world"! In God nothingness deified, the will to nothingness sanctified!...That the strong races of northern Europe have not repudiated the Christian God certainly reflects no credit on their talent for religion – not to speak of their taste.[215]

We can see what Nietzsche is seeking to do. The change is momentous in terms of culture. He is trying to lose accountability to God, and a sense of human humility and meekness. He does not like the culture of the Jews and the Church. He cannot abide seeking and submitting to the will of God, prayer and piety. Above all he hates a Redeemer who takes human suffering on himself and is seemingly defeated on a cross. The idea of the Son of God suffering out of love of sinners sticks in his throat.

Surely, above all god would be powerful. Nietzsche's answer is to move outside the business of living in relation to God. We ourselves must create god. We must become Superman, the figure of power who is able to remake the world and affirm life. So Superman is born. Life is found in the will to power and supremacy. Superman is primordially Nordic. He is a creature of power and action, not of thought, faith and repentance. He is the self-willed philosophical origin of the political "superpower".

Right from the beginning Nietzsche saw the implications of his position. Morality was an old conception which needed to be removed and replaced by the expediency of wielding power. "We sail away right over morality." We were beyond Good and Evil and the Quest for Truth. Moreover, we needed a new conception of freedom. This was not a liberal, democratic kind of freedom where people were worried about treading on one another's toes. No, it was the freedom of the *warrior*, typified in Julius Caesar. "*First* principle; one must need strength, otherwise one will never have it. – those great forcing houses for strong human beings, for the strongest kind there has ever been, the aristocratic communities of the pattern of Rome and Venice, understood freedom in precisely the sense which I understand the word "freedom"; as something one has and does *not* have, something one *wants*, something one *conquers*....[216] This is self-possessed power, free of all God-given constraints. It is the power to rule, to change, to conquer and it is completely different from the Christian "sick-house".

Actually, this idea of toughness reflected a fundamental failure in many rich families as boys were separated from the intimacy of their fathers. Hardness was inculcated in elites throughout Europe at public schools, academies, military schools and officer corps training units. Often young boys faced distant fathers, were brought up by servants and governors, or sent away. Luxury led to the absence in the upper classes of good intimate family life. The problem is revealed most acutely in Nietzsche himself. His father was a Lutheran minister who shared great love and intimacy with his son, but then began suffering blackouts, had a brain tumour and died when Nietzsche was five years old. He then lost his younger brother of two. We can only guess what the loss of his brother and father did to him. If God had killed his dear father, then Nietzsche was going to kill God. His substitute deity was going to be power, and the will to power was the drive in life. Another figure conveys the same lesson. Bismarck complained that his mother was hard and cold towards him, and then "In early childhood I was sent away from home, and never again did it seem like home to me." In the holidays when he longed to come home, his mother sent a note saying that he must stay in Berlin... "My mother was fond of society and troubled herself very little about us..."[217] When he came to govern the nation Bismarck was hardened to conquest and dominance. Thus, the whole culture of the established classes, no less in British public schools, reflected dysfunctional rich families and the early emotional damage to kids who learned to fend for themselves. It was the stiff upper lip, learning to cope without gentleness, facing bullying and becoming like Flashman. It was these emotionally stunted people who led the culture of militarism which Nietzsche promulgated and spread it around the globe.

Nietzsche's quest was spiritual. It is reflected in Wagner's great recall of the pagan Nordic gods and superheroes. It was part of a search for men especially to find themselves and be strong in Nature; the women were shadowy figures or a bit like Brünnhilde. The West looked to the warrior. The Spartans were back in fashion being painted and fêted. Conquering was the stuff of boys' education. Thousands of young Germans went out hiking and hostelling to become imbued with this natural strength. It was contrasted with the cunning and complexity of Jewish customs and thought and led eventually to anti-semitism. It was also anti-democratic. Its appeal was to natural, charismatic leaders, and against democracy, committees, the influence of ordinary people and consultation. It was also militaristic. The attitude fused with the power of the gun, the battleship, the bomb, the tank, chemical weapons, howitzers and all the other instruments of war to deliver domination and to execute the threat – Do what we demand or you will die. That is the real belief in power, the power to control. It was what the Fascists and Nazis had in excess.

**What about Non-fascists? The Half-belief in Power.**

Yet the rest of Europe was not completely different. All of Europe had a half-belief in power, seen significantly in the acquisition of empires, the transport, selling and use of slaves and the control of trade. You make weapons because you come to believe in power. The idea had been fed for decades by the arms industry and then a world-wide war. After four years of world war and the manufacture of countless millions of weapons, this view of power was in people's minds and hands like it had never been before in human history. War reduces relationships to crude calculations about ammunition, the ability to kill and to survive. One of the most important facts about the Second World War was that it came after the First. Soldiers had learned militarism in millions in the Great War; they had had to believe in power and this belief did not suddenly disappear, though it was deeply discredited.

It was elitist, and elites thought this way as a validation of their own superiority. It is odd that people actually believe that because they have guns or bombs, they are superior. Another similarly odd belief is in the superiority of height. The rich who ate well were taller than the poor who did not and the tall looked down on the short, or used a horse to achieve the same effect, and the mere act of looking down was deemed superiority. So we intellectually construct superiority. There are those who rule and then there are the rest – the foot soldiers and the cannon fodder. Britain, Germany, the United States, France, Italy, Scandinavia, Japan and Australia all developed this same secular worship of power. This was the era when those deemed defective were bumped off by their superiors. It was reflected in technology. The power of the fast car, of flight reflected it. We had an Air *Force*. Struggle was good. Fighting was purifying. Here the Life Force makes its entry. The Christian God is renamed as the Great Power.

Many people, especially those out of contact with the Christian God and unwilling to say, "Thy will be done." accepted a secular theology of power - "My will be done". Might is right. Imperial rule is the way of things. This ethos seeped into the West. It fitted with the culture of Empire and especially with the newly emerging weapons' technology. Might is right is trite, but it infused the thinking of millions.

**The Ruling Class: Pulling the Strings of Fascism.**

Yet, most popular thought about fascism stays mesmerized by the jackboots, Nuremburg rallies, the evils of the Holocaust and the obvious later power of the Fascist regimes. However, that ignores the character of most of the Fascist and Nazi leaders. They were ignominious - Hitler in prison, Mussolini a war deserter – and opportunists - who created a party organization of power out of nothing, or rather, because in reality, nothing comes from nothing, they required backing which would make them powerful. And the people with power in the twenties and thirties were the powerful, the ruling class, the industrial, banking, military class (flushed with profits from the Great War). It was this group that helped the Fascists towards and even into power. Without their support the Fascists could not have succeeded.

There were five reasons for the ruling class's use of and support for Fascism. First, they needed to keep control of politics now the new mass voting working class parties were coming through, especially to protect the rich against heavier levels of taxation. They had to encourage the masses to believe in elitism. Second, they needed to stop revolutions, like the one in the USSR, which would threaten their wealth and even their lives. Third, they needed to protect their capital and keep the workers in their place, to prevent unions eating into profits and their economic privileges. Fourth, they needed to protect the military against disarmament. Fifth, they needed to protect banking and finance against controls and any policies which would lead to the erosion of wealth. These reasons cohered into support for groups who would help this agenda. It turned out differently in each country, but the underlying drive was the same. The old establishments could no longer hold their own against the much larger working class groups and then needed help from another populous group against socialism, democracy and disarmament. This they found in a new war-worn underclass of soldiers.

**The War Traumatized Underclass Generation.**

War Veterans are an ignored group. We focus on them when they were fighting on the Somme or in the Dardanelles, but what of them afterwards? There were millions of them living on for decades. They had been, to various degrees, changed and traumatized on a vast scale. People who have faced death, seen their colleagues die, been gassed, injured, faced attack with bullets, mortars and bombs are deeply stressed. Murder is not only the most serious of crimes, but it is also presumably the most distressing to witness or be forced to carry out. The First World War meant time in the trenches for millions with mud and gangrene. On the eastern front soldiers faced months of fighting in freezing conditions. There was famine and starvation on a vast scale, and injuries were even more numerous than war deaths, and often meant incapacity for life. Nor was this all. Spanish flu, which broke out between January 1918 and December 1920 killed between 50-100 million people world-wide, with war conditions and deprivation contributing to it being the worse epidemic ever. That enormous tragedy also hung over the world. Many of the millions who went back home after the war were coarsened, angry, withdrawn, grieving and close to exploding. Many worked out their own way of coping, but others were often out of work, injured, and still living the horrors of war – being gassed, living in trenches, experiencing mass fatalities and rotting corpses. No-one recovers from seeing a rat eat a dead comrade.

Millions of men were affected by post-traumatic stress disorder (PTSD). We now know much more about this. It can involve clinical depression, anxiety states, phobias, obsessive-compulsive disorders, sleeplessness, bi-polar disorders, alcohol and drug abuse, psychotic and other debilitating states. Some are protected from these by their own psychology. Many are not. PTSD involved a profound demographic legacy. The war lasted from 1914-1918, (although the Russian Civil War prolonged it for another couple of years.) For most of the young men involved in it, this was the period when they would normally be learning a trade, marrying and forming their lives. Instead, they often faced recession and joblessness, not least because the man-labour to form many enterprises was now not available. They were left looking at the future with no jobs, appalling memories and the inability, psychologically and practically, to build their own families. This group of men was a damaged cohort who could create political and social disorder for the next twenty or so years. They had learned a trade, but the trade they had learned was fighting.

For example, many German men were raw. The paintings of Georg Grotz convey the era of the 1920s with deep awareness and accuracy. As Grotz himself said: "My drawings expressed my despair, hate and disillusionment, I drew drunkards; puking men; men with clenched fists cursing at the moon. . . . I drew a man, face filled with fright, washing blood from his hands. . . I drew lonely little men fleeing madly through empty streets. I drew a cross-section of tenement house: through one window could be seen a man attacking his wife; through another, two people making love; from a third hung a suicide with body covered by swarming flies. I drew soldiers without noses; war cripples with crustacean-like steel arms; two medical soldiers putting a violent infantryman into a strait-jacket made of a horse blanket. . . I drew a skeleton dressed as a recruit being examined for military duty. I also wrote poetry."[218] Grotz was a faithful artist of his tragic era.

There was also the role of atrocities. The German "rape of Belgium" resulted in over 6,000 civilian murders and great acts of horrific violence and abuse. The evil of the Turkish massacre of the Armenians where thousands were burned, drowned, raped and shot resulted in deaths estimated at between 600,000 and 1,500,000. Perpetrators and victims lived with the evil. Wherever, there was conquest and victory, atrocities occurred. Robert Graves pointed out in *Goodbye to All That* (1929). "For true atrocities, meaning personal rather than military violations of the code of war, few opportunities occurred - except in the interval between the surrender of prisoners and their arrival (or non-arrival) at headquarters. Advantage was only too often taken of this opportunity. Nearly every instructor in the mess could quote specific instances of prisoners having been murdered on the way back. The commonest motives were, it seems, revenge for the death of friends or relatives, jealousy of the prisoner's trip to a comfortable prison camp in England, military enthusiasm, fear of being suddenly overpowered by the prisoners, or, more simply, impatience with the escorting job." All those who had seen atrocities were affected; those who knew of them, were complicit in, or had themselves, murdered, raped, killed, attacked, ignored suffering, saved their own skin to let others die, or merely faced the horror of mass killing were traumatized or hardened to various levels which left their souls in shreds, or armoured in silence.

People who have fought and lost, who have this overwhelming knowledge that it was all for nothing, often have an especial kind of anger and bitterness. This was the state of those who were left behind after fighting. If the world could survive until 1940 without further trauma, this vast problem group would be through to late middle age and less likely to cause damage. *But the world did not quite make it.* Rather this group of people was manipulated by capitalist and munitions groups who wanted to create a bulwark against the socialist tide which was sweeping Europe. They became cheap mercenaries who could be hired for a pittance to march and attack socialist meetings in the twenties and to rule the world in the thirties. We are following a cohort through from one destruction to the later one. The old attitude, learnt in the revolutions of 1848, of using the military to oppose radicalism again moved to the centre of the stage. Chaos could be created through rampant street riots and then cleared up through proper armed soldiers. The war veterans fitted this role exactly. Especially if they were paid and equipped, they could be guaranteed to create the chaos which would make the new workers' democracy impossible. Anyone with some ready funds could dole out a few marks or lire a day and have a make-shift army. The foot soldiers who would build Fascism against the threat of Socialism and Communism were available as young traumatized men in the early twenties and as older unemployed men in the early thirties. They were the class who, if paid, would fight against the workers and democracy. The long-term the consequences were to be disastrous, as we see in the next three chapters.

# Chapter Nineteen: Fascism in Italy, Japan, France and Britain.

## Helping Mussolini Strut to power.

Mussolini is often seen as the founder of modern Fascism, but it is important not to take him too seriously. He had a great gift of marching in two directions at nearly the same time. He came to power in 1922, but his earlier life was somewhat different. John Gooch notes: "Having returned to temporary exile in Switzerland in December 1903 partly in order to avoid conscript service, he bowed to his mother's wishes eleven months later and came back to fulfil his military obligations under the terms of a general amnesty for military deserters proclaimed to celebrate the birth of prince Umberto."[219] Military deserter or soldier? Both, actually. He became a passable soldier.

He also flipped easily from radical socialist to arch capitalist. By background he and his family were radical socialists, and he first came to prominence as a Socialist – as editor of the newspaper, *Avanti*. Mussolini's public position and that of his Socialist bosses was Republican, for the workers, against Italian involvement in war and for confronting Italian capitalism. His private position was that he needed attention, liked women and wanted to be rich. Italian Socialists had organized a General Strike in 1903 and were critical of the right wing nationalism being pushed by Italy's rich elites, especially in the war declared against the Ottoman Empire in September 1911. As Richard Samuels notes, "A young Benito Mussolini, then the most energetic of anti-war maximalists, railed against those who had co-operated, and had them expelled from the party… For his efforts, Mussolini was rewarded with the editorship of *Avanti!*, the main newspaper of the Italian Socialist Movement, a perch from which he garnered national attention." [220] It was promotion by bluster. Shortly before the Great War broke out his headline in *Avanti!* thundered "Down with the War!" So Mussolini was an anti-war socialist even as the First World War arrived. It is important to get the full flavour of Benito's principles.

> War, he declared, was the "maximum exploitation of the proletarian class" Further, he argued that "to declare war against nations with whom Italy was allied for over thirty years and until yesterday... would be repugnant to the Italian conscience [and would constitute a] stab in the back"[221]

Samuels adds, "Then, without warning Mussolini took out his own dagger." The anti-war socialist became the pro-war militarist and suddenly stabbing became a good thing. We could add that he was now also in favour of manufacturing daggers. The real question is who was pulling the strings and paying the very loud piper? Benito came with strings, or bellows, attached. Who were Mussolini's backers?

The change was sharp. In October 1914 Mussolini the anti-war socialist suddenly had a confrontation with *Avanti* Socialists about his new policy of entering the war and left the newspaper almost instantly. Within a few weeks he had started up *Il Popoli d'Italia,* helped practically by Fillipo Naldi, an experienced journalist who did the writing while Benito talked. It became the rival newspaper to *Avanti* - pro-military, "irredentist", meaning Italy wanted to lay claim to any territory where there were Italians (especially Trieste), and for strong re-armament. It was a true volta-faccia. Mussolini now backed war against Austro-Hungary, and wanted to be an ally of France and Britain. He had been bought off and then bought on. The new newspaper, as Filippo Naldi revealed in 1960, was funded to the tune of half a million lire, with sales guaranteed by its backers, and soon it was selling like hot pizzas. These several backers made Mussolini's new paper and the new Fascist movement possible.[222] Who might they be?

**Ansaldo, the Arms Company, and Mussolini's other backers.**

The biggest was the munitions' company, Ansaldo, owned by the Perrone brothers, which became the most successful arms company in Italy. The Perrone brothers had also bought *Il Messaggero* which became a vociferous advocate of intervention, and *Il Popolo* under Mussolini was expected to back the War and did. Earlier, Ansaldo had a link with Armstrong to help its battleship building programme get under way, forming a subsidiary company Ansaldo Armstrong, with Admiral Augusto Albini as President. The main company aimed to produce everything from the steel through to the finished weapons even though the standard of its output was questionable; sometimes its steel was of poor quality and the weapons were not always reliable. Nevertheless, it became the Italian success story of the First World War, dominating munitions production. Its main rival was the firm Terni which had links with the German backed bank Banca Commerciale. Therefore, if Italy entered the War *against* Austro-Hungary and Germany, Terni would be compromised and Ansaldo would be able to dominate the munitions industry. Against all his previous "principles" and at exactly the right time Mussolini backed the War in *Il Popolo d'Italia* and received support from Ansaldo. Both Mussolini and Ansaldo prospered. Its workforce grew during the war from 6,000 to 80-100,000 employees, an increase of fifteen times in four years, working on all kinds of weapons and receiving rich government contracts to produce aircraft, ships and artillery. The Perrone brothers wanted the unions tamed and the peace movements quashed, and so they were - by Mussolini's thugs. They also got capital from abroad through the Banco di Sconto, which Ansaldo and Ivla, a steel producer, had bought. Money came especially from France, who had an interest in having Italy on their side. Obviously, Mussolini a "short, inflated mercenary with a mouth" was the rather noisy puppet and Ansaldo and others pulled the strings. When Mussolini finally came to power the arms company was rewarded by 400 million lira of state funding; it was pay-back time. [223]

Other Mussolini backers were the Italian Edision Company, Fiat, which at this stage made aircraft, machine guns, trucks and ambulances, the Unione Zuccheri and the banks. The motives were partly to keep socialism in check and also to promote the War, which at that stage was unpopular. Many others wanted to stay neutral - the Catholic Church, the Socialists and most ordinary people - with good reason. As Gallo reports, when Italy entered the War, on average "almost thirteen hundred men were put out of action every day". Most of them died.[224] The Italian experience of the War was dreadful. Most of the time they were losing against Austro-Hungary, but Mussolini had to interpret it as the time of Italy's glory

Another backer of Mussolini, uncovered recently by Peter Martland, was Britain's secret service, MI5, which at this stage was just a few people forming an intelligence community, mainly to track down German spies in England. However, it did also get involved in making sure that Italy came into the war on the side of Britain and France. Samuel Hoare at this time was head of the Italian branch, and a hundred agents were sent to Italy for this purpose; presumably there were plenty of volunteers wanting a wartime holiday in Florence and Rome. Hoare knew Benito was a person who could be bribed and from 1917 agreed to pay him £100 a week, a small fortune then, to back the alliance and strengthen the pro-war groups.[225] Martland suspects Mussolini spent much of the money on his mistresses. In part this funding of Mussolini was to help Britain's war, but in part it was an expression of the anti-socialist attitudes of the British establishment. Samuel Hoare, MP for Chelsea, was part of a rich banking family, a member of the Anti-Socialist Union and thoroughly out of sympathy with left wing pacifism. Mussolini, it seems, had also signed up to the Anti-Socialist Union. The workers were well organized, but less good on weapons. They had a solid Socialist movement intent on democracy, higher wages, freedom from war and proper taxation of the rich and other similar outrageous ideas. Once Mussolini and his thugs had learned to beat up socialists, they kept on trying it. He had found the niche which would propel him into power.

**How to use Fascist Thugs.**

The pattern continued after the Great War. Recruiting squads of thugs and returning soldiers to beat up socialists won Mussolini increasing support. Alongside Ansaldo, other capitalists, scared of the solid union, socialist and peace movements, backed him. Rural landowners found this was also the way to keep farm workers in their place, and they too funded the Fascists. The basic model was set. The munitions people and the capitalists, flush with money, used groups who were paramilitaries to attack the socialists and pursue them. The groups helped create the chaos which they then declared only they could sort out, and gave the establishment an excuse for ignoring democratic processes. It became easy to forge a coalition between the Fascists who blustered and attacked and the militarists and industrialists who wanted a right wing command economy, often called state corporatism. This model, with some variations, emerged throughout the world militarized by the Great War. Other right wing groups looked to Benito.

These ex-soldiers, the Arditi, were worked into a frenzy by Benito Mussolini. They were promised that Italy was theirs. They did not know the money he was receiving, as suffering and brutalized, they were given a shirt uniform and a dagger and paid a basic wage each day they went out on the streets. On 21st March 1919 sixty followers of Mussolini, mainly Arditi, gathered in Milan and formed the *Fascio Milanese di combattimento*. Benito's message was that the war won at the front must be carried on in the country. Two days later he dedicated the movement to the war veterans and told them "to sabotage the election campaigns of all parties by whatever means..," and eliminate the socialists. This they did on 15th April, shooting and clubbing them down in a big march and then destroying and setting fire to the *Avanti* offices of his old socialist comrades. Mussolini enjoyed the sweet sense of revenge against the socialists who had "deserted *him*" and declared this to be a spontaneous uprising of the people. He found he could beat up opponents and destroy democracy, and the capitalists loved him.[226] Money flowed and his girth grew. Socialism had been successful in the USSR and strong in most of the countries of the west, and it was dangerous. It dared to treat ordinary people as equal to capitalist leaders. Fascism, funded by the rich, would see it off. So the earliest example of Fascism was underway. Benito strutted to power using this rabble of soldiers, and murdering those who denounced his violence. He was to act as a prototype for many who would follow him and for the backers who wanted socialism defeated.

**Fascism in Japan.**

In different countries, the way in which militarism played into the creation of Fascism varied. We have already seen how the military came to dominance in Japan. The Japanese munitions' industry got underway with help from the British companies of Armstrong and Vickers and other western arms manufacturers. When Mitsubishi wanted to develop aircraft they approached Sopwith in Britain and the Junkers Aviation Company in Germany. In most of these areas the Japanese did not stop with imports, but aimed to develop their own industrial expertise to a level which matched or improved on the West. They were competent engineers and manufacturers. The victory over Russia in 1905 sealed the seeming success of this policy and the arms companies continued to grow. As with Russia much of the industrialization was associated with arms, funded of course by the State's military budget. The Japanese companies retro-engineered, using existing models to develop their own designs.

The major industrial companies, known as *Zaibatsu,* became the dominant force in Japanese national life, competing with the more democratic direction in Japanese politics. They were on the inside of the Japanese state and by and large they were able to control events in their direction. The development of cars around 1911 was not because they were conceived as commercial vehicles, but because the importance of military trucks in warfare became apparent. The Zaibatsu did not need to come to power; they were already in power.

In the First World War Japan supported the Allies but much of its energy was directed towards moving into China and Korea to create its own empire. A great military expansion took place. The war in Europe gave them the green light to do what they wanted nearer home. Already at this stage a military Fascist vision was in place and groups were intent on making Japan into a conquering nation. The democratic parties seemed in control for much of the 1920s, although there were set-backs. Hara Takashi, the first commoner and party-based Prime Minister was assassinated on 4$^{th}$ November, 1921, a typical Fascist "solution". That ended one hope for stable democracy. Other democratic movements seemed for a while to be shaping Japanese politics, but there was another Fascist efflorescence. A formative group, "Omotokyo", believed the Japanese were to dominate the world, and in January 1917 it prophesied that there would be a war between Japan and America in which the Japanese would triumph. In chilling anticipation, it was already looking forward to the Second World War. "Omotokyo" had 25,000 believers by 1919 and 150,000 by 1921 and this included some 500 military officers.[227] There were Fascist ideologues like Ikki Kita, Shumei Okawa and Mitsugi Nishida who saw a central role for the military in the development of Japan and commanded a lot of support. The Japanese Fascists knew they were in conflict with democracy and were happy to use assassination to achieve their ends. If there was a politician who seemed to thwart their military aims, they killed him. In this context there was little need for Japanese munitions' companies to engineer support for their products; there was an automatic state demand.

The militarism became more extended because the Japanese now had an empire. By the end of the First World War, the Japanese controlled a population of fifty million in Korea and southern Manchuria generating a lot of revenue. As the military were in control of these areas, they largely had freedom from political accountability and funding. Army leaders were used to being their own masters and making decisions in relation to these territories. If they were challenged by the politicians, they appealed to the Emperor, claiming they were subject to him alone, and usually got their own way. Thus, by the 1930s normal democratic politics was sufficiently undermined to make the Japanese establishment largely militarist. There was no possibility of controlling the expansion of a military-dominated vision arising from groups like Omotokyo. Against this background the Manchuria crisis which upset the great 1932 Geneva Disarmament Conference becomes immediately understandable. The pity is that the western powers did not perceive the firmness necessary to stand against this military junta at the time.

Given this militarism, politicians accepted that the expansion of armaments was necessary to maintain and defend the colonies. The dominance of the arms manufacturers was now guaranteed and Japan kept a standing army of 300,000 men with a commitment to modernizing its equipment. The Japanese manufacturers began creating the best weapons available and moved smoothly into being dominant. The *Zaibatsu* were manly the four big companies - Mitsui, Mitsubishi, Sutitomo and Yasuda with newcomers like Nissan and others also moving into arms production. They had dozens of subsidiary companies and became a central and highly subsidized part of the Japanese economy, making all kinds of weapons to a high level of competence. Because Japan had little coal and oil, the expansion of electricity production was undertaken and controlled by the Zaibatsu. Their influence over the politicians was complete.

The relationship between the military and the Zaibatsu munitions companies was interesting. Sometimes they were in tension. Makiyo Hori in a careful analysis comes to the following overall conclusion.

> There was a conflict between the military and the zaibatsu. The latter, as we have shown, had never been subordinated to the former. Rather, they secured and expanded their position through the struggle over electrification. The *zaibatsu* had not anticipated the military's attack; but, nonetheless, they won on all strategic points. And quite unlike the European situation, big business in Japan did not finance fascism. Rather they were financed by fascism through compensation funds from the Government. By 1945 the funds which had passed from the state to the owners of the electrical industry amounted to 1,394,207,749 yen. The Nihon Hassoden Company functioned as the keystone supporting the total war economy despite the confusing managerial duality under which it was placed by the Electrical Power Agency.[228]

The munitions' companies were so central to the operation of the Japanese state that they had little problem in selling their arms or in increasing their capital base, and this process accelerated throughout the thirties. At this time about four thousand of the top Zaibatsu leaders owned half of all the shares in Japan.[229] It was an enormous concentration of money and power. A billion yen goes a long way. With the military out of political control, the strike on Pearl Harbour becomes easily understandable. Mitsubishi were building light, long distance strike aircraft just so that this kind of attack was possible. Again, the formative power of the weapons' industry is evident and obvious, turning the culture further towards belief in war.

**French Fascism.**

Fascism occurred throughout the world after the First World War, and it had a similar character in each country. French Fascism was also militaristic, looking back to the First World War, using uniforms, marching, fighting and identifying an enemy. Behind it were rich people, often from munitions companies, iron and steel companies and banking, who needed war and disorder. The rich did not like the unionization of the workers who by wage demands were threatening the erosion of their profits. They were also frightened by socialism, especially after the Russian Revolution in 1918, which suggested they could lose all their accumulated wealth and even their heads. It was strongly nationalist and it distrusted Democracy, ordinary people getting the vote. It looked instead to an elite who could make decisions the old way using a capitalist/ military/ political fusion of interests.

In France there were veterans' organizations which morphed into "ligues" which operated on the normal pattern of marching, initiating riots, and beating up socialists. They peaked in two periods, the mid 20s and the mid 30s, and various "ligues" reflected the normal complexity of French political life. One important one was "Le Croix de Feu" headed up by Francois de La Rocque, a First World War hero. Many commentators focus on the politics, marches and conflicts with socialism, but Robert Soucy in *French Fascism: the Second Wave 1933-39* looks at who financed these movements. He notes a police report which links Francois de

Wendel, the steel manufacturer and President of the Comité des Forges (which was the combined munitions group including Schneider-Le Creusot) to the funding of le Croix de Feu. The report adds the following assessment.

> But if Monsieur de Wendel considers the Croix de Feu disciplined and well organized, representing the only force capable of matching the strength of the left, his doubts about Colonel de La Roque's qualities as a head of state are no less, and he wonders if he would be up to resolving the difficult problems he would face after the installation of a dictatorial regime. That is why it is said that Monsieur Wendel intends, at the right moment, to replace the leader of the Croix de Feu with a man who enjoys greater prestige in the country and who also has the favour of the army.[230]

So Wendel at the centre of the great combined French munitions enterprise was the putative king-maker. Everyone knew where the Comité des Forges stood; it was the centre of the munitions lobby and used to getting its way. Wendel was going to give Pierre Laval a chance for a while but was mainly looking towards a dictatorship and expecting to choose the most suitable one, not necessarily Colonel de La Roque. This was where power lay in interwar France. The strings were ready to be pulled. At the beginning of 1936 militias were outlawed by the Blum Popular Front Government and France closed down the possibility of a Fascist coup, but it was a close run thing on exactly the same pattern – militias funded by the rich munitions people as Italy and Japan.

**Mosley and British Fascism.**

In Britain Fascism was slower to develop, but not mainly because we were decent chaps. We were not invaded during the Great War and faced less trauma. Also significant was Lloyd George's control of munitions during the War which meant the arms companies did not have vast profits to throw around and buy support. They also faced flat demand in the twenties and had considerable financial difficulties, so much so that Montagu Norman at the Bank of England made secret loans to help Vickers and Armstrong in their merger and to support Beardmore, Armstrong and Vickers survive.[231] The State always finds a way of looking after the arms industry. There was also not the same level of class aggression, partly because Britain was not defeated, had a democratic Labour movement, and the General Strike of 1926 did not produce violent confrontations. There was an early version of Fascism, a Mussolini copy-cat group, actually called the British Fascisti, but it did not catch on. Actually, that is not quite accurate. It was formed in 1923. William Joyce, later "Lord Haw Haw" of "Jairmany calling, Jairmany calling" fame, was a founder member. He became Hitler's voice to Britain during the War when he was not widely popular. There were a couple of Generals, a Brigadier General, an Admiral, Lords, Barons, Earls among them. The ethos was anti-Communist, to protect the landed gentry and the Conservative Party and to fight the unions. When the General Strike in 1926 turned out to be a peaceful protest, the quasi-military stance seemed a bit silly, and the movement waned in the late twenties.[232] So there was not the same impetus for class warfare and funding Fascist thugs on the streets for a few years in the twenties. Yet, Fascism did emerge with Mosley's British Union of Fascists.

Oswald Mosley was a minor aristocrat. He was expelled from Sandhurst, went into the forces in the First World War but was injured flying while showing off to his family. He spent much of the rest of the War at a desk in the Ministry of Munitions. He was elected as Conservative MP for Harrow in 1918 and began a political career marked by unusual movements across parties. In May, 1920 he married Lady Cynthia Curzon, second daughter of Lord Curzon, Foreign Secretary between 1919 and 1924. So Mosley was now among the elite of the Conservative Party, but had a row with the party over Ireland and became an independent for the next two elections. In 1924 when the Labour Party was about to come to power, he joined it, and, after losing his seat, was elected for Smethwick in Birmingham in 1926. During this time he worked out a policy of state corporatism involving trade protection and public works to address unemployment. He then fell out with the Labour Party and formed his own party, the New Party, for the October,

1931 election when a National Government was returned. This merged into the growth of the British Union of Fascists in October 1932, at the same time as the failure of the Geneva Disarmament Conference. It soon had 50,000 members, was backed by the *Daily Mail* and led by a dynamic ex-Labour MP. Lord Rothermere, owner of the *Mail*, was friends with Mussolini and Hitler. At a big Fascist rally in Olympia on the 7th June, 1934 hecklers including Margaret Jameson, Vera Brittain, Dick Sheppard and Aldous Huxley, and they had the honour of being forcibly evicted. There was a famous confrontation in Cable Street where the Fascists marched to be met by a solid wall of local people, socialists and peacekeepers until the police cancelled the march. The Fascist/Socialist confrontation was becoming dominant in British politics.

Mosley's private life was not great. He had adulterous relations with his wife's younger sister, his stepmother-in-law, Grace Curzon, and with Diana Guinness, née Mitford, whom he later married at Goebbels' house in Berlin with Hitler present. Like Adolf, Oswald had problems shaving. His first wife died at the age of 33 of peritonitis, possibly feeling neglected after he had taken up with Diana Mitford. Mosley sported the normal fascist repertoire of extreme rhetoric, smart black uniform, and examine my armpit.

His blackshirts went on the streets and he enjoyed a big following among the British aristocracy, including dukes, barons, generals, newspaper magnates, knights and MPs. As the Times reported, "On New Year's Day 1934 was formed the January Club, whose object is to form a solid blackshirt front. The chairman Sir John Squire, editor of the London Mercury said that it was not a fascist organisation but admitted that 'the members who belonged to all political parties were for the most part in sympathy with the fascist movement'. The January Club held its dinners at the Savoy and the Hotel Splendide. The *Tatler* shows pictures of the club assemblies, distinguished by evening dress, wines, flowers and a general air of luxury. The leader is enjoying himself among his own class"[233] The members of this club were: Colonel Lord Middleton, General Sir Hubert De La Poer Gough, director of Siemens and Enfield Rolling Mills, Vincent Cartwright Vickers, a large shareholder in Vickers, but a largely harmless man who wrote a book, "The Google" for kids and thought about banking. Lord Lloyd, former Governor of Bombay, the Earl of Glasgow, a landowner, Major Nathan, a Jewish Liberal MP for Bethnal Green, Ward Price, a *Daily Mail* correspondent who later met and reported on Hitler regularly, Wing Commander Sir Louis Grieg, Director of Handley Page (who developed a bomber in WW1), members of the Mosley set, Count and Countess of Munster, Major Metcalfe, a Commander in Chief in India, Sir Philip Magnus, a Conservative historian, Sir Charles Petrie, the Hon Rennell Rodd of Morgan Grenfell and Ralph Blumenfeld, Chairman of the *Daily Express* and founder of the Anti-Socialist Union. At this stage under the influence of Robert Forgan, the BUF was not anti-Jewish. Later, through William Joyce it became much more so. This group was establishment people, worried by Socialism, attached to the military, banks, landowners, Conservatives, but not, or no longer, in positions of top political influence.

Nevertheless, the BUF appealed to the wider establishment. A few names of supporters will make the point. Let me introduce the Duke of Hamilton, the Duke of Buccleuch, the Duke of Bedford, the Duke of Wellington, the Earls of Mar, Errol and Portsmouth, Viscount Rothermere, owner of the *Daily Mail*, Viscount Nuffield, owner of Morris Motors, Baron Brockett, Baron Arnold, Baron Norman - Montague Norman, Governor of the Bank of England. So are you surprised that the Governor of the Bank of England was a Fascist? We continue. Baron Redesdale and the three Ladies Mitford, Lady Curzon, Lord and Lady Liverpool, Lord Erskine. Of course, it also had Captains, Admirals, Brigadier-Generals, Majors, Colonels, Lieutenant-Colonels, group Captains, Air Vice-Marshalls and Major Generals in the line-up, wanting more support for the military along with a closer relationship with Nazi Germany. The BUF got funding from Hitler, but in the mid 30s the funding from Rothermere and this aristocratic set dried up and the movement lost strength in the 1935 election. It was an example, by failure, of the importance of money to the success of Fascism. It continued as a pressure group for supporting Hitler in Britain, even into the

Second World War. Then, as we now know, the George Pitt-Rivers group was opened up by John Bingham of MI5 and broken under Churchill's orders. Pitt Rivers was Clementine Churchill's cousin, so the Nazi sympathizers were getting a bit close to home.

This link became even more intriguing when, during the War Rudolf Hess, the Führer's deputy, flew over to Britain on the 10th May, 1941 to try to meet with the Duke of Hamilton, the senior Duke in Scotland, (in case you are interested in ducal seniority). He was one of the leaders of this group not averse to ousting Churchill and ending the fight with the Nazis. Fortunately, Hess faced the seclusion of the British aristocracy. He had to try to find Dungavel House in the middle of a grouse moor a hundred miles across the Scottish borders where the Duke was thought to be in residence and receiving guests, but Hess did not quite make it in his daring plane flight. As David Evans pointed out, it was a highly competent flight. He finished twelve miles out, parachuted down, injured himself, was carted off to hospital, identified and then taken to prison. We do not know how the Duke would have received him otherwise, perhaps, "Just dropped in? Do pull up a chair, Rudolf. Now someone said you don't like Churchill and were thinking of a change." So this rather aristocratic group continued to be of some significance. Yet the overall conclusion has to be that it was not politically decisive. It did not quite link the strongest political and economic groups.

**The Engine of Fascism.**

Fascism was an ideology constructed from racism, a belief in power, nationalist obsession, and military might. Yet the examples in this chapter show, and Germany and the United States will continue the theme, the operational key to Fascism was the money that funded it, especially the donations from the munitions people and the anti-socialist capitalists, landowners and bankers. They were able to afford uniforms, cars, offices, meetings, guns, and especially pay enough for fighting men to go out on the streets and take control. Some of this money was international, as the financial capitalists and rich arms manufacturers bestowed support on those who might suit their purposes, like Ford, but much of it was national and local. The Fascists became leaders because they could hand out money passed on to them. Often, the marching thugs were war-damaged people used to carrying out an agenda imposed by others. The underlying racism was destructive; the business of teaching people to hate was nasty and manipulative, but the real arrogance lay in those who were prepared, like Undershaft, to pay the piper and call the tune of this evil movement. We see strong echoes of the process which surrounding the Geneva Disarmament Conference. Disarmament needed to be defeated, either in the Conference Hall or on the streets and this group would pay for it. The munitions/military/ industrial/banking complex had a leaning towards war and militarism; it worked for them, and it had brought them material wealth and power. Wherever Fascism travelled, the process of funding was the driver. As we shall now see, it was no different in Germany.

# Chapter Twenty: Those behind the Nazi War Machine.

## Hitler's Origins.

The early development of the Nazis is well known. They arose from groups of soldiers returning from defeat in the Great War. They were told that Germany had been stabbed in the back by the Jews, a dreamt-up excuse for the devastating mess the German military had inflicted on the population. In reality it was the vast militaristic enterprise of Krupp, the Kaiser and the German military which had failed, even on its own terms, but also in a world-wide level of destruction and especially the intense suffering in Germany. Those who take the sword will perish by the sword. Yet, the munitions/military system passed the blame. So the Jews were "really" to blame for Germany's defeat, and the military, or some of it, continued in its own self-belief. The soldiers came home, but were emotionally lost. Grosz describes them thus: "Yes, there was freedom of speech, but people had been used to marching for years, so they simply went on marching, be it less straight, less smartly than before. For years they had obeyed orders; now they went on marching, but no-one gave the orders…yet."[234] It was out of this group of lost men that National Socialism was born. They needed any explanation to suggest that their sacrifices were not in vain, and to make some sense of the last four years of fighting and death. They clutched at this false artifact of the Jewish stab in the back. They lived in illusion. In reality the war was pointless and most of the sacrifices were empty – two rows of soldiers being mowed down by one another to no purpose at all. We have to sanctify war deaths, because otherwise loved ones would go mad.

In the chaos after the Great War, with socialists looking for a radical change, soldiers were paid a daily wage to oppose and beat up Communists and Socialists marching on the streets. The Kapp Putsch in March, 1920 gave Hitler his model. These street fighters would have a gun or a club and would be paid a basic sum to go out and break up any organization of the workers. A year or two after the War many of these people found better things to do, but Hitler with the single talent of rabble-rousing carried on with the model. He recruited men who would be his gun-touting supporters and would be paid for doing a day's bad work. Where did the money come from?

Hitler himself was without money, and lived parsimoniously in his early life. The money to finance this rabble had to come from somewhere. Many of the ex-soldiers had nothing else to do, but they needed some kind of subsistence, and Hitler needed to run a paper, hire halls and create some kind of momentum. In Munich some of it came from a few local rich families, keen to keep the workers in their place, and Hitler learned a sycophantic charm for the rich donors, bending and scraping to bring in the cash; his body language with the forward lean conveys it exactly. At the same time the need to keep socialism at bay scared the rich into giving. They helped him get going, an important stage, but they were small players.[235] Who were his major supporters?

**Hitler and Henry Ford – Some Detective Work.**

They were quite surprising. For example, Henry Ford was reported in the *New York Times* of 20th December, 1922, as possibly having links with Hitler. This seems extraordinary and far-fetched, so early and across such a big cultural gap. How could a jumped-up little corporal have links with the world famous Henry Ford in 1922? What does the NYT say? It cited the *Berlin Tagesblatt*. The headlines are: ***Berlin hears Ford is backing Hitler. Bavarian Anti-Semitic Chief has American's book and portrait in his office. Spends money lavishly. One German Paper appeals to the United States' Ambassador to make an investigation.*** At first it seems thin; a journalist saw a picture of Henry Ford in Hitler's private office and multiple copies of Ford's anti-semitic book on the table. Clearly Hitler might be a fan of Henry Ford, especially after Ford's four volume publication, *the International Jew; The World's Foremost Problem*, published between 1920-22. Hammer, a German nationalist organization, printed news of Ford's anti-Semitism as early as January 1921 and translated the first volume of *The International Jew* in the summer of 1921.[236] So, then, Hitler and his circles would know about Ford from translation in 1921 and find an international echo for their anti-Semitism. That in itself is serious, but gives no evidence of Ford's support of Hitler. It begs the question of whether Ford actually did. The *New York Times* article said he denied it.

Sutton, whom we look at shortly, uncovers more direct evidence given in the actual 1923 Beer Hall Putsch trial. It is given by Auer, Deputy President of the Bavarian Diet, presumably quite a reliable witness.

> The Bavarian Diet has long had the information that the Hitler movement was partly financed by an American anti-Semitic chief, who is Henry Ford. Mr. Ford's interest in the Bavarian anti-Semitic movement began a year ago when one of Mr. Ford's agents, seeking to sell tractors, came in contact with Diedrich Eichart, the notorious Pan-German. Shortly after, Herr Eichart asked Mr. Ford's agent for financial aid. The agent returned to America and immediately Mr. Ford's money began coming to Munich.

This seems to be public information in a democratic body. Dietrich Eckhart was, of course, the one who saw Hitler as Germany's saviour and helped pump up the Führer's bulldozer ego. He later edited the Nazi newspaper Völkischer Beobachter and wrote the lyrics of "Germany Awake", the Nazi anthem. Mr. Ford's agent was probably W.C. Anderson, who after the Beer Hall Putsch got the sack because Ford's support for Hitler made business difficult for the burgeoning multi-national.[237] Clearly this statement gives a provenance for the route of the contact and suggests that the fact was common public knowledge.[238] It becomes plausible.

Other bits fit. Germany at this time was going through massive inflation and dollars from abroad would help explain the conspicuous wealth of Hitler's office and cars. Moreover, Ford sitting in Detroit being asked by Anderson for funds for a fellow anti-Semite fits better than more direct contact. In many ways Henry Ford does not add up. He made pacifist statements and then made weapons. Probably, he was surrounded by hangers on who used his name and played his tunes. When the funds proved a commercial liability, then Anderson and Hitler were dumped. One is therefore inclined to believe that Ford was tossing some considerable money at Hitler for a couple of years. Later in 1924 with Hitler in prison Kurt Lüdecke was sent directly by Hitler to request funding from Ford. This would have been a costly move if the Nazis had not already got some money and hoped some more would be forthcoming. Perhaps Lüdecke returned empty handed. He and Röhm were able to get weapons by other routes. So, this incident seems to show Hitler's ability to tap influential rich sources of support. He was a man happy to bow and scrape before the powerful, if they would give him their backing, as sometimes they did. This incident also shows the principled opposition to Hitler's Fascist practices in Munich. The *Munich Post* had shown in a long series of articles how violent and vicious Hitler was, and their offices were destroyed in the Munich Putsch for their pains.[239] Hitler, in precarious control of his troops and attacking the legitimate Government, miscalculated and was imprisoned. He could not have survived long-term without later funding from the rich capitalist/nationalist/militarist network who believed that they could use him for their purposes. He was a puppet who learned to pull the strings that made him.

**Fritz Thyssen.**

Another benefactor was Fritz Thyssen. He was very big - a businessman in charge of the biggest German steelmaking firm. His father, August, had moved to the centre of First World War German munitions production, producing a vast output and becoming very rich – growing to become the rival of Krupp. Fritz dominated the firm in the inter-war period. At the end of the War he hid a lot of his money in the Netherlands to avoid losing it and soon had his factories operating again, though, as we shall see, he needed more capital. After the War he was expansionist, taking over other companies until in 1928 he headed up Vereinigte Stahlwerke AG, a massive conglomerate dominating German and European production of steel. It employed some 200,000 workers and Thyssen was therefore at the centre of the biggest German industrial enterprise. During all this time he was trying to reform his industrial empire which was expanding, brilliantly organized, depended in Swedish Iron Ore, and incurring debts for yet more capital expenditure. Primarily, he was a great industrialist addressing the growth of steel production with continuous innovation and organizational improvement. But he was also politically engaged and had attitude. When the French invaded the Ruhr in 1923 Thyssen led the resistance to them, was arrested, imprisoned and fined. As a result he became a kind of nationalist hero. If you wanted financial and political support from anyone in German industry it would be Fritz Thyssen.

Thyssen was big, and Hitler was small, but he was not out of sight. He had cobbled together a movement, became the dominant leader and set about growing by quite successfully portraying that he was bigger than he was. The *New York Times* article of 20/12/1922 conveys what the movement was like this early.

> His spacious headquarters in Munich are splendidly furnished and his organization employs a host of highly paid lieutenants and officials. Last Sunday Hitler reviewed the so-called Storming Battalion attached to his organization, numbering about 1,000 young men in brand new uniforms and all armed with revolvers and black-jacks, which, however, they carried concealed. Naturally, peaceful citizens ask who has paid for these uniforms and arms, who defrayed the heavy expenses of the six meetings Hitler held the same day in all parts of Munich and who paid for the two powerful, brand-new autos in which Hitler and his staff hurried from and to the meetings.

The Nazis in 1922 were somewhat impressive, and these funds may have come from Ford and they conveyed legitimacy and support. Hitler who thought automatically in terms of hierarchy and power, would want more. Adolf early on was quite keen to rouse the workers – hence the National Socialist label. But he was keener to get money and financial backing, and, as with Mussolini, buttering up rich industrialists by using stormtroopers to beat up socialists became the dominant direction of the movement. He, too, could be bought. It was a technique which gave him the resources he needed to grow his evil, narcissistic movement.

The key event for Thyssen was the January 1923 French invasion of the Ruhr which was an attack upon Thyssen's industrial empire, and a requirement that coal and steel be provided to the French to replace the unpaid reparations. Thyssen imprisoned was an icon of the humiliation of Germany. As the summer dragged through, the Deutschmark plunged into hyperinflation in September and the economy teetered. The Right looked for those who would stand against France and also repudiate the Weimar Republic's passivity which Nationalists saw as selling out to the French. Thyssen was the man; he wanted to stand for the pride of Germany and as he was taking his stand, he would hear of a Corporal down in Bavaria who was doing the same thing. They were in contact in the summer, through Ludendorff, another focus of anti-French feeling, and with the Munich Putsch in December and especially Hitler's oratory in his trial, Adolf would come over as a leader supporting Thyssen's passionate nationalist stance. He had contacts through Ludendorff and Goering, heard him speak once, presumably before the Putsch and Adolf's incarceration, and as a result would see Hitler as a natural, though junior, ally. The very rich Thyssen handed over a small fortune to the struggling movement especially because the inflation around the French Invasion of the Ruhr was destabilizing Thyssen's great industrial combine, and he respected Hitler's denunciation of the Treaty of Versailles. As Ford's donations disappeared, Thyssen's more than filled the gap.

Some 100,000 gold marks passed to Hitler in 1923 and eventually probably about a million marks went to the Nazis from Thyssen before they came to power in 1933 in further tranches, and so it was a very substantial contribution in holding the National Socialist Deutsche Arbeiters Partei (NSDAP), the Nazis, together, especially during its lean years. Later, Thyssen had a book ghost written by a journalist entitled, *I paid Hitler*, acknowledging he had contributed a lot, but it is frustrating for what it did not say and was really also an exercise in attempted self-exoneration. He had backed Hitler and lifted him towards national plausibility. Hitler was one of the political hobbies of a very rich man, but rich men should be careful of their hobbies. Thyssen was funding stormtroopers, a militarist and a man of hate against the Weimar Republic and its perceived compromises. Sometimes the Munich Beer Hall Putsch, when Hitler jumped up on a table and began haranguing the spectators before being bundled off to prison, is treated as a bit of a joke, but it was a significant attempt to control Bavarian politics and set National Socialism off on a national stage. Eventually, it would succeed.

**So where was Krupp?**

It is important not to see the history of this time through hindsight, as a general movement towards the coming to power of the Nazis. Indeed, the Nazi focus is misleading. Fritz Thyssen probably spent very little time thinking about Hitler, and the real power bases at this time were those who had run the First World War. Chief among them were the great munitions/industrial combines, like that of Thyssen, but all of them were pursuing slightly different selfish agendas and not acting in concert to bring the Nazis to power until around 1932. For example, Krupp showed no early interest in Hitler. Gustav von Bolen Krupp was used to courting the Kaiser and was quite a snob. Bertha was even more cutting about the jumped-up little Corporal. Moreover Krupp's company policy was quite complex; they were heavily in debt, borrowing from a number of sources including America. Harold James biography brings this out well.[240] They were bailed out by the devaluation of the mark and then with help from the German government. They succeeded in maintaining a workforce of 50,000 or more. In part, they were substantial non-military producers, back producing railways and other heavy civilian engineering products. But they were also part of Seeckt's clandestine Russian operation, had taken over Bofors in Sweden to continue military production through them and were looking for military expansion, especially after 1929 when civilian demand contracted.

Krupp was focused on the military elite and government, scheming towards big state arms orders in the future. Hitler was merely uncouth and beneath his consideration almost until the time that he came to power, and so there were no links between Krupp and the Nazis. At one stage Hitler visited the Krupp works, hoping for some recognition and contact, but was studiously ignored and left signing the Visitors' Book thereby trying to show his goodwill. Right at the last moment, a day before Hitler became Chancellor Krupp advised President Paul von Hindenburg against it, but was overridden. Suddenly he changed when he realized that Hitler in power meant unlimited arms production. He instantly became a sycophantic supporter, poured funds into Hitler's coffers, and lined up the Krupp Empire to work for total re-armament. During the later War the firm of Krupp murdered thousands of people through overwork and appalling treatment, the evil within the company matching the evil direction of the Nazi State. Krupp was therefore not one of the progenitors of Hitler, but he and his son Alfried were committed to burying Versailles and the idea of disarmament.

**Alfred Hugenberg, die Deutschenationale Volkspartei (DNVP) and Hitler.**

But even concluding that Krupp did not directly aid Hitler is too strong, as the figure of Alfred Hugenberg shows. He was an important entrepreneur in the Krupp empire, an economist, with a far better moustache than Hitler, who in 1909 was appointed Chair of the Krupp Supervisory Board as well as having a central role in the finance of the company. He helped steer the Krupp Empire through the Great War, and was one of the central Kruppianer.

In 1918 Hugenberg took up a strong Nationalist line. He had helped found the Aldeutscher Verband, the Pan German League, before the First World War. This was Social Darwinist Racism, believing in the Aryan Race and seeing the Poles as some kind of threat to German racial purity. Hugenberg, partly because he was part of the rich, Krupp-linked establishment, was far more successful politically than Hitler and the Nazis. He created a media empire, initially of newspapers, and then also of film. German newspapers were quite local and depended on syndicated input from national news organizations for their more general coverage. Hugenberg set up a system which allowed him to disseminate columns to about 1,500 newspapers and create a massive opinion-swinging empire while at the same time continuing to make money. As well as being an ardent militarist and nationalist with a hatred of the Poles and the Jews, Hugenberg was also politically engaged after the Great War, backing the Deutschenationale Volkspartei, the German National People's Party, (DNVP) which was the strongest German quasi-fascist party of the twenties, overshadowing the Nazis. They received 19% of votes in the 1924 election.

They were anti-Polish, anti-Jewish, anti-Catholic, anti-Socialist, anti-Republican and anti-Quated, full of the old German establishment. Their great intellectual contribution in the early 20s was to say that the appointment of the eminent and capable Walter Rathenau to the post of Foreign Minister was an insult to German "honour", presumably because he was a well-educated and highly competent Jew. On the basis of this argument they assassinated him on the 24th June, 1922 proving their intellectual superiority. In October 1922 in another triumph of political thought they decided against advocating assassinations on the grounds that they might get caught. Their third triumph was to ask that Admiral von Tirplitz, whom we have met earlier, be made German Chancellor on the grounds that he could steer a ship and remained an avid supporter of German dominance. They were a nuisance to the ordinary, decent, democratic parties of the Weimar Republic. The DNVP was full of people who could scream and shout and Hugenberg gradually became the most reliable and richest figure in this rabble in the late 20s. All of this time Hitler and the Nazis were a smaller version of Hugenberg and the DNVP, as Hitler's moustache was of Hugenberg's. In 1929 Hugenberg and Hitler began to co-operate, giving Hitler more publicity and gradually, partly because he was a far more effective orator, Hitler was able to push the DNVP out of the nest and eat up the support of the militarists, racists and munitions people who had supported it. The career of Hugenberg shows again the crooked line from Krupp and munitions to German Fascism, and suggests that Hitler was a symptom as well as a cause of German Fascism.

**The Army and Munitions.**

The army was similar. The main development of the armed forces was led by Hans von Seeckt who was Commander of the Armed Forces in the 1920s. He was determined to reinstate German military prowess, and knew that arms production was the key. He had strong covert links with the munitions people and meticulously planned the new weapons he would need with the manufacturers against the requirements of the Treaty of Versailles. He organized its survival and strengthened the programme for the Reichswehr which was very self-contained, a "state within a state". The key again here was the military-industrial complex, rather than the Nazis. In September 1921 von Seeckt negotiated a deal with with Leonid Krasin for German aid to the Soviet arms industry. German financial and technological aid to the tune of 75 million Reichsmarks were given to the Soviet arms industry through a company called CEFU for the production of aircraft, tanks, artillery shells and poison gas. This allowed the German munitions companies to develop technologically, despite being disarmed by Versailles.[241] They were colluding with the state who would become their worst enemy.

Georg Grotz describes being at a reception at the Russian Embassy in Berlin, with caviar and drinks. High ranking German and Russian officers drank to each other. "They raised their glasses, clicked their heels, and said 'Prosit, comrade.' It was surprising to see how they resembled each other…. For a few minutes the rigid, impenetrable face of General von Seeckt appeared in the crowd. His monocle seemed glued to his face, his grey moustache cut like a brush, his carp mouth arrogantly closed. His incredibly slender waist looked corseted."[242] The iron will to pursue militarism with anybody, even with Communists, was dominant in the German High Command and they worked intimately with the munitions people. They murdered those who would report to the disarmament inspectors what was going on. Von Seeckt was not going to mess with a jumped up Corporal leading a band of thugs. He was out to plan the next generation of advanced weapons, although he was relatively powerless in the 1920s because of the disarmament provisions. So the arms manufacturers and military danced together to the tune of death.

Nevertheless, General Erich Ludendorff, who really led the German prosecution of the First World War and was a fervent anti-Jewish, anti-Christian nationalist linked up with the early Nazi Party, and gave it much credibility. He took a leading role, though he was projected somewhat unwillingly into the Beer Hall Putsch by Hitler. So there were pockets of Nazi support, but they were only part of a larger munitions/militarist agenda, and by no means in charge of events. The negotiations for worldwide disarmament were beginning at the same time.

**American Banking/Munitions/Industry and the Nazis.**

The link between American industry, munitions and finance and the Nazis cannot be ignored. One statement of it is Anthony Sutton's *Wall Street and the Rise of Hitler*. Sutton was made into a pariah figure because he showed how much Wall Street contributed to the Second World War. During the late 40s, 50s and 60s all the links of the allies with the Nazis tended to be obscured from orthodox history for obvious reasons. People just did not boast of backing Stalin or Hitler. Yet the evidence is clear. American finance and industry helped the Nazis and German munitions profusely. And, moreover, this was not merely incidental - profits first, and forget about the politics, but because the dominant American industrial/banking/munitions groups had strong sympathies with Fascism. The overall picture is described in October 1936 by the American Ambassador, William Dodd in an influential letter to Roosevelt from Berlin.

> Much as I believe in peace as our best policy, I cannot avoid the fears which Wilson emphasized more than once in conversations with me, August 15, 1915 and later: the breakdown of democracy in all Europe will be a disaster to the people. But what can you do? At the present moment

> more than a hundred American corporations have subsidiaries here or cooperative understandings. The DuPonts have three allies in Germany that are aiding in the armament business. Their chief ally is the I. G. Farben Company, a part of the Government which gives 200,000 marks a year to one propaganda organization operating on American opinion. Standard Oil Company (New York sub-company) sent $2,000,000 here in December 1933 and has made $500,000 a year helping Germans make Ersatz gas for war purposes; but Standard Oil cannot take any of its earnings out of the country except in goods. They do little of this, report their earnings at home, but do not explain the facts. The International Harvester Company president told me their business here rose 33% a year (arms manufacture, I believe), but they could take nothing out. Even our airplanes people have secret arrangement with Krupps. General Motor Company and Ford do enormous businesses [sic] here through their subsidiaries and take no profits out. I mention these facts because they complicate things and add to war dangers.[243]

The structure of this strong business inter-relationship needs some background. The First World War left the world profoundly different. There are three important structural facts to take into account. Crucially, the United States had lent Britain, France and Italy enormous sums to finance the First World War and their purchases of weapons and ships. The normal estimate is about $9.5 billion in an era when billions were rare. In addition there were vast wartime profits. Britain moved from having a great external surplus of capital to effectively none at all and it needed to pay back. France and Italy were in the same position. At the end of the War the United States sought to make sure that there was no defaulting on the debt. J.P. Morgan handled much of the debt with Britain often for other banks, and it was pay-back time. The Americans were quite firm about it. Enormous sums of money therefore moved from Britain, France and Italy to the United States. The Federal Reserve

Board had been formed during the First World War partly to handle the organization of this debt, and in part the return to the Gold Standard was a way of making sure that the value of these debts was not reduced.

Second, Britain, France and Italy were intent on using German war reparations as a way of meeting this vast amount of debt. The amount of reparations was larger, some $30 billion, and there are debates as to whether this was possible or difficult for Germany, begun by Maynard Keynes and carried on by others. Keynes wrote a book, *The Economic Consequences of the Peace,* after the Versailles Conference which spelt out the danger of trying to humiliate Germany, and the difficulty of the Germans meeting the reparations payments with a battered economy and the danger that this vengeance was merely setting up another bloody confrontation. Others have questioned whether the burden was so great, but Keynes wisdom is largely validated. Revenge, including economic revenge, keeps alive the hatred of war and gave Hitler the kind of leverage he needed. The history of reparations, including the French invasion of the Ruhr, was a history of total failure at restoring trade and peace and one which pandered to the kind of viciousness the Nazis wanted to practice as well as creating the economic despair that gripped millions of ordinary Germans.

It also set up the third side of the triangle, because American bankers flush with money began investing in Germany, (and in the USSR) and they were not always careful where the money was placed. Indeed, the loans went a long way towards recreating the kind of military revival that then followed. There is a lot of literature showing the links of American money into the companies contributing to the German munitions industries and fuelling the rise to power of the Nazis and the atrocities of the Holocaust. The American banks included not just the Morgan group linked in with Britain and France. A rival group including the Rockefeller, Harriman, Kuhn-Loeb banks, was more strongly linked into lending to Germany, Russia and Eastern Europe. So, in the early and mid 1920s Germany wanted to borrow funds. The obvious link was made and the United States began lending to German companies, became involved with them, creating multi-national operations which did a lot to shape the direction of the Nazi regime. In 1924 this was regularized by the Dawes Plan which slowed down the reparations and tried to establish a stable German banking and economic system. Something like $1.5 billion went from the United States to Germany during this period. It was big international investment of an entirely new kind.

**Harriman, Bush, Thyssen and the Nazis.**

These American links were crucial. We have looked at the tie between Thyssen, the great Vereinigte Stahlwerke AG Company and the Nazis. For Thyssen to build such a great steel empire from the ruins of the war required capital beyond Germany's resources. Moreover, he wanted to move money around, launder it, and operate enterprises through front companies. In 1918 he needed a home for his enterprises which was out of the reach of war opponents and other hostile groups. Further, his steel manufacturing business was, of course, intimately related to arms manufacturing. Before Fritz Thyssen met Hitler, he had already met two Americans, Averill Harriman and George Walker Bush, who set up an investment bank which would service Thyssen's industrial development and move funds around in the way Thyssen wanted. He knew it would be at a cost – American banks did not lend for free. But Thyssen was expanding rapidly and creating a steel cartel which was dominant and would bring in big profits later, and so debts were fine. A three way banking operation was set up. The Bank Voor Handel en Scheepvaart N.V. at 18 Zuidblaak in Rotterdam, Holland was founded immediately after in 1918 with H.J. Kouwenhoven and D.C. Schutte as managing partners, initially to hide Thyssen's wealth and ownerships. It was linked to the August Thyssen Bank of Germany (formerly von der Heydt's Bank A.G.) and these were linked with the Union Banking Corporation of New York. This was the bank that linked the Harriman banking family into the Thyssen empire.

The Harriman family were big money. They had made large profits through gaining control of Union Pacific Railroad which was able to monopolize transport for many products and raw materials during the War. It is widely accepted that old man Harriman (E.H.) made a lot of money by selling watered down, fraudulent, railroad stock. Even Theodore Roosevelt disapproved of him. Morality did not preoccupy the family. During the War they were effectively printing money by transporting munitions and raw materials at their own designated prices. Their lucre initially went into the Rockefeller bank, the National City Bank. That left them well positioned after the First World War, when they were about the fourth richest family in the States with well over $100 million. Then the gold plated baton had passed from old man Harriman to his two sons Averill and E.R or "Bunny" Harriman. Averill struck up a relationship with an older Missouri deal-making magnate called George Herbert Walker, the man who gave the Walker Cup to golf. Walker, Bert to his friends, and Averill quickly took advantage of the situation at the end of the War; they were the people who got international banking with Germany underway – fixing deals across the Atlantic and opening up the vast US private wealth for investment in Germany and the USSR. In 1920 the family acquired a half stake in the Hamburg-America Shipping Line at a knock-down price. This was no small acquisition, but the biggest shipping line in Germany. The company made well-designed posters; Nick and Sarah have one on the wall next door. Magically, the Harrimans also purchased the German ships which had been confiscated by the United States at the end of the War, presumably for a knock-down price as well, and suddenly they had half-ownership of a big shipping line in the Atlantic and other areas of trade. The Harrimans were running banks, shipping lines, and investing wherever money was to be made. They were archetypal mega-capitalists, lending in Germany before other American banks thought of it. Through links between the three banks the Harriman family was prepared to, and did, bankroll the Thyssen empire in its growth. These links were not distant, but also ideological, in that both were in favour of big money, hated and were scared of socialism, and were in favour of fascist type groups who could be bought and defeat socialism on the streets.

Enter at this time Prescott Sheldon Bush, son of our old friend Samuel Bush who had been doling out arms contracts at the end of the First World War. Prescott, at Yale, linked with Bunny Harriman. After his japes there and in the War, he went off to do a number of nondescript jobs. His time finally arrived when he married Dorothy Walker in August 1921. He had two links into the Harriman set – through Bunny and Dorothy. Perhaps, Prescott Bush owed more to nepotism than ability. After a few years of preparatory work he became Vice-President of the Harriman Bank in May 1926 with his father-in-law, Bert Walker, as the President. By now this was a bank moving big funds into steel, raw materials and shipping not only in Germany, but also into eastern Europe and Russia. Prescott and Bunny went off to run Union Banking Corporation and link up closely with Fritz Thyssen. Much of the web literature, apart from pointing out how the Bush dynasty has succeeded in shredding a lot of the evidence that could be most damning from this period, focusses on Prescott Bush as the progenitor of two suspect American presidents and as someone dealing with the Nazis. Let us examine this latter charge. The Harrimans, Walker and Prescott Bush were working for Thyssen and Thyssen was a dominant patron of Hitler and his crew, and a leading nationalist and capitalist. He partly moved the ranting Hitler from powerlessness to political effectiveness by giving him the money to employ unemployable stormtroopers to attack Socialists, Jews and Communists. They were paid a pittance, but they were paid, and a good deal of the money came through Thyssen, who was rich and a lot richer through the Harriman connection, especially in the late twenties. Here was the money which helped Hitler survive and grow after 1923. Prescott Bush was there in and would know which camp he was in. When Hitler came to power the link with the Nazis became stronger still and was an intimate economic and military relationship. In the early 1930s Thyssen persuaded other military industrialists to support Hitler to the extent of helping him to power. At this stage the Harriman Bank and Prescott Bush moved to being the primary American bank of the Nazis. The knowing accommodation to the Nazis must have been strong. The Harrimans and Prescott Bush knew with whom they were dealing and would have had a clear idea of what was going on, including the anti-Semitism. They were not fussy. Thyssen, Hitler and the other Nazi leaders were their partners. He who sups with the devil needs a long spoon and both Thyssen and the Harriman/Bush group had hold of the spoon, and it got warmer.

There is a post-script on Thyssen. After the War he was tried for being a Nazi supporter and employing Jews as slave labour in his factories. He was let off most charges and agreed to pay 500,000 DM as compensation for the "mistreatment" of Jewish people, an enormous amount considering that Thyssen had had, as he declared, almost all of his assets taken away by the Nazis when they eventually imprisoned him half way through the War. But he did not go to prison. One wonders whether the facts that Allen Dulles had been his lawyer and the Prescott Bush/Harrimans had been his banking partners had anything to do with it. He died in 1951 and miraculously his wife later set up the Fritz Thyssen Foundation with capital of 100,000,000DM. She must have found some money down the back of the sofa.

**Other Links.**

This is a chapter of financial links. A legion of books have focussed on Hitler and the Nazis and many others tainted with the association. Yet the focus here is not on personal links, but the solid economic ties with the munitions/military/banking sector. Munitions companies need conflict. Banks lend for weapons. US Banks had financed the First World War. Peace and stability devastate arms sales. They were all against Communism. These strategic issues gave the Nazis the political space to squeeze through to power. The links were not just with the Harrimans and Thyssen, but with a whole range of other industrialists, bankers and munitions people. So, for example, Samuel Prior, was on the board of Union Banking corporation with Prescott Bush and Bunny Harriman, but he was also Executive Director of Remington Arms, part of the Rockefeller Empire and one of the chief arms producers of the Great War. As US Senate investigators uncovered, the rifles

Hitler's Brownshirts and Blackshirts were given came from the American firms Remington and Thompson. They came in through barges on the Sheldt to Antwerp and then overland into Germany. That American producers provided the means for Hitler's thugs to dominate the streets shows the complicity of these groups in the ascent of the Nazis.

A similar link was with the activities of Friedrich Flick, a co-leader of the Vereinigte Stahlwerke with Thyssen, very rich, and a highly active supporter of the Nazis, who worked with Prescott Bush to extend the influence of the steel empire. Flick was sentenced to seven years in prison at the Nuremburg trials but served only three, before he was let out and rapidly became again one of the richest men in Europe. One of the charges at Nuremburg is set out below and gives a flavour of the munitions and industrial support for the Nazis.

> Count Four claimed that between 30th January, 1933, and April, 1945, the accused Flick and Steinbrinck committed war crimes and crimes against humanity as defined by Article II of Control Council Law No. 10, in that they were accessories to, abetted, took a consenting part in, were connected with, plans and enterprises involving, and were members of organisations or groups connected with, murder, brutalities, cruelties, tortures, atrocities and other inhuman acts committed by the Nazi Party and its organisations, including principally Die Schutzstaffeln der Nationalsozialistischen Deutschen Arbeiter-partei (the S.S.) whose criminal character, purposes and actions were established and enlarged upon by the International Military Tribunal at Nuremberg. The accused Flick and Steinbrinck were members· of a group variously known as "Friends of Himmler", "Freundeskreis" ("Circle of Friends") and the " Keppler Circle", which throughout the period of the Third Reich, worked closely with the S.S., and frequently and regularly with its leaders and furnished aid, advice and financial support to the S.S. This organisation (" Friends of Himmler") was composed of some 30 German business

> leaders and a number of the most important S.S. leaders, including Himmler himself. The business members of the Circle represented Germany's largest enterprises in the fields of iron, steel and munitions production, banking, chemicals and shipping.
>
> The Circle was formed early in 1932 at Hitler's suggestion by his economic Adviser, Wilhelm Keppler. The Circle met regularly up to and including 1945 with Himmler, Keppler and other high Government officials. Each year from 1933 to 1945 the Circle contributed about 1,000,000 marks a year to Himmler to aid financially the activities of the S.S.[244]

So these interlocking relations added up to a powerful establishment used to getting its own way through money, and happy to use and relate to groups like the Nazis. Again, the old pattern was there. Munitions companies, including the company that supplied most of the steel for the weapons, pushed the economy in a militaristic direction and promoting the Nazis to effectiveness. Of course, they did not actually want the Holocaust, or Blitzkrieg, but there were used to closing their eyes to these possibilities, or at least squinting. They were just making easy, but deeply costly, money.

**I.G. Farben and the Rockefeller Empire.**

Another of these links was the relationship between the Rockefeller Empire and I.G. Farben. This company was a massive combine created by the coming together of six powerful chemical companies involved in dyes, film, explosives, chemical gas production and fuels. They were involved in poison gas production in the Great War. The Farben group was brought together by Hermann Schmitz in 1925 and by 1939 had become the biggest chemical enterprise in the world. Given the German recession of the early 30s, that level of growth needs explaining. It must have had substantial outside capital and it came mainly from America. Badische Anilin, Bayer, Agfa, Hoechst, Weiler-ter-Meer and

Griesheim-Elektron, all themselves big, were the companies that merged. Farben developed an aggressive culture, forming industrial alliances, making deals and moving towards military output. Especially in the 1930s I.G. Farben moved into explosives, poison gas and fuels for military vehicles and aircraft. It was a combine which fiercely backed Hitler in 1933, although one charge, that it knowingly provided Zylon B gas for the gas chambers seems not to be accurate. Ten thousand prisoners worked at its main headquarters in Frankfurt and most of them were murdered through the process of forced labour. It provided 400,000 Reichsmarks to Hitler's slush funds in early 1933 smoothing the route to power. Then it worked to prepare itself for war in a highly systematic way, working out all the chemical processes which would be needed in the next war. It was a deeply corrupt and evil organization.

One of the usual charges was that Standard Oil, part of Rockefeller's empire, gave I.G. Farben a lot of the materials, processes and raw materials needed to prosecute the Second World War. Again Anthony Sutton gives the picture.

> The process for manufacturing tetra-ethyl lead essential for aviation gasoline, was obtained by I. G. Farben from the United States, and in 1939 I.G. was sold $20 million of high-grade aviation gasoline by Standard Oil of New Jersey. Even before Germany manufactured tetra-ethyl lead by the American process it was able to "borrow" 500 tons from the Ethyl Corporation. This loan of vital tetra-ethyl lead was not repaid and I.G. forfeited the $1 million security. Further, I.G. purchased large stocks of magnesium from Dow Chemical for incendiary bombs and stockpiled explosives, stabilizers, phosphorus, and cyanides from the outside world. In 1939, out of 43 major products manufactured by I.G., 28 were of "primary concern" to the German armed forces. Farben's ultimate control of the German war economy, acquired during the 1920s and 1930s with Wall Street assistance, can best be assessed by

> examining the percentage of German war material output produced by Farben plants in 1945. Farben at that time produced 100 percent of German synthetic rubber, 95 percent of German poison gas (including all the Zyklon B gas used in the concentration camps), 90 percent of German plastics, 88 percent of German magnesium, 84 percent of German explosives, 70 percent of German gunpowder, 46 percent of German high octane (aviation) gasoline, and 33 percent of German synthetic gasoline.

Clearly if you are that interested in explosives and poison gas, the American directors of I.G. Farben (US) should have been suspicious. They were Edsel Ford, obviously of Ford, H.A. Metz - Bank of Manhattan, C.E. Mitchell - Federal Reserve Bank, Herman Schmitz – Bank of International Settlements, Walter Teagle – Federal Reserve Bank and Standard Oil, New Jersey, Paul Warburg Federal Reserve and Bank of Manhattan and W.E. Weiss – Sterling Products. Bank of Manhattan, Standard Oil and even the Federal Reserve Board were, of course, Rockefeller fiefdoms. The Bank of International Settlements, led in Britain by Montague Norman, was another institution happy to connive at Farben's direction. These members of the western financial elite had a fairly intimate knowledge of what I.G. Farben was about, but as long as it was profitable business, they were happy to go along with it, partly out of solidarity with all who were willing to keep socialism and democracy at bay.

Nor could they really plead ignorance. Walter Teagle, the Chairman, and William Farish, the President of Standard Oil worked closely with Hermann Schmitz of I.G. Farben and others. Standard Oil had about $120 million invested in Nazi Germany and it knew what its money did. Teagle undertook to supply the Nazis with tetraethyl lead, without which German planes would not be able to fly. He flew to London and arranged for £15 million of the substance to be supplied by Ethyl, a subsidiary of British Standard. It was sent to Göring from London, and in a short while the bombers were flying back bombing London. Teagle knew what he was doing.

**American Funding of the Nazis after they come to power.**

When Hitler came to power, the wasps came to the honey-pot. The expansion in his military budget was extraordinary. The German military budget of 1 billion marks in 1932 expanded to four billion in 1933, 10 billion in 1936, 17 billion in 1938 and a vast 38 billion in 1939 when it equalled more than half the German State budget and a lot of this expenditure was borrowed and provided a bonanza for the munitions companies and their supporting industries. When Hitler was first Chancellor a lot of industrialists, bankers, politicians, rich people and aristocracy thought that he was a very good idea – spending lots, borrowing lots, keeping the workers in their place and getting rid of the Communists. This chimed with a lot of Americans. The head of International Telephone and Telegraph, Sosthenes Behn, immediately travelled to Germany to congratulate Hitler on coming to power. Soon ITT were in the German aircraft business producing Fokker planes. Du Pont was in there through the family control of General Motors and Opel. Irénée du Pont was obsessed with Hitler's views from quite early on. Edsel Ford was anti-Semitic and also invested in Nazi Germany to the tune of $17.5 million. Ford produced the 5 ton military trucks which were the carthorses of the German war effort. He regularly remembered Hitler's birthday and sent him 50,000 Reichmarks to buy a present – quite touching really. Overall some $475 million was invested in Germany by the time of Pearl Harbour. When it looked as though Britain was losing the war, this group continued to supply Germany and was quite aggressive in their pro-Nazi and anti-British propaganda. Once you have backed one side, you have to see it through to victory.[245]

Because Hitler was borrowing on such a large scale, banking was crucial, and this is when the Union Banking Corporation came into its own. On the Nazi side, Hitler's Economics Minister, Hjalmar Schacht wanted a centralized trade channel to co-ordinate all German purchases with the United States, including those of arms.

On the other side the Harrimans wanted a monopoly of trade with the Germans, and in May 1933, shortly after the Nazis had their feet under the table, Hjalmar Schacht, also a consummate banker, arranged a deal with the Harriman family bank channelling all trade through them. The Harrimans formed a consortium of a hundred and fifty major companies and so the monopoly deal was sealed – at one end Thyssen, the other munitions companies and the Nazis, and at the other end, the Harrimans. John Foster Dulles, who at this stage was acting as lawyer for a number of Nazi involved companies including I.G. Farben, sealed the deal. Averill's cousin Oliver headed up the Bank and Prescott Bush was soon on the Board of this company. It seems he was under some financial pressure from the Wall Street Crash and the subsequent German slump and this new development came as a personal financial relief. Prescott was busy with his head down funnelling money backwards and forwards to Germany *beyond* the time when they were at war with the States. Other banks were linked with Germany. Chase Manhatten had strong links with Schröder bank, and the Bank of International Settlements in Switzerland held some £378 million of Nazi gold with Americans moving money about through its channels. Soon it was boom time again as exports headed to Germany supplying the vast need for weapons and Germany's debt was processed by the bankers. Amazingly, this pattern continued into the War up to Pearl Harbour and the United States' declaration of war against Germany. On 25th March, 1942 William Farish of Standard Oil pleaded "no contest" to charges of criminal conspiracy with the Nazis and was fined $5,000 – not a lot for a naughty very rich boy. John Rockefeller Junior said he did not know this trade was going on, an obvious lie. The Harrimans and Prescott Bush were traitors funding activities against their own Government, and the assets of the Harriman bank were confiscated, but both escaped the publicity that Farish had. "Us at war with Germany? Sorry, didn't notice." Rich traitors are OK. The big mystery is how Bush and others were reimbursed after the War, but we jump ahead.

More support for the Nazis was at hand. The large French munitions company of Schneider-Creusot owned the big Skoda arms producing plant in Poland. Hitler coveted it and Skoda was quick to move over to producing arms for the Nazis and to co-operate with them, an astonishing move for a French company. The munitions/ banking/ industrial elites of the West were, as before, happy to invest in war and wait for its bonanza profits.

**Historical Revision**

All of this gives us a very different picture of the Nazis from the ideological focus on an independent movement. Before they came to power, they were a small party with pretensions. They grew through stormtroopers, financed and equipped mainly by the munitions people. They received support both from the German munitions companies and indirectly from the American munitions/banking sector. These groups, using Fascism as a tool to support their greed and their hatred of socialism, allowed the Nazi Party to survive and then challenge for power. It was even American guns which created chaos in the streets of Germany in the early 1930s. We tend to be mesmerized by Hitler's speeches, the goose-stepping troops and the might of German arms, but the rearmament of Germany did not suddenly come from no-where. It had a munitions industry largely moribund for thirteen years, apart from the subterfuges worked out by von Seeckt and Krupp. The economy had suffered deeply under reparations and the recession. It had a small military until Hitler came to power with low levels of equipment. It needed big money. It was German industrial-military and American funding which made this development possible, and these investors were far from unaware what they were doing. Hitler and his minions were used to create a munitions boom which again had to end in war.

After the Nazis came to power a vast munitions system based on revived German companies and extraordinary American loans allowed Hitler to generate the military base he wanted. This was munitions' based Fascism. It reflected arms producers, banks and industrialists who would make money out of war, and did not look through to the world-wide devastation which actually followed. Always we look at the leading Nazis – at Hitler, Göring,

Goebbels, Himmler and their henchmen, while ignoring the clever, rich people who thought they could run the show and make money. We see the monkey, but ignore the organ grinder. Yet, really this great conglomeration of wealth, munitions, banking and anti-socialist ideology was the driver to start the Second World War, and much of the impetus came from the States. American financial capitalism had more to do with the arrival of the Second World War than appeasement. The same groups led towards war in Japan with the Zaibatsu, in Italy with Ansaldo and others. Shortly, we shall see the impact of Du Pont in the States.

Often the link between the First and Second World Wars is painted as fairly inevitable. The Treaty of Versailles punished Germany and sooner or later Germany would retaliate. Yet, in contrast to this view, we can see that there were multiple possibilities of avoiding the Second World War. Repeated attempts at disarmament could have succeeded, ruling out bombing, submarine, tank and battleship aggression and making international trust normal. Great statesmen worked for peace. Especially, the great 1932 Geneva Disarmament Conference could have adopted the Hoover Plan and contracted weapons and tensions world-wide. Even when Hitler came to power, there was no reason why he should have been given the financial and military resources through which to carry out his intense militarization. Yet, behind this whole long failure lie the munitions companies and bankers undermining peace and disarmament while funding and supplying weapons to raise tension and the likelihood of conflict. They also engineered Fascism to suit their purposes. They made Hitler's car and he drove away with it. The makers of weapons generate wars, and again in 1939, as in 1914, this proved to be the case.

# Chapter Twenty One: The American Fascist Coup Attempt.

## American Fascism?

The title of this chapter is written with reluctance, because it will lose some American readers instantly. How could the United States have a Fascist coup attempt when it is the home of democracy? It is silly to link the world's greatest democracy with the label Fascist, when the United States saved the world from Fascism. That is a fair and undeniable point. But all facts are sacred. Fascism also constituted an important tradition in American politics after the First World War and there *was* a Fascist coup attempt in 1934. The great munitions companies and bankers were rich with pickings from the Great War. They were the richest people in the world and wanted to establish *their* kind of economy; in part it involved making weapons and funding armament. We have already seen the banking links to Germany and the fight against disarmament. But it went further than this. They were, in part, militarists and Fascists and when Europe was swept by Fascism in 1933-4, in America, too, the big financiers/munitions people looked to a Fascist coup.

A whole set of attitudes were involved – fear of socialism and democracy, low taxes for the rich, anti-unionism to keep wages down, state corporatism (wanting the state to back big industry as in Japan and Italy), expecting direct access to government and requiring the protection of their money. Fascism, they thought, could deliver this. It was the new modern way forward, and a military coup was the route in Italy, Japan, and through the storm-troopers in Germany. This tendency was strong in the late twenties and thirties, when Fascism had not yet been blackened by the Holocaust. The munitions' people and the bankers had enormous power and wealth after 1919. They got rid of Wilson and made sure that the United States stayed outside the League of Nations and its disarmament provisions. They mounted the Red Scare against Communism. They poured cash and expertise into the USSR and

Germany, encouraging especially the growth of munitions. The boom in the late 20s gave them a great sense of power and some arrogance. For a decade, until the Great Depression they oiled Republicans into power and had their own way up to the crash of 1929. They encouraged racism, either directly as with Henry Ford's strong anti-Semitic campaign, or through the Eugenics movement backed by the Harrimans and Rockefellers. The growth of the KKK to several millions in the early 1920s also fitted this overall quasi-Fascist agenda, and it too had rich backers.

Fortunately, this tendency was addressed in part and could not fully take hold. The anti-Black and Catholic agendas of the KKK were partly seen off. The political establishment was never fully won by the Right. Working class voters in their millions were added to the electorate and were unionized. As people moved west it also became impossible for an east-coast establishment to control them and their politics. Moreover, immigrants were not interested in external aggression or militarism, because they were forging a new life in a new land. They were also immune to racism, because in the United States the majority was ethnic *minorities* – Irish, Germans, Scots, English, Dutch, Scandinavians, Russians, Jews, Italians, Mexicans, Spanish, Japanese, and many, many more. Indeed, the irony in the United States is that the *natives,* the Indians, have had the toughest time of all. Moreover, the dynamism of the United States economy, with oil, cars, steel, civil engineering and factory output soaring meant that there were plenty of competitors for the munitions industry. Everyone knew that the United States could produce the weapons if they were needed, and because of its sheer size, economic dominance and geographical isolation, it faced no real threats. For all of these reasons the ideology of Fascism with its emphasis on conquest, race hate, a centralized political leadership, controlling democracy and militarism was not easily going to dominate American politics. Yet, the munitions/banking/industrial elite had a good go. They still tried to set up their system for ruling the world. They were used to getting their own way. They knew they were the most powerful people on the planet and they wanted control of the political system.

Britain, France, Italy, the USSR, Argentina, Brazil, Japan, Turkey, countries in South America, Israel and many other countries had Fascist parties and moved in this direction, but in terms of size and influence none of these countries touched the United States. Military fascism was a lot more normal in the 20th century than we like to admit and operated in most democracies. In Britain was not just Mosley's Fascism, but also large sectors of the aristocracy who liked Mussolini and Hitler and were frightened by ordinary voters; they didn't go on marches because they couldn't keep in step, but they were there in spirit, whether it was gin or whisky. Fascism was the ordinary reaction of capitalist/military groups around the world, fearful of workers and the example of the Russian Revolution. As we have seen, the military-industrial-financial complex had become a universal phenomenon, and it was certainly there in the United States. The great plutocratic families like the Rockerfellers, Du Ponts, Harrimans, with others like the Bushes hanging on at the edges, owned the companies that could provide the weapons – the bombers, fighters, ships, guns and explosives - to the United States' Government and many others throughout the world. Keeping this kind of empire afloat is very difficult. You need a set of political and business policies which allows it to happen and you cannot leave the outcome to chance. The Du Pont Company, gorged on explosives money in 1919, suddenly found that nothing was exploding. What was it to do?

**Dinner with the Du Ponts and Prohibition.**

It is time to meet the Du Ponts. As we have already seen the family had made a lot of money during the Great War. At the same time there were wrangles in the family for control, and eventually the three brothers, Pierre, Irenée and Lammot came out on top. They were all chemists, trained at MIT, the Massachusetts Institute of Technology, and superb businessmen and capitalists. They were joined by another, John J. Raskob and presented a formidable foursome. They were into building a vast business empire, and after the War, they diversified into fibres, dyes, paints and other useful products of the chemical industry. But they did not retreat from explosives, although the market had contracted. It might grow again, especially if it was encouraged. They took over Remington Arms, itself a large gun-making company, just in case. So they remained munitions people. But after the Great War, flush with money, Du Pont also took over General Motors and made it into an automobile company even bigger than Ford. Pierre ran GM for a while and then handed it over to Alfred Sloan who was also part of the inner coterie. So they dominated three industries at a world-wide level – munitions, cars and chemicals. The Du Ponts were hyper-big.

Let's get a bit more personal. Pierre was quiet, ambitious and had a limp; Irenée was aggressive and shot his mouth, Lammot technical and efficient and Raskob was a quiet wheeler-dealer on a big scale. We note they were, of course, all men. The Du Ponts could afford to invite you to dinner. Robert Burk describes their domestic life thus:

> With their positions of immense economic power secure by the early 1920s, each of the Du Pont inner circle lived the lavish life of a modern-day feudal lord, complete with large estates and elaborate personal amusements. Among the family's *twenty four* different estates in Delaware and southeastern Pennsylvania, Pierre resided at Longwood in Chester County, Pennsylvania, some seventeen miles north of the company's Wilmington headquarters. Reflecting his love of landscaping and horticulture, the estate contained a thousand acres of Japanese waterfalls, trees, exotic plants, sunken gardens, and six greenhouses for rare tropical species. Pierre's private refuge also included a 1200 seat open-air theatre for private entertainments, immense multi-level fountains highlighted by beams of coloured lights, a transplanted Norman bell tower, and a 10,000 pipe organ which required fourteen railroad cars to ship to Longwood. To play the instrument, Pierre hired Firmin Swinnen, the organist of Antwerp Cathedral. Within a splendid estate that rivalled Versailles in grandeur, he resided in a comparatively modest thirty room mansion at its center,

staffed by over one hundred servants and protected by a $7 million life insurance policy that barred him from flying his private plane.[246]

We resist the temptation to reflect on the aesthetics of the estate, or to wonder what three servants per room do, or to weep because Pierre could not fly his own plane because of his insurance policy; it was an easy drive into New York in some limousine or other. The main estate reflected a serious commitment to wealth and there were other houses and apartments wherever they were needed. Perhaps, rather than changing the sheets, he just moved house. Irenée's main house had seventy rooms, slightly bigger, but he only had a sixty-foot yacht, while Lammot's was a seventy-six-foot craft.

If, after dinner, the talk turned to politics, the Du Pont line would be clear. They did not trust the popular democratic vote, because ordinary people just did not know what politics is about, and popular parties were even more suspect. Pierre doubted if one per cent of voters were properly qualified to vote. "On this account I believe it would be better to discourage voting rather than encourage voters to exercise their rights."[247] Broadly speaking, they, the Du Ponts, were the obvious people qualified to run the country, but since the Constitution didn't quite run like that, they were more interested in particular leaders who might fit with their perception of things. They expected to choose the President from within their group, and largely that was what happened in the twenties. They were also in favour of the corporate state. The leaders of industry were the people with the expertise to guide the economy in the proper way. If political leaders would look to them, then the United States would be properly governed. This was similar to the attitudes in Italy, Japan and Germany, but in the States these great corporate leaders could be expansive and expect to shape things.

As Burk's important study, *The Corporate State and the Broker State*, points out, this attitude was first tried out in the mid-1920s in relation to the prohibition issue. The choice was interesting. Pierre Du Pont scarcely drank alcohol and insisted that his workers were sober in their work and private lives. But Pierre had worked out that even a small sales tax on alcohol would bring in enough revenue to cut taxes on the rich *and* improve the public finances. Although taxes for the rich fell anyway, this issue became an obsessive one with Pierre, Irenée and Roskob. Their driving ambition was to protect their wealth, not to get drunk, and they attacked prohibition and became "Wets". Beginning in 1926 they took over the AAPA, the Association Against the Prohibition Amendment, ploughing in hundreds of thousands of dollars, paying the one dollar subscription for thousands of members and generating a mass movement from their own pockets. At this time the Drys, led by the Anti-Saloon League, had dominant support in the Republican Party and also among the public. Anyone who had seen alcoholism, especially among ex-servicemen, welcomed the fall in alcohol addiction. It is surprising how much popular support Prohibition had – this is usually ignored in later interpretations of what was going on. Of course there was bootlegging, but the solution to bootlegging was properly to enforce the law. The Wets had an uphill task but in seven years the Du Ponts had overthrown the Amendment by using their wallets.

The history of this process is a book it itself, but essentially the Du Pont Group learned a method in politics. You pay to mobilize a lot of people, effectively buying their support and then pressure government to do what you wish – a kind of cash-backed populism or rent a vote majority. This was not the only method. The Du Ponts were also used to direct access to the top politicians. They sponsored them, often with a hefty donation. The politicians who got this kind of help included Herbert Hoover, Al Smith, especially backed by Raskob, and even Franklin D. Roosevelt (to the tune of $100,000). At this time the Du Ponts were a bit fed up with the Republicans (who were stronger on Prohibition than the Democrats), and instead were trying to take over the Democrats. Indeed, by 1929 Raskob had become so involved in Democratic Party politics that he was Chairman of the Democratic National Committee, throwing a million dollars into its party coffers. He expected the Democratic Party to function largely as he saw fit, trying to select the candidates he would back and running the

Democratic Party as he would Du Pont or General Motors. He established a central organization for the Party and modernized it as well as handling its big debts. In August 1929 Raskob took a bit of time out to organize the construction of the Empire State Building in Manhattan to get ready for King Kong's occupation a few years later. Then came the Great Depression. Really, the Du Ponts did not make a great success of running the Democratic Party; they were a bit too prickly for party politics and the unions were also Democratic and wanted a say in things. The Du Ponts were not bridge builders or political fixers, because they were too used to running their own show autocratically. So, although they carried on with this policy until, say, late 1933, it did not really work.

**The Du Pont's were not Depressed.**

The Du Ponts faced the Wall Street Crash with some equanimity. After all, they largely owned their companies, and were not left with handfuls of worthless speculative shares. As Raskob pointed out, it was merely a good time to buy cheap shares. They had some losses, but those could be covered by reduced tax-payments. In November 1929 Pierre Du Pont and John Raskob sold one another $4.5 million shares and then sold them back in January 1930; Pierre promptly netted a $600,000 cut in taxes from the transaction. With an income of over $30 million in 1929 Pierre did not really need the help. Nevertheless, the Great Depression changed things quite drastically. Demand for cars and chemicals fell. But, especially, a vast group of workers began to complain at unemployment, and blamed the financiers, Wall Street and capitalism for the crisis in the American economy. Socialism seemed to be re-emerging and they faced a political crisis.

All of this focussed for the Du Ponts in the Democratic Party. By now Raskob was more or less running the Democratic central organization. But that did not mean he controlled the Party. As the time for nominations for the 1932 Presidential Election drew near, Governor Franklin Roosevelt of New York seemed the strongest candidate, but he was weak on ending prohibition, Pierre's obsession, when the campaign to repeal it was coming to a climax.

Pierre even saw the Du Ponts as in charge of a state-sponsored, regulated alcohol monopoly, another industry which he could completely dominate. Roosevelt's economic policies seemed unsafe and even anti-capitalist. By now, too, Raskob was exposed in his role as Chair of the Democrats. He was charged with seeking one-man control of the Party, of dictating the platform, choosing the candidate and intending to run the administration if a Democrat was elected. Actually, this was more or less what he and the Du Ponts were trying to do. They wanted an industrial elite to run the country, a benign state corporatism. At one stage Raskob had wondered if he could be the candidate, choose himself, so to speak, but that was really too pushy and would not work. Then the preferred candidate was Al Smith, an experienced politician and very much part of the Du Pont camp. Yet in the Democratic Convention at the end of June 1932, Smith, Raskob and his group were defeated and Roosevelt was nominated as Democratic candidate. Raskob was livid. His words to Jouett Shouse, Chair of his executive committee were: "the scum, in the way of the radical element, has just come to the top and will be skimmed off in pretty vigorous fashion at the proper time."[248] – no deep commitment to democracy there. Raskob had been outplayed by Roosevelt and was left hanging out to dry. He even had to finance a lot of the debts of the Democratic Party which would help Roosevelt to wage a successful campaign. Pierre was happier because Roosevelt at the last moment had endorsed repeal of prohibition. He began to plan who might run the liquor industry after repeal, but he was aware that he did not own Roosevelt.

Franklin Roosevelt was elected in November, 1932 by a landslide and would begin in office in March, 1933. Around the same time the great Geneva Disarmament Conference had finally failed, although Roosevelt had sent a letter trying to rescue it. Hitler had a reduced vote but was straining towards power as Chancellor, by now backed by Krupp, Thyssen and a powerful group of industrialists and American bankers. He became Chancellor in February, 1933 and began to crush all opposition just as Roosevelt took up the presidency. Mussolini made a pact with Britain, France and Germany, signed in July. Fascism was in the air, but Roosevelt was President.

**The United States Elite.**

The United States at this time was run by an East coast elite. Of course, the great push westward had been underway a long while – the gold rush, farming expansion, big Californian cities and the extraction of raw materials, but these people, either immigrants or the children of immigrants were not built into American politics, except in the grass roots organization of the Democratic Party and through unions. The eastern elite was still in charge. We are shortly looking at a massive confrontation between Franklin D. Roosevelt and the finance/munitions/business elite, but these people moved in the same circles. So, for example, Roosevelt's son began to go out with Ethel Du Pont, the daughter of Pierre's cousin Eugene in April 1933 and she was at the White House for Christmas 1933. The people we are concerned with interlocked at a number of different levels – munitions, banking, fear of communism and socialism, anti-unionism, family ties, Ivy League colleges, control of newspapers, Washington politics, state politics, international investment, movements like the American Legion and philanthropy. There were rivalries and intrigues, and each group pursued its own particular focus. We have seen how the Harriman bank focused on Thyssen and German investment; the Rockefellers were stronger in Russia, Morgan in England and so on. But they came and went in social events, public events, dinners and concerts, forming their views and above all trying to protect their way of life. For them the threat was Communism and Socialism, and Fascism was their natural ally. But Roosevelt was slightly different.

It is time for a little geography. This business elite were concentrated in New York, or more precisely in lower Manhattan, mainly around the area where Broadway met Wall Street. Here there was the Singer Building, the tallest skyscraper in the world when it was built, made out of the sewing machine business which turned the whole world into clothes makers. By 1913 the company was producing three million sewing machines a year. But the Singer business did not only make sewing machines. It had also produced guns in the Civil War and in the First World War Singer factories in New Jersey, Glasgow and Russia produced cannon, guns and other munitions. That was where the money for the Singer building also came from.[249] 120 Broadway was just next door, an imposing double fronted building, where the Du Ponts and others did their business. Just further down near Broad Street was the J.P. Morgan headquarters and the Stock Exchange, which was to go mad at the end of October, 1929, was close by. This was the great skyscraper building era as all these financiers built lush offices, began to use lifts and enjoy lunches with a view and talked through business over drinks. It was here that the deals were done and the schemes were hatched.

By now the elite were in a big political fight and it looked as though Roosevelt might be on the other side. After the Wall Street Crash there was considerable public anger at the rich capitalist cabal. First, the ethos of business was tarnished; the losers rightly did not trust the grinning and complacent winners. Then, these groups were vastly rich and enjoying excessive lifestyles while others were in extreme poverty. Third, business and finance were seen as an unstable system, with wildly fluctuating markets which did not supply jobs and incomes for ordinary workers. Moreover, the filthy rich - the merchants of death, the financiers and the mega businessmen – did not care about the poor, migrant, unemployed masses looking for a livelihood. Socialism reared "its ugly head", or more accurately, it became a live political option, the more so when the USSR was presenting a growth rate of 5-10% and a highly successful economy. They were threatened, or at least they thought they were.

These rich families sitting around in their large houses or lush corporate headquarters did not respond by doing nothing. They also were not fussy about the methods they used. One lawyer we shall meet later was John W. Davis. His level of operation is recorded in this short note. "During the Great Depression, John Davis represented name partner Louis Levy of the New York City law firm of Chadbourne, Stanchfield & Levy, later named

Chadbourne & Parke. In spite of Davis's vigorous defense, Levy was disbarred after helping get Judge Martin Manton a $250,000 loan, which was never repaid, from American Tobacco's ad agency at the same time American Tobacco faced a lawsuit before Judge Manton." Defend bribing a judge – no problem.[250]

**The American Legion.**

Part of our story is the American Legion. This was formed in 1919, under an initiative by Theodore Roosevelt's son, to bring together both the US expeditionary army and also the reserves after the War. In many ways it was admirable, trying to look after veterans properly as they returned. It obtained decent pensions for those who fought and addressed their shell shock and other traumas. It did not back any political party directly, but had an ethos which included "one hundred per cent Americanism". It was patriotic, and this was quickly interpreted as being anti-communist. Within a week of being formed an American Legion group in Centralia, Washington State, decided to attack the hall of the radical group known as International Workers of the World, IWW, or the "Wobblies" as they were also known. The attack was not as straightforward as they had hoped. The Wobblies had guns and, when the hall was stormed, shot and killed four veterans. An outraged mob then lynched one of the offenders. Indeed, the word "lynched" emerged because the mangled body went off in Jim Lynch's van. That confrontation set the tone nationwide. The American Legion was against Wobblies, Communists and those who were Bolsheviks. They were, in fact, the natural allies of the East Coast capitalist elite who moved in to run the Legion. As early as 1923 they praised Mussolini as an example of the way to thwart the left and in 1930 Mussolini was invited to come and speak at its Convention.

Much of the rest of the Legion was run by an establishment which was closer to the American elite. Perhaps the kingpin was Colonel Grayson Murphy, who had served in the First World War, including working with "Wild" Bill Donovan and the newly formed Red Cross. He travelled about and was savvy about what was happening in Italy and elsewhere. He was also one of the New York financial elite. He co-founded the American Legion and then funded the New York Branch, probably the biggest which required no small contribution. The Legion was an organization where those who paid the money did tend to call the tune. Murphy was seriously rich; he was an investment banker, on the boards of Anaconda Copper Mining Company, Guaranty Trust Company, New York Trust Company, Bethlehem Steel, Goodyear Tire & Rubber, New York Railways, Fifth Avenue Coach Co., and Chicago Motor Coach Co. He rubbed shoulders with the Morgans and Rockerfellers, had a lot of money in these companies and attended meetings to make sure the profits came in. If he wanted to do things, he paid out and did them. Grayson Murphy was thus politically tuned and was a close, long-time friend of Pierre and Irenée Du Pont and John Raskob. He was one of the Du Pont inner circle.

He and Pierre Du Pont worked intimately together on repealing prohibition in the AAPA at least from 1926 and Grayson Murphy often acted as the AAPA's spokesman. When Prohibition was finally defeated on the 5th December 1933, (note the date) after the big celebration dinner at the Waldorf-Astoria in the evening, Pierre Du Pont said to him: "We may have to resort further to this method of change at a time when our representatives fail - to carry out the will of the people." We can imagine Pierre's slight sneer when the reference was made to "the will of the people" for they were already planning what this action might be.[251] The inner informal committee agreed with the idea of "the formation of a group. Based on our old membership in the association [to repeal Prohibition], which would, in the event of danger to the federal Constitution, stand ready to defend the faith of the fathers." In other words, they were looking to direct action against the "unconstitutional" Roosevelt. There were other American Legion people. One of them was William (Bill) Doyle. He was Commander of the Massachusetts American Legion, another member of its inner circle, rather less important than Grayson Murphy. Another was Gerald MacGuire, who was a member of the Connecticut American

Legion, who worked for Grayson Murphy at a $100 a week as a bond salesman. He was effectively Grayson Murphy's man, running around doing his business.

**General Smedley Butler.**

One of the heroes of the American Legion was General Smedley Butler whom we now meet. He had an outstanding war record going back to the Boxer Rebellion. He had received two Medals of Honour, and numerous other awards for bravery, including saving his comrades under fire. During his career he received sixteen medals including five for bravery. Old Gimlet Eye's reputation was untouchable, especially to his fellow soldiers. He was also plain speaking and honest. An important incident, which should have been noted by the financial elite, took place in 1931. A friend of Butler's had recounted how a car he was in with Mussolini had run over a child in the street. Butler's friend screamed in anguish, but Mussolini's response was to tell him that he shouldn't scream; it was only one life and the affairs of state could not be stopped for one life. Butler told the story in another context and concluded that Mussolini was not to be trusted. "How can you talk disarmament with a man like that?" was the rhetorical question. The comment was reported back home by an Italian diplomat present at the meeting and when Mussolini heard about it, he gesticulated and created a diplomatic storm. To avoid creating offence President Hoover then forced Secretary of the Navy, Charles Adams to court-martial Butler, the first officer to be so arrested since the Civil War. The plans for the court-martial rightly provoked a great outcry, and Butler, a Republican, also got support from Roosevelt who at the time was Governor of New York. Eventually, both Hoover and Adams backed down. This event left Butler slightly at the edge of the American Legion and its leadership, but well aware of Roosevelt's integrity.

But another event put him centrally in the frame. In late July 1932 when Hoover was still President a bonus bill was going through Congress to increase the pensions of veterans and a so-called "Bonus Army" of unemployed veterans gathered in

Washington to help the Bill through. The Bill passed in the House of Representatives but was defeated in the Republican dominated Senate. At this stage there were 10,000 angry veterans who had set up a shanty town on the banks of the Anacostia River, and Butler came over to speak to them. Wolfe describes the situation thus:

> He [Butler] urged them to fight on. "If you don't hang together, you aren't worth a damn," he said. "They may be calling you tramps now, but in 1917 they didn't call you bums.... When you go home, go to the polls in November, lick the hell out of those who are against you. You know who they are.... Now go to it." The crowd roared. Butler stayed with the veterans, talking to them through the night and into the next day. As he prepared to leave, he warned them against allowing their frustrations to well over into violence: "You are all right as long as you keep your sense of humor...." The next day, Hoover ordered Gen. Douglas MacArthur to drive the veterans from Washington at bayonet point, unleashing violence against the unarmed "army". The nation was stunned.[252]

Butler emerged from this as the army's champion, while MacArthur was the villain. Again the sense was of Butler's genuine support for the veterans. He invited them to come to his house anytime for a night's hospitality, but explained that he could not get them a job. He was widely respected as an honest, warm soldier who was on the side of those he led, and was trusted to the hilt by the veterans.

**The Inauguration of FDR.**

During early 1933 all kinds of things were going on. Hitler had just come to power, and international business, especially munitions related business, flocked to him to sell weapons. Du Pont bought up Remington Arms, presumably because it was clear that weapons sales to Germany would be strong. Possibly the Company had already been supplying Hitler's storm-troopers with guns, or started to after the take-over. Suddenly the inhibitions on military production since the Great War were broken and American money and business moved in to exploit the market, allowing Hitler to expand unchecked. On 15th February, 1933 Giuseppe Zingara attempted to assassinate Roosevelt, but failed when a women deflected his gun and another person was killed. Zingara was an Italian immigrant who settled in Paterson, NJ, not far from New York, but who was in Miami, Florida, when Roosevelt was also there in a motorcade giving a talk. The FBI under Edgar Hoover hardly investigated the case before Zingara went to the electric chair. If Roosevelt had died, John Garner would have become president. He was an anti-union, anti-prohibition and largely anti-New Deal politician whom Roosevelt accepted on the ticket after he came second in the primaries. The Du Pont/Morgan cabal would probably have controlled the Presidency and Fascism would have had unimpeded dominance in the late 20th century. It was that close.

Roosevelt was inaugurated on the 4th March, 1933 after a landslide victory in the election, and in his speech the words we remember are "the only thing to fear is fear itself" – a good line after you have nearly been assassinated. Actually, the whole speech is awesome and biblical in emphasis. He addressed the depression and capitalism thus:

> Primarily this is because the rulers of the exchange of mankind's goods have failed, through their own stubbornness and their own incompetence, have admitted their failure, and abdicated. Practices of the unscrupulous money changers stand indicted in the court of public opinion, rejected by the hearts and minds of men.
>
> True they have tried, but their efforts have been cast in the pattern of an outworn tradition. Faced by failure of credit they have proposed only the lending of more money. Stripped of the lure of profit by which to induce our people to follow their false leadership, they have resorted to exhortations, pleading tearfully for restored confidence. They know only the rules of a generation of self-seekers. They have no vision, and when there is no vision the people perish.

> The money changers have fled from their high seats in the temple of our civilization. We may now restore that temple to the ancient truths. The measure of the restoration lies in the extent to which we apply social values more noble than mere monetary profit.
>
> Happiness lies not in the mere possession of money; it lies in the joy of achievement, in the thrill of creative effort. The joy and moral stimulation of work no longer must be forgotten in the mad chase of evanescent profits. These dark days will be worth all they cost us if they teach us that our true destiny is not to be ministered unto but to minister to ourselves and to our fellow men.

It is crystal clear that this is war on financial capitalism – words like "stubborn", "incompetent", "failure", "abdication", "unscrupulous", "indited", "outworn", "false leadership", "self-seekers", "the mad chase of evanescent profits" make it clear. Roosevelt knows these people, for he too was one of the elite, and these are not the words you use of your friends. His opposition is principial. He was clear that financial capitalism was ideologically dead, and the route out was work and service. He is biblical. "They have no vision, and when there is no vision the people perish." He points to the example of Christ for his deepest authority. As Christ threw out the money-changers from the Temple, so these money changers are to be evicted and flee. There could be no more powerful statement to the whole nation of the eviction of the capitalist elite.

More than that, in what came to be known as the First Hundred Days in an avalanche of activity Roosevelt set about re-invigorating the economy. First he tackled banking. Credit was being squeezed, mortgage foreclosures were rampant because the banks would not lend (or were lending to Germany and the USSR). Roosevelt in part opened up credit. Then he gave a quarter of a million young men direct employment, set up the Tennessee River Authority, the National Recovery Administration, the National

Industrial Recovery Administration, the National Labor Board, and took America off the Gold Standard so that he could print money and carry out an expansionist economic programme. It was an amazing programme of economic revitalisation. At this stage the American business and financial elite was being outplayed. Roosevelt had secured the nomination over the Du Pont's Al Smith. He had pointed out their moral bankruptcy, set up multiple Government initiatives and communicated directly to the people through his fireside chats, circumventing the capitalist control of the press. But, he was not inviting enemies. He still needed the great companies to help run the economy, and drafted them on various boards. Moreover, he was also proceeding with repeal of prohibition which kept Pierre Du Pont onside at least through to the summer of 1933, but really the Manhattan business elite were seething. They were seeing the reins of power slipping away from them, and rather than running the system, they had a President who was prepared to attack them and rein in the biggest businesses the world had ever known.

The attack was partly carried out through hearings carried out through the Senate Banking Committee in the summer of 1933 with Ferdinand Pecoria as special counsel. Pecoria exposed J.P. Morgan. On the 25th May, the lead headlines in the *New York Times* were "Morgan paid No Income Tax in 1931 and 1932; Neither Did His Partners." That went down really well with the tax-paying masses and led to a lot of criticism of the New York elite. Next day it was "Morgan's Foreign Financing Detailed."[253] He was not best pleased, and the whole banking sector was weakened by this public exposure. Roosevelt used the attacks to make sure that the bankers could not attack his policies for extending credit and expanding the economy through government action. An open letter in the *New York Times* of 31st December, 1933 from John Maynard Keynes also backed up this policy. Again the financial elite were on the back foot, intellectually and in terms of their refusal to pay their fair share. Roosevelt and the people were in charge holding the elite to account.

**The First Move in the Fascist Plot.**

The Fascist plot against Roosevelt is one of the most successful cover-ups in modern history. Few Americans will have heard of it, because it occurred at the time when the elite controlled the press and dominated the media. Because the capitalist elite were so close to power, they could close down any publicity in relation to it. It was also meant to be a plot – secret – until the public were presented with a fait accompli. In the end it did not happen. It was stitched together, emerging, and in the end not workable. Let us take it through its various stages. It is often known as "the Business Plot".

The first stage occurred in the summer of 1933, when it was clear how radical Roosevelt's political agenda was. Two people came to General Smedley Butler with a proposition. On the 1st July Gerald MacGuire, an employee of Grayson Murphy, and Bill Doyle, of the Massachusetts American Legion, met Butler and asked him to run as National Commander of the American Legion. They came in a Packhard limousine with a chauffeur. We have to have a good grasp of the people involved. Gerald MacGuire was sent by Grayson Murphy whom we have already met. He made it clear to Butler that Grayson Murphy looked after him well. We could add that alongside being very close to the Du Ponts, Murphy was also close to J.P. Morgan. He was a Director of Morgan's Guarantee Trust Bank and the New York Trust Company also largely owned by Morgan, and he had gone to Italy to arrange loans for Morgan with Mussolini, and so he had easy going relations with the Italian Fascist Party and knew the way they functioned. He would know about Fascist dictatorships. With the support of Grayson Murphy and others and with Butler's reputation, the latter would be likely to be "elected" to the post. The American Legion's membership at this time was over a million and it had a powerful public and political presence. Why did these dear people want him to become Commander of the American Legion?

They arranged to meet Butler again on the 3rd or 4th July, 1933. They came in the same limousine. Their agenda became clearer. The idea was that Butler would go to the National

Convention as an ordinary veteran. There would be two-or three hundred other veterans planted in the audience, and they would stampede for Butler to make a speech. MacGuire already had the speech to hand, a typewritten speech which he proposed Butler read at the convention. It urged the American Legion convention to adopt a resolution calling for the United States to return to the Gold Standard, so that when veterans were paid the bonus promised to them, the money they received would not be worthless – slight scare tactic there. Really, the capitalists were going to benefit from returning to the Gold Standard. Butler was suspicious and pointed out that veterans could not afford the $200-300 dollars needed for travel and accommodation in Chicago. MacGuire said *they* would pay and showed Butler bank deposits of $42,000 and $64,000 which were set aside for the American Legion plot.[254] The main backers were Grayson Murphy and Robert Sterling Clark. Butler at this stage had become fed up with MacGuire, who was obviously operating for others and a bit out of his depth. He asked to see one of the principals. There was another meeting on 1st September, 1933 when Butler said he was not going to carry on meeting with MacGuire when the latter threw a bundle of $18,000 on the bed in a typical, but futile, gesture. Butler held back and waited.

Then, Sterling Clerk who was heir to the great Singer fortune, based on sewing machines and munitions visited Butler and had dinner with him and his wife. This was a stage closer to the central plotters. Butler vaguely knew him from the past, because he had served with Butler in the Boxer Rebellion and directly knew the General's prowess and reputation within the forces. Butler explained why he was not able to come to the convention under this kind of staged process and Clark accepted it. Under examination later MacGuire admitted that Sterling Clark had handed over $30,000 to him at a dinner in the bankers' club at 120 Broadway, which might have been to buy some bonds or something or other, and his money holdings exactly matched what Butler had said were available to the plot. Clark was also into horse racing and art collecting. Later in 1954 his horse, "Never Say Die" won the Epsom Derby at 33-1 with the young Lester Piggott as jockey. Obviously

Sterling Clark would be keen to get Butler on board. The third figure involved was the Morgan Attorney, John. W. Davis, whom we have already met defending bankers who bribe judges. He wrote the speech that Butler was supposed to give to the American Legion Conference. J.P. Morgan would, of course, be against leaving the Gold Standard and facing the likelihood that its loans would decrease in value. His was a corporate interest.

If we evaluate this first phase in the summer and autumn of 1933, it is clear that this is not yet a coup attempt, but a move to get the American Legion to reverse Roosevelt's move from the Gold Standard. MacGuire was obviously a minion, working for Grayson Murphy, part of the Du Pont inner circle, Sterling Clark and the J.P. Morgan Group. They would be in contact, talking funding and establishing the plan of using the American Legion to attack Roosevelt's movement from the Gold Standard. More than this, we can guess that this plan was hatched at or near 120 Broadway, NY, where the Du Pont and Morgan people were based and others linked to the plot were found. It hosted the exclusive bankers' club on the top three floors. Number 120 shed its big shadow on the Singer Building, not unknown to Sterling Clark, and Grayson Murphy was just down the street at 25 Broadway. These were business buddies, meeting over expensive food. Within a while this part of the plot would date as returning to the Gold Standard became impractical and the fixing would move on.

**The Fascist Heat Rises.**

During the spring of 1934 several trends were underway. First, the gulf between Roosevelt and the business elite grew wider. Roosevelt, it was clear, had a principled opposition to this group and its attempted direction of the American State. He developed his power base and was clearly not going to be in the pocket of the business elite. Rather he was seen as anti-business, radical and socialist because he had exposed them through New Deal economics. Second, the structure of the Du Pont family changed. Pierre, by now, had the reward of the full repeal of prohibition, and through ageing drew back from political involvement. The more confrontational Irenée moved into the arena fully to work with Raskob. Third, the business/banking/munitions elite grew much more interested in both Mussolini and Hitler now organizing a military state based on American loans. They had active business contacts. General Motors, largely owned by the Du Ponts, also owned Opel, after an investment of some $30 million and around this time they began negotiating with the Nazis about making military trucks and creating an open door for investment. J.P Morgan had lent Mussolini $100 million and was looking after his investments. Gerald Maguire spent the Spring travelling round Europe looking at the Fascist groups in Italy, France and Germany at Grayson Murphy's behest and was considering the lessons they might have for veterans organization in the States. He was reporting back to Sterling Clark, Grayson Murphy and Smedley Butler on what he found. Meanwhile the Morgan, Mellon and Harriman groups were extolling the kind of government Mussolini had, describing it as "democratic". So, a Fascist agenda was very much in the air.

But, finally, the munitions issue burst on the public agenda. The book, *The Merchants of Death,* written by H. C. Englebrecht and F.C. Hanighen was published. Please read it. It documented in dispassionate detail the way in which the munitions companies had contributed to the fomenting of the Great War and included many of the contributions of the Du Ponts and others to the process. At this point on 8th February, 1934 Senator Nye introduced a resolution to the Senate for a Committee to investigate this process. It was adopted in mid-April and so the Du Ponts knew that in the future they were going to be grilled by a Senate Committee on their war profits and arms selling. Undoubtedly this move was also approved by Roosevelt as a way of keeping the heat on the group which had now effectively become his enemies. The Committee was well organized. Its legal assistant was a chap called Alger Hiss, who became a hate figure for the Du Pont-Morgan people. Senator Nye was fearless. Senator Homer Bone on the committee charged that Boeing had made 68% profit on navy business and 90% on army contracts.[255] During the summer of 1934 the Nye Committee, or the

Special Committee on Investigation of the Munitions Industry, began its research and called the key figures for hearings; so the whole munitions community knew what was coming and they knew the power of public exposure. The Du Ponts and others were more than a little nervous. Something needed to be done.

During the summer Irenée Du Pont especially was looking around for another organization to oppose Roosevelt more directly than the American Legion. There was a lot of discussion. A formal organization was needed which would carry out the DuPont/Morgan agenda. It was first suggested as "The National Property League", "The American Federation of Business" and "Defenders of the Constitution." and finally by John W. Davis, who had written Smedley Butler's proposed speech to the American Legion, as "The American Liberty League" in a letter to John Raskob. The Du Pont's backed Jouett Shouse, an old friend of Pierre's, as the President. The new organization was to be a great pseudo-popular campaign backed by Du Pont money to defeat Roosevelt and turn the tide against the New Deal. Timing is important. Shouse informed Roosevelt on 15th August, 1934 of its formation suggesting he had nothing to fear from it, trying to disarm opposition to the idea. But the Roosevelt camp knew what it was up against; within a couple of weeks it had spread publicity about this new tycoon-backed pressure group. They labelled it the "Stop Roosevelt Campaign" and publicly linked it with Raskob, Irenée Du Pont, John W Davis and Jouett Shouse.[256] It was an enforced "coming out" and the public response was quite hostile because they now had an idea of what was going on. Cartoons said "Protect the poor billionaires" and showed Du Pont dollar bills as the new kind of money. So the full frontal opposition to Roosevelt was known and the secrecy was blown open to the public. Despite vast quantities of money, expensive meetings, campaigns, leaflets and all the other techniques of what was really a mass media pressure group, the Liberty League was seen from the start largely for what it was – the tool of a lot of plutocrats seeking their own interests and trying to throw normal democracy into an elitist fascist rule which would keep the people in their place.

**The Fascist Plot to oust President Roosevelt**

At the same time another covert scheme was underway. This was for an engineered "spontaneous" Fascist coup. There was to be a march on Washington by half a million veterans to unseat Roosevelt and replace him with the stooge of the plotters. Grayson Murphy, Sterling Clerk, and others were centrally involved. Probably there were discussions throughout the Du Pont/ Morgan group sounding out the possibility. On the 22nd August, 1934 Gerald MacGuire saw Butler again and told him of the proposed plot. He had been on a fact-finding trip to Brussels, Rotterdam, Amsterdam, Hamburg, Copenhagen, Berlin, Prague, Leipzig, Vienna, Munich, Zurich, Basle, Geneva and Paris looking at European Fascism and noting new movements in the Netherlands and elsewhere. He had primed Butler by sending him a number of cards. He outlined the plan. There was to be a march on Washington by 500,000 veterans, many, of course, linked to the American Legion, to occupy the White House, declare Roosevelt too ill to govern and take over the Government. General Smedley Butler was to lead the march, and the ex-soldiers would be armed, and Remington Arms would equip them. By this time Remington Arms was owned by the Du Ponts, so the Du Ponts must have agreed to this. The march would lead to Roosevelt being declared sick and unable to govern and being replaced by General Hugh Johnson, as a stand-in President. MacGuire also stated that the move was backed by $3,000,000. Obviously, it was scaled up from the earlier plot.

The choice of General Hugh Johnson was interesting. He had a good military record, and then worked with Roosevelt and became head of the Roosevelt's National Recovery Administration. While there he collaborated closely with Pierre Du Pont, and it was clear that the two had a lot in common. Hugh Johnson was attracted by the model of Mussolini, where a political leader worked closely with the barons of industry to bring about industrial growth. He was sacked by Roosevelt in September, 1934, possibly because FDR had an inkling of the take-over. Johnson's role suggests that the Du Ponts were in on the plot; the Remington Arms link suggests the same. At this time MacGuire saw Paul French, who had been Butler's Secretary and was now a reporter, whom Butler used to corroborate his story. French took down in detail the discussion he had with MacGuire. James Van Zandt, later a long-time Republican Congressman, confirmed that he too had been approached by the Wall Street plotters, after being warned by Butler that it would happen. Van Zandt said that Colonel Theodore Roosevelt Jnr, former Legion Commander, Hanford MacNider and General Douglas MacArthur had also been approached.[257]

The plot was revealed when Butler informed the House of Representatives Un-American Activities Committee of what had happened, approaching Senator John MacCormack. The Committee might also have heard that something was afoot. Hearings began in November and the Committee interviewed Butler, MacGuire and French and checked out information with others who had been mentioned. We do not have all the records, because they have been destroyed of all sensitive material by someone later. The Committee also declined to interview any of the really powerful backers and MacGuire had to carry the main burden. His interrogation reads hilariously. He tried to forget everything, and pretend that he and Doyle happened to meet and just turned up at General Smedley Butler's by accident because a chap called Jack phoned him, and they then thought of the American Legion idea, but the Committee had his bank records and other evidence which required him to admit what Butler had said was accurate in dozens of points. The final report of the House of Representatives Committee was as follows.

> In the last few weeks of the committee's official life it received evidence showing that certain persons had made an attempt to establish a fascist organization in this country. No evidence was presented and this committee had none to show a connection between this effort and any fascist activity of any European country. *There is no question that these attempts were discussed, were planned, and might have been placed in execution when and if the financial backers deemed it expedient.* (My italics)

> This committee received evidence from Maj. Gen. Smedley D. Butler (retired), twice decorated by the Congress of the United States. He testified before the committee as to conversations with one Gerald C. MacGuire in which the latter is alleged to have suggested the formation of a fascist army under the leadership of General Butler.
>
> MacGuire denied these allegations under oath, but your committee was able to verify all the pertinent statements made by General Butler, with the exception of the direct statement suggesting the creation of the organization. This, however, was corroborated in the correspondence of MacGuire with his principal, Robert Sterling Clark, of New York City, while MacGuire was abroad studying the various forms of veteran organizations of Fascist character.[258]

This clear conclusion, however, was met by two other developments. First the Committee had members who were closer to the business elite and they closed down the issue. Second, because the business elite controlled the newspapers, they were able to marginalize and pooh-pooh it in the Press. The *New York Times* abruptly changed its story and cut reporting the evidence. It is amazing that the Morgan/Du Pont/Rockefeller controlled press was able to talk out the plot to the extent that it has largely disappeared from American history. Most Americans do not know of this attempted Fascist coup in their country by big business. Media control almost works. However, with the plot exposed in Congress, it immediately lost any chance of success, and all linked with it protested their innocence. Roosevelt was safe.

**Roosevelt Wins for a Time.**

Roosevelt knew what he was up against, and was very careful to make sure that this group could not muster enough power to threaten him and American democracy. Indeed, the elite business group had a hard time of it. The Nye Committee exposed the Du Pont's profits from arms, their shady deals and their contributions to war and they received a lot of bad publicity. Roosevelt went further and passed the 1935 Neutrality Act which refused the selling of arms to belligerents. It was especially aimed at sales to Italy and Germany because Roosevelt had assessed the dangers of Fascism. Sadly, there were ways round the Act. For example, it did not cover trucks and oil, and as a result Texaco, Standard Oil, Ford, General Motors and Studebaker used this loophole to supply Franco in the Spanish Civil War, so that by 1939 he owed $100 million to America. Of course supplying weapons to countries not yet at war was not forbidden, and these flowed to most of the potential belligerents of the Second World War, as we have seen. When Hitler began the process of heavy armament, the munitions industry picked up, and the great world arms manufacturers of every country were in business again. Technically, Roosevelt was in control, but actually the genie was out of the bottle and the munitions interest was in the ascendant.

Roosevelt remained under attack. In the 1936 Presidential Election campaign he was faced by a Republican Party which was largely controlled by the American Liberty League and the Du Ponts who poured money into the election campaign to the tune of $850,000, while a further $500,000 was raised by the Liberty League. Yet, Alf Landon, an oil millionaire and Governor of Kansas was defeated overwhelmingly. In his campaign Roosevelt was outspoken against the Fascist tendencies of his opponents. He was such a popular and dynamic campaigner that Landon was defeated in the largest landslide in history, losing every state but Maine and Vermont. It was also a large political defeat for the Du Ponts, losing both money and public credibility. With that background, American Fascism experienced a political defeat in the States which closed down the overt political option, especially when Hitler and Mussolini had done their work, but with the Second World War another level of militarism was to emerge. You didn't need to organize a Fascist Party and try to take over the State. Thereafter, militaristic fascism in the States operated behind the scenes and away from democratic glare. It was *in* executive government, the Pentagon, the CIA and the Cold War industries that the munitions people found their home.

**So, was Appeasement the Problem?**

The overall conclusion of this section on Fascism involves a major revision of the standard popular understanding of the source of the Second World War. Following Churchill, we are asked to conclude that appeasement towards the Nazis and under-arming led to the Second World War. If we had re-armed properly and early enough, the War would have been prevented. *Appeasement,* especially around the time of the Munich Agreement in September, 1938 allowed the Nazis to march to war, There is no doubt of Hitler's bullying and the Allies lack of opposition in the late thirties; in that location Churchill was right, and importantly so. But a longer perspective allows us to see the agenda of the munitions' companies and bankers in breaking the move towards disarmament and peace in the twenties and early thirties. They encouraged the groups that became Fascist in Italy, Japan, Germany and less successfully in France, the United States, Britain and elsewhere. These groups, evident world-wide, were linked to the great munitions and banking corporate structures of the First World War, the richest groups in the world. These interests had made money out of conflict and were not averse to putting war back on the agenda. They thought they could run their money-making show and were happy to contribute to puppets like Mussolini, Hitler and others who liked weapons. They succeeded in generating war in China, Spain and then the Second World War.

They were often stronger than the politicians. We have seen how narrowly Roosevelt, a colossus who saw the problem, won. In Europe their establishment of capital, banking, land, munitions and militarism defeated the peacemakers. The financial/munitions elite was frightened by democracy and socialism and would back whomever was necessary to keep these ways at bay. The British Conservative Party thwarted the move for peace at the great Geneva Disarmament Conference, even helping Hitler come to power when his appeal was weakening. Thus, this combined weight of the munitions/banking/industrial sectors' opposition to disarmament and support of Fascist groups and regimes was the dominant cause of the Second World War. They were producing and selling weapons, funding militias and encouraging the emergence of belligerent Fascists and a permanently militarised world economy. This was no accident.

We think of the Second World War as a great irrational blot on twentieth century history, as something that cannot make sense except in the tortured workings of Hitler's mind, but we ignore the group for whom war is rational and necessary – the arms manufacturers. They provide the means for which war has to be the end, and if they will the means through their business activities, they will the end. Again in the Second World War, as in the First, the logic of promoting arms won its way. Millions were sacrificed to an industry that again became the greatest on the planet. Two World Wars – Same Cause. But the cost and stupidity of this route should bring us all up short. As Pete Seeger later sang, "Where have all the young men gone? Long time passing. Where have all the young men gone? Long time ago. Where have all the young men gone? Gone for soldiers every one. When will they ever learn? When will they ever learn?" We yearn to answer, "Yes, we learn."

## PART VI: 'ARMING THE WORLD – THE SECOND WORLD WAR.

*Wars allow the munitions people unlimited success. The Second World War, which for the munitions industry was well under way by 1935 saw ten years of exponential expansion into far and away the greatest industry on earth. Once this position was established it would not easily be relinquished. This was not the war to end all wars, but the beginning of yet a higher level of world militarization which would in part be permanent.*

# Chapter Twenty Two: The Second World War – the fully armed world economy.

### The Scale of World War.

There are many books written on the narrative of the Second World War, which, we say in hope, was the biggest in human history. Here we will not try to cover the events of the conflict, but only some background points. World population in 1940 was an estimated 2,300 million. Outside South America most of that population found itself engaged in the War.[259] Even in South America many countries entered the War and even contributed troops after Pearl Harbour. The War was largely a total world war, absorbing populations even when they were not directly fighting. The populations of China, the USSR, India, Japan, the Philippines, Africa, Europe, North America and other areas were wholly or substantially taken up with the War, with munitions, transport, troop support, food provision, economic support, medical and health/injury support, the administration of war and so on. It is a crude calculation, but if we say that three quarters of the world's population were directly engaged with the war as their main daily concern, and they were fighting for half on the full war time of six years, i.e, three years, then some 14 trillion hours were absorbed by the war, the greatest waste of human effort ever. It was longer than the First World War by some 50% and thus a more permanent experience. Some servicemen were not demobbed until 1946 or 1947. This duration and scale of war, a pedestrian point compared with the narratives and deaths of the event, remains one of its most important aspects. It drummed war into world consciousness.

The fighting forces are broadly estimated at over 100 million, say 5% of the world's population, or 10% of all men. They got used to fighting. For many it was the job they learned. It was normality, although an horrific one. Most people, most of the time learn from experience. They often do not have the luxury of reflecting on experience when survival, work, getting food and looking after others takes up most of their time. They also received the same repetitive message – the enemy must be defeated. It was more total, backed by radio, than in any other war, and propaganda had come on a lot since 1914. There was no question in this war of soldiers rebelling in the trenches. We tend to ignore the picture of the soldier sitting with a fag in his fingers relaxing, but when he was not fighting, he was still a soldier, and the fag was his reward. It was free and cigarettes, too, could kill those who smoked.[260]. The uniform was the badge of national uniformity, and men were "conscripted" to the armed forces to carry out the script the Government was following.

The costs were vast. Sober casualty estimates amount to some 60 million killed in war, a further 25 million dying in war-related famine and disease. The 85 million deaths total amounts to 3.5-4.0% of the total world population. Of course, many of these were "civilian" rather than military, as people were killed by bombing and the other devastations of war. It is not easy to establish those who were injured. In the USSR and Germany twice as many were injured as killed, and elsewhere, usually, there were more injured than slain. In Japan, because of the nuclear bombs the effects were often delayed. Perhaps another 4-5% of the world population was injured. The suffering represented by these figures is beyond reporting, but there is another effect which they have. The families of these people, dead and injured, deeply need to know that there was some deep purpose to their sacrifices, as indeed, there was, because the Nazis and Fascists needed to be defeated. Nothing could undo that truth. Nevertheless, often this meant that the psychological state of the people involved was frozen away from issues of peace and disarmament. Historically, they could not get beyond the War and 1939 to consider the problems of militarism. More deeply, the idea that all this business of war might be unnecessary was unthinkable. The death of millions, in and because of battle, was the ultimate sacrifice, and sacrifice always has to make sense.

**The Defeat of Peacemaking – The Great Volte-face.**

There is some reflection needed here on the ways we think in everyday life about war, about what went on in our heads in relation to the Second World War and militarism. Let us step back and recall the Great Head Swivel. For a while in the 20s and 30s, after the "War to end all Wars", the munitions people were rightly identified as having encouraged that war and were deeply distrusted. They were "merchants of death", using war to reap their own profit. The evidence emerged of deals, the promotion of conflict and of the attempts to scupper all attempts at peace and disarmament. From the Covenant of the League of Nations through to the Great Geneva Disarmament Conference there were concerted attempts by the world's statesmen to put an end to the trade in arms and its results in terms of wars. There was a strong moral grasp of the horrors of killing people, that the Great War should never have happened, that the soldiers of all nations were pawns in a killing spree which dishonoured their bravery and sacrifice. Indeed, in the 1930s this awareness quickened. In the States the Nye Commission and the astonishing revelations of Englebrecht and Hanighen's book, the *Merchants of Death*, made people suddenly aware of what Krupp, Schneider, Du Pont and the others had been about. For the companies concerned, it was frightening to be so put in the spotlight.

In Britain, Philip Noel-Baker tried to do the same thing. His text, *The Private Manufacture of Armaments* identified the munitions people as a primary generator of war. The issue was clearly put. The Prefatory Note to Noel-Baker's book by Lord Cecil, the great worker for peace sets it out:

> The subject of this book is one of great importance. At a time when every decent citizen should be striving his utmost to maintain peace, there exists a great industry with branches in every country and having capital running into hundreds of millions of pounds, whose interest is to promote war. This book shews that not only is such a state of things in principle indefensible, but in practice it leads to deplorable and dangerous results. The argument is temperately stated and rests on a great accumulation of evidence. Everyone who cares for peace should read it, and I cannot doubt that impartial readers will be convinced that Private Manufacture of Armaments should be brought to an end without further delay. CECIL. London. 25th August, 1936.

Every word is weighed, and even in 1936 most people would fully agree with it. Lord Cecil has been working for disarmament for seventeen years to address this great scar on humanity. He was now urgent, following the Peace Ballot, and watching Europe career towards war.

Noel-Baker provides the detailed content. He knows how the threat of war builds up. Let us hear him.

> Ever since the League of Nations came to life in 1920, Private Arms Firms have been employing again the methods they adopted in the years before 1914. They have been soliciting orders; bribing Ministers and officials, selling arms in whatever market they could find; playing governments off against each other; subsidizing armaments propaganda; purchasing and otherwise influencing the Press; creating scares and panics that keep the peoples in a state of constant anxiety and alarm. We have seen them scoffing at the League of Nations; joyfully proclaiming that Disarmament is dead; supplying arms for the conduct of Covenant-breaking wars; spreading the doctrine that great wars must follow small ones, that "Pacts" are only "scraps of paper," that safety lies in National Armaments alone. We know that their financial and industrial power creates a constant pressure

> for the increase in armaments, however little political reason for such an increase there might be. We know that, once the process of armament expansion is begun, it gathers increasing momentum as the volume of vested interests is increased. The chance of fortunes on the Stock Exchange brings in other "influential men" to increase the pressure. More and more "Prosperity" is founded on increased preparations for the destruction of human happiness and wealth..... What is needed, therefore, is some world-wide change which will end these evils in every arms-producing country in Europe and the world.[261]

No more understanding of the situation was needed. The evil of the munitions process was grasped by all of these people working for disarmament and peace and by millions of the public. Sober thinking people everywhere understood that this was the truth.

Then suddenly events, especially those surrounding Nazi Germany and Japan, pulled the carpet from under them. All the arguments in the world were defeated by rampant Nazi, Italian and Japanese militarization, aided by the financial capitalism of America and Europe, undermining the political process of peace. The arms companies of France, Britain and the United States happily fell in line. Suddenly Geneva was in ruins and the munitions agenda was totally driving events. It was all too late. In 1938 the Moral Rearmament movement swept the western world, but it was ineffective in preventing the great conflagration. Hitler was in power and from nearly nothing was being funded and armed, not just by his own nation, but by America and even Britain. The world has "missed its opportunity". Suddenly, this moral attitude was defeated by rampant militarism not because it was wrong, but because it was buried by events which people of the time could not understand. Neville Chamberlain, blinking with his silly bit of paper, symbolizes this incomprehension. Just when people were overwhelmingly for peace, the career towards war happened through the military-industrial complex. Cecil and Noel-Baker had lost.

**The Really Great Depression**

Richard Overy in *The Morbid Age* and *The Road to War* charts the depression surrounding the unfolding events on that road, state by state, and the condition of hopelessness that gripped the world. They had the prospect of disarmed peace in their hands and suddenly it slipped through their fingers, and they did not understand why, or who had brought about the change, for the merchants of death, aside from Irenée du Pont and a few others went about their job much more quietly. From, say, 1934 it was largely downhill all the way in mind-numbing incomprehension. Seemingly, the world's great statesmen, working together, were unable to prevent another Great War turning up. The mood became one of fatalism and a grim determination to defeat Fascism. Churchill moved from being an outdated military colonialist to the supreme realist, showing the futility of appeasement and the need to arm. The world was heading for the great crash; it had had the tools for understanding why, but the munitions/military and financial interests were now driving the train running out of control. From 1934 the momentum towards war was increasing and in no time at all, aside the excruciating sight of Neville Chamberlain waving a scrap of paper, we crashed into the Second World War, the most evil in history, when millions were gratuitously or purposefully killed, and it took over part of our souls. It cost the world some 85 million deaths, perhaps the same again in injuries and disability and trillions was lost as economic activity was warped towards death and destruction.

At the end of the War, accompanied by an avalanche of mass media propaganda on all sides, the lesson was not that armament and war should be avoided, but that we should arm and win. We thought about winning for five years and then our thinking was reduced to two words which were supposed to cover every eventuality: - "Remember Hitler". If there was no-one remotely like Hitler in sight, and usually there was not, then there was a toothbrush moustache just below the horizon. We forgot how Hitler and Fascism were constructed in the twenties and how the munitions people fought back against disarmament and won.

Despite the horrors caused by militarism, the political lesson was to be strong, to arm to the hilt, and let the military/munitions/political establishment rule our minds. The munitions people were the good guys again, helping us to sleep at night. We had the scare to end all scares in the Cold War. Munitions kept us safe. The munitions people won and then set out to make the peacemakers oddballs and even traitors.

In this new old world, there was an orchestrated agenda. Disarmers were seen as reds, spies, enemies. We accepted nuclear weapons as good. Nobody was really allowed to question militarism and the whole system was sewn up for decades. All the understanding that had accumulated about the dangers of munitions was sublimated as the weapons' people slipped smoothly from the War into the Cold War. They were in charge. We moved from Spitfires to carpet bombing to missile systems, from the London Blitz to Hiroshima and Nagasaki to Mutually Assured Destruction and we had to believe that weapons were always necessary. Every new weapon system was trumpeted as success. Disarmament became a disloyal idea, for just when it had full intellectual justification, it was swept away by all-out war. The *evil* of appeasement was the only thought good citizens were allowed to have and our minds were frozen for us. After the Second World War there was no talk about the War to end all wars, but the defeatist assumption was that war, including cold war, was normal. The real victor in the Second World War was not the Allies, but the militarists and munitions' people, because again they were accepted as normal and they were now inside the system. All the earlier contributions to understanding militarism and Fascism were ignored, as the proto-Fascist bankers and munitions people made themselves squeaky clean and went on to run the post-war establishment, ruling us with fear.

**The Dominant World Industry.**

The drama of the Second World War is so momentous that we tend to focus mainly on the evil of the Nazis, the great battles and Hitler's defeat. We turn over in our minds the millions who died in the greatest slaughter in human history and it will not go away. We look at Nazi totalitarianism, the horrors of the Holocaust, the politics, and more recently at ordinary people's war experiences. This chapter is not a magisterial study of the Second World War, but merely looks at the bits that are sometimes left out.

One area is obvious, but especially ignored. In Germany, the United Kingdom, France, Italy, Japan, the USSR and the United States, still now the dominant arms manufacturers, a vast system of arms manufacturing and military engagement grew up which claimed some 30-40 and even 50% of the economy's total output. The machine guns, bombs, shells, U-boats, planes, tanks, howitzers, mines and torpedoes which dished out this death were all made. The world economy was militarized. *Arms became the biggest of big businesses, the greatest industry on earth.* The scale of expansion is breathtaking. The munitions expenditure of the great powers trebled in 1940 over pre-war levels. Then it nearly doubled again in 1941 and doubled again in 1942 before further big leaps in the next two years. Overall it was a seventeen fold increase in munitions output from immediate pre-war levels to $94 billion in 1944. Of course, total military expenditure was even greater than this. In the United States in 1944 the military budget was between 37.8% and 45% of GDP, depending which measurement you use, the highest level ever.[262] Never had war production occurred on this scale. Munitions became by far the dominant world industry for more than a decade. We need to understand that this was a transformation of the world economy. What do you buy? You don't buy food, or houses, or cars; predominantly you buy weapons, soldiers and the ability to fight. The process was intimately locked into government; the munitions industry finally moved to the inside track. This was a pervasive personal system of relationships, commitments, rewards and benefits inside the State. Ordinary people did the fighting, but the militarists were walking the corridors, and some of them knew what it took to get rich and stay rich. It was the same military/industrial complex whether in the USSR, Japan, Germany, France or the United States; this reality transcended capitalism or communism.

The War was longer, more total and more strongly committed to military equipment than the First World War had been. Money was thrown at anything which was needed to win the war. Ordinary industries were militarized – military clothing, aircraft, vehicles, boots, cigarettes, entertainment and food became part of the military machine. As a result the world economy made a move into militarization greater than had ever occurred before, largely immune from price competition. These were industries involving planes, warships, radar, communications, intelligence, aircraft, tanks, shells, bombs, missiles and guns with heavy investment which pumped out new technologies every six months; they needed new factories, research, machine tools, transport systems, raw materials and labour fast; the US Government paid for them. The whole direction of economic development was being changed in a military direction, as a large tanker swings round driven by a small rudder to move through the seas for a long time straight ahead. When a policy is strongly in place for ten years, from 1935 to 1945, it does not easily change course.

An underemphasized part of the picture of the Second World War is the colonial engine of the Nazi munitions industry, because they had now morphed. Occupying territory allowed the arms system to expand in two key ways. First, it could take over, or convert, factories used for munitions and heavy industry in France, Czechoslovakia, Poland, Russia and all the other occupied territory. Skoda, Schneider and other big munitions units became immediately available, or with supervision from I.G. Farben, Krupp and other German companies could be used to make components or other military needs. This meant a rapid, absolute gain for German munitions. Second, forced labour was used on a massive scale, sometimes linked to concentration camps and sometimes by shipping national workers to arms factories where they could be used, and sometimes used up, dead from forced labour. A total number of about 15 million such workers were employed by the Nazi regime during the War under the direction of Todt and then Albert Speer, the real organizational driver of the Nazi regime. They included Italians towards the end of the War. Of course, the implementation of this policy depended on the German munitions companies which each became imperial enterprises directing production throughout the new German Empire. So, the great munitions empire flourished for a few short years parasitic on the intense suffering of millions which we dare not study.

Another part of this pattern was the military take-over of science and academic technology, already underway in the First World War, but now pushed to even higher levels in Britain, Germany, the United States, the USSR and other countries. This was a redirection of world science on an enormous scale. Engineering was for planes, tanks, submarines. Physics was for nuclear weapons and radar. Chemistry was for explosives. Metallurgy was for tanks, guns, the frames of fighters and bombers and armour. Geography was for bombing and planning wars. Earth sciences were concerned with getting or denying access to raw materials. Mathematics was for secrecy and code breaking; everyone knows about Bletchley Park and Alan Turing, but, of course, it was going on everywhere. Statistics were for overall war strategy. The whole direction of science and technology was militarized in the States, Japan, Britain and the USSR. Everywhere scientists were expected to do military research as part of their national duty. For some it might be a matter of conscience, but they could always be shot. Scientists were excused military service, because they were more valuable in the laboratory. The resultant change was so big that we do not notice it; world science is still militarized. Science is not neutral; substantially it is militarized. It is one of the most unacknowledged transitions in scientific history veneered over by the supposed neutrality of science and even technology. Some 750,000 top scientists are still engaged in military-related research. Neutron bombs do not come out of sheds in the bottom of the garden. Arms companies and government defence departments provide money for research. As the Concise Oxford Dictionary says: "boffin *n.esp. Brit.colloq* a person engaged in scientific (esp. military) research. [20th century coinage]" The word seems first to have been used around 1945. Academic science claimed disinterestness and neutrality, but its neutrality *was* military.

Much of this vast militarization stuck as interests clung onto the enterprises, technologies, science, management styles and cultural attitudes they had learned during this period of war. The concrete had been poured and it set, difficult to knock down in 1945, and often to be lived with later.

**The USSR and the Second World War.**

Early in the Second World War the USSR had a non-aggression pact with Germany. This allowed Poland to be partitioned between the two States, but mainly it allowed the USSR to avoid the early years of the war, as did the USA before Pearl Harbour. During this time, the Russian munitions system, aided by a long period of earlier industrial expansion in the coal and steel industries, kicked into huge levels of output, aided by strong central direction of the labour force. Stalin had seen this coming from the early to mid-30s. From September, 1940 the USSR was fairly clear that it was directly in Hitler's sights and moved its factories back into its hinterland in one of the greatest geographical movements of industry in history. In June 1941 the Nazis moved to hit the USSR and the great Barbarossa push on Leningrad, Moscow and the Ukraine began. As Wikipedia notes, it was the largest military operation in human history involving 600,000 motorized military vehicles. There were roughly ten million troops fighting, twenty thousand tanks, fifty thousand military aircraft and perhaps 120,000 field guns. Either side poured newly constructed munitions into the fight furiously, so that we may never know the final numbers. In parentheses we recognize how much ordinary productive output was destroyed in another useless war. For four years the most ferocious confrontation of the Second World War took place on the Eastern Front. Yet in 1941 the USSR had the highest level of munitions output of any of the powers and it remained ahead of Germany until the final frenetic push in 1944. By December, 1941, the Germans were forced to retreat from Moscow. From September, 1942 until February, 1943 the USSR defended Stalingrad, finally successfully, and then fought the Germans in the greatest tank battles of the War. By the end of 1943 the Soviet forces had retaken most of the territory taken in the German offensive and in turn began to move into its own counter-offensive. This part of the Second World War saw vast quantities of munitions used and destroyed. The USSR had been attacked and had fought back heroically with levels of production of tanks, planes and guns greater than Germany, whose commitment to output was complete. Overall Soviet munitions production increased tenfold from $1.6 billion before the War to $16 billion after the War. Given the German invasion these are amazing figures. The USSR had become, of necessity, and par excellence, a militarized economy.

We think of Stalin as a dictator, and Russian militarism as his product, but that may not be the best way of thinking of it. Russian was industrialized into militarism; it never really knew another system of modern industrial production because the five years plans morphed into this great munitions explosion from about 1935. It had to be done. Hitler was not going to cosy up to Communism. The USSR's preparation for war was all-absorbing; it was its industrialization. Mark Harrison estimates that the defence burden in 1943 was 60% of overall government spending and 30% of net material product.[263] Aided by United States' technologies and factory development, these were the outstanding production systems of Europe, better than the German factories. Once these great munitions systems were established, with party people in high paying jobs, they had a momentum of their own and acted just like a western business establishment, protecting their interests and making sure that weapons stayed paramount. This, rather than Stalin, may largely explain the USSR's militarism.

The munitions factories had strong links with the Army, Navy and Air Force who wanted to guarantee that they also grew and flourished. They become what Eisenhower later called the military-industrial establishment. Generals can be told what technologies they need. Scare stories about the opposition can emerge. The compulsive benefits of technological superiority can be advanced. Show, and faked, weapons trials can be carried out. The politicians can be charged with not defending the people. It is the system that grows, and Stalin and the other politicians were partly passengers in the taxi that was being driven by the USSR's military-industrial complex. Stalin had invested in a vast munitions industry, because he knew the USSR would need defending against the Fascist regime in Germany sooner or later. He was not able to dismember this great edifice once the Second World War was over. He had enough reminders of Western antipathy towards the USSR in the presence of Churchill, the nuclear bombs, later in the McCarthyite scare in the States and the slowness of the Allies to open a second front.

Yet, again, no country suffered like Russia in the Second World War. Some twenty five million Russians died, about a third of the total deaths in the War. The British talk about El Alamein, where they faced a few divisions of the German army, but the Russians had about a *hundred and fifty divisions* attacking them. Stalin pleaded with Churchill to open a second front, but from June 1941 until June 1944, apart from Anzio, the Russians faced the overwhelming force of the Germans. Interestingly, in July, 1942, 60,000 people demonstrated in Trafalgar Square to demand that the Allies open a second front to take some of the pressure off the Russians. Ordinary people could see how unfair it was. The Russians carried the weight of the war against the Nazis. Their armies grew. They produced and procured whatever weapons they could and fought against the mighty German advance. They were brutalized by the process, and later were out for the kind of revenge which war breeds and for the absolute end to the possibility of German attack. The great march through Poland and Eastern Germany as the Nazi war machine finally collapsed was a vindication of their great suffering. It was giving the Russian people what they above all deserved in terms of the spoils of war. They too had learned militarism and the relative poverty of the masses would finance it. But primarily the munitions and military establishment would carry on the system that had been built in the late 1930s and 1940s into the post-War era. At the end of every war it is the military who need to be defeated, and usually they are not because they have citadels of power and influence inside the political system. The USSR merely followed this model like everyone else.

**The United States War Machine controls Roosevelt.**

The productive capacity of the United States at this time was enormous, and moreover its munitions industry, already great, expanded exponentially. By now these companies were not novices, but knew exactly what they wanted. They knew of Roosevelt's hostility during the New Deal, and they were not going to have any soft socialist control exercised over them in their munitions output. On the face of it Franklin Delano Roosevelt was the most powerful President the United States has ever had, serving four terms and marking the failure of American capitalism after the Wall Street crash with the New Deal policies for which he is famous. Yet, capitalists have the habit of not being defeated. In 1939-40 when it was clear that the United States needed to move over to a war footing, Roosevelt was defeated by military capitalism. They took control and developed a system of vast profits, grabbing government contracts and making sure that their people ran the show. A few sentences from a study by Cochran convey the euphoria of the munitions people.

> "It was not that Roosevelt wanted to turn the show over to the money changers..The corporation executives and their numerous satellites, who jammed the cocktail bars, hotel dining rooms and reception suites, and entertained with a lavish hand, and who with their elegantly sheathed ladies turned Washington into a composite of Louis XIV's Versailles and San Francisco during the Gold Rush, could and did demand that mobilization took place on their terms. They not only had the country over a barrel, as a government report put it, but with the aid of their press associates, reversed the language of political discourse to their advantage. War mobilization was defined solely in the light of their special interests." [264]

The munitions companies made sure that the Vinson-Tramnell Act which limited their profits was suspended, but they went further. Roosevelt had given way on a whole range of other demands by the munitions companies, but he wanted an excess profits tax which would keep some control on arms' company profits. The munitions companies effectively called a strike in the summer of 1940; they would not produce arms until Roosevelt gave way, and give way he did, so that their bonanza was guaranteed, even if their patriotism was not. Then, in addition, the business community got their people in position for the vast system of military procurement until in 1943-4 half of the American economy was geared to munitions and war. The munitions firms could more or less do what they liked.

Typical, for example, were the "dollar-a-year men". Because government salaries were not high enough many of those who came in to the federal munitions agencies and the Pentagon were paid a nominal dollar a year by government and retained their status and salary with the arms company they came from. If you were *paid* by Boeing and dishing out American arms contracts, which company would you award them to? While working for Government on arms, they were still actually working for the munitions companies from whom they received vast rewards as the contracts were doled out. It was hardly a recipe for independent procurement.[265] The profits went way beyond those directly involved in munitions as the aluminium, steel, rubber, magnesium, copper and lead industries cashed in on wartime demand.[266] The merchants of death were back in business but this time with the label "the merchants of victory".

The people who technically ran the show varied. The control was initially maintained by the military in a variety of boards – the Office of Production Management (OPM), the Office of Price Administration and Civilian Supply (OPACS), the Supply Priorities and Allocation Board (SPAB) and the War Production Board (WPB) but Charles Wilson of General Electric and other military producers and dollar-a-year military men were soon in on the act and the military were profligate in their demands. In his study Gregory Hooks describes Edward Stettinius at OPM as giving "the services an unlimited quantity of forms signed in blank."[267] Fill in what you want and we will pay! They were coteries of businessmen and politicians who gathered round the honey pot, and they inhabited both the Republican and Democratic parties. John Simkin has done careful work on some of them. Tommy Corcoran was one, initially an advisor to Roosevelt. He formed relationships with George and Herman Brown, Alvin Witz, Root McKenzie, Henry Kaiser, Stephen Bechtel, John McCone, John Prescott Bush and other businessmen. They had politicians Sam Raeburn, Lyndon B. Johnson, Albert Thomas and Francis Biddle in their pockets.[268] These businessmen picked up big munitions contracts engineered by Corcoran and others. Many of them were not properly delivered.

New companies came through. The Bechtel-McCone collusion was one of the most interesting in the military-industrial complex. They were given a secret contract for a refinery and pipeline from the Norman Wells oilfields to Alaska. The amount of the contract ballooned from $35 million to $134 million, but the pipeline *never worked* because the pipes were the wrong size and pumping was very expensive. It was abandoned after a year as inoperable, but McCone and Bechtel pocketed the inflated $134 million including a guaranteed 10% profit over "costs". Even better was the McCone-Bechtel factory at Willow Run, Alabama. It is not to be confused with the Ford Willow Run factory in Detroit which turned out thousands of aircraft. This one was a virtual factory that manufactured nothing. Eight thousand employees clocked in every morning to a building somewhere in a field and then went home until they came back in at 5 o'clock to clock out. They were supposed to be making aircraft, but they just forgot to build any. A suit was filed in July, 1943 against Bechtel-McCone, but it turned out that the contract did not specify any actual output to which the company could be held. Though the scam was discovered, Bechtel and McCone were not prosecuted. Later the General Accounting Office told a House Merchant Marine Committee investigation that the company had made $44 million with an investment of $100,000 and that it was paid $2.5 million to take over a shipyard which cost $25 million with materials in it worth $14 million. Read that again.These deals made business success easy. Laton McCarthy estimates that McCone and Bechtel made $100 million profit on an investment of $400,000 during the War, a 25,000% profit.[269] It was like getting someone else to print money for you. Bechtel and

McCone also flourished after the War, especially under Eisenhower when they majored on nuclear weapons. Now there's another lucrative industry. Perhaps they did not bother to build a lot of the nuclear bombs either – we hope we shall never know.

This business success was not unrelated to the fact that McCone became Chairman of the Atomic Energy Commission with a budget of billions and then, surprise, surprise, Director of the CIA between 1961 and 1965. Bechtel became one of the dominant companies in the nuclear weapons' industry. It was an incestuous business - pigs in the armoured trough. Weapons contracts meant vast profits for all of them.[270] Some in Congress tried to uncover the corruption surrounding Corcoran and others, but they could not; enquiries were shelved and sidelined. It was probably the biggest example of munitions and corruption you could find, but it occurred close to the centre of the Federal Government, and the cover-up was easy. Other politicians on the outside went along with the wider system; it was called pork barrel politics. It was your job as a Senator or Congressman to make sure that some good contracts came to your State or district. Then you would get financial support at elections. This pattern was especially strong in Dixieland. Thus the system of contacts with politicians and Federal Government employees, links with defense, business cartels, and so on was in place. The Government paid up and the businesses sometimes got the job done. The military corporate state by the end of the War was super powerful, rich and well placed enough not to be sidelined. Why bother with fascist coups when the system coughed up anyway?

Again, we must face the sheer scale of the transformation. Gerald Nash looks at the way the War completely changed the western United States. His assessment is as follows: "In four short years it accomplished a reshaping of the region's economic life that would have taken more than forty years in peacetime... a vast network of military installations such as army camps and supply depots. The presence of more than three million military personnel...one of the largest was the supply depot at Ogden (in Utah) when they spent $100 million for permanent facilities... the historians of Utah's defense installations have estimated that altogether the federal government spent about $650 million building military facilities in the state during the war. In addition, Congress authorized another $259 million for privately operated defense plants. Of the latter the Geneva Steel works and the Remington Arms Ordnance plant were the largest.. the total effect of these varied scientific complexes was to direct several more billions of dollars into the West..." [271] This militarized economy helped shape the West. Universities depended on military research. Aircraft companies like Consolidated Vultee, Douglas, Lockheed, North American Aviation, Boeing and Northrop majored on military aircraft and the underlying demand for aluminium was military. This, not the Gold Rush, definitively shaped California. Such a vast economic enterprise did not end with the surrender of Japan. Moreover, at the end of the War there was another bonanza. These factories were mainly built by government money and therefore owned by government, but at the end of the War, the Federal Government had no more use for them, and they had to be "sold" off. Actually, they were more or less given away for a pittance by Averell Harriman and others to their industrial and banking friends in another murky operation that has scarcely been examined. It was one of the biggest give-aways in history, easier profits than printing money. Here you are, have a factory – 90% off!

**The American Fascist Connection.**

When I was young and naïve, I though some people won wars and other people lost them. I did not realize that, like bookmakers, there are some people who set out to win whoever wins or loses. And no-where was this more true than in munitions. Since the First World War multi-nationals, mainly American, had developed operating in a lot of different countries. Here we look at the continued contribution to the Nazi War effort made by American multinationals. Partly, they were happy producing for both sides and partly they were Nazi sympathizers. Earlier links with the Nazis continued into the War and posed a continual threat to Roosevelt and indeed to the Allies victory in the War. Roosevelt was fighting two wars – one against the Nazis and Japanese, and another against the capitalist leaders including Ford, Du Pont, Rockefeller, Walter Teagle and William Parish of Standard Oil, New Jersey, Sosthenes Behn of ITT and David Sarnoff of the giant radio Corporation of America. Broadly speaking Ford, Du Pont, General Motors, Chase Bank, New York and Chase National Bank, Standard Oil, ITT and RCA wanted to carry on trading with Hitler and to protect their assets in Nazi-dominated Europe irrespective of the conflict. They were quite prepared to do deals with the Nazis which would continue their world-wide dominance, and the Nazis were also prepared to co-operate provided they got the supplies they needed, and American support of their war effort. This process is documented by Charles Higham in *Trading with the Enemy: An Expose of the Nazi-American Money Plot* (1983). It is clear that this is not conspiracy theory, but what happened, attested in government documents, congress, the press, addressed by members of Roosevelt's Government, and the subject of continual Government tension. The Bank for International Settlements (BIS) presided over by the Nazis Hjalmar Schacht and Emil Puhl smoothed movements of money from the Rockefeller and Morgan banks and helped Hitler used looted gold. It was backed by Montague Norman of the Bank of England who at one stage helped with Nazi looted gold. The Chase National Bank also serviced Nazi dealings from its Paris branch throughout the period of Nazi occupation, so all the payments could flow smoothly. Göring paid $11 million in 1941 for oil from Standard Oil, and the oil continued to flow into 1944, largely under the pretext of supplying Spain, a supposed neutral country, which then passed the precious oil on to Germany. The United States State Department knew this was happening, but because Standard Oil also supplied the US navy and army with oil, and Standard Oil threatened to be awkward, they could not touch them. Through another American, William Davis, Mexican oil was also made available to the Nazis. He set up U-boat refuelling bases throughout the Caribbean. Very convenient. It was surprising they were not allowed to stop off in Miami for a holiday as well.

There were other schemes. I.G. Farben, led by Hermann Schmitz wanted American investment and sales and set up a German-American company. When the War came this firm melted into General Aniline and Film (GAF) which was really still the German company, but with American directors it appeared American. It was not without hutzpah. Among other things the company made Agfa film and offered government spy groups and the U.S. Army film for their information gathering strategic expeditions. They then offered to process the films for the army, keeping their own copies and sending them to Berlin: I spy on my film and you on yours. Repeatedly, Morgenthau tried to get his hands on the half billion dollar assets of GAF, but was thwarted by its American backers. Native American companies were also nice to Hitler. Both Ford and General Motors had good agreements with the Nazis protecting their factories and assets while producing war vehicles for them. Once the Brits bombed a Ford factory in occupied France; they had not realized that you were not supposed to destroy *American assets* producing for the Nazis; Ford decided not to protest and keep that one quiet, but the message was conveyed that certain factories were off-limits. You could not be quite sure during this period who your friends were. Joseph Kennedy, father of John F. and Bobby, was quite happy to scheme with the Germans even while he was United States Ambassador to Britain. That was really bad manners. And, of course, the Windsors were looking to Fascism as well. In summary, both Churchill and Roosevelt throughout the War had a lot of trouble with the Fascist sympathizers around the munitions/banking/ industrial elites of their home countries.

There were key figures in Roosevelt's team including Henry Morgenthau, Harold Ickes, Norman Littell and others who fought this process of collaboration by exposing the companies involved, but often with difficulty. Government Ministers were backing the other side. One example was the Attorney General, Francis Biddle, who was out to sack Littell, and in November, 1944 under pressure Roosevelt had to dismiss him for insubordination because he was exposing the dealings of these companies with the enemy. "The referee has blown the whistle. Well, send him off the field then." As

Higham records, " Just before Roosevelt died, the ailing President asked to see Littell, who recalls that in a charged meeting in the Oval Office he told the young man he would like to have seen Biddle impeached for treason but the difficulties were too great in his grievous physical condition. Littell asked Roosevelt why Biddle, of all people, was a judge at Nuremberg. Roosevelt did not reply."[272] One of the greatest untold stories of the war is the way the dying Roosevelt on principle both strongly resisted these Nazi links, but also when necessary worked with the capitalists prepared to make money from their connections to Hitler, in order to win the War. Sadly by the time he died, they were deeply inside government.

**The Interesting Japanese Military Economy.**

Japan is another powerful example of total wartime militarization, but then, of total de-militarization. In this, it is a beacon of light for disarmament. We have already seen how Japan was introduced to military production by the British and had become a formidable naval power. She trained her army in conjunction with the German military academy, especially through Jakob Meckel and this element in the Japanese Government grew in power, aided by the Zaibatsu companies. There was also strong opposition to militarism within Japan. Kei Hara was chosen as Prime Minister in 1918 with the rallying cry of "militarism is dead." Sadly three years later he was dead, and not militarism. By the 1930s there was a strong and largely dominant militarism in the Japanese State as the Manchuria incident showed. On 15th May, 1932 the Japanese Prime Minister was assassinated by eleven young naval officers and the military eventually assumed total control. Thereafter it became one of the most strongly militarized economies in the world to devastating effect. In an interesting study by Bisson, *Japan's War Economy,* written in 1945 he charts the way the Zaibatsu retained control of the operation of the war right the way through making sure that they were funded for and directed the whole vast munitions project.[273] We have to record that 20 million Chinese died as a result of the Japanese invasion of their country, far and away the heaviest loss of the War excepting the Soviet Union. Further millions died in the Japanese imperial attack trying to dominate eastern Asia. Behind this conquest was an astonishing level of militarization, led of course by the great Zaibatsu corporations. Akira Hara suggests that 87% of central government expenditure in 1944 was military expenditure which amounted to an amazing 57% of GDP.[274]

Given this total case of militarization, even more astonishing is the reverse process. Japan in 1945 was completely forbidden weapons. It had to undertake an intense process of enforced demilitarization. It had suffered a total defeat, albeit of its own making, overwhelming levels of damage and the effects of the two atomic bombs on Hiroshima and Nagasaki, which continued long after the end of the war in deaths and contamination. At the end of the War Japan had no armed forces or munitions and became an entirely civilian economy. Did it suffer from this demilitarization? No. After a few years, by contrast, it flourished. Now it had to make useful things like cameras, ships, motorcycles, consumer durables and cars which it did with consummate designs and high reliability. The post-war recession was deep but by the early 50s the economy was emerging into the highly technical civilian economy which has been such a success in the post-war world.

No country has faced the level of demilitarization faced by Japan at this period, and it shows the way transition to a military free economy, with all its bonuses of resources, manpower and non-military research and technological development can occur with a far stronger economy as a result. Japan had no military, absorbing 3-10% of its income, teaching people to march up and down and manufacturing destruction. Nobody attacked it. As a result it has become one of the richest of the world's economies. Because there were no arms-manufacturing companies, the pressure towards militarism also disappeared, and Japan has been a peaceful and largely peace-seeking country, until the last decade or so, when it has joined the club again. Remember Japan. If Japan could do it after the intense traumas of the Second World War, then the transition can be easy for the rest of us.

**The Problem with Winning.**

Japan, Germany and Italy were required to demilitarize. The problem with the Allied victors and their vast military and munitions machines was that they were not. Never before in the history of the world had such vast military machines existed, especially in the United States, the USSR and Britain. The suggestion here is that the Cold War was mainly caused by the self-perpetuating drive for these vast military machines to continue, not by the ideological differences between East and West. Indeed, we shall see that those ideological differences were exaggerated in order to perpetuate the militarized confrontation between the USSR and the USA. The Cold War was needed to keep the great weapons companies and the military in business. They were prepared to spook us all to hang on to their system of output. But like Japan and Germany we could have become successful peaceful economies.

# Chapter Twenty Three: The Second World War inside our heads.

## Democracy or Propaganda?

During and after the Second World War the victors maintained an exceptional level of propaganda about the war and its meaning. The story was simple and Churchillian. Hitler and the Nazis were evil. Late in the day, just in time, through the heroic warnings of Churchill, we had woken up to the Nazi menace. Hitler conquered Europe and was held at bay during the Battle of Britain by British bravery. Then after Pearl Harbour the United States entered the war, and with the help of Russia, Hitler was defeated and we won, defending democracy for humankind. Then Stalin turned out to be evil, like Hitler, and we needed the Cold War, led by the super-power America, to successfully defend the free world. We must fight for freedom and democracy from strength; that is the only way to see it and if you don't see it that way you may well be a traitor. Every person on the planet was taught this story in one way or another, and it is re-enforced decade after decade.

It contains less than half-truths; let us fill in what is left out. First, for fourteen years after 1918 peace and disarmament could have prevented the Second World War. Second, the arms companies were allowed to reorganize into selling and promoting arms to create chaos first in China and then Spain and Europe. Third, the League of Nations was poorly supported by British Conservative Governments in its attempts to obtain disarmament and peace, and the 1932 Disarmament Conference was severely undermined by Sir John Simon and British coolness towards the United States. Fourth, Hitler, Mussolini, and other Fascist quasi military groups were paid and encouraged by capitalists and munitions companies out to undermine democracy and socialism with state corporatism. Fifth, Hitler and the Nazi Government were largely funded by American financiers so that they could have an armaments-led boom which prepared them for 1939. Sixth, in the East another munitions sponsored Fascist Movement in Japan attacked China and then

Pearl Harbour. This brought the United States into the War, despite the close business ties of the United States both with German and British munitions. Seventh, the USSR bore the brunt of the War, losing 25 million people and fighting single-handed against the main German attack. Eighth, if the Nazi Government could have been prevented from coming to power, a vast and evil cataclysm on all sides empowered by weapons could have been avoided. Eight, the Second World War left us shadowed in the continued militarism of the Cold War for several decades. These points have been forgotten and erased.

When the War was over, the British people were not Churchillian. They voted against the Conservatives and for a Socialist Government which had been thoroughly for peace in the pre-war era and was reasonably friendly to Russia. America had the McCarthyite era, the Red Scare, and was controlled by the Pentagon and the munitions people into a Cold War. The Soviets were cast as the new enemy in an engulfing tide of propaganda, much of it lies, even thought she had been our ally, although Stalin similarly had his own post-war militarism which he did not dismantle. In the longer term the Churchillian and American good guy superpower myth was to rule the world. Meanwhile the United States, the USSR, Britain, France and other countries carried on needless aggression throughout the world. There are some points to debate here, and we are not suggesting that the wartime heroism of the Allies was not real, but it is possible that this account reflects the work of a range of better historians than the self-validating structure of the Churchillian myth, right through he was in addressing the Nazi menace.

**Popular History.**

Popular history is forged in another way than through detailed books. The Second World War was especially taught through films. It was transmitted in schools, but also through comics, toys and films. It is built into events, though personalities, corporate groups, stories, uniforms and through what the establishment wishes to convey. The popular history of the Second

World War was formed in all these ways in an avalanche of popular propaganda. We know it was fought by cheeky chappie working class British soldiers with a cigarette just in their lip and also by an upper class stiff upper lip smoking a pipe. The normal narrative was simply the story that we won; that was the right thing and any deeper lessons were to be ignored. But above all the popular history of the Second World War was constructed to solve the problem we identified earlier. We had to know that all the deaths, all the fighting, was not in vain, was not pointless. And, of course, it was not. Hitler was evil. The Holocaust was an abomination. We were fighting, to use a biblical phrase, "for righteousness sake" so that some measure of good could prevail. There was a point to the war, and to the deaths and injuries of our citizens. That, of course, is true, and will not be gainsaid, certainly not here. This remembrance of the Second World War has integrity and honesty, and the sacrifice of the armed services is to be honoured. Yet, it is the immediate truth, not the full truth. If somebody throws a baby into a swimming pool and it is rescued by an heroic pool-side figure, the full truth is not only the rescue; we should also know that babies should not be thrown into swimming pools. The reality of the hideous deaths, the waste, the numbing of soul, the validation of murder, the long term stupidity of the whole militaristic enterprise pushed by the munitions people – all of these were sublimated in popular history.

War became glorious. In Britain it was the Dambusters, the Battle of Britain, the Bridge on the River Kwai, St Paul's in the Blitz and a pattern of heroism. We had won *for* democracy, decency, the rule of law, moral values, the British way of life, Christian values, and the common humanity of all, by fighting. The dead had given their lives for us. Remembrance Services solemnized the event so that it is still with us, a measure of our democracy and decency. But we were not all decency. Sometimes, we Brits were nasty, smug and inaccurate. We diminished the significance of the USSR and even the United States in the War. *We* won the War. Americans were late in the War, overpaid, oversexed and over here. The USSR, of course, was evil. Our nationalism was the lens through which the Second

World War was to be seen – a slight distain for the French, self-righteousness towards the German people - square-jawed in comics and really all Nazis - and an oblivion towards our own militarism and cruelty. We were the good guys. Kids played with guns, soldiers, bombers, battleships or tanks, and machine gunned one another in playgrounds. The whole process would gradually become sloppily comfortable to us, like well-word slippers, as the War drifted into history and became Dad's Army or 'Allo, 'Allo. Never would the underlying question be asked: Should this war have taken place?

It was justified especially in media fiction. Westerns gave a parable for the War. The Lone Ranger sorted things out every week with a gun for years. John Wayne, Gary Cooper, James Stewart, Robert Mitchum, Rock Hudson, Paul Newman, Burt Lancester, Yul Brynner, Lee Marvin and many others drummed the genre into our heads during the 50s, 60s and 70s. Thought he didn't make it to the top billings, Ronald Reagan's philosophy of life was formed around the Western and the cowboy hat. The good guy sorts out the bad guy with a gun. That's the way it is, folks. Don't ask any more questions.

Of course, for the Germans and Japanese it was more complicated. They had to face the fact that their dead had fought in vain for evil regimes, and they did face these realities. They were wrong and we were right. For us, British, the deeper issue of whether militarism, capitalism and nationalism had generated an unnecessary war was now hidden. Disarmament was unthinkable for most. Churchill, reds under the bed, fear and the word, "Appeasement" answered all questions about the war, and we descended into routine militarism. Defence was necessary. If we could produce better weapons than the others, then we were safe. We had to defend the Commonwealth and the Empire. And the weapons makers were now hidden in and supported by government. The process of procurement became quiet and well-oiled so that ordinary people did not have to think about it anymore. Finally, militarism became patronizing. We are doing this for your good. Now go away and let us get on with it. Don't worry your silly little heads about it; that's our job. They were the professionals. The job of the voters was just to support them and avoid another war through appeasement.

**Films in our head.**

Probably most people think about the Second World War through films. They have been a great war industry. If we look at the Second World War films alone, separating us from questioning war in terms of the understanding in the twenties and thirties, we face an avalanche. The Dam Busters, Cruel Sea, Bridge on the River Kwai, Saving Sergeant Ryan, Casablanca, Dirty Dozen, The Eagle has Landed, The Longest Day, Pearl Harbour, Schindler's List, Where Eagles Dare, Midway and hundreds of other films are stitched into our brains. Indeed, this visual history is so powerful and so fully with us that it is worth looking at a list of the number of films about World War Two produced in each decade since it occurred.

**Number of films about the Second World War.**[275]

| | |
|---|---|
| **1940s** | **286** |
| **1950s** | **214** |
| **1960s** | **216** |
| **1970s** | **127** |
| **1980s** | **113** |
| **1990s** | **87** |
| **2000s** | **174** |
| **Total** | **1217** |

This vast output conditions our minds and the number of war films has not abated, especially recently. They focus on action, killing, suspense, heroism, espionage, loyalty, friendship, victory, defeat, tragedies, conflicts, and address a lot of important issues, but none of them seems to focus on munitions and the people who make the weapons. War and arms usually have to be presumed, because the war is already underway. The munitions people drop from our awareness. After 1937 or so, they are just the good guys, making Spitfires. The result of this vast media bombardment, backed up by TV output, is to push more strategic and ultimate questions out of our mind. The War is a given. When we see weapons, they are validated by the war which is already going on. We dwell with the horror of large-scale war, often with a sense of intellectual helplessness, but that never allows the background question to be addressed: Did these weapons and the businesses behind them precipitate the War and the millions of dead? "What? Remember Hitler."

**Toeing the Line.**

The result of this intense period of required loyalty to the idea of war was an incredible level of conformism to seeing war as necessary. Everything was involved. To question it was to question our armed forces and the sacrifices they had made. To question war and militarism was to fly in the face of Churchill, the greatest Briton, and the argument he had won for ever at the time of Chamberlain and Munich and then at the Battle of Britain. It was to challenge the history of Britain which was formed by Nelson, Wellington, Clive, Montgomery, Bomber Harris and the Few of the Battle of Britain. Everyone, except a few eccentrics like Donald Soper and Bertie Russell moved over to sanction military strength, a belief in developing superior weapons, and the need for defence as the first call on the government's budget. On the whole, the Church of England remained the established supporter of the military, with military chaplains, military services, regimental flags in churches and an inability to challenge any military adventure the Government might undertake except in muted terms. Universities questioned nothing until a Peace Studies programme was set up in 1973 at Bradford University, nearly 30 years after the end of the Second World War. Politicians were scared of being seen as disloyal if they challenged anything of the military establishment. So the whole structure was in place with powerful psychological pressure to conform. Anti- nuclear movements were seen as (vain) protesters against an establishment, fit only to be carted off to prison for a night to cool off.

This has not yet gone. Sometimes it seems that we still do not have the emotional space to think beyond accepting war as normal. We have seen so much war that it has become domesticated, part of our lives, we live with it. We expect another James Bond movie. He will win. He brings the Queen to the Olympics. We have media-viewed the War without participating. Even the most violent scenes of war are screened in our minds. The blood is never real. We will not be called up to fight. Mentally, we have handed over to Jack Hawkins, James Stewart, Humphrey Bogart and the boys, and we know that we won, and so we do not need to question war any more. There are computer war games that millions of boys play, thinking instinctual, rapid killing and fighting. Kids handle toy guns as a normal part of growing up. Most people's mental equipment does not allow weapons and war to be questioned. This mindset, this brainwashing, we all live in, holding us from really considering the disarmament of the world. Since 1945 it has lasted another seventy years undiminished in popular culture with war gaming, films and media reporting of the necessity of fighting.

**The Permanently Armed World System?**

My life, like billions of others, has been lived totally in the permanently armed world system. By and large we have not been allowed to question it, to consider whether there is another way. Over the full span something like two hundred million war-related deaths have occurred, and the horrors we have looked at have continued right down to the present. It is the longest failed experiment in modern history, still held in place by half-baked arguments and self-righteous patterns of blame. But really it is held in place by the agenda of the arms companies, and their need to sell weapons world-wide to countries who imbibe the mantra that arms guarantee peace. The world had become enthralled to the direction which was charted by Krupp, Armstrong, Vickers, Skoda and the other arms companies. They set out to arm the world and the politicians were not principled and canny enough to prevent their agenda from ruling. By 1945 the system was so strong that it continued under its own momentum, even with the end of the Second World War.

In the next two volumes we consider these years, marked by their own wars, international tensions and patterns of blame, and consider how this nonsense holds sway over us. Yet, it need not. It can change. The way of peace and disarmament is open before us in a crowded, interdependent planet where wars and terrorism are even more senseless. It requires a plan of world disarmament which is clear, and sees the job which was not done in 1932 through to the end with wisdom and the ability to defeat the agendas of the militarists. There is the iron condition which the Bible supplies. Swords must be turned into ploughshares and spears into pruning hooks, so that *we learn war no more*. The plan would require, say, a 10% cut a year in all militaries for a decade, carefully policed by the UN, until all national armies are gone. We look at this more thoroughly in the second book *War to Peace.* We could, with principled wisdom and a commitment to peace and mutual justice close down this vast waste of life and resources in a decade, so that nation speaks peace unto nation and neither is there war any more. Jesus said, after the resurrection, "My peace I leave with you." It is with us and it is not difficult to work and rest in it. It is time we recognized that peace is never *against* any one. Peace is easier than war. With God's help, peace is with us *and* them. It does not allow the construction of enemies, so that a vast industry may prosper by selling the instruments of death. The possibility is open to us. So let us do it. We each sign up for gentle peace throughout the earth by the ordered elimination weapons to shake hands and never point weapons.

## THE SHORT VERSION: WAR OR PEACE?

## -THE LONG FAILURE of WESTERN ARMS

**Volume One: Manufacturing the First World War.**

(This is a heavily shortened version of the text of book one of *War or Peace?* and is here to give you a feeling for the book's fuller argument. Obviously, such a précis has to exclude most of the historical evidence.)

Wars come round like winter. They have led to the death of about two hundred million people in the last hundred years and a similar number of serious injuries – say a tenth of the world population in the twentieth century. We have been conditioned to be fatalistic towards them. The 1914 War, the War to End all Wars, resulted in millions horribly killed and maimed, and widows and statesmen determined to end this horror. They tried, but after a decade and a bit they failed, and since then we have accepted that war is more or less inevitable. Year after year new ones arrive. But humanity produces wars, and perhaps the time has come to review and rethink our military history. We arm, but seldom pull back to consider whether all of this is necessary and why it has happened.

Yet, wars can be understood; they have human causes. Perhaps we can learn from history and the other resources available to us. We manufacture and go to war, but 2014-2018 is a pertinent time to think about the treadmill we have been on since a century ago when the whole world first went to war. Here we consider why wars have happened so often in the modern era, and especially look at one cause of war which was perceived by many statesmen, historians and military people to be the key a century ago. We may, especially if we open up ignored parts of our history, be able to see where we have gone wrong and address it. To carry out this review we need to stand back and see the big picture over a hundred and fifty years – that is why this book is long. War has been the biggest mistake in world history and we need to end it in our crowded, interdependent world as humankind grows to ten billion people. We have had enough sorrow and mourning, and we can do better.

**1. Modern Militarism.**

Conflict has often been shaped by weaponry in human history. Chariots, cavalry, gunpowder, muskets, swords, longbows, cannon and other weapons have shaped eras of world history. War was always motivated by greed, revenge, the hope of political power and the desire to control and enslave, but these motives are further empowered by weapons. In the modern era there has been a new driving force - the industrial production, sale and promotion of arms - and it has changed the impetus towards war. A soldier in hand to hand fighting is different from one with a machine gun mowing down troops. Modern warfare is dominated by technical weaponry, and a new breed of industrial companies have made, marketed and sold these weapons as guaranteeing military success. Great arms companies have grown; they needed a good war every five or ten years. By and large, they got them. They were, and are, avid proponents of militarism and - although they do not publicise it - war. In the nineteenth century Armstrong, Krupp, Schneider, Skoda, BSA, Vickers and other companies spread militarism by selling weapons, training armies, bribing and initiating scares. They sold weapons to anyone, but normally to the top politicians and military people, and set out to arm state after state to fight wars and trained them to use their weapons. Now that kind of militarism is world-wide and accepted as normal.

**2. The Messages of Power.**

This process was no mere accident, but the deliberate accumulation of power of the arms manufacturers. A set of seductive messages were sent out. Weapons meant you could win wars. Arms gave you peace and security. [Slight contradiction there.] The status of every state was ranked by its military power. [Still, the five countries with the largest military expenditures are the permanent members of the UN Security Council, except France has just moved down to sixth below Japan.] If your neighbour was arming you could not trust him. You must more powerful than all of your neighbours to protect your people. [Another munitions win-win.] New arms technologies were the way forward and would always win wars. National patriotism was embodied in the military.

Even though these messages often failed or produced catastrophe, they were kept in place through dogma, induced fear, scares, misrepresenting opposition as enemies, political influence, control of the media and scape-goating opponents. Arms companies controlled newspapers and set up pressure groups. If a country was not afraid of war, its neighbours could be armed. These dogmas spread and were absorbed by politicians who became puppets of the arms companies' agenda, especially after 1870. Like Bernard Shaw's fictional arms manufacturer, Mr Undershaft, they paid the piper and called the tune.

**3. The War Habit.**

In the late 19th century wars became a habit. British weapons won colonial wars to extend the Empire. France, Germany, Belgium, Spain and America also looked to empire. American companies manufactured guns to shoot the Indians. The Crimean War (1853-56) was the first European War when firing weapons – rifles and cannon – obviously got the better of horse and sword. The American Civil War (1861-5) involved American citizens shooting one another; about three quarters of a million died. These and other wars produced a bonanza of arms sales for these developing companies in America and Europe. In 1870 Krupp's cannon were decisive in the Franco-German War. Gradually there grew a collusion between the arms manufacturers and the state. You pay us and we will win your wars – Krupp and the Kaiser, Armstrong and British Naval Supremacy, and Schneider-Le Creusot had this kind of relationship with the French Government.

But these companies also exported. Armstrong gave the Japanese a navy from the Tyne and in 1904-5 they defeated Russia, who then sought weapons from France and Britain, so both Japan and Russia militarised. Insidiously, weapons were spreading the habit of war across the world.

**4. The Arms Companies steer the politicians.**

The arms companies began to shape political responses. They pushed for military expansion, ran scares, bribed leaders to buy weapons, pushed new technologies, organising competitive arming and operated inside politics. Around 1890 the major countries of Europe began competitively arming. They had the habit of empire, achieved by mowing down natives and establishing control. This came to be seen as a European right, aided by weapons. Soon the arms companies were in the ascendency. The Cabinet got rid of Gladstone in 1993 when he was opposed to more naval spending. Sir John Fisher was later removed as First Sea Lord when he did not order enough battleships. An arms manufacturer, Mulliner, fabricated false stories of German arms expansion, eventually provoking a public scare around the slogan, "We want eight (Dreadnoughts) and we won't wait." The growth of arms fostered by the arms companies, and the militarily-created mistrust among European states, became the dominant impetus towards the Great War, the First World War.

**5. The Defeat of Peace.**

In the late 19th century there were a variety of peace movements, often Christian ones drawing on the Anabaptist tradition. They became more articulate, especially when Leo Tolstoy became their clearest advocate. He and others pointed out that mass murder could not be legitimised by war, that soldiers obeying orders to kill were being trained into barbarism, that Europe was wasting vast amounts on soldiers and weapons, and that political leaders like the Kaiser were vain and unprincipled, using militarism to subdue ordinary people and claim unlimited loyalty. It was a devastating attack which had a lot of effect. In the 1890s some Christians called Doukhobors were called to serve in the Russian army. Instead of doing what they were told, they made a bonfire of their weapons and had a party. They were killed and persecuted by the Tsar, but many of them migrated to Canada with Tolstoy's help.

As a result of this pressure an International Peace Conference was called in the Hague in 1899 by the Tsar, whose conscience was possibly affected by Tolstoy and the Doukhobors, to discuss disarmament and peace. The Conference established the Red Cross and principles of decency in war but did not get far on world disarmament, partly because Britain was gearing up for another Boer War at the time. Other later Peace Conferences were weakened by the arms companies and military. In the end, whipping up antagonistic patriotic fervour was able to defeat moves for trust and peace and hasten the Great War. In this War Austro-Hungary was the enemy of Serbia. Russia was the enemy of Austro-Hungary and the friend of Serbia. France was the friend of Russia and the enemy of Austro-Hungary. Germany was the friend of Austro-Hungary and the enemy of Russia and so it went on. We learned, as the arms manufacturers had taught us, to find human enemies and lose the ability to think peace. Arms production expanded out of control and a World War followed.

**6. The Great War Comes.**

After the event, most of the statesmen of the era saw the build-up of weapons as the major cause of the Great War. In the three decades before 1914 arms expenditure by the great powers grew at about 10% a year. Lord Grey, British Secretary of State for Foreign Affairs between 1905-15 put it thus: "The moral is obvious; it is that great armaments lead inevitably to war." There were four arms races going on in the decade before 1914 fuelled by the arms companies – the British-German naval race, the French-German armies, the German-Russian armies, and the east European confrontations involving Russia, Turkey, Austro-Hungary and Serbia. One of them, the last as it happened, was going to trigger a war. Even the row between Austro-Hungary and Serbia which immediately started the War centred on the Skoda Arms company trying to push an arms deal on Serbia. The evidence for the arms companies as the major architects of the War was accepted by most people. After the horrors of the trenches, they sought to make it the

War to End All Wars. A strong disarmament movement started addressing the munitions industry - the merchants of death.

But the arms manufacturers had become powerful. The munitions companies win in every war. The Great War had several effects apart from devastating Europe with tens of millions of deaths and injuries.

1. It pushed military spending up from about 2-3% to about 25% of total European expenditure.
2. It created bonanza time for the arms producers who expanded, made big profits and became even more dominant.
3. It was financed by loans which sent the German economy crazy after the War and left Britain and France in deep debt to the United States.
4. It made the United States into the major world arms producer with companies like Du Pont and Remington pouring arms into Europe.
5. It brutalized Russia and Germany who both lost, facing internal chaos.
6. It caused the Russian Revolution and continued wars through 1919 in eastern Europe.
7. It created economic devastation, malnutrition and an horrific flu pandemic killing some further 50 million people.
8. It birthed Fascism.
9. It wasted a trillion man-hours of work and destroyed an inestimable amount of resources, property and capital.

All wars strengthen the arms companies, and the end of the Great War left a lot of very rich munitions companies facing an acute recession in their industry. . .

**7. The War to end all Wars.**

In 1918 people and statesmen were appalled that a generation of the young in Europe and elsewhere had been murdered in warfare. They wanted to end war and the accumulation of weapons by systematic international disarmament.

These principles were written into the Treaty of Versailles and were meant to be carried out by all nations in the League of Nations. President Wilson saw the kind of change of principle needed to defeat the old order of militarism, and with Lord Cecil and others led a crusade to implement it. He was undermined by the militarists back home, and the United States withdrew from the League of Nations. They also organised a "red scare" against socialism. The Treaty of Versailles punished Germany and levied heavy reparations to pay some of the costs of the French and British wars. After the War there was suffering, family breakdown and economic chaos, but gradually the world tried to address the evil it had created. A generation of statesmen worked for world disarmament - to end military distrust and war, and to sort disputes through the League of Nations throughout the twenties and into the thirties.

**Part Two: Pulling the Strings of Fascism.**

**8. The Defeat of Disarmament and Peace.**

The major countries of the world, including the USSR, worked towards disarmament in a conference in Geneva in 1926 and then in 1932. By the time of the great January 1932 Geneva Disarmament Conference half the population of the world through various groups and agencies had petitioned for world disarmament. A strong disarmament package proposed by President Hoover was backed by most of the states of the world including the USSR. If it had been accepted, it is highly likely that Hitler would not have come to power. But it, and other proposals, became mired in detailed discussion among military personnel and those against disarmament. The arms companies sent agents along to the 1926 and 1932 Conferences to disrupt them by rumour and misinformation. Japan invading Manchuria and that war was fermented by western arms sales. The British and French military, and the British Conservative Party, were obstacles to an otherwise overwhelming world movement for disarmament. Roosevelt could not rescue it. Disarmament was defeated and the militarists won.

Hitler came to power in January, 1933, a process which a successful Geneva Conference in 1932 would have prevented.

**9. Fascism as the Creation of the Arms Companies.**

There was another thread in this story. After the Great War arms manufacturers were out of favour and out of work. Their industries went into recession. The companies, still rich, needed a way of getting militarism back into politics. Fascism is a wicked ideology involving a crude faith in a leader and strong racist, military and nationalist appeals. Usually we focus on the political leaders but ignore the factor that strengthened their hand. After the Great War brutalised soldiers were often out of work. The arms companies paid them to beat up socialists and create mayhem, strengthening the need for the military. Thus, Fascism was substantially funded and encouraged by the munitions' people.

It began in the Great War with Mussolini, who converted from Socialism to a rabid frog-marching nationalism on being given funds by Ansaldo, the Italian arms firm intent on keeping Italy in the First World War. He came to power in 1922.

In Japan the Japanese mega-companies, the Zaibatsu, took over from Armstrong and Vickers as the arms and naval companies, and they, with the military, came to shape an out-of-control military regime, a Fascist state and the defeat of democracy.

In Germany Hitler was supported by Thyssen of the massive steel and arms conglomerate and by Henry Ford, who was anti-semitic. They and others paid for the storm-trooper thugs to disrupt democracy long before he was close to power. Later other arms companies came on board. So the power of Fascism was fed by munitions' money and equipment which financed thugs on the streets. Often the thugs were ex-soldiers, maddened by the Great War. It was this backing which gave Hitler even the chance of success.

**10. British and American Fascism.**

British arms companies had less power after the Great War partly because Lloyd George kept careful control of their profits during the War. As a result, British Fascism was weaker and centred more on the rich aristocracy. Nevertheless, Mosley and others had influence.

In the United States four trends took place. American financiers, especially the Harriman Bank, with Prescott Bush as a key figure, financed Thyssen and other German companies sympathetic to Fascism; they were secondary funders of the Nazi movement. Second, after the Wall Street Crash many big companies including Ford equipped the USSR with the most modern tank and aircraft factories in exchange for gold. The USA militarized the USSR, seemingly with few ideological problems. Third, once Hitler came to power American companies and banks poured resources into Germany as it re-armed, allowing it to move from a largely unarmed depressed state in 1932 to a world military power in 1939. Fourth, Du Pont and other right wing companies tried to organize an American Fascist coup in 1934 to topple Roosevelt. It was foiled by General Smedley Butler, and Roosevelt was able to keep the Du Ponts away from political power. Nevertheless, American money strongly backed Nazi re-armament, and Prescott Bush was still funding them when Pearl Harbour was attacked.

**11. Too late...**

In the mid 1930s there were several developments which showed the public the power of the arms companies. The book, *The Merchants of Death* by Englebrecht and Hanighen (1934) exposed the power and manipulation of the arms companies leading to the Great War. Philip Noel Baker's *The Private Manufacture of Arms* (1936) was a similar work showing the way they had run events. The Nye Commission in the States exposed the dealings of the American arms companies and how much they had made out of war contracts. In 1935, in a Peace Ballot in the UK, over 90% of the eleven million respondents voted for the abolition of arms manufacture for profit and for disarmament. Yet all these moves against arms companies and re-armament were too late as money and resources poured into the Nazi regime and worldwide rearmament. Again, great armaments were leading inevitably to another World War.

**12. The Second World War.**

The Second World War was the greatest triumph for the arms producers ever. The world economy was focussed on their industry. This time military expenditure ratcheted up to 40% or more of GDP over much of the globe and weapons' manufacture became the world's biggest industry by far. The USSR was industrialised on arms manufacture and carried the greatest weight of the brutalising conflict, losing 25 million people. The United States became a gigantic war machine and the arms companies were back inside government, determined never to be dislodged. In Britain, France, Germany, Japan and many other countries weapons' manufacture dominated the economy alongside fighting. Another raft of new weapons arrived – fighters, bombers, tanks, radar, missiles, aircraft carriers and finally nuclear weapons. The War was, we hope, the biggest waste in history, killing some 60 million people directly, and 25 million more through war induced famine and sickness/ It injured a similar number. It involved 100 million troops and wasted perhaps 14 trillion work hours and cost tens of trillions of dollars. Expressed another way, let us say it wasted twenty years of world economic development. By 1945 the military-industrial complexes were in control in the United States, the USSR, Britain, France and the other allied countries. They were destroyed in Germany and Japan. The Western arms companies learned from their exposure as the "merchants of death" to be political insiders and operate quietly behind the scenes within government; they have stayed that way ever since. They also wrapped themselves and their enterprise in unquestioning patriotism.

**13. The Permanently Armed World.**

In 1945 because the Western and USSR militaries and arms companies had become insiders to government, they were able to perpetuate an armed state, partly by creating the Cold War, and partly by picking up the business of selling weapons worldwide until other wars and areas of conflict built up. Sadly, most populations had become so inured the war and the idea of defence, that the permanent armed world became normal creating continual tension and wars and establishing the biggest waste on the planet. This is examined in parts 3 and 4.

Yet, disarmament and peace is waiting to happen as it was before both World Wars. It would have been eminently sensible, saving tens of billions of wasted years of work and trillions of damage. Peace is not an ideal, but practical and sensible compared with the devastating mess of war after war. It is a beatitude, good for us, and the agenda of swords into ploughshares needs us first to see clearly the way the makers of arms have operated and the spiritual fight needed to address them.

**Postscript.**

This book was written merely because someone had to do it; no-one has painted the long historical picture of arms-led militarism and held it up to question for about seven decades. The issue of why we arm and whether it makes sense has been closed down by the military/ industrial/ political establishments who want to presume it is necessary. But it is not. Gradually, the insanity of the whole enterprise pushed by the munitions people has opened up. These two books merely organize that material further without assuming the innate reasonableness of militarism, war and mass slaughter - assumptions which have sat over the west since 1945. It tries to decontaminate our thinking. The conclusions do not even seem controversial once the matter has been given some thought. I give apologies that the material centres on the British and American myths of militarism; that partly reflects the linguistic base of the author, but perhaps also identifies the stronghold of this myth in its world-wide formation. There are further levels of analysis of the formation of militarism through arms companies which these studies do not cover. This research and writing has not depended on any external funding or institutional links.

A number of people have personally oriented me to the issue over the years. They include - my parents, Alec and Doris, and as I now realize, my uncles, Jim, Will, Eric, John and John. Paul Blake at the CNS, Philip Noel-Baker, Charles Raven, Joan Robinson, Bob Goudzwaard, David Alton, John Stott, Bruce Kent, Alan Kreider, friends in the Movement for Christian Democracy and Thinknet people. Ron Clements, Bill Pickering, David Evans, Bruce Wearne and Jock Stein all helped more recently. Warm thanks to them, especially to Ron. There are also many other peacemongers in the public square from whom I've learned much over the years. My deepest debts in relation to the theme are to Leo Tolstoy in his later writings, whom I also thank, and centrally, of course, to the life and teachings of Christ. He is the world's greatest teacher, and more, and the book really just unpicks his one sentence of warning, "Those who take the sword, perish by the sword." Elaine, my wife, has been with it all, has encouraged, critiqued and edited the writing, been patient, given the space, and suggested important improvements - a massive for better contribution.

The library work has been mainly at Cambridge University Library, down the Footpath, and I thank the staff there. There are important background dependencies on Wikipedia, BBC Radio News and *The Guardian* for decades of reporting and Neville Williams, Philip Waller and John Rowatt's *Chronology of the Twentieth Century* for checking dates. The book, of course, depends on the work of hundreds of other people not directly acknowledged and is highly unoriginal. The time has come for the role of munitions to be out in the open, and the West's craven acceptance of militarism to be challenged, as it is by all kinds of groups, and this is a contribution to their case.

Others have tackled aspects of the issue of war or peace more directly, with far greater courage, and have given their lives for peace. It would therefore be invidious to say more about this contribution, except to hope it further opens the world's journey towards disarmament and peace on God's good terms.

Alan Storkey, Coton, Cambridge 2015.

## WAR TO PEACE. Book Two: The Fully Armed World System and its Downfall.

**PART VIII. ENSURING THE MILITARY SUCCESSION.**

24. Victory and Defeat for Peace.
25. We need a Cold War.
26. The American Military Establishment.
27. The Tragic Korean War.

**PART IX. WEAPONS DO NOT WORK.**

28. The Rise and Fall of Chemical Weapons.
29. The Rise and Fall of Nuclear Weapons.
30. Missiles – from Rockets to Star Wars.
31. The United States teaches the world terrorism – the three pronged attack.

**Part X. THE SYSTEM IN PLACE: THE ARMS ESTABLISHMENT.**

32. Eisenhower and the Military-Industrial Complex.
33. The Great Colonial Debacle.
34. Kennedy, Johnson, Nixon and the Vietnam mistake - oops.

**Part XI. UNASSAILABLE DOMINANCE?**

35. Getting rid of a President - Carter has to go.
36. Thatcher, the Falklands and British Aerospace Corruption.
37. Reagan and the Arms Mafia.
38. The USSR Military-Industrial collapse and the end of the Cold War.

**Part XII. AFTER THE COLD WAR: MANUFACTURING ENEMIES.**

39. Keeping in Business: The First Iraq War.
40. The Clinton Interlude and a bit of Ethics.
41. George W. Bush and the Afghan War.
42. We need another War against Eyraq

43. A look at Western Institutionalised Militarism
44. Backing a Losing Streak.

**Part XIII. LEARNING FROM HISTORY.**

45. Re-viewing our History
46. The Honour of the Military and the Stupidity of Militarism.

**Part XIV. CHRISTIANITY AND MILITARISM.**

47. Christianity and Militarism.
48. The Old Testament – Swords into Ploughshares.
49. The Rock Solid Peace of Jesus Christ.

**PART XV. WE CAN DISARM THE WORLD.**

50. The Time has Come: Closing down the Military-Industrial Complex.
51. We can Disarm the World and live in Peace.

# Chronology.

(Wars and Aggression in bold. Peace in Italics.)

**1820s. Little warfare in Europe outside Greece after long Napoleonic wars. Craft industries making guns and swords cut back after the sixteen years of European war. Ottoman Empire weakens. Spain and Portugal lose colonies and face internal collapse. Britain carries on accumulating colonies and industrialises around railways, cotton etc..**

**1820-22 Ecudorian War of Independence against Spain.**
**1821-9 Spanish attempt reconquest of Mexico and Cuba, but fail. Mexico independent.**
**1821-32 Greek War of Independence. Massacres on both sides.**
**1821-3 Ottoman-Persian (Iran) War.**
**1822 – February to 1823 November Brazilian War of Independence from Portugal.**
**1823-31 First Anglo-Ashanti War. British attack Ashantis from the Cape.** *In 1831 Sha River accepted as border.*
1824 **British attack Burma.**
1825 **26/12 December revolt in Russia against new Tsar Nicholas I.**
**1825-30 Java War between Dutch and Prince Diponegoro. 200,000 die. Dutch win.**
1826 Ten year old Alfried Krupp becomes head of failing Essen works.
1827 **20/10 Battle of Navarino in Greek war of Independence. British, French, Russians against Turkish fleet.**
1828 Firm of Naylor, Hutchinson, Vickers and Company comes into being in steel production
1828-34 **Portuguese Civil War.**

**1830s. Industrialisation in Britain ahead of most other countries in Europe. Reform in Europe with a series of revolutions against autocratic regimes. European industrialisation gets underway. Colonial conquests. United States wars with the Indian Tribes as immigrants head west. Ottoman Empire weak. Beginnings of industrial arms production.**

1830 **July Revolution in France replaces Charles X with constitutional monarchy of Louis Phillippe.**

1830 25/8 Belgium breaks from Kingdom of the Netherlands. Establishes independence.

1830 **29/11 Polish November Uprising in Warsaw against Russia crushed by Russian Imperial Army.**

1831 Royal Enfield Small Arms Factory threatened with closure.

**1830-47 French conquest of Algeria from Ottoman control.**

**1831-2 Baptist war in Jamaica. 60,000 mainly Baptist slaves led by pastor to rebel seeking emancipation. Brutally put down by plantation owners. Emancipation in 1833.**

**1831-3 Ottoman-Egyptian War for Syria. Ottomans defeated..**

**1833-9 Civil War in Spain.**

**1834-6 Britain fights Xhosa, murders Chief Hintsa.**

1835 Samuel Colt's revolver patented.

1836 Schneider-Le Creusot munitions company founded.

1838 Alfried Krupp goes to Sheffield to find out how to make good steel.

**1838 Battle of Blood River between Boers and Zulus.**

1839 27/3 British opium supplies confiscated in China.

**1839 July. Beginning of Opium Wars.**

**1840s. US WARS WITH INDIAN TRIBES. COLONIAL WARS. OPIUM WAR. 1848 Revolutions. European Conservatives want weapons to put down rebellions. Railway expansion increases demand for iron and steel.**

1840 Ernst Benzon becomes agent for Vickers.

1840 **June. British Indian Army arrives in China to start Opium War. Modern muskets and cannon defeat Chinese.**

1843 Treaty of Nanking. China pays indemnity to Britain, cedes Hong Kong for 150 years and opens four ports to Britain.

1843-6 **New Zealand Land Wars as settlers take land from Maoris.**

1845-6 **British East India Company wars against Sikhs.** Partial subjugation of Punjab.

1846-8 **United States invasion of Mexico. Mexico cedes** New Mexico and California.

1847 Prussia receives first Krupp steel cannon.

1848 20/3 Polish uprising against Russian and Prussian control.

1848 French Revolution. Paris uprising against Conservatives who had overthrown Louis Philippe. Universal suffrage 2/3. Economic difficulties. Louis Napoleon III comes to power Second Empire.

1848 March. Uprisings in Prussia, Baden, Palatinate for more liberal regimes.

1848 24/7 Italian uprising against Austrian control. Squashed.

1848 Austro-Hungarian Hapsburg Empire has revolution and counter-revolution.

1849 →**United States - Apache wars.**

**1850s. First steel industrial cannon come onto world market. Armstrong and Krupp get going. TAIPING REBELLION – CHINESE CIVIL WAR 20-30 MILLION DIE. CRIMEAN WAR and other wars open up demand for weapons. First moves to iron ships. Birmingham and other weapons centres flourish.**

**1850-64 TAIPING REBELLION. Chinese Civil War. Lead by Hong Xiuquan, copied west, rich, dissolute. 20-30 million die. European arms companies supply weapons. Krupp gets going on cannon. Bessemer steel starts.**

1850-52 Eighth Xhosa War. British led by inept Governor Sir Harry Smith.

1851 Massive Krupp steel ingot at Crystal Palace exhibition.

1852 Anglo-Burmese War British East India Company takeover.

1853 July. Tsar Nicholas sends troops into Ottoman-Empire controlled Moldavia and Wallachia.

1853 United States enforces commercial treaty on Japan with warships.

1854-6 **CRIMEAN WAR. High demand for weapons. Defeat for cavalry by musket fire. 500,000 die.**

1854 25/10 Charge of the Light Brigade. Later "Thin Red Line" routed Russian Cavalry charge. Superiority of musket over cavalry charge twice shown.

1854 December. Sebastopol deaths described by Tolstoy.

1854 Over the next decade 4 million gun barrels were proved in Birmingham.

1855 Paris World Exhibition.

1855 Armstrong produces first breech-loading cannon.

1856 **END OF CRIMEAN WAR.**

**1854-73 Miao rebellion against Qing Dynasty 4 million deaths.**

1856 Bessemer steel.
1856 Krupp gets order for 200 cannon from Egypt.
1856-1860 **SECOND OPIUM WAR.** Armstrong cannon used. Anglo-French against China.
1857 American railway crisis.
1957 5/11 Naylor, Vickers suspends payments
1858 French launch La Gloire – iron plates on wooden hull.
1858 Armstrong wins cannon competition over Whitworth.
1858 Remington 1858 revolver would become one of the main weapons in the American Civil War.
1859 Armstrong enters employ of Government. Knighted.
1859 Skoda works founded by Waldstein family.
1859 January Krupp gets order of 300 cannon from Wilhelm I of Prussia.

**1860s AMERICAN CIVIL WAR promotes European munitions exports and leads to big changes in weapons technology in the States. Allows more continual weapons manufacture. Armstrong established at Elswick making cannon. Breech-loading guns. Vickers get going. Austro-Prussian War begins to show dominance of steel cannon. Birmingham Small Arms world leader. Clear world domination by western industrial arms.**

1860 Britain launched HMS Warrior an iron hulled ship.
1860 **END OF OPIUM WAR.**
1861-65 **AMERICAN CIVIL WAR. Munitions technology developed rapidly. Ironclads. Rifled cannon. Minié ball. Repeating weapons. Colt. Remington. Smith and Wesson. Springfield and Enfield Rifles. Gatling Gun. Imports from Europe. One million died.**
1861 Springfield Model 1961 most widely used rifle in American Civil War, followed by Enfield 1853.
1861-5 Birmingham sends 800,000 guns to American Civil War. Arms both sides.
1862 Krupp opens Bessemer Steel furnace.
1862 October. Elswick Government gun contracts terminated. Armstrong moves over to working at Elswick permanently.
1862-3 British Government approaches Krupp to buy guns when Armstrong deal becomes complicated.

1863 BSA sell 50,000 rifles to Ottoman Empire.
1863 Armstrong gun used extensively in New Zealand Wars.
1863 TNT invented by German chemist, Julius Wilbrand, to be used as a dye..
1864 Geneva Convention addressed treatment of the wounded and captured. Henri Dunant and Gustave Moynier.
1864 Japan intimidated by combined British, French, Dutch fleet.
1864 Armstrong selling guns to Italy. Armstrong provides weapons for Egypt, Spain, Turkey.
1865 British began using breech-loading rifles.
1865 **END OF AMERICAN CIVIL WAR.**
1865 Krupp supplies artillery to Austro-Hungary.
1866 **PRUSSIAN WAR AGAINST AUSTRO-HUNGARY. Attacked by Krupp cannon.**
1864-70 Weapons exports encourage War of Triple Alliance agianst Paraguay.
1866 Von Roon tries not to get Krupp to sell guns to Bavaria.
1866 Prussia invades Austria with Krupp cannon.
1867 17/4 Vickers and Sons incorporated. Tom Vickers steel maker. Edward the entrepreneur.
1967 Armstrong builds first iron-clad battleships for Austria.
1867 1/4 Paris International Exhibition opens 9 million visitors.
1867 Dynamite invented.
1868 BSA largest small arms producer in Europe.
1869 Tolstoy's *War and Peace* published
1869 Emil Skoda buys Pilsen works and creates big munitions company and steelworks.

**1870s FRANCO-PRUSSIAN WAR. British firm of Armstrong moves into steel battleship construction and Krupp takes off on cannon production after Franco-Prussian War and has close links with the Kaiser. Munitions firms move close to European governments. Countries buying best European weapons begin to win wars against their rivals and are encouraged to fight.**

1870-1 **FRANCO-PRUSSIAN WAR. Krupp cannon defeat Napoleon III at Sedan. Bombardment of Paris. Success of Krupp cannon leads to vastly expanded production. Workforce grows to over 10,000.**

1870 Armstrongs link with Gatling.
1871 British begin making torpedoes.
1874 *Brussels International Conference for codification of war.*
1875 Military humiliation of Japan.
1876 **GREAT SIOUX WAR**. General Custer. Many Sioux and Cheyenne wiped out with Springfield rifles.
1877 Great Schneider steam hammer built at Le Creusot.
1877-78 **RUSSO-TURKISH WAR**. Romania, Serbia, Montenegro independent of Ottoman Empire. Turkey buys British and American rifles. German artillery.
1877 British annexes Transvaal because it wanted control of diamond mining. Resented by Boers.
1879 **ANGLO-ZULU WAR**. Bartle Frere starts it. British lose to Cetshwayo initially then recover.
1879 **WAR OF THE PACIFIC** between Chile, Peru and Bolivia. Chile win with British ships.
1879 Tolstoy's *Confession* published.

**1880s British Naval Construction begins to dominate world markets and European military rivalry becomes entrenched. British Imperialism in Southern Africa. FIRST BOER WAR. Maxim gun. Naval panics used to bring in orders, but play on people's fear. Kaiser and Von Tirpitz face Brits showing off navy, want one too.**

1880-1 **BASUTO GUN WAR**. Basutoland independent. Bartle Frere (again) tried to subdue it. Asked natives to give up their guns, bought in the Orange Free State. They would not. Defeated Brits through guerrilla tactics.
1880-81 **FIRST BOER WAR**. Defeat of Cetshwayo allowed Boers to oppose British. British soldiers dressed in red so that they could easily be shot. Brits lose battles of Laing's Nek, Schuinschoogte and Majuba Hill. *Gladstone now Prime Minister sued for peace.*
1881 **SUDAN WAR.** Mahdi's revolt in Sudan.
1883 Armstrong linked with Mitchell in new public company. Builds new yard at Elswick.
1884 2.48 million men under arms (armies and navies) in major powers[276].
1884 Maxim Gun Company formed by Vickers.
1884 18/1 Gordon leaves Britain to fight Mahdi.

1884 18/2 Gordon in Khartoum. Siege begins. First British Naval scare.
1885 25/1 End of Siege of Khartoum.
1886 Gold discovered in Witwatersrand.
1886-90 Military tension between Spain and Portugal. Armstrong supplies.
1887 Vickers commit fully to armaments.
1887 Queen's Golden Jubilee Review of Navy at Spithead.
1887 Vickers link with Nordenfeld guns and submarines.
1887 Japan starts buying battleships from Armstrong and Vickers for first class navy.
1888 Maxim gun licence to manufacture granted to Krupp.
1888-9 Second British Naval Scare.
1889 Naval "panic" against France. Naval Defence Act pushes up British naval budget to £22.5 million.
1889 5-6/8 Kaiser Wilhelm and Admiral Von Tirpitz guests at Spithead Review of the Fleet.

**1890s** ***Peace Movements gain coherence under Tolstoy's influence. Gladstone's warning about European militarism.*** **CHILEAN CIVIL WAR. Rival British and German naval companies set up their interest groups.** ***Hague Peace Conference defeated from carrying out any signifiant disarmament.***

1890-93 Military tension between Chile and Argentina. Armstrong supplies battleships.
1891 Chilean Civil War between the Army and the Navy after period of heavy military expenditure. The Navy won, largely with British ships.
1891 2/5 Great Royal Navy Exhibition Chelsea
1892 Jackie Fisher appointer Comptroller of the Navy.
1892 Another naval panic against France gets underway.
1893 22/6 MHS Victoria and Camperdown collide. Third Naval Panic.
1893 Tolstoy's *The Kingdom of God is within You* published.
Gladstone resigns refusing to agree an increase in Naval Budget. Warns of generating a European conflagration.
1893-5 John Brown build 8,000 ton armour forging press and rolling mill. Cammells also into arms.
French-Russian dual alliance.

1893 Leo Tolstoy's *The Kingdom of God is within You* addresses militarism and non-violence.

1894 11/12 British Navy League formed by naval forms and supporters.

1894 October. Harvey Syndicate to keep up munitions prices among Vickers, Armstrong, Krupp, Schneider, Dillinger, Bethlehem, Carnegie etc.

1896 **First Armenian massacres carried out by Turkey.**

1896-7 British Naval Estamates £22million, up £3mn.

1897 Parsons set up full production steam turbines.

1897 Schneider 75mm Field Gun first produced. Technical lead. 15 rounds a minute up to 5 miles.

1897 Vickers becomes totally armaments company and builds battleships integrated. Using Barrow shipyards by taking over Naval Construction and Armaments Company Limited..

1897 Vickers fully take over Maxim-Nordenfeld.

1897 Mass export of Birmingham rifles to Afghanistan militarises tribesmen.

1898 *Dum dum bullets outlawed because they were inhumane.*
1898The *Flottenverein,* the German Navy League formed to promote German Navy by Victor Schweinburg. Modelled on the British Navy League.

1898/9 *Over 7,500 Dukhobor pacifists go to Canada freed from prison, funded by Tolstoy's novel Resurrection.*

1899 ***Hague Peace Conference.*** *Set up by Nicholas II of Russia. Aim not to increase arms or budgets for a while and then to reduce them. 26 States. Conventions to settle disputes peacefully, and properly conduct war on land and at sea. Prohibition of chemical gas weapons. Britain does not co-operate Boer Wars and colonial wars.*
**Philippine Uprising against United States Occupation**.

1899 Work starts on the War Office in Whitehall.

1899-05 **Somali Jihad against Britain, Italy and Ethiopia.**

**1900 BOER WAR. BOXER UPRISING. SOMALI JIHAD. PHILLIPINE UPRISING DEFEATED BY COLONIAL UNITED STATES. British use Concentration Camps in South Africa. German Naval law passed. European armies grow.**

1/1 **Britain grabs direct control of southern Nigeria.**

**24/1 Boer victory at Spion Kop.**

**28/2 British relief of Ladysmith from Boers.**

5/3 *Kruger peace offer to British.* Turned down.

7/4 US power in the Philippines extended.
30/4 Hawaii becomes US territory.
**17/5 British relief of Mafeking.**
12/6 Second German Naval Act aims at a fleet of 38 battleships in 20 years.
**13/6 – 14/8 BOXER UPRISING against Europeans in NE China.**
**July-August. International western force defeats Boxers in China.**
6/10 Kruger denied audience by Wilhelm II
16/10 Salisbury and Conservatives returned in Kharki election.
17/10 Von Bulow is German Chancellor.
**November British concentration camps in South Africa.**
6/11 William KcKinley, Republican, re-elected President.
9/11 Russia in Manchuria negotiates with Chinese.
14/12 Secret French-Italian agreement on North Africa.
3.34 million men under arms in major powers[277]

**1901 BOER WAR. BOXER UPRISING. SOMALI JIHAD. PHILLIPINE UPRISING. Queen Victoria dies. Russia has underlying instability because of Tsarist autocracy.**

**January. Kitchener attacks Boers in scorched earth policy.**
22/1 Queen Victoria dies. Kaiser present at her death. Edward VII accedes to throne.
**28/2 Boer War peace negotiations fail. British refuse amnesty.**
March. Russian riots.
20/5 End of US military rule in Cuba
June. Morocco seeks French, German, British agreement.
12/6 Cuba becomes a US protectorate.
July. *Abraham Kuyper Government formed in the Netherlands. Tries to mediate in Boer War, refused. Dutch concern at British behaviour.*
**7/8 Kitchener issues ultimatum for surrender to Boers.**
*September Anti-militarist demonstrations in France. Anti-Drefusards pro militarist.*
6/9 President McKinley shot. Teddy Roosevelt succeeds.
7/9 *Peace of Beijing.* China to pay indemnity to western powers for Boxer uprising.
25/10 Joseph Chamberlain makes anti-German speech.
18/11 Panama Canal discussed US-Britain.

**1902 BOER WAR (UNTIL JUNE). BRITAIN BECOMES UNPOPULAR IN EUROPE. SOMALI JIHAD. PHILIPPINE UPRISING AGAINST UNITED STATES RUTHLESSLY CRUSHED. GERMAN/BRITISH NAVAL BLOCKADE OF VENEZUELA. BRITAIN ATTACKS TIBET. Britain isolated by its treatment of Boers, Concentration Camps and imperial dominance.**

20/1 Britain forms Treaty with Japan.

Vickers acquire Beardmore's Glasgow armour plating.

26/3 Cecil Rhodes dies.

**31/3 British Forces in Tibet mow down Tibetans with Maxim machine guns.**

12/4 Kitchener begins to push Boers towards a peace proposal.

15/4 Sipoyagin murdered in Russia. Peasants' revolt suppressed.

31/5 *End of Boer War. Peace of Vereeniging.*

28/6 renewal of triple Alliance between Germany, Austria and Italy for six years.

28/6 *US buys control of the Panama Canal.*

30/6 Colonial Conference in London backs Imperial Preference Tariffs.

11/7 Lord Salisbury retires as British Prime Minister, succeeded by Arthur Balfour.

9/8 Coronation of Edward VII and Queen Alexandria in Westminster Abbey

16/10 Roosevelt ends US coal strike.

1/11 Franco-Italian Entente. Italy neutral if France attacked

7/12 Joint British, German and Italian blockade of Venezuela to enforce debts arranged by Kaiser and Edward VII.

**11/12 Britain attacks Tibet under influence of Curzon using trumped-up reason.**

18/12 First meeting of Committee of Imperial Defence.

**1903 RUSSIA-JAPAN HARDEN ATTITUDES. BRITISH-FRENCH ENTENTE CORDIALE. SOMALI JIHAD. CONGO ATROCITIES. END OF VENEZUELA BLOCKADE. BRITISH ATTACK ON TIBET. Serbia emerges as an unstable military regime.**

1/1 Edward VII holds Durbar At Delhi.

13/2 End of Venezuela Blockade. US concern about Monroe Doctrine.

February. Casement Report of atrocities in the Congo against African and Indian labourers by traders.

**15/3 British forces complete conquest of Northern Nigeria.**
April. Britain and France oppose German construction of Baghdad Railway.
April. Bezobrazov is appointed as Russian Secretary of State. Adopts more hard-line policies in the Far East against Japan.
May. **Public campaign against atrocities in Congo.**
May. Edward VII visits Paris and opens up possibility of more positive political relationship.
10/6. Trappen, Skoda's Director, tries to push through arms sale with Serbia.
10/6. King of Serbia Alexander I and his wife assassinated. Dragutin Dimitrijevic, leader of the Black Hand movement in the military first emerges in Serbia.
6-9/7 Britain and France begin discussions on Entente Cordiale.
20/7 Pope Pius X elected.
25/7 Arthur Henderson elected to Commons in by-election.
**August. Lord Curzon prepares invasion of Tibet. Younghusband's force moves in and starts fighting. Maxim guns.**
August. At London Congress Russian Social Democrats split into Mensheviks (Democrats, Whites) led by Plecharov and Bolsheviks (Militarists, Reds) led by Vladimir Illich Lenin.
12/8 Japanese interchanges with Russia over Manchuria.
16/9 Franz Joseph unifies Austro-Hungarian Army.
18/9 Joseph Chamberlain resigns from Balfour Government over Imperial Preference.
October Anglo-Russian tensions over Persia.
20/10 Britain gives deciding vote for Alaska joining US rather than Canada.
18/12 United States Treaty with Panama gives them Canal Zone.

**1904 SOMALI JIHAD. JAPANESE-RUSSIAN WAR STARTS. BRITAIN MASSACRES TIBETANS, THEN CONQUERS TIBET. European powers maneouvring for alliances. United States under Roosevelt becomes dominant new world power.**

**8/2 Japan attacks Russia and then declares war.**
**March Massacre in Tibet using Maxim guns to mow down Tibetan forces.**
April. Naval Expenditure £42 million. Naval Expenditure on new construction fell slightly.

**1/5 Japan defeats Russian army at Xinyizhou.**
May. Cheaper cross Atlantic rates means more than a million a year going to the United States.
**12/9 Britain wins in Tibet, forces Treaty on Tibetans "ramming it down their throats". Tibet to pay indemnities for having been attacked by the British. Well, fair's fair.**
3/10 Secret Spanish-French Agreement to control Morocco.
October. Jackie Fisher becomes First Sea Lord and begins to get rid of substandard battleships.
21/10 Russian Fleet bound for Japan mistakes fishing vessels on Dogger Bank for Japanese fleet, sinks one vessel. British indignation. Hague Court settles compensation.
8/11 Theodore Roosevelt (Republican) elected United States President. Stronger imperial and military policy.
23/11 Russian negotiations with Germany for an alliance break down because Russia has prior loyalty to France. Russian-French arms deals through Schneider and banks.

**1905 SOMALI JIHAD. JAPANESE-RUSSIAN WAR – RUSSIA DEFEATED. Tsar weakened even further – attempted Russian revolution. Fall in British budget for naval construction, but Fisher lays down Dreadnought. Russian defeat leads to big arms deals with France and Britain for better weapons. Anti-Jewish pogroms in many Russian cities. New British Liberal Government raises hopes of stronger containment of arms and navy. Japan subdues Korea.**

2/1 Russia surrenders Port Arthur to the Japanese.
22/1 "Bloody Sunday" in St Petersburg where crowd led by priest are fired on outside the Winter Palace.
**19/2 – March. Battle of Mukden – Russian army defeated and Japanese control Manchuria.**
3/3 Tsar Nicholas agrees to wide-ranging reforms.
31/3 Kaiser Wilhelm visits Tangier to test French attitudes and Entente Cordiale. It holds.
30/4 British and French hold discussions on military co-operation.
May. German-French tensions over Morocco.
**27/5 Battle of Tsushima – Russian Baltic Fleet destroyed.**
Spring Arthur Lee, Civil Lord of the Admiralty, talks about using first strike against Germans. Reported in German and raises fear and zenophobic reaction.
*7/6. Norway decides to separate from Sweden. It goes ahead peaceably.*

**28/6 Mutiny on battleship Potempkin. Naval unrest at defeat and military pressure on Tsar Nicholas. Re-arming begins.**
*George Bernard Shaw's Major Barbara hits the stage.*
5/9 Treaty of Portsmouth between Japan and Russia. Japan disappointed by result of Treaty. Russian fleet two thirds destroyed and Tsar faces rebellion at home. Russia removed as a naval threat.
Balfour's reduction in naval estimates. Britain builds four ships and Germany builds two.
Fisher moves over to Dreadnought naval strategy.
10/11. First Dreadnought laid down.
**18/11 Japan begins to exercise control over Korea. Emperor of Korea forced to sign Treaty giving Japan control over foreign policy.**
*5/12. Liberals form British Government under Henry Campbell-Bannerman. Move away from armaments. Grey becomes Foreign Secretary.*

**1906 Mulliner starts scare. Bribery outlawed. Fisher's Naval Recession in Britain to get more advanced ships. Dreadnought launched.**
Schneider sells guns to Bulgaria.
March Von Tirpitz, under threat of resignation, gets promise of response to Dreadnaughts
No orders for Coventry Ordnance Works.
British Corrupt Practices Act.
May. Mulliner communicates to Admiralty and War Office "vast German scheme of expansion."
5/6 Third German Naval Bill gives Tirpitz some increases in battleship construction.
27th July 50% cut in Britain's capital ship construction estimates announced.
November. Germany plans widening of the Kiel Canal to take Dreadnought type battleships.
December. Dreadnought launched. Fisher's programme of Dreadnought construction underway.
4/12 Number of workers at Woolwich Arsenal cut by a third in favour of private interests.

**1907 Hague Peace Conference meets and fails to broker disarmament.. Failure to co-operate by Germany and other military powers, backed by munitions' people. In November Germans announce naval expansion.**

19/2 **WAR – HONDURAS, NICARAGUA, EL SALVADOR UNTIL DECEMBER**

***15/6-18/10 Hague Peace Conference. Attempt at stopping arms race fails. Germany opposes naval limitation.***

Triple Alliance of Germany, Austria and Italy renewed for six years, though Italy reluctant.

Deutsche Waffen and Munitions Factory inserts ads describing the great advance in French Army machine guns, then uses these ads to get bigger government orders for their machine guns.

25/7 Japan has full control of Korean Government.

Summer. Successful flights of Zeppelins up to 200 miles.

18/11 Germans announce 25% increase in naval building plans over the next five years.

Cammell Laird struck off list of contractors for Navy and Army

31/8 Russia moves towards alignment with Britain and France.

/12 Lenin leaves Russia until 1917.

16/12 US Fleet of sixteen battleships goes on round the world tour.

**1908 Year of increasing British German tension. The Kaiser is a problem. Mulliner still gets nowhere with his scare until the Summer.**

1/2. King Carlos of Portugal and Crown Prince murdered in Lisbon.

14/2 Kaiser's letter to Lord Tweedmouth assuring him that the German Navy was no threat.

4/3 Colonel Repington accuse Kaiser of trying to influence Naval policy.

6/3. Cambell-Bannerman retires as liberal Prime Minister and is replaced by Asquith.

14/6. German Navy Bill proposes four new Dreadnaughts.

/6 Mulliner-Blatchford public campaign against German naval expansion gets underway.

16/7 Lloyd George, Sir Edward Grey and Count Paul Metternich meet and discuss German Navy. Metternich points out the naval building is public as set out in Navy Bill. There is no secret building. Points out spy scares and press distortions.

August. Lloyd George visits Germany. Von Bülow keeps him away from the Kaiser. Sees Zeppelin catch fire. Bethmann-Hollweg talks of ring of iron of France, Russia, Britain.
20/8 Leopold II hands over Congo to Belgium from being a personal fiefdom.
16/9 Russia agrees Austrian annexation of Bosnia and Herzegovina and Austria agrees to opening of Dardenelles to Russian warships.
25/9 Casablanca incident between Germany and France.
Autumn 1908 Cabinet told of Mulliner's claims.
27/10 Kaiser's indiscrete *Daily Telegraph* interview.
3/11 Taft beat William Jennings Bryan in United States' Presidential Election.
November Mulliner gets hearing from Generals and Admirals, but they do not trust him.
10-11/11 German Reichstag debates Kaiser's Daily Telegraph interview. Anger at Kaiser and Britain.
3.99 million men under arms in major powers.[278]
No orders in Coventry Ordnance Works

**1909 Dreadnaught scare. "We want eight and we won't wait." German concern about misinformation. Sultan of Turkey deposed. Lloyd George Budget.**

1/1. Slight decline in employment figures at Krupp's over previous two years.
9/2 Germany and France sort out Morocco tension.
February. Mulliner interviewed by Imperial Defence Committee, by Cabinet in presence of Fisher and Jellicoe and sees McKenna. Cabinet Committee appointed to investigate. Concludes later that Mulliner is "completely inaccurate".
2/3 Powers intervene to prevent an Austro-Serbian War.
March – Mulliner panic in the press.
12/3 "We want eight and we won't wait." panic leads to acceptance of large naval estimate for eight Dreadnaughts.
22/3 Asquith condemns panic as unscrupulous misrepresentation of the situation in Commons. Grey says that he accepts that Germans do not intend to accelerate their programme.
9/4 Great powers recognize Austro-Hungarian annexation of Bosnia-Herzogovina.
27/4 "Young Turks" depose Sultan of Turkey. Is succeeded by his brother Mohammed V who rules until 1918.

29/4 Lloyd George's "People's Budget"
17/6. Nicholas II and Wilhelm II meet.
14/7 Bethman Hollweg is German Chancellor after von Bülow.
24/7 Aristide Briand forms new ministry after Clemenceau.
25/10 Japan imposes dictatorship in Korea after murder of Prince Ito.
30/11 House of Lords throws out Lloyd George budget by 350 to 75.

**1910 British Constitutional Reform of Lords. International tensions fall. Death of Tolstoy. Re-election of Liberals. Edward VIII dies.**

15/1 British General Election over Lloyd George's Budget, Lords' Reform results in reduced Liberal majority.
20/2 Boutros-Ghali, the first native Prime Minister of Egypt, a Christian Copt, is shot by Nationalist.
31/3 Dissolution of Greek Military League.
27/4 "People's Budget" of Lloyd George passed.
6/5 Edward VIII dies. Succeeded by George V.
26/5 Pope Pius X encyclical angers Germans by criticisms of Luther and Reformation.
27/5 Prussian diet rejects reform of suffrage.
4/7 Russo-Japanese agreement on Manchuria and Korea.
22/8 Japan annexes Korea.
7/9 Hague Court arbitrates US-Britain over Newfoundland.
4/11 Nicholas II and Wilhelm II agree over Baghdad railway.
20/11 Leo Tolstoy dies.
12 British election again returns Liberals and guarantees passage of Parliament Bill and Home Rule for Ireland.

**1911 Parliament Act passed. Agadir Crisis increases tension and hardens relationships between Germany and France, Britain and Russia. Russian Prime Minister assassinated. French-Russian rapprochement.**

17/1 Attempted assassination of Aristide Briand in French Chamber of Deputies.
23/2 French vote for two more battleships.
24/2 Reichstag passes expanded army bill.
27/2 Resignation of Aristide Briand's ministry.
23/5 London Imperial Conference.
26/5 Reichstag allows former French territory Alsace Lorraine relative autonomy.

22/6 Coronation of George V.
1/7 German gunboat to Agadir starts Agadir Crisis.
10/7 Russia notifies Germany of its support for France.
21/7 Lloyd George comes out against Germany on Agadir. Metternich is recalled to Berlin.
31/8 French-Russian military conversations.
14/9 Assassination of Stolypin, Russian prime minister.
9/10 Launch of George V super Dreadnaught.
23/10 Churchill moves to the Admiralty.
4/11 Agadir Crisis formally brought to a close. German climbdown.
12/12 George V holds great Delhi Durbar.
30/12 Vickers bribes Admiral Matsumoto for sale of battle-cruiser, Congo. Against 1906 British Corrupt Practices Act

**1912 Republic in China. Suffragettes. Socialists strong in Germany. Woodrow Wilson elected US President. BALKAN WAR.**

2/1 Socialists strongest party in Reichstag elections.
10/1 Poincaré succeeds Caillaux as French Prime Minister.
12/2 Manchu Dynasty ends. Republic in China.
14/3 Taft forbids shipment of arms to Mexico.
19/3 Tom Mann arrested for inciting soldiers to mutiny.
28/3 British Women's Franchise Bill rejected.
15/4 Titanic goes down.
22/5 Reichstag adjourned following Socialist attacks on the Kaiser.
30/9 Bulgarian and Serbian armies mass for attack on Turkey.
17/10 **BALKAN WAR.** Turkey, Bulgaria, Serbia.
26/11 Lansbury loses Bow election on women's suffrage.
3/12 **END OF BALKAN WAR.**

**1913 Heavy military build-up across main European Powers. Churchill's "Naval Holiday" rejected. SECOND BALKAN WAR. King of Greece assassinated. MEXICAN CIVIL WAR.**

5/1. Von Jagow becomes German Foreign Minister.
21/1 Aristide Briande becomes French Prime Minister.
18/2 **MEXICAN CIVIL WAR BREAKS OUT.**
4/3 Wilson becomes US President.
18/3 French Senate rejects PR and Briande resigns.
30/5 Peace treaty after First Balkan War.

26/6 Bulgaria signs defensive treaty with Austro-Hungary.
30/6 **SECOND BALKAN WAR STARTS. BULGARIA – GREECE AND SERBIA.**
30/6 Reichstag passes bill to fund large increase in army.
10/7 Russia declares war on Bulgaria.
12/7 Turkey re-enters war.
30/7 **SECOND BALKAN WAR ARMISTICE.**
1/8 Krupp Bribery trial involving Pfeiffer and Brandt giving inside information on contracts and bribing state officials.
21/10 Churchill suggests naval holiday to try to get escalation of naval rivalry under control. Rejected both in Germany and Britain.
1/11 German military mission to Turkey to help them improve army.
8/11 Brandt of Krupp convicted of bribery
13/12 Britain and France oppose German-Turkish military convention.

**1914 THE GREAT WAR. Events leading to the outbreak of the Great War. July assassination of Franz Ferdinand. Start of WWI 4.60 million men under arms in major powers, after mobilisation this rises to 8.43 million.** [279]

8/1 German General Otto Liman von Sanders becomes inspector-general of Turkish army.
15/2 Franco-German agreement on Baghdad railway.
14/3 Turkish-Serbian Peace Treaty
20/3 Curragh Mutiny near Dublin against action in Northern Ireland.
April. Deutsche Waffen and Munitions Factory/Steyr Works in Austro-Hungary deliver 200,000 German designed rifles to Serbia. They would shortly be used against Austro-Hungary.
May. Large delegation from Krupps invited to and inspects Beardmore's Armaments and Shipbuilding Company heavy gun making.
25/5 Irish Home Rule Bill passed in Commons.
15/6 British-German Agreement on the Baghdad Railway
**28/6 Archduke Franz Ferdinand and his wife assassinated in Sarajevo by Gavrilo Princip, a Serb.**
5/7 Germany promises support to Austro-Hungary for any conflict with Serbia, the Kaiser's "Blank cheque".

6/7 Kaiser checks with Krupp abour readiness for war.
8/7 Ulster resists Home Rule.
20-29/7 French President Poincaré visits Russia.
23/7 Austro-Hungary issues ultimatum to Serbia.
24/7 *Edward Grey proposes four power mediation of Balkan Crisis, but Serbia appeals to Russia.*
28/7 Austro-Hungary declares war on Serbia.
30/7 Jean Jaurès is murdered in Paris.
August. Widening of the Kiel Canal to allow Dreadnought battleships passage completed.
**1/8 GREAT WAR STARTS. Germany declares war on Russia who is already mobilized against Austro-Hungary.**
**4/8 Germany declares war on France and invades Belgium and France.**
**4/8 Britain declares war on Germany.**
**23/8 Japan declares war on Germany.**
**23/8 The British Expeditionary Force starts its retreat from Mons. Germany invades France.**
**26-28/8 Germans defeat Russians at battle of Tannenberg in East Prussia.**
**5/9 Battle of the Marne slows German advance.**
**September. Churchill suggests capturing the Dardanelles.**
**29/10 Turkey enters war on German side.**
**17-18/9 Western Front established through from Switzerland to North Sea.**
**5/12 Mussolini repudiates Socialism.**
**12/10 First Battle of Ypres.**
***24/12 CHRISTMAS TRUCE called by Pope Benedict XV.***

**1915 THE GREAT WAR. Gallipoli failure. Germans win on Russian Front. US tensions with German subs. ARMENIAN MASSACRES. Lloyd George becomes Minister of Munitions. US lends Britain $500 million for arms.**

**3/1 Germans start using gas.**
**18/1 Japanese ultimatum to China.**
**19/1 First German zeppelin raid in East Anglia.**
**30/1 First German submarine attack.**
**4/2 German submarine blockade announced.**

**19/2 Naval attack on Dardanelles starts. Churchill in favour. Fisher, now First Sea Lord, did not like it. Ten month BATTLE OF GALLIPOLI.**
**18/3 Three allied battleships sunk in Dardanelles.**
**8/4 Armenian massacres start in Turkey.**
**22/4 German offensive. Second Battle of Ypres**
**22/4 Germans use chlorine. Allied gas attacks within six months.**
**25/4 Gallipoli landings British, French, Australians and New Zealanders.**
***26/4 into May WOMEN'S CONGRESS IN HAGUE 1200 delegates demand END TO WAR AND INTERNATIONAL LAW ENSURING PEACE.***
**26/4 Secret Treaty to tie Italy on Allies side. Mussolini paid by British Secret Service.**
**7/5 Germans sink Lusitania killing 1200.**
**14/5 Insurrection in Portugal against military ruler.**
**15/5 Fisher resigns on Dardanelles policy.**
**26/5 Asquith re-orders coalition with Lloyd George as Minister of Munitions. Lloyd George begins total re-organisation of munitions output.**
27/5 Height of **TURKISH MASSACRE OF ARMENIANS**.
3/6 Russian Southern Front collapses.
9/6 William Jennings Bryan resigns as President Wilson moves towards war.
*23/6 German Social Democrats manifesto argues for negotiated peace.*
27/7 Revolution in Haiti.
**29/7 US Marines land in Haiti. Stay for 34 years.**
**5/8 Germany captures Warsaw and moves East.**
**6/8 More Gallipoli landings. Not successful.**
*12/10 Nurse Edith Cavell executed by the Germans for aiding British and French soldiers.*
15/10 J.P. Morgan organizes and co-ordinates $500 million loan to Britain and France.
28/10 Briand forms ministry in France.
13/11 Churchill resigns after the failure of the Gallipoli landings.
21/11 Italy agrees not to make a separate peace.
3/12 Joseph Joffre becomes French Commander in Chief.

15/12. Unmasking of US Navy League as a general sales-promotion bureau for munitions and steel groups.
19/12 Haig becomes British Commander in Chief.
21/12 William Robertson becomes Chief of Staff.

**1916 GREAT WAR CONTINUES. BATTLES OF VERDUN AND SOMME. Tank Warfare Starts. Easter Rising in Ireland. BATTLE OF JUTLAND. Wilson re-elected President. Lloyd George becomes Prime Minister. German Peace Note. Conscription in Britain.**

27/1 Labour Conference votes against conscription.
**21/1-18/12 all year. BATTLE OF VERDUN. Germans and French suffer about 400,000 casualties each.**
29/2 British Black List of firms not to be traded with.
**2/3 Russians advance into Turkey**
15/3 Von Tirpitz resigns as Secretary of State for the Navy.
17/3 -4/4 Clyde strike of munitions workers.
24/3 Passenger ship Sussex sunk by German sub. US passengers.
27/3 Allied War Conference in Paris.
13/4 In States Bethlehem Steel bribes newspapers to oppose Government steel armour plant rather than Bethlehem's factory.
**24/4 Easter Uprising in Dublin by Irish republican Brotherhood and Sein Fein.**
5/5 German pledge not to sink boats without warning.
**31/5 -1/6 Battle of Jutland between British and German Fleets. British lost more ships but German fleet corralled in habour.**
**13/6 General Smuts defeats Germans in Tanzania.**
**18/6 Russians victory at Cernowitz.**
**1/7- 19/11 BATTLE OF THE SOMME. British and French casualties 620,000 and German casualties 450,000.**
**27-30/8 Romania and Italy join Allies and declare war on Germany and Austro-Hungary.**
**15/9 British use tanks in Somme offensive.**
*7/11 Woodrow Wilson re-elected to Presidency on "He kept us out of the war" slogan.*
**28/10 Germans deport 60,000 Belgians to work in Germany.**
November. Setting of Solzhenitsyn's novel. November 1916.
7/12 Lloyd George becomes Prime Minister after Asquith forced to resign.
*12/12 German Peace note to Allies about negotiation rejected.*
*20/12 President Wilson's peace note to both sides.*

23/12 Anger over refusal to bomb Comité des Forges iron ore basin and blast furnaces at Briey near Thionville even though they we vital to the German war effort because the company wanted them back unbombed at the end of the War.
31/12 Rasputin murdered

**1917 GREAT WAR. Russian Defeat. White and Red (October) Revolutions. United States enters the War.**

22/1 Wilson's "Peace without victory" appeal for an armistice.
Winter foods shortages in central Europe.
1/2 Germans unrestricted submarine warfare.
3/2 US liner sunk by submarine.
1/3 Zimmerman telegram proposing German link with Mexico to attack the United States.
8/3 US Marines land in Cuba to occupy it.
8-14/3 the February Revolution, white revolution, against Tsar.
15/3 Tsar Nicholas II abdicates.
16/3 Germans withdraw in West to Hindenburg Line.
**6/4 President Wilson calls sessions of Congress and the United States declares war on Germany.**
Lenin publishes "The State and Revolution"
**April. Allied advances on western front.**
**17/4 munities in French forces.**
**30/4 Lloyd George oders admiralty to use convoys.**
**14/6 American Expeditionary Force arrives.**
**12/7 Germans use mustard gas. 160,000 casualties.**
**14/8 China declares war on Germany and Austria.**
**1/9 German offensive on eastern front.**
**14/9 Kerensky declares republic.**
22/10 Congress of Soviets passes resolution for armistice.
2/11 Balfour, British Foreign Secretary issues Balfour declaration on home rule for Israel.
**7/11 (26th October in Russian Old style calendar) Russian Revolution. Lenin and Bolsheviks seize Winter Palace in St Petersburg.**
*26/11 Russian Soviet Government offers armistice.*
*29/11 Lord Landsdown letter to Telegraph suggesting compromise peace with Germany rejected by Lloyd George.*
5/12 German/USSR Treaty of Brest-Litovsk discussed

**1918 FINAL YEAR OF GREAT WAR. First World War ends in Novemberafter heavy fighting in western front.. The War to end all Wars. Resentment at the rich munitions manufacturers who had made money out of the deaths of millions. Russian Revolution. Churchill Minister for War.**

*8/1 President Woodrow Wilson identifies 14 points for world peace later used in League of Nations Covenant.*

28/1 Red Army founded.

*3/3 Bolsheviks sign Treaty of Brest-Litovsk to get out of War. Cede territory to Germans.*

3/3 Russian Capital moves from Petrograd (St Petersburg) to Moscow.

**21/3 – 17/7 Ludendorff's German Spring Offensive on Western Front. The big bulge. Germans push towards Paris. Krupp's Big Bertha used to shell Paris.**

1/4 Royal Air Force founded.

14/4 Foch is Supreme Commander of all Allied Forces.

**1/5 Germans occupy Sebastopol.**

**15-17/7 Second Battle of Marne halts German Advance.**

**18/7 Allied counter-offensive against Germans – fast after 8th August.**

**8/8 Allies break German line.**

**29/9 Ludendorff approaches Allies for Armistice.**

**24/10 Collapse of Austro-Hungarian army on Italian Front.**

**26/10 Ludendorff resigns.**

4/11 Allies sign armistice with Austro-Hungary.

11/11 Armistice signed between Allies and Germany. **END OF THE GREAT WAR.**

13/11 USSR annuls Brest-Litovsk treaty..

18/11 Kolchak and others form White challenge to Bolsheviks.

29/11 Socialist Revolutionary Forces in Germany suppressed.

1/12 Allied Occupation of Germany starts.

14/12 British General Election. Conservatives dominate Lloyd George led Government.

*14/12 Woodrow Wilson arrives for Versailles Peace Conference.*

30/12 Spartacists found German Communist Party.

**1919 The Versailles Conference and Peace. AFGHANISTAN WAR OF INDEPENDENCE. RED/WHITE RUSSIAN CIVIL WAR. The Red Scare. The Great Munitions Recession. Churchill fights the Reds.**

*3/1 Herbert Hoover is Director-General of Commission for Relief and Reconstruction of Europe.*

5-15/1 In Spartacist (Communist) uprising in Berlin Karl Liebknecht and Rosa Luxembourg shot.

5/1 German Workers Party formed. Hitler attends.

*18/1 Versailles Conference opens. Clemenceau chairs it.*

19/1 German elections won by Social Democrats (38%) and Centre Party (19%).

*25/1 Proposals for founding the League of Nations accepted at the Versailles Peace Conference. Covenant of the League of Nations Para5 of Article 8 declares grave objections to the manufacture of weapons by private companies.*

3-9/2 Denikin's White Army routs Bolsheviks in Caucasus.

6/2 Weimar National Assembly convenes Ebert becomes President.Scheidemann forms ministry of Social Democrats and Centre Party.

*14/2 Woodrow Wilson lays League of Nations Covenant before Versailles Conference.*

21/2 Kurt Eisner, Bavarian Prime Minister, is assassinated in Munich.

28/2 Senator Lodge begins campaign against League of Nations in the States.

**10/3 Riots in Egypt put down by British.**

15/3 American soldiers meet in Paris and found the American Legion for veterans.

23/3 Mussolini founds Fascist Party.

4/4 Philippines demands independence from USA.

April United states bomb plot uncovered to mail 36 bombs to figures on the Right.

8/4 Red Army enters Crimea.

**13/4 Amritsar Massacre of Indians by Gurkhas in British Army.**

30/4 Japan given Shandong. China leaves Versailles Conference.

1/5 Mayday marches in States put down by troops. Beginning of Red Scare

**1/5 Red Army begins counter-offensive against Whites.**

1/5 Bavarian army captures Munich from Communists.

3/5 **AFGHANISTAN WAR OF INDEPENDENCE AGAINST BRITAIN BEGINS.**

7/5 Peace terms imposed on Germany. Reparations. Territory losses.

2/6 Eight bombs explode in American cities, one of them outside house of Palmer, Attorney General where the bomber was killed. Red Scare. Palmer raids. Palmer said Revolution would occur on 1st May, 1920.

**3/6 Churchill's support of White armies in Archangel.**

19/6 Mustafa Kamal resist allies plans for Turkey.

20/6 German Chancellor Scheidemann falls for opposing Peace Treaty. Gustav Bauer forms cabinet.

Summer. Woodrow Wilson gradually loses debate on League of Nations. He is ill.

*28/6 German Representatives sign peace treaty in Hall of Mirrors, Versailles.*

27-31/7 Race riots in Chicago and throughout US including lynchings.

11/8 Weimar Constitution set up.

**2/9 Denikin's white army enters Kiev.**

25/9 Wilson on speaking tour suffers stroke.

27/9 Churchill's British troops in Archangel withdraw.

October-December White armies defeated.

**1920 Germany in chaos. Guns on the streets. Resentment to armistice terms. RUSSIAN CIVL WAR THROUGHOUT YEAR. RUSSIAN WAR WITH POLAND. Post-war recession in United States and Europe..**

1/5 Predicted "American revolution" fails to materialize. Red Scare fades.

*10/1 Ratification of the Treaty of Versailles. League of Nations comes into existence with 29 members immediately, others follow, but not the United States and China.*

16/1 US Eighteenth Amendment for Prohibition of Alcohol passed.

16/1 US votes against joining the League of Nations.

28/1 Turkish national assembly established.

26/2 League of Nations takes over Saar region.

13-17 /3 Kapp Putsch in Berlin backing Kaiser tries military take-over in Germany.

Thompson in US invents submachine gun..

27/3 Bauer is succeeded by Hermann Müller as German Chancellor.

**6/4-17/5 German troops suppress rebellion in Ruhr, French troops occupy area. Fritz Thyssen acts as nationalist rallying figure.**

23/4 Turkish National Assembly finally opens in Ankara with Mustafa Kamal as President.

20/5 Assassination of President Carranza of Mexico. Huerta becomes provisional President.

4/6 Treaty of Trianon between Allies and Hungary imposes limits on Hungary's armed forces and reparations.

6/6 German elections show swing away from Social Democrats and Centre Party towards extremists.

12/6 Republican Convention chooses Harding for Presidential and Coolidge for Vice-Presidential candidate.

5/7 Democratic Convention nominates Cox for Presidency and FDR for V-P.

6/7-12/10 **RUSSIAN WAR WITH POLAND.**

8/7 Britain annexes Kenya.

September. Half a million Italian steel workers occupy factories and seek to run them.

16/9 Wall Street bomb frightens capitalists. Merely building explosives.

September League of Nations Brussels Economic Conference.

*12/10 Russian Polish Peace Treaty* **ENDS RUSSO-POLISH WAR.**

27/10 League of Nations moves to Geneva.

2/11 Harding becomes President and Republicans dominate in US elections.

16/11 **END OF RUSSIAN CIVIL WAR.**

23/12 Partition of Ireland Bill passed

**1921 GREEK-TURKISH WAR. Gustav Krupp begins secret rearmament working on weapon designs. French invasion of Ruhr. Reparations lead to hyperinflation of the Mark. Social Democrat-Centre Party coalition weakened. Fascist Party strengthens in Italy. Washington disarmament Conference cuts navy of US, Britain and Japan.**

1/1 Greek offensive starts **GREEK-TURKISH WAR.**

16/1 Aristide Briand is French Prime Minister.

24-29/1 Paris Conference of Allies fixes German reparations.

9/2 State opening of Central Parliament in India.
27/2 Riots in Florence between Communists and Fascists.
4/3 Warren Harding becomes US President.
21/3 treaty of Riga between Russia and Poland.
23/3 Invasion of Ruhr because Germany fails to pay reparations.
28/3 Independent Labour Party in Britain refuses to affiliate with Communists.
1/4 Turkish victory over Greeks
12/4 Harding declares US will play no part in League of Nations.
27/4 German reparations liability 132 billion gold marks.
5/5 Allied Supreme Council warns that failure of Germany to accept reparations will lead to occupation of Ruhr.
10/5 German Cabinet Crisis. Wirth, Centre Party becomes Chancellor. Accepts ultimatum.
14/5 35 Fascists elected in Italy.
24/5 Foundation of UK British Legion.
7/6 New Northern Ireland Parliament opened.
8/7 De Valera accepts Irish/British truce.
11/8 United States invites powers to conference on Far East and the limitation of armaments.
12/8 Silesian dispute between Germany and Poles referred to League of Nations.
29/8 – 16/12 State of Emergency declared in Germany.
30/9 French troops evacuate from Ruhr.
November Mark falls to 330 Marks per US Dollar.
*12/11 Washington Conference on Disarmament limits navies of USA, Britain, France, Italy and Japan, signed 29/12.*

**1922 German mark begins to move into freefall. GREEK-TURKISH WAR. Lord Cecil's proposal for general disarmament. IRA in armed uprising in Irish Free State. IRISH CIVIL WAR. Fascists in power in Italy. USSR finally comes together. Alfred Hugenberg, of Krupps, organises press agency supplying more than 1000 German newspapers.**

15/1 Michael Collins First Prime Minister of Irish Free State.
13/1 Allies Conference in Cannes decides to postpone Germany's reparations payments.
*1/2 Washington Arms Conference treaties restrict poison gas and submarine warfare.*
11/2 Nine power treaty to secure China's independence.
*15/2 International Court of the Hague holds its first ever session.*

28/2 British Government announces its desire to recognize Egypt as an independent State.
6/3 US prohibits sales of arms to China.
March. Geddes Axe cuts military and other expenditure.
18/3 Gandhi gets six years imprisonment for civil disobedience.
16/4 Germany and Russia resume normal trading arrangements.
26/5 Lenin suffers first stroke. Struggle for succession by Stalin, Trotsky etc.
16/6 Irish Free State election. Pro-Treaty candidates win and the IRA then takes areas under armed control. **IRISH CIVIL WAR.**
24/6 Walter Rathenau murdered by anti-semitic nationalists.
28/6 IRA hold hostages in Dublin. Heavy fighting there until 5/7
31/7 General Strike in Italy. Fascists seize power in some cities.
18/9 Hungary admitted to League of Nations.
*27/9 Resolution XIV of the third assembly of the League of Nations backs reduction of arms in relation to security.*
13/10 **END OF GREEK-TURKISH WAR.**
19/10 Conservatives withdraw from coalition after 1922 Committee meets. Lloyd George resigns.
24/10 Mussolini demands place in Italian Government.
28/10 Fascist March on Rome. Mussolini is asked to form coalition government and become Prime Minister. **FASCISM ARRIVES IN POWER.**
1/11 Kemal Pasha proclaims Turkish Republic and abolishes Sultanate.
1/11 **CHINESE CIVIL WAR STARTS.**
17/11 Conservatives under Bonar Law win General Election.
30/12 Final establishment of USSR.

**1923** ***LEAGUE OF NATIONS PREPARES TREATY OF MUTUAL ASSISTANCE IN WHICH A WAR OF AGGRESSION IS AN INTERNATIONAL CRIME WITH GUARANTEES OF MUTUAL ASSISTANCE.*** **FRENCH MILITARY OCCUPATION OF RUHR. END OF IRISH CIVIL WAR. German Mark suffers hyper-inflation. CHINESE CIVIL WAR FERMENTED BY JAPAN. Hitler's Putsch fails – imprisoned.**

11/1Germany fails to meet reparations payments. French occupation of the Ruhr underway.
14/1 Fascist squads in Italy form into army militias.

3/3 US Senate rejects proposal to join International Court of Justice.
21/3 US declines to recognize Russia unless it acknowledges debts etc.
30/4 Eamon de Valera brokers **END TO IRISH CIVIL WAR.**
20/5 Stanley Baldwin becomes British Prime Minister.
19/6 Baldwin and Mellon sign British-US Convention on war debt.
6/7 USSR Constitution formally adopted.
24/7 Treaty of Lausanne between Greece and Turkey leads to 1.5 million Greeks moving from Anatolia to Greece. Resented.
2/8 US President Harding dies, succeeded by Calvin Coolidge.
6/8 Gustav Stresemann forms coalition in Germany.
31/8 Mussolini bombards and occupies Corfu.
1/9 Japanese earthquake kills about half a million people.
10/9 Irish Free State admitted to League of Nations.
15/9 Inflation pushes German bank rate up to 90%.
14/9 Primo de Rivera becomes Dictator in Spain.
27/9 State of Emergency in Germany because of hyper-inflation.
28/9 Ethiopia admitted to League of Nations.
*29/9 League of Nations submits draft Treaty of Mutual Assistance to its member governments.*
1/10 Black Reichswehr coup fails in Germany.
26/10 London British Empire Conference gives more rights to dominions.
**8-9 /11 Hitler's Munich Putsch linked with Ludendorff fails. Hitler imprisoned.**
20/11 Mark drops to 4 trillion to the dollar. New currency introduced - the Rentenmark.
6/12 Conservatives lose seats in British General Election backing protection. Labour 191 seats..

**1924 Death of Lenin. Minority Labour Government in Britain under Ramsey McDonald make moves towards peace. Hitler in prison, but only until December. Mussolini and Italian Fascists in power. CHINA CIVIL WAR. Moves towards disarmament. Zinoviev letter forgery allows Conservatives back in power. American Investment in the German Economy builds. Of the replies to the League of Nations Treaty of Mutual Assistance 18 agree and 11 demur. Not enough to implement.**
21/1 Death of Lenin.

23/1 Ramsey MacDonald leads minority Labour Government in Britain.
1/2 Britain recognises USSR.
*23/2 Britain reduces reparation recovery duty on German exports to 5%*
1/4 Hitler sentenced to five years. In prison until December. Writes *Mein Kampf.*
6/4 Fascists win election in Italy with intimidation.
14/4 British-Soviet Conference in London.
4/5 German Reichstag elections. Nationalists (95 seats) Communists (62) Social Democrats (100) Centre Party (65) Nazis win first seats (32).
10/5 J Edgar Hoover appointed to head Federal Bureau of Investigation.
10/6 Mussolini bumps off Socialist opponent Matteotti.
30/6 Hertzog, Nationalist Party, succeeds Smuts.
3/7 MacDonald refuses to sign Treaty of Mutual Assistance prepared by the League of Nations which provided for disarmament and military assistance to any nation which might face aggression. Britain backed away because it might need troops in the Empire.. A pity.
*16/7 The Dawes Plan removes reparations from contention.French leave Ruhr and give a series of concessions to Germany tonormalize relationships.*
*6/8 Lausanne Treaty for re-establishing world peace comes into operation.*
30/8 German Reichsbank becomes independent of government and introduces a new German Mark.
1/9 Dawes Plan comes into operation.
5/9 military junta takes power in China.
*2/10 Geneva Protocol for the peaceful settlement of international disputesis proposed at the League of Nations. If the protocol is ratified the Disarmament Conference is to open on 15th June,1925.*
9/10 British Parliament dissolves.
25/10 British Foreign Office leaks the "Zinoviev Letter", a forgery sent by white Russians, to throw the election against Labour. McDonald fails to address it, because he is on the road giving speeches and it hits the Labour vote.
29/10 Conservatives win British election with 200 majority.
4/11 Calvin Coolidge (Republican) wins US Presidential Election.

4/11 Stanley Baldwin forms Conservative Government with Austen Chamberlain as Foreign Secretary, Churchill as Chancellor of the Exchequer.
21/11 Baldwin cancels Treaties with USSR negotiated by Labour.
7/12 Social Democrats (131 seats) biggest party in German elections. Nationalists (103) and Centre Party (69) also do well. Nazis 14 seats.
20/12 Hitler released from prison.

**1925 Locarno Treaties guaranteeing main European borders. Hindenburg becomes German President. Stalin ousts Trotsky. Mussolini is dictator. Mein Kampf published. League of Nations arbitrates in disputes. Strong American investment in Germany. Wall Street buoyant.**

3/1 Mussolini takes dictatorial powers.
11/1 Frank Kellogg becomes US secretary of State.
15/1 Hans Luther (Independent) becomes German Chancellor. Gustav Stresemann is Foreign Minister.
20/1 British-Chinese Treaty of Beijing.
29/1Lloyd George becomes Liberal leader.
***12/3 Sir Austen Chamberlain informs the League of Nations that Britain refuses to sign the Geneva Protocol for the settlement of international disputes. Backs out of international peace process. .***
3/4 Britain back on the gold standard.
25/4 Hindenburg becomes President of Germany.
*4-7/6 Geneva Conference on arms traffic and poison gas. Protocol prohibiting use of gas and arms trafficking discussed and agreed by 131 states.*
*8/6 Britain and France accept German proposal for a security pact to guarantee German-French and German Belgian borders.*
**26/6 Greek coup.**
*13/7 French troops begin evacuation of the Rhineland.*
*October. Greece crosses Bulgarian border – referred to League of Nations. Greece withdraws.*
***25/9 League states that an aggressive war is an internal crime and asks for preparation on a Conference for the Reduction and Limitation of Armaments.***
*5-16/10 Locarno Treaties guaranteeing European borders, especially French, Belgian, Czech, Polish, German borders set up.*
*12/11 US- Italian agreement on the latter's war debt.*

27/11 Aristide Briand forms ministry in France..
*1/12 Locarno Treaties signed in London.*
*12/12 League creates the Preparatory Commission for the Disarmament Conference.*
*15/12 Greece agrees to penalties imposed by League of Nations for Bulgarian invasion.*
*16/12 League rules in favour of Iraq.*

**1926 British General Strike. Geneva Disarmament Conference. Arms Companies organize to disrupt agreements. Germany joins League of Nations. CHINESE CIVIL WAR. Opportunity for Disarmament Momentum passes, Conservatives negative.**

3/1 In Greece Pangalos becomes dictator and then is elected President.
8/1 Ibn Saud king of Arabia and establishes dynasty rule
*14-20/1. Denmark, Norway, Sweden and Finland agree pacific resolution of all disputes.*
10/2 Germany applies for admission to League, blocked by Spain, Brazil who want seat on Council.
7/4 Assassination attempt on Mussolini fails.
24/4 Berlin Treaty of friendship and neutrality between Germany and USSR.
3-12/5 British General Strike grows out of coal strike. Right musters to defeat it.
12-14 /5 Coup led by the army in Poland.
*18-26/5 Geneva Preparatory Disarmament meeting takes place. US attends. Limited progress made. M. Loudon is Chairman.*
**31/5 Army coup in Portugal.**
10/6 Spain announces withdrawal from League of Nations but then rescinds.
5/6 British-Turkish acceptance of League ruling on Mosul.
15/7 Aristide Briand's ministry falls – financial crisis because franc is overvalued..
**22/8 Military coup in Greece.**
6/9 Chiang Kai-shek becomes dominant in China.
*8/9 Germany accepted into League of Nations and Spain leaves in huff.*
*24/9 League asks Preparatory Commission to speed up so that the Disarmament Conference programme is available at the beginning of 1927 so that the Conference can take place before September, 192.*
19/10 Stalin expels Trotsky and Zinoviev from Politbureau.

November. Italy becomes a Totalitarian Fascist State. Other parties closed down.
17/12 Cabinet crisis in Germany.
*Allied Disarmament Commission leaves Essen.*

**1927 Some disarmament moves. Buoyant arms companies back in business. CHINESE CIVIL WAR. Kellogg Pact for the renunciation of war suggested. American boom gives wide economic growth.**
31/1 Allied military control of Germany ends.
January. Shanghai Defence Force dispatched to China to protect Shanghai subjects in Chinese Civil War.
3-13/2 Revolt in Portugal against military dictatorship of Portugal of General Carmona.
February. Lloyd's brokers underwrite arms being sent to China, breaking embargo.
29/1 German Cabinet crisis resolved. Wilhelm Marx becomes Chancellor.
31/1 Allied military control of Germany ends.
April Quomintang strengthens position.
12/4 Chiang Kai-shek begins purging Communists from Quomintang.
*21/4-26/5 Divergences between the British and French delegations prevent the disarmament Conference programme from being formed.*
2-23/5 Geneva economic conference aimed to address high tariffs and cartels.
*20/6 Britain, USA and Japan confer on naval disarmament but no agreement. Ends in failure. Shearer, the arms company agent,helps to destroy possible treaty.*
2/9 Mustafa Kamal empowered to nominate all candidates. Turkish totalitarian state governed by People's Party.
16/9 Hindenburg dedicating the Tannenburg memorial, repudiates German responsibility for the Great War.
*26/9 Eighth Assembly of the League of Nations insists on the Disarmament Conference going ahead. Creates a Commission of Arbitration and Security.*
*30/11 Litvinov proposes complete disarmament at Geneva .Benes chairs Commission of Arbitration and Security.*
14/12 Britain recognises Iraq's independence and recommends their membership of League.

*17/12 Kellogg suggests pact renouncing war as an instrument of national policy.*

**1928 Attempt to make sure all international conflicts are settled peacefully by Kellogg-Briand Pact. US markets take off into speculation. Hoover President. Buoyant world economy.**

*28/3 Military Service in France cut to a year.*

*15-24/3Preparatory Commission decide that the USSR suggestion of complete disarmament cannot be implemented.*

*April Kellogg-Briand work on treaty outlawing war proceeds.*

22/4 French elections. Right wins majority.

Salazar becomes Minister of Finance in Portuguese dictatorship.

3-11/5 Clashes between Chinese and Japanese troops in North east China. Japan occupies part of Shandong.

20/5 German election. Social Democrats 153, Centre 62, Communist 54 etc. Nazis 12. 28/6 Herman Müller, Social Democrat, becomes new German Chancellor.

19/7 King Faud's coup in Egypt. Parliament suspended.

2/8 Italy signs twenty year treaty of friendship with Ethiopia. With friends like that...

*27/8 Kellogg-Briand Pact outlawing all recourse to war and providing for pacific settlement of disputes is signed by 15 major nations including the United States. Major breakthrough.*

*26/9 Kellogg-Briand Pact enacted by League of Nations.*

1/10 Stalin moves to a centrally directed economy and five year plan concentrating on heavy industry.

6/10 Chiang Kai-shek is elected President of China.

7/10 Herbert Hoover is elected President of the United States

**1929 Series of moves towards peace and disarmament. Kellogg-Briand Pact backed by similar agreements. May election returns Labour - Arthur Henderson British Foreign Secretary. Young Plan sorts reparations. Wall Street Crash in October sends world economy into Depression.**

5/1 Alexander I establishes Yugoslavian military dictatorship.

5/1 America wide treaty of arbitration of disputes signed.

6/2 Germany accepts Kellogg-Briand Treaty.

9/2 Litvinov Protocol renouncing war in Eastern Europe.

20/5 Japan leaves Shandong Peninsula.

30/5 British election. Labour returned with Ramsey MacDonald as Prime Minister – Arthur Henderson as Foreign Secretary. Labour has 287 seats, but only four months before the crash..

*24/7 Kellogg-Briand Pact comes into force.*

27/7 Aristide Briand becomes French Prime Minister.

*6/8 Young plan sorts reparations. Allies agree to evacuate Rhineland by June, 1930.*

*11/8 Iran and Iraq sign Treaty of Friendship.*

14/9 US joins International Court.

19/9 Wall Street reaches peak.

24-29/10 WALL STREET CRASH signals start of Great Depression. Loans to Germany from the US fall suddenly.

13/11 Basel Bank for International settlements set up to deal with reparations under the Young Plan.

**1930 World in Depression. Final Withdrawal from Rhineland. Nazi breakthrough in polls. South American military coups.**

28/1 In Spain Primo de Rivera replaced by General Damaso Berenguer.

18-24/2 Geneva tariff conference does not get far because of Wall Street crisis.

12/3 Mahatma Gandhi begins civil disobedience with salt march.

30/3 Brüning – Centre Party becomes German Chancellor.

3/4 Ras Tafari becomes ruler of Ethiopia as Haile Selasse

*22/4 London Conference on Naval Disarmament limits cruisers, submarines of UK, US, France, Italy and Japan.*

30/4 Mussolini announces naval programme of 29 vessels

17/5 Young Plan to address reparations in force.

30/6 Last troops leave Rhineland.

21/7 Maxim Litvinov becomes USSR Foreign Minister.

25/8 Military coup in Peru.

6/9 Military coup in Argentina.

**14/9 German elections. Social Democrats 143, Nazis 107, Communists 77, Centre Party 68, National People's Party 41, Other 137. Nazis major on Anti-Versailles sentiment.**

*2/10 League of Nations adopts Convention of Financial Assistance for a state which is the Victim of aggression.*

14/10 Attempted Fascist coup in Finland.

6/11-9/12 League of Nations accepts draft proposal for the Disarmament Conference.

17/11 Geneva Economic Conference discusses world recession. Hitler pays visit to Krupp works, ignored, but signs visitors' book.

**1931 Great Depression. American firms look to the USSR for exports, including of arms factories. European banks in crisis. MANCHURIA CRISIS JAPAN-CHINA. Labour Government falls.**

2/1 Schleicher changes Defence Department rules to allow Nazis and only Nazis to man arsenals and defence depots.

12/1 Allies military control committee for Germany is dissolved – too soon.

*27/1 Council of the League of Nations decides that the Geneva Disarmament Conference of the League should start on the 2nd February, 1932.*

27/1 Pierre Laval becomes French Prime Minister.

28/2 Oswald Moseley sets up British Union of Fascists.

11/5 Collapse of European banks begins with Credit Anstalt in Austria.

*23/5 Arthur Henderson, Uncle Arthur, appointed president of the Geneva Disarmament Conference. As British Foreign Secretary he would have been able to orientate British policy for disarmament.*

*20/6 Hoover proposes year moratorium on reparations repayments.*

28/6 Left wing parties win large majority in Spain

July. May Committee proposes stringent British cuts to address a possible Budget deficit of £129 million.

9/7 Hitler and Alfred Hugenberg of the German National Party agree to co-operate. Hitler has access to Hugenberg's vast media empire.

13/7 All German banks close in collapse.

24/8 Ramsey MacDonald resigns. Labour Party splits into cutters of welfare and those in favour of temporary deficit. MacDonald becomes Prime Minister in National Government with Conservatives. Labour out of power and split.

13/9 Fascist Coup in Austria fails.

**18-19/9 Mukden incident begins Manchuria Crisis.**

**18/9 Japan begins siege of Mukden and occupies parts of Manchuria. Army is operating more or less autonomously. Encouraged by the arms companies. JAPAN-CHINA MANCHURIA WAR**

*22/9 China brings Japan before League of Nations. Japan manages to prevent a decisive decision from being made and continues its infiltration of China. China should have been supported. This case is going on through the Geneva Disarmament Conference.*
27/10 British General Election over whether cuts suggested by Civil servants should be introduced. Ramsey MacDonald is persuaded to head a National Government made almost entirely of Conservatives. Labour slaughtered and most of the pro-disarmament MPs disappear. 473 Conservatives, 52 Labour. MacDonald Prime Minister, Neville Chamberlain Chancellor, Sir John Simon Foreign Secretary, Stanley Baldwin Lord President of the Council. Lord Cecil loses strong backing for disarmament.
11/12 Japan leaves gold standard.
Krupp joins SS

**1932 Great Geneva Disarmament Conference close to success and then fails. Roosevelt elected President. MANCHURIA CRISIS. CHACO WAR. January. Japanese advance into Manchuria.**
7/1 Germany under Brüning discontinue reparations.
7/1 US note on Manchuria undercut by Britain. Failure of League of Nations to handle Japan properly because of rivalry between Britain and US. Defeat for League of Nations on Kellogg-Briand procedures.
26/1 Hitler speaks to 650 industrialists in the Düsseldorf Industrial Club
***2/2 GENEVA DISARMAMENT CONFERENCE convenes - 60 states gather. Opened with overview from Lord Cecil who then retired from formal role in the Conference.***
***February Opening statements on disarmament by major nations. Sir John Simon, now Foreign Secretary makes statement broadly in line with Cecil's position, but weak..***
***Early March. Land, Political, Naval, Air, National Defence Expenditure Commissions sit, but Committee work which does not forward Conference agenda and merely raises problems.***
9/3 Japanese control of Manchuria established.
***19/3-11/4 Conference prorogued because of German Presidential Election and Easter holidays. Momentum lost.***
10/4 Hitler defeated by Hindenburg in Presidential Election.
13/4 Brüning orders the Nazi SS and SA should be dissolved after they had created a wave of violence.

*11/4 Gibson requests urgent discussion of American proposal.*
*13/4 Grandi (Italy) argues strongly for cutting aggressive heavy weapons.*
*20-22/4 Conference votes for a qualitiative cutting of weapons of aggression without deciding how much. Back to Committees.*
*26/4 discussion pushed back into Committees in each area.*
*/5 No discussion of issues of principle because of French domestic preoccupations.*
*10/5 Committee on chemical and biological weapons set up.*
15/5 Murder of Japanese Prime Minister, Tsuyoshi Inukai, by military.
Military are running Japan.
30/5 President Hindenburg withdraws support from Brüning.
1/6 Brüning replaced by Von Papen as Chancellor.
6-11/6 Report on offensive weapons adopted.
*Summer. Geneva Disarmament Conference stalls on detailed discussions of different kinds of weapon. Shearer and other agents sow distrust.*
14/6 Von Papen rescinds order that the SS and SA should be dissolved.
15/6 Bolivian attack on Paraguay. **BOLIVIA – PARAGUAY CHACO WAR JUNE 1932 – JUNE 1935.** Two League of Nations members in conflict.
*16/6 -9/7 Lausanne Conference on Reparations. Final reparations settlement accepted by Germany. Hinders work at the Disarmament Conference from taking place, but*
*22.6 Hugh Gibson puts President Hoover's Proposal on the table looking for a one third cut in all major offensive weapons and promising immediate US compliance in cutting its weapons by large specified amounts.*
*2/7 delegation asks Henderson to work through the Summer to complete job on Hoover's proposals.*
*7-8/7 Thirty delegates from around the world strongly back the Hoover Plan.*
*14/9 Germany withdraws temporarily from Disarmament Conference demanding equality of armaments.*
*11-20/7 Discussion on final document including absolute prohibition of aerial bombing. Beneś Resolution adopted by eight powers and put through to Commission.*
*20-23/7 Discussed and passed by Commission by 41 votes to 2 (Germany and USSR against) Eight delegations abstain –*

*Austria, China, Turkey, Hungary, Italy, Bulgaria, Afghanistan and Albania.*
*Herr Nalodly explains that Germany will return to the Conference when she has full equality of rights in disarmament.*
*23/7 Agreement at Conference by 49 to 1 (China against) for a truce in armaments.*
**31/7 German Reichstag election. Nazis win 230 seats and are biggest Party, Social Democrats 133, Centre 75, Communists 89, National People's Party 37 Others 44. Inconclusive German election because neither Nazis nor Social Democrats would enter coalition. Hitler presses to be Chancellor but turned down by Hindenburg. Von Papen leads minority coalition.**
**28/8 German Government submits Memorandum on Equality of Rights to the French Government.**
1/9 Peru attacks Leticia in remote Colombia. Colombia sends fleet.
*4/10 League of Nations Commission on Control of armaments begins its work.*
*10/11 Baldwin's speech on war, total disarmament and aerial bombing.*
6/11 Another German Reichstag election. Nazis 192 seats; Social Democrats 121;Centre 70; Communists 100; National People's Party 52 Others 45. Nazis lose 38 seats and begin to wane.
**8/11 Roosevelt elected US President over Hoover in landslide.**

**1933 Year of Failure. Hitler becomes German Chancellor. Roosevelt's New Deal. CHACO WAR. American Fascist Coup against Roosevelt is first planned. Japan gets away with it. Disarmament Conference in Disarray. Nazis consolidate.**

4/1 Meeting at home of Baron Kurt von Schroeder between von Papen and Hitler to present possibility of a joint government to business leaders. Hindenberg approached to allow Hitler to be Chancellor.
**30/1 Hitler appointed German Chancellor.**
7/2 Oxford Union motion, "This house will in no circumstances fight for King and Country." carried easily.
15/2 Giuseppe Zangara assassination attempt on Roosevelt foiled.
24/2 Lytton Report re-affirms that Manchuria belongs to China. Japan withdraws from League over Manchuria.
27/2 Reichstag fire used by Hitler for attack on Communists.

**4/3 Roosevelt inaugurated. "The only thing to fear is fear itself" Attack on "moneychangers in the Temple". Begins New Deal, "hundred days" of measures to reinvigorate the American economy.**
10/3 Zeletsky Bribery scandal in Roumania organising Skoda tax evasion of vast scale.
25/3 Colombian fleet takes reprisals against Peru at Güeppi.
March. Organisations of ex-soldiers with 8 million members world-wide including British Legion send 5000 delegates to Geneva with resolution to suppress private manufacture and traffic in arms with effective mutual international control.[280]
1/4. Nazi persecution of the Jews starts.
April Gustav Krupp meets privately with Hitler.
19/4 Roosevelt removes US from gold standard.
27/4 Trade agreement between Britain and Germany.
31/5 Armistice between Japan and China, forcing China to retreat to just north of the Great Wall.
20/6 Army coup in Siam/Thailand.
1/7 MacGuire and Doyle contact General Smedley Butler about taking over the American Legion.
4/7 MacGuire and Doyle see Butler again.
1/8 MacGuire's third meeting with Butler. Dollars on the bed.
6/8 Vickers-Armstrong Airplane Agent, Lander, deported from Turkey for trying to mess up Turkish airplane manufacturing.
August Vera Brittain's *Testament of Youth* published.
1/9 Butler sees Sterling Clark, head of Singer Empire, declines to attend convention.
14/10 Hitler withdraws from Geneva Disarmament Conference and League of Nations.
25/10 Fulham East Pacifist by-election.
12/11 In German elections Nazis get 92% of the vote amid intimidation.
29/11 Roosevelt sets up Federal Alcohol Control Commission – excludes Pierre Du Pont
5/12 Repeal of prohibition. Du Ponts talk of new organisation.

**1934 Militarism and Fascism now largely free from constraints in Germany and Japan. Fascist Movements elsewhere. CHACO WAR. AMERICAN FASCIST COUP PLAN AGAINST ROOSEVELT by Du Ponts and others. German arming underway with American help.**

7/1 6,000 German pastors defy Nazis saying they will not be muzzled.
11/1 homes of defiant pastors raided.
8/3 Baldwin creates four new air force squadrons and begins re-armament.
29/3 German defence estimates up a third. Vast expansion in air force.
6/4 418 Lutheran pastors arrested.
February ? Du Ponts acquire Remington Arms which have already supplied Nazi stormtroopers.
18/4 Hitler names von Ribbentrop Minister for Disarmament. Ha. Ha. Ha.
2/5 Meeting between Hitler, General Motors and Opel to develop cars. Over next four years GM workforce in Germany grew from 17,000 to 27,000.
11/6 Geneva Disarmament Conference ends in failure.
28-30/6 Night of the Long Knives. Purge of SA and military.
4/7 Advertisement for Tiger Moth supplied to Norway, Sweden, Denmark, China, Japan, Persia, Poland, Spain, Portugal and Germany.
9/7 Himmler in charge of German concentration camps.
2/8 von Hindenburg dies. Hitler makes himself President. Confirmed 19/8 in popular plebiscite.
15/8 American Liberty League formed. Gerald MacGuire asks General Butler to lead Fascist coup against Roosevelt.
16/9 Anti-Nazi Lutherans protest in Munich.
26/11Karl Barth gives himself up to Nazis.
29/12 Japan denounces 1922 and 1930 naval treaties and 5-5-3 ratios with Britain and United States.
Publication of H.C.Englebrecht and F.C. Hanighen *Merchants of Death* has immense influence.
**14/12 Abyssinian Government reports Italian incursion to League of Nations.**

**1935 Great popular ferment for peace, but too late. Germany receiving massive US investment for rearming. Stalin creates industrial munitions system with help from US, runs purge of opposition. Mussolini invades Ethiopia. Haile Selasse appeals to League of Nations. Weapons industry expands.**

13/1 Saar votes for incorporation into Germany.
17-19/1 Stalin purge against Zinoviev and others. Thousands arrested.
1-3/2 British-German Conference in London to discuss Germany's re-armament.
22/2 Italian troops go to North Africa.
16/3 Germany repudiates disarmament clauses in Versailles Treaty and introduces conscription.
11-14/4 Italy, France, Britain protest against German rearmament and agree to act together against Germany.
*14/7 "Peace Ballot" signed by nearly 12 million people in Britain. Over 90% voted for the manufacture and sale of weapons for profit to be prohibited by international agreement.*
*14/7 Peace Pledge Union formed after mass rally in Albert Hall.*
15/9 Nuremberg Rally
8/10 George Lansbury resigns as Labour party leader on pacifist grounds.
9/12 Hoare/Laval Pact gives in to Mussolini's occupation of Ethiopia.

**1936 Japan military and Fascist. ITALY ANNEXES ETHIOPIA. No League of Nations Opposition. SPANISH CIVIL WAR. GUERNICA. Du Ponts set up Liberty League to oppose Roosevelt. Churchill's views accepted and British rearmament.**

16/2 Spanish elections give outright victory for Left-wing Popular Front.
**26/2 Military rebellion in Japan ousts Prime Minister.**
7/3 Germany occupies the Rhineland.
5/5 Italy annexes Ethiopia
21/5 Austria becomes one party state.
17/7 Munitions industry in France is nationalised.
**17/7 General Franco starts SPANISH CIVIL WAR. JULY 1936-MARCH1939.**
Autumn Du Ponts use Liberty League and back Alfred Landon and Republicans with nearly a million dollars
5/10 Jarrow unemployment March.
3/11 Roosevelt re-elected President.

**1937 SPANISH CIVIL WAR- GERMAN, ITALIAN AND RUSSIAN INVOLVEMENT. FULL JAPAN-CHINA WAR BEGINS. FULL-SCALE REARMAMENT.**

6/1 Roosevelt renews Neutrality Act.
Feb: French arms firm Schneider-Creusot nationalised.
Feb Congress Party win Indian elections.
27/2 French rely on Maginot line.
27/4 Guernica bombed in Spanish Civil War. Picasso's painting.
6/5 German airship Hindenburg explodes.
12/5 George VI coronation.
26/5 Egypt joins League of Nations.
28/5 Chamberlain becomes Prime Minister. Eden Foreign Secretary.
June. Stalinist purge of German sympathisers.
3/6 Windsor marries Mrs Simpson in France.
June. Germany and Italy involved in Spanish Civil War.
**7/7 JAPAN-CHINA WAR JULY 1937-SEPTEMBER 1945.**
17/7 British-German naval agreement.
28/7 Japan seizes Beijing.
August-November Battle of Shanghai. Japanese rampage.
3/9 National Council of Labour says European War not inevitable.
25-8/9 Mussolini visits Hitler in Berlin.
1/10 Franco leads nationalists.
17-21/11 Halifax visits Hitler.
11/12 Italy withdraws from League of Nations.

**1938 War looks inevitable. AUSTRIA INVADED BY NAZIS UNOPPOSED. JAPAN-CHINA WAR. SPANISH CIVIL WAR. Austria unifies with Germany. British-Italian Pact not worth paper it is written on. Neville Chamberlain goes to Munich – another piece of paper. Kristalnacht in Germany.**

4/2 Hitler becomes German Commander in Chief. Von Ribbentrop Foreign Minister and Keitel Chief of Staff.
12/2 Austrian Chancellor Schuschnigg humiliated by Hitler. Ordered to appoint Nazi to government.
20/2 Chamberlain tries to link with Italy. Ignores Roosevelt. Eden resigns.
9/3 Austrian Plebescite announced.
12/3 German troops in Austria. On 13th Austria becomes part of Germany.

28/3 Japanese install puppet government in Nanjing.
10/4 Radical Socialist Government in France.
16/4 British-Italian Pact. British recognize Italian control of Ethiopia, dumps Haile Selasse.
17/4 Fascist plot in Roumania.
24/4 Move towards Sudenland annexation.
3/5 Hitler visits Mussolini.
June. **JAPAN WINNING IN SINO-JAPANESE WAR.**
19/7 George VI visits Paris.
15/9 Hitler tells Chamberlain he will annexe Sudatenland.
7/9 League of Nations says Japan aggressor in China. What kept them?
29/9 Munich. Chamberlain's bit of paper. "Peace in our time"
1/10 **GERMANY OCCUPIES SUDATENLAND.**
2/10 Japan withdraws from League of Nations
6/10 Italy passes anti-semitic legislation. Condemned by Pope.
9/11 Nazi Kristallnacht attacks on Jews.
6/12 French-German pact on involiability of existing frontiers. Adolf gave his word.

**1939 GERMANS OCCUPY BOHEMIA AND MORAVIA. NATIONALISTS WIN SPANISH CIVIL WAR. Nazi-Soviet Pact. Nazi pressure on Poland. START OF SECOND WORLD WAR. JAPAN WINNING IN SINO-JAPANESE WAR.**

10/1 Halifax and Chamberlain to Rome to woo Mussolini.
27/2 Britain and France recognize Franco.
15/3 **HITLER OCCUPIES BOHEMIA AND MORAVIA.**
28/3 **REPUBLICANS SURRENDER – END OF SPANISH CIVIL WAR.**
7/4 **ITALY INVADES ALBANIA.**
22/5 Hitler-Mussolini 10 year Pact of Steel.
23/8 Nazi-Soviet Pact.
25/8 British-Polish Treaty of mutual assistance.
1/9 **GERMANY INVADES POLAND.**
**3/9 BRITAIN AND FRANCE DECLARE WAR ON GERMANY. START OF SECOND WORLD WAR.**
14/9 **CHINA HOLDS JAPAN IN SINO-JAPANESE WAR.**
**17/9 USSR INVADES POLAND**
**28/9 POLAND PARTITIONED BY GERMANY AND USSR.**

4/11 Roosevelt sets up cash and carry arms deal for Britain and France.
30/11 **USSR INVADES FINLAND.**

**1940 SECOND WORLD WAR. Japan has military dominated Government. GERMANY INVADES DENMARK AND NORWAY. CONQUERS FRANCE, BELGIUM AND THE NETHERLANDS. BATTLE OF BRITAIN. POLISH JEWS INTERNED. HOLOCAUST STARTS.**

12/3 **FINLAND DEFEATED.**
**9/4 GERMANY INVADES DENMARK AND NORWAY.**
7/5 Chamberlain resigns and is replaced by Winston Churchill as Prime Minister.
10/5 **GERMANY INVADES THE LOW COUNTRIES**
13/5 Churchill's "blood, sweat, toil and tears" speech.
**26/5-2/6 EVACUATION OF BRITISH TROOPS FROM DUNKIRK**
**5/6 GERMANY PUSHES INTO FRANCE**
**10/6 ITALY DECLARES WAR ON BRITAIN AND FRANCE.**
**26/6 USSR OCCUPIES ROMANIA**
**3/7 BRITAIN SINKS FRENCH FLEET.**
**10/7 START OF BATTLE OF BRITAIN**
18/7 Britain closes Burma Road for Japan.
15/8 **RAF DOWNS 180 GERMAN PLANES.**
**23/8 BLITZ OF LONDON BEGINS**
**3/9 US sells Britain 50 destroyers.**
**Sept. HEAVY BRITISH SHIPPING LOSSES.**
**12/10 HITLER POSTPONES 'OPERATION SEA LION' AND USES HEAVY BOMBING AGAINST BRITAIN**
5/11 Roosevelt re-elected.
**11/11 BRITAIN CRIPPLES ITALIAN FLEET.**

**1941 PIVOTAL YEAR IN SECOND WORLD WAR. GERMANY INVADES THE USSR. PEARL HARBOUR. USA ENTERS THE WAR. HOLOCAUST.**

6/1 Roosevelt's Lend-Lease Bill allows arms to be transferred to Britain and Allies.
**30/1 SOUTH AFRICA DRIVES ITALY FROM KENYA.**

**12/2 ROMMEL FACES BRITISH TROOPS IN NORTH AFRICA.**

**March. USSR agrees to support Turkey against German invasion.**

**6/4 German ultimatum to Greece and Yugoslavia. INVASION OF BOTH.**

**10/5 Rudolf Hess flies to Scotland to try peace deal to get rid of Churchill.**

**10/5 HOUSE OF COMMONS BOMBED.**

**27/5 *BISMARCK* SUNK**

**8/6 BRITISH INVADE SYRIA**

**22/6 GERMANY INVADES USSR "OPERATION BARBAROSSA" STRONG GERMAN ADVANCE**

**8/9 GERMAN SEIGE OF LENINGRAD LASTS TWO YEARS - UNSUCCESSFUL**

29/9 Beaverbrook and Averell Harriman go to Moscow to plan war supplies.

1/10 Germans advance on Moscow.

**24/10 GERMANS CAPTURE KHARKOV**

13/11 ***ARK ROYAL* SUNK..**

**7/12 JAPANESE ATTACK ON PEARL HARBOUR.**

**8/12 USA AND BRITAIN DECLARE WAR ON JAPAN..**

**11/12 GERMANY AND ITALY DECLARE WAR ON THE USA.**

16/12 German retreat from Moscow begins as winter sets in.

**26/12 USA AND BRITAIN FORM ALLIANCE WITH CHINA.**

**1942 SECOND WORLD WAR. (30%) NAZIS PLAN FULL DESTRUCTION OF EUROPEAN JEWS. SECOND WORLD WAR BEGINS TO SWING TOWARDS ALLIES. USSR TAKES BRUNT OF GERMAN ATTACKS. STALINGRAD. EL ALAMEIN**

15/2 Surrender of Singapore and 70,000 troops to Japanese.

28/3 British air force bombs Lübeck and destroy medieval city.

8/4 Second Front partly promised to USSR in 1942, but really not practical.

**"Bataan death march" in Philippines after surrender to Japan. 10,000 killed.**

18/4 **GERMAN SPRING OFFENSIVE IN USSR.**

26/5 British-USSR 20 year alliance signed in London.

30/5 **"THOUSAND BOMBER" RAID AGAINST COLOGNE.**

4/5 Four Japanese carriers sunk in Battle of Midway.
28/6 **ROMMEL WINS AT TOBRUK**. British retreat towards El Alamein.
June Roosevelt and Churchill agree secret development of atom bomb.
27/7 60,000 demonstrate in Trafalgar Square for opening of Second Front to take pressure off Russia.
August. Anglo-Canadian raid on Dieppe fails.
3/10 De Pont agrees to build Oak Ridge uranium separation Plant.
20/10 All assets of Union Banking Corporation organized by Bunny Harriman, Prescott Bush and Thyssen representative seized because they were dealing with the enemy.
**CONTINUOUS SLAUGHTER OF JEWS IN CONCENTRATION CAMPS**
23/10 **BATTLE OF EL ALAMEIN**. Rommel pushed back.
18/11 German advance in Caucasus stopped. **GERMAN ARMY TRAPPED IN STALINGRAD.**
2/12 Enrico Fermi constructs first controlled nuclear chain reaction.
2/12 Pure uranium for use in bomb produced in United States

**1943 SECOND WORLD WAR. (30%) HOLOCAUST MASS MURDERS. GERMAN ARMY SURRENDERS AT STALINGRAD. ALLIES ADVANCE THROUGH NORTH AFRICA AND INVADE ITALY.**

11/1 China-British treaty renouncing British territoral rights in China.
16/1 Hanford, Washington chosen for Du Pont's big plutonium facility.
23/1 **ALLIES ADVANCE ACROSS N. AFRICA.**
14-25/1. Casablanca Conference agrees North Africa then Sicily.
Feb. **GERMANS RETREAT BEFORE SOVIET ARMY.**
13/4 Germans announce mass grave of Poles at Katyn Forest, a 10-20,000 massacre by USSR.
16/5 **DAM BUSTERS RAID**
3/6 De Gaulle forms National Liberation Committee.
July **US and UK SATURATION BOMBING OF HAMBURG.**
4/7 **KURSK USSR-GERMAN TANK BATTLE.**
10/7 **ALLIES INVADE SICILY**
August US/UK Quebec Agreement on nuclear weapons.

3/9 **ITALY UNCONDITIONAL SURRENDER. GERMANS FIGHT ON.**
**Oct. GERMANS IN RETREAT IN EASTERN EUROPE AND ITALY.**
**November-December. Tehran Conference. Leaders plan "Operation Overlord" for May.**

**1944 SECOND WORLD WAR. (35%of world economy militarised) HOLOCAUST MASS MURDERS. MUTUAL HEAVY AIR RAIDS. SOVIET ADVANCE. NORMANDY LANDINGS.**

400,000 Hungarian Jews gassed.
20/1 **RAF BOMBS BERLIN.**
**27/1 END OF SEIGE OF LENINGRAD.**
February Bohr/Frankfurter discussion with Roosevelt on nuclear controls with Russians.
April Bohr persuades Anderson, Cherwell and Smuts on nuclear talks with Russians.
**19-26/2 HEAVY GERMAN AIR RAIDS ON LONDON.**
**6/3 US DAYLIGHT BOMBING OF BERLIN.**
**April MORE HEAVY BOMBING OF GERMAN CITIES.**
16/5 Bohr meets Churchill who wanted to keep Russians out.
**11/5 ITALIAN BREAKTHROUGH AGAINST GERMANY.**
**11/5 GERMANS RETREAT FROM SEBASTOPOL.**
**6/6 ALLIED INVASION OF EUROPE. OPERATION OVERLORD. NORMANDY LANDINGS.**
13/6 First V1 flying bombs land on London.
July Bretton Woods Conference founds IMF. Keynes' influence.
3/7 **BIG USSR OFFENSIVE, 150,000 GERMANS CAPTURED.**
25/8 Romania moves from Germany to Russia.
2/8 Gipsy Camp at Auchswitz liquidated.
1/8-2/10 **WARSAW UPRISING** unsupported by Russians
26/8 Bohr meets Roosevelt – positive towards approaching Stalin.
9/9 Bulgaria moves from Germany to USSR.
9/9 Averell Harrison's negative report from Moscow.
18/9 Churchill meets Roosevelt at Hyde Park. Closes possibility of nuclear discussions with Russia. Bohr to be silenced.
7/11 Roosevelt re-elected President. Truman Vice-President rather than Henry Wallace.
12 Himmler tries to cover himself in relation to the Holocaust.

Dec. **GERMANS FIGHT BATTLE OF THE BULGE.**

**1945 SECOND WORLD WAR ENDS IN EUROPE. ATOMIC BOMBS ON JAPAN British Labour Government. Death of Roosevelt. Machinations for a Cold War. START OF CHINESE CIVIL WAR BETWEEN KUOMINTANG-COMMUNIST**

Spring. Germany produces tabun lethal gas

12/1 **SOVIET POLISH OFFENSIVE STARTS.**

14/1 **US HALTS GERMAN BATTLE OF BULGE OFFENSIVE.**

4-11/2 Yalta Conference between Roosevelt, Stalin and Churchill planning German unconditional surrender, formation of UN, Russia will enter war on Japan after German surrender.

13-14/2 **SATURATION BOMBING OF DRESDEN**. 60,000 killed.

9-10/3 **US INCENDIARY BOMBING** burns a quarter of Tokyo. 84,000 killed in first attack. More later.

1/4 **OKINAWA CAPTURED**. 49,000 US dead. 110,000 Japanese dead.

12/4. President Roosevelt dies and is succeeded by Harry Truman.

25/4 Founding Conference of UN.

28/4 Mussolini shot.

30/4 Hitler shoots himself.

2/5 Berlin surrenders to the Soviet Army.

8/5 **VE DAY. FULL SURRENDER OF GERMAN STATE TO ALLIES.**

**END OF SECOND WORLD WAR IN EUROPE.**

31/5 Use of Atom bomb against Kyoto and Tokyo vetoed by Stimson and Truman.

12/6 Franck report suggests demonstration use of atom bomb on barren island.

16/7 first test of Atom bomb at Alamogordo. No international observers invited.

17/7 Potsdam Conference – Stalin, Truman, Churchill, Attlee on occupation of Germany.

26/7 Labour landslide in UK election. Attlee replaces Churchill as Prime Minister.

26/7 Last ultimatum to Japan. No warning of Atom bomb.

August. **DEFEAT OF JAPAN IN CHINA.**

6/8 US plane drops atomic bomb on Hiroshima.
8/8 USSR declares war on Japan and moves into Manchuria.
9/8 Nagasaki bombed.
**AUGUST START OF CHINESE CIVIL WAR BETWEEN MAO AND CHIANG**
11/8 Suggestion that Emperor of Japan will not have to go.
14/8 **JAPAN SURRENDERS.**

**SECOND WORLD WAR ENDS.**

2/9 Ho Chi Minh proclaims Democratic Republic of Vietnam.
6/9 Communist influenced Korean People's Republic proclaimed, but US establish military control.
20-23/9 India demands self-government.
24/10 United Nations Charter ratified. It includes disarmament and the regulation of armaments. US refused to prohibit production.
20/11-31/8/1946 Nuremburg trials.

# Index

AAPA (Association against the Prohibition Amendment) 346, 352
Aberystwyth University Students Union 274
Adams, Charles 353
Addams, Jane 132, 260
Admiralty 81, 86-7, 90, 142
Afghanistan 48-9
Africa 50-2
American Civil War 17,
American Defense Society 195
American Legion 193, 351-3, 359, 360, 363
American Liberty League 362-6
Anabaptists 115-8
Anderson, W.C. 317
Anglicans 127-8, 359
Anglican Pacifist Fellowship 219
Ansaldo 301-2, 339
Anti-Socialist Union 312
Anti-Saloon League 373
Appeasement 278-80, 367-8, 374
Arditi 304
Argentina 46-7
Arms Cause Wars 52-61, 63-6, 170-2
Arms Companies 9-10, 15-17, 18-32, 41-95, 170-2, 220-4, 229-31, 231-7, 248-49, 276-7, 375-6
Arms Syndicate 23, 31-2
Armstrong, William 26-8, 43, 68
Armstrong-Whitworth 40, 43-6, 81-3
Assassination 49, 106
Attlee, Clement 271
Atrocities 112, 133, 297-8
Austro-Hungary 19, 53, 58, 58, 63, 106-112, 146,159-60
*Avanti* 300

Baetens, Freya 136
Baldwin, Stanley 246, 265-6, 270, 272-4
Balfour, A.J. 90, 92
Bank of International Settlements 337, 386
Banking and arms 22-3, 63, 190-4, 336-8
Barbarossa 379, 381
Battleships 27-33, 35-38, 41-5, 77-92, 95-99, 263-4
Beer Hall Putsch (1923) 316-8
Behn, Sosthenes 336
Beresford, Lord Charles 82-3, 89, 92
Bevan, Nye 246
Biddle, Francis 388
Birmingham 8, 15-16, 48, 50, 251
Bismarck, Otto von 19, 180, 293

Bisson, T.A. 391
Black, Jeremy 220
Bloomsbury Group 80-1
Boeing 361-2
Boer War, Second 20, 50-1, 56, 74-6, 125
Bofors 163
Bolsheviks 207-9
Bone, Sen. Homer 361-2
Bowman, Maurice 269-70
Boxer Rebellion 359
Brazil 46-7
Briande, Aristide 245
Bribery 44, 69, 137-139
Bradford University Peace Studies 397
Britain 15-17, 20, 26-31, 33-40, 41, 42-5, 47, 51, 52-94, 98, 106, 109-10, 125-29, 139-40, 153-7, 168-69,
Brittain, Vera 219, 257, 312
British Empire 9, 31, 36-7, 48, 70, 100-1, 159
British Navy League 70, 78-9, 91
British Union of Fascists (BFU) 310-14
Broadway 349-51, 360
Brockway, Fenner 129
BSA (Birmingham Small Arms) 16, 92
Brüning, Chancellor Heinrich 254, 261-2
Bryan, William Jennings 162
Bush, Samuel Prescott 198-199, 330-4, 343
Bush Sam 197-99
Buckeye Steel Castings 197
Butler, General Smedley 353-4, 358-60, 362-5
Buxton, Noel 128
Burk, Robert 344-5

Cammell-Laird 85, 86-92
Campbell-Bannerman, Henry 56-7, 78, 82-3
Canada 121
Carnegie, Andrew 194
Cavell, Edith 195
Carlton Club 154
Cecil, Lord David 233, 280-3, 373-4
Centre Party (Germany) 130
Chamberlain, Neville 282, 373
Charge of the Light Brigade 14-15
Chase National Bank 214, 387
Chase Manhattan Bank 337
Chassepot Rifle 21
Chile 46,
China 46, 76,
Christianity 97,119-125, 134-37, 168-9, 178-183, 220, 257-8, 270-1, 354-5, 397
Christmas Truce (1914) 133-6
Chilwell (Notts.) 148, 157

China 9, 76, 234-6, 246-9, 389
Church of England 126-7, 255-6, 259, 270-1
Churchill, Winston Spencer 59-60, 64, 91, 155, 174-5, 209-12, 221, 245, 279-81, 283-4, 394
Clark, Robert Sterling (Singer) 359-60
Cochran, Bert 382
Cole, G.D.H. and Margaret, 238, 284-5
Comité des Forges 68, 310
Communism 147, 208-9
Concentration camps 76-7
Congo 51
Conrad, Joseph 51
Conscientious Objectors 130
Concentration camps 76
Conservative Party 60, 76-7, 240-4, 266-9, 311, 394
Corcoran, Tommy 384
Coventry Ordnance Works 85-88
Crimean War 12-15, 21
Crusade of European Youth for Disarmament 261
Crystal Palace Exhibition 12, 19,
Curzon, Lord 66, 311
Curzon, Lady Cynthia 311

*Daily Mail* 90, 94, 140-1, 243, 312
*Daily Telegraph* 107
Davis, John W. 351-2, 361
De Wendel, François 309-10
"Defence" Expenditure 60, 63-43, 77, 79, 153-60,217, 221-2,
Democratic Party (US) 347-9
Denikin, General 211
Dingman, Mary 260
Disarmament 172-9, 226, 264-9
Dodd, William 326
"Dollar a year men" 384
Donovan, Wild Bill 353
Doukhobors 123, 126
Doyle, William 353, 359
Dreadnought (HMS) 73, 80-2, 87
Dreadnought Panic 73-4, 85-93
Dulles, Allen 332
Dulles John Foster 338
Dumont, Charles 267
Du Pont family 197, 201, 278, 343-54, 362-8, Pierre 343, 362, Irenée 343,363, Lammot 343

East Dereham 94
Eden, Sir Anthony 268
Egypt 18,
Eichart, Diedrich 318
Einstein, Jacob 258

Empires 148-9, 180
Empire State Building 348
Enfield Rifles 16-17, 50
Engeringhe, Steenberghe 260
Englebrecht and Hanighen (*Merchants of Death*) 18, 1 40-1, 251-2, 284, 362, 372
Esher, Lord 89
Esperanto 131
Espionage Act (US.1917) 133

Farish, William 336, 338
Fascist Parties 288-90, 301-15, 340
Fawcett, Millicent 76
FBI 261
Federal Reserve Board 194
Fenton, Roger 14
Fellowship of Reconciliation 131
Fiat 303
Films (WW2) 395-6
First Hundred Days (Roosevelt) 356-9
Fisher, Jackie 34-6, 79-126
Fleet Review 36-7
Flick, Friedrich 333
Flu epidemic 147
Fogarty, Michael 260
Forbes, Archibald 23
Ford, Henry 314, 317-9, 336-7
Forgan, Robert 313
Fox, George 118
"Four Minute Men" 197
France 13, 18-19, 39-40, 58, 63-5, 67-8, 78-9, 107, 131, 139-40, 190-1, 255, 309-10, 320
French Revolution 7, 10
Franco, General 288-90
Franco-Prussian War (1870) 20, 21, 23-25
French, Paul 365
Fried, Alfred 132

Gallo, Max 302
Gatling gun 49, 189
Gandhi, Mohandas Kamarachand 123-4, 258, 280
Garner, John 355
Geddes, Eric 156
General Analine and Film (GAF) 388-9
General Motors 345, 362
Geneva Disarmament Conference (1932) 240-85
Geneva Protocol 246
German hyperinflation 160-1
German Naval League (Flottenverein) 70, 97-99
German Social Democrats 105-6, 132-3, 255-6
German National People's Party 323-5

Germany 11-12, 18-22, 23-5, 30-1, 53-4, 59, 63-6, 73-4, 81, 147, 149, 159-65, 190-1, 254-6, 261, 273, 279-80, 291-4, 311-3, 315-339, 360, 366, 374-8, 391-2, 396
Gibson, Hugh 264
Gladstone, William Ewart 34-41, 56, 62
God 1340, 180-183, 257, passim
Goebbels 312
Gold Standard 359-60
Göring, Herman 336
Grandi, Signor 265
Great Depression 202, 247-8, 347-57
Grenfell, David MP 267
Grey, Lord Edward 61-2, 258
Grötz, Georg 298, 316, 325

Hague Peace Conference (1899) 125-6, 189-90
Hamilton, Duke of 314
Hankey, Sir Maurice 245, 276-7
Hardie, Kier 30-1 144, 158-9
"Harvey Steel Cartel" 23, 31
Hamburg-America Shipping Line 330
Harriman Bank 198, 201, 329-32, 338, 343
Harriman, Averill 329-31, 387
Harriman, Bunny 329
Harrison, Mark 380
Hebblethwaite, Margaret 46
Henderson, Arthur 246-8, 258-261, 267
Hess, Rudolf 314
Higham, Charles 337
Hiss, Alger 361
HMS Camperdown 37-9
HMS Victoria 30, 37-9
Hitler, Adolf 270, 273-4, 284, 286, 291, 316-40, 367-8, 389
Hiroshima and Nagasaki 390
Hoare, Sir Samuel 304
Hodgkin, Henry 132
Holocaust 175, 394
Hollman, Friedrich 98
Hood, Thomas 9
Horses 52
Hough , Richard 34-5
Hope, Captain Arthur 247
Hoover, Edgar 355
Hoover, President Herbert 248, 264-9, 353
House of Representatives' Un-American Activities Committee 364-5
Hori, Majiko 308
Hugenberg, Alfred 323-5
Huxley, Aldous 312

ICI 222
Idealist/Realist debate 175-7

I.G. Farben 160, 327, 334-7, 338-9
*Il Popolo d'Italia* 303
im Thurn, Donald 245
International Congress of Women (1915) 138-9
International Court 228
International Union of Catholic Women's League 260
International Workers of the World (Wobblies) 351
Invasion of the Ruhr 321
Italy 63, 68, 265, 288,301-4

January Club (Fascist) 312-3
Japan 42-5, 78, 233, 249-55, 306-9, 389-92
Jaurès, Jean 130-1
Jenkins, Roy 40
Jerusalem 13
Jesus Christ 117, 120, 122, 124, 130-1, 136, 170, 181-4, 221, 356, 399
John Augustus 258
John Brown Shipyard 85, 232
Johnson, General Hugh 363
Jones, Morgan MP 254
Joyce William (Lord Haw Haw) 311, 313
Joynson-Hicks MP 141

Kennedy, Joseph 388
Keppler Circle 333-4
Keynes, John Maynard 170-1, 328, 357
Kharki Election 76-7
Kidd, Miss M.W. 262
Kiel Canal 83
Kitchener, Lord 76, 142
Kitching Carolyn 262-3
KKK 342
Krupp (Alfried) 10-12, 18-27, 55-6, 71-2, 76, 86-7, 96-9 (Fritz) 100-101, Margarethe 100 (Gustav) 101, 129, 160-3, 231-2, 322-3
Kuyper, Abraham 182

Labour Party 241-5, 247-8, 272-3, 283, 311
Lamb, Richard 266
Landon, Alf 366
Lansbury, George 131, 258, 272-3
Laval, Pierre 310
Lawrence, Sir Herbert 232
Le Croix de Feu 309-10
League of Nations 139, 221-2, 226-31, 235-41, 249-54, 255-74 276 372-3
Lenin, Vladimir Illich 207-213
Liberty Bonds 195
Liebknecht, Karl 105, 133, 144
Liege guns 51, 53
Littell, Norman 389-9
Live and let live 136

Lloyd George, David 56-8, 73-4, 93, 110-11, 155-6, 167-8, 225, 258, 268, 310
London Peace Congress 124-5
London School of Economics 275
López, Solano 47
Lüdecke, Kurt 319
Ludendorff, General Erich 147, 326
Lusi, Joe 51
Luxembourg, Rosa 105, 130
Lynch, Jim 351

MacArthur, Gen A. 50
MacArthur, General Douglas 50, 354, 364
MacCormack, Sen. John 364
MacDonald, Ramsey 130, 235-6, 242-5, 259, 261, 271
McGonagall, William 38-9
McKenna, Edward MP 142
McKinley, President 49-50
Manchester University Students' Union 275
Manchuria Crisis 236-8, 249-55, 307
Manhattan 349-50
Manufacture d'Armes 21
Mauser rifles 20-1, 75
Maxim, Hiram and guns 29, 66-7, 100
Mellon, Edwin 361
Methodists 260, 271
Metternich, Count 93
MI5 304
Militarism 42-173, 180-4, 277-9, 289, 316, 339-40, 374-80, 390
Milner, Lord 75
Ministry of Munitions 155-8
MIT 343
Mitchell, Charles 27-8
Mitford, Diana 312
Mitsubishi 308
Morgan, Barbara 107-8
Morgan, J.P. 193-7, 202, 327, 350, 352, 358-63, 365
Morgenthau, Henry 388
Mosley, Oswald 310-14
Mulliner, H.H. 73, 85-93
Munich 317-9
*Munich Post* 319
Mussolini, Benito 260, 265, 301-5, 351, 353, 358, 361, 363
Murphy, Col. Grayson 351-3, 358-9, 361

Naldi, Filippo 302
Nansen, Fridtjef 246-7
Napoleon III 19, 68
Napoleonic Wars 7-8
Nash, Gerald 385-6
National Aerial Defence Association 83, 93

Naval Conference (1927) 234-6
Naval lobby 30-41, 59-60, 231-5
Nazi Party 255-6, 269, 274, 291-2, 314, 316 326-40, 377-8
Neutrality Act (1935) 365-6
"Never say Die" (Epsom) 359
*New York Times* 317-8, 320, 357, 365
Nicholas, Tsar 58, 88, 108, 122-3, 204-5
Nicholson, Harold 268
Nietzsche, Frederick 291-5
Nightingale, Florence 14
Nobel, Alfred 133-4
Nobel Peace Prize 132, 134
No Conscription Fellowship 131
Noel-Baker, Philip 16, 46, 235-6, 252, 277-9, 371-3
Norman, Montagu 310-11, 387
Nuremburg Trials 333-4, 389
Nye Commission 192-3, 223-6, 235, 361-2, 365, 371

Oerlikon factory 163
Omotokyo 307
Opel 361
Ottoman Empire 13, 36, 69, 173
Overy, Richard 374
Oxford University 30
Oxford Union Debating Society 274

Paraguay Wars 46-7
Paris 10, 19, 22, 24, 47, 58, 119, 141-2
Pasitch, Serbian Premier 113
Passy, Frédéric 119, 131
Patriotism 149
Peace Ballot 282-3
Peace Movements 115-144, 165-71, 180-8, 257-62, 267, 270-72, 371-3
Peace Pledge Union 221
Pearl Harbour 45, 369, 392
Pecoria, Ferdinand 357
Penn, William 118
Philippine Wars 49-50
Pig War 108-10
Pitt-Rivers, George 314
Ponsonby, Arthur 62, 130, 258
Ponsonby Rules 139, 243
Pope Benedict XV 135-8
Power 291-7
Prohibition 345-6, 360
Propaganda 392-8
Prussia 18, 142
PSTD 297-300
Prior, Samuel 332
Price, Ward 313

Puhl, Emil 387

Quakers 123, 131-2, 264

Rascob, John J. 343, 346-8
Rathenau, Walter 324
Raven, Charles 258
Red Scares 196-8, 343-5, 352-5, 393
Remington Arms 190, 332-3, 344, 354, 363
Rendel, James, George, Stuart and Hamilton 27
Republican Party 346, 366
Reves, Emory 144
Reynolds, David 280
Rist, Charles, 160
Roberts, Lord 76-7
Roberts, Samuel MP 90
Rockerfeller (Frank) 199 (David) 217, 335 (John, Junior) 338, 343, 352
Rhodes Cecil 74-5
Roosevelt Franklin D. 326, 346-9, 353-89
Roosevelt Inauguration 355-6
Roosevelt, Theodore 127-8, 164, 191-2, 197
Rothermere, Lord 141-2, 312
Rothschild, Lord 29, 69
Royal Naval Exhibition 30
Ruling Class 296-7
Russia 13-14, 22-3, 39-40, 53-4, 58, 63-5, 112-5, 141-2, 146-7, 190, 203-19, 265, 378-81
Russell. William Howard 14
Russell, Bertrand 258, 398
Russian Orthodox Church 121-2
Russo-Japanese War 44-5, 78, 127, 204

Salisbury, Marquess of 76-7
Samuels, Richard 301
Schacht, Hjalmar 337-8, 387
Schmitz, Hermann 387
Schneider-Le Creusot 19, 21-34, 54, 68, 76, 155, 269
Schröder Bank 338
Science and Militarism 378
Serbia 108-14, 146
Sevastopol 14
Shaw, George Bernard 55-6
Shearer, William 234-5, 277-8
Sheffield 11-13, 28-9
Sheldon, George 200
Sheppard, Dick 258, 312
Shouse, Jouett 348, 362
Siegmund-Schultze, Friedrich 132
Silvertown Munitions Factory 156-7
Simkin, John 383-4
Simon, Sir John 248-51, 262-9, 271-3, 277

Singer Company 349-50, 359-60
Sloan, Alfred 344
Skoda 108-10
Smith, Al 348
Smith, Sara 251
Smith-Dorien, General Sir Horace 136-7
Smuts, General 70, 123
Snowden, Philip 130
Social Darwinism 180-1, 287
Socialism 105-6, 158-9, 171, 209, 347
Soper, Donald 258, 398
Soucy, Robert 309
Spanish Civil War 367
Stalin, Joseph 212-8, 380-1
Standard Oil, New Jersey 327, 335
Stehr Arms Company 110
State Corporatism 290-1
Stettinus, Edward 383
Stimson, Henry, 248
Stresemann, Gustav 245
Suffragettes 242
Sutton, Anthony 216-7, 318-9, 326, 335-6
Suttner, Bertha von 133-4

Takashi, Hara 306
Tardieu, André 268
Teagle, Walter 336-7
Tennyson, Alfred Lord 15
Terni Arms Company 303
Ten Commandments 13
Thompson, Robert 28
Thyssen, Fritz 160-2, 319-22, 329-33
Tibet 66-7,
*The Times* 28, 86, 233-4
*Times of India* 48
Tolstoy, Leo 14, 103-5, 120-6, 132, 205-6, 208-9, 213, 258
Trade Unions 261
Trafalgar Square 381
Trevelyan, Charles 130
Trotsky, Leon 211-12, 213-14
Tsaritsyn 204
Turkey (Ottoman Empire) 17, 46, 69, 147

Undershaft 55, 83, 115
USSR (see also Russia) 207-19, 265, 379-81
United States 9-10, 42-3, 48, 154, 163-9, 187-202, 215-9, 251-2, 264-9, 326-340, 341-68, 378-9, 382-389
United States War Department 198-9
Utah 385-6

Vansittart, Sir Robert 252, 268, 271, 276-7
Vereinigte Stahwerke A.G. 319-22
Versailles Treaty (1919) 165-9, 255-6, 325
Vickers Arms Company 29, 44, 67-8, 74, 77-8, 93, 156, 204, 231-3, 236, 269, 310, 312-3
Von Falkenhayn, Erich 111
Von Forstner, Lieutenant 106
Von Klass, Gert 232-3
Von Moltke, General 57, 107-9
Von Papen, Fritz 106-7, 274
Von Schleicher, Kurt 274
Von Seeckt, Hans 325-6
Von Suttner, Bertha 132
Von Tirpitz 36-7, 68, 71-2, 84, 91, 97-115, 129

Wall Street 202
Walker, George Herbert 330-1
War, causes of 30-2, 45-6, 53-72, 114-5, 149-51, 342-3
War costs 77, 148, 151-5, 160-1, 377-8, 370-2, 391
War and Debt 159-60, 194-6, 256
War Office 16, 155-6
War to end all Wars 169, 175, 371
Warburg, Paul 336
Washington Naval Agreement 233-6
Weimar Republic 322, 324
Welby, Lord 74
Wells, H.G. 258
Westerns 395
White, Sir William 28
Whitworth, Sir Joseph 27
Wilhelm I 18-20, 23, 97
Wilhelm II 36-7, 57-8, 71-2, 88-9, 90-107, 115
Wilson, Hugh 249
Wilson, President Woodrow 134-5, 166-9, 191, 264
Witt, John 197
Women's Peace Initiatives 124,131-5, 138-9, 260-1
Wooley, Mary, 262

Younghusband 66
Ypres Battle 136-7, 146

Zaberne Affair 105-6
Zacharoff, Sir Basil 18-20, 30-1, 44, 55, 67-8, 204
Zaibatsu 306-9, 389-90
Zeppelin, Count 94
Zingara Guiseppe 355
Zinoviev, Gregori 2134, 243-5
Zinoviev Letter 243-5

## Endnotes:

1 Douglas Tate "Birmingham gunmakers and the Napoleonic Wars" (California: Safari Press, 1997) 49

2 William Manchester *The Arms of Krupp 1587-1968* ( London: Michael Joseph, 1968) 67-72.

3 Harold James *Krupp: A history of the Legendary German Firm* (Princeton University Press, 2012) 87

4 David Williams *The Birmingham Gun Trade* (Gloucs. The History Press, 2005)

5 Philip Noel-Baker *The Private Manufacture of Arms* (London: Victor Gollantz, 1936) [henceforth PMOA] 76

6 Gibb's painting is in Stirling Castle.

7 H.C. Engelbrecht and F.C. Hanighen *Merchants of Death* (New York: Dodd, Mead &Co., 1934) ch 4

8 William Manchester ibid. 106-114

9 J.D.Scott *Vickers: A History* (London: Wiedenfeld and Nicholson, 1962) 32

10 Peter Batty *The House of Krupp* (London: Secker and Warburg; 1966) 76-7

11 Gert von Klass *Krupps: The Story of an Industrial Empire* [trans. James Cleugh] (London: Sidgwick and Jackson, 1954) 59

12 Gert von Klass ibid. 67-8

13 J.D. Scott ibid. 86-7

14 Daily Post 30-31/10/1870

15 Marshall J. Bastable "From Breechloaders to Monster Guns: Sir William Armstrong and the Invention of Modern Artillery 1854-1880" *Technology and Culture* Vol 33 No 2, April, 1992 pp217-224

16 J.D. Scott ibid. 31

17 See John T. Flynn *Men of Wealth* (Von Mises Institute) 337-372 for a good biography.

18 Mike Dash "The mysterious Mr Zedzed: the wickedest man in the world." (Smithsonian 2012)

19 http://www.e-book.com.ay/electionspecial04.htm 04/11/2007 p4

20 This section mainly relies on Richard Hough *First Sea Lord* (London: George Allen and Unwin, 1969) 92-107

21 Richard Hough ibid. 104

22 Dudley Bahlman (ed.) *The Diary of Sir Edward Hamilton* 1885-1906 (Oxford: Clarendon Press, 1972) 236 quoted in Roy Jenkins *Gladstone* (London: Macmillan, 1995) 610

23 ibid. 247 also quoted by Jenkins

24 Richard Hough ibid. 99

25 Encyclopedia Brittanica 1959 Japan

26 Noel-Baker PMOA 184

27 Dirk H.R. Spenneman *British Naval Heritage in Micronesia: tangible*

*evidence of the armament trade from 1890-1937* Albury:URL:http:/marshall.csu.edu.au/Marshalls/html/UKNaval/UKNaval.html

[28] Noel-Baker PMOA 150-57

[29] *Encyclopedia Britannica* 1959 Russo-Japanese War.

[30] Noel-Baker PMOA 184-5

[31] Margaret Hebblethwaite *Paraguay* (Bucks; Bradt, 2010) 13, 288

[32] *Times of India* 18th December, 1897 and 28th May, 1898.

[33] *Arms and Explosives* quoted in Noel-Baker PMOA 109

[34] See, for example, Arnaldo Dumindin *Philippine-American War 1899-1902* PhilippineAmericanWar.webs.com

[35] http://www.littlegun.be/arme%20belge/a%20a%20site%20belge%20gb.htm

[36] John Sinclair Henry Campbell-Bannerman *Dictionary of National Biography*, 1912 Supplement. 307

[37] Sir Henry Campbell Bannerman Albert Hall, 21st December, 1905. Noel Baker PMOA 418

[38] David Lloyd George *War Memoirs* Vol I.

[39] Walter Roch *Mr Lloyd George and the War* (London: Chatto and Windus, 1920) 30-1

[40] Winston Churchill *The World Crisis 1911-14* (London: Thornton Butterworth, 1923) 39-40

[41] Francis Neilson *How Diplomats Make War* (New York: Huebsch, 1915) 125

[42] Lord Grey of Falloden *Twenty-five Years* Vol.I 91-2 quoted in Noel-Baker PMOA 19

[43] Hansard. Commons 3rd August, 1914.

[44] P Jacobson *The Economist* 19/10/1929 Armaments supplement.

[45] Mike Dash ibid.

[46] T. Hunt Tooley "Merchants of Death Revisted: Armaments, Bankers and the First World War" *Journal of Libertarian Studies* (Vol. 9 No. 1 Winter 2005) 39

[47] Clive Trebilcock *The Vickers Brothers* (London: Europa, 1977) 45-9

[48] Ex-Kaiser William II *My Memoirs 1878-1918* (London: Cassell, 1922) 230

[49] Quoted in W.T.Stead The Review of Reviews vol. XLII 1910 227-232 http://www.attackingthedevil.co.uk/reviews/lloydgeorge.php

[50] Royal Commission on the Private Manufacture of and Trading in Arms 1936 quoted in Noel-Baker PMOA 439

[51] Noel-Baker PMOA 445 Hansard 17/3/1914

[52] Fred Morton "Slave Raiding and Slavery in the Western Transvaal after the Sand River Convention" *African Economic History* (20) 1992: 99

[53] Willie Havenga "The Big Guns of the Boer War"

http://ezinearticles.com/?Big-Guns-Of-The-Boer-War&id=484444

54 Clive Trebilcock *The Vickers Brothers* (London: Europa, 1977) 83

55 ibid. 68-73

56 ibid. 64

57 Noel-Baker PMOA 458

58 http://iconicphotos.wordpress.com/2010/01/03/the-dreadnought-hoax/

59 Churchill, Winston S. *The World Crisis 1911-14* (London: Thornton Butterworth, 1923) 104

60 ibid 34

61 Noel-Baker PMOA 444

62 See John Brown plc history.

63 This section is mainly dependent on Noel Baker PMOA 449-510

64 PMOA 463

65 Again Noel-Baker PMOA 464

66 *The Times* 17th February, 1934

67 World Battleship List: German Dreadnoughts compiled by Andrew Toppen http://www.hazegray.org/navhist/battleships/germ_dr.htm

68 These figures were verified by the Chairman of Krupp's, and John Leyland , editor of The Navy and co-editor of Brassey's Naval Annual.

69 *The Daily Mail* 15th December, 1909

70 Noel-Baker PMOA 441

71 Noel-Baker PMOA 412-6

72 ibid 37

73 ibid 37

74 Noel-Baker PMOA 504-5

75 David Clarke Scareships over Great Britain: the airship scare of 1909.

76 Reported in Chicago Tribune 34/10/1908

77 Gert von Klass Krupps: the Story of an Industrial Empire (London: Sidgwick and Jackson, 1954) 216-240

78 Ibid 234

79 Noel-Baker PMOA 435-444

80 Grand Admiral Von Tirpitz *My Memoirs* Vol II (London: Hurst and Blackett, 1920) 318

81 Leo Tolstoy *The Kingdom of God is Within You.* (London: Walter Scott, 1894) trans. A Delano 212-4

82 Militarism in Germany and the Zabern Affair (1917 account)

83 Franz von Papen *Memoirs* (translated by Brian Connell) (London: Andre Deutsch, 1952) 8-9

84 Barbara Morgan "Operational Leadership: the case of General Helmuth von Moltke (The Younger)" (US Naval War College, 2001) 14

85 Jonathan A. Grant *Rulers, guns and money: the global arms trade in the age ofimperialism* (Harvard University Press, 2007) 200

[86] http://www.carbinesforcollectors.com/yugo_serb.html

[87] "Serbian quick firing field artillery" http://www.bulgarianartillery.it/Bulgarian%20Artillery%201/Testi/T Serbian%20QF%20Field%20Artillery.htm

[88] Walter Roch *Mr Lloyd George and the War* (London: Chatto and Windus, 1920) 14

[89] Times newspaper cutting from Vienna Correspondent. No date.

[90] George Fox, *The Journal of George Fox* , edited by John L. Nickalls (Cambridge: Cambridge Univ. Press,1952), p. 67.

[91] Quoted in Leo Tolstoi *The Kingdom of God is within you* (London: Walter Scott, 1984)129-30

[92] Leo Tolstoi *Works Vol IX My Confession* (NY:Fred DeFau, 1898) 12

[93] Ibid. Selected texts.

[94] Rosamund Bartlett *Tolstoy: A Russian Life* (London: Profile, 2011) 364-382

[95] Lyof Tolstoi *The Kingdom of God is Within You* (London: Walter Scott, 1894) 257

[96] J. E. Cookson *The Friends of Peace. Anti-War Liberalism in England* 1793-1815 (Cambridge University Press, 1982) 884

[97] Keith W. Clements "Baptists and the Outbreak of the First World War" Baptist Quarterly. www.biblicalstudies.org.uk/pdf/bq/26-2_074.pdf

[98] Stewart, William *J. Keir Hardie* (London: ILP, 1921)347

[99] http://www.thefreelibrary.com/British+official+attitudes+regarding+anti-war+protesters+in+two+World...-a0128103343

[100] Michael Clinton "The French Peace Movement in Transnational Perspective" http://gwyneddmercy.academia.edu/MichaelClinton/Papers/412377/

[101] e.g. Ellen Lovell Evans *The German Centre Party* 1870-1933 (Carbondale and Edwardsville: Southern University Press, 1981) 114

[102] (ed) Chatfield, Charles *Peace Movements in America* (NY: Schocken, 1973) 40

[103] http://www.1914-1918.net/truce.htm

[104] http://wwi.lib.byu.edu/index.php/Pope_Benedict_XV's_Peace_Proposal

[105] http://www.catholicpeacefellowship.org/downloads/BenedictXV_Gibbon s.pdf

[106] Freya Baetens "The Forgotten Peace Conference: the 1915 International Congress of Women" (Max Planck Encyclopedia of Public International Law ;2010)

[107] H.C. Englebrecht and F.C. Hanighen *The Merchants of Death* (New York: Dodd, Meade and Co. 1934) ch 10

[108] Hansard HC Debate.8/8/1914

[109] Reves, Emery *The Anatomy of Peace* (New York: 1946) 126

[110] President Eisenhower in an interview with Harold Macmillan, London,

1959 cited in Chatfield 39

111 T. Hunt Tooley "Merchants of Death Revisted: Armaments, Bankers and the First World War" *Journal of Libertarian Studies* (Vol. 9 No. 1 Winter 2005) 42

112 Philip Haythornewaite *The World War One Source Book* (London: Arms and Armour, 1992) 87

113 All from B.R.Mitchell *European Historical Statistics* (London: Macmillan, 1981)

114 Winston S Churchill *The World Crisis Vol.II 1915* (London: Thornton, Butterworth, 1923) 311

115 J.D.Scott *Vickers: A History* (London: Weidenfeld and Nicholson, 1962) 390

116 David Lloyd George *War Memoirs Vol. 1* (London: Odhams Press, 1933, 38) 360

117 Woodward Llewellyn *Great Britain and the War of 1914-18* (London: Methuen, 1967) 461-67

118 Keir Hardie Spartacus Schoolnet biography

119 Emrys Hughes *Keir Hardie* (London: Lincolns-Prager, 1950) 79

120 ibid 1499

121 *Les Finances de Guerre de l'Allemange* by Charles Rist (1921)

122 Fred Rogers Fairchild "German War Finance – A Review" in (ed) Larry Neal *War Finance Vol III* (Aldershot: Elgar, 1994) 106-121 reviewing Charles Rist *Les Finances de Guerre d'Allemagne*

123 Quoted in Peter Batty *The House of Krupp* (London: Secker & Warburg, 1966) 145

124 Noel-Baker PMOA 200-7

125 Quoted in (ed.) John Kirshon *Chronicle of America* (Missouri: JL Publishing,1989) 589

126 http://wwl2.dataformat.com/Document.aspx?doc=30758

127 the phrase is from Beard, Charles and Mary *The Rise of American Civilisation* (NY:Macmillan, 1930) 688

128 Jan Willem Schulte Nordholt *Woodrow Wilson: A Life for Peace* (Berkeley, University of California Press, 1991) 404

129 Keynes, John Maynard *The Economic Consequences of the Peace* (London, Macmillan, 1920)

130 Solzbacher, William *Peace movements between the Wars* (Lampeter: Edwin Mellon Press, 1999) 28

131 Lord Grey of Falloden *Twenty Five Years* (NY: Stokes, 1925) 91-2

132 Walter Roch Mr Lloyd George and the War (London:Chatto and Windus, 1920) 47

133 Alexander Bing *Wartime Strikes and their Adjustment* (NY: 1921) 293

134 Senator Nye speech July 1939 ?

135 Gerald Nye N.Y.Times speech 16th Feb. 1936.

[136] H.C. Engelbrecht and F.C. Hanighen *The Merchants of Death* 1934 (NY: Dodd, Mead and Co, 1934)

[137] See Jerry N. Markham *The Financial History of the United States* Vol. II (NY: M.E.Sharpe, 2002) 69-79

[138] John Witt witt_eastman_draft_11-04-03.wpd

[139] Benedict Crowell and Robert Forrest Wilson *The Armies of Industry: Our Nation's Manufacture of Munitions for a World in Arms* 1917-1918 (New Haven: Yale University Press, 1921) 166

[140] "National Register of Historic Places: Old Hickory" US Dept of Interior 6

[141] Bernard Baruch *Report of the War Industries Board – March 1921* (New York: Prentice Hall, 1941) 42

[142] Bernard Baruch *Members of the War Industries Board Organisation* (Washington: US W.I.B., 1919)

[143] Tolstoy "Sevastopol in May".

[144] Bertram D Wolfe *Three Who Made a Revolution* (Middlesex: Pelican, 1966) 704-7

[145] Bertram D Wolfe ibid. 419-20

[146] ed. M.R. Werner *Stalin's Kampf* (London: Jarrolds, 1940) 28

[147] quoted by Ian Grey *The First Fifty Years: Soviet Russia 1917-67* (London: Hodder and Stoughton, 1967) 127-8

[148] Winston S. Churchill *The World Crisis: The Aftermath* (London: Thornton Butterworth Limited, 1929) 250

[149] Winston S. Churchill ibid. 246

[150] Walter Scott Dunn *The Soviet Economy and the Red Army* (Westport, Conn: Praeger/Greenwood, 1995) 19

[151] (ed.) M.R.Werner *Stalin's Kampf* (London: Jarrolds, 1940) 230

[152] Summary of items in Anthony Sutton *The Best Enemy Money can Buy.* http://vho.org/aaargh/fran/livres10/SUTTONbest.pdf

[153] Walter Scott Dunn ibid. 22

[154] F. Jay Taylor *The United States and the Spanish Civil War* (NY:Octagon, 1971) 180 also quoted in the New York Times 17/10/1937.

[155] ibid. 181

[156] Vera Brittain *Letters from a Lost Generation* (London: Abacus, 1998)

[157] Jeremy Black *Warfare in the Western World 1882-1975* (Indianapolis: Indiana University Press, 2002) gives a fuller account of these conflicts in the first 90 pages

[158] Good summary in Anthony B. Chan *Arming the Chinese:The Western Armaments Trade in Warlord China 1920-1928* (Vancouver: University of British Columbia Press, 1992) 61

[159] https://www.mtholyoke.edu/acad/intrel/nye.htm

[160] Lloyd George, David *War Memoirs Vol.II* (London: Odhams, 1936) 1593

[161] Quoted in Philip Noel Baker PMOA 104

[162] Quoted in Philip Noel Baker PMOA 105 Vickers-Armstrong News May 1928

[163] Gert von Glass *Krupps: The Story of an Industrial Empire* (London: Sidgwick and Jackson, 1954) 361

[164] Public Papers of the Presidents: Hoover archives. 193 6/9/1929

[165] *The Times* 6/7/27

[166] Report of the Special Committee on Investigation of the Munitions Industry (the Nye report), U.S. Congress, Senate, 74th Congress, 2nd Session, February 24, 1936 p3-13

[167] Nye Munitions Hearings Report 24th Feb 1936.

[168] Englebrecht and Hanighen *Merchants of Death* ch16

[169] G. D. H. And M. Cole *The Intelligent Man's Guide to Europe Today* (London:Gollancz, 1933) 714

[170] *Re-armament: How the Government's policy affects the Investor* (Financial News, February, 1936)

[171] FCO "The Zinoviev Letter of 1924: A Most Extraordinary and Mysterious Business" http://issuu.com/fcohistorians/docs/history_notes_cover_hphn_14. 48-50

[172] The main text and the most penetrating is Lewis Chester, Stephen Fay and Hugo Young *The Zinoviev Letter* (London: Heinemann, 1967)

[173] Hansard 2/2/1932 and 3/2/1932

[174] Hansard 5/2/1932.

[175] http://hansard.millbanksystems.com/lords/1932/dec/08/manufacture-of-and-trade-in-arms

[176] Sara R. Smith *The Manchurian Crisis:1931-1932: A Tragedy in International Relations* (NY: Columbia University Press, 1948) 235-7

[177] Englebrecht ibid. Ch 16

[178] Noel-Baker PMOA 211-17

[179] Hansard 27/2/1933

[180] Noel-Baker PMOA 513

[181] *The London Gazette* 26th February, 1932 1293

[182] Philip Noel-Baker's account in *The First World Disarmament Conference 1932-33* (Oxford: Pergamon, 1979) informs this and the subsequent text.

[183] Ibid 45

[184] Noel Baker *The First World Disarmament Conference* (Oxford:Pergamon, 1979) 73

[185] John Eppstein *The Catholic Tradition of the Law of Nations* (London: Burns, Oates and Washbourne, 1935) 183

[186] Catholic Women's League, Australia. Brief History of WUCWO

[187] Michael Fogarty *Motorways Merge: The new Challenge to Christian Democracy* (Ware: Christian Democrat Press, 1999) 12

[188] William Solzbacher *Peace Movements between the Wars; One man's work for peace* (Lampeter, Wales: Edwin Mellon, 1999) 209-13

[189] Carolyn J. Keating *Britain and the Geneva Disarmament Conference* (London:Palgrave Macmillan, 2003) 55

[190] Philip Noel-Baker The First World Disarmament Conference (London:Pergamon, 1979) 79

[191] Herbert Hoover *The Ordeal of Woodrow Wilson* (London: Museum Press, 1958)

[192] Presidential Papers, President Hoover 22/6/1932

[193] Richard Lamb *The Drift to War* (London W.H.Allen, 1989) 71

[194] Hansard 8/7/1932.

[195] Peace History Conference 29/3/2008 "The 1932 League of Nations Disarmament Conference at Geneva" Lecturer unnamed.

[196] Ibid.

[197] Wikipedia: Sir John Simon

[198] Hansard. House of Commons. Cmnd 2334 13/5/1932

[199] Maurice Baumont *The Origins of the Second World War* (translated by Simone de Couvreur Ferguson) (New Haven: Yale UP, 1978) 28

[200] http://hansard.millbanksystems.com/lords/1932/dec/08/manufacture-of-and-trade-in-arms

[201] Noel-Baker *The First World Disarmament Conference 1932-3 and why it failed* (London: Pergamon Press, 1979) 120

[202] http://www.fsmitha.com/h2/ch19.htm

[203] Letter from Hankey to Cecil 18th August, 1925, quoted in Noel-Baker *The First World Disarmament Conference* 22-3

[204] Ibid. 13-21.

[205] Noel-Baker PMOA 365, 257-65

[206] Noel-Baker PMOA 367-9

[207] Hansard 25/5/1932

[208] Bernard Feld quoted in Philip Noel-Baker *The First World Disarmament Conference 1932-33 and why it failed* (Oxford: Pergamon, 1935) 11

[209] David Reynolds *Churchill – In control of History* (London: Penguin, Allen Lane, 2003)

[210] Winston Churchill *The Second World War* Volume 1 (London: Cassell, 1948) 52-70

[211] Reynolds. Ibid 138-141

[212] Letter Churchill to Lord Robert Cecil 1/9/1944 (British Library display)

[213] G D H and Margaret Cole *The Intelligent Man's Review of Europe Today* (London: Gollancz, 1933) 740

[214] This is an edited summary and elaboration of the Wikipedia "List of Fascist Movements by Country".
http://en.wikipedia.org/wiki/List_of_fascist_movements_by_country

[215] Nietzsche, Friedrich *Twilight of the Idols/The Anti-Christ* translated by

R.J. Hollingdale (Harmondsworth, Middx.; Penguin, 1990) 140

216 ibid 104

217 Emil Ludwig *Bismarck* (London:George Allen and Unwin, 1927) 25-8

218 Friedrich, Otto *Before the Deluge.* (USA: Fromm International Publishing Corporation. 1986) 37

219 John Gooch *Mussolini and his Generals: The Armed Forces and Fascist Foreign Policy 1922-1940* (Cambridge: University Press, 2007) 5

220 Richard J. Samuels *Machiavelli's Children: Leaders and their legacies in Italy and Japan* (Ithaca: Cornell University Press, 2003) 111

221 Ibid 112

222 Max Gallo *Mussolini's Italy;Twenty Years of the Fascist Era* (London: Abelard-Schuman, 1973) translated by Charles Lam Markman 39

223 Wikipedia. The Economy of Italy under Fascism.

224 Gallo ibid. 49

225 See Martland's forthcoming study of Sir Samuel Hoare and Guardian 13/10/ 2009

226 Gallo 69-73

227 Makiyo Hori *The Roots of Japanese Fascism:Continuities, Crisis and the Ideology of Kita and Okumura*(Cambridge: University Library – presented by the author, 1995) 31-2

228 Ibid 101

229 Kozo Yamamura *The Economic Emergence of Modern Japan* Vol. 1 338.

230 Robert Soucy *French Fascism: The Second Wave 1933-39* (Yale UP, 1995) 126-7

231 Edward Packard "Whitehall, Industrial Mobilisation and the Private Manufacture of Armaments 1918-36" (LSE PhD thesis, 2009) 149-174

232 http://en.wikipedia.org/wiki/British_Fascists

233 *The Times*, 22/3/1934

234 George Grosz *An Autobiography* [translated by Nora Hodges] (London: Macmillan, 1983) 150

235 James and Suzanne Pool *Who Financed Hitler* (London: Raven, 1971) gives the fuller story.

236 Stephan Link Rethinking the Ford-Nazi Connection p141 http://www.ghi-dc.org/files/publications/bulletin/bu049/bu49_135.pdf

237 Glen Yeaden, John Hawkins *The Nazi Hydra in America* (California: Progressive Press, 2002)

238 Anthony Sutton *Wall Street and the Rise of Hitler* (1976) Chapter Six

239 Sara Twogood The Munich Post: Its undiscoved effects on Hitler

240 Harold James *Krupp: History of the Legendary German Firm* (Princeton University Press, 2012)

241 Hans von Seeckt Wikipedia.

242 George Grotz *An Autobiography* (New York: Imago/Macmillan, 1983) 156

[243] Edgar B. Nixon, ed., *Franklin D. Roosevelt and Foreign Affairs,* Volume III: September 1935-January 1937, (Cambridge: Belknap Press, 1969), p. 456 quoted in Anthony Sutton Wall *Street and the Rise of the Nazis* Introduction.

[244] Law Reports of Trials of War Criminals UN War Crimes Commission Vol IX (London: HMSO, 1949) 5

[245] A strong source of this material is Charles Higham *Trading with the Enemy: An Exposé of the Nazi-American Money-Plot 1933-49* (London: Hale, 1983)

[246] Robert F. Burk *The Corporate State and the Broker State: The Du Ponts and American National Politics 1925-1940* (Cambridge, Mass: Harvard University Press, 1990) 8-9

[247] Burk ibid. 18

[248] Burk ibid. 100

[249] http://singermemories.com/guns-sewing-machines/

[250] http://www.fundinguniverse.com/company-histories/davis-polk-wardwell-history/

[251] Burk ibid. 10

[252] L Wolfe "Morgan's Fascist Plot and How it was Defeated- Part II" American Almanac. 4/7/1994

[253] Ibid.

[254] Special Committee on Un-American Activities, House of Representatives, Seventy-Third Congress, second Session at Washington D.C. December 29, 1934, Hearings No.73-D-C-6 Part One (United States Government Printing Office.105730 Washington DC : 1935

[255] http://www.historylink.org/index.cfm?DisplayPage=output.cfm&File_Id=5628

[256] Burk ibid.140-2 and especially cartoons on the following pages.

[257] Jules Archer *The Plot to Seize the White House* (1973) 176

[258] 74th Congress House of Representatives Report, pursuant to House Resolution No. 198, 73d Congress, February 15, 1935. Quoted in: George Seldes, *1000 Americans* (1947), pp. 290–292

[259] See Wikipedia: Participants in World War II

[260] Interestingly, German scientists identified the link of cancer to smoking and the Nazis clamped down on it heavily. They got that right.

[261] Noel-Baker 558-9

[262] Using Mark Harrison's figures in "Resource Mobilization for World War II" Economic History Review (1988) 172 and Hugh Rockoff's in (ed.) Mark Harrison *The Economics of World War II* (Cambridge University Press, 1998) 83

[263] Mark Harrison "The Soviet Union; the defeated victor" in (ed.) Mark Harrison *The Economics of World War II* (CUP 1998) 276-7

[264] Bert Cochran *Harry Truman and the Crisis Presidency* (NY: Funk and

Wagnalls, 1973) 11-12

265 Gregory Hooks *Forging the Military-Industrial Complex: World-War II's Battle of the Potomac* (Chicago: University of Illinois Press, 1991) 100

266 Cochran ibid. 110

267 Hooks ibid. 166

268 John Simkin "Assassination, Terrorism and the Arms Trade: The Contracting out of American Foreign Policy 1940-2006" The Education Forum: Controversial Issues 2006

269 Layton McCartney *Friends in High Places* (NY: Ballantine, 1989)

270 ibid.

271 Gerald D. Nash *World War II and the West: Reshaping the Economy* (Lincoln and London: University of Nebraska Press, 1990) 1-8

272 Charles Higham *Trading with the Enemy: An Exposé of the Nazi-American Money Plot 1933-1949* (London: Robert Hale, 1983) 153

273 T.A. Bisson *Japan's War Economy* (NY: Macmillan, 1945)

274 Akira Hara "Japan: Guns before Rice." In (ed.) Mark Harrison *The Economics of World War II* (CUP, 1998) 257

275 Wikipedia List of World War Two films

276 Noel-Baker *The Arms Race* (London: Atlantic books, 1958) 40

277 Noel-Baker *The Arms Race* 40

278 Noel-Baker *The Arms Race* 40.

279 Noel-Baker *The Arms Race* 40-1

280 Noel-Baker PMOA 82-3

Made in the USA
Charleston, SC
12 June 2015